SAGE was founded in 1965 by Sara Miller McCune to support the dissemination of usable knowledge by publishing innovative and high-quality research and teaching content. Today, we publish over 900 journals, including those of more than 400 learned societies, more than 800 new books per year, and a growing range of library products including archives, data, case studies, reports, and video. SAGE remains majority-owned by our founder, and after Sara's lifetime will become owned by a charitable trust that secures our continued independence.

Los Angeles | London | New Delhi | Singapore | Washington DC | Melbourne

Indian Constitution

Indian Constitution

Text, Context and Interpretation

Bidyut Chakrabarty

Professor in Political Science, Department of Political Science, University of Delhi

SAGE | TEXTS

Los Angeles | London | New Delhi
Singapore | Washington DC | Melbourne

First published in 2017 by

SAGE | TEXTS

SAGE Publications India Pvt Ltd
B1/I-1 Mohan Cooperative Industrial Area
Mathura Road, New Delhi 110 044, India
www.sagepub.in

SAGE Publications Inc
2455 Teller Road
Thousand Oaks, California 91320, USA

SAGE Publications Ltd
1 Oliver 's Yard, 55 City Road
London EC1Y 1SP, United Kingdom

SAGE Publications Asia-Pacific Pte Ltd
3 Church Street
#10-04 Samsung Hub
Singapore 049483

Published by Vivek Mehra for SAGE Publications India Pvt Ltd, typeset in 10/13 pts Minion Pro by JMV Design Solutions, Chandigarh 31-D, Delhi and printed at Sai Print-o-Pack, New Delhi.

Library of Congress Cataloging-in-Publication Data
Name: Chakrabarty, Bidyut, 1958- author.
Title: Indian Constitution : text, context, and interpretation / Bidyut Chakrabarty.
Description: New Delhi, India ; Thousand Oaks, California : SAGE Publications Inc., [2017] | Includes bibliographical references and index.
Identifiers: LCCN 2017006697 | ISBN 9789386446107 (pbk.)
Subjects: LCSH: Constitutional law—India. | Constitutions—India. | Law—India—History. | Freedom of religion—India. | India. Constitution. | Secularism—India. | Democracy—India.
Classification: LCC KNS1750 .C425 2017 | DDC 342.5402—dc23
LC record available at https://lccn.loc.gov/2017006697

ISBN: 978-93-864-4610-7 (PB)

SAGE Team: Amit Kumar, Indrani Dutta, Priya Arora, Suhag Dave and Ritu Chopra

Brief Contents

Detailed Contents

List of Abbreviations

AASU	All Assam Students Union
AJGAR	Ahir, Jats, Gurjars and Rajputs
ASOSAI	Asian Organization of Supreme Audit Institutions
BJP	Bharatiya Janata Party
CAG	Comptroller and Auditor General of India
CDP	Community Development Programme
CLM	Commissioner for Linguistic Minorities in India
COPU	Committees on Pubic Understandings
CSE	Centre for Science and Environment
CWG	Commonwealth Games
DPSP	Directive Principles of the State Policy
GATT	General Agreement Trade and Tariff
HSRA	Hindustan Socialist Republican Army
IA & AD	Indian Audits and Accounts Department
IIM	Indian Institute of Management
IMDT	Illegal Migrants (Determination by Tribunal) Act
INTOSAI	International Organization of Supreme Audit Institutions
ISC	Inter-State Council
JP	Jayaprakash Narayan
NDA	National Democratic Alliance
NDC	National Development Council
NES	National Extension Service
NGOs	Non-governmental Organizations
OBCs	Other Backward Classes
PDP	People's Democratic Party
PIL	Public Interest Litigation
PIO	Persons of Indian Origin
POTO	Prevention of Terrorism Ordinance
PPP	Public–Private Partnership
PRIs	Panchayati Raj Institutions
RWAs	Residents' Welfare Associations
SAI	Supreme Audit Institution of India
SAPs	Structural Adjustment Programmes

SCs	Scheduled Castes
STs	Scheduled Tribes
ULBs	Urban Local Bodies
WTO	World Trade Organization

Preface

This is not a book on the Constitution of India per se, but one on constitutional democracy in India, which means that the former needs to be understood not in isolation but as integral to the entire constitutionalizing processes. In view of being primary to India's constitutional democracy, the 1950 Constitution no longer remains a compilation of rules and regulations, but a living organism sustaining and consolidating democratic values and also a structure of governance upholding them. The Constitution is pre-eminent and the supportive institutions of governance seem to be mere actors, governed by what the Constitution set for them. Unlike the Westminster model of democracy where Parliament is sovereign, the Indian founding fathers preferred the US form of democratic governance, privileging the Constitution over other institutions of governance. There is also a puzzle here since the Indian Constitution favours a hybrid system, which means that it redefines parliamentary authority in conjunction with the Constitution being sovereign. This is persuasively explained by reference to the unfolding of federalism in specific historical perspectives: While the US emerged as a federation following the decision whereby the erstwhile independent States abdicated their sovereignty for unity, federalism in India was an offshoot of what is known as 'the unpackaging of the Empire', whereby constituent states of British India were given power and authority in the new constitutional set-up which they lacked in the past.

The book is not a conventional study of the Constitution of India; it is a study that also seeks to understand the unfolding of the Constitution in the context of a rapidly changing India in response to indigenous and exogenous influences. This is accomplished in a three-fold academic strategy of dwelling on (a) how the constitutional provisions evolved out of fierce debates in the Constituent Assembly, (b) the actual constitutional provisions and their expansion by way of amendments and (c) the judicial pronouncements leading to reinterpretation and reconfirmation of some of the fundamental constitutional values and principles.

A challenging task no doubt; it has been made possible by the help that I have received from my friends, colleagues, family and, of course, my students both in India and in another campuses where I have had a chance to teach. My doctoral students, Dr Prakash Chand of Dyal Singh College, Delhi University and Ms Subha Sinha of Shyama Prasad College, Delhi University were always helpful. Professor Ujjwal K Singh of my Department contributed to my understanding of the Constitution by drawing my attention to some of the important judicial verdicts which are critical in reconceptualizing the changing texture and also the nature of the 1950 Constitution of India. I shall be failing in my duty if I do not recognize the contribution of the Librarian of the University of Delhi, Dr DV Singh who, by procuring a number of relevant texts, made my task, as an author, much easier.

The main purpose of this book is to place before the readers a text which is both informative and provocative. Informative because it deals with the actual constitutional provisions and provocative because it goes beyond the conventional style of understanding the Constitution by being sensitive to other multiple inputs which usually escape attention in a conventional mode of academic exercise. Once the book serves these twin purposes, I will have achieved my goal as an author.

I thankfully acknowledge the contribution of the reviewers for having drawn my attention to certain aspects of constitutional studies which escaped my notice. The book would not have been the same without their critical inputs.

The book would not have hit the stands without the cooperation of people at SAGE, especially Mr Amit Kumar and Ms Indrani Dutta. Without their unflinching support to the project, it would not have been possible for me to complete the text. I salute their concern for me as an author. Let me also express my gratitude by saying further that both Amit and Indrani deserve appreciation in view of being highly professional in their interaction with the authors, which is now a rarity. I am also thankful to Mr Vivek Mehra for his care for the authors, which explains why the SAGE is a safe home for authors across the world. Keep it up Vivek!

Last but not the least, the role of my family has always remained critical in transforming me from a mere reader to an author. Our kids, Barbie and Pablo, may not have developed a professional eye to assess their Baba's intellectual babies, but, by always being supportive whenever I am glued to the computer, they also have contributed in my academic feat. By being critical and supportive, my wife, Sanchita, plays a role that a wife usually discharges when her husband winkles-in forgetting the world around him!

Bidyut Chakrabarty
Delhi, 2017

About the Author

Professor Bidyut Chakrabarty is currently a faculty at the Department of Political Science, University of Delhi, India. He earned his PhD from London School of Economics (LSE) and has been associated with teaching and research for more than three decades. He has taught in some of the most prestigious educational institutes such as LSE, UK; Indian Institute of Management (IIM) Calcutta, India; Monash University, Australia; National University of Singapore, Singapore and Hamburg University, Germany.

Professor Chakrabarty has authored five textbooks for SAGE India: *Indian Government and Politics* (with Rajendra Kumar Pandey, 2008), *Modern Indian Political Thought* (with Rajendra Kumar Pandey, 2009), *Public Administration in a Globalizing World* (with Prakash Chand, 2012), *Indian Administration* (with Prakash Chand, 2016) and *Public Policy* (with Prakash Chand, 2016).

Introduction

I

A constitution is the backbone of democracy for securing people's participation in governance. By developing a conducive system based on well-defined rules and regulations, a constitution also becomes an effective means to create an environment for the evolution of a supportive mindset. In conceptual terms, the idea is articulated as 'the constitutional morality', which is a driving force behind the success of a constitution. Thus, having a perfect constitution does not necessarily mean that it is going to achieve the goal for which it is created; what is also needed is an environment in which the values and principles that a constitution seeks to build receive adequate nourishment and backing. What is emphasized here is the concern for the values on which the constitution is based. It is easier said than done, though this is most fundamental to a constitution seeking to chart out a definite course of action for a collectivity. Upholding this view, Arthur James Balfour, in his introduction to Walter Bagehot's classic *The English Constitution*, most categorically stated:

> Constitutions are easily copied, temperaments are not; and if it should happen that the borrowed constitution and the native temperament fail to correspond, the misfit may have serious results. It matters little what other gifts a people may possess if they are wanting in those which, from this point of view, are of most importance. If, for example, . . . they have no natural inclination to liberty and no natural respect for law; if they tolerate foul play, if they know not how to compromise or when; if they have not that distrust of extreme conclusions which is sometimes misdescribed as want of logic; if corruption does not repel them; and if their division tend to be either too numerous or too profound.[1]

What was thus required was to develop corresponding 'habits' to support the constitution that the Constituent Assembly was engaged in making. It was nonetheless a difficult but not an insurmountable task, as Begam Aizaz Rasul, a Muslim woman member in the Constituent Assembly from the United Provinces, mentioned. According to her, while being reeled under autocratic regimes over centuries, it would be initially difficult for the Indians to 'adopt the democratic form of government [deriving its

[1] Arthur James Balfour's introduction to Walter Bagehot's *The English Constitution* (Oxford: Oxford University Press, 1928), p. xxii; cited in AG Noorani, *Constitutional Questions in India: The President, Parliament and States* (New Delhi: Oxford University Press, 2000), p. 13.

sustenance] from the people who will make India's destiny'; with their sincerity and commitment to the democratic cause, 'India's democratic constitution will become an example for the rest of the world to imitate'.[2] The argument hinges on the familiar concern that democratic constitution survives and thrives on a complementary set of people who are adequately inspired by the values that it represents. Values do not emerge out of a vacuum; they are the product of what BR Ambedkar defined as 'constitutional morality', an idea he had developed by drawing on the conceptualization of George Grote, the famous classicist, as propounded in his classical study of Greek history in the late eighteenth century. According to Ambedkar, a constitution by itself is just an inanimate object which comes to life once it is complemented by constitutional morality. While being engaged in the making of perhaps the lengthiest of the available constitutions, Ambedkar always held constitutional morality as most critical to its success in developing an ideologically persuasive system of governance for all, regardless of class, caste or religious barriers. Drawing on Grote, Ambedkar, the chairman of the Drafting Committee, invoked the idea in support of his contention that without constitutional morality no constitution, however solid in its ideological foundation, would survive the test of time. What is constitutional morality then? Quoting Grote, he suggested that it meant

> a permanent reverence for the forms of the constitution, enforcing obedience to authority and acting under and within these forms, yet combined with the habit of open speech, of action subject only to definite legal control, and unrestrained censure of those very authorities as to all their public acts combined, too, with a perfect confidence in the bosom of every citizen amidst the bitterness of party contest and the forms of the constitution will not be less scared in the eyes of his opponents than his own.[3]

This long quote from Grote's writings was surely an aid to Ambedkar when he defended a liberal democratic framework of constitutional governance in India, though he was aware that it was difficult to instil a sense of constitutional morality in India because democracy which 'complements constitutional morality . . . is only a top-dressing on an Indian soil which is essentially undemocratic'.[4] In the absence of constitutional morality, the operation of the constitution, no matter how carefully written, 'tends to become arbitrary, erratic and capricious'.[5] How to make the constitution an effective instrument of governance in such circumstances, asked Ambedkar? He was in favour of detailed provisions in the constitution to scuttle efforts at derailing it and challenging the fundamental constitutional values from which it derived its sustenance. In his defence, he argued that 'one can take the risk of omitting from the Constitution details of administration and leaving it for the Legislature to prescribe them . . . if the people are saturated with Constitutional morality such as the one described by Grote'.[6] As is evident, Grote provided Ambedkar with an intellectual justification for a liberal constitution in a context in which basic liberal values of human dignity were brutally bypassed in favour of perhaps the most ruthless form of social segregation. So, the idea of constitutional morality was a powerful device, which allowed Ambedkar to knit together liberal constitutional principles despite strong opposition by the Gandhians in the Constituent Assembly, who insisted that 'instead of incorporating Western theories the new Constitution should have been built upon

---

[2] Begam Aizaz Rasul (United Provinces), 8 November 1948, *Constituent Assembly Debates*, Book No. 2, p. 305.

[3] BR Ambedkar, 4 November 1948, *Constituent Assembly Debates*, Book No. 2, p. 38.

[4] Ibid., p. 39.

[5] Andre Beteille, 'Constitutional Morality', *Economic and Political Weekly*, 4 October 2008, p. 36.

[6] BR Ambedkar, 4 November, 1948, *Constituent Assembly Debates*, Book No. 2, p. 38.

village panchayats and district panchayats'.[7] For constitutional morality to strike organic roots, Ambedkar insisted on the obedience to

> constitutional methods of achieving our social and economic objectives [which meant that] we must abandon ... the method of civil disobedience, non-cooperation and satyagraha [because] when constitutional methods are open, there can be no justification of unconstitutional methods ... and sooner these unconstitutional methods are abandoned, the better for us.[8]

There are two important points that Ambedkar kept on harping: on the one hand, he was confident that without strong values of constitutional morality, a constitution ceased to become an effective and meaningful instrument of governance; this entails, on the other, the idea of being accommodative and respectful of differences, which means that being different did not justify discrimination or separation. Rajendra Prasad, the President of the Constituent Assembly had an identical concern which he expressed in his speech just before the endorsement of the constitution by its members by saying that 'successful working of a democratic constitution requires in those who have to work it willingness to respect the view point of others, capacity for compromise and accommodation'.[9] Ambedkar too conceded by emphasizing that 'the capacity for compromise and accommodation' remained one of the fundamental pillars of constitutional democracy, which needed to be nurtured by the future generations and political parties; otherwise, the edifice of India's democratic governance would, in no time, crumble down. In his speech in the Assembly on 25 November 1949, he expressed his feelings by persuasively arguing that

> the working of a Constitution does not depend wholly upon the nature of the Constitution. The Constitution can provide only the organs of State, such as the Legislature, Executive and Judiciary. The factors on which the working of these organs of the State depend are the people and the political parties they will set up as their instruments to carry out their wishes and politics. Who can say how the people of India and their parties will behave? Will they uphold constitutional methods of achieving their purposes or will they prefer revolutionary methods of achieving them? ... It is, therefore, futile to pass any judgment upon the Constitution without reference to the part which the people and their parties are likely to play.[10]

According to Ambedkar, the codification of the rule of law does not, by itself, ensure good governance; they need to be translated meaningfully into policies without being prejudiced or tilted to pursue partisan interests. Ultimately, it is the people who remain most critical in constitutional governance; the institutions of authority, such as the legislature, executive and judiciary, will function in accordance with the constitutional stipulations, provided they are made to function in keeping with the fundamental constitutional values.

---

[7] Ibid., p. 38.
[8] Ibid., p. 38.
[9] Rajendra Prasad, 26 November, 1949, *Constituent Assembly Debates*, Book No. 5, p. 993.
[10] BR Ambedkar, 25 November 1949, *Constituent Assembly Debates*, Book No. 5, p. 975.

II

There were serious differences of opinion among the members on whether the Constituent Assembly had the right to draft a constitution for sovereign India. The argument was defended by suggesting that (a) it was not representative in character since the Assembly was constituted by restricted franchise and (b) it was convened not by the national or any provincial assemblies but by the British government who regarded it merely as a conference of the delegates of the major political parties. It was, thus, not surprising that MA Jinnah, the architect of Pakistan, never recognized the Assembly as a sovereign body capable of producing a constitution for the country; the situation was further complicated by the decision of a section of the Muslim League not to participate in the proceedings of the Assembly. According to an estimate, only about 10 per cent of the Indians voted in the 1946 provincial elections, as voting right was based on property and educational qualifications. The chief commissioners' provinces and excluded areas within the Governors' provinces were not allowed to participate in the election; only half of the members who came from the princely states were elected from their legislatures and the remaining half was nominated by the ruler. In the light of the methods of the composition of the Assembly, the argument that it was an elitist forum gains credibility.

The issue was raised by several members by highlighting that the Assembly lacked legitimacy to produce a constitution for independent India since it was not representative of the people for whom the constitution was to be prepared. One of the first salvos was hurled by Damodar Swarup Seth of United Provinces. He believed that 'a constitution-making body of a free country should be able to claim that it represents the will of the entire people of that country. [Since the Assembly] cannot claim to represent the whole country, it has not right whatsoever to embark on this exercise'. Elaborating his point of view, he further mentioned:

> At most it can claim to represent 15 per cent of the population of India who had elected the members to the provincial legislatures. The election too, by virtue of which the members of this Assembly are here, was not a direct one; they are here by virtue of indirect election. In these circumstances, when 85 per cent of the people of the country are not represented in the House and when they have no voice here, it will in my opinion a very great mistake to say that the House is competent to frame a Constitution for the whole country.[11]

The argument was very clear: the Constituent Assembly lacked the legitimacy to articulate the voice of the country because of the immanent limitations due to the way it was constituted. Since it was not representative of the majority of the people, the entire exercise was dubbed as 'un-democratic and elitist'. Hence it deserved to be scrapped, as Seth further argued by underlining 'the unrepresentative character of the Assembly'. The contention did not, however, persuade the majority of the members. Challenging Seth, Bal Krishna Sharma of United Provinces questioned the fundamental premise of the statement made by his colleague, Seth. According to him:

> The argument that we are the representative of fifteen percent of the population and that the representatives of eighty-five percent of the population are not with us and therefore we do

[11] Damodar Swarup Seth (United Provinces), 5 November 1948, *Constituent Assembly Debates*, Book No. 2, p. 212.

> not have the right to make the Constitution is a fallacious one because (a) nowhere in the world can a model constitution be constituted ... and (b) we are the representatives of the will, emotions and ambitions of the people, and in this capacity representing the whole of India; we are framing the constitution on this basis which is not representation on mere numbers.[12]

The crux of the argument hinges on the fact that the representativeness of the Assembly cannot be conceptualized in absolute terms; it has to be assessed with reference to the context in which the Assembly was constituted. Despite not being representative in contemporary terms, the fact that the Assembly upheld the popular zeal and aspirations had supported its claim of being representative of the people. Furthermore, this was the pattern that was followed in the preparation of other democratic constitutions. By drawing attention to the way the American Constitution was produced in the 1786 Philadelphia Conference, BR Ambedkar strongly refuted the charge of his colleagues who strove to undermine the endeavour by saying that since 'the Constitution has been framed by the people who are not the true representative of the general masses ... it will neither be accepted by them nor will work permanently'.[13] For Ambedkar, the argument was without substance, as he defended by comparing the deeds of the US Constitution-makers with those of India's Constituent Assembly. He mentioned:

> As most members know that the Constitution of the United States of America ... was drafted by a very small body [comprising] representatives from 13 States [who] met in a small conference in Philadelphia. Therefore if these 13 representatives say that what they did was in the name of the people, on their authority, basing on it their sovereignty, ... I personally myself do not understand unless a man was on absolute pedant, that a body of people 292 in number represent this vast continent, in their representative capacity, could not say that they are acting in the name of the people.[14]

Ambedkar defended the point of the Constituent Assembly being representative in character on the basis of his faith in one of the core principles of representation being practised in indirect democracy, which proclaims that the representatives represent those who elected them. Conceptually, this is valid since this was perhaps the best possible option available at that particular historical juncture. It is true that the Assembly members were elected by a very limited franchise, though they were ideologically tuned to India's Independence; hence they appeared to have had the legitimacy to represent the rest of the countrymen. By referring to the Philadelphia Conference that framed the American Constitution, he reinforced his argument to confirm that what the Constituent Assembly did was not an exception but conformed to the pattern. There was possibly a personal aspect to his argument: he did not want to miss this opportunity to create a liberal framework of constitutional governance which, he strongly felt, was necessary in a society heavily prejudiced against the so-called untouchables due to their social origin. With a liberal constitution in place, this could be stopped once and for all. Hence, not only did he challenge the efforts towards undermining the entire exercise of the Assembly for allegedly being unrepresentative, he also created a

---

[12] Bal Krishna Sharma (United Provinces), 5 November 1948, *Constituent Assembly Debates*, Book No. 2, pp. 214–15.
[13] Damodar Swarup Seth (United Provinces), 19 November 1949, *Constituent Assembly Debates*, Book No 5, p. 694.
[14] BR Ambedkar, 17 October 1949, *Constituent Assembly Debates*, Book No. 5, p. 455.

strong group within the House to defend his point of view. As a result, the voice that was raised against him lost its steam in no time.

III

The Constituent Assembly was convened on 9 December 1946. It was handicapped from the very beginning since the Muslim League decided to boycott the Assembly as it was contrary to the League's political objective of creating an independent state for the Muslims. The withdrawal of the League was a source of sadness, but did not seem to affect the strength of the mind that the framers had evinced. For them, it was a great responsibility that they were about to shoulder. Jawaharlal Nehru articulated the feeling by stating that

> we who meet here under a heavy sense of responsibility—responsibility not only because the task which we have undertaken is a difficult one or because we presume to represent vast numbers of people, but because we are building for the future and we want to make sure that that building has strong foundations, and because, above all, we are meeting at a time when a number of disruptive forces are working in India pulling us this way or that way, and because, inevitably and unfortunately, when such forces are at work, there is a great deal of passion and prejudices in the air and our whole minds may be affected by it. We should not be deflected from that vision of the future which we ought to have, in thinking of the present difficulties.[15]

Here too, Nehru set the tempo of the effort that was required to be undertaken for such a gigantic task. This was a task for the future of the nation and needed to be accomplished with great care. His was a persuasive speech that not only inspired the members but also clarified to them the nature of the responsibility that they were asked to shoulder. The first major step that the Assembly undertook was the adoption of the Objective Resolution which 'seeks to show how [the founding fathers] shall lead India to gain the objectives laid down in it [and] . . . also to give a live message to India and to the world at large to show [what they] have resolved to accomplish by framing a Constitution of their choice'.[16] The Resolution had eight interrelated parts, each focusing on critical aspects of collective existence which the constitution was meant to protect. Primarily, the Objective Resolution contained a list of exalted socio-economic goals that the framers so assiduously aspired to fulfil during the battle against colonialism and its aftermath. Tuned to 'the nation's dream and aspiration', the Resolution[17] runs as follows:

1. This Constituent Assembly declares its firm and solemn resolve to proclaim India as an independent Sovereign Republic and to draw up for her future governance a Constitution;
2. Wherein the territories that now comprise British India, the territories that now form the Indian States, and such other parts of India as are outside British India and the States as

[15] Jawaharlal Nehru, 28 April 1947, *Constituent Assembly Debates*, Book No. 1, pp. 374–75.
[16] Jawaharlal Nehru, 13 December 1946, *Constituent Assembly Debates*, Book No. 1, pp. 58–59.
[17] Ibid., p. 59.

well as such other territories as are willing to be constituted into the Independent Sovereign India, shall be a Union of them all; and

3. Wherein the said territories, whether with their present boundaries or with such others as may be determined by the Constituent Assembly and thereafter according to the Law of the Constitution, shall possess and retain the status of autonomous Units, together with residuary powers and exercise all powers and functions of government and administration, save and except such powers and functions as our vested in or assigned to the Union, or as are inherent or implied in the Union or resulting therefrom; and
4. Wherein all power and authority of the Sovereign Independent India, its constituent parts and organs of government, are derived from the people; and
5. Wherein shall be guaranteed and secured to all the people of India justice, social, economic and political; equality of status, of opportunity, and before the law; freedom to thought, expression, belief, faith, worship, vocation, association and action, subject to law and public morality; and
6. Wherein adequate safeguards shall be provided to the minorities, backward and tribal areas, and depressed and other backward classes; and
7. Whereby shall be maintained the integrity of the territory of the Republic and its sovereign rights on land, sea and air according to justice and the law of civilized nations; and
8. This ancient land attains its rightful and honoured place in the world and make its full and willing contribution to the promotion of world peace and the welfare of mankind.

Being the foundation of the discussion leading to the making of the constitution, the Objective Resolution has three major components. The first part relates to the aim of the exercise that the founding fathers were to undertake soon to draft a constitution for independent India. It is clearly articulated in the first point of the Resolution. The goal of the exercise was to, in other words, develop a solid foundation for India to grow as a sovereign republic. It is also interesting to note here that despite having agreed to be in the Commonwealth, the framers were influenced by the idea of republicanism, which means that the head of the State was to be elected. With their endorsement of republicanism, the founding fathers left no doubt that, unlike Australia or Canada, India would become a republic. Second, there is a categorical statement in Item Number 4 that the sovereign power rests with the people and all the institutions of governance derive their existence as part of India's constitutional democracy from the *demos*. Perfectly in tune with their commitment to democracy, the planners of the constitution affirmed their faith in people being the sole repository of substantial authority. Only then, a true democracy was likely to emerge, which would not be a mere copy of the available forms of democratic forms of government but an improvement, thus claimed Nehru who further argued that 'in any event whatever system of Government we may establish here must fit in with the temper of our people and be acceptable to them.'[18] It was further endorsed by Alladi Krishnaswami Ayyar, who reaffirmed the sentiment by saying that 'the constitution of sovereign independent India is the concrete expression of the will of the people of India as a whole conceived of as an organic entity . . . and the authority of the rulers can rest ultimately on will of the people concerned.'[19] Fundamental here is the idea that in a true democracy, the source of authority remains with the *demos* and that can never be wished away. The third aspect of the Resolution is about certain critical attributes of the democratic polity, which are distinctive and place the democratic form of governance in a different

[18] Ibid., p. 62.

[19] Alladi Krishnaswami Ayyar (Madras), 19 December 1946, *Constituent Assembly Debates*, Book No. 1, p. 142.

class altogether. The constitution was to secure justice to all regardless of one's social and economic locations and political predilections. In order to realize democracy in its undiluted form, the constitutional recognition of these values is of utmost importance. It was also hinted that mere codification of rules directed to fulfil the constitutional aims might not be an effective means unless they were endorsed by a supportive mindset. The apprehension was justified and GB Pant of United Provinces replied by saying that the elaborate constitutional provisions would, in the long run, create an environment for a conducive mindset to grow. The final component deals with the mechanism for protecting the minority rights, for the strength of a constitution is contingent on this aspect; if the constitution fails to safeguard the interests of the minorities, goes the argument, the claim that India is a democratic country will become a false one. As GB Pant expressed:

> The question of minorities everywhere looms large in constitutional discussions. Many a constitution has foundered on this rock. A satisfactory solution of questions pertaining to minorities will ensure the health, vitality and strength of the free State of India that will come into existence as a result of our discussion here. . . . So far, the minorities have been incited and have been influenced in a manner which has hampered the growth of cohesion and unity. But now it is necessary that new chapter should start and we should all realize our responsibility. Unless the minorities are fully satisfied, we cannot make any progress; we cannot even maintain peace in an undisturbed manner.[20]

The concern for the minorities seems to have assumed tremendous significance following (a) the endorsement of the Pakistan plan on the basis of the two-nation theory whereby Hindus and Muslims were projected as separate nations and (b) the withdrawal of the Muslims League from the Constituent Assembly since the Muslims felt that it was meant to frame a constitution for 'Hindu India'.

On the whole, the Objective Resolution are about an ideational concern which the founding fathers had shared with one another before they embarked on the gigantic task of preparing an acceptable constitution for India. There were serious difficulties: on the one hand, the unity of India as an independent polity was at stake, given the existence of many princely states which needed to be integrated with the mainland to make it a one unit; the feelings of the minorities were also to be assuaged, on the other, to make them feel being part of the country, not under compulsion but by being drawn to the ethos of Indian fraternity. The main concern of the founding fathers was to guarantee 'full freedom to its various sections to have themselves whatever administration they liked and . . . give them full freedom in their social and religious affairs'.[21] What is distinctive here is the fact that despite the agony of partition, the planners for India's constitution did not seem to nurture any ill-feelings towards the minorities; instead, they took upon themselves the responsibility of making the minorities feel comfortable in independent India since they, according to the planners, were as much a part of India as anybody else. The most revealing statement was made by S Radhakrishnan of United Provinces on 20 January 1947, who seems to have laid out a solid conceptual foundation in this regard by proclaiming that

> we are not here asking anything for a particular community or a privileged class, We are here working for the establishment of Swaraj for all the Indian people. It will be our endeavour to

[20] GB Pant (United Provinces), 24 January, 1947, *Constituent Assembly Debates*, Book No. 1, p. 331.

[21] PD Tandon (United Provinces), 13 December 1946, *Constituent Assembly Debates*, Book No. 1, pp. 66–67.

> abolish every vestige of despotism, every heir loom of inorganic tradition. We are here to bring about real satisfaction of the fundamental needs of the common man of this country, irrespective of race, religion and community. It is therefore essential that our bugle call, our trumpet-sound, must be clear, must give the people a sense of exhilaration, must give the suspicious and abstaining a sense of reassurance that we are here pledged to achieve full independence of India where no individual will suffer from undeserved want, where no group will be thwarted in the development of its cultural life.[22]

The constitution was not just about the rule of law but was also a tool for building an inclusive society in the real sense of the term. Keeping in view the obvious constraints due to India's socio-economic and political uncertainties following the 1947 Great Divide on the basis of unbridgeable communal schism, Radhakrishnan devoted his attention to address the individual wants as well as cultural alienation of a collectivity which, he felt, would provoke further cracks in India's socio-economic fabric.

In a nutshell, the Objective Resolution seem to have charted a specific course of action drawn on certain ideological preferences that the founding fathers articulated during their campaign against colonialism. For them, it was a great challenge since the constitution was to serve a future nation. Furthermore, that their goal was clearly futuristic also gave them an advantage of not being governed by immediate compulsions; it means that since the Assembly members were placed in circumstances where they had no axe to grind, they had an obvious advantage which allowed them to be absolutely insulated from the petty or partisan aims. BR Ambedkar, thus, emphasized that 'the Constituent Assembly in making a constitution has no partisan motive. Beyond securing a good and workable constitution it has no axe to grind. In considering the articles of the constitution, it has no eye on getting through a particular measure.'[23] The impartiality that the Constituent Assembly had shown was simply impossible for the future parliaments, since they had to address the partisan interests of those who chose them as their representative. As Ambedkar clarified:

> The future parliament, if it met as a Constituent Assembly, its members will be acting as partisans seeking to carry amendments to the Constitution to facilitate the passing of party measures which they have failed to get through parliament by reason of some article of the Constitution which has acted as an obstacle in their way. . . . That is the difference between the Constituent Assembly and the future parliament. That is the reason why the Constituent Assembly though elected on limited franchise can be trusted to pass the Constitution by simple majority and why the parliament though elected on adult suffrage cannot be trusted with same power to amend it.[24]

The argument has substance. The founding fathers were entrusted with the task of developing a constitutional design for future India. Given their obvious suffering during colonialism, it was quite natural for them to create a system that would work for the country as a whole. In other words, in their efforts to build a system of governance for independent India, they acted like statesmen who were charged with a historical responsibility of modelling India as a democratic polity. The Objective Resolution and Nehru's elaborate

[22] S Radhakrishnan (United Provinces), 20 January 1947, *Constituent Assembly Debates*, Book No. 1, pp. 269–70.

[23] BR Ambedkar, 4 November 1948, *Constituent Assembly Debates*, Book No. 2, p. 43.

[24] Ibid., pp. 43–44.

exposition of what India, as an independent nation, should aspire for left enough ideological inputs for the members in the Assembly to build their arguments to their favour. Since the Assembly had 'no axe to grind', as Ambedkar mentioned, it was possible for the members to rise above partisan interests while being engaged in formulating appropriate constitutional provisions for a stable political order in future India.

IV

While Nehru laid down the ideological foundation of the constitution, BR Ambedkar created a blueprint by identifying the areas of concerns that needed attention. In a detailed speech on 4 November 1948, he elaborated both the form of government and the form of the constitution that India was going to have after the conclusion of the deliberations in the Constituent Assembly. At the outset, he explained that the constitution was framed by taking into account the inputs from various committees that were appointed to look into the specific areas of socio-economic concerns. The draft constitution consisted of 315 Articles and three Schedules which made Ambedkar comment that 'the Constitution of no country could be found to be so bulky as the Draft Constitution'.[25] It is true that the 1950 Constitution of India is perhaps the most exhaustive constitution, framed by taking into consideration the best constitutional practices that were followed in other constitutional democracies in the world.

Ambedkar's speech focuses on two important aspects of the constitution: (a) the form of the government and (b) the form of the constitution. As regards the first, namely the form of the government, Ambedkar categorically suggested that Constitution of India favoured a government, the head of which happens to be the President. Unlike the American presidential form of government, the Indian system approximates to that of the British system, which means that the head of the government is a titular head like the British monarch. There is, however, a difference: the Indian President was to be elected, unlike the British head of the government who holds the post hereditarily. The President is, according to Ambedkar,

> the head of the State and not of the Executive. He represents the Nation but does not rule the Nation. He is the symbol of the nation. His place in the administration is that of a ceremonial device on a seal by which the nation's decision are made known.[26]

Therefore, constitutionally, the President is the head of the government, which means that government functions are carried out in his name though he/she does not have substantial power because he/she is bound by his/her ministers; the duly elected government cannot be dismissed as long as it commands a majority in the Parliament.

The second important part of the speech is about the form of the constitution. In a very candid way, Ambedkar elaborated the features of the constitution. First, it is a federal constitution with dual sets of government, one at the union level and the other at the state level. According to him, the proposed constitution is 'a federal constitution in as much as it establishes what may be called a Dual Polity [consisting of] the Union at the Centre and the States at the periphery each endowed with sovereign powers to be

[25] Ibid., p. 31.

[26] Ibid., p. 32.

exercised in the field assigned to them respectively by the Constitution'.[27] This is a dual polity with a single citizenship which entails that 'every Indian has the same rights of citizenship, no matter in what State he resides'.[28] In a stark contrast to the American system of constitutional governance, the Indian version

> can be both unitary as well as federal according to the requirements of time and circumstances. In normal times, it is framed to work as a federal system. But in times of war, it is so designed as to make it work as though it was a unitary system. Once the President issues a Proclamation of [Emergency] which he is authorised to do under the Constitution, the whole scene can become transformed and the State becomes a unitary state.... Such a power of converting a unitary State no federation possesses. This is one point of difference between the Federation proposed in the Draft Constitution, and also other Federations we know of.[29]

According to Ambedkar, the draft constitution justified the conversion of a federal state into a unitary one since it was needed to address the untoward circumstances; otherwise, it was absolutely federal which means that '(a) any invasion by the federal government in the field assigned to the States and vice versa is a breach of the Constitution, and (b) such breach is a justiciable matter to be determined by the judiciary only'.[30] That India was to be a genuine federation was reinforced by the means and methods whereby India will have a federation and, at the same time, will have uniformity in all the basic matters which are essential to maintain the unity of the country. The means adopted by the draft constitution are three: '(a) a single judiciary, (b) uniformity in fundamental laws, civil and criminal, and (c) a common All-India Civil Service to man important posts'.[31] Structurally, the proposed constitution has both the elements of being a federal and unitary constitution at the same time. This is a unique feature that was justified by reference to the context in which it was being framed and also the politico-ideological preferences (which were tilted in favour of the Westminster form of constitutional democracy) of the founding fathers.

What is most important in any stable constitutional democracy is, as Ambedkar endorsed, the spirit of constitutional morality which is articulated as reverence to those critical ideological values which are fundamental to a constitution. Without constitutional morality in place, no constitution succeeds in fulfilling its ideological mission. Furthermore, there should be a compatibility between the form of administration and the form of the constitution. According to him, 'form of administration must be appropriate to and in the same sense as the form of the Constitution'[32]; otherwise, it is perfectly possible, warned Ambedkar, 'to pervert the Constitution, without changing its form by merely changing the form of the administration and make it inconsistent and opposed to the spirit of the Constitution'.[33] This was a clear possibility in the absence of constitutional morality which was not instinctively formed but 'has to be cultivated',[34] as Ambedkar strongly felt. A difficult task indeed, because 'democracy in India is a top-dressing on an Indian soil which is essentially undemocratic'.[35] What is emphasized here is the fact that

---

27 Ibid., p. 33.
28 Ibid., p. 34.
29 Ibid., pp. 34–35.
30 Ibid., p. 35.
31 Ibid., p. 37.
32 Ibid., p. 38.
33 Ibid., p. 38.
34 Ibid., p. 38.
35 Ibid., p. 38.

without developing a democratic mindset appreciative of constitutional morality, no system of constitutional democracy can succeed.

One of the indices of constitutional democracy, according to Ambedkar, is the safeguards provided for minorities. Appreciating the members of the Constituent Assembly for having devised a set of safeguards for them, he further noted that the majority needed to be trained to accept the minorities as integral to a multicultural India. Unless the minorities were taken into confidence, the aspirational dream of the founding fathers of making India a true constitutional democracy would become futile, felt Ambedkar. On the basis of the analysis of the events in Europe, he warned that since 'minorities are an explosive force which, if it erupts, can blow up the whole fabric of the State'.[36] What was thus required, as Ambedkar had elaborated, was to develop a mindset that is appreciative of the minorities as a significant part of India's existence as a democratic polity. Drawing upon his conceptualization of social endosmosis (which means intermixing between majority and minority, regardless of social origin, economic strength and political preferences), he insisted that it was for the communal majority

> to realize its duty not to discriminate against minorities. Whether the minorities will continue or will vanish must depend upon this habit of the majority. The moment the majority loses the habit of discriminating against the minority, the minorities can have no ground to exist. They will vanish.[37]

Ambedkar's concern for the minority needs to be contextualized. Following the acceptance of the partition of India between two independent dominions, it was imperative for the founding fathers to be sensitive to the minority issue. It was clear that the Pakistan campaign gained momentum not only because it was engineered by the Muslim League leadership but also because it received spontaneous support from Muslims who seem to have been alienated from the majority Hindus, especially in Bengal and Punjab. In order not to escalate the communal strife, it was judicious on the part of the majority, felt Ambedkar, to address the concerns of the minority, which would complement the nationalist effort towards building a stable constitutional democracy in India.

With Ambedkar setting the tone of the discussion, there were other members in the Assembly who also came out with their own assessment of the draft constitution. For M Ananthasayanam Ayyangar, it was 'an absolutely democratic Constitution [because] it vests the sovereignty of the people and enables them to continue to exercise that sovereignty in full'.[38] With the abolition of untouchability, the Constitution of India endorsed the principles of social justice, and hence 'there is no discrimination between one individual and another due to their birth'.[39] In response to the accusation that the proposed constitution was 'a mere copy of the 1935 Government of India Act', Ayyangar refuted the charge by saying that it was framed to control 'a subject nation', whereas the draft constitution was meant to realize the democratic aspiration of a free nation.

The Gandhians were unhappy with the Constitution because it was not based on what the Mahatma stood for. While reviewing the Constitution, K Hanumanthaiya of Mysore argued that 'we wanted the music of Veena or Sitar, but here we have the music of an English band. That was because our constitution

---

[36] Ibid., p. 39.
[37] Ibid., p. 39.
[38] M Ananthasayanam Ayyangar (Madras), 18 November 1949, *Constituent Assembly Debates*, Book No. 5, p. 662.
[39] Ibid., p. 662.

makers were educated that way'.[40] Being critical of the Constitution, which was not based on Gandhian principles, he further noted that

> the constitutional structure ought to be broad-based . . . [and] should be built from the bottom and should taper right up to the top. What has been done is just reverse. The pyramid has been reversed [which led to a situation in which] . . . the initiative from the Provinces and State and from the people has been taken away and all power has been concentrated in the Centre. This is exactly the kind of Constitution Mahatma Gandhi did not want and did not envisage.[41]

The Constitution, in Hanumanthaiya's opinion, was neither federal nor democratic; it was centralized and appreciative of unitary tendencies which, he apprehended, would harm the country in the long run. The top-down form of administration that the Constitution favoured was not at all appropriate for India, given the diversity that was embedded. In its place, what was required was decentralized administration in which people from the grassroots, from all walks of life, could participate, something that Gandhi always insisted for realizing democracy in governance.

To conclude, a perusal of the debates in the Constituent Assembly confirms that it was Ambedkar who had prevailed over his colleagues in so far as the nature of the proposed Constitution of India was concerned. Not only did he play a critical role in its making, he also steered the discussion in the Assembly by setting its tone in accordance with his firm belief in the fundamental principles of liberal democracy of the Western variety. The Assembly debates also underline that it was divided between the Gandhians and their bête noire, following the viewpoints that Ambedkar, Nehru and their colleagues endorsed. It is also true that the Gandhians failed to persuade the Assembly to accept their specific suggestions based on Gandhi's insistence on making the village as the basic unit of governance. Nonetheless, the fact that Part IV of the Constitution of India contains some of the Gandhian ideas, especially those regarding the panchayati raj governance at the grassroots, also reveals that their effort was not entirely futile; the constitutionalization of the Gandhian mode of rural governance in 1992, following the adoption, particularly of the Seventy-Third Amendment Act, is a further testimony to the fact that what the Gandhians had initiated in the Constituent Assembly was not wasted but had set in motion the processes for democratic decentralization as perhaps an appropriate model of governance at the grassroots.

V

This book is not just a study of the Constitution of India, it is also an attempt to analyse the processes of constitutionalizing India. In other words, it is argued here that the provisions of the Constitution do not make sense unless they are conceptualized in the perspective in which they are articulated in the form of legal stipulations. The idea that is being conveyed here is the need for comprehending the actual provisions with reference to the processes in which they are shaped in directional terms. This is also a very complex task, for it involves a careful reading of multiple social, political, economic and, of course, ideological inputs, which were articulated in the form of provisions in the Constitution of India. It is true that finally these provisions were given a specific shape by the members of the Constituent Assembly after having

[40] K Hanumanthaiya (Mysore), 17 November 1949, *Constituent Assembly Debates*, Book No. 5, p. 616.
[41] Ibid., pp. 616–67.

intensive deliberations on the floor of the Assembly. The process that followed was elaborate, since the members dealt with each and every aspect of governance in independent India.

The Constituent Assembly debates are a useful source to understand the mind of the constitution-makers. There is no doubt that their being born and raised in colonized India had its obvious impact on how they conceptualized the design of governance, which was appropriate to realize their exalted socio-economic and political goals. Moreover, the fact that a section of the Muslim League did not participate in the deliberations was also a source of weakness for the Assembly; one point of view remained unrepresented. And, the fact that there was hardly a serious disagreement among the members also support the contention that the Constitution of India is an offshoot of consensus and accommodation. On the surface, this may seem so; but, a careful reading of the deliberations reveals that it was not so because there were occasions when the opponents were either silenced or not allowed to press an argument beyond a point. Several amendments were rejected, not because they were constitutionally untenable but because the dominant section within the Congress seemed to have held contrary points of view. Hence, it is fair to argue that the Constitution of India represented the views of the majority of the Assembly members who, in their best of intentions, contributed to its making in little less than three years during the most tumultuous period of India's political history.

This book endeavours to capture the complex processes leading to the making and finalization of the Constitution of India. The purpose is thus two-fold: along with a detailed analysis of the provisions, the aim is also to understand how they evolved to attain their present form. In three interrelated sections, the task is pursued and accomplished. Comprising four chapters, Section A deals with those foundational values that informed the founding fathers while being engaged in framing the Constitution of India. Chapter 1, thus, dwells on the politico-ideological roots which were critical to the framers; it is argued here that the 1950 Constitution of India represents a combination of efforts that had begun long before the Constituent Assembly met in 1949. A follow-up of this chapter is Chapter 2, which dwells on the principles that are enshrined in Part IV of the Constitution, enumerating Directive Principles of State Policy. Chapter 3 focuses on the distinctive nature of the Constitution with reference to the values that are pre-eminent; this is also a narrative in which an attempt is made to highlight the distinctive politico-ideological characteristics of the Constitution. Chapter 4 is a summary of the discussion of the issues that figured in these chapters, done through the reference to the basic features of the Constitution. On the whole, the aim in Section A is to acquaint the readers with those driving ideological forces that remain critical in nurturing constitutional democracy in India, appreciating the rule of law and due processes.

Section B provides further elaboration of the aforementioned concern by dwelling on how the vision of the founding fathers was articulated in the form of provisions in the constitution. There are 12 chapters, each with a distinctive focus. Since ethics in governance was a major concern of the framers, it is necessary to deal with this aspect at the very outset in this section. Chapter 5 is about ethics in governance. How is this articulated in the Constitution and also in parliamentary practices in general? The concern is to develop value-based politics in India. Chapter 6 extends the discussion by an in-depth analysis of the basic structure of the debate with reference to the multiple judicial pronouncements, especially since 1973. The chapter draws on the idea that basic structure is critical to the survival of the Constitution. For a democratic polity, citizenship is an important area of concern. How the framers address this issue is the crux of Chapter 7, which needs to be read along with Chapter 8 that deals with language, another area of concern in a multicultural society like India. Besides drawing upon the constitutional provisions relating to citizenship in India and the language issue, these two chapters also concentrate on other related legislative interventions that were made to ensure India's distinctive socio-cultural characteristics. Chapter 9 is about reservation, which is also a tool for social justice in a context where socio-economic discrimination is an age-old phenomenon. In order to address gender inequality and injustice, several steps were taken and are being continuously pursued in India. Chapter 10 is an endeavour towards both conceptualizing and comprehending the issues that are critical for gender justice and equality. Chapters 11 and 12 provide an elaborate discussion of secularism by making reference to its historical antecedents and also the relevant judicial pronouncements. For the framers, it was an obvious choice to sustain India's multicultural persona; it was endorsed by the judiciary in a number of judgements, which reinforces the argument that secularism continues to remain an area of concern. That federalism was an obvious choice for the founding fathers was evident in the discussion in the Constituent Assembly. Chapter 13 discusses the provisions relating to federalism and also those pertinent judicial verdicts that reiterate the concerns of the founding fathers and also those who presided over India's destiny as an independent polity. Chapter 14 concentrates on emergency provisions which were incorporated in the Constitution to maintain constitutional democracy in India. These provisions are exceptional in character and can be invoked only under exceptional circumstances in which the constitutional fabric is seriously challenged and constitutional values are threatened to be bypassed. Chapter 15 deals with Article 370 of the Constitution of India; the purpose here is to understand the distinctive texture of India's federalism through a reference to Article 370, which was meant to provide constitutional guarantee for Jammu and Kashmir, in view of the peculiar historical circumstances in which this princely state of the British India became part of India after the British withdrawal. One of the important means of sustaining constitutional democracy is to hold elections at regular intervals and this is the concern of Chapter 16. By focusing on the Election Commission of India, this chapter provides a threadbare discussion of an institution that holds a pre-eminent position in India's constitutional democracy.

The last section, Section C, is about those instruments that the Constitution recognizes as integral to the maintenance of constitutional democracy in India. The section has five interdependent chapters beginning with Chapter 17 that deals with relevant constitutional provisions for the judiciary. Being the custodian of the Constitution, the judiciary in India, the Supreme Court of India, the High Courts in the provinces and other lower courts play a very laudable role in sustaining the constitutionality of the Constitution. Dealing with the amendment procedures, Chapter 18 makes an attempt to comprehend the relevant constitutional provisions and their manifestations in a series of steps that were undertaken to address the newer socio-political concerns. In Chapters 19 and 20, an elaborate discussion is made to understand two important institutions of constitutional governance in India: the role of the Comptroller and Auditor General as a watchdog of constitutional democracy has been dealt with in Chapter 19, while Chapter 20 makes an attempt to understand the role of Governor as a constitutional agency, responsible for maintaining 'federal balance' within the well-set constitutional parameters. The last chapter, Chapter 21, is about grassroots democracy. Here, too, an endeavour is made to conceptualize grassroots governance in India with reference to the arrangement that the Constitution prefers. By dwelling on the distinctive role and nature of the panchayati raj governance, the chapter also places the experiment in the wider context of constitutional democracy in India.

Written in a textbook mould, the book is both a study of the Constitution of India with reference to the provisions of the Constitution and an effort at conceptualizing constitutional democracy in India with reference to the role that the Constitution plays. What is unique in this exercise is also the endeavour to develop two fundamental arguments that are useful to grasp the distinctive nature of constitutional democracy in India. By dwelling on the historical evolution of constitutional democracy in India, the book makes the first argument by suggesting that the peculiar texture of India's constitutional democracy needs to be understood with reference to how it evolved first in the context of British colonialism and later when India became politically independent. The second argument draws our attention to the distinctive structural characteristics of the Constitution of India, which is also organic to the prevalent socio-economic and political circumstances. As the Constitution provides a framework for governance, the aim here is to understand the Constitution not merely as a compilation of rules and regulations but also as a living organism being continuously adjusted to the rapidly changing milieu, in which newer ideas, demands and concerns are being articulated through deliberations, negotiations and, of course, contestations.

There is a methodological issue which needs to be spelt out to situate the book in the wider theoretical concern for constitutional democracy as a persuasive conceptual category. The aforementioned arguments are made and pursued by reference to the processes leading to the framing of the 1950 Constitution of India. This is one aspect though. The other aspect dwells on how the Constitution responds to the changing socio-economic milieu, which allows us to look into the judicial pronouncements on major socio-economic issues. For instance, our understanding of reservation in India or secularism shall remain skewed unless one has a holistic understanding of these issues with reference to both the constitutional provisions and the judicial verdicts. Each chapter of the book is structured accordingly. This is methodologically useful, for it will enable us to comprehend the constitutional design that has evolved in India both by drawing upon the provisions and also by judicial interventions as and when the court of law is asked to ascertain justiciability of legislative decrees. On the whole, the book is an attempt to understand the constitutional stipulations as well as their unfolding in the context of rapidly transforming socio-economic circumstances in a globalizing India.

Section A
FOUNDATIONAL VALUES

Introduction to Section A

A constitution is an ideational project in which ideas get articulated in various provisions, which are primarily directional. The ideas have multiple sources: they are both indigenous and derivative. As the chapters in this section show, the 1950 Constitution of India draws on the core principles of the philosophy of Enlightenment as much as those being derivative of the indigenous intellectual tradition. It is therefore not surprising that in contrast with BR Ambedkar, who insisted on making individual the basic unit of governance, the Gandhians argued strongly in favour of establishing the village-centric system of governance. Arguments and counter-arguments made by the members in the Constituent Assembly provide useful inputs to understand how, finally, Ambedkar's preferences were privileged over those of the Gandhians. Ambedkar had won and the Gandhians failed to mobilize enough support for village swaraj. With the passing of the Seventy-Third Amendment Act in 1992, which constitutionalized the Gandhian idea of panchayati raj governance at the grassroots, the Constitution endorsed the scheme which was not accepted by the founding fathers at the dawn of India's Independence.

This section is thus very important. With four interrelated chapters, it deals with the evolution of the constitutional practices, norms and values over a historical period of time. The primary aim here is to acquaint the readers with those relevant ideas that seem to have informed the processes leading to the making of the Constitution in 1949. Furthermore, the section also dwells on the principles constituting the Directive Principles of State Policy (Part IV), which played a crucial role in charting out a completely different constitutional path for India by adequately emphasizing some of the neglected socio-economic values towards building 'a fair' society. Chapter 4 is a summary in the sense that it puts in one place the critical features of the Constitution which need to be kept in view to understand its distinct texture.

Chapter 1

Historical Roots of the Constitution of India

Learning Objectives

- To understand the 1950 Constitution of India with reference to its conceptual roots and historical antecedents
- To identify the important benchmark events that critically influenced the Constitution
- To assess the nature of the Constitution in the light of the changing socio-economic milieu

The 1950 Constitution of India is drawn on the fundamental liberal values which flourished during the long colonial rule. Liberal ideas were articulated both by the British liberals and their Indian counterparts. While the former was paternalistic in their attitude, the latter held liberalism as perhaps the only empowering ideological design of governance which was appropriate for India. In contemporary scholarship, three important types of liberalism have been identified: colonial liberalism, nationalist liberalism and radical liberalism. Drawn by their paternalistic concern for the colonized, the colonial liberals contributed to the consolidation of a system of governance which would prepare Indians to appreciate rule-driven administration. Although they differed in their assessment of the situation in India, they agreed that colonialism was beneficial to the rise of India as a well-governed polity in due course. While they strongly felt that representative democracy was certain to flourish in Australia and America given identical civilizational identity, India was simply incapable of self-government, argued one of most influential liberal thinkers, JS Mill, because of the lack of social homogeneity. Nonetheless, liberal ideas of limited government and the rule of law, equality before law and education as a means of social empowerment were gradually introduced in India in the wake of the colonial rule. A careful study of the British rule in its initial phase suggests liberalism created a space for the growing involvement of the Indians in administration. Two substantial events changed the course of colonialism: (a) the founding of the universities of Calcutta, Madras and Bombay helped develop an articulate opinion of the educated Indians on the British rule. It captured the growing discontent among the Indians who always remained, for obvious reasons, peripheral in administration. (b) The inauguration of the Indian National Congress in 1885 created a new platform to ventilate the grievances of the ruled. This also became a forum for the Indians to articulate demands for better rule. The outcome of which was the 1892 Indian Councils Act. As the Act underlines, its aim was

> to widen and expand the functions of the Government of India, and to give further opportunities to the non-official and native elements in Indian society to take part in the work of the

> Government, and in that way, to lend official recognition to that remarkable development both of political interest and political capacity that had been visible among the higher classes of Indian society since the Government of India was taken over by the Crown in 1858.[1]

The Act provided for the enhanced membership of the Councils. It was mandatory for the government to consult the representative bodies and institutions, approved by the government, before selecting nominees for the Councils. Besides legislative powers, the Councils were also empowered to pull the Executive on financial matters though it had no power to either revise or reject decisions on this matter. However, the growing weightage of the Councils is indicative of a sea change in the colonial rule. As Morley, the Secretary of State, articulated, 'there are two rival schools of thought, one of which believes that better government of Indian depends on efficiency, and that efficiency is, in fact, the end of British rule in India. The other school, while not neglecting efficiency, looks also to what is called political concessions'.[2] This declaration laid one of the foundational principles of the British administration in India. As a first step, a Royal Commission was appointed in 1907 to look into the administration that seemed to have lost its viability in the context of growing discontent among the ruled. The aim of the Commission was to provide an administration which was adapted to the changed social, economic and political realities of India. While recommending the corrective measures, the Commission was guided by the following factors: (a) the difficulties of ruling the vast sub-continent from a single headquarter and the inevitable failure in the statesmanship and efficiency in administration; (b) the difficulties of applying uniform schemes of development for the provinces which are socio-culturally diverse; (c) to instil a sense of responsibility among those engaged in provincial and local administration and (d) to strengthen the colonial rule by educating people in the values of strong administration. On the basis of the recommendation of the Commission, a bill was introduced in 1908 which became the 1909 Morley–Minto Reforms. As a political scheme seeking to strengthen colonial rule in India, the 1909 Act introduced a profound change with long term effects in representation of communities in Councils. This is the beginning of a trend that gradually unfolded, as will be shown further by dwelling on the legislative steps that gave impetus to the steady growth and consolidation of representative institutions in India. By drawing on the ideational inputs that inform the processes of constitutionalizing India, the chapter substantiates the argument that the Constitution of India is an outcome of a long-drawn battle of ideas in which both the colonialists and their opponents had participated. The chapter is thus both an endorsement of the argument as well as an endeavour to pursue further research in constitutionalizing India.

Nationalist and Radical Liberals

Liberalism reached the Indian shore through the colonial liberals who however had strong reservation about its application in India. Nonetheless, they inspired the early nationalists who were politically baptised through those texts which articulated the liberal approach to politics and governance. Liberalism gained hegemony in part because of 'the Anglicization of public life'.[3] The political ideas of JS Mill, Herbert Spencer,

[1] The text of the Act is available at http://www.sdstate.edu/projectsouthasia/loader.cfm?csModule=security/getfile&PageID=861833 (accessed 25 May 2016).

[2] The statement of John Morley is quoted from DA Hamer, *John Morley: Liberal Intellectual in Politics* (Oxford: Oxford University Press, 1968), p. 111.

[3] CA Bayly, *Recovering Liberties: Indian Thought in the age of liberalism and empire* (Cambridge: Cambridge University Press, 2012), p. 346.

August Comte, among others were spread to the English educated classes through English and later vernacular newspapers, books and pamphlets. The influence was so well-entrenched that even the Indian National Congress had no qualms to openly appreciate the British rule because it purportedly drew on the fundamental ethos of liberalism. In its eleventh annual session, Indian National Congress thus declared:

> To England, we look for inspiration and guidance [because] English history has taught us those principles of freedom which we cherish. . . . We have benefitted by the education that we receive and by the material civilization which annihilates time and distance, and brings us together to feel a common interest in our own elevation under a vivifying influence of a literature and a history, the like of which the world has not known in the past for its triumphs in the emancipation of mankind.[4]

However, the delegates were highly disappointed since colonialism in India had already manifested in its most brutal form. Hence, they made an appeal to the rulers 'to gradually change the character of her rule in India, to liberalize it, . . . so that in the fullness of time, India may find itself in the great confederacy of free states, English in their origin, English in their character [and] English in their institutions'.[5] So, the main concern was to imbibe the spirit of liberalism in governance. Their main ideal was their representation in the legislature. The demand was continuously made by the Congress since it would allow the Indians to voice their concerns in legislative forums. While justifying the demand, Dadabhai Naoroji, a prominent moderate liberal, strongly argued for expansion of representation to include Indians in the legislature. As he stated:

> What makes us proud to be British subjects, what attaches us to this foreign rule with deeper loyalty than even our own past Native rule, is the fact that Britain is the parent of free and representative government, and, that we, as her subjects and children, are entitled to inherit the great blessing of freedom and representation. . . Britain would never be a slave and could not, in her very nature and instinct, make a slave. Her greatest glory is freedom and representation, and as her subjects, we shall have these blessed gifts.[6]

What Naoroji had initiated was reinforced by his successors, such as Pherozeshah Mehta (1845–1915), Surendranath Banerjea (1848–1925) and GK Gokhale (1866–1915), who also insisted that institutions of representation were seen as the *sine-qua-non* of human freedom. They were also persuaded to believe that it was possible for them to express their views freely in public forums since colonial rulers drew on liberalism. 'It is under the civilizing rule of the Queen and the people of England', thus argued Naoroji, 'that we regularly meet, unhindered by none and are freely allowed to speak our minds without the least fear and least hesitation'.[7] In a similar vein, he further admired British rule as follows:

> We understand the benefits [that] the English rule has conferred upon us; that we thoroughly appreciate the education that has been given to us, the new light which has been poured upon

[4] 'Report of the Eleventh Indian National Congress', held at Poona in 1895, p. 3. http://dspace.gipe.ac.in/xmlui/handle/10973/17997 (accessed 20 March 2017).

[5] 'Report of the Eleventh Indian National Congress', p. 13.

[6] Chunilal Lallubhai Parekh, ed., *Essays, Speeches, Addresses and Writings of the Honourable Dadabhai Naoroji* (Bombay: Caxton Printing Works, 1887), p. 321. https://ia802608.us.archive.org/30/items/essaysspeechesa00paregoog/essaysspeechesa00paregoog.pdf (accessed 19 August 2016).

[7] Parekh, *Essays, Speeches, Addresses and Writings . . .*, p. 332.

> us, turning us from darkness into light and teaching us the new lesson that kings are made for the people and not people for their kings; and this new lesson we have learned amidst the darkness of Asiatic despotism only by the light of free English civilization.[8]

A careful reading of the early nationalists' intervention reveals that they upheld liberalism to the hilt since they were convinced of its utility as an empowering ideology for the colonized. Hence they insisted on constitutionalism, gradual reforms and an appeal to the English traditions which helped build the liberal ethos as integral to governance in Britain. The arguments that the early nationalists made in favour of liberalism had two complementary components: on the one hand, what it entailed was their concern for political transformation following the fundamental principles of liberalism; their critique of the British rule in India was, on the other hand, drawn on the fact that it had failed, to a significant extent, 'to live up to its own mission as the bearer of liberal and modern institutions and values in India'.[9] They were appalled, in other words, because 'Britain was failing to complete the appointed role, as evidenced by its selfish economic and political policies in India, and by its distrust of the very class that it had brought forth'.[10] What was basic to their arguments was the effort to articulate liberalism in spirit and content and they felt discontented since the British rule in India was not adequately liberal.

Notwithstanding the debilitating effect of colonialism in India, the early liberals seem to have found the British rule most conducive for the growth of a liberal society in India. In their perception, representative institutions and free press were always identified as critical to the material and moral progress of a country which was plagued by archaic customs and primordial social values. As Surendranath Banerjea noted, 'the three great boons which we have received from the British Government are High Education, the gift of a free press and local Self-Government. . . . But High Education is the most prized, the most deeply cherished of them all. It is High Education which has made local Self-Government the success that it is admitted to be. It is again High Education which has elevated the tone of the Indian press'.[11] In the creation of a liberal India, the institutional changes were as much critical as the change of the prevalent mindset that had undergone a massive transformation with the introduction of English education, the early nationalists claimed. By recognizing the immense utility of English education, the Deccan Sabha thus exhorted that 'the greatest gift [of the British rule] has been to bring within our reach the blessing and benefit of English education which has helped us to avail of and assimilate the civilizing elements which accompany and distinguish [the rule by the British parliament].[12] This was an unqualified appreciation of how the English education contributed to the consolidation of liberal ideas in society. It was strongly felt that efforts towards building a liberal society were likely to fail unless it was complemented by a conducive mindset which was possible only by accepting English education. Being critical of political liberals and social Tories, MG Ranade, another vocal liberal, thus stated:

> You cannot be liberal by halves. You cannot be liberal in politics and conservative in religion. The heart and head must go together. You cannot cultivate your intellect, enrich your mind,

---

[8] Parekh, *Essays, Seeches, Addresses and Writings . . .*, p. 333.

[9] Sanjay Seth, 'Rewriting Histories of Nationalism: The Politics of "Moderate Nationalism" in India, 1870–1905', *American Historical Review* 104, no. 1 (1999): 104.

[10] Seth, 'Rewriting Histories of Nationalism', p. 104.

[11] Surendranath Banerjea's presidential address, 1902, Indian National Congress in AM Zaidi, ed., *Congress Presidential Addresses*, Vol. 2 (New Delhi: Indian Institute of Applied Political Research, 1985), p. 118.

[12] 'Address of the Deccan Sabha', p. 9. Cited in Seth, 'Rewriting Histories of Nationalism, p. 113.

> enlarge the sphere of your political rights and privileges, and, at the same time, keep your hearts closed and cramped. It is an idle dream to expect men to remain enchained and enshackled [*sic*] in their own superstition and social evils, while they are struggling hard to win rights and privileges from their rulers. Before long these vain dreamers will find their dreams lost.[13]

On another occasion, Ranade emphasized the importance of a strong state, guided by the rule of law in combatting the well-entrenched social evils. In other words, he was in favour of a strong state which was necessary to establish a liberal social format as well. The argument was forcefully made when he stated that 'the history of the suppression of infanticide and Sati shows that these institutions which had grown as excrescences upon the healthy system of ancient Hindu society, were checked and can only be checked by the strong arm of Laws, and once they are denounced as crimes they disappeared from the face of the country'.[14] Justifying state intervention as legitimate, he further argued:

> The diseased corruptions of the body cannot and should not be dealt with in the same way as its normal and healthy developments. The sharp surgical operation and not the homoeopathic infinitesimally small pill is the proper remedy of the first class of disorder and the analogy holds good in the diseases of the body politic as well as the material body in dealing with the parasitical growth of social degeneration.[15]

Two important ideas stand out: first, the early liberals were persuaded to believe that unless there were adequate institutional back-ups, the Westminster form of liberal democracy would remain elusive. Their insistence on having those institutions was thus a natural choice. Secondly, they were also aware of the fact that without supportive value systems, not only would the liberal institutions fail to strike organic roots in India they would also become merely cosmetic.

While the moderate liberals pursued a policy reconciliation within the British rule, their extremist counterparts championed violence, if necessary, to harm the ruler. Their idea of swaraj approximated to self-government of the liberal variety though the extremists felt that 'as long as the source of power is situated in Whitehall there cannot be even a beginning of the democratic processes'.[16] What was basic in their politico-ideological campaign was the demand for freedom which would facilitate the formation of a political system of their choice. Hence it was suggested that the new system involved 'the abdication of the right of England to determine the policy of the Indian government, the relinquishment of the right of the present foreign despotism to enact whatever law they please, the abandonment of their right to tax the people according to their own will and to spend the revenues of the country in any way they like'.[17] Their aim was to form a government according to what the people of India thought which was evident in what Lala Lajpat Rai mentioned by saying that 'in order to be free we must form, guide and control the national will in such a way as to make it irresistible'.[18] What was unique in the extremist

---

[13] Address by MG Ranade in The Second Social Conference, Allahabad, 1888, in *The Miscellaneous Writings of late Hon'ble Mr. Justice MG Ranade* (New Delhi: Sahitya Academy, 1992), p. 88.

[14] Ranade, *The Miscellaneous Writings*, p. 81.

[15] Ranade, *The Miscellaneous Writings*, pp. 81–82.

[16] Lala Lajpat Rai, *Ideals of Non-Cooperation* (Madras: Ganesh and Company, 1921), p. 50.

[17] Bipin Chandra Pal, *Swadeshi and Samaj: The Rise of New Patriotism* (Calcutta: Yugayatri Prakashak Limited, 1954), p. 55b.

[18] Rai, *Ideals of Non-Cooperation*, p. 98.

perception was their belief that sovereignty rested with the people. Unlike the moderates, Aurobindo, one of the most vocal extremists, made his preference very clear by stating that 'only by becoming responsible to the people and drawn from the people can the government be turned into a protector instead of an oppressor'.[19] Appreciative of liberal democracy since it drew its sustenance from the people, he reinforced his argument as follows:

> The only effective way of putting an end to executive tyranny is to make the people and not irresponsible Government the controller and paymaster of both executive and judiciary. The only possible method of stopping the drain is to establish a popular government which may be relied on to foster and protect Indian commerce and industry conducted by Indian capital and employing Indian labour. This is the object which the new politics, the politics of the twentieth century, places before the people of India in their resistance to the present system of Government, not tinkerings and palliatives, but the substitution for the autocratic bureaucracy, which at present misgoverns us, of a free constitutional and democratic system of government and the entire removal of foreign control in order to make way for perfect national liberty.[20]

Despite their strong criticism of the colonial rule which led to devastations in India, the extremist thinkers expressed their keenness in adopting a liberal democratic system of governance for two reasons: first, liberal democracy was perhaps one of those forms of government which derived its strength from people; the fact that it nurtured popular sovereignty attracted the extremists regardless of the fact that it had evolved in Britain. Secondly, the idea appears to have swayed the extremist thinkers presumably because of their personal experience of the system of governance that existed in England during their stay as students or otherwise; they thus believed that liberal democracy was not only a libertarian ideology, but also appropriate for meaningfully translating popular sovereignty in spirt and content.

There are therefore reasons to believe that the early liberals helped create some of the conditions for the rise and consolidation of India's political democracy. Supportive of the democratic institutions that articulated liberalism in practice, they also contributed to develop a space in which debates over the feasibility of a system of governance that owed its sustenance from liberalism. What is however paradoxical was the fact that their concern for class interests, including property rights clouded their vision for social democracy. As a result, they, despite being critical of inequality during colonial rule, failed to provide a conceptually persuasive analytical framework for combatting well-entrenched poverty which also had social roots. This confirms the argument that liberalism in India was contextually constructed which means that the classical British liberal ideas were 'deconstructed and reassembled to reflect Indian conditions and structures of thought'.[21]

While the early liberals were keen to build the institutional fabric of the nation since it was, in their perception, unavoidable to realize the fundamental liberal ethos, the radical liberals, especially Jyotirao Phule (1827–90) and BR Ambedkar (1891–1956) strongly argued for rearranging of the prevalent social systems to avoid birth-driven discrimination. Influenced by Thomas Paine's *Rights of Man*, Phule was persuaded to believe that since 'the creator has bestowed upon all men and women equal religious and

---

[19] Aurobindo Ghose, *The Doctrine of Passive Resistance* (Calcutta: Arya Publishing House, 1948), p. 11. https://books.google.co.in/books?id=LL9JAAAAMAAJ&printsec=frontcover#v=onepage&q&f=false (accessed on 20 August 2016).

[20] Ghose, *The Doctrine of Passive Resistance*, pp. 15–16.

[21] Bayly, *Recovering Liberties*, p. 346.

political liberties,... [they] should therefore have equality before law and equality of opportunity for entry into the civil service or municipal administration'.[22] Anticipating some of the ideas that BR Ambedkar was to articulate in future, he attributed social discrimination to Brahmin domination in Hindu society. Being critical of MG Ranade for his appreciation of 'Hindu tradition', he maintained that this was a ploy to retain a discriminatory social arrangement in which *sudras* (untouchables) would always remain subservient to the upper caste, particularly Brahmins. His appreciation of the British rule was governed by his firm belief that it was meant by 'the Creator to rescue the *sudras* from slavery [and hence he urged upon them] to exploit the golden opportunity given by the British rule to get themselves emancipated from Brahman domination'.[23] What Phule suggested was further developed by BR Ambedkar who, while challenging the existent heritage-dependent hierarchical social order in India, also welcomed the British rule for being liberal in its approach to governance. He was a vocal supporter of positive constitutional and political discrimination in favour of the untouchables. BR Ambedkar created and also expanded normative spaces involving not just equality, liberty and rights but also self-respect and dignity for the historically disadvantaged segments of the population. There is a caveat here because Ambedkar's notion of constitutional liberalism can be said to have redefined its basic thrust by insisting on the group autonomy and dignity (and not merely individual autonomy and dignity) against coercion, whatever the source—the state, society or any other institution. It was an effort that was translated into reality in the 1950 Constitution of independent India which created a template for liberty, equality and fraternity regardless of class, clan and ethnicity. By interrogating the foundational values of Hinduism that tended to justify social inequality, Babasaheb gave a voice to the critique that subjected the sociologically justified caste divisions to a thorough scrutiny. In his conceptual framework, the human agency remained central, which also reflected a Deweyan emphasis on the role of human beings in the making and unmaking of the world that we live in. It was thus perfectly compatible with his overall ideological position when he declared that 'do not depend ... for the abolition of caste slavery upon God or Superman. Your salvation lies in political power and not in making pilgrimages and the observance of fasts. Devotion to scriptures would not free you from bondage, want and poverty'.[24] Central to his argument was a belief in human efforts in reconceptualizing social mores and values which were contrary to liberal interpretations of human civilization. While defending liberalism, Ambedkar also introduced a unique moral and political framework in public reasoning which owed much to the European variety of Enlightenment paradigm combining social virtues (such as benevolence, compassion and tolerance) with scepticism and reason and the American variety of republican values. The idea of every person having the right to life, liberty, free speech and pursuit happiness—and the duty of the state to ensure that they were not violated remained critical in Ambedkar's understanding of liberalism which had clear contextual roots. Being 'an eclectic thinker'[25] who was also sensitive to the social brutalities that he suffered due to his birth as a Mahad, he supported 'vigorous state action to empower the untouchables and lower castes',[26] which, however, ran counter to the fundamental ethos of classical liberalism. Nonetheless, there are imprints of English liberal idealists, like TH Green (1836–82) and LT Hobhouse (1864–1929) who insisted on community, individual welfare rights and an activist state. Although

[22] Rajendra Vora, 'Two Strands of Indian Liberalism: The Ideas of Ranade and Phule', in *Political Thought in Modern India*, eds. Thomas Pantham and Kenneth Deutsch (New Delhi: SAGE, 1986), p. 107.

[23] Vora, 'Two Strands of Indian Liberalism', p. 108.

[24] Address of BR Ambedkar to a felicitation function, Bombay, 4 March 1933. Reproduced in *Ambedkar Speaks*, ed. Narendra Jadhav, Vol. 1 (New Delhi: Konark Publisher Pvt. Limited), p. 422.

[25] Bayly, *Recovering Liberties*, p. 305.

[26] Bayly, *Recovering Liberties*, p. 310.

he drew on multiple philosophical traditions within liberalism, he devised his own model of state-driven social transformation in which his own experiences of humiliation because of the accident of birth remained critical. Hence it is fair to argue that Indian liberals, including the radical liberals, reinvented what they derived from their understanding of British liberalism in the Indian context. The shift from constitutional liberalism of the early nationalist era to 'the quasi-socialistic communitarianism of 1900 and after'[27] is illustrative here. It is therefore not odd to find that by championing the idea of secular freedom and equality, Gandhi set in motion an ideological search that was not exactly derivative of classical British liberalism. It was an idea that was creatively interpreted in the context of the struggle that he led in South Africa and later in India against the denial of the basic rights of freedom and equality because of the deviant nature of a so-called liberal state. The Mahatma posed a clear challenge to the typical Western articulation of the basic values of liberalism that justified racial stereotypes by drawing on the Christian ideas of the value of individual, early bourgeois idea about the transition from a state of nature to civil society, and the ideas of progress that informed industrial capitalism, among others. By evolving his critique of liberalism on the obvious logical fallacy of the way the exponents of exploitation viewed liberalism, Gandhi powerfully challenged the regimes (in South Africa and India) that simply failed to be liberal because they clearly deviated from the classical liberal creed.

A thorough analytical scan of the multiple traditions of liberalism that figured prominently in the writings and also deeds of the nationalists in India reveals that liberalism remained a critical ideological force. Beginning with the moderate liberals in the early part of India's nationalist movement to Gandhi, Ambedkar and their partners, liberalism did not seem to have lost its appeal despite being conceptualized differently in different phases of India's struggle for freedom. There is no denying the fact that liberalism appealed to the Indian nationalists in the context of the Anglicization of the public life which was reinforced possibly because it became an empowering ideology in their battle against colonialism. It was further strengthened by the constitutional designs that evolved in the wake of the British rule in India, as will be shown below, which, by creating a template of governance, seem to have governed, to a significant extent, the nationalists' preference. The end result was that despite having drawn on contrary ideological perspectives, the nationalists and their bête noire upheld liberal constitutional values while seeking to pursue their respective political aims.

Major Designs Towards Constitutionalizing India

The Constitution of India had both colonial and nationalist imprints. By devising mechanisms of sharing power with their Indian counterparts, the colonial rulers set in motion processes of constitutionalizing India which drew its inspiration from the fundamental ethos of British Enlightenment. There were concerted efforts by the alien state, in other words, to conceptualize constitutional governance within the theoretical framework of liberalism. The inevitable outcome was the growing support for the Westminster model of democracy as perhaps a panacea for all troubles that the colonized had to face. Despite occasional challenges to liberal democracy by those who did not seem persuaded, parliamentary democracy had prevailed over other ideological options since Indian National Congress and its allies were convinced of its effectiveness as a form of governance for India. How was it possible? At one level, the increasing acceptance of liberal democracy was an offshoot of the British initiatives to involve the Indians in

[27] I borrow this expression from CA Bayly who developed the idea in his *Recovering Liberties*, p. 346.

administration which was primarily a colonial strategy to weaken the efforts against colonialism. This was further strengthened by those nationalist leaders, from the moderates to Gandhi and Jawaharlal Nehru who, unlike the former, demanded complete independence, who, by being ideologically baptised in liberalism during their growing-up years, appeared to have found its merit which was strong enough to sway them for what they stood for. This book thus makes two arguments: first, the structure of governance that evolved during colonialism and its aftermath was drawn on the fundamental principles of liberal democracy that was rooted in the efforts that the colonial government undertook as a strategy by dispersing power; in other words, the idea had gradually percolated down to the grassroots presumably because it generated a hope among a sizeable section of the colonized who now became part and parcel of colonial governance. Second, the fact that the leading nationalists accepted liberalism as an empowering ideology strengthened its base in India; it was therefore not surprising that the moderates who never pressed for complete independence and their opponents converged by being appreciative of liberal constitutional values which also confirms that the British-initiated processes of constitutionalism continued to remain critical whenever the nationalists articulated their preferences for a specific kind of constitution.

Keeping these two arguments in view, the book thus proposes to pursue the discussion in two complementary parts: on the one hand, there will be an analytical account of all the legislative endeavours that the colonial government adopted to efficiently manage administration in the context of the growing disenchantment of the colonized with colonialism; on the other, the discussion shall also be devoted to explore on the other, the nationalist alternative which, despite having been drawn on contrasting political perspectives, was not radically different in tenor presumably because of the nationalist faith in liberalism as a libertarian ideological design.

Major Initiatives by the Colonial Government

Colonialism expanded its control in India in two distinct ways: first, by tactfully following the divisive *divide-et-impera* strategy that created and sustained the schism between the two major communities of Hindus and Muslims. The British strategy worked favourably because of the socio-economic differences that separated these two communities. In course of time, the divide-and-rule formula not only consolidated the British rule in India, but also created conditions for the politically underprivileged sections to rise as meaningful partners in governance. So, it cut both ways: on the one hand, the chasm between communities, based on genuine socio-economic differences as well, made the task of governance easier for the ruler; this also, on the other hand, led to a process whereby the peripheral communities became a powerful political voice in the nationalist struggle for Independence. Second, drawing on the classical liberal-democratic tradition, the British ruler introduced several legal steps to consolidate the empire by gradually opening up administration to the Indians. Along with the application of force, the British government also adopted various reform schemes to inject constitutional values that shaped the nationalist campaign to a significant extent. It will therefore not be incorrect to suggest that the British rule survived in India with least coercion because of the role of the Indian collaborators in defending the empire. Except in the context of the 1942 open rebellion, the collaborative network of support had never shown signs of collapse. The adoption of various reforms by the British government created conditions in which Indians felt attached with the imperial rule that finally disintegrated due to its internal contradictions and also the growing nationalist consolidation opposed to a foreign rule. Focusing on the landmark constitutional designs during the British rule, this chapter is an analytical discussion on the British politico-legal strategies to consolidate the Raj. These designs, undoubtedly concessions to the ruled, were also devices to weaken the nationalist agitation as and when it became a serious threat to the government. In other words, while the British liberal tradition may have contributed to the constitutional reforms, one cannot deny the growing strength of the nationalist campaign, Gandhian or otherwise, that forced the British to introduce measures to defuse crisis.

An uncritical look at the selective, but major, landmark constitutional initiatives during the colonial rule may lead one to conclude that these were initiated by the British for the Indians. Hence the spirit of nationalism is underrated. If one goes beyond the surface, what is evident is that the inclusion of Indians in administration was but an outcome of the British effort to defuse popular discontent. Hence the argument that every constitutional drive was initiated by the Raj is totally unfounded. History reveals that there were situations which forced the British authority to adopt measures to control agitation. For instance, the Congress campaign in the 1880s contributed a lot to the introduction of the 1893 reforms. Behind the 1909 Morley–Minto Reforms lay the *Swadeshi* Movement and revolutionary terrorism. Similarly, the 1919 Montague–Chelmsford Reforms were attempts at resolving crises that began with the Home Rule League and climaxed with the 1919 Rowlatt Satyagraha and the Non-cooperation Movement of 1910–21. To a large extent, the Gandhian Civil Disobedience Movement (1930–32) accounted for the introduction of constitutional measures seeking to involve Indian politicians in public administration.

Furthermore, the interpretation of these constitutional designs remains partial unless linked with the broader socio-economic and political processes in which they were conceptualized. An attempt to analyse the structure and dynamics of constitutional politics without reference to the broader social matrix and economic nexus is futile because the politic-constitutional structure reflects economic and social networks, religio-cultural beliefs and even the nationalist ideology which impinged on the organized world of administrative and constitutional structure. So, an urgent and unavoidable task for an analyst is not to completely ignore the broader socio-economic context but to ascertain its relative importance in shaping a particular constitutional initiative. For instance, the 1932 Communal Award was believed to have been initiated by the British to expand political activity among the Muslims in Bengal and Punjab. But, as studies have shown, it was also a concession the British was forced to grant in order to make the maintenance of the Empire easier.[28] The sharing of power with the native elites was thus prompted by considerations other than merely British initiatives.

The evolution of colonialism in India will continue to remain an interesting area of research for a variety of reasons. Prominent among them is certainly the process in which colonialism sustained its grip in India by creating a strong collaborative network and also by successfully pursuing a divide-and-rule strategy to scuttle efforts at unifying socio-economically separated communities. The strength of British colonialism lies in the fact that unlike their European counterparts, the British rulers expanded and also maintained their presence not merely by coercion, but also by creating circumstances in which they emerged as the best possible option by the Indians who remained highly divisive due to various socio-economic and political reasons. The constitutional landmarks that we have discussed earlier are a clear testimony to those imperial efforts that defused opposition rather easily on most occasions. What was distinct about British colonialism was its success in welding a significant section of the population to the system of governance that the British introduced. It was possible perhaps due to its triumph in ideologically moulding people towards liberal political values and ethos. Barring the militant nationalists, most of the nationalists were

[28] I have shown this in my 'The communal award of 1932 and its implications in Bengal', *Modern Asian Studies*, Cambridge, 23, no. 2 (1989).

content with the method of three Ps (petition, prayer and protest) until the rise of Gandhi who radically transformed the complexion of anti-British confrontation.

These landmark constitutional experiments had a role in permanently dividing major communities in India on the basis of religion and other socio-economic denominations. Both the Hindus and Muslims redefined their identities through a process of contestation of vision, contestation of beliefs and contestation of history. The period between 1909 and 1947, when major constitutional experiments were undertaken, sharply shows the mutation in the formation of Hindus and Muslims as communities opposed to each other in the political arena. What was distinctive about this period was the growth of the communities as political units always in a permanent adversarial relationship with the members of the 'other' community. This was further consolidated following the introduction of the communal electorate in the 1937 provincial elections. With the acceptance of the principle of majority, Muslims automatically became the most powerful community in Bengal and Punjab by their sheer demographic strength. In other words, religious identity as a demographic category became probably the single most crucial criterion in determining the distribution of governmental power in these Muslim-majority provinces. The 1935 Government of India Act reiterated the divide-and-rule strategy by formally recognizing that Muslims needed to be treated separately as a distinct, but neglected minority in India. This was a decisive constitutional intervention because not only did it establish the principle of majority as sacrosanct in democracy, it also made the Muslims self-conscious of their critical importance in governance in India. It is now possible to argue that the 1935 Act definitely shifted the centre of political activity in Bengal to the east of the province. Not by virtue of any inherent superiority of the Muslims but simply because in a democratically elected legislature, as a contemporary report underlines, 'the weight of numbers tells and the teeming millions of East Bengal—sixty percent of their being Muslims outweighed in point of numbers the more educated Hindus of the South, West and extreme north of the province'.[29] The migration of power to the countryside took place in the context of a major realignment in the social bases of political power.

The 1935 Government of India Act was certainly a powerful constitutional intervention that the colonial rulers seriously made to accommodate the nationalist zeal within, of course, the colonial administrative format. This is also illustrative of efforts at legitimizing the growing democratic aspirations of the ruled in India through a constitutional device. Interestingly, the 1935 Act remained the strongest influence during the making of the 1950 Constitution for free India. Some 250 Clauses of the present Constitution were, in fact, lifted from the Government of India Act. Although the political system of independent India draws its sustenance from universal adult franchise and political sovereignty, rules are undoubtedly derived from its colonial past. The most striking provisions that the Constitution of India derived from its 1935 counterpart are 'the Emergency provisions' that enable the President to suspend the democratically elected governments and fundamental rights of the citizens.

There is no doubt that the post-colonial state in India inherited its habits of governance from colonial practices. And, its *weltanschauung* (world view) is based on 'the mixed legacies of colonial rule' that upheld rule of law, bureaucracy, citizenship, parasitic landlords, modern political institutions and 'two-track tradition of protest and participation'.[30] What accounts for relative stability for colonialism in India was certainly its ability to adapt to the changed socio-political circumstances and also the gradual but steady 'internalization' of domination by the subjects of colonial rule, which provoked an analyst to characterize

---

[29] India Office Records, London, Tyson Papers, Eur E 341/41, John Tyson's note, 5 July 1947.

[30] Subrata Mitra, 'Constitutional Design, Democratic Vote Counting and India's Fortuitous Multiculturalism' (working paper, South Asia Institute, Heidelberg University, November 2004), 29–34.

colonialism as 'an intimate enemy'[31] because the dominated imagined the virtues of being dominated for their own betterment. Colonialism was thus not seen as an absolute evil but complementary to India's rise as an independent nation in future. The statement may not be politically correct. Nonetheless, it can safely be argued that colonialism provided critical impetus to various processes that finally resulted in serious political mobilization against imperialism in India. Whether nationalism or democratization—they had their roots in the long history of colonialism, and in this sense colonialism remained a significant force behind the rise of India as an independent nation in 1947.

Major Nationalist Initiatives

One of the first serious endeavours in this direction was made in the 1927 Madras Congress that sought to evolve constitutional governance in India. Known as the Swaraj Constitution, it was also an outcome of a series of discussion involving several political parties, including the Muslim League. Realizing that without consensus among the major communities, no effort towards making a constitution was likely to succeed, an attempt was made to frame a resolution in such a way as to create confidence among them, especially the Muslims. The resolution that the Congress had adopted was thus explicit in stating that

> having regard to the general desire of all political parties in the country to unite together in settling a Swaraj Constitution, and having considered the various drafts submitted to it and the various suggestions received in reply to the Working Committee's circular, [the Madras Congress] authorizes the Working Committee ... to draft a Swaraj Constitution for India on the basis of a Declaration of Rights, and to place the same for consideration and approval before a special convention ... consisting of the All India Congress Committee and the leaders and representatives of the other organization ... and elected members of the central and provincial legislatures.[32]

On paper, it was a grand design though it did not succeed because of the failure of the Congress to counter the apprehension of the Muslims that they were likely to be marginalized in the proposed constitutional arrangement although the Committee assured that no community would be allowed to dominate over other. Asserting that the aim was not to 'give domination to one over another but to prevent the harassment and exploitation of any individual or group by another [the Committee insisted] on the fullest guarantee of religious liberty ... [and] cultural autonomy'.[33] In order to establish group rights in its most substantial form and content, the Committee argued for 'joint or mixed electorates' and discarded Separate Electorates completely 'as a condition precedent to any rational system of representation'.[34] Characterizing Separate Electorates as 'bad and harmful for the growth of a national spirit',[35] the Committee also marshalled arguments to suggest that Separate Electorates ended up creating a permanent fissure between the minority

[31] Ashis Nandy, *The Intimate Enemy: Loss and Recovery of Self Under Colonialism* (1983, reprint, Delhi: Oxford University Press, 1989).

[32] The resolution is quoted in *The Nehru Report: The Anti-separatist Manifesto*, Vol. 1 (New Delhi: Machiko & Panjathan, 1928), p. 25.

[33] *The Nehru Report*, 1: 35.

[34] *The Nehru Report*, 1: 36.

[35] *The Nehru Report*, 1: 36.

and majority community. Hence it was argued that 'under Separate Electorates, the chances are that the minority will always, have to face a hostile majority, which can always, by sheer force of numbers, override the wishes of the minority'.[36] The aim of the Nehru Committee was to counter the League's insistence on special constitutional protection to the Muslims by guaranteeing Separate Electorates which was never appreciated given its obvious divisive character. Nonetheless, special care was taken to protect cultural autonomy of the minorities which, felt the Committee, was needed to sustain India's socio-economic diversity. So, the conceding of group rights was not a concessional measure but a politically contrived design for the sake of sustaining the national spirit.

The 1928 constitutional draft, prepared by the Motilal Nehru Committee was finally rejected due to lack of consensus. Nonetheless, it was one of the first serious endeavours that the Indian nationalists had undertaken to constitutionalize India following the fundamental principles of liberalism which unfolded in the wake of the British rule. In order to realize these principles in public life, the Committee admitted having imitated the British system of governance which was evident in its submission that recommendations were not 'original'. The Committee was said to have been content 'to follow models which have been tried and tested in other parts of the world and which even the framers of the Montague–Chelmsford constitution professed to follow'.[37] The Committee, however, maintained that the proposed constitution was not exactly derivative of the available constitutions, since in drawing up the Constitution, it 'deliberately declined to be overcome by one type or the other'. Aware of India's peculiar socio-economic circumstances, the members strove to provide 'for the development of fullest possible provincial life compatibly with national interests'.[38] Another bone of contention was the minority rights which figured prominently in the Report which introduced group rights in the shape of cultural and religious rights of minorities partly to allay the fears of the religious minorities that they would be swamped in a Hindu-dominated India, partly to stave off the demand for separate electorates, and partly to devise a principle that helped the Congress to regulate intergroup relations.[39] Similarly, the Committee recommended for adult suffrage despite strong criticism even by the Congress. Two points of criticism were made: first, it was argued that without being adequately educated, the voters would fail to exercise franchise 'intelligently'; second, in view of the vastness of the country and the lack of transport, it would be difficult, if not impossible, for the voters to go to the booth to exercise their rights, which would make the system redundant. To counter these arguments, the Committee retorted that 'the repeated exercise of the right to vote is in itself a powerful educative factor'.[40] And, it was further argued that 'the average Indian voter understands his business and [that he] can form an opinion that affects him directly'.[41] What was unique about the Nehru Report was an attempt to conceptualize group rights in a liberal way since it also endorsed individual rights by insisting on adult suffrage. This was a revolutionary step which also confirms the nationalists' concern for creating a constitutional arrangement on the basis of their understanding of liberal constitutionalism.

Dissensions surfaced as soon as the Nehru recommendations were made public. Even Jinnah who appreciated Motilal's effort in drafting a constitution for united India rejected the recommendations demanding that the residual powers should rest with the provinces rather than the centre to scuttle the

[36] *The Nehru Report*, 1: 36.

[37] *The Nehru Report*, 2: 62.

[38] *The Nehru Report*, 2: 65.

[39] Neera Chandhoke pursues this argument in her 'The Political Consequences of Ethic Mapping' (discussion paper no. 14, Crisis State Development Research Centre, LSE, mimeograph, December, 2005), 12–14.

[40] *The Nehru Report*, 2: 67.

[41] *The Nehru Report*, 2: 67.

rise of a unitary and authoritarian Hindu-dominated state. Other Muslim groups joined hands and in January 1929, an All Parties Muslim Conference met in Delhi agreed to abandon the Report that hardly addressed the Muslim concern. While Muslims dissociated from the Report as it was far from their expectations, there were dissidents even within the Congress. Led by Jawaharlal Nehru and Subhas Chandra Bose, a powerful faction within the Congress formed 'Independence India League' that demanded complete independence rather than dominion status as suggested by the Nehru Committee. While elucidating the difference between dominion status and independence, Nehru stated that dominion status 'envisages the same old structure, with many bonds visible and invisible tying us to the British economic system: [complete freedom] gives, or ought to give us, freedom to erect a new structure to suit our circumstances'.[42] Critical of those defending dominion status, Nehru further argued:

> For them the problem is one of changing colour of administration, or at most having a new administration . . . [and] not a new state. . . . They can only conceive of a future in which, they or people like them will play the principal role and take the place of the English high officials.[43]

The 1928 Calcutta Congress thus saw an open split between those who defended dominion status and those who advocated complete independence. It was more or less a foregone conclusion that in view of the growing importance of the radical section within the Congress, it had no alternative but to insist on complete independence. With the acceptance of the complete independence resolution in the 1929 Lahore Congress, it was decided to boycott the legislature and the Congress members were asked to resign. Furthermore, the All India Congress Committee was authorized to launch civil disobedience, including non-payment of taxes wherever it deemed appropriate. Gandhi rose as the undisputed leader and was made the sole authority to decide the time and manner of the launching of the Civil Disobedience Movement.

Like the 1928 Motilal Nehru constitutional draft, the 1945 Sapru Committee also prepared a constitutional design following the fundamental ethos of liberalism. Here too, the institutional arrangements that Indians had inherited as colonial subjects were accepted as integral to the making of a liberal constitution for India. Admitting that it was the British initiatives that led to the consolidation of liberal democracy in India, the Committee had begun its recommendations by quoting Montague's famous declaration in the House of Commons on 20 August 1917 which corroborated the idea by declaring that

> the policy of His Majesty's Government, with which the Government of India are in complete accord, is that of the increasing association of Indians in every branch of the administration and the gradual development of self-governing institutions with a view to a progressive realization of responsible government in India as an integral part of the British Empire.[44]

This was not a favour that the British government extended, but was the outcome of the challenges that the ruling authority was apprehending in view of the growing discontent. It was a powerful strategy to seek to quell the circumstances that were quite volatile as the nationalists were being regrouped under

---

[42] Jawaharlal Nehru, *An Autobiography: With Musings on Recent Events in India* (London: John Lane the Bodley Head, 1941), p. 418.

[43] Nehru, *Autobiography*, p. 417.

[44] *Constitutional Proposal of the Sapru Committee, 1945* (Bombay: Padma Publications, 1945), p. 10.

charismatic Gandhi. The idea was also appreciated by a hardcore colonialist, like Curzon who found the suggestion most appropriate since, as he argued:

> With the modern ideal of nationalism and self-determination making in the circumstances of the times so strong an appeal, the peoples of countries such as India attached much more importance to being governed, even though not so well-governed, by themselves, than they did to being even superbly governed by another race.[45]

By referring to the early British initiatives, the Sapru Committee justified that the idea of self-government was nothing new; instead, it was perhaps a natural outcome of the British endeavour towards constitutionalizing India in a liberal democratic format. On the basis of this understanding, the Committee built its argument for a constitutional structure that drew on the fundamental ethos of liberalism. Here too, the members appear to have been persuaded by his erstwhile colleagues who prepared the 1928 Nehru Report which, despite having accepted dominion status within the Empire, also defended self-government. Being favourably disposed towards the Westminster form of liberal democracy, they thus insisted that 'the future of India lies in adopting a democratic constitution and taking all the risks which a change from the present system of government to a state of real democracy must involve'.[46] Similar to its 1928 counterpart, the Committee strongly argued for adult franchise with a proviso that under the existing circumstances 'it may be excusable to give communities divided on religious lines the right to a fair and adequate share of opportunities for service in the legislature and of executive power'.[47]

The Constituent Assembly (1946–49) and Its Role

Seeking to lay out the background for the Constituent Assembly that drafted free India's Constitution, it is conceptually pertinent to focus on two specific constitutional steps that the British government undertook just on the eve of the 1947 transfer of power. While the 3 June Plan set out the agenda for the transfer of power, the 1947 Indian Independence Act translated that into reality. Framing a constitution for independent India was not an easy task. Beginning with the 1942 Cripps Mission, the idea of involving Indians for drafting their constitution was being debated. Although the 1946 Cabinet Mission enthusiastically supported the formation of a constituent assembly to prepare the constitution for free India, its members were convinced that 'a solution involving the partition of the Punjab and Bengal would be contrary to the wishes and interests of a very large proportion of the inhabitants of these Provinces'.[48] Nonetheless, the subcontinent was partitioned and two independent nations—India and Pakistan—were born in 1947. The Constituent Assembly for India met, for the first time, on 9 December 1946 and in less than three years, the Constitution of India was produced and was adopted by the nation on 26 November, 1949. Besides elaborating the processes that led to the making of the Constitution, this chapter draws on the socio-economic and political circumstances of the era and also on the philosophical predilections of the founding fathers to delve into the riddle as to why India's Constitution incorporated some of the

---

[45] Curzon's statement of 20 August 1917 in the House of Commons in response to Montague's declaration is cited in the *Constitutional Proposal of the Sapru Committee*, p. 11.

[46] *Constitutional Proposal of the Sapru Committee*, p. 325.

[47] *Constitutional Proposal of the Sapru Committee*, p. 326.

[48] MV Pylee, *Constitutional Government in India* (reprint, London: Asia Publishing House, 1963), p. 127.

draconian provisions of the 1935 Government of India Act despite being opposed to it when it was introduced.

The outcome of the 1947 India Independence Act was the inauguration of two new nations. India became free on 15 August 1947. A new era dawned and Jawaharlal Nehru captured that moment in his famous 'tryst with destiny' speech as follows:

> At the stroke of the midnight hour, when the world sleeps, India will awake to life and freedom. A moment comes, which comes but rarely in history, when we step out from the old to the new, when an age ends, and when the soul of a nation, long suspended, finds utterance. It is fitting that at this solemn moment we take the pledge of dedication to the service of India and her people and to the still larger cause of humanity.[49]

While Nehru was optimistic, his colleagues were not so given the multiple sources of discontent that the newly emerged nation was likely to confront. Apprehending that political freedom, by itself, made no sense unless it was articulated to bring about radical changes in governance which was possible once the sources of social, economic and political discontent were completely eradicated. Hence Rajendra Prasad, the President of the Constituent Assembly, exhorted:

> India needs today nothing more than a set of honest men who will have the interest of the country before them. There is a fissiparous tendency arising out of various elements in our life. We have communal differences, caste differences, language differences, provincial differences and so forth. It requires men of vision, men who will not sacrifice the interests of the country at large for the sake of smaller groups and areas and who will rise over the prejudices which are born of these differences.[50]

The scene does not appear to be as gloomy as it was made out to be, as he immediately pointed out that 'successful working of democratic constitution requires in those who have to work them willingness to respect the view point of others, capacity for compromise and accommodation'.[51] He was also persuaded to believe that it was not difficult to achieve since 'we have been able to draw this Constitution without taking recourse to voting and division in Lobbies'.[52] Nonetheless, social diversity of India was 'a real, if awkward, fact [which] simultaneously provoked pride in India's civilizational fecundity and plurality, and a fear in its centrifugal potential'.[53] India's Partition in 1947 was a testimony to a situation when communal schism was resolved only with the vivisection of the country. One cannot therefore ignore the context in which specific efforts towards constitutionalizing India were made. In other words, what was initiated by the colonial rule in the name of constitutional governance and also those parallel attempts that the nationalists made towards that goal need to be understood with reference to the contemporary democratic politics. Constitutionalism is conceptualized as organically linked with the prevalent socio-economic

---

[49] Jawaharlal Nehru's 'Tryst with destiny' speech, delivered at the dawn of independence in India on 15 August 1947. Quoted from B Shiva Rao, ed., *The Framing of India's Constitution: Select Documents*, Vol. 1 (reprint, New Delhi: Universal Law Publishing Co., 2004), pp. 558–59.

[50] Rajendra Prasad's address in the Constituent Assembly on 26 November 1949, *Constituent Assembly Debates*, Book No 5, p. 993.

[51] Ibid., p. 993.

[52] Ibid., p. 993.

[53] Uday S Mehta, 'Indian Constitutionalism: Crisis, Unity and History', in *The Oxford Handbook of the Indian Constitution*, eds. Sujit Choudhury, Madhav Khosla and Pratap Bhanu Mehta (New Delhi: Oxford University Press, 2016), p. 53.

context. There is a point of view however suggesting that it was a design for 'political exclusion of the masses'[54] which both the colonial rulers and their opponents endorsed while articulating their responses for constitutionalizing India. Despite having contrasting political objectives, the colonizers and the colonized were hardly different in their approach to the masses given their 'shared political language of exclusion [which] was intrinsic to constitutional reforms'[55] that were undertaken so zealously during colonialism and its immediate aftermath. As their ideological goal was identical, the nationalists were persuaded to accept that 'in order to achieve any measure of self-government, they had to adopt a language of representation, one that fundamentally agreed with the colonial government that large masses had yet to be tutored in the art of self-government'.[56] It is true and the argument draws heavily on this, that there existed two worlds: organized and unorganized; in the former, the appeal of constitutionalism was significant while the latter remained peripheral due to complex socio-economic reasons explaining their exclusion. However, the situation had undergone a sea change with the arrival of Gandhi who tried to bridge the gulf between the organized and the unorganized words for a nationalist goal. There were other ideological forces representing the interests of the peasants, workers and other marginalized sections of society which also became prominent in struggles which were also directed against socially entrenched vested interests. The point here relates to the argument emphasizing the dialectical interconnection between democratic politics and constitutionalism. Hence, India's constitutional history is not one of absolute consensus but one that represented a series of conflicts around myriad social, economic and political issues. The proposed study will approach the concern at two levels: at one level, it will probe into the nationalist efforts that favoured Westminster form of liberal democracy which they justified as an appropriate mode of governance because (a) it was meant to realize what they had imbibed by virtue of being part of the Empire that drew on the Philosophy of Enlightenment and (b) it also had a nature appeal to them since they were nurtured in that tradition. At another level, the study will look into those areas of conflict which reveals, on the one, that the nationalists hardly spoke in one language, and also introduced them, and on the other hand, to areas which would have, otherwise, escaped their attention. As will be shown in the text, this is true to the efforts that the nationalists and their bête noire undertook to seek to conceptualize governance in India in liberal theoretical mould. For instance, with the increasing importance of Muslims as an independent political entity, it was unavoidable for both the British government and Congress nationalists not to take into account their special politico-ideological needs while devising the 1935 constitutional design for India; in a similar vein, the 1945 Sapru Committee paid significant attention to the communal question though within the nationalist framework to allay the fear of the minorities of being marginalized in what they characterized as Hindu-dominated India.

The Constituent Assembly and the Making of the Constitution

The making of free India's Constitution by the Constituent Assembly over a period of little less than three years is reflective of the efforts that the founding fathers undertook to translate into reality the nationalist

---

[54] Arvind Elangovan, 'Constitutionalism, Political Exclusion and Implications or Indian Constitutional History: The Case of Montague–Chelmsford reforms (1919)', *South Asian History and Culture*, 2016, p. 14.

[55] Elangovan, 'Constitutionalism', p. 14.

[56] Elangovan, 'Constitutionalism', p. 14.

and democratic aspirations of an independent polity following decolonization. Furthermore, while the Constitution is a continuity at least in structural and procedural terms, it was also a clear break with the past since the 1950 Constitution drew on an ideology that sought to establish a liberal democratic polity following the withdrawal of colonialism. There can be no greater evidence of the commitment to constitutionalism and rule of law on the part of the founding fathers than the Constitution that they framed despite serious difficulties due to partition. The commitment to liberal democratic values, as the Constituent Assembly proceedings suggest, remained paramount in the making of the Constitution.

Set up as a result of negotiations between the nationalist leaders and the members of the Cabinet Mission over the possible constitutional arrangement in the post-war India, the Constituent Assembly was not, it is argued, convened 'by any national provisional government but by the British government [to bring together] the delegates of the major political parties'.[57] The task of the Constituent Assembly was to draft a constitution for India. The Objective Resolution that Jawaharlal Nehru moved was, according to Ujjal Singh of Punjab, 'an expression of the pent-up emotions of the millions of this country'.[58] While defending the Objective Resolution, Nehru argued strongly for democracy and socialism: he strongly defended 'democracy' as the most appropriate system of government that 'fit in with the temper of our people and be accountable to them'.[59] Similarly, socialism, he firmly believed, would bring about economic democracy to India. For him, political independence was futile unless it was supported by democratic governance and socialistic vision. Hence he was critical of the princely states that were reluctant to relinquish monarchy for democracy. As a true democrat who had no doubt that socialism was the ultimate solution for India's stark poverty, Nehru set the tenor of the discussion in the Assembly by providing a philosophical layout for free India's Constitution. Nonetheless, the political context in which the Constitution was being deliberated was full of uncertainty because of (a) Hindu–Muslim rivalry and (b) reluctance of most of the princely states to join independent India. While the former led to the dismemberment of India following the British withdrawal in 1947, the latter necessitated threat or application of coercion, on occasions, to geographically unify India by bypassing the claim of the existing rulers of the princely states. By staying away from the Assembly, the Muslim members clearly stated their preference for Pakistan that gained momentum especially after the adoption of the 1940 Lahore resolution. The 1946 Calcutta and later Noakhali riots confirmed the Congress apprehension that it was possibly strategically correct to accept partition to avoid further bloodbath. What was clear when the Constituent Assembly met for drafting the Constitution was that Pakistan was inevitable and a strong state was required to fulfil its socio-economic goals.

The Outcome

Despite being appreciative of India's pluralistic social texture, there was a near unanimity among the Assembly members for a strong state.[60] Even those who were critical of the Emergency provisions also defended a centralized state to contain tendencies threatening the integrity of the country. Emergency provisions in the Constitution were justified because 'disorder' or 'misgovernance' endangers India's

[57] Shibanikinkar Chaube, *Constituent Assembly of India: Springboard of Revolution* (Manohar: New Delhi, 2000), p. 49.

[58] Ujjal Singh (Punjab), 17 December 1946, *Constituent Assembly Debates*, Book No. 1, p. 104.

[59] Jawaharlal Nehru (Uttar Pradesh), 13 December 1946, *Constituent Assembly Debates*, Book No. 1, p. 62.

[60] Mohit Bhattacharya, 'The Mind of the Founding Fathers', in *Federalism in India: Origins and Development*, eds. Nirmal Mukarji and Balveer Arora (New Delhi: Vikas Publishing House, 1992).

existence as 'a territorial state'. Such concerns could only have reflected, argues Paul Brass, 'another kind of continuity' between the new governing elite and the former British rulers, namely 'an attitude of distrust' of the ordinary politicians of the country and 'a lack of faith' in the ability of the newly franchised population to check 'the misdeeds' of their elected rulers.[61] Nonetheless, the fear of 'disorder' was probably the most critical factor in favour of the arguments for a centralized state despite its clear incompatibility with the cherished ideal of the nationalist leaders for a federal state. BR Ambedkar's contradictory stances on federalism, for instance, thus may appear whimsical, independent of the circumstances. In 1939, Ambedkar was clearly in favour of a federal form of government for its political viability in socio-culturally diverse India.[62] By 1946, he provided a radically different view by saying that 'I like a strong united Centre, much stronger than the Centre we had created under the Government of India Act of 1935'.[63] While presenting the final report of the Union Powers Committee, Jawaharlal Nehru also argued in favour of a strong state when he stated:

> We are unanimously of the view that it would be injurious to the interest of the country to provide for a weak central authority which would be incapable of ensuring peace, of coordinating vital matters of common concern and of speaking effectively for the whole country in the international sphere.[64]

As is evident, federalism did not appear to be an appropriate structural form of governance in the light of the perceived threats to the existence of the young Indian nation. Hence the constitution-makers recommended for a strong centre because the constitutional design of a country is meant to serve 'the normative-functional requirements of governance'. The Constitution was to reflect 'an ideology of governance' regardless of whether they articulate the highly cherished ideals of the freedoms struggle that a majority of the Assembly members nurtured while participating in the freedom struggle. As GL Mehta believed that 'we have to build up the system on the conditions of our country [and] not on any abstract theories'.[65] In the same tune, Alladi Krishnaswamy Ayyar argued that 'our constitutional design is relative to the peculiar conditions obtaining here, according to the peculiar exigencies of our country [and] not according to a prior or theoretical considerations'.[66] In the making of the Constitution for governance, they were guided more by their views on state craft which would surely have been different without the traumatic experience of partition and communal bloodbath preceding the inauguration of the Constitution in 1950. Hence one can safely suggest that 'hard-headed pragmatism and not abstract governmental theories' was what guided 'the architects of our Constitution'.[67]

Yet, it was not the entire Assembly that wrote the document. It was clearly the hard work 'of the government wing of the Congress, and not the mass party' and the brunt of the task fell upon 'the Canning Lane Group [because] they lived while attending Assembly sessions on Canning Lane'.[68] There is another dimension of the functioning of the Assembly which is also instructive. According to Granville Austin, Indian's constitutional structure is perhaps 'a good example' of decision making by consensus and

---

[61] Paul Brass, 'India, Myron Weiner and the Political Science of Development', *Economic and Political Weekly*, 20 July 2002, p. 2132.

[62] BR Ambedkar, *Federation versus Freedom* (Poona: Gokhale Institute of Politics and Economics, 1939).

[63] BR Ambedkar, 17 December 1946, *Constituent Assembly Debates*, Book No. 1, p. 102.

[64] Report of the Union Powers Committee, 20 August 1947, *Constituent Assembly Debates*, Book No. 1, p. 58.

[65] GL Mehta, (Western India States Group), 21 August 1947, *Constituent Assembly Debates*, Book No. 1, p. 78.

[66] Alladi Krishnaswami Ayyar (Madras), 23 November 1949, *Constituent Assembly Debates*, Book No. 5, p. 839.

[67] Bhattacharya, 'The Mind of the Founding Fathers', p. 89.

[68] Granville Austin, *The Indian Constitution: Cornerstone of a Nation* (Delhi: Oxford University Press, 1966), pp. 17, 317.

accommodation, which he defends by examining the debates on various provisions of the Constitution.[69] Scholars however differ because given the Congress hegemony in the Assembly, views, held by the non-Congress members were usually bulldozed. As SK Chaube argued that at least on two major issues—political minorities and language—both these principles were conveniently sacrificed. As regards political minority, there was no consensus and the solution to the language was, as Austin himself admits, 'a half-hearted compromise'.[70] By dubbing the Assembly as 'a packed house', the shrunk Muslim League expressed the feeling of being alienated from the house. Even Ambedkar underlined the reduced importance of the Assembly since on a number of occasions, as he admitted, 'they had to go to another place to obtain a decision and come to the Assembly'.[71]

Decision by consensus may not be an apt description of the processes of deliberation. But, as the proceedings show, there was near unanimity on most occasions and divisions of opinion among the Congress Party members who constituted a majority were sorted out politically. As Ambedkar admits, 'The possibility of chaos was reduced to nil by the existence of the Congress Party inside the Assembly which brought into its proceedings a sense of order and discipline. . . . The Party is therefore entitled to all the credit for the smooth sailing of the Draft Constitution in the Assembly'.[72] As Shiva Rao informs, on a number of controversial issues, efforts were made to eliminate or at least to minimize differences through informal meetings of the Congress Party's representatives in the Constituent Assembly.[73] If the informal discussion failed to resolve the differences, 'the Assembly leadership . . . exercised its authority formally by the Party Whip'.[74] As is evident, in the Constituent Assembly, no attempt was made to force decision, the accent being on unanimity presumably because 'the leaders were alive to the fact that the constitution adopted on the Principle of majority vote would not last long'.[75] It was not therefore surprising that Rajendra Prasad, the President of the Constituent Assembly preferred to postpone debate and allow them to work out agreed solutions rather than take a vote that might, as he apprehended result 'in something not wanted by anybody'.[76]

Two important points emerge out of the preceding discussions: first, the making of the Indian Constitution was a difficult exercise not only because of the historical context but also due to the peculiar social texture of the Indian reality that had to be translated in the Constitution. The collective mind in the Assembly was defensive as a consequence of the rising tide of violence taking innocent lives immediately after partition. Second, the founding fathers seem to have been obsessed with their 'own notion of integrated national life'. The aim of the Constitution was to provide 'an appropriate ordering framework' for India. As Rajendra Prasad equivocally declared on the floor of the Assembly, '[p]ersonally I do not attach any importance to the label which may be attached to it—whether you call it a Federal Constitution or a Unitary Constitution or by any other name. It makes no difference so long as the Constitution serves our purpose'.[77] On the whole, a unitary mind produced 'an essentially unitary constitution doused with a sprinkling of

[69] Austin, *The Indian Constitution*, pp. 311–21.

[70] Austin, *The Indian Constitution*, Chapter 12 (Language and the Constitution: The Half-hearted Compromise), pp. 264–307.

[71] *Hindustan Times*, 27 November 1949.

[72] BR Ambedkar, 25 November 1949, *Constituent Assembly Debates*, Book No. 5, p. 974.

[73] Shiva Rao, *The Framing of India's Constitution*, Vol. 5 (New Delhi: Universal Law Publishing, 2004), p. 835.

[74] Austin, *The Indian Constitution*, Chapter 12, p. 315.

[75] Rajni Kothari, *Politics in India* (reprint, New Delhi: Orient Longman, 2005), p. 107.

[76] Rajendra Prasad's press statement, *Hindustan Times*, 29 December 1949.

[77] Rajendra Prasad's statement, made after the Constitution was inaugurated on 26 of January 1950, *The Times of India*, 29 January 1950.

permissive power for a highly supervised level of constituent units'.[78] This was not the goal of the nationalists and, of course, their leader, Mahatma Gandhi, who always stood for decentralized village republic. Besides confirming that constitutionalism in India was not entirely derivative, this assumption directs our attention to the argument that the Indian Constitution was 'cosmopolitan' in character not only 'in its fidelity to the universal principles of liberty, equality and fraternity' but also due to fact that its text and principles, its values and its jurisprudence were drawn from 'the major cross-currents of global constitutional law'.[79]

Concluding Observations

Constitution making is an arduous task, more so in a socio-culturally diverse society like India. As is argued earlier, the Constitution was the culmination of a process in which contrasting ideas converged to evolve an acceptable set of principles for a socio-culturally and economically diverse population. The account is historical too because the ideas that became pre-eminent in the Constituent Assembly had their roots in the tumultuous days of India's freedom struggle in which various waves of thought were also discernible. By arguing that the Constitution of India was the outcome of a complex ideational battle in different phases of India's struggle for freedom, the book challenges the conventional notion that it is merely a mindless, if not haphazard, borrowing of constitutional provisions and practices prevalent elsewhere. The argument supporting the contention that the Indian Constitution is a borrowed doctrine seems vacuous given the fact that it is also a break with the past. One of the most significant break was to constitutionally recognize the principle of representative government in its unalloyed form through universal adult suffrage, an ambition that the nationalists had been nurturing since the adoption of the 1928 Motilal Nehru Report. Besides the emergent need of tackling contingent circumstances following the partition which created a strong demand for the continuity of the available colonial administrative machinery, the founding fathers also felt the need of a strong administration to translate into reality their ambitious plan of transformation. It has thus been persuasively argued that '[w]hile continuity was sought in the service of the break in this way, the claim of break itself was called upon to justify certain continuities'.[80] A careful study of the arguments that were marshalled in favour of incorporating mechanisms and institutions from the colonial era confirms the point.

A cursory look at the processes that influenced constitutionalism in India reveals that there are three critical areas—social justice, liberal constitutionalism and group representation—in which an ideational battle took place involving those who were responsible for charting out a specific course for India's constitutionalism to follow. The aim here is primarily to understand how these ideas were articulated in a series of efforts which culminated in the Constituent Assembly when the founding fathers sat together to make a constitution for independent India in a historical perspective which is both derivative and context-driven: derivative because it was drawn on liberalism that had no parallel in India, and context-driven since Indian socio-economic and ideational reality did not seem to favour liberal socio-economic and political practices. A daunting task indeed, the exercise will not only be intellectually refreshing but also allow us to conceptualize the making of India's Constitution in a completely new perspective.

---

[78] Bhattacharya, 'The Mind of the Founding Fathers', p. 103.

[79] Sujit Choudhury, Madhav Khosla and Pratap Bhanu Mehta, 'Locating Indian Constitutionalism', in *The Oxford Handbook of the Indian Constitution*, pp. 4–5.

[80] Sandipta Dasgupta, '"A Language which is Foreign to Us": Continuities and Anxieties in the Making of the Indian Constitution', *Comparative Studies of South Asia, Africa and Middle East* 34, no. 2 (2014): 240.

Review Questions

1. **Critically evaluate the legislative inputs that influenced the 1950 Constitution of India.**
2. **In what respects it will be correct to say that the Indian Constitution draws on the philosophy of Enlightenment? Elaborate your response.**
3. **What are major nationalist inputs which the founding fathers took into account while being engaged in the framing of the Constitution? Elaborate.**
4. **How far it is correct to say that the Constitution of India was made in the past but articulated in the Constituent Assembly? Elaborate your response.**
5. **Critically evaluate the 1919 Montague–Chelmsford reform scheme as a constitutional design.**
6. **Critically evaluate the 1858 Queen's Proclamation from the point of view constitutionalizing governance in India.**
7. **Critically assess the importance of the 1928 Motilal Nehru Committee report as a significant input for the Constitution of India.**
8. **How was the Constituent Assembly constituted? Was it democratic? Elaborate your response.**
9. **'The Constitution of India was an outcome of accommodation and consensus'. Do you agree? Elaborate your response.**
10. **Is the Constitution of India democratic in nature and character? Elaborate your response.**

Chapter

2

Directive Principles of State Policy (Part IV of the Constitution of India)

Learning Objectives

- To understand why the Directive Principles of State Policy are important in a constitutional design
- To comprehend why the founding fathers insisted on Directive Principles of State Policy
- To evaluate the importance of these principles, despite not being non-justiciable, in constitutional governance in India

The Directive Principles of State Policy (DPSP) is a vision document which was carefully crafted by the founding fathers of the Indian Constitution. It reflects the ideal constitutional formula of achieving historical consensus in post-colonial India which had to achieve freedom from social and economic inequalities on the one hand and removal of monopoly over political power, on the other, through effective empowerment of teeming half naked millions by means of decentralization of democratic process and articulation of the general will. In fact, the promises made during the freedom struggle to the dumb semi-starved millions, to use Gandhi's phraseology, and the declarations made time and again (that political independence for the country would have no meaning if the starvation and exploitation of the millions were not ended) had aroused massive societal expectations from the political elites of independent India. The Constituent Assembly of India, having been under tremendous pressure to ensure socio-economic justice within the framework of a liberal democracy which is explicitly visible in the Constituent Assembly debate over primacy to individual rights versus societal rights came out with a non-justiciable constitutional recipe, namely DPSP which was to act as fundamental principle of governance. Most of these Directives intend to establish the socio-economic democracy, which is succinctly enumerated in the Preamble. Granville Austin considered these directives as a decisive politico-constitutional tool for bringing about social revolution. According to him:

> By establishing these political obligations of the state, the members of the Constituent Assembly made it the responsibility of future Indian government to find a middle way between individual liberty and the public good, between prescribing the privileges of the few and bestowing benefits on the many in order to liberate the powers of all men equally, for constructions of common good.[1]

[1] Granville Austin, *The Indian Constitution: Cornerstone of a Nation* (New Delhi: Oxford University Press, 1966), p. 52.

For the founding fathers, these principles, by nature, were non-justiciable directional steps representing their aspired dreams. With Vallabhbhai Patel, as it chairman, the Fundamental Rights Sub-committee thus recommended that

> we have come to the conclusion that in addition to justiciable fundamental rights, the constitution should include certain directives of State policy, which, though not cognizable in any court of law, should be regarded as fundamental in the governance of the country.[2]

Their primary concern was to build an egalitarian society which was a distant dream then. Nonetheless, by insisting on the inclusion of these principles in the future constitution, they felt that they left enough inputs for the posterity to guide India's destiny towards the goal that they set for themselves. These are not mere pipe dreams, but are realistically designed modes of organizing governance for public well-being, as history of constitutional democracy in India has, so far, shown. Given the importance of the DPSPs in governance, the chapter concentrates on how they evolved and became integral to India's policy designs. By dwelling on their rising salience, the chapter also makes an argument suggesting that despite not being enforceable, the DPSPs remain one of the fundamental pillars of constitutional democracy in India that is being constantly reinvented in response to newer socio-economic demands. The argument appears to have gained precedence in the light of the Seventy-Third and Seventy-Fourth Amendment Acts of 1992 which, by making panchayati raj governance part and parcel of India's governance now, radically altered its political texture.

Historical Antecedents

If we go through the constitutional history of socio-economic rights in the modern state system it becomes crystal clear that the enunciation of socio-economic policies came into existence as a regular feature in the constitutions drafted in post-war years as they intended to secure not only political justice for the individuals alone but also aimed at securing socio-economic justice for the society as a whole. Although the constitution was meant to act an instrument for socio-economic well-being of the people, its approach and methods differ from one place to another. In other words, there is hardly a pattern which perhaps confirms the importance of the context in which a constitution is made. The 1921 Constitution of the Principality of Liechtenstein[3] and the 1931 Constitution of the Spanish Republic, both professing Roman Catholic Christianity are illustrative here. The Constitution of Liechtenstein directed the state that the supreme duty of the State was to ensure the public welfare on the basis of its 14 principles relating to education, public health, industrial and agricultural labour, public utilities, natural resources, currency, credit and taxation, poor relief, social insurance and reform of the legal systems. However, the Spanish Directive was an improvement on the Liechtenstein directives in the sense that it broad-based the 'directives' as it included matters relating to family and culture apart from social and economic matters. The inclusion of social and economic policies, for the first time found a distinct place in the Constitution

[2] Vallabhbhai Patel to the President of the Constituent Assembly, 25 April 1947, reproduced in the *Constituent Assembly Debates*, Book No. 1, p. 373.

[3] The Constitution of the Principality of Liechtenstein, passed by the Diet of Principality on 24 August 1921 was approved by the reigning prince, Johann II on 2 October 1921 and finally signed on behalf of the prince on 5 October 1921.

of Ireland which came to force on 29 December 1937.[4] In fact, it made a significant contribution to the historical legacy of constitutional enactments as it made a clear-cut distinction between 'Fundamental Rights' relating to personal rights and other rights relating to the family, education, private property and religion and Directive Principles of State Policy, which contains social and economic matters. Commenting upon the probable infeasibility of such distinctive articulation of directives in the Irish Constitution, Donald O'Sullivan observed that

> large sections of the new Constitution consist of declarations of homiletic character concerning personal rights, and the family, education, private property, religion, and directive principles of social policy. Many of these are so vague that they could not possibly be impleaded in the courts and it is difficult to see what purpose they serve in such document.[5]

However, compared to other constitutions of the world, the inclusion of a chapter on the directives in the Constitution was a break with the past in the realm of constitutionalism as it clearly demarcated the rights as justiciable and non-justiciable which was earlier an unknown feature. Moreover, the title given to the provisions of this chapter as Directive Principles of State Policy and their being non-justiciable in character not only enlarged the scope of the 'Directives' but also its applicability.

The Indian Paradigm

It is worthy to note here that the adoption of DPSPs in the Constitution of India no doubt has inputs from several sources but the major influence has undeniably been the Irish Constitution. The function of the provisions contained in the 'Directives' is to give a particularly solemn sanction and status to the principles which are regarded as of great importance. With regard to the content, it may be said that no model 'Directives' could be set for the adoption by all countries. The most that could be done is to lay down generally acceptable objectives. It is also pertinent to mention that apart from adaptation of contemporary Western political and social philosophy there are many principles which are inherently Indian, particularly the ones relating to panchayats, cottage industries, prohibition, protection against cow slaughter, and protection of scheduled castes, scheduled tribes and other backward classes. In a very candid assessment of the DPSPs, KC Wheare thus argues:

> As these principles cannot be enforced in any court, they amount to little more than manifesto of aims and aspirations. In this matter of declarations of rights and of directives of State Policy, the Indian Constituent Assembly has followed the Irish Constitution and European practice rather than less colorful and more legalistic documents which serve as constitution for other members of the Commonwealth. One thing is certain. If these declarations of liberal principles, strange as they may seem in a legal document to British eyes, help the Indian Constitution on

[4] Declaration embodying a programme of social, economic or cultural reform also found a place in the Constitution of the Irish Free State (Saorstat Eireann) Act of 1922. Articles 10 and 11 related to free elementary education and the nationalization of the natural resources of the country.

[5] The views of Donald O' Sullivan are cited in KC Markandan 'Fundamental Rights vis-à-vis Directive Principles of State Policy', in *Indian Political System*, eds. MP Singh and Himanshu Roy (New Delhi: Gyanda Prakashan, 1995), p. 121.

> its way and assist people in working their government, they are more justified. This is the biggest liberal experiment in the Government of men by themselves that has ever been tried.[6]

The debates in the Constituent Assembly on the chapter containing DPSPs seem to be useful to understand clearly the ideological perspective in which the members argued their respective points of view either in favour or against these principles. Christened initially as 'the Fundamental Principles of Governance' by the Advisory Committee on Fundamental Rights, they later became the Directive Principles of State Policy which was also a source of discomfort to some members.[7] There were prominent individual members who hailed the constitution makers for having incorporated the DPSPs while others did not find the effort worth pursuing since they were non-enforceable. It is true that the founding fathers did not allow their differences to be unbridgeable, and hence it was agreed upon that this chapter of the Constitution needed to be kept as 'a conscience keeper' for governance for future India. This was the sentiment which came out very unambiguously in the debates in the Assembly.

By not being persuaded to concede that these principles are 'useless because they have not biding force in law', BR Ambedkar thus elaborated his defence by stating:

> What are called Directive Principles is merely another name for Instrument of Instructions,... which were issued to the Governor-General and to the Governors of the Colonies and to those in India by the British Government under the 1935 Act. The only difference is that they were instructions to the Legislature and Executive.... Wherever there is a grant of power in general terms for peace, order and good government, it is necessary that it should be accompanied by instructions regarding its exercise.[8]

So, these principles were no foreign to the founding fathers. In view of their salience in governance, they were 'welcomed', as Ambedkar mentioned. Being critical to constitutional values, these principles were thus justifiably incorporated in the Constitution, as Ambedkar further argued by underlining:

> Whoever captures power will not be free to do what he likes to do with it. In the exercise of it, he will have to respect these instruments of instructions which are called Directive Principles. He cannot ignore them. He may not have to answer for their breach in a Court of Law. But he will certainly have to answer for them before the electorate at election time. What great value these directive principles possess will be realized better when the force of right contrive to capture power.[9]

In his perception, in two ways, these principles were to play a significant role in governance: on the one hand, they, by insisting on those cardinal principles of democracy, would not allow the system of governance to slip away from the fundamental precepts of constitutional democracy in India; they would also strengthen, on the other hand, democratic rule for if they were ignored by the rulers, the electorates would

---

[6] KC Wheare, 'India's New Constitution Analysed', *Allahabad Law Journal* 21 (1950): 18.

[7] HV Kamath of Central Provinces and Berar expressed his resentment in his speech in the Assembly on 19 November 1948, *Constituent Assembly Debates*, Book No. 3, pp. 474–75.

[8] BR Ambedkar, 4 November 1948, *Constituent Assembly Debates*, Book No. 2, p. 41.

[9] Ibid., p. 41.

punish them when they asked for votes. So, the DPSPs were integral to democratic governance in India which would both instil democratic values and inculcate a mindset supportive of democracy in the country.

Ambedkar's argument did not auger well with some of the leading members of the Assembly. The opposition built their viewpoints by insisting that these principles needed to be enforceable, and if that was not 'the desired option', they could easily be deleted. As Kazi Syed Karimuddin (Central Provinces and Berar) expressed the feeling of being disappointed by saying:

> If this Constitution is not laying down these principles for being enforced in a court of law, or if they are not binding on the State, they are meaningless. . . . [T]hese principles should be embodied in the Constitution as Fundamental Rights and that a scheme embodying these principles should be brought into operation within ten years. . . . They should be made Fundamental Principles of State Policy.[10]

The idea is very clear. Given the fact that these principles are directed to attain the values that the founding fathers aspired, they needed to be included as a part of the chapter containing Fundamental Rights. As a nationalist, Karimuddin was also not willing to include 'the Instrument of Instructions' which was colonial in character, and hence he raised the point by stating that 'if [they] are from colonial rule, why should they find a place in the Fundamental Principles to be embodied in the Constitution'.[11] He was supported by Mahboob Ali Baig Bahadur of Madras who endorsed the argument that Karimuddin had advanced by insisting that 'this chapter should not have a place in the Constitution since [it] reflects the desire of the members [belonging to the Congress] to placate the electorate saying [that] we have framed a Constitution in which we have made these provisions which are as good, if not better than the principles and programmes of some other party, say the Socialist Party'.[12] With a blatant political motive of the dominant majority, Baig Bahadur thus asserted that 'this is very wrong . . . and on account of the fact that they cannot be enforced they are useless and they had better be deleted'.[13] This was the sentiment which KT Shah (Bihar) also shared. Insisting that the word 'directive' should not be taken out of the Constitution, he felt that

> in the absence of any such mandatory direction to those who may have the governance of the country hereafter, it is quite possible that all these things for which we have been hoping and striving all these years may have come to pass, at any rate within our life time. This is an attitude which no lover of the people would care to justify, would dare to justify.[14]

What is evident here is the concern of democracy being diluted by not agreeing to incorporate these principles in the justiciable segment of the proposed constitution. While summarizing the argument, Shah defended the point that unless these principles were mandatary in governance, they would certainly enhance 'the cosmetic beauty of the constitution' but would become futile for building constitutional democracy in India in its true spirit and substance. Hence TT Krishnamachari (Madras) characterized this part of the Constitution 'as a veritable dustbin of sentiments [that] . . . seems to be sufficiently resilient

[10] Kazi Syed Karimuddin (Central Provinces and Berar), 19 November 1948, *Constituent Assembly Debates*, Book No. 2, p. 473.
[11] Ibid., p. 473.
[12] Mahboob Ali Baig Bahadur (Madras), 19 November 1948, *Constituent Assembly Debates*, Book No. 2, p. 489.
[13] Ibid., p. 489.
[14] KT Shah (Bihar), 19 November 1948, *Constituent Assembly Debates*, Book No. 2, p. 479.

as to permit any individual of this House to ride his hobby horse into it'.[15] What caused a division among the members was the decision of keeping these principles in the non-justiciable part of the Constitution since that would, as they believed, serve no substantial purpose.

The arguments supportive of making the directives judicially enforceable did not however find many takers in the Assembly. In fact, Ambedkar's supporters outnumbered the opponents since their principles were considered to be useful for protecting and also strengthening those critical values which built a solid foundation for democratic governance. This was most categorically stated by M Ananthasayanam Ayyangar when he said that 'these are principles which the Government must keep in mind, whatever government may be in power, and they must be carried out. We have incorporated them in the Constitution itself because we attach importance to them'.[16] Ayyangar also argued for a clear demarcation between the DPSPs and Fundamental Rights by insisting that 'to classify them as Fundamental Rights as in Part III would be to take away the difference between the one set and the other, and making all the rights justiciable, which, in the nature of things, is impossible'.[17] For him, instead of being carried away by sentiments, what was required of the members was to be 'practical' because 'we cannot go on introducing various provisions here which any Government, if it is indifferent to public opinion, can ignore'.[18] Being confident that a democratic nation was a shield against abuse of power since the people remained the final arbiter which he articulated by saying that 'it is the public opinion and the strength of public opinion that is behind a demand that can enforce these provisions'.[19] According to him, mere constitutional guarantee was not adequate to sustain democracy; what was required utmost was an alert public opinion that unfolded in a particular way every time the rulers faced the electorates. Hence he concluded by emphasizing that 'once in four years, election will take place, and then it is open to the electorate not to send the very same persons who are indifferent to public opinion. That is the real sanction and not the sanction of any court of law'.[20] In continuity of the argument that Ayyangar offered, Shibban Lal Saksena of the United Provinces held the view that with the introduction of these values in governance, this chapter

> gives such a guarantee that it will surely be open to every legislature to point out when an act is brought before the Assembly that it is in conflict with the principles laid down in this Chapter. So, the mere fact that they are being included in the Constitution shows that every legislature will be bound to respect these directive principles in the Constitution and therefore, any act which offends the directive principles shall be *ultra vires*.[21]

For Saksena, the chapter of DPSPs constituted an important segment of the constitution which was to ensure constitutional democracy in India. Hence he concluded that 'this chapter is not merely a chapter of pious wishes, but a chapter containing great principles ... which will govern the policy of the State and ... will therefore ensure to the people of the country the realization of the great ideals laid down in the preamble'.[22] Pursuing the point that Saksena made in support of this chapter, Mahavir Tyagi of United Provinces appreciated the clause by adding that 'this chapter is of great importance [because] ... this is

[15] TT Krishnamachari, 24 November 1948, *Constituent Assembly Debates*, Book No. 2, p. 583.
[16] M Ananthasayanam Ayyangar (Madras), 19 November 1948, *Constituent Assembly Debates*, Book No. 2, p. 475.
[17] Ibid., p. 475.
[18] Ibid., p. 475.
[19] Ibid., p. 475.
[20] Ibid., p. 475.
[21] Shibban Lal Saksena (United Provinces), 19 November 1948, *Constituent Assembly Debates*, Book No. 2, p. 482.
[22] Ibid., p. 482.

the only chapter which translates into practice our aim of securing Justice, Equality and Fraternity. [Furthermore], this is the only chapter that accommodates all the revolutionary slogans [and] it is the pivotal point in the Constitution'.[23] Given the critical importance of this chapter in fulfilling the fundamental ideological aims of the founding fathers, Tyagi insisted that 'this chapter must be made very strong [in order to fulfil their aspired objective of] promoting the welfare of the people by securing and protecting a social order in which justice, social, economic and political shall inform all our institutions'.[24] Like his colleagues, Saksena and Ayyangar, Tyagi also felt that for democratic governance to strike roots in India, the DPSPs had a critical role to play. In that respect, they needed to be incorporated in the Constitution.

As the discussion held earlier shows, despite some opposition, a large section of the Assembly members was in favour of including DPSPs in the constitution. The Assembly however witnessed another series of arguments and counter-arguments when these principles were presented as non-justiciable. It was BN Rau, one of the prominent constitutional advisors, who initiated this debate when he placed the suggestion of the Cabinet Mission in favour of justiciable and non-justiciable rights. In consonance with the Irish constitutional design of dividing two classes of rights, Rau recommended the division of rights in two parts, Part A and Part B: while the former dealt with the Fundamental Rights of State Policy which meant DPSPs, the latter with the Fundamental Rights. Here too, there were members who felt that the distinction was apt as the proposed DPSPs were merely intended as 'a guide and directive of state policy'. According to some of the members, the distinction was arbitrary since DPSPs were also critical to governance, and hence they argued strongly for their inclusion in the justiciable part of the constitution. The matter was resolved with the publication of the report of the Advisory Committee on Fundamental Rights, chaired by Vallabhbhai Patel. In its report which was placed before the Assembly on 30 March 1947, Patel, by ruling out the demand for making these principles enforceable, stuck to the distinction though in his formulation these principles were defined as Fundamental Principles of State Policy which later became DPSP.

According to the first set of DPSP as framed on 30 March 1947 by Sub-Committee, it was resolved that 'the principles of social policy set forth in this part are intended for the general guidance of the appropriate legislatures and governments in India (collectively called as the State hereafter). The application of these principles in legislation and administration shall be the care of the State and shall not be cognizable by any court'.[25] On the next day, 31 March 1947, the Sub-committee however decided to insert the following Preamble to the Directive Principles of Social Policy: 'the principles of social policy set forth in this part are intended for the general guidance of the State. The application of these principles in legislation and administration shall be the acre of the State and shall not be cognizable by the court'.[26]

The members adopted provisions based on BN Rau's draft highlighting that the state should raise the level of nutrition and the standard of living of the people and to promote international peace and just dealings between nations.[27] Certain changes and counter-changes were made during the next several weeks, but in general the first stage of drafting the Directive Principles was over. The Minorities Sub-Committee suggested two changes in the Clause relating to non-justiciable rights as framed by the Fundamental Rights Committee. Two other changes effected by the Advisory Committee in the list of non-justiciable rights recommended by the Fundamental Rights Sub-committee were (a) Clause 33 was

[23] Mahavir Tyagi (United Provinces), 19 November 1948, *Constituent Assembly Debates*, Book No. 2, p. 492.
[24] Ibid., p. 493.
[25] Minutes of the Fundamental Rights Sub-Committee meeting of 31 March 1947. President's collection.
[26] Minutes of the Fundamental Rights Sub-Committee meeting.
[27] Clauses 9, 10 and 12, Supplementary Report.

given the subtitle Preamble and the rest a subtitle Principles and, (b) the substitution of the words 'are not' for the words 'shall not be' in the second sentence of the Clause 33.[28]

The second stage in the framing of the principles took place on the Assembly floor in November and December 1948 during the debate on the Drafting of Constitution. Interestingly, it appears from the debate that two major concerns emerged towards the draft: one that the Directives did not go far enough towards establishing a socialistic state and the other that they should have placed greater emphasis on certain institutions. Some Assembly members sought to make the promotion of cottage industries a government responsibility and make it a duty of state to prevent the slaughter of cattle and to improve animal husbandry and agriculture. In the Assembly, Ambedkar admitted 'a considerable amount of feeling'[29] in favour of government encouragement for cottage industries forced him to accept an amendment placing the promotion of cottage industries in the Directive Principles.[30] The provisions pertaining to the improvement of agricultural and animal husbandry techniques and the prohibition of cow slaughter was also added. The prohibition of liquor and harmful drugs (e.g., opium) also became a fundamental principle of governance. Furthermore, what was most striking was the reluctance of the members to accord judicial protection in case these DPSPs were infringed. This was strange also since the Nehruvian socialism seemed to have been endorsed over other ideological priorities by most of the members. And, yet amendments to that effect were either withdrawn or voted down; the Congress also did not appear to be very keen on this, as was evident in several meetings that were held to discuss the constitutional issues. As a result, the opinion in favour making these principles justiciable never gained adequate strength that explains why they were included in Part IV which was a non-justiciable segment of the constitution.

Nonetheless, the debate on this issue is very useful to comprehend the arguments that were put in favour of different points of view that surfaced; the discussion will also help us understand how a specific kind of mindset was privileged for developing a system of governance which was functionally strong and not inhibited by narrow ideological considerations. This was evident because there was, as mentioned earlier, hardly a consensus on this issue. As a result, for some, the chapter entails 'pious expressions and pious superfluities'; it is 'vague' and a 'drift', according to some; for some, it was 'a cheque on a bank payable when able'; another opinion took it to be analogous to 'an election manifesto' and hence it had no place in the Constitution; and yet, there was another view suggesting that since it was specifically meant for a particular section of the people, it was invariably 'undemocratic' and opposed to parliamentary democracy which justified its complete deletion from the Constitution.

Many of the dissenters in the Assembly did not appreciate the distinction between justiciable and non-justiciable nature of the rights since the aim of these sets of rights remained identical. These two parts of the constitution cannot be separated, argued Thakur Das Bhargava by saying that 'Fundamental Rights and Directive Principles ... are the soul of the Constitution, and we cannot establish the Ramrajya, advocated by Mahatmaji [Gandhi] unless we make the Fundamental Rights and the Directive Principles our guiding star and work according to them'.[31] Insisting that Directive Principles were critical to eradicate

[28] Clause 33: The principles of policy set forth in this part are intended for the guidance of the state. While these principles shall not be cognizable by any court, they are nevertheless fundamental in the governance of the country and their application in the making of laws shall be the duty of the State'.

[29] BR Ambedkar, 23 November 1948, *Constituent Assembly Debates*, Book No. 2, p. 535.

[30] Article 43 of the Constitution; the Amendment that Dr Ambedkar accepted was moved by TA Ramalingam Chettiar (Madras), 23 November 1948, *Constituent Assembly Debates*, Book No. 2, p. 532.

[31] Thakur Das Bhargava, 18 November 1949, *Constituent Assembly Debates*, Book No. 5, p. 686.

some of the major socio-economic sources for discrimination responsible for inequality in India, Somnath Lahiri of Bengal pursued the point by strongly arguing that

> it is rather difficult to make a distinction between what are justiciable rights and what are not. For instance, when we make a provision that people should have right to work, that is, unemployment should not exist in our country, it would be a social right. If you make it an inalienable provision of our fundamental rights, naturally it will have to be justiciable. Similarly, take the question of nationalization of land. If one wants to say that land belongs to the people and to nobody else that would be a social and fundamental right no doubt.... It will also be a justiciable right.... Therefore, it is rather arbitrary to make any distinction between what is justiciable and what are social and economic rights.[32]

Being opposed to the distinction, Lahiri also felt that the design itself was in contravention of the fundamental ethos of democracy. By putting some of the inalienable rights as non-justiciable, the proposed constitution

> takes away rights that we fought for [and] ... this is a thing against which Indians have been entertaining bitterest feelings and they been agitating against this from the Congress and every other platform.... This is a thing against which every patriotic Indian is up in arms [because] ... in the heart of heart every Indian feels that in a free India in order that people may feel freedom and act up to it, there should not be constraints of any kind to deprive them of their rights.[33]

For Lahiri, the distinction was thus unwarranted because it served neither the purpose for which the freedom fighter fought for freedom nor creates a democratic society in which people enjoyed freedom in its undiluted form. This sentiment was shared by his colleague in the Assembly, Promatha Ranjan Thakur of Bengal, who also felt that this 'artificial' distinction was a deterrent for realizing the socio-economic objectives that India's freedom stood for. He was clueless as to 'why economic fundamental rights were not included in the justiciable rights [since] ... economic rights are essential while framing a country's Constitution and they also must be made justiciable'.[34] Thakur was not a lone voice; the same concern was expressed by Renuka Ray of West Bengal who was persuaded to believe that the sources of socio-economic discrimination remained so long as the property owners received legal protection from the state. Hence she was not supportive of 'adequate compensation' in case a person was deprived of his property because it would harm the aim of the Constitution. In order to make the country socio-economically even, she thus recommended:

> The provision for compensation for property, ... taken by the State for public purposes in accordance with law should be under directives and not under rights which are justiciable and enforceable in the court of law [because] ... it is not right that we commit the future to the economic structure of the present.[35]

[32] Somnath Lahiri, 29 April 1947, *Constituent Assembly Debates*, Book No. 1, p. 403.
[33] Ibid., p. 404.
[34] Promatha Ranjan Thakur (Bengal), 29 April 1947, *Constituent Assembly Debates*, Book No. 1, p. 403.
[35] Renuka Ray (West Bengal), 9 November 1948, *Constituent Assembly Debates*, Book No. 2, p. 357.

Both Ray and Lahiri upheld similar views, namely, in order to achieve equality, the directives needed to be given adequate legal protection; mere articulation of these principles in the Constitution was not a guarantee that they would be respected. In that respect, the inclusion of these principles as non-justiciable rights was an attempt to deflect the main issue because without adequate judicial defence they would cease to be effective constitutional values.

Member's also expressed their view that in absence of provisions in this chapter making it obligatory it was quite possible that none of these provisions might ever be realized in a lifetime.[36] A strong opinion was thus expressed by Krishna Chandra Sharma of United Provinces by saying that despite the fact that

> we have directive principles [whereby] the State shall endeavour to find work and employment for all, we will be restrained to implement the provision since it belongs to the non-justiciable part of the Constitution. The State does not take the responsibility to make the people work, on the principle that he who does not work, neither shall he eat. This is simply not acceptable. We should have provision for enforcement of work for able-bodied citizens.... In the directive principles ... there is no legal obligation imposed on the State to fulfil the rights given in the Constitution [and] ... we should make a provision that any law made in contravention of these principles shall be ... void.[37]

Critical of the directives for being merely directional and not mandatary, Sharma reflected a concern that some of his colleagues had also shared, as is evident from the earlier discussion. They were not persuaded to accept the distinction between justiciable and non-justiciable rights since it was, as they felt, framers' escape route to avoid their constitutional obligations to the future India. Despite having made their point forcefully and also persuasively, they failed to convince the majority of the Assembly members who seemed to have endorsed the arguments that Ambedkar made in favour of separating the non-justiciable rights from the justiciable ones. In his detailed response on 19 November 1948, Babasaheb made a strong case for this distinction by arguing that

> the word "directive" ... should be retained because it is understood that in enacting this part of the Constitution, the Constituent Assembly ... is giving certain directions to the future legislature and the future executive power which they will have. If the word "directive" is omitted, ... the intention of the Constituent Assembly in enacting this part will fail in its purpose.[38]

So, it was made clear that these principles were just directional to the future administrators and law makers. The chairman of the Drafting Committee had thus no doubts about the purpose of this chapter in the Constitution. The DPSPs are mere directives for governance which are not legally binding. Despite not being mandatary constitutional rights, these principles served useful purposes, as Ambedkar strongly felt when he said:

> It is not the intention to introduce in this part these principles as mere pious declarations; it is the intention of this Assembly that in future both the legislature and the executive should

---

[36] KT Shah (Bihar), 19 November 1948, *Constituent Assembly Debates*, Book No. 2, p. 479.
[37] Krishna Chandra Sharma (United Provinces), 5 November 1948, *Constituent Assembly Debates*, Book No. 2, p. 230.
[38] BR Ambedkar, 19 November 1948, *Constituent Assembly Debates*, Book No. 2, p. 476.

> not merely pay lip service to these principles enacted in this part, but that they should be made the basis of all executive and legislative action that may be taken hereafter in the matter of governance of the country.[39]

For Ambedkar, the choice was very unambivalent. Directive principles needed to be there in the Constitution despite not be being mandatary just for giving directions to the future legislature and executive. Based on what they wanted to ideally achieve, the founding fathers left enough space to the prospective governors to shape governance in accordance with the principles that were included in this chapter of the proposed constitution. True, they were not made legally binding, and yet they entailed those constitutional and ideological values which were critical for the evolution and also consolidation of democratic governance in future India. Hence, it was admitted in the Preamble to the Fundamental Principles of Governance (that later became DPSPs), which stated:

> The principles of policy set forth in this part are intended for the guidance of the State. While these principles are not cognizable by any court, they are nevertheless fundamental in the governance of the country and their application in the making of laws shall be the duty of the State.[40]

There was hardly any ambiguity in Ambedkar's assessment of Fundamental Principles of Governance. They were fundamental in the sense that they upheld those values which one could not afford to ignore if one was keen to realize constitutional democracy in its true form and substance. From the discussions in the Constituent Assembly, the following points emerge in respect of the Directive Principles of the State Policy:

1. That the directives are like instruments of instructions to the legislature and the executive and as such could be justified for inclusion in the Constitution;
2. That the directives cannot or will not be ignored by any responsible government or any legislature elected on the basis of universal adult suffrage for the sanction behind them is not the courts but the electorate;
3. That the directives lay down the ideals of economic democracy.

Typologies of Directive Principles

Broadly speaking, there are two major sources of DPSPs: some of the principles seem to have been drawn from the Gandhian concern for equality, especially by devising mechanisms to uplift the poorest of the poor; there were also principles which had clear socialistic roots in the sense that they seek to create an egalitarian society by appropriating some of the means that were employed in the erstwhile Soviet Union.

There are 16 Articles of the Constitution (Articles 36–51) that deal with the DPSPs. Based on their concern for common well-being, the founding fathers included a wide range of provisions which were

[39] Ibid., p. 476.

[40] Appendix A, appended with the letter that Vallabhbhai Patel (the chairman of the Committee on Fundamental Rights) wrote to the President of the Constituent Assembly on 25 August 1947, *Constituent Assembly Debates*, Book No. 1, p. 375.

reflective of what they aspired to in case the situation was propitious. Hence these principles entail those areas of human activity which the state should take care for creating equality in its most undiluted form and substance. The state is, in other words, expected to undertake those activities which are tuned to the goals for socio-economic development. Broadly speaking, these Articles can be clubbed under three major categories in the light of the objectives that they seek to fulfil: *Socialistic principles*, *Gandhian principles* and *Liberal-democratic principles*.

Socialistic Principles

1. Article 38 sets out the objectives that the chapter envisions in two Clauses:
   According to Clause 1, 'the State shall strive to promote the welfare of the people by securing and promoting as effectively as it may a social order in which justice, social, economic and political shall inform all the institutions of the national life'.
   Clause 2 stipulates that 'the State shall, in particular, strive to minimize the inequalities in income and endeavour to eliminate inequalities in status, facilities and opportunities, not only amongst individuals but also amongst groups of people residing in different areas or engaged in different vocations'.
2. As per Article 39, which is meant to bring about meaningful socio-economic changes, the State shall direct its policy towards securing
   a) adequate means of livelihood to all citizens;
   b) a proper distribution of material resources of the community for the common good;
   c) prevention of concentration of wealth to the common detriment;
   d) equal pay for equal work for both men and women;
   e) the protection of the strength and health of workers and avoiding circumstances which force citizens to enter a vocations unsuited to their age or strength, and
   f) the protection of childhood and youth against exploitation or moral and material abandonment.
3. Article 41 insists that the state shall make effective provisions for securing 'the right to work, to education and to public assistance in cases of unemployment, old age, sickness and disablement, and in other cases of undeserved want'.
4. According to Article 42, the state is responsible, to the extent it is possible, for securing 'just and humane conditions for work and for maternity relief'.
5. As Article 43 mentions, the state is 'to secure, by suitable legislations or economic organization or in any other way, to all workers, agricultural, industrial or otherwise, work, living wage, conditions of work ensuring a decent standard of life and full employment of labour and social and cultural opportunities'. This obligation of the state in this regard was expanded in 1976 with the adoption of the Forty-Second Amendment Act which suggests that the state shall take steps, by suitable legislations or in any other way, to secure the participation of workers in the management of undertakings, establishments or other organizations engaged in any industry'.
6. Article 45 insists that the state 'provides, within ten years of the commencement of the Constitution, free and compulsory education to all children up to the age of fourteen years'.
7. According to Article 46, it is the responsibility of the state to promote, with special care, the educational and economic interests of the weaker sections of the people, especially the Scheduled Castes and Tribes'.
8. Article 47 bestows the responsibility on the state to secure the improvement of public health and the prohibition of intoxicating drinks and drugs.

Gandhian Principles

1. In order to devolve power to the grassroots units of governance, Article 40 states that the state needs to take steps to organize village panchayats as effective centres of governance.
2. In order to make agriculture and other related ancillary works attractive, Article 48 underlines that the state 'shall endeavour to organize agriculture and animal husbandry on modern and scientific lines and shall, in particular, take steps for preserving and improving the breeds and prohibiting the slaughter of cows and calves and other milch and draught cattle'.

Liberal-democratic Principles

1. In order to erase social disparities between religious communities, Article 44 stipulates that the state shall 'endeavour to secure a uniform civil code throughout India'.
2. Article 49 makes the state responsible for protecting all monuments of historic interest and national importance.
3. As per Article 50, the state shall take steps 'to separate the judiciary from the executive in the public services of the State'.
4. To address the founding fathers' concern for international peace and security, Article 51 thus suggests that the state shall strive to 'maintain just and honourable relations between nations, foster respect for international law and treaty and obligations in the dealings of organized people with one another, and encourage settlement of international disputes by arbitration'.

Annotation

Reflective of the desire of the founding fathers for realizing some of the exalted socio-economic objectives, these DPSPs continue to act as a conscience keeper since they are not justiciable. Nonetheless, by emphasizing these principles, the framers seemed to have set certain constitutional conditions which were expected to be respected by the future policy makers. As history has shown, there were numerous occasions when these principles acted decisively in cases when the State privileged DPSPs over Fundamental Rights. The Indian judiciary too endorsed the preferences as they were stepping towards building an egalitarian society. Their importance cannot thus be belittled in governance. Being most perceptive of the future, the DPSPs thus become a significant ideological pillar of India's constitutional democracy.

These principles also direct our attention to a specific kind of functioning of the Constituent Assembly which was hailed as a forum for building consensus. Seeking to accommodate different, if not conflicting, points of view over multifarious socio-economic and politico-ideological issues, the founding fathers seem to have been receptive to various kinds of opinions arising out of even contrasting ideological perspectives. That was never a source of discomfort or bitterness among them; instead, they were welcome as they represented India's true socio-economic texture of being a microcosm of diverse views and perspectives. In fact, this became a source of strength because it was believed that out of dialogues among those who always privileged India's collective existence over one's regional identity would emerge possibly the most meaningful, if not the best, politico-ideological options for governance. It is therefore not surprising that BR Ambedkar thus characterized the DPSPs as a harbinger for economic democracy which, if implemented in its true substance, would usher an era of undiluted happiness. The sentiment was expressed by MC Chagla, a former chief justice of India, when he said that 'if all these principles are fully carried out, our country will indeed be a heaven on the earth'.[41] Despite not being judicially enforceable, the constitutional importance of these principles can never be undermined since they continue to inspire the policy makers for significant socio-economic changes in India.

In view of the intensive debates in the Assembly that followed once the DPSPs were placed for discussion, there is no denying that, notwithstanding their colonial roots, (as they were the erstwhile instrument of instructions), these principles were upheld zealously by the founding fathers for being directional to the rulers. It was strongly felt by the members regardless of ideology that the DPSPs needed to be made strong if the exalted goal of making the country free from hunger, want and socio-economic prejudices was to be realized. A beacon light for the future decision makers, these principles would not only sustain constitutional democracy but also help combat social, economic and politico-ideological discrimination in future India.

Constitutional Amendments and DPSPs

As was expressed in the Assembly, the DPSPs became a yardstick in designing policy priorities in independent India. In order to fulfil the ideological goal of eradicating socio-economic discrimination, the Constitution was amended on several occasions. Of all these Amendments, the 1976 Forty-Second Amendment Act and Forty-Fourth Amendment Act of 1978 seem to have radically altered India's constitutional texture by privileging DPSPs in decision making. In the changed socio-economic and political environment, some of the ideas of Part IV of the Constitution were considered to be most useful in significant social restructuring which was required to create a society of equality.

The Forty-Second Amendment Act, 1976

Adopted during the Emergency (1975–77), the Forty-Second Amendment Act was also characterized as a ploy to strengthen the draconian rule that evolved following the proclamation. Nonetheless, it was also hailed as a significant constitutional step towards realizing some of the socialistic goals that the founding fathers had held as their aspirational ideological goals. It is evident in the formulation of the Act which, in categorical terms, highlights that

1. If the impediments to the growth of the Constitution are not removed, the Constitution will suffer a virtual atrophy. The question of amending the Constitution for removing the difficulties which have arisen in achieving the objective of socio-economic rejuvenation, which would end poverty and ignorance and disease and inequality of opportunity, has been engaging the active attention of government and the public for some years now.
2. The democratic institutions provided in the Constitution are basically sound and the path for progress does not lie in denigrating any of these institutions. However, there could be no denial that these institutions have been subjected to considerable stresses and strains and that vested interests have been trying to promote their selfish ends to the great detriment of public good.
3. It is, therefore, proposed to amend the Constitution to spell out expressly the high ideals of socialism, secularism and integrity of the nation, to make the Directive Principles more

[41] Quoted in GG Mirchandani, *Subverting the Constitution of India* (New Delhi: Abhinav Publications, 1993), p. 48.

comprehensive and given them precedence over those fundamental rights which have been allowed to be relied upon to frustrate socio-economic reforms for implementing the Directive Principles. It is also proposed to specify fundamental duties of citizens and make special provisions for dealing with anti-national activities, whether by individuals or associations.[42]

The Forty-Second Amendment was a remarkable piece of legislation with significant constitutional implications for governance. Besides inserting the word, 'socialist' in the Preamble to the Constitution of India, this Act had also added, similar to the Constitution of the erstwhile USSR, an independent article, Article 51A, identifying 'fundamental duties' for the citizens of the country. What was most remarkable was the legal stipulation to the effect that DPSPs were to be privileged in case they came in conflict with the Fundamental Rights, enshrined in Part III of the Constitution. For the ruling dispensation, led by Indira Gandhi, it was necessary since socialism did not 'indicate collectivism, but the offering of equal opportunities to all through socio-economic reforms'.[43] The aim was to adopt socio-economic measures to realize the socialistic goals that Part IV of the Constitution stipulated. Two Articles were inserted: Article 39A insists that the State is under obligation 'to ensure that opportunities for justice are not denied to any citizen by reason of economic or other disabilities'. In tune with the pledge for justice that the Preamble takes, this Article is complementary to the entire effort. Seeking to translate the ideological goal of making the workers integral to the management of industries and other undertakings, Article 43A creates a legitimate space for them. This was also justified in recognition of the endeavour for involving the workers in running the industries which was clearly a part of the socialistic design of governance.

The Forty-Fourth Amendment Act, 1978

The importance of the DPSPs was ascertained again in 1978 with the adoption of the Forty-Fourth Amendment Act which was hailed as an effective step 'to ensure to the people themselves an effective voice in determining the form of government under which they were to live'. The objectives were very clear, as the Act states:

1. Certain changes, which would have the effect of impairing its secular or democratic character, abridging or taking away fundamental rights prejudicing or impeding free and fair elections on the basis of adult suffrage and compromising the independence of judiciary, can be made only if they are approved by the people of India by a majority of votes at a referendum in which at least 51 per cent of the electorate participate.
2. In view of the special position sought to be given to fundamental rights, the right to property, which has been the occasion for than one amendment of the Constitution, would cease to be a fundamental right and become only a legal right. Necessary amendments for this purpose are being made to Article 19 and Article 31 is being deleted. It would, however, be ensured that the removal of property from the list of fundamental rights would not affect the right of minorities to establish and administer educational institutions of their choice.[44]

---

[42] 'The Preamble to the Forty-Second Amendment Act, 1976'. http://indiacode.nic.in/coiweb/amend/amend42.htm (accessed 27 November 2016).

[43] Indira Gandhi's speech in the Lok Sabha, *Hindustan Times*, New Delhi, 2 September 1976.

[44] 'Forty-Fourth Amendment Act, 1978'. http://indiacode.nic.in/coiweb/amend/amend44.htm (accessed 27 November 2016).

The outcome of the Forty-Fourth Amendment Act was the insertion of Clause 2 which became a part of Article 38 which underlines:

> The State shall . . . strive to minimize the inequalities in income, and endeavour to eliminate inequalities in status, facilities, opportunities, not only amongst individuals but also amongst groups of people residing in different areas or engaged in different professions.

Here too, the idea is very clear: in order to eradicate inequality, the ruling authority has, if backed by the required numerical strength in Parliament, every right to amend the Constitution. Inclusion of Clause 2 in Article 38 is just a step towards that though it has been criticized for being prejudiced against the property owners. As DD Basu commented:

> This innocently-looking amendment is to be read along with elimination of the Fundamental Right to Property. They have paved the way for confiscatory taxation and for equalizing salaries and wages for different vocations and different categories of work, which would usher in a socialistic society, even without resorting to nationalization of the means of production.[45]

Be as it may, the Forty-Fourth Amendment Act is complementary to an ideological preference which ran contrary to those supportive of the right to property. The argument that this amendment was directed to attain economic democracy was persuasive and was not so strongly challenged; as a result, Clause 2 of Article 38 became integral to the Constitution of India shaping a specific design of constitutional governance encouraging economic democracy.

Operational Dynamics

Despite finding a prominent place in the Constitution the journey undertaken by the DPSPs in more than six decades of its inception has generated a lot of heat due to legal wrangling between the Parliament and the Supreme Court on the issue of primacy of fundamental rights. This unfortunate scenario has been a by-product of two provisions of the Constitution; while, on the one hand, DPSP has to be applied in enactment for governance, it ought not to violate any provisions of the fundamental rights, on the other. Several laws enacted to implement DPSP to bring about socio-economic changes have been declared ultra vires on the ground that that they violate the fundamental rights. In cases like Champakam Dorairajan (1951) and several other instances in which the respective High Courts had adjudicated, it was pronounced clearly that the state was not authorized to enact a law to implement DPSPs by overriding the fundamental rights. This led to First Amendment Act (1951) which tried to limit the right to private property. It also inserted Articles 31A and 31B along with thirteen land reform acts in Schedule Nine so that judicial scrutiny in the name of protecting fundamental rights can be legally safeguarded. However, the judicial decision in the case of *Shankari Prasad Singh Deo v. the Union of India and State of Bihar* and *Bela Banerjee v. State of West Bengal* again forced the Parliament to adopt the Fourth Amendment Act (1955) to rule out the possibility of granting adequate compensation out of judicial purview. What drove the State to go for such an amendment was its concern to accord legitimacy to a large number of social welfare legislations,

---

[45] DD Basu, *Introduction to the Constitution of India* (22nd edition, Gurgaon: LexisNexis, 2016), p. 164.

meant to eradicate socio-economic inequality. The tug of war, however, continued unabated. In *Mohd. Hanif Qureshi and others v. the State of Bihar and Others* (1958), the Supreme Court intervened when the ban on cow slaughter was challenged as it contravened the Right to Freedom guaranteed under Article 19 (1) (g). It was argued that because the ban was designed to give effect to Article 48, and because DPSPs were critical to governance of the country, a right-based challenge to such legislation was unconstitutional. Being categorical in its preference for rights in Part III, the Court observed:

> A harmonious interpretation has to be placed upon the Constitution and so interpreted it means the State should certainly implement the directive principles but it must do so in such a way that its laws do not take away or abridge the fundamental rights.[46]

Similarly, while deciding the constitutional validity of the 1957 Kerala Education Bill which intended to provide free and compulsory education to children (as per Article 45) and challenged the fundamental rights of the minority communities to establish educational institutions of their choice as per Article 30 (1). In its 1958 verdict, the apex court held that DPSPs were subservient to the Fundamental Rights, which it articulated as follows:

> The directive principles of State Policy have to conform to and run as subsidiary to the Chapter on Fundamental Rights.... There can no manner of doubt that our Constitution has guaranteed cherished rights of the minorities concerning their language, culture and religion. These concessions must have been made to them for good and valid reasons. Article 45, no doubt, requires the State to provide for free and compulsory education or all children, but there is nothing to prevent from discharging that solemn obligation through Government and aided schools and Article 45 does not require that obligation to be discharged at the expense of the minority communities. So long as the Constitution stands as it is and is not altered, it is, we conceive, the duty of this Court to uphold the fundamental rights and thereby honour our sacred obligation the minority communities who are of our own.[47]

As per the judiciary, the DPSPs were not to be allowed to override the fundamental rights since it was contrary to the fundamental ethos in which the Constitution was articulated. Nonetheless, the idea that DPSPs were also critical to governance and thus could not be altogether ignored was also an important aspect of judicial pronouncement that gained acceptance. However, The politico-judicial honeymoon in the name of 'harmonious construction' soon came to an end with the pronouncement of the Supreme Court in the Golaknath case (1967) whereby it not only obliterated the distinction between the 'constitutional law' and 'statutory law' but also declared the First (1951), Fourth (1955) and Seventeenth Amendment (1964) Acts as null and void. This judgement virtually made fundamental rights 'sacrosanct'. Similar position was taken by the Supreme Court in Vajravelu case (1968), Metal Corporation case (1969) and the Bank Nationalization case (1970). Once again, in order to nullify the restrictive role of these judgements on Parliament's prerogative of unfettered power to amend the Constitution including fundamental rights, Twenty-Fourth and Twenty-Fifth Amendment Acts (1971) were passed. An important provision of the

---

[46] *Mohd. Hanif Qureshi and Others v. the State of Bihar and Others*, 1958. http://judis.nic.in/supremecourt/imgs1.aspx?filename=525 (accessed 27 November 2016).

[47] *The Kerala Education Bill v. Unknown*, 1959. https://indiankanoon.org/doc/161666/ (accessed 27 November 2016).

Twenty-Fourth Amendment Act (1971) was an insertion of a provision which stated that 'no law containing a declaration that it was for giving effect to such policy shall be called in question in any court on the ground that it does not give effect to such a policy'. The Parliament also piloted Twenty-Ninth Amendment Act (1972) to put two land reform acts of the Kerala state in the Ninth Schedule of the Constitution. As was expected, these provisions did not last long since the Supreme Court in the Kesavananda Bharati case (1973) declared them unconstitutional by devising a new legal dictum of 'Basic Structure' of the Constitution. With the consolidation of constitutional authoritarianism following the 1975–77 Emergency Proclamation, the Parliament passed the Forty-Second Amendment Act (1976) whereby an attempt was made to reinvigorate the DPSPs by bringing about fundamental change in the operative relationship between Fundamental Rights and the DPSPs. It accorded legal primacy and supremacy to the DPSPs over fundamental rights to equality, freedom and property. Such an endeavour on the part of the Parliament received further strength by the Forty-Fourth Amendment Act (1978) which abolished the Fundamental Right to Property. Thus, an important legal hurdle was sought to be removed which had legally been exploited as a stumbling block in the path of realization of ideals of DPSPs. In the Minerva Mills case (1980), the Supreme Court, once again, established the supremacy of the fundamental rights. Though the apex court had accepted the subordination of fundamental rights under Articles 14 and 19 to Clauses (b) and (c) of Article 39 on the one hand, it also declared, on the other, that subordination of the Fundamental Rights to the DPSPs as a whole (as effected by the Forty-Second Amendment Act) is ultra vires as it violated one of the basic structures of the Constitution.

From Supremacy to Compatibility

The post-Emergency articulation of several critical issues by NGOs relating to common concerns, such as environment, bonded labour, transparency, education, free legal aid and empowerment of weaker sections and so on have had definite positive impact on the judicial behaviour which was reflected in many proactive pronouncements. It is also alleged that by being excessively proactive, the judiciary appears to have usurped legislative and executive authority while seeking to implement the DPSPs. This has been achieved by the judicial acceptance of the fact that the Fundamental Rights and DPSPs are nothing but integrated constitutional scheme for realizing the cherished ideals of Preamble. This approach of judiciary was clearly formulated by Justice Hegde in the 1969 *Chandra Bhavan Boarding and Lodging v. the State of Mysore* case. He wrote:

> Part IV of the Constitution is designed to bring about the social and economic revolution that remained to be fulfilled after independence. The aim of the Constitution is not to guarantee certain liberties to only a few of the citizens but for all. The Constitution visualizes our society as a whole and contemplates that every member of the society should participate in the freedoms guaranteed. To ignore Part IV is to ignore the substance provided for in the Constitution, the hopes held out to the Nation and the very ideals on which our Constitution is built. Without faithfully implementing the Directive Principles, it is not possible to achieve the Welfare State contemplated by the Constitution. A society like ours stepped in poverty and ignorance satisfying the minimum economic needs of every citizen of this country. Any Government which fails to fulfil the pledge taken under the Constitution cannot be said to have been faithful to the Constitution and to its commitments.[48]

[48] *Chandra Bhavan Boarding and . . . v. the State of Mysore and Another*, 29 September 1969. https://indiankanoon.org/doc/1801637/ (accessed 27 November 2016).

Despite having endorsed the importance of DPSPs as instruments for substantial socio-economic changes, Justice Hegde was also aware that his arguments lack judicial endorsement since these principles were not justiciable. Nonetheless, they were recognized as critical to governance, both by the members of the Constituent Assembly and judiciary in post-Independence India. This was the sentiment that he articulated as follows:

> Provisions contained in Part III and Part IV ... are complementary and supplementary to each other. The mandate of the Constitution is to build a welfare society in which justice, social, economic and political shall inform all the institutions of our national life. The hopes and aspirations aroused by the Constitution will be belied if the minimum needs of the lowest of our citizens are not met.[49]

In the 1993 Unnikrishanan case, the court reiterated similar sentiments and said, without mincing words, that the Fundamental Rights and Directive Principles are supplementary and complementary to each other, and not exclusionary of each other, and that the Fundamental Rights are but a means to achieve the goals indicated in Directive Principles.[50] Since then, it appears to have become a practice in Indian judiciary which tends to pay adequate attention to the DPSPs while articulating its responses to cases dealing with threats to Fundamental Rights. This was evident again in 2012 *Union of India v. the State of Rajasthan* and 2014 *Pramati Education & Cultural Trust and Others v. Union of India and Others* when the apex court held that 'in order to achieve the constitutional goals of equality of opportunity and social justice, set out in the Preamble of the Constitution', Fundamental Rights should not be construed as 'absolute' and they needed to be understood in the light of the values, articulated in the DPSPs.[51] Being complementary to each other for realizing constitutional democracy in India, the DPSPs and Fundamental Rights are therefore integral to constitutionalize India in a specific ideological fashion. This was most clearly articulated by V Krishna Iyer who, in a 2012 judgement, pronounced:

> The social philosophy of the Constitution shapes creative judicial vision and orientation. Our nation has, as its dynamic doctrine, economic democracy sans which political democracy is chimerical. We say so because our Constitution, in Parts III and IV and elsewhere, ensouls such a value system and the debate in this case puts precisely this soul in peril.... Our thesis is that the dialectics of social justice should not be missed if the synthesis of Part III and Part IV is to influence State action and court pronouncements. Constitutional problems cannot be studied in a socio-economic vacuum, socio-cultural changes are the source of the new values, and sloughing off old legal thought is part of the process of the new equity-loaded legality. A judge is a social scientist in his role as constitutional invigilator and fails functionally if he forgets this dimension in his complex duties.[52]

---

[49] *Chandra Bhavan Boarding and ... v. the State of Mysore and Another.*

[50] *Unni Krishnan JP and Others ... v. the State of Andhra Pradesh and Others*, 4 February 1993. https://indiankanoon.org/doc/1775396/ (accessed 27 November 2016).

[51] *Pramati Education and Cultural Trust and Others v. Union of India and Others*, 6 May 2014. http://supremecourtofindia.nic.in/outtoday/41505.pdf (accessed 27 November 2016).

[52] *State of Karnataka and Shri Ranganatha Reddy*, 1977. http://supremecourtofindia.nic.in/outtoday/wc40012.pdf (accessed 27 November 2016).

It is clear that the old arguments privileging Part III of the Constitution do not seem to have the constitutional validity to the extent it was assumed in the past. Instead, the constitutional provisions need to be interpreted in the light of the socio-cultural changes of the present era. In determining the scope and ambit of the DPSPs, the Court may not entirely ignore them and should adopt the principles of harmonious construction so as to give effect to both as much as possible. In the implementation of the statues also, the Court is constitutionally responsible to ascertain that the spirit in which the DPSPs were incorporated in the Constitution received adequate attention. Despite not being exactly enforceable, these principles are thus directional in the sense that they guide policy priorities and also lay out the vision in which judiciary is expected to interpret the justiciability of the executive designs and legislative feats. Hence it is argued:

> The Directive Principles . . . inform the content of fundamental rights; they do not determine them. The fundamental rights continue to embody concepts, and concepts themselves not only have determinate meaning, but also have the core', as the judicial pronouncements confirm.[53]

The DPSPs cannot thus be undermined in the light of the changes in India's socio-political texture; they continue to provide powerful conceptual, and also practical, inputs to the decision makers and also to the judiciary when it is called to ascertain the constitutional validity of the government deeds; they are not mandatory, but remain integrally connected with a growing mindset in support of the goals, envisioned in the Constituent Assembly; they are moral precepts which the State cannot afford to ignore especially in the changed socio-ideological milieu. Fundamental here is the idea that DPSPs have grown in importance largely due to the consolidation of those values which are complementary to constitutional democracy in India, and, in that respect, they are as integral as Part III of the Constitution.

Concluding Observations

What is most striking about the DPSPs is that they create a space for confluence of thought in which contrasting view-points seem to coalesce. A cursory look at the trajectory of its unfolding in India confirms the argument. As was evident, the members of the Constituent Assembly supported, in unison, the inclusion of this chapter with the hope that this would pave the way for significant socio-economic change by creating a complementary mind-set. It was argued in the Constituent Assembly that 'the idea behind the Directive Principles is to emphasize the way in which we want the country to function'.[54] Despite not being justiciable, these DPSPs were ideologically strong enough, it was thus believed, to build a society, free from discrimination and social prejudices. It was therefore not surprising that Ambedkar warned that if these principles were bypassed by the future rulers while being involved in governance the electorates were unlikely to spare them. Since the demos remain critical to democracy, Ambedkar's cautionary note in the Assembly seems to have struck a unity in the Assembly and notwithstanding fierce debates, this chapter was thus readily accepted even by those dissenters who were reluctant to make them non-justiciable. The near consensus among the members is usually attributed to their belief that the DPSPs, by being instruments of instruction, provide the State with adequate inputs to accomplish the unfinished task that

[53] Gautam Bhatia, 'Directive Principles of State Policy', in *The Oxford Handbook of the Indian Constitution*, eds. Sujit Choudhury, Madhav Khosla and Pratap Bhanu Mehta (New Delhi: Oxford University Press, 2016), p. 658.

[54] L Krishnaswami Bharathi (Madras), 22 November 1948, *Constituent Assembly Debates*, Book No. 2, p. 525.

the founding fathers had left for the posterity. These Directives were meant to further the goals of social revolution by creating conditions necessary for this. In an eloquent way, Austin thus mentioned:

> In the Directive Principles, . . . one finds an even clearer statement of the social revolution. They aim at making the Indian masses free in the positive sense, free from passivity engendered by centuries of coercion by society and by nature, free from abject physical conditions that had prevented them from fulfilling their best selves.[55]

These principles thus represented a source of optimism and great hope for the founding father who also realized that mere political freedom was not adequate for the nation to be independent in its substantial sense. Furthermore, they also epitomized a clear confluence of thought stemming from multiple ideological perspectives in which India's future was sought to be conceptualized in the aftermath of the British withdrawal. As well as the Gandhian model of socio-economic regeneration, these Directives upheld socialistic principles which created a legitimate space for the workers to participate, as partners, in the management of the industries where they work. As history has shown, this is not now uncommon to see the workers as integral to the decision making in industries. It is also true that there are areas which hardly received attention, so far, due to variety of socio-economic and political reasons which are indicative of the fact that the present milieu does not seem to be conducive to address them. Nonetheless, it can be fairly argued that DPSPs fuelled multiple socio-economic campaigns directed towards transforming the stifling socio-economic circumstances seeking to cripple human endeavours.

As has been shown earlier, the DPSPs continue to remain vibrant constitutional devices. Beginning with the First Amendment Act in 1951, these directives seem to have provided the prevalent governments with adequate constitutional justifications for change. Of these amendments, the Forty-Second Amendment of 1976 and Forty-Fourth Amendment Act of 1978 seem to have been most critical in charting a different course of history for the DPSPs. In both these Amendments, these Principles were privileged over Fundamental Rights in case of a clash between them. The court also became sensitive to the changed ideological priorities of the ruling dispensation which was reflected in major legal stipulations. It has also been thus seen that the judiciary did not seem to be reluctant to uphold the DPSPs in preference to the Fundamental Rights, enshrined in the enforceable part of the Constitution. This is the context in which the idea of Fundamental Rights being interpreted in the light of the DPSPs gains ground. Three reasons are offered to justify this: first, since DPSPs meet 'the public interests', they are privileged by the court over Fundamental Rights; second, if the legislation is not clearly directional, the court tends to interpret laws in such a way as to accord priorities to the DPSPs; third, as the DPSPs embody some of the fundamental human values which are also implicit in the Fundamental Rights, enshrined in Part III of the Constitution, the court justifies its take on the laws as being tuned to the core of constitutional democracy.[56] It is now more or less well accepted that for the judiciary, Part III does not seem to be exactly sacrosanct since they are not absolute and need to be interpreted in keeping with the values and ideological goals that the DPSPs seek to attain.

The argument supporting the harmonious relationship between Fundamental Rights and DPSPs is conceptually persuasive though it is constitutionally ultra vires to Article 21 of the Constitution restricting the judicial interpretation by the procedure established by law. As soon as the court got an opportunity, it had overruled the legislative stipulations affecting fundamental rights. The beginning was made in the

[55] Austin, *The Indian Constitution*, p. 51.

[56] Drawn on Bhatia, 'Directive Principles', p. 661.

1967 Golaknath case by stating that the Parliament cannot abrogate Fundamental Rights on any pretext. In 1973, the apex court reiterated its stand in the famous Kesavananda case by confirming that Parliament was not authorized to take away Fundamental Rights since they were a part of the Basic Structure of the Constitution. Nonetheless, it was also argued that there existed no 'potential dissonance between fundamental rights and directive principles',[57] as they are like 'a twin formula for achieving a social revolution which is the ideal the visionary founders of the constitution set before themselves'.[58] While prefacing its pronouncement in the 1980 Minerva Mills case, the court held almost an identical view by suggesting that

> there can be no doubt that the intention of the Constitution makers was that the Fundamental Rights should operate within the socio-economic structure or a wider continuum envisaged by the Directive Principles, for then only would the Fundamental Rights become exercisable by all and a proper balance and harmony between Fundamental Rights and Directive Principles secured.[59]

For the founding fathers, Fundamental Rights and DPSPs constituted a solid foundation for a new India where poverty, hunger and social prejudices were completely alien. Instead of choosing one for the other, they endeavoured to creatively blend the ideas emanating from these two complementary chapters of the Constitution. Hence its was further argued in the Minerva Mills case that

> together, they are intended to carry out the objectives set out in the Preamble of the Constitution and to establish an egalitarian social order informed with political, social and economic justice and ensuring dignity of the individual not only to a few privileged persons but to the entire people of the country including the have-nots and the handicapped, the lowest and the lost.[60]

The court's aforementioned argument may direct one to accept the constitutional validity of the DPSPs over Fundamental Rights since they represented certain values which the founding fathers so assiduously nurtured. There are also judgements showing that court is in favour of striking a harmony between Part III and Part IV of the Constitution. But when the court was asked to ascertain the justiciability of DPSPs, it hardly had wavered given the categorical constitutional directions which were further made clearer in multiple judgements. In the Minerva Mills case of 1980 in which the court appreciated the importance of the DPSPs, and yet it held, for instance, that the objectives laid out in Part IV of the Constitution could not justify overriding Fundamental Rights. In an unambivalent way, the apex court thus stated that 'to destroy the guarantee, given by Part III, in order purportedly to achieve the goals of Part IV is plainly to subvert the Constitution by destroying its basic structure'.[61] Explicitly stated, the 1980 judgement is a powerful intervention in India's constitutional history for more than one reasons: first, it confirmed that provisions in Part III need to be read in the light of the DPSPs, and second, it also laid out that Fundamental Rights required to be upheld since they are an integral part of the basic structure of the Constitution.

---

[57] Pratap Bhanu Mehta, 'The Inner Conflict of Constitutionalism: Judicial Review and the "Basic Structure"', in *India's Living Constitution: Ideas, Practices Controversies*, eds. Zoya Hasan, E Sridharn and R Sudarshan (New Delhi: Permanent Black, 2002), p. 198.

[58] *Kesavananda Bharati v. the State of Kerala*, 1973. https://indiankanoon.org/doc/257876/ (accessed 28 November 2016).

[59] *Minerva Mills Ltd and Others v. the Union of India*, 1980. https://indiankanoon.org/doc/1939993/ (accessed 28 November 2016).

[60] *Minerva Mills Ltd and Others v. the Union of India*.

[61] *Minerva Mills Ltd and Others v. the Union of India*.

REVIEW QUESTIONS

1. **Why are the Directive Principles important for constitutional governance? Elaborate.**
2. **How are they defined in constitutional lexicon? Elaborate.**
3. **'Directive Principles of State Policy represent constitutional values which hardly have any contextual relevance'. Do you agree? Elaborate your response.**
4. **Critically evaluate the provisions of Part IV of the Constitution of India.**
5. **Why these principles are characterized as 'directive' and not 'instructional'? Elaborate.**
6. **What are the arguments that you can marshal to make the provisions of Part IV of the Constitution enforceable? Elaborate your response.**
7. **Why did the Parliament privilege the Directive Principles of State Policy? Elaborate.**
8. **What role did the Supreme Court play in reinventing the Directive Principles of State Policy? Elaborate.**
9. **'The Directive Principles of State Policy was a constitutional instrument without much substance'. Do you agree? Elaborate your response.**
10. **In what respect, the provisions in Part IV of the Constitution are linked with the basic structure doctrine? Elaborate your response.**

Chapter 3

Constitutional Democracy in India[1]

Learning Objectives

- To understand constitutional democracy as a conceptual category
- To comprehend how constitutional democracy had evolved in India
- To unfathom the processes leading to the rise and consolidation of constitutional democracy in India

Constitutional democracy in India is a colonial legacy. In order to consolidate its rule, the colonial government devised various politico-ideological strategies during its long governance. These strategies were both coercive and persuasive: while the former is obvious and does not require explanation, the latter represents an endeavour on the part of the rulers to accommodate the Indians in public administration through various constitutional means. Drawing on the classical liberal-democratic tradition, the British ruler introduced several legal steps to consolidate the empire by gradually opening-up administration to the Indians. Along with the application of force, the British government also adopted various reform schemes to inject constitutional values that shaped the nationalist campaign to a significant extent. It will therefore not be incorrect to suggest that the British rule survived in India with least coercion because of the role of the Indian collaborators in defending the empire. In other words, the rulers' concern for constitutional governance was not reflective of their commitment to the values of Enlightenment, but became a necessity to take the steam out of the nationalist agitation. Constitutional democracy was thus not a gift, but a context-driven outcome which however gained ground in India presumably because it developed organic roots in the country. As history demonstrates, governance in India was couched in the liberal democratic format in phases. With the adoption of the 1861 India Council Act, the process had begun that ushered in an era of constitutional democracy in India. True, the colonial rulers held the de facto authority though the space that was given to the indigenous elites in administration made them aware of how the state functioned. In other words, it was a training ground for the Indian masters who now had an opportunity to be integrally connected with governance. What is striking to note is the fact that even the staunch nationalists who fought tooth and nail against the British for freedom also endorsed, rather enthusiastically, constitutional democracy as perhaps the most appropriate form of governance for

[1] This chapter is drawn on the chapter 15 of my book entitled *Modern Indian Political Thought: Text and Context* (New Delhi: SAGE, 2009), which I wrote in collaboration with Dr Rajendra Pandey.

an extraordinarily diverse country like India. Not only did they endorse constitutional democracy through their participation in governance during the British suzerainty, they also zealously adopted this when India became free. It is therefore not surprising that a majority of those who partook in the making of the Constitution of India spoke in a language that drew on their commitment to liberal democracy; they felt strongly that for India to survive as a unit liberal democracy was the only available option. Arguments for constitutional democracy were readily accepted by the nationalist elites and their supporters presumably because it made them relevant to governance even when India was not politically free.

With the consolidation of constitutional democracy in India, the other forms of governance had hardly had a chance to flourish; it became pertinent to India's political culture. This suggests that the British rule laid the foundation of constitutional democracy in India which was further strengthened by the nationalists both during their struggle against colonialism and also in the aftermath of decolonization. What is surprising to notice is the continuity of more or less an identical structure of governance which consolidated colonialism even in independent India. The Constituent Assembly which framed free India's Constitution unequivocally endorsed liberal democracy as the guiding principle which gets reflected in the provisions. It is thus argued that the 1950 Constitution of India is liberal in character and spirit.

In conceptual terms, constitutional democracy draws on the constitution-driven structure of governance which also establishes the supremacy of the constitution. This is contrary to the Westminster form of democracy in which Parliament reigns supreme, but similar to the US democracy where the constitution is supreme. What it signifies is the fact that constitutional democracy that evolved in India was not a carbon copy of what existed during colonialism but a creative blending of the prevalent politico-ideological traditions that had also flourished during her political servility and its aftermath. Nonetheless, the fact remains that the 1950 Constitution of India that upheld constitutional democracy in India had drawn on the past constitutional stipulations seeking to consolidate colonialism. It can thus fairly be argued now that the journey that had started in 1861 with the approval of the first Council Act continues in India even today since constitutional democracy is being appreciated regardless of the fact that it fails to articulate democracy in its true form and actual substance. Fundamental here is the point that the Constitution remains the core of governance in the sense that it not only stipulates how public rule is to be structured and articulated but also what is to be done to realize democracy in a meaningful manner. In other words, by being in the driver's seat, the Constitution thus holds the spirit of governance which, if undermined, will immediately take the kernel out of constitutional democracy.

Since constitutional democracy in India has a long history, it cannot be properly understood without reference to the past when it was conceptualized and made operational. By concentrating on the trajectory of the unfolding of constitutional democracy in India, this segment of the book delves into those constitutional designs and stipulations that created conditions for its growth and consolidation. These designs, undoubtedly concessions to the ruled, were also devices to weaken the nationalist agitation as and when it became a serious threat to the government. In other words, while the British liberal tradition may have contributed to the constitutional reforms, one cannot deny the growing strength of the nationalist campaign, Gandhian or otherwise, that forced the British to introduce measures to defuse crisis. The aim here is to understand constitutional democracy as a context-led design which was simultaneously a colonizing design from the British point of view and also a libertarian mode of politics in the nationalists' perception.

Colonialism expanded its control in India in two distinct ways: first, by tactfully following the divisive *divide-et-impera* strategy that created and sustained the schism between the two major communities of Hindus and Muslims. The British strategy worked favourably because of the socio-economic differences that separated these two communities. In course of time, the divide-and-rule formula not only consolidated the British rule in India, but also created conditions for the politically underprivileged sections to rise as meaningful partners in governance. So, it cut both ways: on the one hand, the chasm between communities, based on genuine socio-economic differences as well, made the task of governance easier for the ruler; this also, on the other hand, led to a process whereby the peripheral communities became a powerful political voice in the nationalist struggle for Independence. Second, drawing on the classical liberal–democratic tradition, the British ruler introduced several legal steps to consolidate the empire by gradually opening up administration to the Indians. Along with the application of force, the British government also adopted various reform schemes to inject constitutional values that shaped the nationalist campaign to a significant extent. It will therefore not be incorrect to suggest that the British rule survived in India with least coercion because of the role of the Indian collaborators in defending the empire. Except in the context of the 1942 open rebellion, the collaborative network of support had never shown signs of collapse. The adoption of various reforms by the British government created conditions in which Indians felt attached with the imperial rule that finally disintegrated due to its internal contradictions and also the growing nationalist consolidation opposed to foreign rule. Focusing on the landmark constitutional designs during the British rule, this chapter is an analytical statement on the British politico-legal strategies to consolidate the Raj. These designs, undoubtedly concessions to the ruled, were also devices to weaken the nationalist agitation as and when it became a serious threat to the government. In other words, while the British liberal tradition may have contributed to the constitutional reforms, one cannot deny the growing strength of the nationalist campaign, Gandhian or otherwise, that forced the British to introduce measures to defuse crisis.

Acts and Reforms

The most distinctive Act that radically altered the nature of the British rule in India was the Act of 1858 which brought the East India Company's century-old rule to an end. The Act provided for the enhanced membership of the Councils. It was mandatory for the government to consult the representative bodies and institutions, approved by the government, before selecting nominees for the Councils. Besides legislative powers, the Councils were also empowered to pull the Executive on financial matters though it had no power to either revise or reject decisions on this matter. However, the growing weightage of the Councils is indicative of a sea change in colonial rule. As Morley, the Secretary of State, articulated, 'there are two rival schools of thought, one of which believes that better government of Indian depends on efficiency, and that efficiency is, in fact, the end of British rule in India. The other school, while not neglecting efficiency, looks also to what is called political concessions'. This declaration laid the foundational principles of the British administration in India. As a first step, a Royal Commission was appointed in 1907 to look into the administration that seemed to have lost its viability in the context of growing discontent among the ruled. The aim of the Commission was to provide an administration which was adapted to the changed social, economic and political realities of India. While recommending the corrective measures, the Commission was guided by the following factors: (a) the difficulties of ruling the vast sub-continent from a single headquarter and the inevitable failure of in the statesmanship and efficiency in administration; (b) the difficulties of applying uniform schemes of development for the provinces which are socio-culturally diverse; (c) to instil a sense of responsibility among those engaged in provincial and local administration; and (d) to strengthen the colonial rule by educating people in the values of strong administration. On the basis of the recommendation of the Commission, a bill was introduced in 1908 which became the 1909 Morley–Minto Reforms. As a political scheme seeking to strengthen colonial rule in India, the 1909 Act introduced a profound change with long term effects in representation of communities in Councils. Once the Muslim League was founded in 1906 there were demands for 'separate electorate' for the Muslims. In his plea to the Governor-General, the Muslim League chief, Aga Khan defended separate electorate for the Muslims on the basis of their 'numerical strength', 'political importance' and 'contribution' which they made 'to the defence of the Empire'. Endorsing the argument, Minto assured Aga Khan that the Muslims 'may rest assured that their political rights will be safeguarded'. So, the 1909 Act is remarkable in the history of representation in India. Muslims were recognized as a separate community and their electoral rights were also guaranteed accordingly. The British policy of 'divide-and-rule' was thus formally articulated. Public administration continued to remain partisan, for obvious reasons. Meanwhile, the nationalist movement gained momentum and the political atmosphere in India changed. The 1909 Morley–Minto Reforms failed to address the genuine grievances of the ruled. Various other acts were enacted to reinforce the repressive system of governance that was articulated by the 1909 Reform scheme.

With the outbreak of the First World War, a change in the attitude of the British government was visible which was largely 'strategic' to solicit the support of the Indians in its war effort. The result was the adoption of the 1919 Montague–Chelmsford Reform scheme which was guided by the committed goal of the government 'to increase association of the Indians in every branch of the administration and the gradual development of self-governing institutions in India'. On the surface, the Reform scheme appears to be novel which drew on the commitment to make public administration India-friendly, as the four major principles that formed the core of the scheme, suggest:

1. There should be, as far as possible, complete popular control in local bodies and the largest possible independence for them of outside control.
2. The provinces are the domain in which the earlier steps towards the progressive realization of responsible government should be taken. Some measures of responsibility should be given at once, and the aim of the British government is to provide complete responsibility to the Indians in their governance to the extent possible under the present circumstances.
3. The Government of India must remain wholly responsible to the Parliament and saving such responsibility, its authority in essential matters must remain indisputable pending experience of the effect of changes now to be introduced in the provinces. Meanwhile, the Indian legislative council should be enlarged and made more representative and its influence in the processes of policy making needs to be enhanced.

There is no denying that the 1919 Act was a politically appropriate strategy in a context when the nationalist movement was growing in importance, especially after the arrival of Gandhi on the scene. Although the administration was guided by the colonial spirit, by involving the loyalist Indians in governance the British rulers provided a new design of public administration in India. In the new dispensation, structural changes in administration were made. The most remarkable step was the adoption of dyarchy. The dyarchy was an administrative device that demarcated functions between those which were to be given to popular control and those which must continue to remain with the British rulers: the former were called 'transferred subjects' and the latter 'reserved subjects'. The Governor-General-in-Council was in charge of the reserved subjects while Governors, acting with the ministers in the provinces, remained supreme in so far as the transferred subjects were concerned.

Despite being unique, the dyarchy was doomed to fail simply because of its ideological roots in colonialism. Even the Alexander Muddieman-led committee which was constituted to examine the functioning of dyarchy concluded that it crumbled because of its inherent weaknesses and dissensions due to the following factors: (a) the demarcation of authorities between reserved and transferred was meaningless since the de facto power always rested with the former; (b) as a result, there was hardly effective dialogue between the provincial ministers and the Governors or the Governor-General; (c) the Indian ministers were further handicapped since Indian civil service officers hardly cooperated with them; and (d) the excessive control by the finance department of the Government of India over the transferred subjects.

As is evident, attempts were constantly made to accommodate the Indians in governance. This was a strategic device to address the resentment among the ruled that worked favourably, at least at the outset, to contain the nationalist agitation. Although the actual power rested with the British authority, dyarchy was a critical step towards administrative devolution that radically altered the complexion of the British power in India that largely revolved around Governor-General-in-Council. Dyarchy empowered the Governors who exercised independence in regard to transferred subjects in the provinces. Furthermore, the involvement of the Indian ministers had introduced changes, though cosmetic in character, in public administration. Apart from gaining experience in administration, the Indian ministers acquired first-hand knowledge of how the administration functioned in most partisan manner. This helped them articulate a nationalist agenda which was now readily acceptable to the people at large since it was experience based. So, dyarchy was very critical to conceptualizing the changing nature of public administration in British India at least in the first two decades of the twentieth century.

The Simon Commission

The appointment of the Simon Commission was a political strategy to divert the attention away from the nationalist resentment due largely to the failure of the Government of India Act, 1919 to provide a responsible government. Headed by John Simon, the Commission with seven members was appointed in 1927 to enquire into the possibilities for further reform in India. Outlining the task for the Commission, the parliamentary declaration thus elaborates that a seven-member commission with John Simon as its chairman was appointed to

> enquire into the working of the system of government, the growth of education, and the developments of representative institutions in British India, and matters connected therewith and to report as to whether and to what extent it is desire able to establish the principle of responsible government, or to extend, modify, or restrict therein, including the question whether the establishment of second chamber is or is not desirable.

The Commission had a three-fold task: (a) to assess the functioning of the system of government that evolved out of the 1919 Government of India Act, (b) to ascertain whether the representative institutions were strong enough to establish a responsible government, and (c) to judge whether the second chamber was desirable or not.

As Indians were excluded from the Commission, most of the political organizations, including the Indian National Congress, decided to boycott. Constituted solely by the British members of the House of Commons and Lords, the Commission was a clear 'negation of imperial promises of consultation with Indians and their incorporation into the decision making-process'.[2] Indians were only to give evidence to

[2] Judith Brown, *Modern India: The Origins of an Asian Democracy* (New Delhi: Oxford University Press, 1985), p. 256.

the Commission that was finally responsible to report to the British Parliament for its decisions about India's future. Lord Birkenhead, the Secretary of State, defended the exclusion because Indians were quite incapable of agreeing on a workable political framework. This provoked mass protest all over the country and as result, the Commission failed to collect enough evidence to suggest an effective political formula. A large number of Congressmen, several splinter groups belonging to various Hindu communal outfits, liberals and also a significant section of the Muslim League, led by MA Jinnah decided to boycott the Commission. The Simon report insisting on making the Governor-General stronger than earlier was immediately rejected by the nationalist opinion irrespective of political differences. Condemning recommendations, the nationalist Shaffad Ahmed Khan thus argued that the Commission

> recommended for a Governor-General who would have become more powerful than Shah Jehan and more irresponsible that Shah Alam. The American conception of irresponsible executive was transplanted in a country which had been cradled in the Parliamentary system and nourished on English constitutionalism. It was not a constitutional scheme which deserved any detailed examination but a jig-saw puzzle and few Indians were capable of appreciating its Chinese mysteries.[3]

Despite having provoked mass protest, as the Commission was greeted with the 'Simon Go Back' slogan as soon as its members arrived in Bombay (now Mumbai), the recommendations were certainly a step ahead in creating a federal arrangement for colonial India. By suggesting reorganization of the British Indian provinces, the Commission unleashed a process that loomed large in the days to come. Although these recommendations were governed by imperial considerations, the idea of bifurcating large states and also to dissociate Burma from India as separate crown colony was welcomed for better governance. Furthermore, by taking into account the princely states, the Commission sought to redefine the contour of the emerging nation that, so far, was confined to the British India. The Commission seemed to have signalled a process whereby the princely states emerged as critical to the British political agenda. It was therefore emphatically argued that the princely states 'are not British territory and their subjects are not British subjects. The relations between each of them and the Paramount Power may be ascertained or deduced from Treaty or other written document, or usage and agreement; but however that may be, the Crown is, in each case, responsible for the state's external relations and its territorial integrity'. This statement reconfirms that the princely states, despite being autonomous, remained extremely vulnerable and their existence was highly dependent on the British support. There were two serious consequences of this statement: on the one hand, this created space for rulers of several princely states to initiate dialogues with the nationalist forces, particularly the National Congress, to consolidate their opposition against the British; this gave the nationalists, on the other hand, an opportunity to expand their influences beyond the border of the British India. It was not therefore surprising that at the 1929 Lahore Congress, the princes were called upon to grant responsible government to the ruled.

The all-white Simon Commission was a watershed in India's freedom struggle for three specific reasons. First, it provoked massive nationalist protest all over the country. Besides 'Simon Go Back' demonstrations, showing black flags and observing *hartals* in various cities, the 1928 anti-Simon protest was 'marked by

---

[3] Shaffad Ahmed Khan, *Indian Federation* (1937), quoted in MV Pylee, *Constitutional Government in India* (second edition, London: Asia Publishing House, 1965), p. 90.

the beginnings of a renewed movement for boycott of British goods'.[4] Simon was greeted by countrywide *hartals* on 3 February, the day he reached. His team confronted massive demonstrations on 19 February when they arrived in Calcutta. The call for the British goods was not only a great success in the city but also forged a unity among the Hindus and Muslims. A major clash with the police at Lahore on 30 October injured Lajpat Rai who succumbed to death on 17 November. Second, on the whole, the anti-Simon campaign was therefore the occasion for the articulation of the nationalist protest in an unprecedented way. The Congress renewed its campaign against vested interests. Vallabhbhai Patel, one of Gandhi's trusted lieutenants, launched a satyagraha campaign in Bardoli against the imposition of land revenue at a time when the cultivation was hard-hit due to lack of adequate monsoon. There was an epidemic of strikes involving jute, textile and railway workers. Led by the Workers' and Peasants' Party, thousands of jute workers of Bengal marched into the 1928 annual session of the Congress and disrupted the deliberations demanding Purna Swaraj. The Bombay textile workers were mobilized by the Textile Labour Union against wage-cuts. In Jamshedpur, the steel workers, led by the local leadership with support from the Congress, forced the management of Tata Iron and Steel Company to concede to some of their demands. Revolutionary activities were vigorously undertaken by several splinter groups in Bengal, Uttar Pradesh and Punjab. The most important group was certainly the Hindustan Socialist Republican Army (HSRA) that struck the headlines for sustained revolutionary activities involving the youth. The Army lost its momentum with the arrest of its leader, Bhagat Singh and his associates. This followed a series of bomb blasts in the Punjab; an attempt to blow-up the train carrying Lord Irwin, the Viceroy; the throwing of bombs in the Punjab Legislative Assembly and assassination of the district magistrate Saunders, as a revenge for the death of Lajpat Rai who succumbed to injuries that he received in a police lathi charge while peacefully protesting against the Simon Commission. The third consequence was no less insignificant. Lord Birkenhead's statement that Indians were incapable of working for an agreeable political framework provoked the Congress to take initiatives for drafting a constitution for the country. The 1928 All-Parties Conference appointed a small committee with Motilal Nehru as chairman and seven other members: Ali Imam, Tej Bahadur Sapru, MS Aney, Sardar Mangal Singh, Shuaib Qureshi, Subhas Chandra Bose and GR Pradhan. It was a committee, based on a consensus among the participants in the conference, as the composition clearly demonstrates. The Motilal Nehru Committee is illustrative of the extent to which nationalism cemented a bond among those opposed to the British rule. This was also a powerful nationalist statement challenging Lord Birkenhead. So, the constitution drafting was not merely a technical exercise, it was also an articulation of the nationalist protest in perhaps the most creative fashion.

The report of the Simon Commission remains 'a monument to a conservative strategy for imperial control'[5] whereas the Motilal Committee report was the first nationalist draft of a constitution for independent India. Primarily the work of two eminent jurists of the period, TB Sapru and Motilal Nehru, the Nehru Report proposed:

> India shall have the same constitutional status in the comity of nations known as the British empire, as the Dominion of Canada, the Commonwealth of Australia, the Dominion of New Zealand, the Union of South Africa and the Irish Free State, with a Parliament having powers

[4] Sumit Sarkar, *Modern India, 1885–1947* (New Delhi: Macmillan, 1983), p. 265.

[5] Brown, *Modern India*, p. 256.

to make laws for the peace, order and good government of India and an executive responsible to that Parliament, and shall be styled and known as the Commonwealth of India.[6]

As is evident, the Report demanded dominion status for India just like other white self-governing dominions within the British empire. Vesting the executive authority in the King, the Report also recommended a constitutional arrangement for uniting the princely states with the British Indian provinces. The status of the provinces was to remain the same and the residual powers were vested in the Central Government that provoked protest even among those sympathetic to the Report. The Nehru Committee revised the 1916 Lucknow agreement with the Muslims and endorsed the principle of joint electorate for the House of Representatives at the centre and the provincial legislatures. There would, however, be no reservation of seats except for Muslims in those provinces where they were in a minority and non-Muslims in the North-West Frontier Province. This also suggests that reservation for Muslims in Bengal and Punjab where they constituted a majority was completely ruled out.

As soon as the details of the Report were made public, the differences of opinion rapidly surfaced. Muslims parted ways since they were denied constitutional guarantee against a possible Hindu-dominated hegemonic state. Even Jinnah who appreciated Motilal's effort in drafting a constitution for united India rejected the Report demanding that the residual powers should rest with the provinces rather than the centre to scuttle the rise of a unitary and authoritarian Hindu-dominated state. Other Muslim groups joined hands and in January 1929, an All Parties Muslim Conference met in Delhi and agreed to abandon the Report that hardly addressed the Muslim concern. While Muslims dissociated themselves from the Report as it was far from their expectations, there were dissidents even within the Congress. Led by Jawaharlal Nehru and Subhas Chandra Bose, a powerful faction within the Congress formed 'Independence India League' that demanded complete independence rather than dominion status as suggested by the Nehru Committee. While elucidating the difference between dominion status and independence, Nehru stated that dominion status 'envisages the same old structure, with many bonds visible and invisible tying us to the British economic system: [complete freedom] gives, or ought to give us, freedom to erect a new structure to suit our circumstances'.[7] Critical of those defending dominion status, Nehru further argued 'for them the problem is one of changing colour of administration, or at most having a new administration ... [and] not a new state .... They can only conceive of a future in which, they or people like them will play the principal role and take the place of the English high officials'.[8] The 1928 Calcutta Congress thus saw an open split between those who defended dominion status and those who advocated complete independence. Two groups agreed to cooperate once the President of the session, Motilal Nehru, devised a formula for reconciliation by suggesting that if the Report was not accepted by the British Parliament by 31 December 1929, the Congress was free to adopt the complete independence pledge and to organize non-violent non-cooperation to achieve it. It was more or less a foregone conclusion that in view of the growing importance of the radical section within the Congress, it had no alternative but to insist on complete independence. With the acceptance of the complete independence resolution in the 1929 Lahore Congress, it was decided to boycott the legislature and the Congress members were asked to resign. Furthermore, the All India Congress Committee was authorized to launch civil disobedience, including

[6] *The Motilal Nehru Report*, August 1928, reproduced in B Shiva Rao, ed., *The Framing of India's Constitution: Select Documents*, Vol. 1 (reprint, New Delhi: Universal Law Publishing Co. Pvt. Ltd., 2004), p. 59.

[7] Jawaharlal Nehru, *An Autobiography: With Musings on Recent Events in India* (London: John Lane, the Bodley Head, 1941), p. 418.

[8] Nehru, *An Autobiography*, p. 417.

non-payment of taxes wherever it deemed appropriate. Gandhi rose as the undisputed leader and was made the sole authority to decide the time and manner of the launching of the Civil Disobedience Movement.

The 1935 Government of India Act

Colonialism and centralization of power seem to go hand in hand though administration in British India underwent changes at least in its content. A change is visible if one follows the evolution of the British Indian State since the adoption of the 1772 Regulating Act. Perhaps the most (and last) significant constitutional measure in India during the British rule is the 1935 Government of India Act that drew on the inputs from the Indian Statutory Commission, the All Parties Conference, the Round Table Conferences and the Joint Parliamentary Committee of the British Parliament. Seeking to establish a federal form of government in which the constituent provinces had autonomous legislative and executive powers, the Act paved the way for a parliamentary form of government in which the executive was made accountable within certain bounds to the legislature. This was also a major experiment in the devolution of power within, of course, the imperial parameters. As the then Viceroy, Linlithgow commented, 'after all we framed the constitution ... of 1935 because we thought it the best way ... to hold India to the empire'.[9] Although the well-espoused federation never came into being, the Act was nonetheless a powerful comment against the integrated administrative system of the colonial variety. A perusal of the Act draws our attention to the following features:

1. Provincial autonomy was recognized by giving the provinces a separate legal identity and liberating them from central control except for certain specific purposes.
2. A federation of India was established demarcating domains between the provincial governments and the federal Central Government.
3. Dyarchy, discontinued in the provinces, was introduced at the centre. Subjects of foreign affairs and defence were 'reserved' to the control of the Governor-General; the other central subjects were transferred to ministers subjects 'safeguards' in the provinces.
4. The federal principle was recognized in the formation of the lower house of the Central legislature though the de facto ruler remained the Governor-General.
5. Separate electorate was retained following the distribution of seats among the minority communities, as devised by the 1932 Communal or MacDonald Award.

The Act was undoubtedly a strategic response to the growing popular resentment against the British rule in India in the context of the war crisis. It was possible that the Act was an outcome of political calculations to win over Indian support for the British war effort. Nonetheless, the Act provided an arrangement whereby ministers were entrusted with specific responsibilities in which they remained supreme though the Governor was given special responsibilities to be discharged in his individual capacity and was also empowered with certain discretionary functions. In case of failure of constitutional machinery, the Governor was constitutionally authorized to take over the administration and suspend provincial autonomy

[9] Quoted in Sekhar Bandyopadhyyay, *From Plassey to Partition: A History of Modern India* (New Delhi: Orient Longman, 2004), p. 326.

if it deemed appropriate. As evident, the Act allowed provincial autonomy only within the parameters, set by the British government. Yet, the 1935 Act was a significant constitutional step towards building India in a federal set-up.

That the Act was basically an imperialist design is evident from the constitutionally guaranteed powers and immunities of the Governor-General. The role of this highest executive authority was indeed unique. He had a dual role. As the Governor-General of British India, he remained supreme in so far as constitutional authority was concerned. For the princely states, he was in charge of the use of the Royal Prerogative and paramount authority that upheld imperial control beyond the border of the British India. The scheme was constitutionally most appropriate from the point of view of the British government since it bestowed complete authority in one institution. In fact, the arrangement was also a convenient device to wrest control from the elected representatives as soon as it was required. So, the federal distribution of power that the Act stipulated was heavily tilted in favour of the Central authority, namely Governor-General that itself suggests that the guarantee of provincial autonomy was possibly a politically expedient device to address the nationalist resentment in a very clever way.

It would, however, be wrong to dismiss the Act as being exemplary of a clear imperialist design since it unleashed a process towards provincial autonomy while responding to the long-standing nationalist demand for sharing power. Introduction of provincial autonomy enabled the Indian ministers to directly involve in administration though they had to function under the overall restriction of colonialism. Hence it was characterized as 'a gigantic constitutional facade without anything substantial within it'. The Act was also a sign of the determination of the British government to warp the Indian question towards electoral politics. By involving Indians in administration, the Act had brought more players in the arena of public administration. There is no doubt that the Act introduced the Indian politicians to the world of parliamentary politics and as a result of the new arrangement, stipulated by the Act, politics now percolated down to the localities which largely remained peripheral so far. The available evidence also suggests that the Act was the price the British paid for the continuity of the Empire. What thus appears to be a calculated generous gesture was very much a politically expedient step. In fact, the surrender of power, though at the regional levels, caused consternation among the votaries of the British power in India who saw an eclipse of British authority in this endeavour.

The Act had 'more enemies than friends',[10] argued VP Menon who played a crucial role in the transfer of power. Its federal design was condemned by almost all political parties, with the exception of National Liberal Party and Hindu Mahasabha. The Congress articulated its opposition in its Faizpur meeting of 1936 by attacking the proposed safeguards and the Governor-General's overriding powers. The Congress also resolved to combat the Act both inside and outside the legislature before it was implemented. Nonetheless, the Congress finally agreed to contest the forthcoming election possibly as a strategy to gain as much as possible by being part of the government. Likewise, the Muslim League justified its participation in the election as possibly the best option under the prevalent conditions despite having condemned the Act as inadequate to establishing 'responsible government'.

Elections to the provincial legislature were held in early 1937. The Congress won a clear majority in Madras, the United Provinces, the Central Provinces and Orissa. In Bombay, it succeeded in winning half of the seats in the provincial legislature and formed the government with the support of a few sympathizers. In Assam and the North-West Frontier Province, the Congress emerged as the single largest party. In Bengal and Punjab, the Congress failed miserably, and the victory of two regional parties—Krishak Praja Party

[10] VP Menon, *The Transfer of Power in India* (reprint, Madras: Orient Longman, 1963), p. 54.

in Bengal and Unionist Party in Punjab—had also shown the failure of the Congress to strike roots in these two Muslim-majority states. While in Bengal, the Krishak Praja Party formed the government after an alliance with the Muslim League, the Sikander Hyat Khan-led Unionist Party constituted the government on its own.

The initial euphoria over the acceptance of office was however short-lived because of the ingrained constraints of working under the overriding imperial authority. One is however baffled because most the political parties, despite condemning the Act from the very outset, participated in the elections and joined the government most enthusiastically. In other words, how could the parties committed to freedom and bitterly critical of the Act agree to work within its framework? This was a paradox of the period that was finally resolved 28 months after the Congress had taken over power in the provinces when the Congress ministries resigned in protest against the reluctance of the British government to spell out its war aim, including the freedom of the colonies. The Act did not survive enough to fulfil its desired goal given the outbreak of the second world war which 'did not give time to its sponsors to stage even a decent burial'.[11] Nevertheless, the 1935 Government of India Act was perhaps the most elaborate constitutional scheme during the British rule that by devising provisions for provincial autonomy sought to tackle the difficulties of governing a highly complex society like India. What is striking about the Act is that it was not only a well-articulated response to India's political diversity, but also the last serious effort to sustain imperial control within the broad liberal parameters of Westminster parliamentary democracy. It is therefore not surprising that the founding fathers while drafting the Constitution could not afford to ignore the Act notwithstanding their critical opposition when it was introduced by the imperial ruler. This itself is an eloquent testimony of the constitutional validity of some of the Sections of the 1935 Act that reappeared in free India's 1950 Constitution either in spirit or letters. The explanation lies in the very nature of India's socio-political circumstances that remained more or less same, if not worse, because of the bloodbath following the 1947 Partition. The constitution-makers were drawn to the Act possibly to articulate their response to the extraordinary circumstances in which the constitutional machinery completely broke down. In this sense, the Act provided critical inputs to those who presided over India's destiny in the Constituent Assembly at a critical juncture of her rise as a free nation.

The Cripps Mission

The war crisis created circumstances in which the British government was forced to negotiate with the nationalist forces in India. With the Japanese conquest of Singapore in February and Rangoon in March 1942, the Indian political situation changed dramatically. Following the rapid Japanese advance in 1941–42, it was believed that 'India's safeguard in the war . . . was lost. After the fall of Singapore, the Bay of Bengal lay open. When Rangoon fell, it seemed as if the tide of Japanese conquest would soon be sweeping into Bengal and Malabar'.[12] Not only was there preparation for evacuation of the British, the Government of India issued an order to the effect that 'in the event of Bengal being overrun by the Japanese, all officers of District rank and below in all departments were to remain at their posts to administer the district for the good of the people under the control of the enemy'.[13] With the increasing military preparedness in

[11] Menon, *The Transfer of Power in India*, p. 57.

[12] R Coupland, *Indian Politics, 1936–1942: Report of the Constitutional Problem in India*, Part 2 (Madras: Oxford University Press, 1944), p. 263.

[13] *Memoirs (TSS) of SG Taylor, Inspector General of Police*, Bengal, 1941–43 (Cambridge: Centre of South Asian Studies), pp. 5–6.

view of the impending Japanese attack, the India Office felt obliged to make some gesture to win over Indian public opinion. The Viceroy did not agree to this idea because, in his views, they [Indian politicians] are entirely ruthless . . . and any further move at this stage will likely to improve India's contribution to the war'.[14] Nonetheless, the political initiative came from the British Parliament in the form of the Cripps Mission, under the leadership of the Labour leader of the House of Commons, Stafford Cripps, that arrived in India in March, 1942 with the task of exploring the possibilities of a political accord between the British, the League and Congress. Stafford Cripps was chosen because of the high esteem in which he was held in Britain and India and also because of his intimacy with Nehru. The plan that the Cripps carried with him included immediate transformation of India, as soon as the war ended, into a self-governing dominion with a Clause conceding the secession of the provinces that aimed at placating the Muslim League. The main features of the scheme that Cripps offered for negotiation with the Congress, Muslim League and other political parties in India:

1. The object of His Majesty's Government was the creation of a new Indian Union which shall constitute a Dominion in the British Commonwealth but in no way subordinate to Britain in any aspect of its domestic or external affairs.
2. Immediately upon cessation of hostilities, steps shall be taken to set up in India an elected body for framing a new Constitution for India.
3. Provision shall be made for the participation of the princely Indian states in the constitution-making body.
4. Any province that is not prepared to accept the new constitution to retain its present constitutional position was to be allowed to have a constitution of its own with the same status as the Indian Union.

Despite the differences of opinion between the Secretary of the state and the Viceroy, the agreement on the appointment of the Cripps Mission was clinched largely due to international pressure. The US President Franklin Roosevelt touched on India's political future in his meeting with the British Premier Winston Churchill in December 1941. Chiang-Kai-Shek, during his trip to India, publicly expressed sympathy for 'India's aspiration for freedom' adding that Britain would as speedily as possible give 'real political power' to the Indian people. Winston Churchill responded to the international demand by suggesting a new policy for India that runs as follows:

> After the war, [the British Government] would work out a new constitution for India. Its main conclusions on the constitution would be (in the nature and procedure for reaching them) an expression of the desire of the people of India as a whole. His majesty's government would accept a constitution so arrived at and would negotiate with the Council in regard to the fulfilment of British obligations.[15]

That the declaration by Churchill was a strategic attempt to convince the Allied Partners was confirmed by LS Amery, the Secretary of State who unambiguously stated that the decision to send the Cripps Mission 'is to answer the charge that our policy in India is inconsistent with our general profession about fighting

[14] Nicholas Mansergh and EWR Lumby, eds., *The Transfer of Power*, Vol. 1 (London: Her Majesty's Stationary Office, 1971), p. 23.
[15] Winston Churchill's statement is quoted in Menon, *The Transfer of Power*, p. 116.

for freedom as well as the even more humiliating charge that if we are prepared to make concession to India now, it is simply the result of a decadent imperialism realizing that the game is up.'[16] The announcement of the Cripps Mission was thus a politically expedient decision to avoid further dent on the British liberal image. However, the draft declaration was certainly a positive drive towards resolving the constitutional deadlock by promising dominion status with the right of secession, a constitution-making body, elected by the provincial legislatures, with individual provinces being given the right not to join it and with princely states being invited to appoint representatives.[17] Linlithgow, the Viceroy, threatened to resign[18] because he was unhappy with the draft declaration which was, he felt, unwarranted during the war crisis. His resignation was not accepted and Churchill convinced Linlithgow by drawing his attention to the effect that the appointment of the Cripps Mission had on the world opinion, especially the Americans by arguing that 'it would be impossible owing to unfortunate rumours and publicity, and the general American outlook, to stand on a purely negative attitude and the Cripps Mission is indispensable to prove our honesty pf purpose. . . . If it is rejected by the Indian parties . . . our sincerity will be proved to the world.'[19] The Cripps Mission was finally withdrawn for not adequately consulting the Viceroy and the Commander-in-Chief Lord Wavell who expressed concern that Cripps was conceding far too real power to the Congress.[20] The negotiation finally failed over the Congress' insistence that Executive Council of the Governor-General needed to be replaced by a National Government. Cripps was unable to accept the demand because it meant constitutional amendment that was impossible during the war time. He tried to persuade the Congress to accept the prevalent constitutional arrangement as 'absolutely temporary' to which the Congress did not subscribe. This was the last nail in the coffin and the Mission was withdrawn. As is evident from contemporary research, Churchill was not keen on its success and sought to sabotage the Cripps effort from the outset. He was afraid that there might be an agreement that would commit the British to withdraw after the war. As soon as he found out that the Congress was insisting on its participation in the wartime government in India, the British Prime Minister immediately sent a telegram to Cripps asking him not to make any commitment regarding the participation of the Indians in the government. The intransigent Viceroy, Linlithgow, proved convenient to Churchill. Stafford Cripps found no support from within the government and the Mission was inevitably withdrawn.[21] In fact, as VP Menon informs, Churchill made it abundantly clear in his speech in the House of Commons that 'His Majesty's Government had not been willing to support Sir Stafford Cripps to the extent to which he himself was prepared to go.'[22] That the appointment of the Cripps Mission was a mere strategy to win the support of the British allies was evident when Churchill congratulated Stafford Cripps on his success in 'proving how great was the British desire to reach a settlement. . . . The effect throughout and in the United States has been wholly beneficial.'[23] The effort was therefore a part of the British propaganda, the aim of which was to address the concern of the Allied Partners. The argument gained acceptance as Churchill himself declared in November 1942 that 'I have not become King's first minister in order to preside over the liquidation of the British

---

[16] 'Linlithgow Papers, Amery to Linlithgow, 17 June, 1942' (London: India Office Records, Mss. Eur. F 125/11).

[17] For details of the Cripps Mission, see RJ Moore, *Churchill, Cripps and India, 1939–45* (Oxford: Clarendon Press, 1979).

[18] 'Memoirs of WHJ Christie (an ICS officer working in the Viceroy's office)' (London: India Office records, Mss. Eur. F 180.9c), p. 11.

[19] *The Transfer of Power*, London, 1971, Vol. 1, Churchill to Linlithgow, 10 March, 1942, pp. 394–95.

[20] *The Transfer of Power*, London, 1970, Vol. 1, A war cabinet telegram to Stafford Cripps, 18 April, 1942, p. 670.

[21] This argument is made by Crispin Bates in his *Subaltern and Raj: South Asia since 1600* (London: Routledge, 2007), p. 157.

[22] Menon, *The Transfer of Power in India*, p. 136.

[23] *The Transfer of Power*, London, 1970, Vol. 1, Churchill to Stafford Cripps, 28 April, 1942, pp. 707–08.

empire'.[24] It is therefore difficult not to suspect, as Sumit Sarkar argued, 'an element of bluff and double-dealing here so far as the British were concerned, though opinions may well differ as to whether Cripps himself was a willing or unconscious agent in this game'.[25]

Stafford Cripps came to India on 22 March and left for England on 12 April. The fate of the Mission was thus sealed in just three weeks. Despite his genuine concern for India's freedom, he failed to convince neither the Congress nor the Muslim League nor his colleagues in the India Office in London. When he returned to England, he was a frustrated soul which is evident in his statement: 'We have tried by the offer that I brought to help India along her road to victory and to freedom. But, for the moment, past distrust has proved too strong to allow of present agreement'.[26] The abrupt withdrawal of the Mission and sudden departure of Cripps led to various kinds of speculation and conjecture. The Congress was persuaded to believe that 'Cripps deceived them in the interests of British propaganda in America'. The Muslim League was not enthusiastic from the outset because the Cripps suggestion for sharing power with the Congress was a critical step to 'stifle in advance its ambition for a separate Muslim state'.[27] Cripps was also criticized for being 'hypocrite' because whenever there was a definite agreement on practical details on the basis of certain principles he always dithered and withdrew his support despite being committed to those principles at the outset. The contemporary press attributed the breakdown of the Cripps negotiation to the intransigent attitude of those who mattered in the India Office in London. The British authority was not willing to part with the empire in India, as the argument goes, and the Cripps Mission was an eye-wash to placate the international opinion condemning the His Majesty's government for its vicious role in India. On the whole, the Cripps Mission became a suspect and instead of bringing the government and nationalist forces together for an amicable solution to constitutional *impasse*, the Mission served to make the gulf unbridgeable. The manner in which the negotiations collapsed tended to strengthen the doubts and suspicion in the minds of the Indian nationalists that 'there was no genuine desire on the part of the His Majesty's Government to part with power'.[28]

The Cripps Mission failed to weld the Congress into collaborative network, and its rejection by the leadership led to open confrontation with the government in the Quit India Movement. Its appointment might have placated the opinion outside India though from the British point of view, it was a hasty and ill-conceived attempt that seemed to have exposed how vulnerable the British government in India was during the war. Gandhi thus characterized the Cripps proposal as 'a post-dated cheque on a crashing bank'.[29] It seems that it also suited Gandhi who, convinced that the British found themselves in a very difficult position, 'was now all set for a fight'.[30] The outcome was the Quit India call on 9 August, 1942. The British government in India became helpless as the Quit India Movement gained momentum. Characterizing the Cripps offer as 'that point at which the British departure after the war became inevitable', Judith Brown thus argues that 'a hasty and ill-conceived attempt in large part designed to placate opinion outside India as well as to attract Indian politicians' cooperation at one of the war's darkest hours became the charter

[24] Winston Churchill speech at the Mansion House, London, 10 November 1942, as reported in the *New York Times* on 11 November 1942, quoted in Bates, *Subalterns and Raj*, p. 155.

[25] Sarkar, *Modern India*, p. 388.

[26] Quoted in Menon, *The Transfer of Power in India*, p. 135.

[27] Quoted in Menon, *The Transfer of Power in India*, p. 121.

[28] Menon, *The Transfer of Power in India*, p. 138.

[29] Quoted in Pylee, *Constitutional Government in India*, p. 122.

[30] Calude Markovitz, ed., *A History of Modern India, 1480–1950* (London: Anthem Press, 2002), p. 385.

for India's freedom'.[31] What was thus defined as a liberal design to address genuine concerns of the ruled led to processes which culminated in India's political freedom.

Reviewing the Argument

Constitutional democracy survives in India while elsewhere in South Asia that had the same colonial legacy it had never a chance to evolve naturally. There are many factors which account for India's distinctive political texture. Although it was avowedly an inheritance from the past it has characteristics which are clearly indigenous. In other words, the Indian version of constitutional democracy is uniquely textured presumably because of the equally unique processes of socio-political churnings following independence along with partition. This is not merely an idea, but also a mode of existence in which India's cultural pluralism is appreciated and respected notwithstanding its limitations in creating a society of equals in socio-economic terms. Constitutional democracy has thus been reinvented in a non-Western context; its sustenance presents us with a paradox that lies in the persistence of abysmal poverty along with serious commitment to democratic governance on the part of the poor. This is a major contradiction which could become an Achilles' heel in the days to come unless it is resolved conclusively. As early as 1949, BR Ambedkar highlighted this aspect of constitutional democracy which was likely to lose its substance unless the sources of economic inequality were completely eradicated. It was evident when he spoke:

> On the 26th of January, we are going to enter a life of contradictions. In politics we will have equality and in social and economic life we will have inequality. In politics we will be recognizing the principle of one man one vote value. In our social and economic life, we shall, by reason of our social and economic structure, continue to deny the principle of one man one value. How long shall we continue to live this life of contradictions? How shall we continue to deny equality in our social and economic life? If we continue to deny it for long, we do so only by putting our political democracy in peril. We must remove this contradiction at the earlier possible moment or else those who suffer inequality will blow up the structure of political democracy which this assembly has so laboriously built up.[32]

Yet, political process or the processes which make democracy function creates a distinct space for various kinds of struggles to seek to correct the imbalance in available economic opportunities. Democracy is a struggle, argues a commentator, 'whose protagonists are at once products of ancient habits and of modern ambitions, who have found in democracy a form of action that promises them control over their own destinies'.[33] The democratic process is thus 'the space that becomes available—contracting or expanding—for the range of resistance people are capable of'.[34] So, the functioning of democracy has not resolved the problems of economic imbalances and yet it has given rise to a new kind of 'democratic progress' constrained, of course, by the existent restricting socio-economic circumstances redefining primordial values in typical modern idioms. The Indian model therefore adds a new dimension to theories of democracy. Despite being an aggregative model, the Indian version has also elements of deliberative

---

[31] Brown, *Modern India*, p. 318.

[32] BR Ambedkar's statement in the Constituent Assembly, 25 November 1949, *Constituent Assembly Debates*, Book No. 5, p. 979.

[33] Sunil Khilnani, *The Idea of India* (London: Hamish Hamilton, 1997), p. 13.

[34] Javeed Alam, *Who Wants Democracy*? (New Delhi: Orient Longman, 2004), p. 25.

democracy simply because even after expressing their preferences through voting, the Indian voters participate in every day struggles against an encroaching state. Electoral participation is certainly a powerful mode that is always being complemented by people's democratic involvement in processes which may not be directly linked with the poll, but may have consequences for its outcome.

Concluding Observations

An uncritical look at these selective, but major, landmark constitutional initiatives during the colonial rule may lead one to conclude that these were initiated by the British for the Indians. Hence the spirit of nationalism is underrated. If one goes beyond the surface, what is evident is that the inclusion of Indians in administration was but an outcome of the British effort to defuse popular discontent. Hence the argument that every constitutional drive was initiated by the Raj is totally unfounded. History reveals that there were situations which forced the British authority to adopt measures to control agitation. For instance, the Congress campaign in the 1880s contributed a lot to the introduction of the 1893 reforms. Behind the 1909 Morley–Minto Reforms lay the *Swadeshi* Movement and revolutionary terrorism. Similarly, the 1919 Montague–Chelmsford Reforms were attempts at resolving crises that began with the Home Rule League and climaxed with the 1919 Rowlatt Satyagraha and the Non-Cooperation Movement of 1910–21. To a large extent, the Gandhian Civil Disobedience Movement (1930–32) accounted for the introduction of constitutional measures seeking to involve Indian politicians in public administration.

Furthermore, the interpretation of these constitutional designs remains partial unless linked with the broader socio-economic and political processes in which they were conceptualized. An attempt to analyse the structure and dynamics of constitutional democracy without reference to the broader social matrix and economic nexus is futile because the politic-constitutional structure reflects economic and social networks, religio-cultural beliefs and even the nationalist ideology which impinged on the organized world of administrative and constitutional structure. So an urgent and unavoidable task for an analyst is not to completely ignore the broader socio-economic context but to ascertain its relative importance in shaping a particular constitutional initiative. For instance, the 1932 Communal Award was believed to have been initiated by the British to expand political activity among the Muslims in Bengal and Punjab. But, as studies have shown, it was also a concession the British was forced to grant in order make the maintenance of the Empire easier. The sharing of power with the native elites was thus prompted by considerations other than merely British initiatives.

The evolution of colonialism in India will continue to remain an interesting area for research for a variety of reasons. Prominent among them is certainly the process in which colonialism sustained its grip in India by creating a strong collaborative network and also by successfully pursuing a divide-and-rule strategy to scuttle efforts at unifying socio-economically separated communities. The strength of British colonialism lies in the fact that unlike their European counterparts, the British rulers expanded and also maintained their presence not merely by coercion, but also by creating circumstances in which they emerged as the best possible option by the Indians who remained highly divisive due to various socio-economic and political reasons. The constitutional landmarks that we have discussed earlier are a clear testimony to those imperial efforts that defused opposition rather easily on most occasions. What was distinct about British colonialism was its success in welding a significant section of population to the system of governance that the British introduced. It was possible due perhaps to its triumph in ideologically moulding people towards liberal political values and ethos. Barring the militant nationalists, most of the nationalists were content with the method of three Ps (petition, prayer and protest) until the rise of Gandhi who radically transformed the complexion of anti-British confrontation.

These landmark constitutional experiments had a role in permanently dividing major communities in India on the basis of religion and other socio-economic denominations. Both the Hindus and Muslims redefined their identities through a process of contestation of vision, contestation of beliefs and contestation of history. The period between 1909 and 1947, when major constitutional experiments were undertaken, sharply shows the mutation in the formation of Hindus and Muslims as communities opposed to each other in the political arena. What was distinctive about this period was the growth of the communities as political units always in a permanent adversarial relationship with the members of the 'other' community. This was further consolidated following the introduction of the communal electorate in the 1937 provincial elections. With the acceptance of the principle of majority, Muslims automatically became most powerful community in Bengal and Punjab by their sheer demographic strength. In other words, religious identity as a demographic category became probably the single most crucial criterion in determining the distribution of governmental power in these Muslim-majority provinces. The 1935 Government of India Act reiterated the divide-and-rule strategy by formally recognizing that Muslims needed to be treated separately as a distinct, but neglected minority in India. This was a decisive constitutional intervention because not only did it establish the principle of majority as sacrosanct in democracy it also made the Muslims self-conscious of their critical importance in governance in India. It is now possible to argue that the 1935 Act definitely shifted the centre of political activity in Bengal to the east of the province. Not by virtue of any inherent superiority of the Muslims but simply because in a democratically elected legislature, as a contemporary report underlines, 'the weight of numbers tells and the teeming millions of East Bengal—sixty percent of their being Muslims outweighed in point of numbers the more educated Hindus of the South, West and extreme North of the province'.[35] The migration of power to the countryside took place in the context of a major realignment in the social bases of political power.

The 1935 Government of India Act was certainly a powerful constitutional intervention that the colonial rulers seriously made to accommodate the nationalist zeal within, of course, the colonial administrative format. This is also illustrative of efforts at legitimizing the growing democratic aspirations of the ruled in India through a constitutional device. Interestingly, the 1935 Act remained the strongest influence during the making the 1950 Constitution for free India. Some 250 Clauses of the present Constitution were, in fact, lifted from the Government of India Act. Although the political system of independent India draws its sustenance from universal adult franchise and political sovereignty, rules are undoubtedly derived from its colonial past. The most striking provisions that the Constitution of India derived from its 1935 counterpart are 'the Emergency provisions' that enable the President to suspend the democratically elected governments and Fundamental Rights of the citizens.

There is no doubt that the post-colonial state in India inherited its habits of governance from colonial practices. And, its *weltanschauung* (world view) is based on 'the mixed legacies of colonial rule' that upheld rule of law, bureaucracy, citizenship, parasitic landlords, modern political institutions and 'two-track tradition of protest and participation'.[36] What accounts for relative stability for colonialism in India was certainly its ability to adapt to the changed socio-political circumstances; also gradual but steady 'internalization' of domination by the subjects of colonial rule, which provoked an analyst to characterize colonialism as 'an intimate enemy'[37] because the dominated saw the virtues of being dominated for their

---

[35] 'Tyson Papers, Eur E 341/41, John Tyson's note, 5 July, 1947' (London: India Office Records).

[36] Subrata Mitra, 'Constitutional Design, Democratic Vote Counting and India's Fortuitous Multiculturalism' (working paper, South Asia Institute, Heidelberg University, November 2004), 29–34.

[37] Ashis Nandy, *The Intimate Enemy: Loss and Recovery of Self under Colonialism* (1983, reprint, New Delhi: Oxford University Press, 1989).

own betterment. Colonialism was thus not seen as an absolute evil but complementary to India's rise as an independent nation in future. The statement may not be politically correct. Nonetheless, it can safely be argued that colonialism provided critical impetus to various processes that finally resulted in serious political mobilization against imperialism in India. Whether nationalism or democratization—they had their roots in the long history of colonialism and in this sense colonialism remained a significant force behind the rise of India as an independent nation in 1947.

Review Questions

1. **Identify and elaborate the distinctive features of constitutional democracy as a theoretical category.**
2. **'Constitutional democracy is both an ideological design and an empirical instrument for governance'. Elaborate.**
3. **Evaluate the importance of the 1927 Simon Commission in constitutionalizing governance in India.**
4. **What are the distinctive features of the 1935 Government of India Act? Elaborate.**
5. **In what respects, the 1942 Cripps Mission is a prelude to the processes leading to the making of the 1950 Constitution of India? Elaborate.**
6. **Is it justified to argue that with the British initiatives at constitutionalizing governance, India would not have become a constitutional democracy? Elaborate your response.**
7. **'Understanding of history is essential to conceptualize contemporary politics'. Elaborate.**
8. **'Constitution represents politico-ideological aspirations of a multitude'. Explain.**
9. **Can the British system of governance be characterized as being liberal? Give reasons to your answer.**
10. **What are the distinctive features of constitutional democracy that had emerged in the wake of the British rule in India? Elaborate your response.**

Chapter

4

Salient Features of the 1950 Constitution of India

Learning Objectives

- To understand the important features of the Constitution of India
- To comprehend them with reference to the socio-economic context in which they evolved
- To evaluate them in a comparative perspective

Constitutionalism in India has a unique history. The initial impetus came from the colonial masters who undertook several steps to constitutionalize India in accordance with their ideological priority. Nonetheless, they laid the foundation of constitutionalism in India. This is one side of the story. The nationalist intervention is another part of the story which also needs to be grasped to understand the complex processes that finally culminated in the making of the 1950 Constitution of India. It is true that the provisions of the Constitution were drafted and fine-tuned by the members of the Constituent Assembly within a period of almost three years between 1946 and 1949. A mere surface reading of the constitutional provisions reveals that it was a borrowed doctrine since it contains almost two-thirds of the provisions that the 1935 Government of India Act had. What needs to be emphasized here is the fact that these provisions were subject to a thorough scrutiny in the Constituent Assembly and they were finally accepted since they conformed to the ideological belief that the majority of the members had held. This means that these provisions received their approval since they were considered appropriate to realize the socio-economic goals that the framers of the Constitution had so dearly nurtured during their struggle for freedom. It is thus conceptually persuasive to suggest that Indian Constitution was an offshoot of a closely-fought ideational battle both during colonialism and its immediate aftermath.

Furthermore, the deep rooting of the ethos and functional vibrancy of democratic life in India may arguably be taken to be the fruition of the long cherished endeavour of the fathers of the Constitution who not only envisioned India to be a modern nation based on the norms of rule of law, secular character of the society, democratic nature of the polity and ordinarily, primacy of the people's fundamental rights over other imperatives of the state; but also made comprehensive and mostly precise provisions in the Constitution to facilitate the march of the nation in the desired direction. The chapter is devoted to an analysis of the salient features of the Indian Constitution encompassing the whole spectrum of vital issues ranging from the spirit of the Constitution as expressed in various Parts highlighting the ideational distinctiveness of its character. Primarily a procedural constitution, the Constitution of India has also features approximating to a prescriptive constitution. In conceptual terms, while the former concentrates of the well-defined procedures to articulate governance the latter emphasizes the foundational principles to guide the government. Drawn on a collective vision, a prescriptive constitution pays less attention to the procedural details since they are usually context-driven. This distinction does not appear to be entirely valid in regard to the Constitution of India since it is a creative blending of both procedure and prescriptive ideological visions. There are certain aspects which besides emphasizing the procedures also delve into those politico-ideological values that are critical in shaping India's constitutional journey. One can certainly make an analytical distinction since both these aspects are intertwined in the Constitution of India. For instance, there is no dispute that the Preamble to the Constitution of India epitomizes that set of values which cannot be bypassed in governance. Another significant part of the Constitution is Part IV which enumerates the DPSP: a collection of socio-politically relevant values, this Part has gradually become most significant in policy making due to the increasing importance of the demos in governance. In order to translate these values in specific operational policies, the Constitution also lays out a structure of governance by creating appropriate institutions with demarcated powers and authority. There are several Parts in the Constitution which dwell on the institutions of governance, like the legislature, executive and judiciary. Just like the Parliament, the executive and judiciary play critical roles in executing the constitutional directions for fulfilling the constitutional goals. Since the chapter has a limited goal of acquainting the readers with the salient features of the Constitution of India, it is confined to those major Parts which are critical to constitutional values and practices in India.

India's Contextual Peculiarities

For several reasons, framing of an acceptable-to-all constitution for free India was an extremely arduous task which the Constituent Assembly shouldered efficiently to produce the longest democratic constitution in the world. First, the partition of the country and the subsequent mayhem in Punjab and Bengal led to a shocking state of nervousness amongst the leaders who immediately set on to devise ways and means to instil in the people the confidence in the governability of the country. Moreover, the onerous task of ensuring the integration of five-hundred plus princely states in the Indian Union appeared quite challenging in view of the ambivalent, if not totally defiant, positions taken by the rulers of the states like Junagadh, Hyderabad and Jammu and Kashmir.

Second, the carving out of Pakistan did not mean the conversion of India into a homogenous country as more than 10 per cent of the total Muslim population of the country was left in India whose religious and cultural identities needed to be protected. At the same time, India itself was home to numerous communities speaking different languages, professing different faiths, practicing different customs, following different traditions and emphasizing different cultures. In the face of such a diverse cultural base of the people, it was indeed a stupendous task to provide for sufficient constitutional provisions to protect the distinct religious and cultural identities of the citizens, without compromising with the unity and integrity of the country.

Third, the tone and tenor of the national movement had aroused a high level of expectations amongst the common people in general and the hitherto marginalized sections of the society like the scheduled casts, scheduled tribes and the other backward people in particular, to experience a new dawn with the inauguration of the constitution of the independent India.

Finally, the spirit of liberal democratic traditions were so strong amongst the majority of national leaders, particularly Nehru, that independent India was bound to usher into a full-blown democracy, irrespective of its preparedness to experience the mass scale of democracy based on universal adult franchise on the one hand, and the lurking dangers to the unity and integrity of the nascent nation from the dynamics of electoral politics on the other. Combined together, these riddles of the constitution making in independent India acted both as challenges as well as opportunities for the constitution-makers to show their fullest constitutional acumen and innovativeness.

Faced with the complex conundrum of meeting out scores of seemingly mutually competing and sometimes contradictory claims on the constitution of independent India, the constitution-makers had to adopt a policy of drafting a lengthy and all-encompassing document which contained not only the classical tenets of a constitution like the provisions defining the powers and functions of the various organs of government at both the union and the state levels, the fundamental rights guaranteed to the people, etc., but also a number of unconventional provisions like the DPSP to make the constitution an instrument of socio-economic change in the country. The constitution-makers, therefore, had to draw on all the available constitutions and other legislative documents to provide for the building blocks to erect the edifice called the Constitution of India. To be precise, the framers banked heavily upon the colonial construction, i.e., the Government of India Act, 1935 to get the foundational base of the Constitution of India which is an ironic epitome of the fact that the framers could not move much away from the system of governance devised by the British for India.

Thus, keeping the core drawn from the Act of 1935, the framers looked upon other constitutions like the American and the Irish to provide for the operational dynamics of not only the democratic system of government in the country through the provisions of Fundamental Rights but also that of the visions of new India, marching on the path of rapid socio-economic transformation through the guiding force of the DPSP. However, the physical structure of the Constitution of India, as drawn from the above mentioned sources, would have remained hollow and infertile, had the breathing spirit to it not been provided by the Objective Resolution, drafted by Nehru himself and approved by the Constituent Assembly on 22 January 1947. Finding its manifestation through the Preamble of the Constitution, which declared the pious goals of the Constitution to secure to all its citizens justice, social, economic and political; liberty of thought expression, belief, faith and worship; equality of status and of opportunity ; and to promote among them all fraternity, assuring the dignity of the individual; this resolution put into black and white the very raison d'être for which the Constitution of India is supposed to come into existence.

With the broad structure and essence of the future polity of the country being obvious, the Constituent Assembly arrived at seven basic decisions pertaining to the nature of the new state, namely, written constitution, federal structure of the polity, republic from of state, parliamentary democracy, membership of the Commonwealth of Nations, secular nature of state and the welfare character of the state. These decisions were, in fact, the cherished dreams of the leadership of the national movement whose fulfilment was sought to be attained through the mechanism of the new Constitution. The various provisions of the Constitution of India appear, in a way, nothing more than the bricks and mortar to facilitate the construction of the structure of a constitutional polity in the country.

Analysing the inherent philosophical moorings of the Indian Constitution, Granville Austin discerns a 'seamless web', consisting of three strands, namely, protecting and enhancing national unity and integrity; establishing the institutions and spirit of democracy; and fostering a social revolution to better the lot of the mass of Indians.[1] Bestowing equal weightage and significance to all the three strands in time and space, Austin asserted the mutual dependence and inextricable intertwinedness of these strands and warns that undue strain on, and slackness in, any one strand would distort the web and risk its destruction and, with it, the destruction of the nation.[2]

---

[1] Granville Austin, *Working a Democratic Constitution: The Indian Experience* (New Delhi: Oxford University Press, 1999), p. 6.
[2] Austin, *Working a Democratic Constitution*, p. 6.

However, despite the mutual dependence and inextricable intertwinedness of the three strands, as stressed by Austin, it may be argued that there appears a certain degree of prioritization amongst the three strands and the framers seemed to be fairly clear on the first things first in the Indian Constitution. Framed with much painstaking perseverance and imbued with the long cherished dreams of the national leaders, the Constitution of India reflected the wisdom of the framers in not only meeting out the challenges at hand like preserving the unity and integrity of the nation, threatened by the communal violence, but also a prophetic vision of heralding in an era of what Gandhi called 'Ramrajya'.

To put it differently, the first and foremost priority of the framers at the time of Independence, and probably afterwards, appeared to be jealously guarding the unity and integrity of the county, for which they were willing to afford so much of unfettered powers to the Central Government even at the risk of rendering the federal set up of the polity meaningless. Apparently, it appears paradoxical that though very few mentions have been made in the Constitution with regard to the unity and integrity of the country, so sweeping powers and unwritten discretion have been provided, in addition to the retention of the colonial constructions like the all India services like the IAS (formerly ICS) and IPS (formerly IP), to the Central Government that it would not be impertinent to argue that the preservation of the unity and integrity of country is the running consideration pervading from the first to the last word of the Constitution.

Having been reassured of the indestructibility of India as a nation, the framers set on to infuse the ethos and spirit of democratic governance in the country, within the broad spectrum of the parliamentary system, based on the sanctities of universal adult franchise. Banking heavily, if not exclusively, on the periodic elections, to be conducted by an independent constitutional body, the framers' trump card, with regard to democracy, turned out to be the classical negative rights of western mould, ensuring for the common people the basic minimum constitutional guarantees through which they can feel as being the citizens of an independent country and enjoy the freedom of not only choosing their rulers but also live a life of their volition, notwithstanding, the traditional character of Indian society and the socio-economic backwardness of the mass of the people. Thus, unlike the absolute value of unity and integrity, democracy did not become an absolute value for the framers who, nonetheless, wished it to underpin the Indian polity and evolve in the course of time.

The value of social revolution, as referred to by Austin, appears only at the last stage of contemplation by the framers, after ingraining fully the other two values of unity and integrity as well as democracy in the Constitution. Though fully aware of the indispensability and unavoidability of a subtle social revolution in the country in order to make democracy meaningful and sustainable, the framers seem to be convinced of the primacy and pivotal position of the other two values, which are bound to become the substructure over which the superstructure of social revolution could be erected.

In sum, undoubtedly, the Indian Constitution appears to be a seamless web characterized by the three strands of the unity and integrity of the country, institutions and spirit of democracy and social revolutionary fervour, yet, the shape of the web does not appear to be circular where it is not possible to figure out the sequence and placing of the particular value. Rather, it may be argued that the shape of the web would probably be pyramidal in which the three values are arranged in the ascending order with the base position occupied by the value of unity and integrity of the nation, the next position accorded to the value of the democracy and finally comes the value of social revolution, in order of their dispensability from top to bottom. In other words, it demonstrates the Venn diagrammatic nature of the Indian Constitution whereby one value resides within the hard shell of the other, paving the way for the realization of the other value only once assured of its own durable existence.

Exploring the Value Preferences

Those who were engaged in the framing of the constitution were guided by their distinct ideological inclinations. Their upbringing and education in colonial India left, for obvious reasons, an imprint on them. It was therefore not surprising that a majority of them remained liberal in their politico-ideological dispensation. Raised in an environment in which the Westminster form of democracy was preferred, they had hardly a choice in favour of any other form of government that had flourished elsewhere. Although the framers had consulted the constitution of the then Soviet Union, liberal constitutionalism seemed to have prevailed over other alternatives presumably because of its organic roots in India due to long colonial rule that drew its sustenance from the philosophy of British Enlightenment.

Since the aim is to comprehend the value preferences of those who contributed to the making of the constitution through sustained deliberations for almost three years, this section is selectively devoted to those Parts that appear to have directed India's journey towards democratizing a former colony. Besides the Preamble to the constitution, Part III (Fundamental Rights), Part IV (DPSP) and Part IVA (Fundamental Duties) laid out those foundational values which informed the constitution. Part XX that deals with the procedures for amendment remains critical to our understanding of the nature of the constitution which is neither exactly rigid nor flexible, but elastic enough in circumstances to be accommodative of newer values and demands reflective of popular aspirations.

The Preamble

The Preamble is often referred to as the soul of the Indian Constitution affording a key to its letter and spirit. Delineating the core concerns of the polity in independent India, the Preamble seeks to express a solemn resolve which becomes the guiding light for the posterity in the country. The American Constitution was the first to initiate with a Preamble. Many countries, including India, followed this practice. The term 'Preamble' which is described as the introduction or preface to the Constitution is nothing but the summary of the constitutional goals. NA Palkhivala, renowned jurist and constitutional expert, called the Preamble the 'identity card of the Constitution'. The Preamble to the Indian Constitution is based on the 'Objective Resolution', drafted and moved by Nehru, and adopted by the Constituent Assembly. It has been revised by the Forty-Second Constitutional Amendment Act (1976), which added three new words 'socialist,' 'secular' and 'integrity.' The text of the Preamble to some extent resembles the language of the Preamble of the American Constitution of 1787 which reads:

> We the people of United States, in order to form a more perfect Union, establish justice, insure democratic tranquility, provide for a common defense, promote the general welfare, and secure the blessing of the liberty to ourselves and our posterity, do ordain and establish the Constitution for the United States of America.

Unlike the Constitution of Australia, Canada or the USA, the Constitution of India has an elaborate Preamble. The purpose of the Preamble is to clarify who has made the Constitution, what is its source, what is the ultimate sanction behind it; what is the nature of the polity which is sought to be established by the Constitution and what are its goals and objectives? These are important questions that need to be asked to understand the value preferences which the founding fathers had upheld while being engaged in framing the Constitution of India. It is also true that they were governed by contextual compulsions, linked with the tumultuous events that followed immediately after the traumatic partition of 1947. Nonetheless, in their effort to constitutionalize India in a liberal–democratic politico-ideological mould, they chose a specific constitutional framework which, they felt, was most appropriate to attain the goal they fought for.

Historical Genealogy

Though, formal journey of the Preamble started with the draft prepared by Sh. BN Rao in his memorandum of 30 May 1947 but it was later reproduced in the Draft of 7 October 1947 which was reformulated during the Constituent Assembly deliberations. In the light of the Objective Resolution which was introduced by Jawaharlal Nehru on 13 December 1946 which was adopted by Constituent Assembly on 22 January 1947 the drafting committee felt that 'the Preamble should not be restricted to defining the nature and the essential features of the new state and its basic socio-political objectives and the subject matters dealt within the Resolution, but also appropriately provided for in the substantive part of the Constitution'. In the framing of the Preamble, Nehru's Objective Resolution played a very significant role; in fact, it would not be an exaggeration to suggest that the ideas and sentiments that figured in the Preamble had their appearance in the Resolution, as is being shown below:

1. This Constituent Assembly declares its firm and solemn resolve to proclaim India as an Independent Sovereign Republic and to draw up for her future governance a Constitution.
2. Wherein the territories that now comprise British India, the territories that now form the Indian States, and such other parts of India as are outside British India and the States as well as such other territories as are willing to be constituted into Independent Sovereign India, shall be a Union of them all.
3. Wherein the said territories, whether with their present boundaries or with such others as may be determined by the Constituent Assembly and thereafter according to the law of the Constitution, shall possess and retain the status of autonomous units, together with residuary powers and exercise all powers and functions of government and administration, save and except such powers and functions as are vested in or assigned to the Union, or as are inherent or implied in the Union or resulting therefore.
4. Wherein all power and authority of the Sovereign Independent India, its constituent parts and organs of government, are derived from the people.
5. Wherein shall be guaranteed and secured to all the people of India justice, social, economic and political; equality of status, of opportunity, and before the law; freedom of thought, expression, belief, faith, worship, vocation, association and action, subject to law and public morality.
6. Wherein adequate safeguards shall be provided for minorities, backward and tribal areas, and depressed and other backward classes.
7. Whereby shall be maintained the integrity of the territory of the Republic and its sovereign rights on land, sea and air according to justice and the law of civilized nations; and
8. this ancient land attains its rightful and honoured place in the world and make its full and willing contribution to the promotion of world peace and the welfare of mankind.[3]

---

[3] Jawaharlal Nehru, The Objective Resolution, 13 December 1946, *Constituent Assembly Debates*, Book No. 1, p. 59.

The Objective Resolution contains all those exalted ideas and value-preferences that the founding fathers had so assiduously nurtured during their fight for freedom. Fierce debates unfolded in the Assembly as soon as it was placed which led Ambedkar to comment that 'the most arduous task before us . . . was to make the heterogeneous mass that we have today take a decision in common and march on the way which leads us to unity'.[4] Ambedkar's apprehension was not unfounded since, besides the withdrawal of the Muslim League from the Assembly, there were groups who, due to their preference for the village swaraj of the Gandhian variety, did not appreciate the liberal democratic mould of governance. As was evident in the Assembly debates, the division was explicit though it never became unmanageable.

In a very perceptive way, Ujjal Singh of Punjab characterized the Resolution as 'an expression of the pent-up emotions of the millions of this country'.[5] He provided a three-fold classification of the Resolution: the first part deals with the declaration of an Independent Sovereign Republic of India; the second part is about the autonomous units having residuary powers with the Union; and the third part commits to the ideas of social and economic freedom and justice and also pledges to provide adequate safeguards to the minorities, backward classes and tribal areas.[6]

The Objective Resolution represented a concern that the framers of the Constitution had shared. For them, the most pressing need was, as Nehru articulated, 'to solve the problem of the poor and starving, and this remains unresolved, our paper constitution will become useless and purposeless'.[7] In a very scathing attack on the critics, he further exhorted:

> There is no group in India, no party, no religious community, which can prosper if India does not prosper. If India goes down, we go down, all of us. . . . But if it is well with India, if India lives as a vital free country, then it is well with all of us to whatever community or religion we might belong.[8]

What it meant was that mere political freedom was not adequate to realize their life-long mission of making India free from poverty, hunger and distress. The ideological pledge that the founding fathers had taken would become vacuous unless it was accompanied by the sincere commitment to weed out the well-entrenched roots of India's age-old socio-economic ailments. This was, therefore, a great responsibility, as Nehru explained:

> Not because the task which we have undertaken . . . or because we presume to represent vast number of people, but because we are building for the future and we want to make sure that the building has a strong foundations [sic], and because, above all of the circumstances when the disruptive forces are adversely affecting our minds. [And] we should not be deflected from that vision of the future which we ought to have, in thinking of the present difficulties.[9]

The Objective Resolution set out the vision for the future polity which was to emerge with the withdrawal of British colonialism. Based on their commitment to liberal democracy, the framers readily accepted the

---

[4] BR Ambedkar (Bengal), 17 December 1946, *Constituent Assembly Debates*, Book No. 1, p. 101.
[5] Ujjal Singh (Punjab), 17 December 1946, *Constituent Assembly Debates*, Book No. 1, p. 104.
[6] Ibid., p. 104.
[7] Jawaharlal Nehru, 22 January 1947, *Constituent Assembly Debates*, Book No. 1, p. 317.
[8] Ibid., p. 317.
[9] Jawaharlal Nehru, 28 April 1947, *Constituent Assembly Debates*, Book No. 1, pp. 375–76.

Resolution as a guiding device. What was however surprising was that the Objective Resolution was completely silent on the Gandhian approach to socio-economic regeneration. The mission was to develop India as a liberal democratic country though the Assembly was not unanimous in its endorsement of the Nehruvian politico-ideological model, as was evident in the Constituent Assembly debates. Liberal constitutional democracy finally triumphed with the support of the majority of the Assembly members who did not seem to be persuaded by the indigenous Gandhian model of governance. It was evident from the very beginning of the proceedings of the Constituent Assembly which witnessed serious debates on each and every provision of the proposed constitution.

Unfolding of the Debate

The Preamble was extensively debated in the Constituent Assembly. The purpose was to ascertain whether the Preamble followed the spirit of the Objective Resolution. As it was made clear at the outset by Ambedkar who stated that it 'embodies what is the desire of every Member of the House [and] that this Constitution should have its root, its authority, its sovereignty from the people'.[10] Most of the members were drawn to the discussion on the Preamble since it was, to them, a core of the constitutional arrangement that independent India was to institute. In her intervention, Purnima Banerjee (United Provinces) expressed the sentiments by saying that 'the Preamble forms one of the most important parts of the Constitution and . . . it stands as a charter of our freedom and as a measure of our success and failures'.[11] There is hardly a difference of opinion and it was more or less unanimous that the Constitution needed to be prefaced by a Preamble which was to highlight the fundamental politico-ideological values for governance. It means that the members agreed that the Preamble was that part of the Constitution where the core constitutional values were incorporated. Hence the Preamble to the Constitution of India was defined as 'the soul of the Constitution, . . . a key to the Constitution, . . . a proper yardstick with which one can measure the worth of the Constitution; . . . it is a superb prose-cum-poem, . . . a perfection in itself'.[12] Here too, what is privileged is the contention that the Preamble is a touchstone to validate, or otherwise, of the constitutional provisions; as constitution's soul, the Preamble contains, in itself, those values which always remain critical to India's constitutional democracy. So, it is not merely a vision document, but one that contains specific directions to the future rulers. In other words, not only is the Preamble a beacon of light it is also a pathfinder for India's constitutional democracy which the founding fathers had preferred while working on the 1950 Constitution of India. Two important points merit attention here: (a) as a preface, the Preamble lays out, for the Constitution of India, its ideological foundations by drawing on those value preferences which the framers opted for making a constitution of their choice; and (b) being a foreword to the Constitution, it also provided a foundation to India's future governance by underlining that sovereignty lay with the people with the statement that we 'do, HEREBY ADOPT, ENACT AND GIVE TO OURSELVES THIS CONSTITUTION' presumably to avoid confusion in this regard.

Reference to the debates of the Constituent Assembly shows that there was considerable discussion in the said Assembly on the Preamble. A number of amendments were moved and were rejected. There are two amendments that attracted serious attention: one by HV Kamath (Central Provinces and Berar) who

---

[10] BR Ambedkar, 17 October 1949, *Constituent Assembly Debates*, Book No. 5, p. 456.

[11] Purnima Banerjee (United Provinces), 17 October 1949, *Constituent Assembly Debates*, Book No. 5, p. 451.

[12] Thankur Das Bhargava (East Punjab), 18 November 1949, *Constituent Assembly Debates*, Book No. 5, p. 684.

argued strongly for the Preamble to begin 'in the name of God'[13] another by M Ananthasayanam Ayyangar (Madras) who felt that the Preamble should start with an invocation to Mahatma Gandhi. Kamath justified his point by suggesting that without divine bless no achievement was possible. In his words, 'without invocation of God, . . . it is like sounding brass and tinkling cymbal.'[14] Hence we should 'consecrate this Constitution by a Solemn dedication to God in the spirit of Gita.'[15] The amendment was a cause of embarrassment. Purnima Banerjee of United Provinces thus opposed the amendment by insisting that 'let us not try to invoke His name; it should not be brought up in this form and the members compelled to vote one way or the other. The flame of God is invoked by every nation upon earth and God is an Impartial Entity and he should be allowed to remain so.'[16] In a similar vein, M Thirumala Rao (Madras) requested Kamath not 'to subject God about whom he spoke in such reverent terms to the vote of the House, and if it comes to vote, it will not be fair to ourselves and to the nation.'[17] The most revealing argument was made by Hriday Nath Kunzru (United Provinces) when he forcefully argued:

> Such a course of action is inconsistent with the Preamble which promises liberty of thought, expression, belief, faith and worship to everyone. How can we deal with this question in a narrow spirit? We invoke the name of God, but . . . while doing so, we are showing a narrow, sectarian spirit which is contrary to the spirit of the Constitution and we should not get distracted now when we have reached the end of a very important stage of our labours.[18]

The Assembly members arrived at a consensus and the amendment was defeated and Kamath expressed his anguish by saying that 'God save India [and] it is a black day in our annals.'[19] What was however established as a result was the endorsement of secular values which were pertinent to constitutional democracy. Divinity, despite being part and parcel of human existence, was presumed to be an anathema in so far as public governance was concerned, and it was firmly established in the arguments that a majority of the Assembly members offered to protect the secular fabric of the Preamble to the proposed Constitution of India.

The other amendment that M Ananthasayanam Ayyangar moved was about an invocation for Mahatma Gandhi in the Preamble. Similar to the Preamble to the Eire Constitution which began with the words, 'In the Name of the Most Holy Trinity. . .', he thus suggested that we should likewise start with the words, 'with the grace and benediction of Mahatma Gandhi, the Father of the Nation.'[20] He did not pursue the amendment because he felt that 'whether his name appears in the Preamble in writing or not, nobody can erase the peaceful and solemn voice of Mahatma Gandhi from our hearts.'[21] Congratulating the members of the Drafting Committee and also those who endorsed the Preamble, he further noted that without their unflinching commitment to constitutional democracy, it would not have been possible to have a constitution with such a clear ideological aim. The message that the Preamble conveyed was unambiguously articulated in the Constitution which

---

[13] HV Kamath (Central Provinces and Berar), 17 October 1949, *Constituent Assembly Debates*, Book No. 5, p. 439.
[14] HV Kamath (Central Provinces and Berar), 19 November 1949, *Constituent Assembly Debates*, Book No. 5, p. 689.
[15] HV Kamath (Central Provinces and Berar), 17 October 1949, *Constituent Assembly Debates*, Book No. 5, p. 440.
[16] Purnima Banerjee (United Provinces), 17 October 1949, *Constituent Assembly Debates*, Book No. 5, p. 438.
[17] M Thirumala Rao (Madras), 17 October 1949, *Constituent Assembly Debates*, Book No. 5, p. 441.
[18] Hriday Nath Kunzru (United Provinces), 17 October 1949, *Constituent Assembly Debates*, Book No. 5, p. 441.
[19] HV Kamath (Central Provinces and Berar), 17 October 1949, *Constituent Assembly Debates*, Book No. 5, p. 442.
[20] M Ananthasayanam Ayyangar (Madras), 18 October 1949, *Constituent Assembly Debates*, Book No. 5, p. 664.
[21] Ibid., p. 664.

> is an absolutely democratic constitution [because] it vests the sovereignty in the people and enables them to continue to exercise that sovereignty in full; . . . besides political sovereignty, the Preamble also secures to the Indians social justice [which means] that there is no discrimination between one individual and another.[22]

The unqualified appreciation by Ayyangar was largely due to the Preamble being attentive to those socio-economic goals which the Mahatma endeavoured hard to achieve. Besides insisting on popular sovereignty, Gandhi also stood out for his uncompromising stance on the issues of social justice, especially his lifelong battle against untouchability. With its declared aim of achieving equality, the proposed Preamble was, as Ayyangar was persuaded to believe, a stepping stone towards attaining the Gandhian objectives.

There were also objections by members when the proposed Preamble excluded the word, independent, while characterizing India as a polity; by defining India as a Sovereign Democratic republic, Maulana Hasarat Mohani charged Ambedkar for being insensitive to the Objective Resolution which preferred to characterize the new nation as an Independent Sovereign Republic. For Mohani, India could not become a republic given Nehru's commitment to remain in the Commonwealth. As he argued, 'India will be a republican dominion. Because if it is a real republic and not a republican dominion, you should have nothing to do with any King or Emperor directly or indirectly in any manner. When once Pandit Jawaharlal Nehru has agreed to remain in the British Commonwealth, I think he has forfeited his right to call India as a Republic'.[23] Despite his forceful defence, Mohani failed to persuade his colleagues and the amendment was defeated giving way to the pledge of making India a Sovereign Democratic Republic.

Analysing the Politico-ideological Aims of the Preamble

A motion was thereafter adopted by the Constituent Assembly that 'the Preamble is a part of the Constitution'.[24] The central idea which emerged after the marathon brain storming sessions was that the Preamble should be in conformity with the provisions of the Constitution and express in a few words the philosophy of the Constitution. After the transfer of power, the Constituent Assembly became sovereign, which was reflected in the words 'give to ourselves this Constitution' in the Preamble which also implies that sovereignty lies with the people.

The original draft of the Constitution which opened with the words' Sovereign Democratic Republic' was enriched by insertion of value loaded words 'Socialist' and 'Secular' on the one hand and the word 'unity' was reinvigorated by inserting 'integrity' by the Forty-Second Amendment Act (1976). The significance of the Preamble of the Indian Constitution lies in the 'We, The people' which explicitly expresses that the ultimate power rests in the hands of the people of India. The expressions state that the Constitution is made by the people and for the people of India. The Preamble lays down the essential goals for every citizen which are justice, liberty, equality and fraternity.

The word 'sovereign' implying internal supremacy and external freedom in decision making and formulation and execution of its policies clearly reflects in unequivocal terms the independent existence

---

[22] Ibid., p. 662.

[23] Maulana Hasarat Mohani (United Provinces), 17 October 1949, *Constituent Assembly Debates*, Book No. 5, p. 434.

[24] *Constituent Assembly Debates*, 17 October 1949, Book No. 5, p. 456.

of the country. Furthermore, the country has a free government which is directly elected by the people and makes the laws that govern the people. The inserted word 'Socialist' which did not find a place in the original draft of the founding fathers implies social and economic equality. In addition equality implies the absence of discrimination on the grounds only of caste, creed, colour, sex, religion, language etc. Besides, social equality also aims at equal status and opportunity for all. The word 'Secular', which was also a bi-product of the Forty-Second Amendment Act of 1976, implies equality of all religions as well as religious tolerance and does not identify any official State religion which upholds that India is not a theocratic State.

The Preamble of the Indian Constitution also puts forth the terms, 'Democratic' and 'Republic'. It means that India should have democratic form of Government. The people of India elect their governments at all the level such as Union, State and the Local Governments by the system of universal adult franchise. India is also a Republic, because it is a country where the Head of the State is elected though indirectly for a fixed tenure. Preamble, therefore, not only indicates the source of the Constitution of India, i.e., from its sovereign people but also states the objectified historical consensus which it seeks to establish and promote.

The Preamble, though, does not contain laws enforceable in a Court, but ideally no law can be enacted or amended in a manner that violates the spirit of the Preamble. Thus, the Preamble of the Constitution of India can rightly be said as the heart and soul of the constitution which must be preserved, protected and promoted by the elected representatives on the one hand and the positive interpretations of the judiciary on the other.

Changes in the Preamble

Though the framers of the Constitution were sagacious enough to ingrain all the vital values underpinning the Indian polity in the Preamble, the government of Indira Gandhi, for obvious political considerations, effected an unnecessary amendment in the original Preamble to the Constitution by inserting the words 'Socialist' and 'Secular' along with the original 'Sovereign', 'Democratic', 'Republic' as well as 'Integrity' along with the original 'Unity' of the nation, through the Forty-Second Amendment on 18 December 1976.

Arguably, the insertion of these words appears unnecessary and unwarranted due to the futility of the purposes they were supposed to serve. Undoubtedly, the dominant faction of the leadership during the national movement, led by Jawaharlal Nehru, was overwhelmingly intoxicated by the mesmerizing characteristics of socialism and would have in all probability gone for steering India on the socialist path of development. If there were any doubts on this count, the matte was finally settled at the Avadi Session of Congress in 1954 by professing India to follow the 'socialistic pattern of society'. Above all, the policy of centralized planned economic development through successive five year plans, initiated by the government of Nehru as well as the unbridled nationalization of the financial institutions by Indira Gandhi, left not even an iota of doubt that India is totally on the socialistic path of economic development.

Similarly, the idea of secularism was probably as deep rooted in the mind-set of the Indian leadership as well as the masses as the idea of democracy. Significantly, as the Indians fought the colonial rulers for Independence, they also became well versed with certain values which though appeared western, became synonymous with the value system of the Indians—two such values being that of democracy and secularism. At the same time, vehemently opposed to the two-nation theory of Muslim League and wary of the creation of a theocratic state of Pakistan in their neighbourhood, the framers of the Constitution were probably so dead sure of secularism being an indestructible characteristic of the Indian socio-political life that they found it absurd to ingrain it in an formalistic sense in the Preamble to the Constitution.

As regards the insertion of the word 'integrity' in the Preamble, it seems obvious that the original phrase—unity of the nation—would have been taken as all inclusive, encompassing the term integrity in its ambit. Alternatively, after passing through the horrifying reality of the partition of the country, the framers appeared to be sufficiently assured that whatever remained of India would, for the times to come, remain integral part of the country, provided it remains united. Yet, in view of the centrifugal tendencies which emerged in the country after a few years of Independence, it would not seem impertinent, if not undesirable, to insert the word 'integrity' in the Preamble to the Constitution. Crucially, the only point of dispute appears to be that the motive behind these insertions was more political, than idealistic or constitutional.

Source of the Authority

The expression 'We the People of India' truly recognizes the people of India as the source of ultimate sovereignty and the fact that the Constitution is the product of the consent of the people. It shows that the Constitution has the roots in the people of India and it derives its authority from the people. It is an embodiment of the fact that the people are the real source of authority and that they themselves have declared India to be 'Sovereign, Socialist, Democratic Republic'. The powers defined by the Constitution with respect to the Centre and the State Governments are not dictated by the former colonial masters or by the princely states or any particular section of the society. The Constitution of India has been framed by the people of India through their representatives in the Constituent Assembly, and can only be modified by the procedure laid down in the Constitution itself. The significance of 'We the People of India' lies in the fact that the Constitution of India eliminates the British king externally and the Indian princes internally, from claiming any vestiges of sovereignty. While the former was explicit, the latter was made to be implicit, as, with the lapse of paramountcy on 15 August 1947, the Indian princes became independent and so sovereign power belonged to them as a matter of inherent right which had to be naturalized by some such declarations.

The Text of the Preamble

The Constitution of India opens with a Preamble. The Preamble to the Constitution of India as amended in the year 1976 reads as follows:

> WE THE PEOPLE OF INDIA having solemnly resolved to constitute India into a
> SOVEREIGN, SOCIALIST, SECULAR, DEMOCRATIC REPUBLIC and to secure to all its citizens,
> JUSTICE – Social, Economic and Political
> LIBERTY – of Thought, Expression, Belief, Faith and Worship,
> EQUALITY – of Status and Opportunity and to promote among them all
> FRATERNITY – Assuring the dignity of the individual and the UNITY and INTEGRITY of the nation,
> IN OUR CONSTITUENT ASSEMBLY this 26th day of November 1949 DOES HEREBY ADOPT, ENACT AND GIVE TO OURSELVES THIS CONSTITUTION.

Analysing the Features

As amended in 1976, the Preamble, unambiguously, exemplifies the broad contours of the Indian political life and serves a number of useful purposes, for, the expressions used in it connote certain fundamental aspects of the polity from which there is no escape for the various stakeholders in the political life of the nation. Being directional, the Preamble to the Constitution of India has the following features which are illustrative of the politico-ideological goals that it is meant to serve:

First, though the use of the phrase, 'We, the people of India', may appear customary, its implications are far reaching for a nascent and fragile nation like India, marching on the unchartered path of democratic governance with competing hopes and aspirations from diverse quarters of the society. Thus, by establishing the sovereignty of the people, the Preamble reduces all other units of governance in the country to a secondary position, robbing from them any possibility of usurping the powers of other units as well as organs of government. At the same time, it also implies that the powers which are given to the government in India are sourced not from the states or any section of society or the former rulers of the Indian states but from the people at large, as a result of which no section of the people can challenge its authority and contend that it is not bound by the authority of the state because it has not accorded its consent to it. More importantly, since the states of the Union were not the party in the creation of the Union, which was created by the people of India, they cannot claim a right of secession from the Union. Therefore, the Preamble not only affords a stable democratic polity for the nation but also solidifies the unity and integrity of the nation.

Second, the Preamble puts in black and white the nature of polity in the county which must conform to the hard earned ideals of sovereign, socialist, secular, democratic republic. Needless to say, the nature of the Indian polity would not have been different from what it is today, had the words 'socialist' and 'secular' not been added to the original Preamble. While sovereignty affords a respectful place of pride to India in the comity of nations, the ideal of democratic republic manifests the basic outline of the nature of polity, guaranteeing the people the fundamental right of choosing their representatives to foster democratic governance in the country. Unavoidably, the mention of India becoming a republic becomes a compulsive requirement in view of the previous incarnation of India as a British Dominion whose head of state would have been the British monarch. Hence, by making India a republic, the framers of the Constitution carried out a crucial, if not total, break from the British suzerainty, even if nominal in practical terms.

Interestingly, despite the urge to make India a socialist country, the subtle and somewhat irreversible departure of the policies of the government from socialism, beginning in early 1990s with the adoption of Structural Adjustment Programmes (SAPs) under the dictates of the international financial institutions, has become most profound today, whereas the ideal of secularism has been so deeply ingrained in the ethos and mind-set of the one and all that it is now professed both formally as well as informally that the demise of secularism in the county may prove to be the demise of India as a nation as well. Thus, it appears to be a story in contrast for the two equally plausible notions of socialism and secularism, inserted into the Preamble with equal vigour, whereby while socialism, appearing an alien transplant in the Indian constitutional framework, fell in disfavour with the rulers of the day, without any rescue efforts by the other organs of the government, the notion of secularism, a long enduring value of Indian socio-cultural life, not only found commanding heights through the judicial pronouncements but also delving deep into the psyche of the people as well as the government alike.

Third, the Preamble presents a wish list outlining the aspirations of the people which they expect the government of India to secure for them. Spelt out in terms of justice, equality and fraternity, these ideals act as the benchmark to guide the policies and programmes of the government in future to cast India into the mould of a welfare state. Leaving no room for ambiguity on the dimensions of justice, the Preamble demarcates that justice needs to be in terms of social, economic and political, to be construed in the broadest sense of the term so that the nature of state in India does not become lop-sided.

The framers were quick enough to supplement the ideal of justice with that of the ideal of equality of status and opportunity to provide for the holistic framework of an egalitarian society in India. In the meanwhile, the Preamble does emphasize the promotion of fraternity amongst the citizens by assuring the dignity of the individual in society. Aware of the propensity of certain sections of society to advocate the subordination of individual dignity to the cause of farcical societal interests, the framers did not mince words to clarify that societal good could be ascertained only by ensuring the individual good in the society. Thus, the framers wished to create a social democracy in India, which, as Ambedkar elaborates, 'means a way of life which recognizes liberty, equality and fraternity which are not to be treated as separate items in a trinity. They form a union of trinity in the sense that to divorce one from the other is to defeat the very purpose of democracy. Liberty cannot be divorced from equality; equality cannot be divorced from liberty. Nor can liberty and equality be divorced from fraternity'.[25]

Fourth, the Preamble makes it amply clear that the unity and integrity of the country is a precondition for the other cherished ideals to become reality in the scheme of things in an independent India. Discounting any scope for tempering with the unity and integrity of the nation, the essence of the letter and spirit of the Preamble conclusively bars all the stakeholders in the nation, be it the individuals, group of people, the state or any other entity, from casting aspersions on the unity and integrity of the country, in case of which the people of India and/or the government of India are enjoined to safeguard the unity and integrity of the nation.

Finally, the utility of the Preamble is discerned in its serving as a beacon light to the higher courts in the country that are called upon to discharge the grand duty of interpreting the Constitution. At the times of interpreting a controversial law or constitutional provisions, where the meaning of the law in point is not clear or ambiguity or uncertainty prevails in the minds of the constitutional lawyers or the judges, the only reference point left to the court is the language of the Preamble through which they persevere to mark out real intention of the framers of the Constitution. It is argued that the Preamble is the repository of the spirit of the Constitution and hence, the only reference point for those engaged in interpreting the constitutional provisions should be the ideals embodied in it.

Preamble: Whether a Part of the Constitution?

Whether Preamble should be treated as part of the constitution or not has been a matter of great debate and discussion not only in India but also in USA. It was opined by the Supreme Court of USA that a Preamble is not an operative part of the Constitution. It indicates only the general purpose for which the people ordained and established the Constitution. It has never been regarded as the source of any substantive power conferred on the government of the USA or any of its department. The Supreme Court of India has laid down in some cases that the Preamble is not an operative part of the Constitution and hence it can never be a source of power. It has limited application and can be resorted to where there is any ambiguity or where the object or meaning of any enactment is not clean. Where the enabling part, i.e., the operative

[25] BR Ambedkar's defence of the constitution of India in the Constituent Assembly, 25 November 1949, *Constituent Assembly Debates*, Book no. 5, p. 979.

part of the Constitution is explicit and unambiguous, the Preamble cannot be resorted to, to control, qualify or restrict. In other words, where the language or provisions of the operative part are clear, full effect should be given to the operative part, even though those provisions appear to contradict the terms of the Preamble. It has thus aptly been argued that: 'Two propositions are quite clear: one that a preamble may afford useful light as to what the state intends to reach; and another, that if an enactment is itself clear and unambiguous, no preamble can qualify or cut down the enactment'.

But in India, proper function of the Preamble is to explain and recite certain facts which are necessary before the enactment contained in an act of the Parliament could be understood. The Preamble is often used to limit the scope of certain expressions used in the Constitution and to throw light on certain facts. Whenever a doubt arises, the Preamble helps in fixing the ambiguity or connotation of the words which can possibly have more than one meaning. In 1950, in the case of *AK Gopalan v. the State of Madras*, it was contended that the Preamble to the Constitution, which seeks to give India a democratic constitution, should be the guiding force in its interpretation and hence any law made under Article 21 of the Constitution should be held void if it offends the principle of natural justice for otherwise the so called 'fundamental rights' to life and personal liberty would have no protection. The majority bench of the Supreme Court rejected this contention holding that 'law' in Article 21 refers to positive or state-made law and not natural justice, and that the meaning of the language of Article 21 could not be modified with reference to the language of Article 21.

In the 1960 Berubari Union Case, the Supreme Court declared that the Preamble is not an integral part of the Indian constitution. Therefore it is not enforceable in a court of law and, further, Preamble had never been regarded as the source of any substantive power conferred on the government or on any of its departments. The court explained that 'what is true about the powers is equally true about the prohibitions and limitations'. It was therefore, observed that the Preamble had limited application. The court laid down that the Preamble would not be resorted to if the language of the enactment contained in the constitution was clear. However, 'if the terms used in any of the articles in the constitution are ambiguous or capable of two meanings, in interpreting them some assistance may be sought in the objectives enshrined in the Preamble'. Being unanimous in their decisions, the constitutional bench delivered a judgement which Justice PB Gajendragadkar articulated by saying that the Preamble of the constitution, is a key to our understanding of the Constitution despite not being its part. In other words, the values that the Preamble represents need to be taken into account while interpreting the Constitution.

In the Bommai case of 1994, the majority of nine Judges laid down that the Preamble of the Constitution is the part of the basic structure of the Constitution. A Proclamation under Article 356(1) is open to judicial review on the ground of violating the basic structure of the Constitution. It laid in the judgement that the proclamation under Article 356(1), which violates any of the basic features as summarized in the Preamble of the Constitution is liable to be struck down as unconstitutional. A further extension of this innovation is that a political party, which appeals to religion in its election manifesto, acts in violation of the basic structure, and the President may impose President's Rule on a report of the Governor that a party has issued such a manifesto. Three of the nine judges have opined that the word 'secularism' in the Preamble of the Constitution is the part of the basic structure of the Constitution.

The Kesavananda Bharati case (1973) was a milestone and was a watershed India's constitutional history. For the first time, a bench of 13 judges assembled and sat in its original jurisdiction hearing the writ petition and they all placed on record 11 separate arguments to defend their points of view. It is not the source of power or the source of limitations for the prohibitors. The Preamble has an important role to play in the interpretation of the provisions of the constitution. Justice Palekar held that the Preamble is the part of the Constitution and therefore is amendable under Article 368 of the Constitution. It is the introductory part of the Constitution and is based on the Objective Resolution of Nehru. It tells about the nature of the state and objects that India has to achieve. There were many judicial interpretation on the issue if the Preamble is the part of the constitution or not? But finally the judiciary in the Kesavananda Bharti case held that the Preamble was a part of the Indian Constitution. Chief Justice Sikri said, 'it seems to me that the preamble of our constitution is of extreme importance and the constitution should be read and interpreted in the light of the grand and the noble visions expressed in the preamble.'[26]

In the Minerva Mills case (1980) the Supreme Court applying Kesavananda principle invalidated the Clauses (4) and (5) of Article 368 inserted by the Forty-Second Amendment Act since they were in violation of the basic structure of the Constitution. Therefore, as it stands today, the Parliament can amend every part of the Constitution, but cannot change the basic structure of the Constitution of which Preamble is an integral part.

In the 1992 Indra Sawhney case, India's apex court drew our attention to the critical importance of the Preamble to the Constitution. Hailing the contribution that the founding fathers had made in constitutionalizing India, the Supreme Court held that the republic was

> founded with the four-fold objective of securing to its citizens justice, liberty, equality and fraternity. Statesman of the highest order . . . belonging to the fields of law, politics, and public life, came together to fashion the instrument of change, the Constitution of India. They did not rest content with evolving the framework of the State, they also pointed out the goal-end and the methodology for reaching the goal. In the Preamble, they elaborated the methodology to be followed for reaching the goal.[27]

Characterizing the Preamble as 'a turning point in history', it was also emphasized by the court that it was also 'a key to the minds of the framers of the constitution'.[28] The argument is very explicit: since the Preamble upholds the fundamental values that the founding fathers nurtured, it provides guidance to the future law makers with reference to what is considered to be constitutionally most appropriate at a particular historical juncture. This has been established by the court more than once. The most significant judicial pronouncement happens to be the Kesavananda judgement of 1973 in which the Preamble was identified as integral to the Constitution of India. Pursuing this understanding of the Preamble, M Hidayatullah further mentioned:

> The Preamble resembles the Declaration of Independence of the United States of America, but is more than a declaration. It is the soul of our Constitution which lays down the pattern of our political society which it states is sovereign, democratic republic. It contains a solemn resolve which nothing but a revolution can alter.[29]

Emphasizing that the Preamble lays-out the politico-ideological directions that the State needs to follow while discharging its social responsibility the apex court privileged the prescriptive characteristics of the Constitution of India over those insisting on its procedure-specific nature. This is a remarkable judicial feat since it both upheld the importance of some of the cardinal values of governance in a democratic setting and firmly established the idea that they can never be bypassed under any circumstances. The Preamble is thus not merely a text with tremendous constitutional importance, it also streamlines processes

[26] *Kesavananda Bharati v. the State of Kerala*, 1973. https://indiankanoon.org/doc/257876/ (accessed 29 November 2016).

[27] *Indra Sawhney v. the Union of India*, 1992. https://indiankanoon.org/doc/1363234/ (accessed 29 November 2016).

[28] *Indra Sawhney v. the Union of India*, 1992.

[29] M Hidayatullah, *Democracy in India and the Judicial Process* (Delhi: Metropolitan, 1982), p. 51.

for democratic governance by stressing those pertinent politico-ideological values which are critically important in this regard.

Reviewing the Argument

Conceptually speaking, a Preamble to a constitution is not just a preface, but a text containing the major constitutional values for guidance. In other words, a Preamble contains a summary of the entire constitution in terms of those fundamental politico-ideological values, expected to be upheld by the policy makers while embarking on policy designs. As is shown earlier, the Preamble to the Constitution of India was framed by the founding fathers after having had fierce debates in the Constituent Assembly; according to them, being the soul of the Constitution, it retains those values which are critical in charting the course of action that the constitution is likely to take. It has also been shown that the Preamble cannot be sacrosanct; it is changed on occasions. Here is an ethical question with serious implications for the constitution. Can the values which are considered fundamental be changed because they do not appear to be relevant, or can new ideas be incorporated in the Preamble to adapt it to the changed socio-economic milieu? A conservative response shall be in the negative, and those subscribing to the view that being organic to a particular society, the Preamble needs to be accommodative of new ideas or dismissive of those principles which are no longer relevant, will hold a completely different point of view. For instance, two expressions—'socialistic' and 'secular'—were not there in the Preamble to India's Constitution in its original form; these were added after a constitutional amendment in 1976, presumably to highlight the significance of these ideas in governance; it is also indicative of the nature of the regime. If new ideas can be incorporated, old ideas can, by implication, be discarded. Is it therefore valid to hold the view that Preamble is sacrosanct? There is no easy answer to this question. What is clear however is that so long as these ideas are integral to the Preamble, they are inviolable, as multiple court judgements have shown. By insisting that the Preamble is part of the Constitution, the apex court has time and again emphasized that the ideas enshrined there can never be bypassed or undermined while assessing the constitutional validity of executive and legislative decisions. Beginning with the 1950 *AK Gopalan* case, the Supreme Court of India has always upheld the importance of the Preamble in assessing whether a particular piece of legislation or an executive feat is justiciable. This is a valid and also persuasive constitutional position so long as there is guarantee for 'procedure, established by law' as per Article 21 of the 1950 Constitution of India which also confirms that in its absence, the situation may not seem to be propitious and favourably tilted for the Preamble. It further means that being the soul of the constitution, a Preamble continues to remain uninfringeable since it is politically endorsed and ideologically defended in a particular socio-economic milieu, the absence of which makes its future uncertain and unpredictable.

Fundamental Rights[30]

The inclusion of a detailed scheme of fundamental rights in the Constitution marks the culmination of a long and sustained desire of the Indians to be bestowed with the basic liberties of free and happy life.

[30] Bidyut Chakrabarty and Rajendra Kumar Pandey, *Indian Government and Politics* (New Delhi: SAGE Publications, 2008), pp. 11–14.

Indeed, the formation of the Indian National Congress in 1885 was, among other things, aimed at ensuring the same rights and privileges for Indians that the British enjoyed in their own country[31] though the first systematic demand for fundamental rights came in the form of The Constitution of India Bill, 1895. The Bill stipulated to secure to all the citizens freedom of speech and expression, right to personal liberty, inviolability of one's house, right to property, equality before law, equality to admission to public offices and right to petition for redress of grievances. However, the idea of Indians being called as the citizens of India was still absent, even in the minds of the prominent Indian leaders, including the leaders of the Congress, who in the wake of the publication of the Montague–Chelmsford Report, impressed upon the British Government for 'declaration of the rights of the people of India as British citizens.' The echo of demands of the Indians for certain fundamental rights was also heard in the draft of the Commonwealth of India Bill, formulated by the National Convention under the inspiration of Annie Besant in 1925.

Thereafter, numerous resolutions were passed and committees were appointed to put forth the perspectives of Indians on the nature and scope of the fundamental rights, aspired by the people of India. Significantly, the Cabinet Mission Plan, while accepting the demand for the Constituent Assembly and the necessity of a written guarantee of Fundamental Rights in the Constitution of independent India, suggested the appointment of an Advisory Committee on the Rights of Citizens, Minorities and Tribal and Excluded Areas, bestowed with the responsibility of preparing a list of Fundamental Rights and also to suggest their inclusion in the Union or the State List. Afterwards, the major boost for the provisions of Fundamental Rights came with the introduction of the Objective Resolution by Jawaharlal Nehru. While adopting the Resolution on 22 January 1947, the Constituent Assembly solemnly dedicated itself to draft a Constitution for the governance of India wherein shall be guaranteed and secured to all the people of India, justice, social, economic and political, equality of status, of opportunity and before law; freedom of thought, expression, belief, faith, worship, vocation, association and action, subject to law and public morality. In the light of the perspective provided by the Objective Resolution, the Constituent Assembly formed the Advisory Committee for reporting on Minorities, Fundamental Rights and on the tribal and excluded areas under the chairmanship of Vallabhbhai Patel and consisting of 53 other members. Streamlining its functions, the Advisory Committee, in turn, set up five sub-committees, one of which was vested with the responsibility of suggesting the blueprint of Fundamental Rights for Independent India. The draft report of the Sub-Committee, accompanied by the explanatory notes on various Clauses of the outline of Fundamental Rights, was circulated to its members who came out with insightful inputs on these Clauses and after consolidation of the views suggested by the members, the final report of the Sub-Committee was submitted to the Chairman of the Advisory Committee on 16 April 1947.

The final shape to the provisions on Fundamental Rights was given by the Advisory Committee. Basing its formulations on the recommendations of the Sub-Committee, the Advisory Committee agreed on the desirability of dividing the rights into justiciable and non-justiciable rights, thereby paving the way for the compartmentalization of the erstwhile Fundamental Rights into two distinct categories of Fundamental Rights and the Directive Principle of State Policy. At the same time, even within the sphere of Fundamental Rights, it was decided to bestow certain rights upon all persons while few rights were to be guaranteed to the citizens only, though the application of the rights was extended to all the states of the country. The report of the Advisory Committee was accepted and adopted by the Constituent Assembly which by way of creating two Chapters, III and IV, made provisions for the Fundamental Rights and the Directive Principles of State Policy, respectively.

---

[31] Granville Austin, *The Indian Constitution: Cornerstone of a Nation* (New Delhi: Oxford University Press, 1966), pp. 52–53.

Originally, the Constitution contained seven Fundamental Rights. But the right to property was repealed in 1978 by the Forty-Fourth Constitutional Amendment during the rule of the Janata Government, reducing these rights to six only which are classified so: Right to Equality (Articles 14–18), Right to Freedom (Articles 19–22), Right against Exploitation (Articles 23 and 24), Right to Freedom of Religion (Articles 25–28), Cultural and Educational Rights (Articles 29 and 30), and the Right to Constitutional Remedies (Article 32). These rights have been protected against undue infringement by the state excepting certain specific circumstances provided under the Constitution, though their amendability has been upheld by the Supreme Court under Article 368 of the Constitution in the Kesavananda Bharti case.

Described, along with the DPSP, as the conscience of the Constitution, by Austin, the Fundamental Rights arguably constitute the soul of the Constitution. However, in material terms, as pointed out by NA Palkhiwala, they constitute the anchor of the Constitution and provide it with the dimension of permanence. The Constitution envisages the Fundamental Rights as the common platform on which divergent political ideologies and practices may meet. They provide the iron framework within which experiments in social and economic changes may be tried out.[32]

These rights, therefore, have been given a much esteemed position in the constitutional law of the country, for, all laws in force in the territory of India immediately before 26 January 1950 and all legislations enacted thereafter, have to conform to the provisions of Part III of the Constitution.

Moreover, the scope of the Fundamental Rights are wide enough to encompass practically all those rights which human ingenuity has found to be essential for the development and growth of the personalities of the citizens of the country. Significantly, the focus of attention of the framers in this regard was on the citizens mainly, if not exclusively, as many of these rights are not guaranteed to the aliens. For instance, the rights contained in Article 15 (Prohibition of discrimination on the basis of religion, race, caste, sex, place of birth or any of them), Article 16 (Equality of opportunity in the matters of public employment), Article 19 (Right to Freedom) and Article 29 (cultural and educational rights) are available to the citizens only. Nevertheless, the best part of the provisions on Fundamental Rights is the fine-tuned machinery to guarantee these rights in practice, as under Article 32 the Supreme Court is given the original jurisdiction to entertain the petition of a person whose fundamental right has been infringement and is empowered with various which can be issued to secure the enjoyment of these rights.

Despite being taken as the bedrock of democratic life in the country, the Fundamental Rights have not been made absolute since several reasonable restrictions have been placed on their enjoyment. Set to secure the public good on the one hand and the unity and integrity of the nation on the other, the reasonable restrictions can be imposed specifically in the interests of the sovereignty and integrity of India, security of the state, friendly relations with foreign states, public order, decency, morality, health etc. and for the protection of the interests of any Scheduled Tribes. Though these restrictions, no doubt, appear to be an attempt on the part of the framers to strike a balance between individual liberty and the social good, in the course of the functioning of the Constitution, it was rightly apprehended that the state might, under the garb of reasonable restrictions, put undue infringement on the enjoyment of these right. Consequently, the endeavour of the Courts in the country has been to a rigorous check on the reasonableness of the restriction, as and when they are imposed to curtail the rights of the people. Proclamation of a state of emergency provides another circumstance when the enjoyment of fundamental freedoms guaranteed under Article 19 may be suspended. Similarly, Article 33 empowers the Parliament not to grant some of the fundamental rights to the persons employed in the armed forces.

---

[32] Cited in VD Mahajan, *Select Modern Constitutions* (New Delhi: S Chand and Company, 1984), p. 70.

Reasonable restrictions notwithstanding, the Fundamental Rights appear to be big restrictions on the legislative, executive and to some extent judicial powers of the state. In making laws, the legislatures must see to it that such law does not in any was infringe any of the Fundamental Rights guaranteed to the people, for, if such law as a whole or any part of it is found inconsistent with any of the Fundamental Rights, it would be declared null and void by a competent court. More precarious is the position of the executive authorities who bear the brunt of the Court when they are found to be acting in an unconstitutional manner. The recent case of the Soharabuddin fake encounter case of Gujarat has proved to be the undoing of several senior IPS officers of the state. The same canon of constitutional propriety applies to the judiciary also as no decision which is in contravention to the provisions of Fundamental Rights can be pronounced by any court in the country, for, if such a decision is delivered, it is bound to be set aside by the higher courts. More importantly, the restrictions of the Fundamental Rights do not apply only on the state agencies but on the private individuals and organizations also. For instance, Article 17 stands for the abolition of untouchability, Article 15(2) prohibits the disability of any citizen in the use of shops, restaurants, wells, roads and other public places on account of his religion, race, sex, or of birth, and Article 23 bars the practice of begging or forced labour in any form. Thus, the state, in addition to obeying the Constitution's negative injunctions not to interfere with certain of citizen's liberties, must fulfil its positive obligation to protect the citizen's rights from encroachment by society.[33]

Fundamental Duties

Impregnating the high sounding and zealously guarded domain of Fundamental Rights with a moderate dose of ethical citizenship responsibilities, the fundamental duties were inserted in the Constitution in 1976 through the Constitution Forty-Second Amendment. Drawn from the Constitution of former Soviet Union and placed in Part IVA of the Constitution under Article 51A, the set of ten fundamental duties are supposed to be only moral exhortation to the citizens of the county to inculcate a sense of patriotic and sensible citizenship, without any legal justiciability.

Though not justiciable and therefore, with little consequence in practical terms, the provision of fundamental duties was opposed by many people who also brought out several inconsistencies in these duties. For instance, one of the fundamental duties ask every citizen of the country to develop the scientific temper and spirit of enquiry but with bulk of the people still illiterate, how is it possible to imbibe the habit of thinking with clarity and precision if they are unable to get the basic inputs of such a thinking. Nevertheless, the fundamental duties have become a part of the Constitution and despite their non-justiciability; they continue to exercise some sort of social and collective restriction on those who are fond of enjoying unfettered rights without discharging even an iota of duty to the society and the nation.

Concluding Observations

Constitution represents a voice that gets articulated in different ways in various provisions. Given the importance of the socio-economic context in shaping the voice, it is fair to argue that there is hardly a universal format of constitution since the context in which it evolves hardly remains static. There is also

[33] Austin, *The Indian Constitution*, p. 51.

substance in the argument that constitution also builds on the prevalent set of values and principles presumably because of their viability in the changed environment. What it means is that a constitution is an articulation of a voice at one level; at another level, it also draws on those constitutional principles guiding a specific state. The Constitution of India that was inaugurated in 1950 is a perfect example of a creative blending of the nationalist voice and the colonial system of governance which drew on a series of legal stipulations, including the 1935 Government of India Act. A cursory look at the provisions of the 1950 text reveals that they had their roots in the colonial designs of constitutionalizing India.

Besides these two major influences, there is another powerful input which is evident if one carefully weaves through the provisions of the Constitution of India. With their exposure to the Western societies, the founding fathers also had access to the ideas and also the constitutional structures elsewhere. This is therefore not a matter of surprise that the Indian Constitution also has imprints of other democratic constitutions either in terms of contributing to the ideational foundation of the constitution or by actually articulating its provisions. As is commonly known, the Preamble to the Constitution of India reproduces the first two sentences of the Preamble to the US constitution. The idea that the constitution belongs to the people and it has to be announced at the outset which the US constitution champions was readily accepted by the framers since it also corresponded with what they felt so passionately during their confrontation with the British. In a similar vein, Part IV of the Constitution enumerating the DPSP is drawn on the fundamental principles that Irish Constitution has incorporated; although these principles are not justiciable, they gradually became instruments for democratization and the establishment of equality in its substantial sense. Characterized as the nation's 'conscience keeper', this Part contributed immensely to the articulation of various legal stipulations empowering the demos and thus contributing to the processes of democratization in the country. For instance, the successful campaign leading the acceptance of the Right to Education (2010) and Right to Food (2013) as compulsory rights had its roots in Article 41 of Part IV of the Constitution. Similarly, the path-breaking Seventy-Third Amendment Act (1992) which constitutionalized panchayati raj governance at the grassroots level draws its ideological sustenance from Article 40 of the same Part. The idea is very clear: by virtue of being sensitive to the needs of the demos, the constitution has to be elastic enough to accommodate the new impetus and demands; otherwise, it will cease to be organic to the prevalent socio-economic and political circumstances.

The fact that the constitutional values and principles are not sacrosanct confirms that it is a living organism which adapts to the constantly transforming milieu. The abolition of the Right to Property (Article 31) is illustrative here. As this right stood in the way of realizing the ideological goal of democratizing the nation, the Forty-Fourth Amendment Act (1978) withdrew the privileges and made the Right to Property a mere legal right which can also be taken away in accordance with law. Here too, the concern was to fulfil a politico-ideological mission that the nationalist leadership so assiduously aspired while being engaged in preparing an appropriate constitution for the country. So, nothing is sacrosanct except the basic structures of the Constitution since they not only form the core of governance but also contribute to the fulfilment of those fundamental constitutional goals which the Preamble to the Constitution nurtures. What is fundamental here is the idea that the constitution and the context are dialectically linked which plausibly explains the changes that are effected to steer the constitutional processes in a new direction.

By arguing that the constitution is not merely an instrument of authority but also a repository of ideas which are tuned to the contemporary socio-economic and political needs, the judiciary reinvents the constitution in accordance with the needs of the day. Given its historical roots in colonialism, Indian Constitution was often criticized for being largely a borrowed doctrine which is not entirely unfounded, and it is perfectly understandable why a powerful section in the Constituent Assembly was not persuaded to endorse the text that had emerged after three years of hard work. Strictly by an emotional yardstick, the charge was plausible though logically this appears to be clearly over-stretched since the 1950 Constitution epitomizes those values which informed the nationalist struggle against foreign domination. It is true that the framers were nurtured in a context in which the British liberal ethos reigned supreme. As a result, not only did they imbibe liberal ideas and values, they were also persuaded to believe in liberal democracy as perhaps the only effective device to create a polity of their desire. The Constitution that came out of deliberations in the Constituent Assembly was thus not drafted in a vacuum but in circumstances when different ideological strands and preferences jostled with one another for supremacy. That liberalism remained the principal ideological plank on which the Constitution was built notwithstanding the well-argued opposition by the Gandhians is a testimony to the processes whereby it prevailed over other ideological alternatives. Being an offshoot of relentless debates and arguments that went on close to three years in the Constituent Assembly, the 1950 Constitution of India cannot thus be said to be entirely a borrowed doctrine because not only was it an outcome of the efforts that the framers had undertaken while defending their respective ideological choices, it also drew on the constitutional practices that colonial state had nurtured to consolidate its rule. What is thus distinctive here is the importance of the processes in which some of the constitutional ideas and practices are privileged as they are complementary to what the founding fathers recognized as useful and self-fulfilling. Fundamental here is the argument that constitution, being a living organism, can neither be entirely derivative nor exclusively indigenous, for it is an outcome of processes drawing on the structure of governance and also the ideas contributing to its articulation and functioning. The 1950 Constitution is not only illustrative here, but also makes a fundamental conceptual point challenging the effort towards dismissing the text for being borrowed from the Western intellectual legacies.

Review Questions

1. **Critically evaluate the fundamental features of the 1950 Constitution of India.**
2. **Write an evaluative essay on the importance of the Preamble to the Constitution of India.**
3. **What are the primary constitutional values that figure prominently in the Constitution of India? Elaborate your response.**
4. **How was the Preamble to the Constitution of India conceptualized in Constituent Assembly? Elaborate your response.**
5. **Is the Preamble to the Constitution of India a part of the Constitution? Give reasons for your answer.**
6. **Critically evaluate the Rights enshrined in Part III of the Constitution of India.**
7. **Why are these Rights, incorporated in Part III of the Constitution of India called Fundamental Rights? Elaborate your answer.**
8. **Critically evaluate Fundamental Duties with reference to their historical roots.**
9. **Are the Fundamental Rights sacrosanct? Elaborate your response with reference to concrete examples.**
10. **A constitution reigns supreme provided it is backed by a complementary political will. Do you agree with this view? Elaborate your response.**

Section B

ARTICULATING A VISION

Introduction to Section B

Being the lengthiest section in this book, Section B is, in one sense, an expansion of Section A because it also deals with the vision that was sought to be articulated by the founding fathers in the Constituent Assembly. There are 12 chapters, each with independent focus. The concern here is to understand those important aspects of constitutional practices, norms and principles which remained most critical in conceptualizing constitutional democracy in India. The effort is directed to acquaint the readers with the parts of the Constitution not merely with reference to the provisions of the Constitution but also by drawing on their historical antecedents and specific judicial pronouncements, showing them in different lights. Along with an elaboration of the provisions, this section also raises theoretical questions that need to be addressed in the wider context of India's constitutional democracy. For instance, a conventional conceptualization of federalism that tends to support the contention that India is not a federal country, and the description of India being 'a union of states' (Article 1 of the Constitution), is a source of grave confusion though there are three lists demarcating domains for the constituent provinces and the Centre. This is a very simplistic understanding of India's federalism because it also epitomizes a uniquely textured hybrid form of governance in which parliamentary supremacy is tempered with constitutional sovereignty within a specific type of constitutional democracy. Similarly, the incorporation of Article 370, which is supportive of a special status of Jammu and Kashmir, a constituent province within federal India, is also a source of confusion unless it is understood historically and with reference to the processes that finally culminated in this erstwhile princely state being included in the Union of India. The section is thus pertinent in comprehending the Constitution of India not merely as a text of rules and regulations but also as an important conceptual aid for understanding constitutional democracy both as a theoretical category and its specific manifestation in India.

Chapter

5

Ethics and Constitutional Governance in India[1]

Learning Objectives

- To conceptualize the dialectics of ethics and constitutional governance in India
- To understand how does ethics shape constitutional democracy in India
- To evaluate the efforts towards making constitutional governance in India ethics-sensitive

In constitutional discourses, ethics in governance seems to have acquired tremendous salience. This is obvious that a constitution survives not by coercion but by consent which is possible only when it is complemented by socio-political values supportive of ethics in governance. A state governs by instruments of authority which derive their sustenance also from the extent to which they are endorsed ethically in a specific socio-political context. The idea is simple, for governance to succeed it needs to be established in a well-defined constitutional framework, the success of which is also dependent on whether it is ethically defensible. Implicit here are two important points: on the one hand, it is argued that ethics and constitution are interrelated and cannot be conceptualized one independent of another; being dialectically construed, the relationship contributes, on the other, to significant politico-ideological processes whereby new indices of constitutional governance are conceptualized and articulated.

Constitution is thus not merely a checklist of provisions tuned to attain specific ideological goals; it is also a driver for processes which are pertinent in articulating a well-defined set of values and principles. What is implied here is the idea that since constitution is a value-driven phenomenon, it helps evolve certain value-preferences which may not have received adequate attention due to specific circumstances. Here too, one needs to conceptualize the constitution–value interface in the dialectical mould since they both influence and draw on each other. Two important conceptual ideas are implicit here: first, it has been proved beyond doubt that the strength of a constitution is not contingent on the instruments of authority, but on how far it organizes governance in accordance with rules and regulations which are free from prejudices to one group or another; secondly, values too need nurturing which is evident since they remain in vogue so long as they are pertinent and meaningful in certain socio-economic milieu.

This history of constitutionalism in India is replete with instances showing that the efforts at constitutionalizing India always drew on the concern for governing India in a direction which, despite

[1] Some of the points are drawn from my book, *Ethics in Governance in India* (Oxford and New York: Routledge, 2016), pp. 192–207.

being driven by the desire for protecting colonial interests, was also guided by the concern for creating and consolidating a constitutional foundation, conducive for ethics in governance as well. It is true that colonialism is out-and-out an extractive ideology; nonetheless, it had, rather in consequences, led to democratization, though in a limited way, of governance as colonial rule had progressed. It is also true that nationalism became a powerful ideology during the freedom struggle had its roots in the visible incompatibility of the British rule in India and the liberal constitutional values and ethos informing the British system of governance. The argument that the British administration was not ethical was persuasively justified by referring to this incongruity which the nationalists, including Gandhi, always highlighted in their opposition to the British colonialism.

A perusal of the debates in the Constituent Assembly reveals that the founding fathers had always believed that a constitution was always an empowering device in a context in which it evolves organically. What is most critical, as per them, was to build the constitution on 'the democratic spirit' of popular governance. This was most explicitly stated by BH Zaidi (Rampur–Banams State) when he mentioned that unless the democratic spirit was inculcated, the Constitution, despite being

> the finest Constitution on earth, is bound to breakdown. What we must work for is the proper democratic spirit, the realization that everyone of us is responsible to see that the country is governed properly along enlightened, progressive and democratic lines; [And], if that spirit . . . is missing, then [India's] constitutional fabric will collapse in no time.[2]

The constitutional fabric needs to be strengthened not by way of fortifying the institutions of governance but by reinforcing the democratic spirit of the governed. This is a part of ethics because once the spirit becomes a part of one's *ethikos*, (the Greek word for 'habit'), it cannot be separated from one's being. What is thus critical here is to evolve complementary ethikos by inculcating those values and ethos in human behaviour which are pertinent to specific constitutional design. Implied here is the argument that being 'a lifeless machine', a constitution acquires life because of the multitude that participates to articulate governance in a particular fashion. Hence Rajendra Prasad, the President of the Constituent Assembly exhorted that in order to make India's constitutional experience meaningful, what we needed was

> nothing more than a set of honest men [sic] who will have the interest of the country before them. There is a fissiparous tendency arising out of various elements in our life. We have communal differences, caste differences, language differences, provincial differences and so forth. It requires men of strong character, men of vision, men who will not sacrifice the interests of the country at large for the sake of smaller groups and areas and who will rise over the prejudices which are born of these differences. We can only hope that the country will throw up such men in abundance.[3]

In so many words, it was stated by Prasad that the success of the constitution was dependent on the commitment to contribute to a prejudice-free India which was possible provided one extended one's commitment to that goal. An objective scan of the Assembly debates testifies that while devising a constitutional design for the country, the founding fathers insisted on the importance of ethics

[2] BH Zaidi (Rampur–Banams), 3 August 1949, *Constituent Assembly Debates*, Book No. 4, p. 145.

[3] Rajendra Prasad, 26 November 1949, *Constituent Assembly Debates*, Book No. 5, pp. 993–94.

in governance which, they strongly felt, was essential for breaking 'the shackles of traditional social hierarchy . . . to usher in a new era of freedom, equality and justice'.[4] In that sense, the Indian Constitution did not only disenable those in power, but also provided opportunities to those who, because of structural constraints, always remained peripheral and marginalized. By drawing on the debates and also those events in contemporary India which are critical to the phenomenon, this segment aims to substantiate the argument that ethics always remains inalienable from healthy constitutional practices. On the basis of an analytical account of the socio-political processes emphasizing the importance of ethics in governance, this segment also defends the contention that independent of ethics a constitution however strong in its ideological lineages is just a compilation of certain rules and regulations without much substance and grit.

The Constitutional Morality

The idea of constitutional morality holds the key in comprehending ethics in governance where ethics is understood as critical moral values shaping a specific mind-set, being appreciative of responsibility and accountability. Given the fact that in democracy, public functionaries are 'trustees of the people'[5], the former is dialectically connected with the latter. The authority exercised by those in governance is thus not arbitrarily exercised, but is conceptually drawn on public interests. For a morally sensitive political order, appropriate laws and rules need to be made, and the public functionaries are also to be imbued with the required moral values allowing the system to remain viable. The concern for public well-being is a key to perfect governance which is conceivable if those responsible for governance are also made to be aware of their constitutional obligations when in power. This is possible in two ways: on the one hand, an alert citizenry will not allow them to be deviant which will be complemented, on the other hand, by stringent laws which will be indiscriminately used to punish if the charge of the abuse of authority is proved. Laws are undoubtedly effective preventive instruments provided they are not short-circuited by the intervention of political bigwigs. It is true that punitive measures are restraining devices; they also create an environment in which civic virtues for upholding the constitutional values are nurtured. The basic purpose is to generate an impulse for constitutional morality as perhaps the most reliable shield against ethics deficit in governance. This was a belief that BR Ambedkar held so dear even when he presented the 1950 Constitution of India to the nation. It was John Dewey of Columbia University who provided him with ideological support in favour of his argument for social democracy which was wider in connotation than political democracy. Like his academic mentor, John Dewey, Ambedkar also believed in the supremacy of the constitutional values in democratic political systems. Mere codification of laws was not enough, as Ambedkar argued, unless 'there is public conscience to behave in accordance with Constitutional provisions [which] is more important that the Constitution itself'. In continuation of the argument, he further stated:

> The principles of democracy are for the people to respect the system of formation of Government, observance of laws, habit of independent thinking and observance of laws of the majority.[6]

[4] Rajeev Bhargava, ed., *Politics and Ethics of the Indian Constitution* (New Delhi: Oxford University Press, 2008), p. 15.

[5] *Ethics in Governance*, Fourth Report, Second Administrative Reforms Commission (New Delhi: Government of India, 2007), p. 19.

[6] BR Ambedkar, lecture in the legislative assembly, Trivandrum, 10 June 1950, reproduced in Narendra Jadhav, *Ambedkar Speaks: Political Speeches*, Vol. 3 (New Delhi: Konark Publishers Pvt. Ltd, 2013), p. 537.

What was critical for the survival of democracy was civility, a Dewey conceptualization that Ambedkar held so dear while discharging his historical role. It called for tolerance, restraint and mutual accommodation in public life. Civility was thus 'a moderating influence which acts against the extremes of ideological politics'.[7] In his perception, without civility, 'democracy becomes defunct' and he was also aware that the lack of a living democratic tradition in India was a serious deterrent in the context of rigid caste hierarchy. To transform a society of caste and communities into one of citizens was not an easy task. Nonetheless, he fulfilled his role by seeking to create 'a sense of constitutional morality' while defending his liberal agenda.[8] Here too, Ambedkar was indebted to a classicist George Grote[9] who he quoted extensively in his speech of 4 November 1948 in the Constituent Assembly. Institutions of governance in a democracy, felt Grote, 'lose salience [unless] there is diffusion of constitutional morality, not merely among the majority of any community, but throughout the whole ... since any powerful and obstinate minority may render the working of a free institution impracticable, without being strong enough to conquer ascendancy for themselves'.[10] By constitutional morality, Grote meant

> a paramount reverence for the forms of constitution, obedience to authority acting under and within these forms, yet combined with the habit of open speech, of action subject to definite legal control and unrestrained censure of those in public authorities ... with a perfect confidence amidst bitterness of party contest that the forms of constitution will not be less sacred in the eyes of his opponents than his own.[11]

This long quote from Grote's writings was surely an aid to Ambedkar when he defended a liberal democratic framework of constitutional governance in India though he was aware that it was difficult to instil a sense of constitutional morality in India because democracy which 'complements constitutional morality ... is only a top-dressing on an Indian soil which is essentially undemocratic'.[12] In the absence of constitutional morality, the operation of the constitution, no matter how carefully written, 'tends to become arbitrary, erratic and capricious'.[13] How to make the constitution an effective instrument of governance in such circumstances, asked Ambedkar. He was in favour of detailed provisions in the constitution to scuttle efforts at derailing the constitution and challenging the fundamental constitutional values from which it derived its sustenance. In his defence, he thus argued that 'one can take the risk of omitting from the Constitution details of administration and leaving it for the Legislature to prescribe them ... if the people are saturated with Constitutional morality such as the one described by Grote'.[14] As is evident, Grote provided Ambedkar with an intellectual justification for a liberal constitution in a context in which basic liberal values of human dignity were brutally bypassed in favour of perhaps most ruthless form of social segregation. So, the idea of constitutional morality was a powerful device which allowed Babasaheb to knit together liberal constitutional principles despite strong opposition by the Gandhians in the Constituent

[7] Andre Beteille, 'Constitutional Morality', *Economic and Political Weekly*, 4 October 2008, p. 42.

[8] Pratap Bhanu Mehta makes this point in his 'What is Constitutional Morality', *Seminar* 17 (November 2010): 17–24.

[9] George Grote (1794–1871), an English radical who wrote the *History of Greece* (four volumes) during 1846–56 period was influenced by liberals like Ricardo, James Mill and Jeremy Bentham.

[10] BR Ambedkar speech before the Constituent Assembly on 4 November 1948, *Constituent Assembly Debates*, Vol. 7, p. 38.

[11] Ibid., p. 38.

[12] Ibid., p. 38.

[13] Beteille, 'Constitutional Morality', p. 36.

[14] BR Ambedkar speech, 4 November 1948.

Assembly who insisted that 'instead of incorporating Western theories the new Constitution should have been built upon village panchayats and district panchayats'.[15]

For constitutional morality to strike organic roots, Ambedkar insisted that the obedience to 'constitutional methods of achieving our social and economic objectives [which meant that] we must abandon ... the method of civil disobedience, non-cooperation and satyagraha [because] when constitutional methods are open, there can be no justification of unconstitutional methods ... and sooner these unconstitutional methods are abandoned, the better for us'.[16] The Gandhian Satyagraha was, according to him, a form of coercion. This is an assessment which probably reflects serious political differences that Ambedkar had with Gandhi since the 1932 Poona Pact which deprived the Untouchables of separate electorates in the 1935 Government of India Act. The defence for his opposition to Satyagraha was based on his commitment to constitutional morality which was a key to the success of the constitution. As one who was influenced by Edmund Burke too, Ambedkar was also convinced that violence could never be a permanent solution to human problems because 'the forceful subjection of any community always leads to resentment [which was enough] ... to cause severe dent to democratic ethos'.[17] Ambedkar thus provided a typical liberal solution by suggesting that the issues of discontent could be resolved by a strong legal system along with the desire to sort out differences through dialogues and deliberations. Besides being appreciative of fundamental democratic means, Ambedkar also found in constitutional morality a powerful means to contain decline of ethics in governance. For him, constitutional morality acquires organic roots in democracy presumably because the latter creates an environment in which public functionaries cannot afford to ignore the public since they owe their existence to them. So, once democracy is strengthened whereby public voice gets reinforced the chances for misuse of governance are likely to be less. The argument insisting on empowering the citizens as perhaps the most effective challenge against ethics deficit can easily be substantiated with the consolidation of public opinion in contemporary India against corruption *per se*, and particularly against forces thriving on corruption. Constitutional morality may not be adequate to contain corruption because it draws on the individual inclination towards ethics-driven conditionalities; but a nation-wide democratic movement involving people cutting across social barriers, as was witnessed recently in the wake of the 2011 Anna Hazare campaign, nurtures not only a mass drive for opposition to corrupt practices, but also creates an environment in which demands for ethics in governance are being forcefully made. It is therefore fair to argue that sustained campaigns against the misuse of public authority is perhaps the best option to organically create a proactive mind-set which will be a deterrent against deviant acts by those involved in governance. This is also an ideologically meaningful design in which the idea of constitutional morality is as critical as the challenges by the masses for evolving an environment insisting on obedience to the fundamental ethical values by the public functionaries while in governance.

Battling Corruption

Corruption seems to be instinctively linked with human nature; so are the efforts to weed out its roots. The dialectical interconnection between corruption and the consolidation of public opinion needs to be understood to conceptualize the phenomenon in a historical perspective. This is articulated in an argument

[15] Ibid, p. 38.

[16] BR Ambedkar speech before the Constituent Assembly on 25 November 1949, *Constituent Assembly Debates*, Vol. 10, p. 978.

[17] BR Ambedkar, speech at the Round Table Conference, London Plenary session, 20 November 1930, reproduced in Jadhav, *Ambedkar Speaks*, Vol. 3, p.107.

that while corruption, in one form or another, has always existed, there have always been well-defined policy measures which have made a significant dent. Implicit here is the fact that corruption cannot be completely ruled out; what is feasible is to contain the incidence by creating an environment in which values of ethics, integrity and morality are deeply rooted. It is true that institutionalized legal means are a deterrent to corruption; they cannot however be adequate to substantially weaken its base unless a propitious environment complements the endeavours. The ideological milieu that the 1975 JP movement had created was translated in the repeal of a large number of draconian laws (codified in the 1977 Forty-Second Amendment Act) through the Forty-Third and Forty-Fourth Amendment Acts in 1978. In other words, the fact that the mounting public pressure resulted in the abrogation of laws supporting authoritarianism also confirms the critical role that social context plays in shaping a specific ideological stance. Similarly, the insistence on a strong Lokpal by those involved in the India Against Corruption campaign of 2011 can also be said to have its roots in the movement that Hazare had launched against the debilitating impact of corruption in India's public life.

There is one fundamental conceptual point here: corruption and decline of ethics are dialectically interconnected; while the former has had 'variegated incidence in different times at different places, with varying degrees of damaging consequences'[18] the latter also unfolds gradually and is thus contingent on specific mind-sets which either remains indifferent or supportive of 'some sort of malfeasance for private enrichment'.[19] There can thus hardly be a universal explanatory model because this interrelationship is also context-driven. For instance, in the erstwhile Licence-Quota-Permit-Raj guaranteeing massive discretionary power to those holding public authority, corruption was considered to be 'the much needed grease for squeaking wheels of rigid administration'.[20] Gradually the idea seems to have lost steam. In the mid-1970s, the efforts towards utilizing government machineries for personal gains provoked mass consternation which was reflected in the 1975 JP movement. Challenging the ideological design of those in power, the campaign for JP's total revolution created, rather instantaneously, a constituency of support in the country presumably because of the abuse of authority by the powerful at the cost of the ordinary citizens. This was the main factor behind the massive campaign that JP had spearheaded in collaboration with political forces with incompatible ideological predilections. By the time when the Anna Hazare led the campaign for the Jan Lokpal Bill in 2011, it was evidently clear that public offices were utilized for personal gains with the revelation of scams involving the transaction of huge financial benefits for those in governance. What is striking is the fact that those who are responsible for managing governance in India tend to be corrupt presumably because of the excessive importance of public authority in India's development trajectory. It is true that state seems to have lost its determining role in economy in contrast with what it had in the earlier dispensation of the state-driven economic development; nonetheless, even in the changed socio-ideological milieu, the Indian state continues to remain a significant player especially in disbursing money for development and also in extending favour to the private operators to initiate business ventures in exchange of kickbacks. The 2G spectrum scam and illegal appropriation of government funds to prepare for the 2010 Commonwealth Games in Delhi are illustrative here. The Hazare movement may not have achieved its goal though it had fulfilled a historical mission by articulating the middle class frustration in the form a nation-wide campaign against corruption.

---

[18] Pranab Bardhan, 'Corruption and Development: A Review of Issues', *Journal of Economic Literature* 35, September (1997): 1320.

[19] Bardhan, 'Corruption and Development, p. 1321.

[20] Samuel P Huntington, *Political Order in Changing Societies* (New Haven: Yale University Press, 1968), p. 386.

There is a continuing thread linking the 1975 JP movement with its 2011 counterpart, led by an army subaltern, Anna Hazare. As shown earlier, in the battle against the derailment of public authority in two different phases of India's recent political history, both JP and Hazare emerged as undisputed leaders holding hegemonic control over the movement for probity in governance. They became, in other words, messiahs to save Indians from crises. By encouraging individual-based leadership, these movements were criticized as undemocratic in character; there was hardly a mechanism to replace the hegemonic individual leaders presumably because of their charismatic ability to guide their massive followers in accordance with what they felt appropriate at the particular historical juncture. This is definitely a bad side of messianism which creates a situation in which the will of the leader is carried forward since he/she has a majority to back his/her claim even at the cost of the constitution and institutions of parliamentary governance. Neither the Constitution of India nor the constitutionally guaranteed institutions can be overturned by the wishes of a majority at a particular time. 'If perchance', thus argues an analyst, we

> accept messianism out of expediency, it would be violating the spirit of the Constitution and undermining democracy. Besides, any such licence will make multiple (quasi-religious) messiahs sprout, who compete and collude, as oligopolists do in the markets for goods, to keep people in thraldom.[21]

Nonetheless, it is fair to argue that the campaigns that JP and Anna Hazare had spearheaded were a product of circumstances in which public frustration reached its zenith. It was possible for them to trigger movements given their unassailable public images. They became messiahs in the absence of leaders who had the Gandhian capability of uniting socio-economically and also ideologically disparate masses for a common cause. One of the reasons which sustained their popularity was perhaps the use of civil disobedience methods and also the invocation of Gandhi who continues to remain ideologically inspiring especially in movements challenging an authoritarian state or tendencies of political authorities towards being authoritarian. So, at a particular point of history, messiahs are required to quell anti-democratic forces despite the fact there is always an implicit danger, as history has demonstrated, in uncritically championing messianism in political mobilization.

Ethics in Governance and Administrative Reforms

Administrative reforms and the concern for ethics in governance are dialectically connected: the latter sets in motion processes which the former articulates in the form of policy decisions. It is true that in order to conclusively address and also resolve contemporary socio-economic and political issues, governance needs to be regularly reinvented; otherwise, it will lose its salience. So, administrative reforms are regular events which are usually undertaken with an ideological, but context-dependent, agenda since administration is also a problem solving tool. This is also an arena of negotiation and contestations which further confirms that politics seem to remain critical in conceptualization administrative reforms. Administrative reforms in India contributed to the articulation of ethics in governance which however was defined differently in different historical phases that India had encountered in her journey as a polity. During the British rule, the issue of ethics did not seem to figure prominently since colonialism had completely different ideological

[21] Prabhat Patnaik, 'Messianism versus Democracy', *The Hindu*, 24 August 2011.

goals which ran contrary to the interests of the 'native' citizens. Nonetheless, it had also initiated processes for reorienting administration in such a way as to given prominence to the prevalent rules of law, and not customs, as was the practice in the preceding years before the British rule was firmly legally established in India. For colonialism to flourish, the change from custom based governance to the one that had derived its sustenance from the well-defined constitutional principles appeared to have been ethically drawn to the Indians who had shown, so far, their habitual obeisance to the royal diktat based generally on customs. As times passed by, the colonial government agreed to accommodate Indians in administration as part of their ideological mission to rule India in accordance with the fundamental principles of the British Enlightenment. This certainly had a political angle which we cannot lose sight of. Nonetheless, the drive towards running the administration on the basis of codified rules and regulations seem to have been derived from the urge to establish ethics in governance. There is no doubt that colonial administration however rule-bound it had been was an exploitative system. Yet, by insisting on a rule-bound governance, colonial administrators did create an environment in which an alternative form of administration was not only conceptualized, but pursued contrary to the whimsical governance that they had inherited once they established their hegemony in India. The fundamental point that governance no longer remained a captive of the ruler, but was dependent on the written laws seems to have instilled the idea that public administration, to remain ethics-bound, needs to be sensitive to the rules and regulations which were meant to serve 'the subjects of the Crown' in accordance with what the colonial rulers had construed as the best possible principles of governance.

Independent India has, as the earlier discussion has shown, different sets of challenges which are both inherited from the long colonial rule and is also drawn on the obvious contextual constraints. The founding fathers had, in order to fulfil their exclusive ideological priorities, prescribed a system of administration which was tuned to the goal of development in accordance with the much-hyped socialistic pattern of society. What did not seem to have received adequate attention from those who had presided over India's destiny at the dawn of India's rise as an independent polity was whether the prevalent administration which the colonial power had bequeathed was sufficiently equipped to handle the administrative issues confronting India following the 1947 transfer of power. India's growth was not satisfactory and the economic model that the democratically elected rulers suggested did not appear to be, it was alleged, suitable. Administration was charged with being prejudiced when several scams broke out in the first quarter of India's existence as an independent nation. Two issues seem to have become preeminent: on the one hand, questions were raised about the integrity of those holding power; the misappropriation of public funds could not have been possible without the complicity of top political bosses. This was, on the other hand, identified as a testimony to the breakdown of India's moral fabric which encouraged individuals and groups to bend rules and regulations to achieve personal ends. Reiterating that ethics in governance was too critical to be neglected, several specific steps were undertaken: the most prominent among them was, as discussed at length in this chapter, was the appointment of the First Administrative Reforms Commission in 1964 which reinforced the argument that the decline of ethics and the increasing incidence of corruption in India were mutually inclusive, an idea that the Santhanam Committee had, most critically, probed in its 1964 report on the prevention of corruption which probably a thorough analytical statement on the linkages between the decline of ethics and serious administrative lapses.

Despite the fact that committees after committees came out heavily against corruption and malpractices in governance, the situation has hardly improved; corruption continues to plague the system. It has thus been argued that the system can be improved once the roots of corruption receive no nourishment which may not be an easy thing to achieve because vested interests are too powerful to disappear so quietly. Administrative reforms in India thus get reduced to mere window dressing since most of the radical recommendations are usually shelved, given its possible adverse effect on the existent power equations, nurtured by the politicians for their personal gain. This is however not to suggest that change is impossible. In fact, history is full of examples to prove otherwise; what innumerable instances from India show is how the release of mass energy for a cause radically alters the texture of a system even in adverse circumstances. While administrative reforms do not seem to be adequately equipped to bring about a complete overhauling of the system since they usually have a limited mandate, they nonetheless articulate those significant inputs which are most critical in assessing the nature of contemporary governance. Indicative of the deterioration of the system, administrative reforms are thus possibly the most powerful steps to recharge its vitality following what is deemed to be appropriate in a specific context. Here lies the importance of administrative reforms at regular intervals to also remind those in authority of their responsibility to exercise power upholding the fundamental ethical tenets of governance.

Administrative reform is a continuous challenge to those seeking to understand the processes of governmental renewal, which derives its impetus from the sense that the existing political and governmental systems do not meet contemporary demands. In other words, administrative reform does not take place in a vacuum and is always inspired by the failure of the prevalent system of governance to respond effectively to the social and political needs of the governed. In the context of 'breathtaking change', bureaucratic institutions that developed during the industrial era seem to be inadequate and the importance of globalization as conceptualization of new issues involving the government and the governed cannot be glossed over in such a scenario. So, a new perspective—underlining the role of market or market-type mechanisms in redefining the nature of governance—has emerged in which administrative reform is articulated. What is new here is a distinctive formulation synthesizing traditions of public administration with contingent changes in public service provision and influences from the private and voluntary sectors. The process, known as the pluralization of state has, as already shown, redefined the contour of reform where the state is just a mere agency along with others involved in public affairs. Administrative reform is thus a practical scheme of governance highlighting a clear theoretical advancement in the discipline of Public Administration.

Administrative change is inevitable because (a) public administration regularly negotiates with the changing priorities of a society of which it is a part, and (b) it seeks to incorporate not only the new administrative techniques but also the ideas that grow out of socio-economic and political churning. The constant governmental renewal thus appears to be the outcome of a search for an appropriate administration keeping pace with the changing reality. So, it would not be wrong to argue that governmental renewal is primarily inspired by 'ideologies, philosophies and policy approaches on which interventions in society are based.'[22] Governance is a legitimizing device of governmental action that is justified by the rationale from which a government draws its sustenance. In a democracy, for instance, the administrative reform is usually articulated in measures reflective of the predominant politico-ideological values. Not only do they provide rationales for governmental action they are also yardsticks for assessing policy alternatives. As is shown, reform efforts in India reveal the extent to which the changing priorities of the political system act decisively in governmental renewal. Whether in the pre-liberalization phase or its aftermath, administration reinvents itself to accommodate the dominant values on which its legitimacy is drawn. Before the onset of globalization, the distinctive feature of public administration was that though despite having nurtured the colonial structure it had successfully injected new dynamism in governmental activities reflective of

[22] Nico Nelissen, Marie-Louise Bemelmand-Videc, Arnold Godfroij and Peter De Goede, eds., *Reinventing Government: Innovative and Inspiring Visions* (The Netherlands: International Books, 1999), p. 18.

a conscious search for an alternative both in spirit and content. Globalization with its ideological package of 'structural adjustment' means an altogether different and intricate external environment seeking to radically alter both the administrative setup and the values on which it is based. Several steps have already been taken to undermine the bureaucratic grip over public administration in India. The recommendations of the Fifth Pay Commission (1997) seem to have upheld this spirit while suggesting several steps at administrative reorganization in India. Changes in administration are, however, mostly cosmetic in nature. So, although the reform efforts have a direction they lack an appropriate ideological backing that appears to have weakened the entire project.

Summarizing the Argument

Governance and ethics are intertwined. A government functions within certain broad moral and ethical parameters, integrally linked with the sociological foundation of the polity in which it is articulated. The importance of ethics in governance has acquired a significant place in contemporary theoretical discussion more so because of the growing decadence in governmental practices largely owing to a decline of ethical values in public life which is perhaps singularly responsible for the rise of 'corruption' in a virulent form. One needs to conceptualize the role of the constitution in this perspective. The question that needs to be asked is whether a constitution is an adequate deterrent to corruption and corrupt practices. A perusal of the growing incidence of corruption in India confirms that the constitutional design for combatting non-ethical practices and behaviour does to seem to be strong enough to contain, if not completely eliminate, their roots. Does this mean that the 1950 Constitution has failed us? There is hardly a conclusive response to this query since the constitution is not sole means to evolve a strong ethics-driven society; it is, at best, a facilitator of the processes which are complementary to the growth and consolidation of forces in support of ethics in public life. The Indian experience of constitutional governance since the 1947 Independence is also a breakthrough in our understanding of constitutionalism as an empowering device which is illustrated by reference to the recognition, for instance, of the dalits as integral to constitutional governance. Implicit here is the idea that the constitution is not merely a compilation of provisions, but also provides a specific socio-economic design for realizing certain aspired politico-ideological goals.

Concluding Observations

Decline of ethics in public life and its inevitable consequences continue to be intriguing to the scholars and policy makers alike. Regardless of ideological differences, opinions converge on the point that corruption is an impediment to national/global growth. So it needs to be effectively combatted to secure the future of human civilization. But who will bell the cat especially if those who are given the responsibility to capture allow the cat to freely roam around! As the present study has shown that public authority breeds corruption and most of the institutional devices seem to have been handicapped given the growing vested interests in governance. Nobody seems to be serious in the containment of corrupt and malpractices presumably because of the selfish motive of those who remain critical in dispensing public services. Corruption is said to have become inevitable in a rigid administration; nothing seems to move unless one dishes out monetary or other benefits in exchange of what one receives from the government. This was the scene in the context of the License-Quota-Permit-Raj, as various studies of how the government functioned have shown. The impact was felt though the social climate was such that no serious campaign was launched to challenge the system that seemed to have encouraged corrupt personnel to abuse public authority for personal enrichment. Attempts were made, as shown in the book, to weed out corruption by creating new public institutions and strengthening the prevalent ones. Despite putting these new mechanisms in place, the results did not seem to have been encouraging which however raises a bigger question by suggesting that without adequately changing the social climate, mere tweaking of the system by creating/strengthening institutions was futile. This is one side of the story; the other side is about the attempts, repeatedly made by the ordinary masses to challenge the system and also the beneficiaries. The 1974–75 Total Revolution campaign by Jayaprakash Narayan (JP) is illustrative here. It was a spontaneous campaign that soon built into a nation-wide mass movement against those who abused authority for fulfilling partisan ideological and also gainful missions. The JP movement may have failed to achieve the goal; nonetheless, by catapulting the issue of corruption onto the centre stage of Indian politics, it had not only built a new political trend, but also created an environment in which people got a voice. The 2011 Anna Hazare-led *India Against Corruption* was a continuity though the context was remarkably dissimilar. Like the 1974–75 JP assault on corruption in public life, the Anna Hazare campaign, despite having succeeded in creating a mass support base, gradually fizzled out without attaining its proclaimed aim of having a Lokpal. But that it triggered a mass momentum against corruption was undeniable. Both these movements reinforced the importance of creating a propitious social climate in which tendencies supporting corruption and corrupt practices are considered anathema for healthy social growth.

There is a final point. Ethics deficit is a contextual outcome, linked with a variety of complex reasons. A constitution is a shield, but may not always be a perfect one since much of its strength is derived from the ethical foundation of the polity in which it evolves. The story of India's constitution reveals that at one level, it was a successful experiment; at another, its success is marred by equally deplorable failure which was manifested in the growing incidence of scams, especially in the last two decades. Does it mean that the constitution has failed its citizens or vice versa; the answer cannot be given in conclusive terms since the scams reflect the failure of 'the men' that the President of the Constituent Assembly referred to in his speech of 26 November 1949 which also entails that constitutional values also need constant nurturing; otherwise, they will die in no time. In other words, unless they were regularly nourished with those complementary socio-economic values, their life span is bound to be highly restricted. There is however another side of the story which also confirms that the constitution does not seem to be a mere document, but a living organism. That there has emerged a parallel system being opposed to scams and other corrupt practices in governance is also a testimony to the growing consolidation of constitutional values in support of a corruption and prejudice-free society. This is where the constitution has succeeded in creating an environment where ethics is privileged and the socio-political forces weakening its foundations are clearly marginalized.

Review Questions

1. **How is ethics conceptualized? Elaborate your response.**
2. **Why is ethics so important in governance? Elaborate your response.**
3. **What are the mechanisms whereby ethics in governance can be instilled? Elaborate.**
4. **How do you define constitutional morality? Elaborate your response with examples.**
5. **Define corruption. Can corruption be weeded-out from a system? Elaborate your response.**

6. **'Governance and ethics are intertwined'. Explain.**

7. **In what respects, concern for ethics and constitutional democracy are inseparable? Elaborate your response.**

8. **How did Jayaprakash Narayan address the concern for decline of ethics in governance? Elaborate.**

9. **'The *India Against Corruption* campaign is reflective of mass disenchantment with governance in India'. Do you agree? Elaborate your response.**

10. **'Constitutional democracy and ethics in governance are dialectically linked'. Explain.**

Chapter 6

The Doctrine of Basic Structure of the Constitution of India

Learning Objectives

- What is the basic structure doctrine?
- How did this evolve in the Indian context?
- In what ways, the basic structure doctrine is critical in conceptualizing the nature of the Constitution of India?

In the constitutional parlance, the basic structure of the constitution entails those distinctive features which form the core of the constitution. Once they are compromised, it would be detrimental to the fundamental character of the constitution. In view of their critical importance in conceptualizing the foundational values on which the constitution rests, these features remain inseparable and can never be belittled for the sake sustaining its basic ideological thrust. This is usually understood in two complementary ways: on the one hand, the constitution evolves out of certain fundamental values and principles which are articulated in the provisions or conventions that also flourish along with specific constitutional practices; there are also, on the other, significant socio-political and economic inputs arising out of the prevalent context with which the constitution is organically linked. Fundamental here is the idea that the doctrine of basic structure of the constitution can never be conclusively defined independent of the context since it is an offshoot of a dialectical interconnection with the context; as a consequence, it cannot thus be articulated as something which is sacrosanct which further means that the features of the basic structure need to be constantly reinvented in response to the demands of the time and space. One has to factor in, in other words, the rapidly transforming socio-economic context to pinpoint what constitutes the basic structure at a particular juncture of India's existence as a democratic polity.

The doctrine of basic structure is conceptually empowering since it also enables us to grasp the foundational basis of democracy. Broadly speaking, in the liberal conceptual mould, there are two major forms of democracy which draws its sustenance from the demos. On the one hand, there is the Westminster form of parliamentary democracy in which it is the parliament which reigns supreme and everything else is subservient; the parliamentary authority is, in principle, unrestrictive and shackle-free, of course, within the ideological boundaries that have been set by the constitutional practices and conventions. The American system of governance provides, on the other, another form of democracy where it is neither the Congress nor the President who holds sovereign authority, but the constitution which remains supreme in so far as the polity is concerned. The idea is very simple: the only source of authority is the constitution and all other institutions of governance derive their constitutional right in governance from the constitution.

The Indian Constitution does not follow either of these formats of governance in its undiluted form. Instead, by creatively blending these two unique constitutional experiences, it articulated a third alternative, namely, a parliamentary democracy in which constitution is made the supreme authority though it took a while to establish that the Constitution cannot be bypassed by any of the institutions of political authority. In such a context, basic structure doctrine assumes tremendous constitutional significance.

In the articulation of the doctrine of basic structure, the Indian judiciary has played a very critical role. Not only has the Indian judiciary acted as a guardian of constitutional democracy in India, it has, by creatively interpreting the constitutional provisions in the context of the changing socio-economic circumstances, evolved a new area of jurisprudence drawing on the 'due process of law' doctrine. The interpretation is not exactly drawn on 'the procedure established by law' which the Constitution of India upholds in Article 21, but on the basis of those values emanating from the social compact epitomizing new politico-ideological concerns. Being a proactive player in India's constitutional democracy, the Supreme Court of India has not only created a new domain of its functioning, it has also initiated significant processes of change by privileging the constitution over the executive and legislature. A new era in India's constitutional democracy has ushered in whereby judiciary does not seem to a mere an interpreter of the legislative acts and executive feats, it also provides powerful inputs to the policy makers. The doctrine of basic structure is therefore a watershed in India's constitutional democracy. With the recognition of the doctrine, it is now established beyond doubt that constitutional supremacy can be relegated under no circumstances. Parliament, despite being the voice of the people, is subservient to the constitution which sets out the parameters for its functioning. In other words, the Parliament has to function within the boundary demarcated by the constitution. This has not been readily accepted by the Parliament, and judiciary, as history has shown, had to confront the legislature, on a number of occasions, for being respectful to the basic structure of the Constitution.

The aim of this chapter is to acquaint the readers with the basic structure doctrine with reference how it emerged in India's constitutional discourses with reference to the major judicial pronouncements since the inauguration of the 1950 Constitution. This is a narrative of judicial ascendancy in India. An offshoot of creative jurisprudence, the doctrine delineates a critical role for the judiciary which is also constitutionally authorized to ascertain whether Parliament is within its limits while discharging its obligation to the governed. Given the massive significance of basic structure in constitutional governance in India, by drawing on some of the major judicial verdicts which are pertinent here, this chapter thus concentrates on how it evolved in India's democratic practices with reference to its integral features.

Historical Antecedents

The root of the basic structure debate can be traced back to the debates in the Constituent Assembly which pondered over the choice between 'the procedure established by law' and 'due process of law' which the US Constitution upholds. The founding fathers favoured the former on the basis of the advice given by Justice Felix Frankfurter of the US Supreme Court to BN Rau; they were persuaded to believe that 'the due process of law' was likely to be a deterrent to the independent functioning of the parliament which was, in their views, not justified in democratic governance where parliament represented the voice of the people; the judiciary being authorized to ascertain the constitutionality of parliamentary acts in accordance with the due process of law would then overpower the parliament weakening thereby the foundation of constitutional democracy in India. The decision provoked a fierce debates. Kazi Syed Karimuddin of Central Provinces and Berar, for instance, did not seem persuaded since he felt that if the constitution incorporated

> the procedure established by law, instead of due process of law, there will be very great injustice to the law courts in the country because as soon as a procedure according to law is complied with by a court, there will be an end to the duties of the court and if the court is satisfied that the procedure has been complied with, the judges cannot interfere with any law which might have been capricious, unjust or iniquitous. . . . As soon as the procedure is complied with, there will, [in other words] be an end to everything and the judges will be only spectators. The clause, as it stands, can [thus] do a great mischief in a country which is a storm centre of political parties and where discipline is unknown. Let us guarantee to individuals inalienable rights in such a way that the political parties that come into power cannot extend their jurisdiction in curtailing and invading the Fundamental Rights laid down in the Constitution.[1]

An apprehension loomed large because it was felt that Parliament was to gag individual freedom since political parties might not be sensitive enough of their obligation to the values of constitutional democracy. Sharing the concern, Krishna Chandra Sharma (United Provinces) also argued:

> The term "without due process of law" has a necessary limitation on the powers of the State, both executive and legislative. . . . What this phrase means is to guarantee a fair trial both in procedure as well as in substance. The procedure should be in accordance with law and should be appealable to the civilized conscience of the community. It also ensures a fair trial in substance, that is to say, that substantive law itself should be just and appealable to the civilized conscience of the community.[2]

Here, the argument for parliamentary supremacy was being questioned by reference to the apprehension that it was likely to be missed in future which was not entirely unfounded as the 1975–77 Emergency experiences demonstrates. Despite forceful arguments, the clause 'due process of law' was not finally accepted since it was believed that 'the clause may serve as a great handicap for all social legislation [and] would allow the judiciary a free hand in devising major policies'.[3] Such an understanding also reveals that 'the Drafting Committee, . . . in suggesting 'procedure' for 'due process of law' was possibly guilty of being apprehensive of judicial vagaries in the moulding of law'.[4] BN Rau's warning that due process was an impediment for Parliament to act, without shackles, for fulfilling mass democratic aspirations seemed to have conclusively settled the issue; and the Constitution incorporated 'the procedure established by law' in Article 21.

It is true that Indian judiciary is constrained to go beyond the constitutional mandate of following the procedure established by law while looking into the justiciability of the policy preferences of the executive and legislative feats. Nonetheless, with the growing acceptance of the idea of basic structure of the constitution which can never be violated, the courts seem to have carved an independent space in constitutional governance in India. The doctrine of basic structure does not provide the judiciary with the authority that the US Supreme Court possesses because of the constitutional guarantee of due process; it however creates a definite space for the judiciary to act in case the Parliament undermines the fundamental constitutional values and principles for the fulfilment of partisan goals and desires. In the changed

[1] Kazi Syed Karimuddin (Central Provinces and Berar), 6 December 1948, *Constituent Assembly Debates*, Book No. 2, p. 843.

[2] Krishna Chandra Sharma (United Provinces), 6 December 1948, *Constituent Assembly Debates*, Book No. 2, p. 850.

[3] Alladi Krishnaswami Ayyar (Madras), 6 December 1948, *Constituent Assembly Debates*, Book No. 2, p. 854.

[4] Ibid., p. 854.

socio-economic environment leading to the consolidation of democratic ethos and values, the basic structure doctrine further constitutionalizes judicial intervention in areas which are considered to be critical for sustaining constitutional democracy in India.

The Basic Structure Doctrine

As is mentioned earlier, the basic structure doctrine is rooted in the processes leading to democratization of governance in India. With the growing public disenchantment with the executive and legislature, the judiciary seems to have emerged as a messiah for constitutional democracy. The beginning of the doctrine is usually traced back to the judicial concern for misuse of power by the Parliament as per Article 368 of the Constitution. With the constitutional guarantee, can the parliament amend any part of the constitution for the socio-economic causes was the question that the judiciary was asked to respond. According to Article 368, Parliament 'may, in exercise of its constituent power, amend by way of addition, variation or repeal any provision of this constitution in accordance with the procedure laid down in this article'. The founding fathers did not seem to have restrictions on Parliament's authority in amending the constitution. For instance, Jawaharlal Nehru argued:

> While we want this Constitution to be as solid and as permanent a structure as we can make it, nevertheless, there is no permanence in constitutions. There should be certain flexibility. If you make anything rigid and permanent, you stop a nation's growth. So, when you pass this Constitution, ... you will ... lay down a period of years ... during which changes to that constitution can easily be made without any difficult process. ... We should not make a Constitution such as some other great countries have, which are so rigid that they do and cannot be adapted easily to the changing conditions. ... Therefore, while we make a constitution which is sound and as basic as we can, it should also be flexible and for a period we should be in a position to change with relative facility.[5]

Nehru was keen to make the constitution flexible to keep pace with the changing world while insisting on making it as 'basic' as was possible under the circumstances. This means that the constitution is to have a ' asic character in politico-ideological terms which can never be compromised. The basic character needs to be sustained. The idea that Nehru offered was made clearer by BR Ambedkar who, while elaborating the procedure for amendment to the constitution, clarified that by eliminating the proviso that the constitution could only be amended by 'a decision, adopted in a convention or referendum', the constitution was made flexible which means that legislature, central and provincial, is empowered to revise the constitution by following simple procedures. This is one aspect of the amendment procedure. The other aspect relates to 'the amendment of specific matters' for which 'the ratification of the State Legislatures is required' along with the condition that 'such an amendment shall be done by majority of not less than two-thirds of the members of each House present and voting, and a majority of the total membership of each House'. He also apprehended that future parliament, being elected on adult suffrage, could be tempted 'to alter the fundamental character of the Constitution ... by acting as partisans seeking to carry

---

[5] Jawaharlal Nehru, 8 November 1948, *Constituent Assembly Debates*, Book No. 2, pp. 322–23.

amendments to facilitate the passing of party measures'.[6] The idea is crystal clear, namely, there are some values which hold the substance of the constitution and they need to be protected and cannot be allowed to be bypassed under any circumstances. Nehru too endorsed the point by suggesting that there were 'specific areas' in the constitution that could be amended by following a rigid procedure.

Two basic points that had emerged in the Assembly seem to have contributed to the formulation of the basic structure doctrine: first, Indian constitution has certain distinctive features which allow it to be distinguished as a democratic constitution; these features are integral and cannot be fiddled with; secondly, since these are core to the constitution, they cannot be allowed to be sacrificed by the parliamentarians for the sake of fulfilling their partisan aims.

Conceptual Roots

In conceptual terms, basic structure entails those values and principles which form the core of a constitution. The doctrine is about certain characteristics which are essential since they define the nature of the constitution and once they are separated, the constitution, by implication, loses its identity. The crux of the argument is that given their critical importance in shaping the politico-ideological characteristics of a constitution, they can never be divorced from the constitution. Although the idea has philosophical roots in some of the classical texts on democracy, federalism and republicanism, it was very clearly articulated in a commentary on the Weimer Constitution in the context of the early phases of Nazism in Germany in the early 1930s. Ernst Rudolf Huber, who is infamous for his support to the Nazi regime since it came to power through election, underlined the importance of constitutional norms in governance which, if bypassed, would lead to the collapse of the constitutional structure in no time. In a very categorical way, he thus argued:

> Every constitution consists of such principles, which determine the totality of the constitutional order and make up "the spirit of the constitution". There is no equality of rank among the numerous provisions of a written constitutional document. The main principles of the common order have clear priority; the remaining legal precepts are derived from them.... One can say of a constitution that it is valid only so long as his core of the constitution maintains its existence. If the core of the constitution is destroyed, then the entire constitution is wiped out, even if individual constitutional precepts of inferior rank continue to be legally valid.[7]

The argument provides us with three important conceptual inputs to articulate the basic structure doctrine: (a) no amendment is permissible if it effectively alters the basic essential principles of the constitution since it means a stark departure from the purpose for which it was framed; (b) if the amendment destroys the foundation values of the constitution, it is unconstitutional and thus uncalled for; and finally (c) if the amendment undermines the basic values of the constitution, it has no intention of revising the constitution but desire to eliminate the constitution. Hence, it is argued that 'if certain fundamental principles, values

[6] The quoted parts of the sentences are taken from the speech that BR Ambedkar made in the Constituent Assembly on 4 November 1948, *Constituent Assembly Debates*, Book No. 2, pp. 43–44.

[7] Ernst Rudolf Huber, 'Constitution' in *Weimer: A Jurisprudence Crisis*, eds. Arthur J Jacobson and Bernhard Schlink (2002), p. 328, quoted in Yaniv Roznai, *Unconstitutional Constitutional Amendments: A Study of the Nature and Limits of Constitutional Amendment Powers* (PhD dissertation, London School of Economics, 2014), p. 119.

and norms ... are seriously altered, the life of the constitution actually comes to an end; from its ashes, a new political regime emerges'.[8] What is explicitly stated here is that once the core values of a constitution are altered, it results in a complete breakdown of the edifice on which the constitution rests which means that the constitution is no longer the same as it was in the past in its original form.

In India, the idea of basic structure is a judicial invention and is attributed to MK Nambyar, a lawyer who pleaded before the Supreme Court in the *IC Golaknath v. the State of Punjab* in 1967. Nambyar owed this idea to Dietrich Conrad, an academic from Germany who delivered a speech in Banaras Hindu University, entitled 'Implied Limitation of the Amending Power' in February 1965. According to Conrad, 'any amending body organized within the statutory scheme, howsoever verbally unlimited its power, cannot by its very structure change the fundamental pillars supporting its constitutional authority'.[9] The idea was further expanded when he argued:

> Could a constitutional amendment abolish Article 21, to the effect that forthwith a person could be deprived of his life or personal liberty without authorisation by law? Could the ruling party, if it sees its majority shrinking, amend Article 368 to the effect that the amending power rests with the President acting on the advice of the Prime Minister? Could the amending power be used to abolish the Constitution and reintroduce, let us say, the rule of a moghul [*sic*] emperor or of the Crown of England? I do not want, by posing such questions, to provoke easy answers. But I should like to acquaint you with the discussion which took place on such questions among constitutional lawyers in Germany in the Weimar period—discussion, seeming academic at first, but suddenly illustrated by history in a drastic and terrible manner.[10]

What Huber had apprehended in the 1930s had resonated in Conrad's assessment of the situation. He also felt that there were certain features in the constitution that could never be abrogated; Conrad also warned that if the Parliament was allowed to undertake such an exercise, it would finally contribute to the growth of an authoritarian state, as it happened in Germany following the disintegration of the Weimer republic.

Judicial Pronouncements

As argued earlier, the basic structure doctrine evolved in India in the course of a series of judicial verdicts, especially since the 1967 Golaknath case. In the history of constitutional laws in India, the idea of basic structure was mooted in the 1964 *Sajjan Singh v. the State of Rajasthan*. While endorsing the right to property, P Gajendragadkar raised a question:

> Whether the basic features of the Constitution under which we live and to which we owe allegiance are to endure for all time—or at least for the foreseeable future—or whether the yard no more enduring than the implemental and subordinate provisions of the Constitution'.[11]

---

[8] Eivind Smith, 'Old and Protected: On the Supra-constitutional Clause in the Constitution of Norway', *Law Review* 44 (2011): 369, quoted in Roznai, *Unconstitutional Constitutional Amendments*, p. 119.

[9] AG Noorani, 'Behind the Basic Structure Doctrine: On India's Debt to a German Jurist, Professor Dietrich Conrad', *Frontline* 18, no. 19 (28 April–11 May 2001). http://www.frontline.in/static/html/fl1809/18090950.htm (accessed 18 December 2016).

[10] Quoted in Noorani, 'Behind the Basic Structure Doctrine'.

[11] *Sajjan Singh v. the State of Rajasthan*, 1964. https://indiankanoon.org/doc/1308308/ (accessed 18 December 2016).

In his note of dissent, JR Mudholkar, another member of the bench, also referred to the concept by stating:

> It is a matter of consideration whether making a change in a basic structure of the Constitution can be regarded as an amendment or would it be, in effect, rewriting a part of the Constitution; and, if the latter, would it be within the purview of Article 368?'[12]

This is the beginning of the unfolding of the conceptual-legal journey of the basic structure doctrine which passes through a series of judicial pronouncements. The purpose here is not to provide a detailed account of the verdicts, but to highlight the points that India's apex court made while laying out the foundation of the doctrine and its essential features by reference to the major court judgements in this regard.

One of the first significant judicial steps in this regard was the 1967 Golaknath case in which the Supreme Court contributed to the articulation of the doctrine. The primary question that the Supreme Court had raised was whether 'in the exercise of the power of amendment the fundamental structure of the Constitution may be changed or even destroyed or whether the power is restricted to making modification within the framework of the original instrument for its better effectuation'. The answer is equally unambiguous: characterizing the Fundamental Rights as 'transcendental and immutable or inviolable', the majority of the judges in the bench held the view that

> (1) the Constitution is intended to be permanent and therefore it cannot be amended in a way which would injure, maim or destroy its indestructible character; (2) the word "amendment" implies such an addition or change within the lines of the original instrument as will effect an improvement or better carry out the purpose for which it was framed and it cannot be so construed as to enable the parliament to destroy the permanent character of the Constitution; (3) the amending power cannot be used to abolish the compact of the Union or destroy the democratic character of the Constitution teeing individual and minority rights; and (4) the fundamental rights are a part of the basic structure of the Constitution and, therefore, the said power can be exercised only to preserve rather than destroy the essence of these rights.[13]

In clear terms, the court held that Fundamental Rights being a part of the basic structure of the Constitution cannot be abrogated. So, the Parliament does not have unrestricted authority to amend any of the rights enshrined in Part III of the Constitution. There was a dissenting note too; Justice Wanchoo of the bench felt that the court's insistence on the basic structure could be an impediment to social progress, as the members of the Constituent Assembly had apprehended. He was thus categorical in asserting that no limitation should be implied on the amending power of the Parliament under Article 368 and

> basic structure would lead to the position that any amendment made to any article of the Constitution would be subject to the challenge before the Courts on the ground that it amounts to the amendment of the basic structure.[14]

---

[12] *Sajjan Singh v. the State of Rajasthan*, 1964.

[13] *IC Golaknath v. the State of Punjab*, 1967. https://Indiakanoon.org/doc/129358/ (accessed 18 December 2016).

[14] *IC Golaknath v. the State of Punjab*, 1967.

Nonetheless, the decision that basic structure cannot be challenged was carried forward as the majority of the bench endorsed the argument. It was now settled that Fundamental Rights were a part of the essential features of the Constitution that needed to be protected and upheld unconditionally. A revolutionary judgement, it, for the first time in India's recent political history, established that Parliament was subservient to the constitution which remained supreme and its authority to amend the constitution was also absolute. The Parliament took the verdict as an infringement in its constitutional rights for being the voice of the people, and hence it adopted legislations to re-establish its absolute authority in law-making. The result was the enactment of the Twenty-Fourth, Twenty-Fifth and Twenty-Ninth Amendment Acts in 1971. While the Twenty-Fourth Amendment Act was meant to abrogate the Golaknath ruling of the court to restore Parliament's unconditional authority in amending the Constitution the Twenty-Fifth and Twenty-Ninth Amendment Acts evolved separate legal tools of safeguarding compulsory acquisition statutes from being struck down for violating Fundamental Rights.

These amendments were put to test for the first time in the 1973 Kesavananda Bharati case in which the Supreme Court, with its full bench of thirteen jurists, probed into the constitutional validity of the Kerala Land Reforms Act, 1963, as amended by Kerala Land Reforms (Amendment) Acts, 1969 and 1971. The decision challenging the Twenty-Fourth Amendment Act was clinched by a majority of seven judges as against six; the court ruled that the Article 368 does not enable Parliament to alter the basic structure of the Constitution; there are three different expressions, basic structure, basic elements and basic features which figured in the judgements. Although the jurists did not conclusively define what constituted basic structure, they left enough inputs to identify those essential characteristics which, according to them, constituted 'the basic structure'. That the apex court avoided defining the basic features categorically was presumably due to the fact that it was not exactly needed and it was also not possible to enumerate them since they were context-driven. The court also held that because 'a particular concept of law cannot be rigidly defined, it does not cease to be a concept of law; principles of natural justice and negligence also cannot be rigidly defined still they are effective concept of law'.[15] In order to further strengthen the argument, the court advanced the point as follows:

> The ultimate purpose of the Constitution is the conservation of utility and integrity of the nation and also the dignity of the individual. This can be assured only by promoting fraternity. Any principle of law which, if taken away from the Constitution, would result into a loss of fraternity and unity and integrity of the nation and dignity of the individual would be considered to be an essential feature of the Basic Structure.[16]

The amending power of the Parliament was conditional and subject to judicial scrutiny to probe whether it had affected the basic structure. While exercising its constituent power under Article 368, the Parliament cannot, the court held, 'damage, emasculate, destroy, abrogate, change' the basic structure or the fundamental framework of the Constitution. The argument was persuasively justified by Justice SM Sikri of the bench who supported the basic structure doctrine as follows:

> Our Constitution is not a mere political document. It is essentially a social document. It is based on a social philosophy and every social philosophy like every religion has two main

[15] *Kesavananda Bharati v. the State of Kerala*, 1973. https://Indiakanoon.org/doc/25786 (accessed 18 December 2016).
[16] *Kesavananda Bharati v. the State of Kerala*, 1973.

> features, namely basic and circumstantial: the former remains constant but the practices associated with it may change. Likewise, a Constitution like ours contains certain features which are so essential that they cannot be changed or destroyed.[17]

This was a powerful argument in defence of the basic structure doctrine. Being essentially a product of consensus, the 1950 Constitution of India was also an offshoot of a bargain by which the diverse groups constituting the Indian polity came together to form the Union. So, it became a social compact which emerged out of processes in which differences were resolved through dialogues and deliberations without fear or coercion. The founding fathers devoted a great deal of energy to consolidate the social compact by way of reconciliation, accommodation and agreements among the socio-economically diverse groups. And, the basic features evolved out of such intensive dialogues among groups holding contrasting points of view. The idea was captured in its true spirit by Justice Khanna who opined:

> Amendment of the Constitution necessarily contemplates that the Constitution has not to be abrogated but only changes have to be made in it. The word "amendment" postulates that the old Constitution survives without loss of its identity despite the change and continues even though it has been subjected to alterations. As a result of the amendment, the old Constitution cannot be destroyed and done away with; it is retained though in the amended form.... Although it is permissible under the power of amendment to effect changes, however important, and to adapt the system to the requirements of the changing conditions, it is not permissible to touch the foundation or to alter the basic institutional pattern. The words "amendment of the Constitution" with all their wide sweep and amplitude cannot have the effect of destroying the basic structure or framework of the Constitution.[18]

There was unanimity among the seven of thirteen judges of the bench that engaged in the Kesavananda Bharati case. The minority view, articulated by a group six jurists, led by Justice AN Ray held that all parts of the Constitution were essential and distinction between essential and non-essential did not seem to be constitutional; they also endorsed the Twenty-Fourth Amendment Act and agreed to the view that Parliament was empowered to amend any part of the Constitution.

The majority verdict in Kesavananda Bharati case upheld the view that there were features which constituted the core of the constitution and could never be abrogated though there was hardly a compact list of basic features; each of the seven judges gave their own lists of essential features which, of course, are fundamental to the Constitution. The lists are exhaustive, as the following shows:

In Justice Sikri's conceptualization, the list should include:

- Supremacy of the Constitution
- Republican and democratic form of government
- Secular character of the Constitution
- Separation of powers between the legislature, executive and the judiciary
- Federal character of the Constitution

[17] *Kesavananda Bharati v. the State of Kerala*, 1973.

[18] *Kesavananda Bharati v. the State of Kerala*, 1973.

According to Justice AN Grover and Justice SJ Shelat, the following two are important:

- The mandate to build a welfare state contained in the Directive Principles of State Policy (Part IV of the Constitution)
- Unity and integrity of the nation

Justice KS Hegde and Justice SN Mukherjea incorporated the following:

- Sovereignty of India
- Democratic character of the polity
- Unity of the country
- Essential features of the individual freedoms secured to the citizens
- Mandate to build a welfare state

Justice Jaganmohan Reddy listed the following:

- Sovereign democratic republic
- Provisions for social, economic and political justice
- Liberty of thought, expression, belief, faith and worship
- Equality of status and opportunity

These are aspects of the basic structure of the Constitution. By identifying the fundamental politico-ideological values and also institutions for constitutional democracy, the court prepared an exhaustive list. In the 1975 *Indira Gandhi v. Raj Narain* case, the court devised a principle to characterize basic structure. Justice KK Mathew argued that whether a particular feature forms part of the basic structure needed to be determined on the basis of the specific provisions of the Constitution. According to him:

> To be a basic structure it must be a terrestrial concept having its habitat within the four corners of the Constitution. What constitutes basic structure is not like a twinkling star up above the Constitution. For instance, the Preamble enumerates great concepts embodying the ideological aspirations of the people, but these concepts are particularised and their essential features delineated in the various provisions of the Constitution. It is these specific provisions in the body of the Constitution which determine the type of democracy which the founders of that instrument established; the quality and nature of justice, political, social and economic which aimed to realize the content of liberty of thought and expression which they entrenched in that document and the scope of equality of status and of opportunity which they enshrined in it. These specific provisions enacted in the Constitution alone can determine the basic structure of the Constitution. These specific provisions, either separately or in combination, determine the content of the great concepts set out in the Preamble. It is impossible to spin out any concrete concept of basic structure out of the gossamer concept set out in the Preamble. The specific provisions of the Constitution are the stuff which the basic structure has to be woven.[19]

[19] *Indira Gandhi v. Raj Narain*, 1975. https://indiankanoon.org/doc/1569395/ (accessed 18 December 2016).

These are very useful inputs to conceptualize basic structure. There are two important aspects that appear to be critical in capturing the core of the doctrine. On the one hand, instead of pinpointing specific characteristics, the court in this instance preferred to identify basic features in terms of the values that inform them—which means that in the conceptualization of basic structure, the supportive constitutional values and principles remain significant. The court also preferred, on the other, to be indecisive possibly because what constitutes fundamental is also context-dependent—which denotes that the list cannot be conclusive presumably because it needs to be revised in accordance with the prevalent socio-economic priorities.

Following the Kesavananda Bharati judgement, the Congress government, led by Indira Gandhi enacted the Forty-Second Amendment Act in 1976 to dilute the basic structure doctrine. The court intervened again and reaffirmed the basic structure in the 1980 *Minerva Mills Ltd v. the Union of India* in 1980. Striking down the authority of the Parliament to repeal any of the features, identified as part of the basic structure, the court ruled that 'parliament cannot, under Article 368, expand its amending power so as to acquire for itself the right to repeal or abrogate the Constitution or to destroy its basic and essential features'.[20] Reiterating the Parliament has conditional authority of amendment, the apex court further argues:

> It has no inherent power of amendment of the Constitution and being an authority created by the Constitution, it cannot have such inherent power but the power of amendment is conferred upon it by the Constitution and it is a limited power which is conferred. Parliament cannot in exercise of this power to amend the Constitution as to alter its basic structure or to change its identity. Now, if, by constitutional amendment, Parliament was granted unlimited power of amendment, it would cease to be an authority under the Constitution, but would become supreme over it because it would have power to alter the entire Constitution, including its basic structure an even to put an end to it by totally changing its identity. Therefore, the limited amending power of parliament is itself an essential feature of the Constitution, a part of its basic structure for if the limited power of amendment was enlarged into an unlimited power, the entire character of the Constitution would be changed.[21]

The Minerva Mills case reaffirms the limited authority of Parliament in so far as amendment is concerned. The court defended the argument by saying that this was likely to change the fundamental identity of the Constitution. As Justice YV Chandrachud of the Supreme Court bench argued, in a rather poetic language, that 'the theme song of . . . Kesavananda Bharati is: amend as you may even the solemn document which the founding fathers have committed to your care, for you know best the needs of your generation. But, the Constitution is a precious heritage; therefore, you cannot destroy its identity'.[22] What is emphasized here is the sanctity of the Constitution that can never be compromised which means that Indian system of governance is neither exactly the Westminster form of democracy nor its US counterpart, but a creative blending of the two.

The limited nature of the amendment power is now an established constitutional principle. And, the Parliament has to respect the basic structure while seeking to enact an amendment to the Constitution. Hence it is argued that 'since the power to amend the Constitution is not unlimited, if changes brought

[20] *Minerva Mills Limited and others v. the Union of India*, 1980. https://Indiakanoon.org/doc/1939993 (accessed 18 December 2016).

[21] *Minerva Mills Limited and others v. the Union of India*, 1980.

[22] *Minerva Mills Limited and others v. the Union of India*, 1980.

about by amendments destroy the identity of the Constitution, such amendments would be void'.[23] In order to pursue the argument, Justice YK Sabharwal Singh who wrote the judgement for the *IR Coelho (dead) v. the State of Tamil Nadu* 2007, thus adumbrated:

> The existence of the power of parliament to amend the Constitution at will, with requisite voting strength, so as to make any kind of laws affecting rights, enshrined in Part III including power of judicial review under Article 32 is incompatible with the basic structure doctrine. Therefore such an exercise, if challenged, has to be tested on the touchstone of basic structure as reflected in Article 21 read with Article 14 and Article 19, Article 15 and the principles thereunder.[24]

Here too, the Parliament is told again that it does not have the absolute power of amending the Constitution at will; it has to be respectful to the essential features of the Constitution which the Supreme Court has upheld in a series of its pronouncements. The doctrine of basic structure has now become 'an axiom [which] is premised on the basis that invasion [by Parliament] in areas, recognized as the basic structure, is not, at all, permissible [because] it is constitutionally *ultra vires*'.[25] The court prevailed over the Parliament and the validity of the basic structure doctrine was ascertained beyond doubt. Whether it undermines representative democracy is an issue that cannot be settled so easily though there is no doubt that by privileging its role as a reliable custodian of constitutional values and principles the court tilted the balance in its favour. Whatever may have been the consequences of court prevailing over the elected representatives, the fact remains that it is possible for the apex judiciary to overturn a series of executive decisions presumably because of the public trust-deficit in the political authority which cannot be brought back so quickly.

Summarizing the Argument

Out of the tussle between the judiciary and executive emerged the basic structure doctrine. It has also evolved largely due to the judicial concern for sustaining the sanctity of the Constitution which is being violated by the executive as and when opportunity arises. The judiciary is not unanimous, of course, in its assessment of the situation as the majority pronouncements show that, on most occasions, the judiciary was divided, and the decision was endorsed by the majority opinion. The only major exception is 2007 *IR Coelho (dead) v. the State of Tamil Nadu* where the apex court approved the contention without being split in their opinion. Nonetheless, in view of its growing importance in reviewing the constitutionality of the executive feats, the basic structure doctrine can be said to have become 'the bedrock of constitutional interpretation in India'.[26] The judiciary–executive interaction has thus become far from being amicable, with each trying to outsmart the other as soon they get a chance.

Despite the disagreement between the judges on what constitutes the basic structure of the Constitution, the idea that the Constitution has a core has always been upheld in the judicial discourse. As the trajectory

[23] *IR Coelho (dead) v. the State of Tamil Nadu*, 2007. https://indiankanoon.org/doc/322504/ (accessed 18 December 2016).

[24] *IR Coelho (dead) v. the State of Tamil Nadu*, 2007.

[25] *IR Coelho (dead) v. the State of Tamil Nadu*, 2007.

[26] Granville Austin, *Working a Democratic Constitution: A History of Indian Experience* (New Delhi: Oxford University Press, 1999), p. 258.

of the doctrine shows, there was hardly a fixed list of 'essential' features; the court keeps on adding to the list. Of course, the jurists while deciding the 1973 Kesavananda Bharati case provided an exhaustive list of items which, they felt, should be the core of the Constitution and were thus to be protected. In its judgement in the 1980 Minerva Mills case, the court privileged the non-justiciable Directive Principles of State Policy since they

> nourish the roots of our democracy, provide strength and vigour to it and attempt to make it real participatory democracy which does not remain merely a political democracy but also becomes social and economic democracy with Fundamental Rights available to all irrespective of their power, position and wealth. The dynamic provisions of the Directive Principles of State Policy fertilize the static provisions of the Fundamental Rights [which] cannot be considered in isolation from the socio-economic structure in which it is to operate.[27]

So, despite not being enforceable, the court held that the rights enshrined in Part IV of the Constitution are relevant in the changed context of massive democratization of governance. By establishing an obvious link between Part III (Fundamental Rights) and Part IV (DPSP), the court seems to have been governed by the Forty-Second Amendment Act (1976) which privileged Part IV rights as they were considered to be effective politico-ideological tools for bringing about the required socio-economic changes for the establishment of 'a socialist republic', which the Preamble to the Constitution announces. This was pursued further in the 1994 SR Bommai judgement of the apex court. Reiterating that

> the Indian Constitution, being a social document, contains the ideals expected by the nation, the apex court while delivering the verdict, underlined that 'federalism, social pluralism and pluralist democracy . . . form the basic structure of our Constitution, [and] . . . if the fabric of pluralism and pluralist democracy and the unity and integrity of the country are to be preserved, judiciary in the circumstances is the only institution which can act as the saviour of the system and of the nation.[28]

Here too, the basic structure doctrine was expanded to include some of the major socio-economic ideals that are pertinent to effect visible socio-economic transformations. It also implies that the executive did not seem to have paid adequate attention to the goal that the Constitution laid out. What is interesting to note is that the court set aside the presidential decree for dismissal of the Karnataka state government not on procedural grounds but on certain constitutional values which represented the basic structure.

In carving out a specific constitutional position for the basic structure doctrine, the judiciary seems to have upheld two important issues which are critical in parliamentary democracy: one substantive and another institutional.[29] Substantively, the rivalry between judiciary and executive has established that the former retains 'inherent power' to review the parliamentary feats to ascertain whether they are constitutionally justiciable. By implication, it means that the parliamentary supremacy is not absolute and subject to judicial review because the court is not only the final interpreter of the Constitution, but also its saviour. The growing ascendancy of the court has serious institutional implication as well. As the scan

[27] *Minerva Mills and others v. the Union of India*, 1980.
[28] *SR Bommai and Others v. the Union of India*, 1994. https://indiankanoon.org/doc/60799/ (accessed 19 December 2016).
[29] The idea is drawn on Austin, *Working a Democratic Constitution*, pp. 258–76.

of the multiple judgements reveal, the court has both won and asserted its institutional rights by challenging the Parliament 'in constitutional matters through the basic structure doctrine'. There was hardly a significant opposition as it was believed that the court 'rescued the democracy strand of the seamless web from those who would have sacrificed it to genuine or pretended social revolutionary intentions'.[30] Nonetheless, it is difficult to arrive at a definite conclusion since the tussle is far from over which is evident in a series of counterattacks by the executive intending to undermine the judicial supremacy in India's constitutional democracy.

Critiquing the Doctrine

The basic structure doctrine seems to have put the two major organs of governance in a collusion mode. The court has appropriated powers which ordinarily belong to the parliament since it represents people. The minority bench in the Kesavananda Bharati case, led by Justice AN Ray endorsed the view that being people's voice, the Parliament remained supreme in India's constitutional governance which, by implication, means that it was authorised to enact legislations in accordance with what was required to fulfil the politico-ideological mission that the elected representatives had. By striking down the Parliament's decision as it is contrary to the basic structure, the Supreme Court appears to have assumed 'a veto power on all constitutional amendments'.[31] Instead of interpreting the amendment clause, the court has, in effect, become the arbiter by suggesting that it will decide whether to permit the legislature to amend the Constitution. The basic structure creates an environment in which 'the constituent power gets transferred from the elected representative of the people to the judges of the Supreme Court', which is a serious threat to constitutional democracy.[32] Highlighting this aspect of the judicial overreach, HJ Kania, the first Chief Justice of India thus remarked that 'in a democratic country, the people make the laws through their legislature. It is not the function of the court to supervise or to correct the laws passed by the legislature as an overriding authority'.[33] In the name of protecting the constitution, the judiciary through its 'self-invented doctrine of basic structure' appears to have 'destroyed the most basic feature of Indian polity, namely the primacy of the people and democracy being a government of the people, by the people and for the people'.[34] The argument is based on a fundamental principle of democracy privileging elected representatives since they articulate people's voice and remain accountable to them whereas the judiciary is neither accountable nor institutionally equipped to capture people's voice; it does not seem to be constitutionally justified because it creates an arrangement contrary to the spirit of parliamentary democracy by allowing concentration of unfettered power in one institution which, incidentally, is not an elected body. This is an endeavour to replace the duly elected representatives by a small, often divided, set of appointed judges to devise policy preferences.[35] Hence, the basic structure doctrine is charged with being an alibi to tread into an area which, from the point of view of democracy, belongs to parliament. In a nutshell, the basic structure doctrine is being challenged as 'an illegitimate infringement on majority rule,

[30] Austin, *Working a Democratic Constitution*, p. 258.

[31] Subhas C Kashyap, *Indian Constitution: Conflicts and Controversies* (New Delhi: Vistara Publications, 2010), p. 246.

[32] Kashyap, *Indian Constitution*, p. 247.

[33] *Hindustan Times*, Delhi, 28 March, 1950.

[34] Kashyap, *Indian Constitution*, pp. 247–48.

[35] NR Madhava Menon, 'Basic Structure after 30 Years', in *The Supreme Court versus the Constitution: A Challenge to Federalism*, ed. Pran Chopra (New Delhi: SAGE, 2006), p. 62.

an attempt to infuse India's constitutional scheme with judicial supremacy'.[36] Being a parliamentary democracy in the Westminster format, the judicial ascendance is ideologically debilitating since it puts hurdles to the elected representatives when they seek to bring about revolutionary socio-economic changes by way of innovative legislations. So, the basic structure doctrine is a retarding means in India's constitutional democracy which is ideologically restrictive and constitutionally contrarian.

Concluding Observations

Conceptually, the basic structure doctrine is justified given the fact that the Indian constitution clearly 'adopted the American model of constitutionalism with limited government and strong judicial review'. Though some elements of the British parliamentary system were 'adapted to the Indian constitution—the composition of the higher executive and effective collective cabinet responsibility'—it is difficult to accept that it entails 'the doctrine of parliamentary sovereignty'.[37] Despite strong critiques, the basic structure doctrine is being continuously expanded and appears to have created a wave in its favour around the world, especially in South Asia. In a 1989 judgement on *Anwar Husain v. Bangladesh*, Justice BH Chowdhury while emphasizing the importance of basic structure argued:

> Call it by any name—basic structure or whatever, but that is the fabric of the Constitution which cannot be dismantled by an authority created by the Constitution itself, namely, the Parliament. ... Because the amending power is but a power given by the Constitution to Parliament, it is a higher power than any other given by the Constitution to Parliament, but nevertheless [*sic*] it is power within and not outside the Constitution.[38]

The basic structure doctrine has also been appreciated by the Supreme Court in Pakistan. In *Al-Jehad Trust v. the Federation of Pakistan* (1996), the court ruled that in order to resolve a conflict between a constitutional provision and a later amendment, the constitution has to be interpreted as a whole, taking into account 'the spirit and basic features of the Constitution'.[39] This was further pursued in a 1997 judgement when the Supreme Court reiterated that the Pakistan Constitution has salient features—federalism, parliamentary form of government blended with Islamic provisions—'which are beyond the amendment power'.[40] Although the basic structure doctrine did not become integral to Pakistan's constitutional law as in India, these are important judgements which created a space for the doctrine more or less on the same arguments which were offered by the Indian Supreme Court.

Notwithstanding the obvious conceptual limitation of the arguments supportive of the doctrine in a parliamentary democracy, there is a powerful defence when it is shown to be an effective means for preventing parliament from being a self-engineered institution of governance. In the Indian context, the doctrine was conceptualized when the executive resorted to constitutional amendments rather indiscriminately to fulfil its political agenda seemingly at the cost of constitutional propriety. The doctrine

---

[36] Madhav Khosla, *The Indian Constitution* (New Delhi: Oxford University Press, 2012), p. 155.

[37] Sudhir Krishnaswamy, *Democracy and Constitutionalism in India: A Study of the Basic Structure Doctrine* (New Delhi: Oxford University Press, 2009), pp. 218–19.

[38] The judgement is quoted in Roznai, *Unconstitutional Constitutional Amendments*, p. 59.

[39] The judgement is quoted in Roznai, *Unconstitutional Constitutional Amendments*, p. 61.

[40] The judgement is quoted in Roznai, *Unconstitutional Constitutional Amendments*, p. 61.

that had emerged in the context of the challenges to the validity of constitutional amendments was thus hailed as a panacea which applied brakes; otherwise, 'the engine of amending power would soon', it was apprehended, 'overrun the constitution'.[41] By insisting on the basic structure, the Supreme Court thus acts as a brake which is required to sustain a healthy balance among the organs of the government. Besides imposing limits on Parliament's amending power, the doctrine also acknowledges that the constitution can be radically changed by the people themselves; it thus emphasizes simultaneously the importance of the elected representatives and 'the democratic pedigree earned by non-representative institutions', including judiciary. The trajectory of the basic structure doctrine confirms that it evolves and gets consolidated when the representative institutions fail to 'maintain democratic essentials' of the country.[42] Hence the importance of the doctrine cannot be so easily dismissed; in fact, it has gained credibility to the extent of being part and parcel of constitutional democracy in India.

In the final analysis, the basic structure is not merely a judicial decision, but a political intervention in governance which was likely to be derailed due to specific socio-political context reportedly leading to the consolidation of anti-democratic and authoritarian forces, especially in the mid-1970s. By raising concerns, the judiciary seems to have created an environment for 'fostering a democratic dialogue around key constitutional principles between the institutions of government'[43] which not only confirms the importance of the principles of checks and balances in constitutional governance but also consolidates democracy as a collective venture. In principle, the doctrine is thus an important aid for keeping the executive within a limit; in practice, however, the judicial intervention through the doctrine of basic structure does not seem to be as fundamental as is construed, which Justice Khanna (who was superseded when his turn to become the Chief Justice of India due probably to his dissenting note in the 1976 Habeas Corpus case) articulated as follows:

> There is no modern instance, it is said, in which any judiciary has saved a whole people from the grave currents of intolerance, passion and tyranny which have threatened liberty and free institutions. The attitude of a society and of its organized political forces rather than of its legal machinery, is the controlling force in the character of free institutions. The ramparts of defence against tyranny are ultimately in the hearts of the people. The Constitution, the courts and the laws can act only as aids to strengthen those ramparts; they do not and cannot furnish substitute for those ramparts. If the ramparts are secure, anyone who dares to tamper with the liberties of the citizens would do so at his own peril. If, however, the ramparts crack down, no convention, no court would be able to do much in the matter.[44]

This is the crux of the matter; no matter how strong the judiciary is while stream-rolling its diktats, its authority can be effective so long as it is held by the people as an effective instrument for fulfilling some of their cherished socio-economic goals. So, in the ultimate analysis, the basic structure doctrine, by itself, does not seem to be an empowering device; that it has acquired the status of being a significant shield against the trespassing by the executive of its constitutionally recognized boundaries clearly authenticates the critical role of the *demos* in charting out definite courses for institutions of governance in a democratic polity. This is where the doctrine stands out.

---

[41] Upendra Baxi, *Courage, Craft and Contention: The Indian Supreme Court in the Eighties* (Bombay: NM Tripathi, 1985), p. 68.

[42] Krishnaswami, *Democracy and Constitutionalism in India*, p. 221.

[43] Krishnaswami, *Democracy and Constitutionalism in India*, p. 215.

[44] Quoted in Michael Henderson, 'Setting India's Democratic House in Order', *Asian Survey* 19 (1979): 955–56.

Review Questions

1. **What is the basic structure in the parlance of constitutional studies? Elaborate.**
2. **How did the basic structure evolve in India? Elaborate.**
3. **How did the Supreme Court of India define the basic structure of the Constitution of India? Elaborate.**
4. **It is difficult to precisely identify the basic structures of the Constitution. Do you agree with this view? Elaborate your response.**
5. **The 1973 Kesavananda Bharati case is a watershed in the evolution of the doctrine of the basic structure. Explain.**
6. **Elaborate two major Supreme Court judgements in the conceptualization of the doctrine of basic structure.**
7. **Does the basic structure doctrine undermine parliamentary sovereignty? Give reasons to your answer.**
8. **'The basic structure doctrine is not merely a judicial intervention but a political intervention as well'. Explain.**
9. **Is it fair to argue that the basic structure doctrine contributes to a hyperactive judiciary in India? Give reasons to your answer.**
10. **The basic structure doctrine is nothing but a means to reinforce the sovereignty of the constitution. Do you agree? Elaborate your response.**

Chapter

7

Citizenship in India

Learning Objectives

- How to conceptualize citizenship as critical to constitutional democracy?
- How did the founding fathers approach and address the issues of citizenship while framing a constitution for independent India?
- To understand how citizenship was reinvented in the context of newer legislative stipulations

Citizens are core to a democracy for variety or reasons. Prominent among them is the fact that they constitute the compact that governs within the well-established and also transparent set of systems. This means that citizens are to articulate their responses while being involved in governance in a format which evolves out of a dialogue. In real terms, citizens become citizens since they agree to remain in the compact by being tuned to the system of governance that they themselves create by way of contestation and also negotiation. Fundamental here is the idea that citizenship is conceptualized both as an outcome and a tool in democratic initiatives and also activities. What is emphasized here is the process whereby citizenship is articulated in a particular fashion. This has two major implications: on the one hand, it is argued that citizenship, if imposed, may not be substantial since it is engineered by outside forces or processes which may just be transitional; it also underlines, on the other, the importance of the processes in which citizenship is both defined and put into practice. In other words, citizenship needs to be understood as an offshoot of a dialectical interaction involving individuals and the context which is also multifaceted.

There are two arguments that receive serious attention in the academic discourse: first, citizenship is not given, but evolves out of complex processes in which history seems to be a critical factor. This is visible in the Indian context. Being a former colony when the 'native' population was deprived of the citizenship rights which were available to the British citizens, the urge for citizenship was obvious. Despite having raised this point repeatedly, the nationalists failed to convince the rulers. It is thus not surprising that when the discussion over citizenship had begun in the Constituent Assembly, the members prefaced their remarks with the anomaly in the British system of governance. Second, it is very difficult to conceptualize citizenship in a straitjacketed formula presumably because it is context-dependent. There are constitutional stipulations which define citizenship and accord citizenship rights accordingly; but there are contingent circumstances in which constitutional rigidity may act as an impediment, and hence the constitution is to be equipped with mechanisms to handle issues arising out of such a situation.

That citizenship is governed by well-defined rules and regulations, or, in other words, the rule of law or the constitution which, despite being driven by codified stipulations, draws on the conventions and widely practised norms as well. The constitution is the source of authority and citizenship is defined and the rights are given to the citizens on the basis of the directions given in the constitution. With regard to any discussion of citizenship, the importance of the constitution cannot thus be belittled since it forms the basis on which citizenship is based. This is a fundamental idea that TH Marshall in his famous treatise *Citizenship and Social Class* (1950) articulated by suggesting that there are three elements in citizenship: civil element (the rights necessary for individual freedom), the political element (the right to participate in the exercise of political power) and the social element (referring to a compact of social rights to enable individuals to self-actualize their full potentials). These three elements are critical to the conceptualization of citizenship in the contemporary era. In simple terms, citizenship entails a bunch of rights which are necessary for the individuals to evolve without constraints. However, these rights are not absolute; the state is also given authority to restrict citizenship rights if it deems appropriate for a wider public cause which needs to be articulated within the constitutional parameters. Citizenship rights are thus determined by the constitution. This is an empowering device and also disempowering at the same time. For instance, when Gandhi fought for equal status for the Indians in South Africa in the early twentieth century, he failed in his mission so long as he articulated his opposition in legal terms; in other words, despite being adequately equipped, he was unable to convince the judges that the government design of treating Indians differently due to racial differences is ultra vires to the rule of law; his success was largely attributed to Indians being politically mobilized for a cause although there is no denying that his protracted legal battle in South Africa helped him earn public support both in England and elsewhere in the Empire.

To begin with, a fair understanding of citizenship in India requires, (a) a thorough probing of the context in which it evolved and which entails a thorough analysis of individual efforts for creating a level playing field for all who are connected with one another by virtue of being a part of the collectivity in a specific polity, and (b) the framing of relevant rules and regulations to translate the constitutional aims and objectives which are again context-driven. In real terms, it means that for an appropriate understanding of citizenship in India, what is needed is to understand, (a) how the constitutional provisions were shaped out of fierce debates in the Constituent Assembly in which the founding fathers participated to evolve appropriate rules in this regard, and (b) to comprehend the processes in the aftermath of constitutionalizing citizenship which also led to changes in the constitutionally guaranteed prevalent system. In a nutshell, being dialectically connected with the prevalent socio-economic context, citizenship cannot be conceptualized in absolute terms, which further confirms that it is theoretically restrictive, if not myopic, if it is sought to be explained in the one-size-fits-in formula.

The purpose here is to acquaint the reader with the processes culminating in the articulation of provisions in Part II of the Constitution of India with reference to their historical genealogy and also the contemporary pulls and pressures due to the transforming socio-economic and political context. In order to defend the argument that citizenship is both constitution-driven and socio-politically constructed, the aim of this chapter is twofold: (a) to draw out the implications of the Constituent Assembly debates to understand how citizenship in India was conceptualized in the backdrop of partition riots, and (b) to briefly discuss the factors which account for the crystallization of a new perspective in which citizenship is being articulated in new light.

Historical Antecedents

The contradictory nature of India's Independence on 15 August 1947 continues to baffle the nationalists and also the scholars, engaged in conceptualizing the historical processes leading to the British withdrawal. Freedom was won, but was marred by the trauma of partition and the mayhem that followed immediately before the transfer of power was formally articulated. Thus India's Independence represents a great paradox of history. The success of the nationalist movement was its failure. Underlying this conundrum—the success and failure of the freedom struggle—lies the roots of the paradox of Independence that further complicated the task that the Constituent Assembly members had undertaken to devise appropriate provisions for citizens and their rights in a very uncertain context due partly to the volatile socio-economic and political circumstances arising perhaps out of a sudden laxity in the administration. The implications were disastrous: partition of India led to a forcible transfer of a large segment of population from India and the newly created Pakistan, and vice versa, as soon as the division of the country was formalized. In actual terms, the 1947 Great Divide forced approximately fourteen million people to cross the newly demarcated borders for being recognized as citizens with the concomitant rights and benefits. It was a real challenge to the founding fathers because they had to accommodate those who suddenly became 'refugees' when they shifted from those areas, located in the new state of Pakistan; it was a challenge also because they had to arbitrate the claims of citizenship in circumstances which were far from being normal and stable. It was not an easy task for the framers of the constitution who devoted a great deal of attention while finalizing the provisions for citizenship in India which made Jawaharlal Nehru to say that 'all these articles relating to citizenship have probably received far more thought and consideration during the last few months than any other article contained in this constitution'.[1] He was right presumably because not only did a majority of the members participate in the debate, they also took active interest in framing 'the right kind of provisions' for those, to be identified as 'proud Indians'.

This was however not the first time when the Indian nationalists had engaged with such a task. In fact, one of the first efforts in this regard was made by the 1928 Motilal Nehru Report which, in Article 3 of the Report, clearly distinguished citizens from foreigners. As it was mentioned:

> The word "citizen" wherever it occurs in this constitution means every person (a) who was born, or whose father was either born or naturalized, within the territorial limits of the Commonwealth and has not been naturalized as a citizen of any other country; and (b) who is naturalized in the Commonwealth under the law in force for the time being.[2]

So, as per the Nehru Report, a person is eligible to become a citizen by birth or being naturalized within the acceptable legal modes. It did not allow 'dual citizenship' since it categorically mentions that one cannot become India's citizen unless one renounces one's citizenship in a different country. Implicit here is a distinction between two contrasting principles of citizenship which is theoretically useful to conceptualize citizenship in India: (a) *jus soli* (birth being the sole criterion for citizenship) and (b) *jus sanguinis* (blood-based descent being a determinant of citizenship). While the former form of citizenship is more inclusive because it also draws on ethno-cultural unity the latter is an expansive design to address the concern arising

[1] Jawaharlal Nehru, 12 August 1949, *Constituent Assembly Debates*, Book No. 4, p. 398.

[2] *The Nehru Report*, August, 1928, reproduced in B Shiva Rao, ed., *The Framing of India's Constitution: Select Documents*, Vol. 1 (Delhi: Universal Law Publishing Company, 2004), p. 59.

out of contingent circumstances. These are however 'a pure type' which is analytically valid, but may not be always appropriate. Nonetheless, they seem to have governed the deliberations in the Assembly to a significant extent. It was BR Ambedkar who initiated the debate on 10 August 1949. Like Nehru, he was also of the opinion that to draft an agreeable provision in regard to citizens was a herculean task. In his words:

> I do not think that any other article has given the Drafting Committee such a headache as this particular article on citizenship. I do not know how many drafts were prepared and how many were destroyed as being inadequate to cover all the cases which it was thought necessary and desirable to cover. I think it is a piece of good fortune for the Drafting Committee to have ultimately agreed upon the draft [that I moved] because this is the draft which satisfies most people, if not all.[3]

The end result of the hard work of the Drafting Committee were the provisions which, felt Ambedkar, were acceptable to most of his colleagues. Before he placed the amendment, he also underlined that these provisions were 'not permanent or unalterable'; they were ad hoc in character presumably because the founding fathers did not subject the future policy makers to the conditionalities confronting them. With these clarifying remarks, Ambedkar presented the formula for citizenship by saying that 'the Drafting Committee has provided for five different classes of people who can, provided they satisfy the terms and conditions which are laid down in this article, become citizens on the date on which the Constitution commences'.[4] These five categories were:

1. Persons domiciled in India and born in India: in other words, who form the bulk of the population of India, as defined by this Constitution;
2. Persons who are domiciled in India but who are not born in India but who have resided in India. For instance, persons who are the subjects of the Portuguese Settlement in India or the French Settlement in India like Chandernagore, Pondicherry, or the Iranians for the matter of that who have come from Persia and although they are not born here, they have resided for a long time and undoubtedly have the intention of becoming the citizens of India;
3. Persons who are residents in India, but who have migrated to Pakistan;
4. Persons resident in Pakistan and who have migrated to India; and
5. Persons who or whose parents are born in India but are residing outside India.[5]

These are well-defined categories of people who were entitled to become independent India's citizens. Being aware that these categories might have left out some group of people, Ambedkar further clarified that 'if there is any category of people who are left out by the provisions contained in this amendment, we have given power to Parliament subsequently to make provision for them'.[6] So, Ambedkar did not foreclose the option of expanding the categories which also suggests his concern for future when citizenship needed to be conceptualized differently, if situation so demanded. In this sense, the conceptualization that he provided appears to have taken into account not only the prevalent but also prospective compulsions

[3] BR Ambedkar, 10 August 1949, *Constituent Assembly Debates*, Book No. 4, p. 347.
[4] Ibid., p. 347.
[5] Ibid., p. 347.
[6] Ibid., p. 349.

which, one could not afford to ignore, to evolve a meaningful and persuasive set of criteria in regard to citizenship.

The Constituent Assembly witnessed heated discussion on the issue of who to become citizens of the country. There were some members who felt that the right to citizenship should not be given so easily, especially to those who had objectionable credentials in the past. The point was raised in response to an amendment that KT Shah (Bihar) moved to decide the course of action in regard to those who initially migrated to Pakistan but returned to India later. Shah's amendment entails that a person

> who has migrated to the areas now included in Pakistan but has returned from that area [to India] since the nineteenth day of July, 1948, shall produce such evidence, documentary or otherwise, as may be deemed necessary to prove his intention to be domiciled in India and reside permanently there.[7]

Shah felt that the proposed provisions of the constitution were soft especially to those who continued to remain indecisive or they were not serious in making a choice either way; they should not be allowed to take Indian citizenship for a ride. This was the sentiment that ran through when he exhorted:

> The privilege of citizenship of India should not be regarded as something very commonplace affair, cheap and easy. It is . . . and it promises to be still more, a great privilege, of which not only those of us who are now citizens may be proud, but even those who may hereafter become citizens of India should also be proud. It was the proud privilege in the days of the Roman Republic for any Roman citizen simply because of that citizenship to regard himself as equal to any King. . . . I hope, the time is coming when the same proud boast may justly be made by Indians, when the citizenship of India will not be merely regarded as a burden of "nativity"—for we were used to be called "natives" in the dead and buried past—but it would be regarded as something to which the rest of the world will look up with respect.[8]

Citizenship was a precious possession, felt Shah, which needed to be treated accordingly. This was an argument that drew on the concern for building one's self-esteem: one should feel proud of being an Indian. Jaspat Roy Kapoor, an Assembly member from Punjab, however, raised a serious objection to the draft provision allowing those who left for Pakistan to come back. Characterizing this provision as 'an obnoxious clause', he thus argued:

> Once a person has migrated to Pakistan and transferred his loyalty from India to Pakistan, . . . he has definitely made up his mind at that time to kick this country for settling in Pakistan. It defies all logic if we allow those persons who went away to Pakistan to come back [because] they went definitely with the intention of settling down there permanently. They gave up their loyalty to this country and they gave their allegiance to the new country of Pakistan. Their migration was therefore complete and absolute and therefore their right of citizenship which they had before their migration is eliminated altogether.[9]

[7] KT Shah (Bihar), 11 August 1949, *Constituent Assembly Debates*, Book No. 4, p. 369.

[8] Ibid., pp. 369–70.

[9] Jaspat Roy Kapoor (Punjab), 11 August 1949, *Constituent Assembly Debates*, Book No. 4, p. 366.

For Kapoor, it was matter of concern since those who left India for Pakistan did not seem to have loyalty to India; hence they should not be allowed. His colleague, PS Deshmukh of Central Provinces and Berar endeavoured to persuade the members not to endorse the amendment saying that this had dangerous consequences for the country because those who are willing to come back could be 'fifth columnists ... [who] might have come here with the intention of sabotaging Indian independence ... or, for selling off their property'.[10] This was an extreme position which did not receive much support in the Assembly. Instead, there were many who sympathized with the argument that because of the uncertain circumstances following partition, many Muslims left for Pakistan. They should not have, argued Thakur Das Bhargava, 'any trouble in being citizens of India, ... and no obstacle should be placed in the way of those persons who have come from Pakistan on account of disturbances and who have left their home and hearth and come to this country'.[11] This should not be treated as a blanket approval for all, as he further noted that those who 'left this country to become citizens of Pakistan with open eyes and with the song on their lips *Hanske Liya Pakistan, Ladke Lenge Hindustan* [we got Pakistan easily and we will take over India by ploy and trick] should not be made citizens of India because they plan to return with ill-intentions'.[12] Basic to the arguments, made by Kapoor and Deshmukh, was a concern for nation building which should not be allowed to be vitiated by elements with dubious antecedents; according to Bhargava who took a middle path by insisting that instead of treating everybody as being motivated, which was unfair, it would be judicious to apply the provision selectively to deny citizenship to those who were likely to be miscreants.

The Constituent Assembly drafted the provisions for citizenship in uncertain circumstances stemming out of partition. It was therefore not odd that most of the interventions by the members focused on the plight of the victims of partition who suffered due to no fault of their own; they became pawns in the game of politics. The members confronted a very difficult situation in which they had to identify appropriate rules and regulations to sustain constitutional democracy in India. Realizing that it was not an easy task and lapses were inevitable, Nehru thus argued:

> I do not think it is possible for you to draft anything, whatever meticulous care you might exercise which could fit in with a very difficult and complicated situation that has arisen, namely partition. One has inevitably to do something which involves the greatest amount of justice to our people and which is the most practical solution to the problem. You cannot in any such provision lay down more or less who you like or whom you dislike; you have to lay down certain principles, but any principles that you may lay down is likely not to fit in with a number of cases. It cannot be helped in any event. Therefore you see that the principle fixed fits with a vast majority of cases, even though a very small number does not wholly fit in, and there may some kind of difficulty in dealing with them. I think the drafters of these proposals have succeeded in a remarkable measure in producing something which really deals with 99.9 percent of cases with justice and practical common sense.[13]

There are two important points that Nehru made: first, being aware that it was difficult, if not impossible, to devise appropriate rules and regulations relating to citizenship due to (a) the unavoidable partition-related uncertainties that India was passing through and (b) the crystallization of contrasting points of

[10] PS Deshmukh (Central Provinces and Berar), 11 August 1949, *Constituent Assembly Debates*, Book No. 4, p. 354.
[11] Thakur Das Bhargava (East Punjab), 11 August 1949, *Constituent Assembly Debates*, Book No. 4, p. 380.
[12] Ibid., p. 381.
[13] Jawaharlal Nehru, 12 August 1949, *Constituent Assembly Debates*, Book No. 4, p. 398.

view in the Assembly, since members held views which ran contrary to that of Nehru and the Congress; the second point is linked with his democratic concern for building consensus which was not always possible; hence one had to be pragmatic which he expressed by saying that if the decision was just and satisfied the majority, it was fine as far as he was concerned. Core to Nehru's argument is the point that since citizenship was an area of fierce contestation for obvious reasons there was a remote possibility of having consensus among the members, as was the case on most occasions.

Constitutional Provisions

Comprising seven Articles (Articles 5, 6, 7, 8, 9, 10 and 11), Part II is about citizenship. Article 5 to 8 confer citizenship on every person who fulfil the following criteria at the time of the inauguration of the Constitution:

1. Domiciled in India and born in India;
2. Domiciled, but not born in India;
3. Domiciled, not born in India but ordinarily resident for more than five years;
4. Resident of India, but migrated to Pakistan after 1 March, 1947, and later returned to India on resettlement permit;
5. Resident of the area, earmarked as Pakistan, but who migrated to India before 19 July, 1948 or who came after that date but had resided in India for more than six months and got registered in the prescribed manner; and
6. Resident outside India but who or either of his/her parents or grandparents were born in India.

As the provisions stipulate, there are three ways in which one can become Indian citizen: (a) by being born and domiciled in India, (b) the migrants from those areas which became Pakistan following the partition and (c) those Indians who were residing abroad. Of these, the first way is more or less universally followed: citizenship is ordinarily given to those born in a country; those who are domicile are also granted citizenship. The second was peculiar to India, as was discussed earlier with reference to the Constituent Assembly debates; it was finally agreed upon with the justification that those who left India and settled in Pakistan as a contingent measure following the political uncertainty in India should be given an opportunity in case they decided to come back. The third way was an effort to bring back those who settled abroad; by allowing them citizenship, the Constitution recognized them as integral to India's constitutional democracy.

While the first part of Part II deals with the guarantee of citizenship, the second part consisting of three Articles (Article 9, 10 and 11) is an expansion of the former. Article 9 provides a sanction in case Indian citizenship is voluntarily abdicated by an Indian citizen in favour of citizenship of a foreign country. Drawn on the universal practice, especially in European countries, the founding fathers endorsed such a stipulation. Article 11 empowers the Parliament to adopt new rules and regulations if it deems necessary while Article 10 is a guarantee of citizenship rights to those holding Indian citizenship as per the constitutional provisions.

In pursuance of Article 11, the Parliament enacted the Citizenship Act of 1955 which was both an endorsement of the available constitutional provisions and also evolved new parameters for citizenship in view of the contingent circumstances in the aftermath of Independence. The Act is a guarantee of citizenship for

1. A person born in India after 26 January, 1950 would become a citizen of India by birth;
2. Anyone born outside India after 26 January, 1950, subject to certain requirements, would be a citizens of India if his father was an Indian citizen at time of his/her birth;
3. Under certain circumstances, certain category of persons could acquire citizenship by registration in the prescribed manner;
4. Foreigners are entitled to get Indian citizenship on application for naturalization on certain conditions;
5. If any territory becomes part of India, the State could, by order, specify the criteria for bestowing citizenship on the people belonging to that part;
6. Citizenship could be taken away by termination, renunciation or deprivation on the basis of clearly-defined government stipulations with intimation to the law-making authority; and
7. A citizen of a Commonwealth country would have the status of a Commonwealth citizen in India in accordance with appropriate executive directions, approved by the law-making authority.

A scan of the 1955 Act demonstrates that citizenship can be acquired in five ways: by birth, descent, registration, naturalization and incorporation of a territory. At one level, the Act appears to have reinforced the criteria and conditionalities that Part II of the Constitution refers to while constitutionalizing citizenship in India; at another, it also carves out new factors which did not receive attention in the past presumably because the situation did not seem to have favoured them. What is most striking in the Act is the stipulation that the executive is empowered 'to determine and certify the citizenship of persons whose citizenship of India is in doubt'.[14] By according a determining role to the executive, the Act seems to have cleared the deck for the Illegal Migrants (Determination by Tribunal) Act (IMDT) of 1983 by the Parliament which was actually a response to the growing political discontent in Assam over the illegal migrants who were charged of having tilted the demographic balance in their favour. That it was directed against a section of the population in Assam was evident, as the Act states:

> Whereas a good number of foreigners who migrated into India across the borders of the eastern and north-eastern regions of the country on and after 25th day of March, 1971, have, by taking advantage of the circumstances of the circumstances of such migration and their ethnic similarities and other connections with the people of India and without having in their possession any lawful authority so to do, illegally remained in India; and whereas the continuance of such foreigners in India is detrimental to the interests of the public of India; and whereas on account of the number of such foreigners and the manner in which such foreigners have clandestinely been trying to pass off as citizens of India and all other relevant circumstances, it is necessary for the protection of the citizens of India to make special provisions for the detection of such foreigners in Assam and also in any other part of India in which such foreigners may be found to have remained illegally.

The Act, instead of being welcomed, was identified as a detrimental step to achieve what was expected to attain. It was an Assam-specific stipulation which was contrary to the established laws on foreigners, especially in the 1946 Foreigners Act which defines a foreigner as a person who is not a citizen of India and onus of proving whether a person is a foreigner or not shall lie on such a person. However, as per the

---

[14] Niraja Gopal Jayal, *Citizenship and its Discontent: An Indian History* (Ranikhet: Permanent Black), 2013, p. 63.

IMDT Act, the burden of proving the citizenship or otherwise rested on the accuser and the police, not the accused. This was a major departure from the provisions of the Foreigners Act, 1946.[15] The Act thus removed 'the burden from individuals suspected of being illegal migrants and placed it on their neighbours who could then file a complaint to report illegal immigrants in their area [which] will now be investigated by the tribunals to ... determine conclusively [the authenticity of the complaint] to undertake further action in this regard'.[16] There are many infirmities in the Act as it was pointed by the Supreme Court which set aside the Act in 2005 by suggesting that it was most impractical of the Acts that had so far been enacted because citizens were unlikely to initiate proceedings for the deportation of the illegal migrants. While making the Act ultra vires to the Constitution, the Supreme Court thus argued:

> Not every person feels that he [*sic*] owes a duty toward the nation and he should initiate proceedings for deportation of an illegal migrant. The applicant also incurs the risk of his own security and safety besides spending time and energy in prosecuting the matter.... This shows how one-sided the provisions of the IMDT Act are. They have been so made that they only result in giving advantage and benefits to an illegal migrant and not for achieving the real objective of the enactment, namely, of detection and deportation of a Bangladeshi national who has illegally crossed the border on or after 25 March, 1971.[17]

The Act was, as per the Supreme Court, doomed to fail since the mechanism was also a suspect for being impractical and also ridden with dangerous implications for those who took the responsibility, if at all, of reporting to the tribunal for illegal immigrants. The political implication of this judgement was obvious: Sarbanada Sonowal who belonged to the Bharatiya Janata Party (BJP) created instantaneously a support base for the party among the Bengali population who so far remained the target of the Congress party. It was not surprising that in the 2016 Assam state assembly election, it was the BJP which trounced the incumbent ruling party which governed the state for two decades.

The Changes in the Citizenship Act

The 1955 Act for citizenship was amended in 1986 which, by adding a new Article 6A, made a special provision for 'citizenship of persons covered by the Assam Accord of 1985'. The Amendment Act guarantees citizenship to (a) those persons of Indian origin who had come to Assam before 1 January 1966 from 'the specified territory' (Bangladesh), including those whose names were in the electoral roll for the 1967 general elections, and who had been ordinarily resident in Assam from the date of their entry shall be 'deemed to be citizens of India from the 1st day of January. And also, those persons of Indian origin who came to Assam from Bangladesh on or after 1 January 1966 but before 25 March 1971, had been ordinarily resident in Assam after their entry, and had been detected to be a foreigner by the Tribunal, constituted

---

[15] Anupama Roy provides an analytical account of the Act in her *Mapping Citizenship in India* (New Delhi: Oxford University Press, 2010), pp. 104–06.

[16] Jayal, *Citizenship and its Discontent*, p. 64.

[17] *Sarbananda Sonowal v. the Union of India*, 2005. http://refugeelawreader.org/en/en/english/section-v-asian-framework-for-refugee-protection/iv3-states-not-party-to-the-1951-refugee-convention/iv32-india/cases-27/8135-the-sarbananda-sonowal-v-union-of-india-2005-5-supreme-court-cases-665-aliens-aggression-illegal-migrants-powers-of-state/file.html (accessed 16 December 2016).

by the Foreign (Tribunal) Order of 1964, could register themselves as Indian citizens. This was a concession to the All Assam Students Union (AASU) who, through a sustained agitation for six long years, convinced the then ruling dispensation, led by the Congress, as critics argue, that 'a marauding infiltration by Bangladeshi nationals from across the border was putting the Assamese language and culture in great danger'.[18] Despite resentments by a section of the population in the state of Assam and elsewhere in India, the tripartite settlement between the Union Government, the Assam government and the AASU leadership on 14–15 August 1985 stopped the violence which justified the concession as perhaps the only option available at that juncture of history.

While the 1986 Amendment seems to have been politically contrived, the 2003 amendment to the 1955 Citizenship Act represented an endeavour to go beyond the conventional domain of citizenship. The amendment was meant to accommodate the Indian diaspora within the fold of Indian citizenship. The Citizenship (Amendment) Act of 2003 introduced 'a version of dual/transnational citizenship for persons of Indian origin (PIO) in the form of Overseas Indian Citizenship'.[19] This amendment should be read with another amendment that was enacted in 2005. While the 2003 revision stipulated for overseas citizens of India the 2005 amendment insists on the maintenance of a national register of Indian citizens and overseas citizens of India. A person of Indian origin may be registered as an overseas citizen of India and will have some justiciable rights like owning property, travelling to India without visa, making investment in business, among others; they, however, are not given voting rights and are also not entitled to contest elections for high elective offices of the State nor they can be appointed as judges or hold any public office or claim equality of opportunity in matters of public employment.

Summarizing the Argument

Part II of the Constitution of India and the 1955 Citizenship Act constitute the core of the constitutional design for citizenship in India. With regard to the former, it was the Constituent Assembly that provided the basic inputs while in regard to the 1955 Act, it was the compulsion of the newly independent nation which was translated into various measures leading to a context-driven conceptualization of citizenship in India. As was shown earlier, the 1955 Act had undergone changes in response to political movements in Assam in the 1980s that resulted in changes in the criteria for citizenship. The role of the judiciary was also very critical, as was visible when the IMDT Act was struck down in 2005 as it was contrary to the fundamental spirit of the Constitution. The 2003 Amendment was an expansion of the rules, already made; by creating overseas citizen of India with the adoption of the 2005 amendment to the Citizenship Act, the chapter on citizenship seems to have complete a full circle.

Concluding Observations

Citizenship was a tricky area of concern not only for the members of the Constituent Assembly but also for those who presided over India's destiny in the aftermath of decolonization. For the members of the Assembly, it was a responsibility that could also be shifted to the future Parliament, according to BR

---

[18] Joydeep Biswas, 'The Starkness of Being Nowhere', *The Hindu*, 10 September 2015.
[19] Roy, *Mapping Citizenship in India*, p. 39.

Ambedkar who said that 'all that we are doing is to decide ad hoc for the time being the question' as to who would be the citizens with the commencement of the Constitution, and 'the business of laying down a permanent law of citizenship has been left to the future Parliament'.[20] The Constituent Assembly did not, in other words, commit to conclusive provisions in this regard presumably because of the volatile socio-political circumstances following the partition. Hence it has been eloquently argued that 'the immediacy and impermanence were dictated by the particular circumstances of the Partition of India in 1947 that shaped these provisions substantially and in their self-conscious temporariness'.[21] Nonetheless, the constitutional provisions in Part II of the Constitution not only define citizenship but also identify the criteria by which one can be a citizen. The design had undergone changes in the context of the Assam agitation in the 1980s which led to the conclusion of the Assam Accord in 1985. The reversal of the IMDT Act of 1983 by the Supreme Court also reveals that issues relating to citizenship always remained contentious. The 2003 and 2005 amendments to the Citizenship Act are a testimony to the contention that citizenship needs to be defined contextually which means that law has to be flexible to the extent of accommodating new demands.

The definition of citizenship and what makes one a citizen of a country are context-dependent, as the trajectory of citizenship in India since the inauguration of the Constitution in 1950 illustrates. One of the striking features of Part II is the provisions for so-called migrants from Pakistan. The founding fathers were divided in their attitude toward those identified as migrants and the debates reveal that they hardly converged presumably because the differences were so stark and unbridgeable. As shown earlier, a fierce debate occurred when the question of accepting those who were coming back from Pakistan after having deserted India was discussed. For a large number of members, it was an insult to the Indian citizenship and hence they should not be allowed to return; there were some who did not appear to hold such strong views and were persuaded to believe that it was a decision under serious predicament on their part, especially in the context of the uncertainty arising out of partition. Interestingly, the same view point was endorsed by the Supreme Court in 1954 when the bench pronounced:

> In October or November, 1947, men's minds were in a state of flux. The partition of Indian and the event that followed in its wake in both Pakistan and India were unprecedented and it is difficult to cite any historical precedent for the situation that arose. Minds of people affected by this partition and who were living in those parts were completely unhinged and unbalanced and there was hardly an occasion to form intentions requisite for acquiring domicile in one place or another. People vacillated and altered their programmes from day to day as events happened. They went backward and forward; families were sent from one place to another for the sake of safety. . . . No one, as a matter of fact, at the moment thought that when he was leaving Pakistan for India or vice versa that he was forever abandoning the place of his ancestors.[22]

The decision was not an easy one for those undergoing emotional stress and mental trauma due to the tumultuous unfolding of events in the aftermath of the partition. This is reflected in the provisions in Part II which did not seem to be as rigid as some of the members of the Assembly expected. In the same

---

[20] BR Ambedkar, 10 August 1949, *Constituent Assembly Debates*, Book No. 4, p. 357.

[21] Niraja Gopal Jayal, 'Citizenship', in *The Oxford Handbook of the Indian Constitution*, eds. Sujit Choudhury, Madhav Khosla and Pratap Bhanu Mehta (New Delhi: Oxford University Press, 2016), p. 163.

[22] *Central Bank v. Ram Narain*, 1954. https://indiankanoon.org/doc/426664/ (accessed 16 December 2016).

vein, the 1955 Citizenship Act incorporated sections which were meant to accommodate the concern of those who failed to decide conclusively one way or the other due to the emotional uncertainty that they confronted due to the sudden eruption of events following the partition.

To conclude, the discussion of citizenship in India underlines two fundamental points: first, it was the 1947 partition of India that critically shaped the constitutional design for citizenship in India. Part II holds the substance of this contention which was further substantiated by the amendments to the 1955 Citizenship Act that followed. Although the Supreme Court had set aside, the controversial 1983 IMDT Act seems to have drawn on the religious divide separating the 'illegal migrants' from the local Assamese which reinforces the argument that religious identity continues to remain a significant marker for citizenship in India. Conceptually significant, the second point captures 'a gradual and subtle shift from the *jus soli* conception of citizenship at the constitution-making stage towards a *jus sanguinis* conception.'[23] Although Part II holds *jus soli* as a determining criterion, *jus sanguinis* has become a defining tool in conceptualizing citizenship with the unfolding of India's trajectory as an independent polity. The argument is substantiated by the State being receptive to the claim of the so-called illegal migrants from Bangladesh or the Hindus in Pakistan for citizenship in the *jus sanguinis* sense. The 2005 Amendment Act further confirms the contention by extending citizenship rights even to the diaspora which was simply inconceivable in the past as the political situation did not seem to be favourable.

Review Questions

1. **What is citizenship? Elaborate.**
2. **How is citizenship conceptualized in the constitutional discourse? Elaborate.**
3. **Define citizenship with reference to the typology that generally is appreciated.**
4. **Who is a citizen in India? Elaborate.**
5. **Critically evaluate the constitutional provisions of Part II of the Constitution of India.**
6. **How does the Constitution of India address the issue of citizenship in regard to 'the certain migrants' from Pakistan? Elaborate.**
7. **Critically evaluate the 1955 Citizenship Act.**
8. **Critically assess the 1986 Citizenship Act.**
9. **The issue of citizenship in India is political too. Do you agree with this view? Elaborate your response.**
10. **Citizenship cannot be conceptualized independent of the prevalent socio-economic and political circumstances. Explain.**

[23] I owe this point to Niraja Gopal Jayal who developed this in her article 'Citizenship', p. 179.

Chapter 8

Language and Nation-building: Constitutional Inputs

Learning Objectives

- To understand the importance of language in building a social compact
- To comprehend how the constitutional provisions relating to language evolved during the making of the Constitution of India
- To conceptualize the critical role that language plays in constitutionalizing a diverse society like India

Constitutionalizing language is one of the trickiest issues in an immensely socio-culturally diverse society like India. During the British period, the issue did not appear to have received adequate attention for obvious reason. The colonial authority did not seem to have held anything against sustaining India's multilingual identity so long as it did not undermine the hegemony of English. With the approval of Macaulay's minutes privileging English, the prevalent Indian languages never became important, for obvious reasons, in the transaction of official business; they, however, remained prominent in the public life and flourished with the nationalist movement. The Indian National Congress strongly held the view that a nation's progress was contingent on its cultural resources which also included the development of languages with their distinct identity not only etymologically but also in epistemological terms. Language needed to be strengthened to develop a strong nation, the Congress believed though in its annual sessions, the business was mostly transacted in English which the Congress leaders seem to have instinctively imbibed. Nonetheless, the importance of well-developed languages, as a marker of national identity, was always strongly felt. A scan of the activities that the Congress had undertaken since 1922 Gaya Congress reveals that the national leadership paid adequate attention to the language issue because it believed that language constituted an important pillar of nationhood. In view of the prevalence of multiple languages which were equally developed, it was difficult for them to make a definitive statement. Nonetheless, the Gandhian concern for sustaining India's distinctive linguistic identity seems to have set in motion the discursive parameters for future debates in this critical aspect of the struggle for political liberation. The idea and argument are crystal clear: language is not merely a mode of expression, it also represents a culture which also helps develop a community with its distinctive traits. Hence the argument that what supplements the evolution and also strengthening of a language also provides a platform for the community, and consequently the nation, to articulate a distinct voice which is certainly context-driven, but culturally charged.

The processes leading to the crystallization of a concern for language need to be conceptualized with reference to the historical milieu in which it gets consolidated. This further confirms that independent of the prevalent socio-economic and political context, the concern is likely to be misconstrued for obvious reasons. One can easily conceptualize this position with reference to India being a colony and its aftermath. During colonialism, the state was ideologically tilted in favour of those modes of governance which were supportive of its distinctive politico-ideological preferences. The nationalists' priorities were also equally unambiguous, namely, political freedom was the main goal with the belief that other nationalist aims were to be fulfilled with India being a free state following decolonization. The scene had however undergone a sea change with the transfer of power in 1947 when the nationalist held the saddles of power, and the concerns that were peripheral in the past became, for obvious reasons, most critical in their design for governance for independent India. It is therefore no surprise that the founding fathers devoted a great deal of energy to delve into some of the significant socio-political issues, including that of language, in the Constituent Assembly. In other words, in their concern for nation-building in a context in which colonialism seems to have left an indelible print, they were extremely careful while charting out the preferred courses for a newly independent nation, like India.

Language always remained an area of serious concern for the nationalists because it was not only an emotive issue, it was also an issue which could trigger alienation among the communities. The situation was further aggravated by the rising importance of the elites who appeared to have been favourably tilted in favour of English given its important historical role as a link language during the nationalist struggle. In other words, despite not being fascinated, a large number of Indians were drawn to English since it was a passport to public jobs and also social respectability among the elites, both Indian and British. With government patronage, English virtually became a *lingua franca* in India, especially among those who were connected with governance. There were two consequences: on the one hand, the sustained loyalty of the Indians to English was certainly one of the major factors impeding the growth of Indian languages since they lacked the market value in comparison with English; it also had a positive consequence, on the other, in the sense that the acceptance of English by the nationalists regardless of region, class, caste or ethnicity led to the evolution of 'a linking language' which acted as a bridge among them despite being socio-culturally diverse.

Given the obvious importance of language which is more than a mere means of communication, the chapter concentrates on those aspects of the debates that the Constituent Assembly witnessed in this regard. Furthermore, since language played a critical role in nation-building in India, the chapter also dwells on some of the significant endeavours that the Indian state had undertaken in the aftermath of the promulgation of the 1950 Constitution.

Historical Antecedents

A cursory look at the trajectory of the nationalist movement reveals that the nationalists held a very distinct view in so far as language was concerned presumably because of its critical importance in nation-building. Gandhi and his colleagues were keen to develop a linking language cutting across linguistic barriers, which the Constituent Assembly took into account while being involved in deciding an appropriate language policy for the country. The task that the Assembly undertook did not seem to be an easy one because (a) there was hardly an Indian language which was acceptable-to-all, and (b) the arguments in favour of evolving Hindi as 'a national' language had hardly had support from the communities located in the southern part of India. The founding fathers were thus drawn to a difficult situation which they handled in an innovative way by drawing on their unique approach to the issue. As the following discussion demonstrates, by being sensitive to India's unique linguistic texture, the framers evolved an equally unique formula which was neither tilted in favour of communal demands nor being blind to the arguments supportive of English as a connecting language. It was therefore sheer pragmatism that finally led to the articulation of specific provisions by the founding fathers in the Assembly which will be discussed further:

That the discussion on language was likely to generate heat was well anticipated by the Assembly which the President of the Assembly, Rajendra Prasad articulated just before the deliberation had begun. Being aware that it was 'agitating the minds of the members for some time',[1] Prasad thus made an appeal to them not to be partisan in their approach to the issue since 'it will have to be carried out by the country as a whole'.[2] The issue was of immense importance which he highlighted by saying that 'there is no other item in the whole of Constitution of the country which will be required to be implemented from day to day, from hour to hour . . . and from minute to minute in actual practice'.[3] Opposing the principle of 'majority-driven decision', he further argued that 'even if we succeed in getting a particular proposition passed by majority, if it does not meet the approval of any considerable section of people in the country—either in the north or in the south, the implementation of the Constitution will become a most difficult problem'.[4] With the setting of the tone of the debate, it was N Gopalaswami Ayyangar who devised a formula to evolve consensus on the language issue. After long drawn debates involving various segments of society, including the press, he deduced that opinion was unanimous in favour of having 'a common language [which] should be used for the official purposes of the Union'. This could be possible 'if we agreed to bid good bye to a language [English] on which, . . . we have built and achieved freedom [which led] some to violently oppose the decision, though, at the end, they agreed to the decision, not without a pang, of course'.[5] Before the idea was placed for debate, Ayyangar elaborated the model that he had in mind which became, later, known as 'the Ayyangar formula' which he expanded by saying that 'we should accept Hindi as the language for all official purposes of the Union under the new Constitution [which] involves that when that decision is adopted, we have to bid good-bye to a language on which many of us have been reared and on the strength of which . . . we have achieved our freedom'.[6] Aware that replacement of English by Hindi could not be done so instantaneously, he subjected the decision to the fulfilment of two 'subsidiary decisions': English language

> shall be kept for a number of years until Hindi could establish for itself a place, not merely because it is an Indian language, but because as a language it would be an efficient instrument for all that to say and do in the future and until Hindi established itself in a position in which English stands today for Union purposes. So we took the next decision, namely that for a period of fifteen years English should continue to be used for all purposes for which it is being used today and will be used at the commencement of the Constitution.[7]

As per the Ayyangar formula, 'the common language for India should be Hindi and the script should be the Devanagari script', and English would be allowed to retain its position as an official language so long as Hindi lacked the linguistic strength that English possessed. In his words:

---

[1] Rajendra Prasad's statement on 12 September 1949, *Constituent Assembly Debates*, Book No. 4, p. 1314.

[2] Ibid., p. 1314.

[3] Ibid., p. 1314.

[4] Ibid., p. 1314.

[5] N Gopalaswami Ayyangar (Madras), 12 September 1949, *Constituent Assembly Debates*, Book No. 4, p. 1319.

[6] Ibid., p. 1320.

[7] Ibid., p. 1320.

> We must admit that [Hindi] is not today sufficiently developed. It requires a lot of enrichment in several directions, it requires modernization, it requires to be imbibed with the capacity to absorb ideas, not merely ideas but styles and expressions and forms of speech from other languages. Hence, it is the duty of the State to promote the development of Hindi so that it may achieve all these enrichments and will in due course be sufficiently developed for replacing adequately the English language which we certainly contemplate should fad out our officially recognized proceedings and activities in due course of time.[8]

As soon as the Ayyangar formula was placed before the Assembly, it naturally provoked a fierce debate separating those supportive of Hindi and those who were its opponents. Algu Rai Shastri of United Provinces was one of the staunch supporters of Hindi being made the official language. Couching his argument in a familiar way, Shastri thus argued that 'English is not our language [which] the elites mastered under compulsion through great labours to serve the alien rulers; if they could master English [which] had been brought by the foreigners', he exhorted, 'it is hard to believe that they cannot master Hindi which is a language of their own country. [When one can] go through such hard toil and labour for mastering English', believed Shastri, 'one will have to put forth much less labour to learn Hindi which is much simpler than English and can, therefore, be learnt with much greater ease than that foreign language'.[9] Being persuaded by the argument that Ayyangar put forward to defend Hindi as a common language, Shastri seems to have been governed by the belief that linguistic unity was core to the national unity and with the departure of the British, it was necessary to strengthen a bond of fraternity among the Indians which appeared to have been considerably weakened due to colonialism.

The arguments for Hindi were however cut into pieces by those who found in the Ayyangar formula an evil design of imposing 'a regional language' on the country as a whole. One of the most persuasive arguments was offered by Shyama Prasad Mookherjee of West Bengal. As he suggested, given the fact that

> India has been a country of many languages, ... it has not been possible for anyone to force the acceptance of one language by all people in this country. [Disturbed by the Ayyangar formula, he further adumbrated that] if it is claimed by anyone that by passing an article in the Constitution of India, one language is going to be accepted by all, by a process of coercion, ... that will not be possible to achieve. Unity in diversity is India's keynote and must be achieved by a process of understanding and consent and for that a proper atmosphere has to be created.... That unity must be achieved by allowing those elements in the national life of our country, which are today vital, to function and function in dignity, in harmony and in self-respect. Today, it stands to the glory of India that we have so many languages from the north to the south, from west to the east, each one of which in its own way, has made contributions which have made what Indian life and civilization are today.[10]

The argument is simple: India's diverse linguistic texture was distinctive of her civilization and existence in the comity of nations. This needed to be protected not by imposing one language on the recalcitrant

---

[8] Ibid., pp. 1320–21.

[9] Algu Rai Shastri (United Provinces), 13 September 1949, *Constituent Assembly Debates*, Book No. 4, p. 1384.

[10] Shyama Prasad Mookherjee (West Bengal), 13 September 1949, *Constituent Assembly Debates*, Book No. 4, p. 1391.

people but by creating an atmosphere in which they held others in high esteem and dignity. Only through consensus, this could be possible, sensed Mookherjee. Hence he argued:

> If I belonged to a province where Hindi is the spoken language, I would have felt proud today of the agreement to which practically all the members of this House have voluntarily submitted themselves by accepting Hindi in Devnagari script as the official language of free India. This is the solid achievement which, I hope, those friends of mine who come from the Hindi-speaking provinces should appreciate.[11]

It was not Mookherjee who was alone in raising a voice of concern. His other colleagues had shared his concern. For instance, PC Chacko of United State of Travancore and Cochin argued the same point more or less following the point of view that Mookherjee had held. Chacko made two arguments in his defence. First, he emphasized:

> A national language can be decided upon only by mutual agreement; it cannot be done by taking votes. No language [as he further underlined,] can be imposed upon an unwilling people, . . . and no nation has ever succeeded in imposing the language of the majority upon the minority. [Secondly, he further stressed that] the national language for a great country like India . . . should be capable of expressing all the needs of modern civilization. Hindi may not be an appropriate language in that respect.[12]

In view of the obvious limitation of Hindi being a common language, Chacko thus recommended that 'English should continue to be used for a period to be fixed and the question of a national language should be left to the future Parliament'.[13] Being critical of the Ayyangar design, which smacked of 'Hindi imperialism', TT Krishnamachari shared the sentiment as follows:

> If we are going to be compelled to learn Hindi . . . I will not be willing to do it because of the amount of constraint that you put on me, [and] . . . will also mean the enslavement of the people who do not speak the language. This will foment further trouble [given the fact that] there are already elements in South India who want separation and it is up to us to tax the maximum strength we have in keeping those elements down, and my honourable friends in UP do not help us in any way by flogging their idea "Hindi Imperialism" to the maximum extent possible. It is up to my friends in UP to have a whole India; it is up to them to have a Hindi-India. The choice is theirs and they can incorporate it in this Constitution, and if we are left out, we will curse our luck and hope for better times to come'.[14]

While Krishnamachari did not seem to have been persuaded by the arguments supportive of Hindi being elevated to a common language, there were powerful voices which strongly defended the claim for Hindi. Not only did they insist on their claim in the Assembly they also campaigned vigorously for mobilizing public opinion in its favour, as it was evident when PD Tandon of United Provinces spoke in a public speech in Delhi on 7 August 1949 by emphasizing that 'those who oppose acceptance of Hindi as the

[11] Ibid., p. 1391.
[12] PC Chacko (United State of Travancore and Cochin), 13 September 1949, *Constituent Assembly Debates*, Book No. 4, p. 1396.
[13] Ibid., p. 1396.
[14] TT Krishnamachari (Madras), 5 November 1948, *Constituent Assembly Debates*, Book No. 2, p. 235.

national language and Nagari as the single national script ... are still following a policy of anti-national appeasement and are catering to communal aspirations'.[15] What Tandon stated had its resonance in the Assembly since a majority of the members, especially from the Hindi-speaking provinces, endorsed the claim for Hindi being made the national language. There were hardly dissenting voices and the so-called Hindi-wallahs acted as a bloc in the Assembly, and, for them, it was a foregone conclusion which led Granville Austin to comment that 'the Hindi-wallahs were ready to risk splitting the Assembly and the country in their unreasoning pursuit of uniformity'.[16] The Assembly therefore witnessed the most heated debates; Hindustani would not have been acceptable since it meant hegemony of a specific language group at the cost of the rest. Despite vehement opposition of the members, particularly from the south of India, an opinion was gradually mobilized in favour of Hindi being accepted as a common language for India. Accepting Hindi 'because it is a compromise solution', Kuladhar Chaliha from Assam also emphasized that he was attracted to Hindustani because he was 'struck by the dignity, flexibility, refinement of style, sweet intonations of that language' which will make it acceptable to all in due course'.[17] Seeking to defend his argument on the basis of the inner strength of Hindustani as a language, Chaliha appears to have set in motion those ideas which gradually gained precedence in the Assembly debates.

One of the most persuasive proponents of Hindustani was Jawaharlal Nehru who spoke convincingly while justifying his choice. As will be shown below, there are three parts of the argument which was made to support (a) why was language important for nation-building, (b) why English was not adequate for this purpose and (c) what could be the best solution under the present circumstances. In his long speech in the Assembly on 13 September 1949, he elaborated his point of view by saying that 'language is the most intimate thing [which] ... makes us aware of ourselves, ... makes us aware of our neighbour, ... makes us aware of our society [and] it makes us aware of other societies also. We have to be careful in choosing a common language especially in our country because it could lead to bitterness in society if ... we are partisan in our choice'.[18] Despite being appreciative of English as 'a great language [that] has done us a lot of good and we have learnt much from it and progressed much', he was not persuaded to argue for its continuity because 'no nation can become great on the basis of a foreign language [which] divides a nation into two strata or more—those who live in thought and action of a foreign tongue and those who live in another world'.[19] This was, he felt, an impediment to the rise of India as a nation. India needed 'a language of the people [and] not a language of the coterie, as English has become'.[20] Notwithstanding the visible contribution of English in India's nationhood, Nehru minced no words while criticizing those who held the forte for English because 'it created a gulf between us who knew English and those who did not know English and that was fatal for the progress of a nation'.[21] What was his suggestion? He made two important suggestions: first, while endorsing the Ayyangar formula supportive of making Hindustani the common language, he argued:

> It has to be done wisely in two ways: by making it an inclusive language and not an exclusive one, and include in it all the language elements in India which have gone to build it up with a

[15] *The Hindustan Times*, 8 August 1949.

[16] Granville Austin, *The Indian Constitution: Cornerstone of a Nation* (New Delhi: Oxford University Press, 1966), p. 292.

[17] Kuladhar Chaliha (Assam), 13 September 1949, *Constituent Assembly Debates*, Book No. 4, p. 1404.

[18] Jawaharlal Nehru, 13 September 1949, *Constituent Assembly Debates*, Book No. 4, pp. 1411–12.

[19] Ibid., p. 1412.

[20] Ibid., p. 1412.

[21] Ibid., p. 1416.

> streak of Urdu or a mixture of Hindustani—not by statute, but by allowing it to grow normally as it should grow; secondly, it is not forced down upon an unwilling people' [because] you just cannot force any language down the people or group who resist that; a foreign conqueror with the strength of the sword might try to do it, but history shows that even he has failed. In the democratic context of India, it is an impossibility. You have to win through the goodwill of those people, those groups in India in the various provinces whose mother tongue is not Hindi. You have to win the goodwill of those groups who speak ... some variation of Hindi, Urdu or Hindustani. If you try, whether you win or not, if do something which appears to the others as an authoritarian attempt to dominate and to force down something then you will fail in your endeavour.[22]

As a pragmatic nation-builder, Nehru, despite being persuaded to accept Hindustani as a common language, did not altogether reject English though he was aware that it led to a schism between 'the English-knowing elite and a large mass of our people not knowing English'. Nonetheless,

> English must continue to be a most important language in India which large number of people learn and perhaps learn compulsorily [because] it is far more important in the world today than it was when the British came here. It is undoubtedly today the nearest approach to an international language; it is not the international language certainly, but it is the biggest and the most widespread language in the world today, and if we want to have contacts with the world as we must, then how are we to have those contact unless we know foreign languages.... It is absurd for us to try to forget what we know or not take advantage of what we have learnt. But it will have to be inevitably a secondary language meant for a relatively restricted number of people.'[23]

As is evident, Nehru creatively blended the claim for a common *lingua franca* with the need for keeping English as it allowed India to remain in contact with foreign countries, especially those belonging to the British Empire where it is spoken. His colleague, Abul Kalam Azad endorsed his concern for a common language, but was not sure of the methods that the Ayyangar formula recommended. According to him, there were

> two great obstacles [which] stand in our way. [The first difficulty was that] there was no national language as such which can immediately take the place of English, [and hence] ... time is needed to evolve it, brush it and polish it. In view of this, none of our languages can all of a sudden claim the position of English.... The second obstacle is the non-existence of a common language in place of English ... which can be that language which is widely read and written alike throughout the whole country. No doubt, the language of Northern India is widely spoken and understood: but, firstly, it is not spoken and written elsewhere, and secondly, the South does not come under its domain. There you will come across only a very small section of population which can express itself in broken Hindi. We have got to admit that so far as language is concerned North and South are two different parts. The union of North and South

[22] Ibid., pp. 1416–17.
[23] Jawaharlal Nehru, 13 September 1949, *Constituent Assembly Debates*, Book No. 4, p. 1416.

> has been made possible only through the medium of English. If today we give up English then this linguistic relationship will cease to exist'.[24]

Like Nehru, Azad was sensitive of the circumstances. It was really a tricky situation: English was not accepted since it represented colonialism and yet its utility in India's growth as a nation could not be disputed. Hindustani did not seem to have received all-round support from the Assembly members; instead, those from the eastern and southern parts of India vehemently criticised the endeavour as being an imposition on them. Nonetheless, the members agreed, at the end, to the Ayyangar formula which endorsed the continuity of English for fifteen years as the official language and the acceptance of Hindustani (in Devnagari script) as the connecting language. Besides the discussion in the Assembly, the issue was thoroughly debated in the Congress Working Committee where Nehru strongly defended the formula since (a) it was possibly the best option under the circumstances and (b) it also corresponded with Gandhi's preference for Hindustani, which represented 'a creative blending of Hindi with Urdu, neither highly Sanskritized, nor highly Persianized nor Arabianized'.[25] For most of the members, the Ayyangar formula was a temporary measure as they felt that future parliament would devise a new design if the existent one appeared inappropriate for the requirements of the new generation. Although there were differences among the members, they were hardly impediments which led to the adoption of the Ayyangar formula. Hence, in his concluding remarks, Rajendra Prasad, the President of the Assembly, while congratulating his colleagues, mentioned:

> The language issue, if it was not resolved the way it had been, would have separated us. Let us imagine what would have happened if the South had not accepted the Hindi language and the Devnagari script. If we had accepted the Swiss formula [which accorded constitutional recognition to three languages, German, French and Italian], we had to recognize as many languages as they are in existence for central administrative purposes to keep together all the provinces and bind them together; this would have caused confusion and put administration in unnecessary hassles.

So, Hindustani in Devnagari script, was accepted because it was certain to create a unity among the Indians which was sadly missing so far. In other words, it was thus believed by the Assembly members that a *lingua franca* was fundamental to the evolution of a nation and it was indigenous in character it would instantaneously bring together disparate communities for the sake of the nation. For Prasad, it was perhaps 'the wisest thing possible' under the circumstances that members had accomplished, which he articulated as follows:

> The language that we shall use in the Centre will tend to bring us together nearer and nearer. ... [I]n place of English we have adopted an Indian language [which] will bring us closer together, particularly because our tradition is the same, our culture is the same, and everything that goes to make our civilization is the same. Therefore if we did not accept this formula, the result would have been either a large number of languages to be used, for the country as a

[24] Abul Kalam Azad (United Provinces) 13 September 1949, *Constituent Assembly Debates*, Book No. 4, p. 1455.

[25] MK Gandhi, 'A Common Script', *Young India*, *Collected Works of Mahatma Gandhi*, Vol. 32, p. 344. http://www.gandhiserve.org/cwmg/VOL032.PDF (accessed 13 December 2016).

whole, or separation of provinces which did not like to submit or accept any particular language under pressure.[26]

This was a stupendous achievement for a young nation like India, Prasad felt, which 'will have far-reaching consequences in building up the country in future'.[27] There were, however, members who accepted the decision with a caution since 'Hindi is a provincial language and there are languages in which literature is far more rich' by saying that the best way of persuading people in the non-Hindi speaking areas 'is not with the strength of vote, ... but by persuasion'.[28] For some like Shrimati G Durgabai (Madras), the agreement over the acceptance of Hindustani was a sacrifice that members made 'for the sake of satisfying the sentiments of friends who have accepted Hindi in Devanagari script. It is no less sacrifice for us', she further added, 'to have had to depart from a principle, which we have all along fought for and lived for. This departure means a very serious inconvenience to us and it is not without a pang that we have agreed to this departure'.[29] So, the imbroglio over language seems to have been resolved as a compromise in which members, after having expressed their reservation on the formula, agreed as perhaps the best option, available at that point of time.

Reviewing the Argument

Volumes V to IX of the Constituent Assembly Debates bear a testimony to the fact that the debates on language in the Constituent Assembly were essentially centred on the following questions:

1. Should India have a national language?
2. Should India settle for an official language rather than a national language?
3. Does India have a *lingua franca* that connects this vast country from east to west, north to south?
4. Should Hindi or Hindustani be declared the official language of the Union?
5. Should English be given the same status of the official language, if so, for how many years?
6. What would be the status of Sanskrit, considered the 'mother language', in India?
7. How should the provincial governments decide on the official languages for the states?
8. What should be the official language in legislature, executive and judiciary?
9. What should be the language for inter-provincial communication, and communication between the Centre and the States?

Finding answers to these questions was never easy, especially when the country was passing through some-never-happened-experience in its history, society and politics. The members of the Assembly in general, and those of the Drafting Committee in particular had to invest much of their collective wit to negotiate with the larger issues concerning Hindi versus English, Hindi versus Hindustani and national language versus official language. As has been alluded to earlier, reaching unique resolutions to these contentious questions, each of which had a strong parochial undertone, always appeared a mission impossible to the Assembly. The members of the Assembly did not attempt the impossible; they did not

[26] Rajendra Prasad, 14 September 1949, *Constituent Assembly Debates*, Book No. 4, p. 1493.
[27] Ibid., p. 1493.
[28] NV Gadgil (Bombay), 13 September 1949, *Constituent Assembly Debates*, Book No. 4, p. 1373.
[29] Shrimati G Durgabai (Madras), 14 September 1949, *Constituent Assembly Debates*, Book No. 4, p. 1428.

lay down in the language provisions of the Constitution that one language should be spoken over all India. Yet they could not avoid giving one of the regional languages a special status, so they provided, not that there be a 'national language', but using a tactful euphemism, that Hindi should be the 'link language of the Union'. Hindi would also be used for inter-provincial communication. For an initial period of fifteen years, however, English was to continue to serve as the official language. After this time, Hindi would supplant English unless Parliament legislated otherwise; English would be retained for uses in courts and for official texts after the expiration of the fifteen year period until Parliament otherwise legislated. The provincial governments were permitted to choose one of the regional languages, or English, for the conduct of their own affairs and the major regional languages were listed in a schedule to the Constitution. Finally, the members also attempted a definition of Hindi, and provided for language commissions to report on the language situation and on how to further the spread of the 'official language'. The language provisions are thus a compromise.

Notwithstanding differences among the members, the Ayyangar formula brought them together for the sake of national unity in a context when this was being threatened following the partition-related violence. This was also a master stroke by the Congress leadership which defended their argument in defence of Hindustani as capable of cementing a bond among the disparate communities in India. The argument had received extra mileage since the Ayyangar formula was prepared by a Congressman from the southern part of India where Hindustani was neither popular nor had an emotional attachment. The fact that it was endorsed by a south Indian who, despite not being a native Hindi speaker, was persuaded by the nationalist arguments in favour of Hindustani, justified the Congress claim that the proposed linguistic design was neither partisan nor driven by sectional interests. A contentious issue was thus resolved through extensive debates in the Assembly finally leading to the articulation of specific provisions for a *lingua franca* in India which will receive attention in the following paragraphs:

Constitutional Provisions[30]

The outcome of the debates in the Constituent Assembly was a broad array of constitutional provisions which have become 'sites of ongoing constitutional contestation in post-independence India'.[31] The majority of the provisions relating to language are contained in Part XVII of the Constitution of India. With four Chapters and nine Articles, this Part deals with (a) language of the Union (Articles 343 and 344), (b) regional languages (Articles 345, 346, 347), (c) language of the Supreme Court, High Courts etc. (Articles 348 and 349), and (d) special directives (Articles 351 and 352). Besides Part XVII, there are important provisions in the Constitution which relate to the linguistic issues. For instance, Article 120 and 210 deal with the language of the legislative proceedings in Parliament and state assemblies respectively. The Right to Freedom of Religion, especially Articles 29 and 30 guarantees the right of the linguistic minorities to protect their languages. Furthermore, the Eighth Schedule, by providing constitutional recognition to eighteen of the Indian languages as official languages, remains a critical part of the provisions guaranteeing the distinct linguistic identity of the provinces. Apart from these explicit provisions, Article 3 is also important in this regard for it provides authority to Parliament to change boundaries of the existing

[30] I have written this section in collaboration with Dr Joydeep Biswas of the Department of Economics, Cachar College, Silchar, Assam.

[31] Sujit Choudhury, 'Language', in *The Oxford Handbook of the Indian Constitution*, eds. Sujit Choudhury, Madhav Khosla and Pratap Bhanu Mehta (New Delhi: Oxford University Press, 2016), p. 180.

provinces and also to create new provinces in case Parliament deems it appropriate. As history shows, this Article has been used primarily to accommodate the demands for linguistic reorganization.

The constitutional safeguards for the linguistic minorities in India are broadly covered under the Fundamental Rights (Part III) and the Official Language (Part XVII). Under the Fundamental Rights, while Articles 29 and 30 provide direct protection to the rights of the linguistic minorities, Article 14, 15 and 16 act as a sort of secondary safeguard, only when interpreted in a favourable manner.

Article 29(1) states that 'Any section of the citizens residing in the territory of India or any part thereof having a distinct *language, script* or culture of its own shall have the right to conserve the same. Article 29(2) goes as 'No citizen shall be denied admission into any education institute maintained by the State or receiving aid out of the State funds on grounds only of religion, race, caste, *language* or any of them.' Article 30(1) says: 'All minorities, whether based on religion or *language*, shall have the right to establish and administer education institutes of their choice'. Article 30(2): 'The State shall not, in granting aid to educational institutions, discriminate against any educational institution on the ground that it is under the management of a minority, whether based on religion or *language*.' (Italics mine)

Even as nowhere therein 'language' is explicitly mentioned, the linguistic minorities may nonetheless take shelter under the expanded connotation of Article 14 (Equality before law), Article 15 (Prohibition of discrimination on grounds of religion, race, caste, sex or place of birth), and Article 16 (Equality of opportunity in matters of public appointment).

Under the Part XVII of the Constitution, the following safeguards for the minor language groups are enumerated.

Article 347: 'On a demand being made in that behalf the President may, if he is satisfied that a substantial proportion of the population of a State desire the use of any language spoken by them to be recognized by that State, direct that such language shall also be officially recognized throughout that State or any part thereof for such purpose as he may specify.'

Article 350: 'Every person shall be entitled to submit a representation for the redress of any grievance to any officer or authority of the Union or a State in any of the languages used in the Union or in the State, as the case may be.'

Article 350(A): 'It shall be the endeavour of every State and of every local authority within the State to provide adequate facilities for instruction in the mother-tongue at the primary stage of education to children belonging to linguistic minority groups; and the President may issue such directions to any State as he considers necessary or proper for securing the provision of such facilities.'

Article 350(B): '1) There shall be a Special Officer for linguistic minorities to be appointed by the President. 2) It shall be the duty of the Special Officer to investigate all matters relating to the safeguards provided for linguistic minorities under the Constitution and report to the President, upon those matters at such intervals as the President may direct, and the President shall cause all such reports to be laid before each House of Parliament, and sent to the Governments of the States concerned.'

Given the justiciable nature of the provisions enumerated under the Part III of the Constitution vide Article 32(1–4) it is but obvious that the State is forcefully encouraging both promotion and preservation of language and script and also is refraining from any kind of discrimination on the ground of language when it comes to the subject of distribution of public outlay to educational institutions. But a reading of some other provisions under the Part XVII of the Constitution gives us an incontrovertible impression that the will of the makers of the Constitution was indeed 'half-hearted'. The Directive for development of the Hindi language under Article 351 of the same Part reads as: 'It shall be the duty of the Union to promote the spread of the Hindi language, to develop it so that it may serve as the medium of expression for all the elements of the composite culture of India and to secure its enrichment. . .'

In the first place, Article 350(A) and 350(B) did not form part of the original Constitution, implying thereby that there was absolutely no mechanism to serve the case of the 'linguistic minority' provided for by the Constituent Assembly. Interestingly enough, the very word 'linguistic minority' is still absent in the 'holy book'. On the recommendation of the States Reorganization Commission these two Articles were inserted into the Constitution vide the Seventh Constitution Amendment Act, 1956. The Special Officer under the Article 350(B) was designated as the 'Commissioner for Linguistic Minorities in India (CLM).' The office of the CLM under the Ministry of Minority Affairs started functioning in July 1957 only.

Notwithstanding the safeguards to the linguistic minorities accorded by the provisions in the Part III and the Articles 350(A and B) taken together, the contents of the Article 351 clearly underline the constitutional bias towards the Official Language' in India for the following reasons: *first*, the language provisions of the Constitution specifically acknowledge the acceptance of Hindi as the dominant language by the Indian state even as it is spoken by slightly over 24 per cent of the citizens at present. *Second*, the State takes unto itself the 'duty' of promoting the spread of Hindi and its enrichment. *Third*, there is a bizarre announcement that one language (Hindi) is capable of being elevated to the status of the single 'medium of expression' for 'all the elements of the composite culture of India'. *Fourth*, the Constitutional provisions are not only overlapping and self-contradictory in respect of linguistic safeguards, they create a peculiar set up in a working democracy where the mighty Indian State with all its resources and forces is sponsoring the dominant language, but still asking its marginalized, disadvantaged, small linguistic minority groups to preserve and promote their endangered language and scripts! Such an uneven battle for cultural assertion could be the classic case of oxymoronic expression in an otherwise accommodative Constitution of India.

Contemporary Developments

A perusal of India's recent political history reveals that the claim for distinctive linguistic status, backed by strong political mobilization, led to the creation of a number of states though the Constituent Assembly never endorsed the idea of linguistic provinces. Article 345 allows the state to adopt, by law, 'any one or more of the languages in use in the State or Hindi as the language or languages to be used for all or any of the official purposes of that State'. This is an indication of the support that the Constitution guarantees if Hindi is adopted as the official language; furthermore, the constitutional authorization to the parliament for the creation of a new province or redrawing of the boundaries of the prevalent provinces is another supportive enactment for those championing the cause of the linguistic minorities. There are instances to show that as soon as issues relating to the selection of official language did not get resolved at the level of the state assemblies, they were immediately sent to Parliament for resolution which later became a demand for a new province. The processes leading to the formation of the erstwhile Andhra Pradesh for the Telugu-speaking people are illustrative here.

A historical account of the commissions that were appointed to address the concern of the linguistic minorities also endorses the fact they were taken to be as the safety valves for defusing crisis. The Linguistic Provinces Commission (also known as Dar Commission since it was presided over by Justice SK Dar) of 1948 was rejected especially in the South as it was seen as clearly prejudiced against their demands for recognition of the languages, being spoken there. This was followed by the constitution of the Congress Linguistic Provinces Committee in 1949 which strongly recommended for the creation of Andhra State (later it became Andhra Pradesh) with the Telugu-speaking people in the erstwhile Madras state. This 1949 Committee led to the formation of the State Reorganization Commission in 1956 which played a critical role in the formation of linguistic states in India. One of the factors that the Commission took into account while recommending for a new state or change of boundary of the prevalent state was language. In order to protect the distinctive linguistic character of the areas, the Commission strongly felt that this was a natural demand of the people and needed to be endorsed for sustaining India's multicultural persona. Following the Commission's recommendations, Parliament created Assam, Bihar, Bombay, Jammu and Kashmir, Kerala, Madhya Pradesh, Madras State (later Tamil Nadu), Mysore State (later Karnataka), Orissa and Punjab. Bombay state was divided, the Gujarati speaking areas were demarcated and Gujarat was born in 1960. Punjab was divided and Haryana was created in 1966.

The formation of linguistic states was a victory of popular will. The Constituent Assembly endeavoured hard to hegemonize India's cultural life by imposing Hindustani which was not even remotely connected with any of the languages in the South of India, and yet, it did not work out, as the past history has shown. A strong political will for linguistic states developed and prevailed over the political machinations of the ruling authority that also did not seem to be terribly favourable to this demand. The movements for linguistic states thus revealed 'an extraordinary depth of popular will, in the consolidation of which … language proved a more powerful marker of identity than caste or religion'.[32] A cursory study of the India's recent political history confirms that the insistence on linguistic identity is, under no circumstances, an impediment to the consolidation of national unity; instead, it contributes to the strengthening of the nation by giving adequate space to the constituent provinces.

Concluding Observations

Part XVII of the Constitution of India is an important segment of the constitutional design of governance that had emerged after intensive deliberations in the Constituent Assembly in which contrasting arguments were marshalled in favour of one opinion or the other. Members were divided, and yet, at the end, they converged on an identical point of view. Several points of view had emerged, as shown earlier, which were never allowed to become divisive presumably because of the effective role that the inner circle within the Congress had played. The discussions in the Assembly were thus kept within the set parameters which no members generally trespassed. As is argued earlier, despite being unhappy with the attempt to impose Hindustani, those who held this argument did not insist to the point of disrupting the flow of the discussion which means that at a certain level the members of the Assembly agreed to the decision that was arrived at following the debates in the Assembly. This also confirms that in spite of holding different, if not contrarian, viewpoints, the members did not mind being in agreement with what came out after fierce debates in the Assembly which further underlines their faith in the democratic processes.

The formation of the linguistic provinces also denotes that the constitutional approach to a contentious issue does not remain static. Whereas the members of the Assembly were keen to consolidate the so-called Indianness by evolving a cementing language, Hindustani, their colleagues in independent India seem to have held a completely different point of view which was reflected in their approval of the creation of linguistic provinces. What explains this variation in approaches is the changed context and also the parameters of governance in a democratic set-up. A democratic polity ceases to be one unless it has mechanisms to effectively address differences and defuse crisis, if differences lead to one. With the recommendations of the State Reorganization Commission in 1956 for linguistic states, the circle was

[32] Ramchandra Guha, *India after Gandhi: The History of World's Largest Democracy* (New Delhi: Picador, 2007), pp. 198–99.

complete which also revealed that the concern for linguistic identity was not, at all, incompatible with the consolidation of a collectivity in the name of a nation.

Part XVII is perhaps one of those chapters which not merely addresses the linguistic issues, it also draws our attention to the so-called silent zones of the Constitution of India. It is therefore not surprising to find that what the Constituent Assembly upheld to sustain India as a unified polity had undergone a sea change following the consolidation of movements in favour linguistic states. Even the linguistic design for temporarily privileging English due to contingent socio-political circumstances, was hardly overturned, but was allowed to remain even after the expiry of the constitutionally-stipulated fifteen years' embargo. English is being continued along with the 22 regional languages, being included in the Eighth Schedule. The reasons are to be located in the political processes that are at work since the inauguration of the 1950 Constitution which further means that the cataclysmic role of the constitutional provisions is likely to be compromised unless they are complemented by politico-ideological processes arising out of a favourably tilted socio-economic and political environment. Part XVII thus stands out for being ideologically innovative and politically vibrant chapter of the Constitution which is both a compilation of relevant provisions and also epitomizes a quest for an appropriate constitutional design to address the concern of a linguistically diverse polity, like India.

Review Questions

1. **Elaborate the provisions in Part XVII of the Constitution of India.**
2. **How did the founding fathers address the question of language in the Constituent Assembly? Elaborate.**
3. **What are the constitutional guarantees for linguistic minorities? Elaborate.**
4. **Why was English preferred as a link language by the founding fathers? Elaborate.**
5. **Critically evaluate the constitutional provisions relating to the creation of provinces on the basis of language.**
6. **The issue of language assumes significance in volatile political circumstances. Do you agree with this view? Elaborate your response.**
7. **What are the arguments, marshalled by the framers of the Constitution of India in favour Hindi in Devanagari scripts? Elaborate.**
8. **What are the counter-arguments, being made by those opposed to Hindi being elevated to being 'a national language'? Elaborate.**
9. **It is difficult to have a national policy on language in India. Do you agree? Elaborate.**
10. **In a socio-culturally society like India, the concern for linguistic rights is obvious. Do you agree with this view? Elaborate.**

Chapter

9

Constitutionalizing Reservation in India

Learning Objectives

- To understand how reservation is a means for social justice
- To grasp how the Constitution of India address the issue of reservation
- To conceptualize reservation in the light of specific judicial verdicts in this regard

Reservation is a tool to ensure equality of status and opportunity. The socio-economic backwardness of communities due to age-old exploitation for reasons connected with well-entrenched social prejudices is sought to be addressed by putting in place multiples schemes of reservation for public jobs and other facilities. The purpose is to bring this socio-economically excluded group at par with other communities. This is, in other words, an inclusive design to fulfil the constitutional promise of creating an egalitarian India. Two important issues with significant socio-political implications surface with the acceptance of reservation as a legitimate means to strike a social balance: on the one hand, with the promulgation of schemes for reservation, it was accepted that there had been exploitation of a specific group of people due to accident of birth, and it was socially justified to keep them socio-economically subservient to the dominant communities. In the changed circumstances, this system was, on the other, not only despised and a strong voice had emerged for its repeal, and powerful arguments, backed by equally powerful social movements and political campaigns, were offered for 'compensatory discrimination' or 'reverse discrimination' whereby the rights of the historically discriminated communities were to be privileged. This appeared 'fair' from the point of establishing substantive equality which was denied to communities due to their specific social lineages. The purpose of this chapter is to conceptualize the arguments of reservation not only with reference to the ideas of the founding fathers which were articulated in the Constituent Assembly but also on the basis of the judicial interventions in this regard. A study of the arguments in its favour and those against reservation reveals that this is an area of fierce contestation then and now in independent India, presumably because of its consequences: it is positive for those being benefitted and naturally negative for those adversely affected.

Historicizing the Arguments

Reservation through affirmative action is drawn on the desire for social justice which is justified in situations where 'exclusion takes the form of discrimination against identifiable groups defined by race, caste, religion, gender or ethnicity'. In such circumstances, it is difficult to enforce 'a law of equal opportunities' which creates conditions for affirmative action. In other words, given the fact that discrimination is historically entrenched, it is perfectly appropriate to uphold positive discrimination 'in favour of the underprivileged or excluded . . . as a corrective to compensate for embedded discrimination'. In real terms, an affirmative action entails

> a set of policies and practices that are used to create equal opportunity and maximum diversity. These target primarily workplaces and educational institutions while using race, caste, gender or ethnicity a factors that must be taken into account when employment or admissions decisions are made. The object is to redress perceived disadvantages attributable to overt institutional or involuntary discrimination.[1]

Fundamental here is the idea that historically defended discriminatory practices seem to have contributed to a situation when discriminatory legislations appear to have become compatible with social concerns. Tuned to the concern for instituting a society of equals, or for the sake of social justice, the argument appears to have been drawn on a wider ideological dispensation for democratic governance.

The phenomenon of reservation or compensatory discrimination received adequate attention from both Gandhi and BR Ambedkar. For Gandhi, social discrimination was necessarily 'a social evil' which could be easily mitigated through 'moral re-education of the upper castes'; while, for Ambedkar, it was embedded in the structured violence and coercion that could be effectively addressed by stern political action, including legally endorsed compensatory discrimination.[2] Ambedkar's perception enables us to conceptualize 'various challenges to homogeneous national identity posed by struggles around various markers of identity (caste, gender, region and so forth) which have contributed to a differentiated entry into the domain of citizenship'.[3] By strongly arguing for 'differentiated citizenship' as perhaps the most effective means to establish equality and fraternity in the liberal sense, Ambedkar thus argued for a political scheme whereby '[u]niversalist ideas of rights had to give way for positive discrimination in favour of the oppressed'.[4] He was the first of the Indian thinkers to have advocated group-differentiated rights by seeking to institute 'special cultural rights for religious minorities, legislative quotas or the downtrodden castes and tribe, and preferential treatment in education and government employment for backward groups'.[5] The idea gained ground in the Constituent Assembly when it discussed reservation for the historically underprivileged sections because of well-entrenched social prejudices. The most revealing of the comments was made by M Ananthaayanam Ayyangar when he stated that 'the first requisite is that all appointments shall be made in the interests of public administration on merit alone. But, having regard to the conditions of our country, there must be some provision in favour of those persons who . . . may not be able to come up to the mark. There must be some limitation to it'.[6] Ambedkar defended the notion of differentiated citizenship in his witness before the Southborough Committee of 1919 and Round Table

[1] Deepak Nayyar, 'Discrimination and Justice: Beyond Affirmative Action', *Economic and Political Weekly*, 15 October 2011, p. 55.

[2] Mark Galanter, *Competing Equalities: Law and the Backward Classes in India* (Delhi: Oxford University Press, 1974).

[3] Anupama Rao, 'Arguing Against Inclusion', *Economic and Political Weekly*, 22 February 1997, p. 428.

[4] CA Bayly, *Recovering Liberties: Indian Thought in the Age of Liberalism and Empire* (Cambridge: Cambridge University Press, 2012), p. 305.

[5] Rochana Bajpai, 'Liberalism in India: A Sketch', in *Liberalism as Ideology: Essays in Honour of Michael Freeden*, eds. Ben Jackson and Mark Stears (New York: Oxford University Press, 2012) p. 75.

[6] M Ananthasayanam Ayyangar (Madras), 24 May 1949, *Constituent Assembly Debates*, Book No. 3, pp. 252–53.

Conference 1932 which received adequate attention by his colleagues in the Constituent Assembly. It will thus not be an exaggeration to suggest that his was a powerful voice in favour of 'a liberal egalitarian framework for addressing group-based inequalities' to create a system of constitutional governance, which, despite being discriminatory, was perhaps the most useful tool of levelling the prevalent socio-economic imbalances for reasons which were never seriously interrogated in the past.[7] In other words, conceptually defensible and politically persuasive, the arguments for group-differentiated rights created a space for compensatory discrimination as perhaps the most legitimate means to weed out the roots of inequality arising out of essentially artificial designs of social engineering, perpetuated by the socio-economically dominant sections.

Historical Antecedents

Embedded discrimination produced strong rationale for reservation in India. BR Ambedkar and his colleagues who were on the same wavelength as him were the main architects of a very persuasive design of reservation in the 1950 Constitution of India. The model that was followed in India had two attributes: the first was an affirmative action in favour of the scheduled castes (SCs) and scheduled tribes (STs); as discrimination was 'embedded in history, caste was the defining basis'. The second was 'proportional reservation' entailing quotas roughly in conformity with their proportion in the total population which was 15 per cent for SCs and seven-and-a half for the STs at that time.[8]

The Constituent Assembly debated the issue of reservation intensively. There were supporters and opponents as well. In order to correct a historical wrong, reservation for the SCs was most appropriate, argued Mohammad Ismail Sahib of Madras. Defending his argument, he further argued that the SCs

> fully deserve it; they are a class of people who have been the victims of oppression and so many difficulties for ages; and, therefore, now when we are emerging into the world of freedom, it is only right that they should also be given the freedom of coming before the world and saying what they want to say.[9]

The sentiment was pursued by Jagat Narain Lal of Bihar who also felt that due to justified socio-economic reasons, the SCs needed reservation in the legislature and also public employment. He defended reservation by saying that 'the Scheduled Castes have been given reservation not on grounds of religion at all; they form part and parcel for the Hindu community and they have been given reservations apparently and clearly on grounds of their economic, social and educational backgrounds'.[10] This is the crux of the argument in favour of reservation which not only seeks 'to interrogate the system of hierarchical social relations [but also] more fundamentally it seeks to alter the social relations along egalitarian lines'.[11] The idea was articulated clearly by S Nagappa in his justification for reservation when he stated that the scheduled castes

[7] Bajpai, 'Liberalism in India: A Sketch', p. 75.

[8] Deepak Nayyar, 'Discrimination and Justice: Beyond Affirmative Action', *Economic and Political Weekly*, 15 October 2011, p. 56.

[9] Mohammad Ismail Sahib (Madras), 25 May 1949, *Constituent Assembly Debates*, Book No. 3, p. 280.

[10] Jagat Narain Lal (Bihar), 25 May 1949, *Constituent Assembly Debates*, Book No. 3, p. 308.

[11] Gopal Guru, 'Social Justice', in *The Oxford Companion to Politics in India*, eds. Niraja Gopal Jayal and Pratap Bhanu Mehta (New Delhi: Oxford University Press, 2010), p. 365.

> are lagging behind other communities due to reasons connected with India's peculiar social history, [and hence] reservation is justified. . . . I am prepared for the abolition of the reservation provided every Harijan family gets ten acres of wet land, twenty acres of dry land and all the children of Harijans are given education, free of cost, upto the university level and given one-fifth of the key posts either in the civilian departments or in the military departments.'[12]

In substance, reservation was upheld by the SC representatives in the Assembly since it was perhaps the only corrective means to weed out the age-old socio-economic discrimination for the community. The SCs needed to be privileged to bring them to the socio-economic level of advantages that the other communities had already reached. This was fair and legitimate. Although a majority of the Assembly members agreed to reservation for the SCs and STs, there were dissenting voices too which drew on the fact that it was going to be appropriated by the well-off sections within these socially underprivileged sections of the SCs and STs. Based on his understanding of social relations in a typical Marxist perspective, Mahavir Tyagi of United Provinces thus elaborated his argument for opposing reservation by saying that advantages of reservations were reaped by

> a selected few belonging to Scheduled Castes. This is not fair [because] it is the individual or family which gets benefitted. Hence, . . . instead of caste [being the basis of] of reservation, it should be class. . . . In place of the Scheduled Caste, the landless labourers, the cobblers or those persons who do similar jobs and who do not get enough to live, should be given reservation for employment and other public benefits. By allowing caste reservation, let us not re-inject the poisonous virus which the Britisher has introduced into our body politics. Instead of Scheduled Castes, minorities be protected . . . on class basis. Let cobblers, washer men and similar other classes be given reservation.[13]

While Mahavir Tyagi insisted on class criteria, ZH Lari (United Provinces) drew attention to the narrow political calculations behind the insistence on reservation of legislative seats for SCs and STs. Since 'there is a suspicion in some minds that possibly we will not be able to overcome the prejudices of the caste', Lari felt, 'some of the members are demanding reservation for SCs and STs'.[14] The apprehension that 'we will not be able to send sufficient number of Scheduled Castes to the Legislature' did not seem to be unfounded given the increasing resentment of the SC members against the Congress for being indifferent to their genuine socio-economic causes. By insisting that instead of giving them reservation 'temporarily', they should be empowered to stand on their own, once they 'are awake, they can decide what is best for them as a community'.[15]

As the above-mentioned deliberations on reservation in the Assembly show, there are three major viewpoints that appear to have guided the members when they supported reservation as a matter of policy. First, it was strongly felt by members regardless of ideological differences that these socio-economically underprivileged communities, SCs and STs, were legitimately entitled to reservation for the sake of common well-being; second, this was possible only through constitutional guarantee since the social prejudices against them remained very strong and possibly well-entrenched, and third, it was also assumed, rather

[12] S Nagappa (Madras), 25 May 1949, *Constituent Assembly Debates*, Book No. 3, pp. 292–93.
[13] Mahavir Tyagi (United Provinces), 26 May 1949, *Constituent Assembly Debates*, Book No. 3, pp. 344–45.
[14] ZH Lari (United Provinces), 25 May 1949, *Constituent Assembly Debates*, Book No. 3, p. 288.
[15] Ibid., p. 288.

implicitly, that with constitutional provisions, which were institutionally backed, the SCs and STs would gradually become integral to India's constitutional democracy. Once they were adequately empowered they no longer required artificial prop like reservation to realize their goal which they could do on their own.

Constitutional Provisions

The Constitution of India recognizes three main beneficiaries of reservation policy: SCs, STs and Other Backward Classes (OBCs). Of these identified castes, the SCs were also given constitutional protection in the 1935 Government of India Act which entailed 'specific benefits' to them. Some of the princely state in pre-independent India allowed the SCs to enjoy extra benefits just to enable them to come to the level of other 'forward' castes. The 1935 Act secluded those caste groups which were considered 'untouchables' in a schedule to the Act; hence they are so named. In contemporary ideological discourses, they are also known as 'depressed classes' while for Gandhi, they were 'Harijans' and BR Ambedkar preferred to identify them as 'Dalits'. Whatever may have been the nomenclature, they have been socially backward and economically marginalized. Hence, they deserved special privileges which the constitution-makers also endorsed and specific provisions were devised accordingly. Similar is the case in regard to the STs who, being the aboriginal, were also given privileges which would help them to self-actualize in a context when contrarians seemed to have put obstacles to their distinct existence. This is a global phenomenon: in the US, the native Americans, popularly known as Red Indians, or in Australia, the aboriginals, or in New Zealand, the Maoris were recognized being distinct communities, and are given constitutional guarantee for privileges which other communities do not have. This does not seem to be unfair in view of the growing importance of the idea of society being inclusive; in such a situation, the idea of 'differentiated rights' does not appear to be non-constitutional. Therefore, the argument for constitutional guarantee for specific segments of the demography is justified from the point of the view creating an inclusive society which is not, at all, tilted in favour of the caste groups which are historically dominant by virtue of the accident of birth. Besides the SCs and STs, there is another caste group, known as OBCs which are also entitled to constitutional privileges in view of their relatively backward socio-economic status within the stratified caste system. The argument for constitutional protection is justified by reference to the fact that despite constituting more than half of India's population, the OBCs have a share of only 5 per cent of public jobs which is not fair; hence the demand for constitutional guarantee for privileges for them. It was conceded, as will be shown below, with the adoption of the Mandal Commission Report in 1990.

The Outcome

Reservation is legitimate to ascertain a level playing for all the communities; no community shall be deprived of the opportunities which are available to everybody regardless of caste, ethnicity, clan or kin. The argument was accepted by the founding fathers, and the SCs and STs received reservation in public employment and other facilities which are deemed to be pertinent for their blossoming as citizens of free India. By following proportional reservation, SCs were given 15 per cent reservation while the share of STs were 7.5 per cent in public jobs and in higher education. With regard to SCs and STs, there are 12 separate Articles in the Constitution of India. These are Articles 15, 16, 46. 164, 330, 332, 334, 335, 338, 341, 342 and 366. Of these Articles, Article 15 seems to be most fundamental in the sense it ensures guarantee of reservation without shackles by stating that

> nothing ... shall prevent the State from making any special provision for the advancement of any socially and economically backward classes of citizens or for the Scheduled Castes and Tribes.

There are also complementary provisions in Part XVI of the Constitution which provides reserved seats to the SCs and STs following the principle of proportional representation. As Article 330 stipulates, the state shall reserve seats in the legislature for the SCs and STs; the number of seats for them

> shall bear, as nearly as may be, the same proportion to the total number of seats allotted to that State or Union Territory ... as the population of the Scheduled Castes in the State or Union Territory or of the Scheduled Tribes in the State or Union Territory.

The arrangement is total, and the Constitution leaves no space for confusion. Initially, it was decided to retain the scheme for reservation for fifty years which was later, with the adoption of the Seventy-Ninth Amendment Act in 1999, expanded for sixty years. The period of reservation was further extended to 2020 by the Ninety-Fifth Amendment Act of 2009.In an attempt to erase socio-economic differences, the Constitution creates an adequately-equipped mechanism for the marginalized groups of people who remain at the bottom of the pyramid because of being born with a specific caste tag or in a tribal family. Politically forward-looking and ideologically empowering, these Articles are a watershed in the unfolding of India's blossoming as a constitutional democracy.

The OBC Reservation

With the promulgation of the Mandal Commission recommendations, the OBCs were entitled to get 27 per cent reservation in this regard. The OBC reservation received constitutional recognition with the acceptance of the Ninety-Third Amendment Act in 2005 which was also validated by the Supreme Court of India in 2008 in the famous *Ashok Thakur v. the Union of India* in 2008. For the apex court, reservation was justiciable and did not violate the basic structure of the Constitution since, as the court pronounced,

> the ultimate objective is to bring people to a particular level so that there can be equality of opportunity. In that context, one has to keep in view the justice and redress principles. There should not be mere equality in law but equality in fact.[16]

The aim is to establish substantive equality cutting across class, caste and clan. This is what the founding fathers had in mind while being engaged in the Constituent Assembly for the constitution. In the court's perception, social backwardness and poverty are linked, hence without eradicating the sources of social backwardness, constitutional democracy in India remains elusive. Caste may not be a good index though historically it has been shown that one's caste identity is indicative of one's socio-economic status in a hierarchical society. In the Ashok Thakur judgement, the Court thus argues:

> Social backwardness is in the ultimate analysis the result of poverty to a large extent. Social backwardness which results from poverty is likely to be aggravated by considerations of their

[16] *Ashok Thakur v. the Union of India*, 2008. http://judis.nic.in/supremecourt/imgs1.aspx?filename=31231 (accessed 6 December 2016).

> caste. This shows the relevance of both caste and poverty in determining the backwardness of citizens. [Since] social backwardness which results from poverty is likely to be magnified by caste considerations.... It is only by directing the society and the State to offer them all facilities for social and educational uplift that the problem is solved.[17]

Reservation for the OBCs is now constitutionally valid. The Ninety-Third Amendment Act (2005) and the endorsement by the Supreme Court in the Ashok Thakur judgement put the scheme beyond question. Here too, what has been emphasized is the idea of differentiated citizenship in which specific groups of citizens are privileged over others for reasons of historical wrongs and which impede the growth and consolidation of an inclusive society. Implicit here is also idea that once the society is made a level playing field for all, it will help all achieve substantive equality. The story of the Ninety-Third Amendment Act remains incomplete without reference to the Mandal Commission's recommendations which argued strongly for OBC reservation for fairness and social inclusion. Insisting on guaranteeing constitutional protection of reservation for the OBCs for the sake of establishing substantive equality, the Mandal recommendations are path-breaking in nature and spirit, as will be shown further.

The Mandal Recommendations

By deciding to implement the Mandal Commission Report, submitted to the Government of India in 1980, the VP Singh government championed, as it were, the cause of the OBCs who constituted 52 per cent of the population. Although the recommendations were accepted by the government in 1990, there were series of attempts in according reservation to what was defined as OBCs. To fulfil a constitutional obligation, as Article 340 suggests, the government of India appointed the First Backward Classes Commission, popularly known as Kalelkar Commission after its chairman in 1953. The Commission submitted its report in 1955, listing about 32 per cent of the population as backward on the basis of caste identity. The Commission also identified 2399 castes as backward. However, Kalelkar rejected the report when he placed the report for presidential assent saying that it would have been preferable to determine backwardness on 'principles' rather than 'caste'. The reservations seemed to have lost its momentum except that nearly all the states constituted their Backward Commission and legalized reservation in public services and educational institutions under state control. The Second Backward Classes Commission, known as the Mandal Commission, appointed in 1978, revived interests in formulating a national policy for OBCs. The Commission suggested that OBCs who form 54.5 per cent of country's population require special concession to correct the social imbalance. But the Supreme Court ruled that 'reservations cannot exceed 50 per cent of the jobs. So the Commission reluctantly agreed to accept 27 per cent jobs for the OBCs though they constitute more than half of India's population. There was also a rider because the Commission also categorically stated that 'candidates belonging to OBCs recruited on the basis of merit in an open competition should not be adjusted against their reservation quota of 27 per cent'. By implication what it means is the fact that if the commission's recommendations are respected, half the posts in the public sector and universities will be filled by people who could not get in on merit, provided they belong to 'the right castes'. As evident, the Mandal formula rests on two premises: (a) the OBCs comprise a very large segment of India's population and (b) their representation (only 5%) in the public sector is abysmally poor.

[17] *Ashok Thakur v. the Union of India*, 2008.

Hence the recommendations ensuring 27 per cent reservations in central jobs and education for the OBCs appear revolutionary. In contrast with the Kalelkar Commission, the Mandal Commission Report 'changed the original philosophy of reservations by clearly identifying the potential of cultural identity as a key strategy for enhancing political influences and thereby seeking subsidies and favours for the entire caste/group.'[18]

Reservations were born out of a concern to remedy injustices which deprived certain sections of an equal opportunity to enhance their status in society. In order to create 'an inclusive Indian identity', the post-Independent Indian leadership favoured 'policies of discrimination' as instruments through which 'to offset the advantage, enjoyed by some, and to equalize opportunities at the starting line.'[19] Seeking to rectify the social imbalance due to the age-old economic deprivations the Mandal formula seeks to give 27 per cent reservation to a total of 3743 OBCs in government jobs. What it therefore means is the promotion of the backward castes that will also be entitled to a much bigger slice of 'an already meager employment cake'.[20] The violent student riots, led primarily by the privileged upper castes that swept the entire north India after the announcement seems explicable in view of the perceptible threat to the upper caste hegemony in the white collar world. South India was hardly affected probably because of the long tradition of non-Brahmin movement there.[21] The incessant violence over the extension of the controversial scheme shows the extent to which the idea of reservation has itself become repulsive to the assertive section of the upper castes. In the immediate aftermath of Independence—reservation was mandatory for the scheduled casters and scheduled tribes as it is directed 'towards advancing social and economic equality'.[22] In 1977–78, the Bihar Chief Minister, Karpoori Thakur introduced 26 per cent reservation for the OBCs. The formula which took into account the economic backwardness as a criterion for reservation provoked a violent outburst in which 118 people were reported to have been killed. Madhya Pradesh government raised reservation from 28 per cent to 32 per cent in 1985 which sparked off violent riots and arson. So, widespread and alarming was the trouble that the government was forced to revoke its decision. Gujarat shared the same fate in 1985 when the Madhavsinh Solanki government fell following the introduction of reservation in promotions of posts in medical colleges. These illustrations draw out the fact that north India has not had a consensus evident in the South.[23] This probably explains why in north India 'the acceptance of the Mandal Commission Report has resulted in condemnation verging on hysteria.'[24]

Whatever the advantages the Mandal formula may have, reservation for the backward castes and for the religious minorities are directed towards maintaining a balance of power in the caste-divided India's social structure. As a scheme striving to strike a balance between the privileged upper castes and the hitherto neglected OBCs, the Mandal recommendation deserves appreciation. In reality, however, the better-off sections of the OBCs would reap the benefit at the cost of the more deserving sections within these castes. To substantiate the argument, let us draw our attention to the caste dynamics in north India. Till the 1950s, domination was enjoyed in the rural areas by the AJGAR (Ahir, Jats, Gurjars and Rajputs)

---

[18] Nitya Rao, 'Social Justice and Empowerment of the Weaker Sections and Gender Rights', in Katharine Adeney and Lawrence Saez, eds., *Coalition Politics and Hindu Nationalism* (London: Routledge, 2005), p. 119.

[19] Niraja Jayal Gopal, *Representing India: Ethnic Divers and the Governance of Public Institution* (London: Palgrave, 2006), p. 191.

[20] Sunanda K Dutta Ray, 'Darkness at Noon: Implications of Student Riots', *The Statesman*, Calcutta, 30 September 1990.

[21] Rosalind O'Hanlon, *Caste, Conflict and Ideology: Mahatma Jotirao Phule and Low Caste Protest in Nineteenth Century Western India* (Cambridge: Cambridge University Press, 1985).

[22] Andre Beteille, 'Caste and Politics: Subversion of Public Institutions', *The Times of India*, Lucknow, 12 September 1990.

[23] VN Srinivas, 'The Mandal Formula: Backwardness—Caste v. Individuals', *The Times of India*, Lucknow, 18 September 1990.

[24] Mihir Desai, 'The Need for Reservation: A Reply to Shourie and Others', *Lokayan Bulletin* 8, no. 4 (1990): 54.

group.[25] They gained remarkably in material terms after the Green Revolution and all of them moved well and truly into modern sector. The intermediate castes, like Kurmis, Koeris, Lodhas and others also benefited but not uniformly, and therefore there is considerable social and economic heterogeneity in each of these castes. Hence, the Mandal definition of 'backwardness' does not appear plausible in view of its obvious limitation of having ignored social and economic heterogeneity among OBCs. As a result, the benefits, meant for the backwards of the OBCs, are likely to be monopolized by the better-off and influential in these castes. In other words, 'the rhetoric of reservation is addressed to the mass of underprivileged, but their rewards are reserved for the affluent upper castes of the OBCs'.[26] MN Srinivas thus argues that 'when a certain caste has political clout it should be excluded from the backward class list; otherwise, the richer members of the higher groups among the backward classes ... will hog the benefits which should have gone to the genuinely deserving backward classes'.[27]

The political imperatives behind reservations are thus apparent. What prompted the ruling elite to accept the Mandal recommendations is probably a well-calculated design aiming at mobilizing the support of the OBC elite. LR Naik, the only Dalit member of the Mandal Commission refused to sign as he felt that the recommendations would placate the interest of the powerful landowning castes within the OBCs as against those who remained at the periphery within this social segment.[28] Despite clear economic gains for the OBCs, there is no doubt that what governed the VP Singh-led National Front government's decision to implement the recommendations were political calculations that surely hinge on the following:

1. Populist vote catching device as the OBC constitute the majority of Indian population.
2. A move to upstage the Haryana leader, Devi Lal who was threatening the VP Singh-led coalition with rural–urban polarization.
3. To shift the focus from the Ram Janmabhumi issue which singularly created a solid vote bank for the BJP especially after the October (1990) Rath Yatra.
4. The realization that it was one issue on which none of the allies of the National Front would be able to openly oppose the government, if presented as a fait accompli.

By virtue of its unique status in the OBC society, its wealth, its relatively high educational level and its hegemony in a majority of caste councils, the OBC upper crust is viewed as the most significant power brokers in the Hindi heartland. So, the Mandal formula, designed to ensure social justice, is virtually a scheme for creating and sustaining a secure vote bank for the National Front government. And, since number counts in franchise today, parties irrespective of ideology strive hard to win the support of caste groups for electoral gains by promises whipping-up caste sentiments. So, if caste has acquired a new lease of life in independent India, this is almost entirely axiomatic because of the increasing use made of it in politics. The decision to implement the Mandal Commission report is just another effort to effectively draw on caste sentiments for victory in elections. The Commission is thus described as 'a caste commission' which is seen 'as a passport to power'.[29] Whatever the future of the reservation plan, the Mandal formula

[25] Chandan Mitra, 'Moulded in Caste: Electoral Patterns in North India Since Nehru', in *Whither India's Democracy*, ed. Bidyut Chakrabarty (Calcutta: KP Bagchi & Co., 1993).

[26] Ashok Guha, 'Reservation in Myth and Reality', *Economic and Political Weekly*, 15 December 1990, p. 2716.

[27] MN Srinivas, 'End of an Egalitarian Dream', *The Sunday Observer*, New Delhi, 12 August 1990.

[28] Chandra Bhan Prasad, 'Mandal's True Inheritors: Reservations Should Go to MBCs (Most Backward Castes), not OBCs (Other Backward Castes), *The Times of India*, 12 April 2006.

[29] CP Bhambri, 'The Politics of Caste Alliance: Alignments on a Caste Basis have Sharpened and Legitimized the Rich–Poor Divide', *The Telegraph*, 23 May 1991.

has polarized the contemporary political forces more sharply than before. So, a mere acceptance of modern secular political idioms does not ensure their sustenance in a society which draws on feudal sentiments and primordial loyalties. It is not therefore strange that elections are conducted on caste calculations, the candidates are nominated on caste ratio, and as a consequence, patronage is likely to be distributed on caste basis and public policies are also to be tilted in favour of the caste support base.

Despite sharp criticism and violent student fury directed against the Mandal Commission Report, the formula deserves serious attention as it strives to correct the social imbalances of centuries inflicted on the downtrodden in the name of the discriminatory *varna* system. Due to peculiar socio-economic transformation in India which had a long colonial past, the benefits, meant for the genuine backwards, are likely to go to the relatively better-off sections within the OBC. So, the Commission's aim of ensuring a greater equality for the OBCs as such is likely to be defeated under the present circumstances. The National Front decision on reservation therefore appears 'mainly a tactful response of a desperate regime to the struggle for empowerment by the oppressed sections of [Indian] society'.[30] Unless it becomes a part of a comprehensive plan for development, the Mandal formula, despite BP Mandal's sincerity and devotion to the OBC cause, hardly makes sense in a situation in which the reservation plain is being utilized primarily for electoral gains.

Mandal II: Reservation for Social Justice or Appropriation by the Creamy Layer?

Reservation in educational institutions is referred to as Mandal II. In August 2005, the Supreme Court abolished all caste-based reservations in unaided private colleges. On 21 December 2005, the Lok Sabha passed the 104th Constitutional Amendment act, 2005 rolling back the Supreme Court judgement by introducing a new clause into Article 15 to allow for reservations for Scheduled Castes and Scheduled Tribes as well as other backward classes in private unaided educational institutions other than minority institutions. In 2006, the UPA Government agreed to introduce 27 per cent reservations for OBCs in Central Government-funded higher education institutions like Indian Institute of Managements, Indian Institute of Technology, All India Institute of Medical Sciences and Central Universities. In other words, the proposed design is meant to introduce 27 per cent 'quota' to all institutions of higher learning. This blanket guarantee for reservations stands in contradiction with the 1992 Supreme Court judgement in the case of *Indra Sawhney v. Union of India* delivered on 16 November 1992 which upheld 27 per cent reservations subject to the exclusion of socially advanced persons/sections (creamy layer) from amongst the OBCs. The Court also directed the government to evolve criteria for identification of this creamy layer. In response to the Court directives, the government appointed a committee which suggested that rules of exclusion applies to children of persons holding different constitutional positions, class I officers and defence personnel who holds the rank of colonel and above. Children of persons with annual income greater than ₹100,000 were also to be excluded. The limit was later revised to ₹250,000 in 2004. The recommendations were accepted and circulated among all ministries/departments of Union and State governments in September 1993, allowing reservations to come into force.[31]

---

[30] Manoranjan Mohanty, 'The Relevance of Reservation', *Lokayan Bulletin* 8, nos. 4–5 (July–October 1990): 143.

[31] Drawn on *The Times of India*, 10 April 2006.

Viewed in a long term perspective, Mandal II is a logical corollary of Mandal I. It takes forward 'the process of transfer of social and political power to majority communities'.[32] In the context of Mandal II, VP Singh thus characterized Mandal as 'a macro-process that has acquired its own dynamics. [Hence,] no matter which party forms a government, it has to take the process further'.[33] It would not be an exaggeration if one thus argues that the centre of gravity in Indian politics is now defined by 'quota politics'.[34] Whatever the implications, reservation through quota translates 'protective discrimination' into reality. In contrast with 'affirmative action' that is practised in the US, it is the combination of quotas and lower eligibility criteria that defines protective discrimination in India.

The Mandal II Arguments

The state can adopt discriminatory measures to favour one group of people against another in a multicultural society. In order to neutralize inequality, the state must provide resources to the underprivileged 'on non-market principles—free education, assured income, nutritious food and health'.[35] The idea of 'recognition' is thus clearly political because it is justified keeping in mind a specific type of power relationship. Can 'reservation' be thus an appropriate scheme to accord 'recognition' to the disadvantaged due to historical reasons? Perhaps yes. A politically 'liberal' society however does not endorse social discrimination because citizenship, conceptually speaking, is 'universal'. Hence 'ascribed' identities are completely disregarded while defining citizens. One may perhaps theoretically defend this position. But, given the peculiar evolution of societies in various socio-economic and political contexts, this position may not appear tenable simply because 'identical' rights for all are inadequate for protecting cultural-minorities. What we therefore require are 'special' rights for minorities who are identified as 'disadvantaged' groups. The argument that justifies discriminatory laws draws on the idea that since citizens are 'differentiated' and thus 'unequal', for obvious reasons, different communities should have different rights as citizens. Based on this logic, theorists of multiculturalism articulate the notion of 'differentiated citizenship'. There are two significant implications of this conceptualization: (a) in contrast with universal citizenship of liberal variety, differentiated citizenship clearly argues for discrimination in favour of cultural minorities as 'justified'; and (b) by taking into account 'the cultural distinctiveness' as a denominator, those championing differentiated citizenship challenges the ideologically charged attempts at 'homogenizing' communities with clear socio-cultural differences.

There is a historical dimension too. Different communities undergo different kinds of social churning processes which affect their progress and development as a social entity. Hence some are 'privileged' and some are 'marginalized'. A society that rejects 'differentiated citizenship' and appreciates universal citizenship seeks to insist that the latter give up their identity and submerge with the majority. This is how a society flourishes. From the multicultural point of view, this position smacks of 'cultural imperialism' because the prism through which a society is uniformly viewed insists on treating un-equals equally. This is clearly a case of cultural imperialism because norms and values of the privileged majority acquire salience given their well-entrenched nature and therefore any opposition to them provokes consternation among those who tend to belittle the importance of historical processes in dividing mankind.

[32] Yogendra Yadav and Satish Deshpande, 'Wrong Route, Right Direction: Reservation Policy Needs to be Fine-tuned', *The Times of India*, 31 May 2006.

[33] VP Singh's press interview, *The Hindu*, 14 June 2006.

[34] Christophe Jaffrelot, *India's Silent Revolution: The Rise of the Low Castes in North Indian Politics* (New Delhi: Permanent Black, 2006), p. 493.

[35] Neera Chandhoke, 'Three Myths about Reservations', *Economic and Political Weekly* 41, No. 3 (10 June 2006), p. 2289.

There are thus strong arguments in favour of reservation in a multicultural country like India. But difficulty arises the moment groups or communities that deserve reservation are identified on the basis of ascribed identity, namely caste. Besides the 1931 census of India, caste was never a criterion in classifying Indian population. So if caste is a defining category, the 1931 index remains critical. This is hardly persuasive because the 1931 census was guided by imperial priorities and may not have reflected India's actual demographic profile. Furthermore, since the criterion of 'backwardness' is historically conditioned it is doubtful whether it remains valid even in the twenty-first century.

Similarly, reservation in higher education seems to be an empty slogan in the light of the fact that seats for scheduled castes and scheduled tribes remain vacant for lack of applicants. Even after more than half a century of reservation for these communities, the number of beneficiaries is abysmally low. The reasons are not difficult to seek. As is evident in the latest educational statistics, released by the Union Ministry of Human Resources Development, while 73 per cent of the SC students quit school before taking the class X final examination, the figures for the ST students (79%) are worse. Interestingly, the drop-out rates are not so high among the children within the class I–IV. Only 37 per cent of the SC students discontinue while 59 per cent of the ST students fall under this category. If contrasted with prevalent high Gross Enrolment Ratio, which is 83 per cent for the SCs and 86 per cent for the STs, the drop-rates reveal the unfavourable socio-economic circumstances in which they are forced to take up odd jobs for mere survival. Since the majority of SC and ST population draw on agriculture for livelihood, these children are roped in for farming once they reach 10–12 years of age.

Given this reality, reservation in higher education makes no sense so long as the drop-out rates in schools are alarmingly high. In order to translate the scheme into practice, what is thus required is to pursue 'the literacy mission' seriously especially among the downtrodden by creating conditions in which benefits for going to school outweighs the forced alternative of working in the field for mere survival. Otherwise, the benefits of reservation continue to be 'uneven' among those who can avail them. The well-placed group of the backward section would be better off with such reservation. It would help only the creamy layer to grab the advantages. Thus the social justice agenda will always remain a distant goal.

It is difficult to suggest a convincing scheme to get out of the imbroglio relating to the reservation issue. In order arrive at a solution one may begin by taking into account most seriously the creamy layer judgement of the Supreme Court. Unless one reviews whether it is appropriate to extend reservation to the creamy layer generations after generations. It makes no sense if the children of the IAS officers, for instance, enjoy reservation simply because of their ascribed social status, even though they, despite their caste identity, are socio-economically better placed than their upper caste counterparts. As the argument goes, 'to allow the undeserving to benefit from reservation is to deny protection to those who deserve to be protected'.[36] So, is the cause of social justice served well if reservation is confined to first generation learners or further? Differentiated citizenship is a powerful device to achieve social justice. But it causes serious social distortion unless it is conceptualized in the affirmative action mould rather than extending a blanket license to those, differentiated merely by virtue of birth.

Concluding Observations

The reservation policy which was initiated as a temporary measure (merely for ten years) gradually became integral to India's constitutional democracy. What is striking that instead of being a tool for empowering

[36] Zoya Hasan, 'Countering Social Discrimination', *The Hindu*, 2 June 2006.

the poorest of the poor, reservation is being used to create and consolidate a vote bank. The mission of evolving an inclusive society that the founding father so assiduously aspired to achieve thus remains distant. Nonetheless, the constitutional guarantee for the SCs and STs set in motion processes of empowerment leading to the breakdown of social barriers in a significant way. Hence it is argued that the supportive provisions are 'social not only it seeks to interrogate the system of hierarchical social relations, but more fundamentally it seeks to alter these social relations along egalitarian lines'.[37] These provisions, adequately backed by constitutional–legal means, create a space where the dominant power structure, supported by the prevalent social relations, is being fiercely challenged by those who so far remain peripheral for historical reasons. In that respect, they are truly revolutionary in character.

Despite having stirred the sensibilities of both the socially advantaged and disadvantaged sections of society, the Mandal initiative is a powerful input that has brought about radical changes in Indian polity and society. The grammar of entitlement has become an integral part of the language of politics in contemporary India. There can be a debate on how to execute the decision, but all political parties are unanimous in accepting the logic and reality of the Ninety-Third Amendment Act (2005) confirming reservation in all institutions of higher learning. The appointment of the Oversight Committee in 2006 to suggest steps to expand the OBC quota without adversely affecting the equilibrium in admission to institutions of higher learning is a strategy to defuse social tension in the country.[38] Yet, the 2006 controversy had also shown 'how entrenched social prejudices remain and how deep runs the hostility to change in areas where it matters the most'.[39] Despite the obvious social implications, social justice in the discourse supportive of OBC reservation redefined deprivation not in terms of lack of economic entitlement, but primarily in terms of 'social disabilities, . . . which were the consequences of social hierarchies, rather than economic arrangements'.[40] Instead of conceptualizing deprivation as being an inevitable outcome of specific socio-economic circumstances, the Mandal formula explained the phenomenon in terms of caste affiliation. The Mandal debate thus has two important consequences: on the one hand, it linked democracy 'instrumentally to social justice' by arguing for quotas for the OBC in public employment and higher education; this will result, on the other, in allowing the OBCs an access to benefits and facilities which were beyond their reach in the past. A group's exclusion or under-representation in institutions of authority is thus seen 'not so much as a consequence of unjust socio-economic inequalities but as its cause'.[41] Conceptually, the argument for OBC reservation may have lapses though it has raised those important social issues which hardly received adequate attention in the past presumably because of the hegemonic grip of the dominant social groups over constitutional governance in India. In that sense, the Mandal debate marks an important shift in the debates and discussions over public justification for reservations. After Mandal, caste as a basis of collective struggle for gaining equality in positions and social status became 'a term of respectable usage' among the marginalized. It is now being seen as 'an empowering device to enhance one's meager entitlements in society'.[42] The shift thus involved a reinterpretation of the nationalist goal of a more equal and just society by empowering the disadvantaged and recognizing the socially denigrated groups in addition to reduction socio-economic disparities. The conceptual mechanism

[37] Guru, 'Social Justice', p. 365.

[38] M Veerappa Moily's press interview, *The Hindu*, 18 June 2006.

[39] Harish Khare, 'Lessons from the New Intolerance', *The Hindu*, 12 April 2006.

[40] Rochana Bajpai, *Debating Difference: Group Rights and Liberal Democracy in India* (New Delhi: Oxford University Press, 2011), p. 234.

[41] Bajpai, *Debating Difference*, p. 261.

[42] Javeed Alam pursues this argument at a greater length in his *Who Wants Democracy?* (New Delhi: Orient Longman, 2006), pp. 9–11.

articulating the redefinition involved, argues Rochana Bajpai, 'a relocation of equality in proximity to democracy on the one hand, and by distancing (but not its dissociation) from national unity, on the other'.[43] However one characterizes the Mandal debate, the reservation policy has nonetheless become 'the fixed point of Indian political life' because different groups have different reasons to support it. It is a soft option for the political elites who, 'reluctant to carry out deep-rooted changes in society would rather opt to enlarge the constituency for reservations in a shrinking state sector and in a declining educational system, than transform ownership of resources in the country'.[44] In other words, by securing the numerically mandated quotas for the OBCs, the Mandal II is a way of avoiding doing the things that really create access to opportunities. Bhikhu Parekh thus laments,

> Social justice has come to be defined almost exclusively in terms of reservations, and the massive programme of redistribution needed to tackle the deep roots of historically accumulated disadvantages has been marginalized. Rather than fight for such a programme, the scheduled caste, scheduled tribe, and OBC representatives in powerful positions use their constituents as a vote bank to promote their own careers.[45]

By deciding to implement the Mandal II reservation scheme, the primary aim of the ruling elite is, suggests a commentator, 'to lure back the traditional voter [and] reservation has [nothing to do with the] balancing [of] society; it has everything to do with winning elections'.[46] The Left political parties extend support to the reservation scheme because in the absence of the implementation of radical 'redistribution programme', it is best 'to stick to constitutionally guaranteed and politically accepted policy of reservation'. Due to peculiar socio-economic circumstances, the reservation policy not only enjoys 'a broad-based support' it has also become what Bhikhu Parkeh characterizes as 'a touchstone of social conscience and an integral part of Indian politics'[47] though 'the churning of Indian politics and society that followed Mandal has [largely] petered into an endlessly involuted conflict of one sub-caste with another [and] most anti-caste movements turn out to be . . . merely anti-upper caste movements [happily excluding] those below them'.[48] Reservation policy may not thus be a fool-proof device in the light of its articulation in contemporary India as a means for creating and strengthening a vote bank although there is no denying that it has unleashed processes of empowerment by making the socially-marginalized sections of society aware of being stakeholders in political processes and governance.

Review Questions

1. **How do you conceptualize reservation as a constitutional design for empowerment? Elaborate.**

2. **Distinguish between reservation and affirmative action with examples.**

---

[43] Rochana Bajpai, 'Redefining Equality: Social Justice in the Mandal Debate, 1990', in *Political Ideas in Modern India*, eds. VR Mehta and Thomas Pantham (New Delhi: SAGE, 2006), p. 335.

[44] Neera Chandhoke, 'Three Myths about Reservations', *Economic and Political Weekly*, 10 June 2006, p. 2290.

[45] Bhikhu Parekh, 'Limits of the Indian Political Imagination' in Mehta and Pantham, *Political Ideas*, p. 443.

[46] Vir Sanghvi, 'The Debate over Reservation', *Hindustan Times*, 30 April 2006.

[47] Parekh, 'Limits', p. 442.

[48] Pratap Bhanu Mehta, *The Burden of Democracy* (New Delhi: Penguin, 2003), p.163.

3. **Is reservation an appropriate means to realize the goals that the founding father had set for themselves? Elaborate your response.**
4. **How did the founding fathers address the issue of reservation in the Constituent Assembly? Elaborate your response.**
5. **Critically evaluate the constitutional provisions relating to reservation in India.**
6. **In what respects, the Mandal Commission report was a revolutionary step towards realizing social justice in its true spirit and substance? Elaborate.**
7. **Critically evaluate the importance of the 1992 Indra Sawhney judgement of the Supreme Court of India in fulfilling a fundamental constitutional objective.**
8. **How do you assess the role of India's apex court in creating a level playing field for all regardless of one's socio-economic locations? Elaborate your response.**
9. **Reservation is a political design. Do you agree with this view? Elaborate your response.**
10. **Reservation and social justice are dialectically interconnected. Do you agree with this view? Elaborate.**

Chapter 10

Gender as Critical to the Processes of Constitutionalization

Learning Objectives

- How is gender conceptualized in constitutional terms?
- How did the founding fathers approach gender while being engaged in the making of the Constitution?
- How it is being re-articulated in contemporary India by legislative design and judicial intervention?

Following the growing democratization, issues such as women empowerment and gender rights have gained massive importance in contemporary political discourses in India. Despite having paid adequate attention, the founding fathers do not seem to have pursued the matter to the extent it was expected, presumably because they had other pressing priorities. The issue thus remained unresolved though it is being continuously raised especially in the wake campaigns for democratizing governance. That women were socio-politically tortured and exploited beyond imagination is an age-old phenomenon. Protests were mounted though the roots were hardly touched, presumably because of the well-entrenched prejudices against gender-neutral governance. In simple theoretical terms, it can be explained in terms of patriarchy being hegemonic in relation to the issues of gender. The aim of this chapter here is to comprehend the complex unfolding of the trajectories leading to the articulation of gender equality as a constitutional goal. As the role of judiciary is critical in sustaining the constitution and the values from which it derives its sustenance, this chapter, by dwelling on some of major judicial pronouncements, traverses a relatively less trodden path in contemporary Political Science scholarship.

Historical Antecedents

The concern for gender equality receives adequate attention in the Constituent Assembly though the members had doubts whether the proposed constitution was well-equipped to develop a constitutional design for this purpose given the well-entrenched patriarchy. Long before the debate started over a common civil code for the country, the Constituent Assembly members referred to this aspect of Indian social reality. In her intervention in the debates over the Objective Resolution, Hansa Mehta (Bombay), for instance, minced no words when she stated:

> The average woman in this country has suffered for centuries from inequalities heaped upon her by laws, customs and practices of people who have fallen from the heights of that civilization

> of which we are all so proud. . . . There are thousands of women today who are denied the ordinary human rights. They are put behind the purdah, secluded within the four walls of their homes, unable to move freely. The India woman has been reduced to such a state of helplessness that she has become an easy prey of those who wish to exploit the situation. In degrading women, man has degraded himself. In raising her, man will not only raise himself but rise the whole nation.[1]

There are two important points that, according to Mehta, merit attention here: first, by understanding gender discrimination in a historical perspective, she laid out the theoretical foundation for discussion on this issue in the Assembly. For her, this was a wrong that had been committed over ages presumably because of the male domination in human society. Second, her suggestion that unless women were taken as equal partners in socio-economic regeneration, the clamour for equality would remain elusive, a humanist-cum-feminist hypothesis that she foregrounded in this argument for gender justice. This was made clear when she further commented that instead of

> asking for reserved seats, quotas or separate political justice . . . what we have asked for is social justice, economic justice and political justice. We have asked for that equality which can alone be the basis of mutual respect and understanding and without which real cooperation is not possible between man and woman. Women form one-half of the population of this country and therefore men cannot go very far without the cooperation of women.[2]

Here too, the argument is clear enough to establish that social prejudices sustained discriminatory gender relations. Unless that was done away with, the efforts towards building a society of equals were likely to be defeated. According to Mehta, it was a particular mind-set that was responsible for the consolidation of such 'a heinous system of social interaction'. There was, of course, an undercurrent in her statement highlighting that substantial changes in regard to gender equality were not possible so long as the prevalent mind-set remained untouched.

The concern for a uniform civil code is integral to that of gender equality. Article 44 insisting on securing uniform civil code is the only constitutional provision which is also not justiciable since it is part of the Directive Principles of State Policy. The Constituent Assembly pondered on this issue though there were no conclusive suggestions, presumably because they did not appear to be critical at the time of the making of the Constitution. Nonetheless, some of the members articulated the concern while pondering over this issue. For some, personal laws were absolutely 'personal' and hence no interference was permissible while there were members who felt that a common civil code was complementary to democratic governance. One of the strong voices against uniform civil code was that B Pocker Sahib Bahadur of Madras. According to him:

> For each community the right to follow their personal laws as regards marriage, inheritance, divorce etc., is fair and thus legitimate, and the state should have no authority to override all these provisions and to have uniformity of law to be imposed upon the whole people on these matters. This is a tyrannical provision which ought not to be tolerated; and let it not be taken

[1] Hansa Mehta (Bombay), 19 December 1946, *Constituent Assembly Debates*, Book No. 1, p. 138.
[2] Ibid., p. 138.

> that I am only voicing forth the feeling of the Mussalmans. In saying this, I am voicing forth the feeling of ever so many sections of the country who feel that it would be really tyrannical to interfere with the religious practices, and with religious laws, by which they are governed.[3]

In a socio-culturally diverse society, the imposition of common civil code was unwarranted since it would erase 'the distinctive character of the communities' comprising the multitude. In a very detailed justification for separate civil code, Sahib Bahadur further argued that this was consolidated over centuries of sustained practices, undertaken by 'many multitudes of communities following various customs for centuries or thousands of years.... What is the purpose served by this uniformity except to murder the consciences of the people and make them feel that they are being trampled upon as regards their religious rights and practices? Such a tyrannous practice ought not to find a place in our Constitution.'[4] This was not the feeling of a particular community, he further underlined:

> There are ever so many sections even among the Hindus who are rebelling against this and who voice forth their feelings in much stronger language than I am using. Hence if the framers of this article say that even the majority community is uniform in support of this, I would challenge them to say so. It is not so. Even assuming that the majority community is of this view it has to be condemned and it ought not to be allowed, because, in a democracy, . . . it is this duty of the majority to secure the sacred rights of every community. It is a misnomer to call it a democracy if the majority rides rough-shod over the rights of the minorities. It is not democracy at all; it is tyranny.[5]

This was a well-articulated view that drew on the clichéd argument that since the communities were distinct in terms of their socio-cultural characteristics, they should not be forced to give up which they had been nurturing over ages. The argument may have validity if it is taken in isolation of the democratic processes; it however loses its plausibility, to a significant extent, if it is conceptualized as complementary to wider concern for democratizing governance. This is what led KM Munshi to argue that uniform civil code was part and parcel of democratic governance. In response to the charge of some of his colleagues that the enactment of a common civil code was 'tyrannical to minorities', he forcefully argued that the characterization of the enactment of common civil code being tyrannical was totally 'unfounded [because] nowhere in advanced Muslim countries the personal law of each minority has been recognized as so sacrosanct as to prevent the enactment of a Civil Code. In countries like Turkey or Egypt, [n]o minority . . . is permitted to have such rights.'[6] Being opposed to discriminatory civil code, Munshi insisted that it needed to be incorporated in the proposed Constitution

> to consolidate and unify our personal law in such a way so that the way of life of the whole country may in course of time be unified and secular. [With the adoption of this] we want to

[3] B Pocker Sahib Bahadur (Madras), 23 November 1948, *Constituent Assembly Debates*, Book No. 2, pp. 544–45.

[4] Ibid., p. 545.

[5] Ibid., p. 545.

[6] KM Munshi (Bombay), 23 November 1948, *Constituent Assembly Debates*, Book No. 2, p. 547.

> divorce religion from personal law, from what may be called social relations or from the rights of parties as regards inheritance and succession.[7]

The separation of religion from personal law was of utmost importance in the interest of building a secular nation in which discrimination around religious axes was an anathema. The need of the day was, as Munshi further argued,

> to unify and consolidate the nation by every means without interfering with religious practices. If however the religious practices in the past have been so construed as to cover the whole field of life, we have reached a point when we must put our foot down and say these matters are no religion, they are purely matters for secular legislation'.[8]

Seeking to demarcate an independent domain for secular constitutional practices, Munshi appears to have anticipated some of the arguments that were made later in independent India. The points that he made are twofold: on the one hand, he allowed no space to religion in deciding secular constitutional design of governance because religion and secularism were incompatible, for obvious reasons; since personal law, based on religion, was contrary to secular constitutional practices, arguments against a common civil code seemed to have been, on the other, overstretched and contrary to the fundamental cannons of democracy.

The clamour for a common civil code was also endorsed by BR Ambedkar who was clueless when some of this colleagues in the Assembly did not support him. Being surprised at this demand since there existed a uniform code of laws covering almost every aspect of human relationship, he was at a loss. While elaborating his point, he further argued:

> There are innumerable enactments which would prove that this country has practically a Civil Code, uniform in its content and applicable to the whole of the country. . . . The only province the Civil Law has not been able to invade so far is marriage and succession [and] it is our intention to bring about that change because . . . this [is] odd for the is simple reason that we have, as a matter of fact, covered the whole lot of the field which is covered by a uniform Civil Code in this country.[9]

Defending the spirit of uniform civil code, Ambedkar argued strongly that the subjects of the Indian state shall have the right 'to claim full and equal benefit of all laws and proceedings for the security of persons and property as is enjoyed by other subjects regardless of any usage or custom based on religion and be subject to punishment, pains and penalties and to none other'.[10] The Constituent Assembly was clearly divided on the issue of personal laws. On the one hand, there was a powerful lobby to protect religious freedom, especially minority interests and there was also a constant demand, on the other, to have a uniform civil code for all, based on liberal arguments for common citizenship. Unable to arrive at a consensus, personal laws of minorities—the whole gamut of family, property, marriage, divorce and adoption rights—were left within the domain of their respective religious strictures. Debates on these issues have also brought out the deep divisions within the women's movement following schism along lines of caste, class and

---

[7] Ibid. p. 547.
[8] Ibid., p. 547.
[9] BR Ambedkar, 23 November 1948, *Constituent Assembly Debates*, Book No. 2, pp. 550–51.
[10] B Shiva Rao, 1967, *The Framing of India's Constitutions: Select Documents*, Vol. 2, p. 89.

community. Whatever the political aims of those pushing these two issues, there is no doubt that both these efforts articulated women's rights as citizen of a modern secular state by challenging particularistic and traditional values of family, religion, culture and community.

Reviewing the Argument

A perusal of the debates in the Constituent Assembly reveal that the members, influenced by the Nehruvian secularism, insisted on a common civil code as this was complementary to constitutional democracy while the Muslim members in particular were not persuaded by this argument because, for them, it was contrary to the Shariat law and the state was not authorized to intervene in one's personal law for the time being. This was articulated by Nazimuddin Ahmad of Bengal who, in unambiguous terms, stated:

> The interference with these matters should be gradual and must progress with the advance of time. I have no doubt [he further added] that a stage would come when the civil law would be uniform; but then the time has not yet come, . . . and the power that has been given to the State to make the Civil Code uniform is in advance of the time.[11]

In view of the fact that time was not ripe for a common civil code, a pragmatic Ahmad apprehended that 'it will lead to a considerable amount of misunderstanding and resentment amongst the various sections of the country'.[12] He thus urged his colleagues 'not to proceed in haste, but with caution, with experience, with statesmanship and with sympathy'.[13] In view of such a sharp division in the Assembly, a majority of the members decided not to pursue the matter since, as they felt, a categorical provision for imposing an identical civil code cutting across communal divisions did not seem to be warranted. It thus avoided the constitutionalization of a Hindu code and left it to the future parliament to legislate on this issue if it felt appropriate. To placate the orthodox Hindu forces and also to defuse tension among the Muslims, the Assembly 'inserted an ambiguous formulation into the constitution as part of the Directive Principles of State Policy which were non-justiciable'.[14] It was readily accepted even by the opponents since these principles were not justiciable and hence could not be legally enforced. So Article 44 seeking to secure 'for the citizens a uniform civil code throughout the territory of India' was a politically expedient design to purportedly evolve a consensus among communal groups with incompatible socio-economic interests.

The issue again came up in 1951 when BR Ambedkar proposed the Hindu Code Bill seeking to protect some basic women rights, viz, the right to divorce, outlawing polygamy, granting of inheritance rights and recognition of inter-caste marriage, among others. Behind Ambedkar's effort to place this bill before Parliament was his vision that women were central to the fight against caste system, that is, the subjection of women is central to the functioning of the caste system. Since women are, as he believed, 'the gateway to the caste system, the Brahminical forces that uphold caste must take control of these gateways in order to perpetuate the system of caste hierarchy and caste oppression'.[15] The need for a decisive juridical

---

[11] Nazimuddin Ahmad (Bengal), 23 November 1948, *Constituent Assembly Debates*, Book No. 2, p. 542.

[12] Ibid., p. 543.

[13] Ibid., p. 543.

[14] Hanna Lerner, 'The Indian Founding: A Comparative Perspective', in *The Oxford Handbook of the Indian Constitution*, eds. Sujit Choudhury, Madhav Khosla and Pratap Bhanu Mehta (New Delhi: Oxford University Press, 2016), p. 66.

[15] Wandana Sonalkar, 'An Agenda for Gender Politics', *Economic and Political Weekly*, 9 January 1999, p. 25.

code that ensures women freedom in marriage, divorce and inheritance is essential because along with the constitutional guarantee for basic social, political and economic rights, 'there must be progressive code which allows for revolutionary change in Hindu society in religious practice'.[16] The Bill was knocked down in the lower house of Parliament. Nehru supported the bill at the outset and later did not appear to be as vocal as was expected to bulldoze the opposition, presumably because it threatened 'the patriarchal social framework'. It was alleged that he buckled in under pressure from orthodox Hindu groups who, he apprehended, had the potential to erode his support base among the Hindu which he could not afford to ignore as the 1952 Lok Sabha poll was imminent.

The debate had again erupted with the approval of Hindu Personal Law in 1956. The Nehru Government was restrained to extend the law's ambit to the Muslim community with the fear of losing their votes for the Congress in future election. A staunch socialist, JB Kriplani was aghast at Nehru's stance of segregating communities in the application of personal law. In a very candid way, he thus mentioned in his intervention in the lower house of Parliament:

> If you want to have divorce for Hindu community, have it, but have it for catholic community as well. I tell you this is democratic way, the other is communal way. It is not Mahasabhites [members of Hindu Mahasabha] who alone are communal, it is the government also that is communal. I charge you with communalism because you are bringing forward a law only for the Hindu community. You must bring it for the Muslim community; take it from me that the Muslim community is prepared to have it but you are not brave enough to do it'.[17]

Sharing an identical view, NC Chatterjee of the Hindu Mahasabha also condemned the Congress government for being subdued because of the adverse political repercussion of uniform civil code. He thus blamed Nehru by saying that 'why not frame, if you have got the courage and wisdom to do it, one Uniform Civil Code? Why are then proceeding with communal legislation?'[18] Rajendra Prasad (who later became India's President) was diplomatic in his response. Instead of questioning Nehru's insistence, he charged him for having 'hurried through the legislation [which] was not warranted since it draws on customs which are ever-changing and ever-growing'.[19] Nehru appears to have been cornered with the barrage of criticism both in the Congress and also outside. Nonetheless, he held the fort by arguing that to his mind, 'the real progress of the country means progress not only on the political plane, not only on the economic plane, but also on the social plane; they have to be integrated all these when the great nation goes forward'.[20] In order to initiate the processes towards evolving a common civil code, he was persuaded to support the Hindu Marriage Act which was approved by the Parliament in 1955. Instead of forcing other communities to accept a common civil code presumably because of the apprehension that it would alienate the Muslims from the Congress, he probably preferred to experiment with the Hindus because he believed that 'the Hindu society which was traditionally dynamic and vibrant [and not] static and inflexible, would be able

---

[16] Ibid., p. 25.

[17] JB Kriplani, 18 June 1956, *Lok Sabha Debates*, Vol. 4, part 2, p. 981, quoted in Reba Som, 'Jawaharlal Nehru and the Hindu Code: A Victory of Symbol over Substance?' *Modern Asian Studies* 28, no. 1 (February 1994): 178.

[18] NC Chatterjee, 26 April 1955, *Lok Sabha Debates*, Vol. 4, Part 2, quoted in Som, 'Jawaharlal Nehru and the Hindu Code', p. 174.

[19] Rajendra Prasad to Nehru, 15 September 1951, reproduced in KM Munshi, ed., *Indian Constitutional Documents: The Pilgrimage to Freedom*, Vol. 1 (Bombay: Bharatiya Vidya Bhawan, 1967), p. 81.

[20] Jawaharlal Nehru's statement in the Lok Sabha, *Lok Sabha Debates*, 26 April 1955, Vol. 4, Part 2, quoted in Som, 'Jawaharlal Nehru and the Hindu Code', p. 181.

to absorb and integrate the changes proposed without any disruption'.[21] Despite vehement opposition by his colleagues, including the resignation of BR Ambedkar, as his Law Minister, by taking the Hindu Marriage Act to its logical conclusion, Nehru is said to have set in motion the processes towards adopting a common civil code in India which however had contrasting legal and constitutional implications because, at one level, it codified Hindu laws, and at another, it also allowed statutorily the diverse customs and usages followed by various sects, communities and regions.

India's socio-political scene did not appear to have changed and the demand for uniform civil code continued to figure in contemporary political discourses. One major intervention in this regard was the 1974 report, prepared by the Committee for the Status of Women in India which also insisted on the implementation of a common civil code as critical to women empowerment. It was thus stated in the Report that 'the chasm between the values of new social order proclaimed by the Constitution and the realities of contemporary India as far as women's rights are concerned remains as great now as at the time of independence'.[22] One of the major factors for such an appalling state of affairs was the failure of the government to push an identical civil code for all the communities. Hence the Committee concluded:

> The absence of a uniform Civil Code in the last quarter of the 20th century, 27 years after independence, is an incongruity that cannot be justified with all the emphasis that is placed on secularism, science and modernization. The continuance of various personal laws which accept discrimination between men and women violate the fundamental rights, and the Preamble to the Constitution which promises to secure all citizens "equality of status", and is against the spirit of national integration and secularism.[23]

Being unanimous in their views, the Committee members thus recommended for 'the expeditious implementation of a Uniform Civil Code'[24] in accordance with the Constitutional directions to ensure equality of status and opportunity. The arguments that they offered were not unique. In a democratic society, separate civil code, they argued, was simply not desirable because it was an impediment towards the growth of the nation as a solid unit. In other words, the constitutional guarantee for separate code for a community does not seem to be logically defensible. A uniform civil code was thus natural, if not inevitable, in a democratic polity.

Legal Interventions

By putting the state's responsibility for introducing a common civil code in the Directive Principles of State Policy which is not enforceable, the Constitution leaves enough space for the judiciary to intervene in the light of the growing demands, made by various groups, for bringing various communities under one civil code though the legislative initiatives to engage with this issue have been 'few and far between'.[25]

[21] Som, 'Jawaharlal Nehru and the Hindu Code', p. 181.

[22] 'Towards Equality', Report of the Committee on the Status of Women in India, Ministry of Education and Social Welfare (Delhi: Government of India, 1974), p. 302. http://feministlawarchives.pldindia.org/wp-content/uploads/towards-equality-1974-part-2.pdf?,.

[23] 'Towards Equality', p. 142.

[24] 'Towards Equality', p. 142.

[25] Flavia Agnes, 'Personal Laws', in *The Oxford Handbook of the Indian Constitution*, p. 915.

The reasons are not difficult to seek because the Constitution is ambiguous on the issue of personal law, and arguments in favour or against are both based on provisions laid in the Constitution. Opposition to reform of personal laws is drawn on 'the freedom of religion and conscience whereas the guarantee to citizens of equal protection from the law and before the law supports a uniform civil code'.[26] Fundamental here is to understand whether rights guaranteed in the Part III of the Constitution can be superseded by personal law. In one of the early pronouncements, in 1954, the Bombay High Court held that since personal laws do not fall within the ambit of 'laws in force' they cannot be declared ultra vires to the rights enshrined in the justiciable Part III of the Constitution. According to this verdict, personal laws were immune from judicial review since scriptures and religious texts were not amenable to judicial interpretation. The controversy over the uniform civil code surfaced again with the 1985 Supreme Court judgement granting financial support to Shah Banu (who once divorced, demanded alimony from her husband) under a provision in secular criminal law. Based on its concern for equality of status, the Supreme Court endorsed the demand for a common civil code by unambiguously stating that

> it is a matter of regret that Article 44 of our constitution is a dead letter. There is no evidence of any official activity for framing a common civil code for the country. A belief seems to have gained ground that it is for the Muslim community to take a lead in the matter of reforms of their personal law. A common civil code will help the cause of national integration by removing disparate loyalties to laws which have conflicting ideologies. No community is likely to bell the cat by making gratuitous concessions on this issue. It is the state which is charged with the duty of securing a uniform civil code for the citizens of the country.[27]

Here too, the basis of the judicial preference for a common civil code is the familiar constitutional direction, available in Article 44 and the overall obvious concern for democratizing rights across communities. In the interest of national integration, it was most desirable and the State needed to take appropriate steps in this regard. But the political texture of contemporary India did not seem to be propitious, as the court clearly stated when it mentioned that

> the legislative competence is one thing, the political courage to use that competence is quite another. We understand the difficulties involved in bringing persons of different faiths and persuasions on a common platform. But a beginning has to be made if the Constitution is to have any meaning. Inevitably, the role of the reformer has to be assumed by the courts because it is beyond the endurance of sensitive minds to allow injustice to be suffered when it is so palpable. But piecemeal attempts of courts to bridge the gap between personal Laws cannot take the place of a common Civil Code. Justice to all is a far more satisfactory way of dispensing justice than justice from case to case.[28]

The Supreme Court seems to have hit the bull's eye. Only with a strong political will of the ruling authority in favour of a common civil code it was possible, as the Court stated very categorically. This verdict provoked

---

[26] Sanghamitra Padhy, 'Secularism and Justice: A Review of Indian Supreme Court Judgments', *Economic and Political Weekly*, 20 November 2004, p. 5031.

[27] *Mohd. Ahmed Khan v. Shah Banu Begam and Others*, 23 April 1985. http://cscs.res.in/dataarchive/textfiles/textfile.2008-07-22.2150472804/file (accessed 2 December 2016).

[28] *Mohd. Ahmed Khan v. Shah Banu Begam and Others.*

the Muslims who characterized this intervention by the Supreme Court as having fiddled with their personal law. The violation of personal law became a rallying point for Muslim political identity. To defuse the crisis, the Rajiv Gandhi-led Congress government hurriedly approved the Muslim Women (protection of rights in divorce) Act in 1986 more or less along the lines endorsed by the Muslim leaders ignoring other dissenting voices. The new law overriding the Supreme Court judgement was defended on democratic grounds. Deference to Muslim opinion on personal law was endorsed by the democratic norm of popular rule and the wishes of a select group of Muslims were identified with the preferences of the majority in the community. Furthermore, the decision was also justified as being compatible with 'the norms of popular sovereignty, the institutions of representative parliamentary government, and the procedures of majority rule within the constraints of a framework of rights'.[29] The Muslim personal law was thus legitimate because it was purportedly a majority opinion and endorsed by an institution (Parliament) with constitutional authority. There is however a contrary point of view which suggests that the government decision to go for such a conciliatory legislation was governed by a clear political calculation of not hurting the patriarchal sentiments of a politically dominated sections among the Muslims, as a former retired bureaucrat, Wajahat Habibullah, confirms. According to him, the Congress government did not contest the Shah Banu verdict because it would 'appear to the Muslim community that the Prime Minister did not regard them as his own'.[30] In what he perceived as 'the defence of their religious right', the Prime Minster would show himself 'worthy of the support that the community had always placed in his family'.[31] It was purely a political calculation that restrained the Congress government from undertaking appropriate steps towards promulgating a common civil code for the communities. It was, in other word, 'the politics of minority accommodation that prevented the introduction of a UCC [Uniform Civil Code] and thus the promotion of modern values'.[32] So, the charge that the ruling party tends not to disturb the applecart does not seem to be overstretched at least in case of implementing the uniform civil code as per Article 44 of the Constitution.

The apex court was again drawn to this issue in 1995 when it was asked to arbitrate in *Sarla Mudgal v. the Union of India*. Here too, Justice Kuldeep Singh was unambivalent in his opinion. Conforming to the popular urge for national integration, he emphasized that uniform civil code was required for national integration, and the minorities, he further stated, should give-up 'their commitment to the two-nation theory and accept reforms in a similar manner as the Hindus and promote national unity'. Since the majority of the Indians had accepted the code, he found it constitutionally incongruent if a select group of minorities remained outside its ambit. Hence the Supreme Court held:

> The government has so far failed to make any effort towards unified personal law for all Indians. The reasons are too obvious to be stated. When more than 80% of the citizens have already been brought under the codified personal law, there is no justification whatsoever to keep in abeyance, any more, the introduction of uniform civil code for citizens in the territory of India.[33]

---

[29] Rochana Bajpai, *Debating Difference: Group Rights and Liberal Democracy in India* (New Delhi: Oxford University Press, 2011), p. 202.

[30] Wajahat Habibullah, 'Deciding Issues of Personal Law', *The Hindu*, 18 October 2016.

[31] Habibullah, 'Deciding Issues'.

[32] Narendra Subramanian, 'Making Family and Nation: Hindu Marriage Law in Early Post-colonial India', *The Journal of Asian Studies* 69, no. 3 (August 2010): 794.

[33] *Sarla Mudgal v. the Union of India*, 10 may 1995. http://judis.nic.in/supremecourt/imgs1.aspx?filename=10742 (accessed 2 December 2016).

The trend continued and the court endorsed the sentiment that for national unity a uniform civil code was a necessity. In the latest judgement in the 2003 *John Vallamattom v. the Union of India*, Chief Justice VN Khare left no confusion when he uttered the following:

> We would like to State that Article 44 provides that the State shall endeavour to secure for all citizens a uniform civil code throughout the territory of India It is a matter of great regrets that Article 44 of the Constitution has not been given effect to. Parliament is still to step in for framing a common civil code in the country. A common civil code will help the cause of national integration by removing the contradictions based on ideologies.[34]

The argument is very explicit. In view of the guarantee, given under Article 44, the State had no difficulty in implementing a common civil code for all. What was suggested in the Sarla Mudgal judgement was reproduced verbatim in this case by saying that a uniform civil code was required for national unity. Implicit here is also the fact that given the acceptance of a common code by the majority of the population, what prevented the other communities from acceding to this was beyond comprehension. Two important ideas were being propagated in this judgement: on the one hand, the court attributed national integration to a common civil code which was also constitutionally endorsed, à la Article 44; the fact that the majority had already accepted the code reinforced, on the other, the claim that it was not undemocratic. What it means is that in view of the majority endorsement, uni-culturalism for the sake of being religio-culturally distinctive does not seem to be a persuasive idea; hence it can be sacrificed for a wider concern for national integration.

Re-reviewing the Argument

The 1950 Constitution does not provide a clearly defined direction and by putting the concern for uniform civil code in the Directive Principles of State Policy, the founding fathers seemed to have avoided being embroiled into unnecessary controversies. As the debates in the Assembly demonstrate, there were arguments on both sides and the dominant section preferred to remain non-committal. Immediately after having assumed power, the Congress leadership also appeared disinclined for legally adopting a common civil code, as Nehru felt, 'at the present moment, the time is not ripe for me to try to push it through'.[35] Nonetheless, strong opinions had built up in its favour. The message of the 1974 report, 'Towards Equality', was explicit. The apex court, in a series of pronouncements, endorsed the idea that uniform civil code was neither unconstitutional nor politico-ideologically untenable, and yet, the idea remains in cold storage since it never received as serious attention as was expected from the law makers. The reasons seem to be located in the constitution itself. Five provisions in Part III (Articles 25, 26, 27, 28, 29 and 30) protect the Right to Freedom of Religion and Cultural and Educational Rights for the minorities. It is from these constitutional stipulations that the religious communities derive the right to be governed by personal law. So, any argument to regiment various ethnic and linguistic groups into a uniform mould could be counter-productive because 'different ethnic, religious and linguistic groups have different traditions and cultures [and] ... their personal laws are based on such variety of traditions and cultures and therefore cannot be

[34] *John Vallamattom v. the Union of India*, 21 July 2003. https://indiankanoon.org/doc/533870/ (accessed 2 December 2016).

[35] Jawaharlal Nehru's statement in the Lok Sabha, 23 April 1954, *Hindustan Times*, 24 April 1954.

obliterated just for the sake of uniformity'.[36] This argument is also too persuasive to be easily dismissed. Similarly, the logic that the Supreme Court upheld in sustaining its argument for a common civil code is also too strong to be kept aside. There is substance when it argues:

> The religious practices, violative of human rights and dignity and sacerdotal suffocation of essentially civil and material freedoms are not autonomy but oppression. Therefore, a unified code is imperative, both, for protection of the oppressed and for promotion of national unity and solidarity.[37]

What the apex court had endorsed seems to have sustained a momentum for a common civil code. In a recent judgement by the Allahabad High Court (December 2016), it has been persuasively argued:

> The Muslim law in India was being applied contrary to the spirit of Koranic laws and the Prophet's teachings. The same misconception vitiates the law dealing with the wife's right to divorce.... The arbitrary and unilateral use of triple *talaq* by Muslim husbands was not in sync with Islamic laws and it was a popular fallacy that a Muslim man enjoys, under the Koranic law, unbridled authority to liquidate marriage. Triple *talaq* is cruel and the most demeaning form of divorce being practised by the Muslim community [and] personal laws of any community could not claim supremacy over the rights granted to individuals by the Constitution. Women cannot remain at the mercy of the patriarchal set-up held under the clutches of sundry clerics having their own interpretation of Holy Quran.[38]

A precarious situation has thus arisen because the constitution is silent and the judicial intervention does not seem to lead us anywhere except amicably sorting out 'the differences of opinion', nurtured by communities to support their contention. The issue remains unresolved and the concern for gender equality which is constitutionally guaranteed does not seem to have received the attention it requires. The argument that personal law is immune from legislative intervention is not sustainable since it stands in contradiction with Article 25 which guarantees the Right to Freedom of Religion 'subject to public order, morality and health and to the other provisions of' Part III of the Constitution. Furthermore, the continuity of the 1867 Portuguese Civil Code in Goa providing equal division of income and property regardless of gender between husband and wife and also between children reinforces the argument that uniform civil code is not a deterrent to communal amity and harmony. So, constitutionally, the demand for a common civil code is justified though it is politically undesirable for the political parties given the fear of losing minority support. Under these circumstances, the only option left is to place the issue for extensive public debate since it is purely a political issue that needs to be settled politically. Laws could be an aid, perhaps powerful, once the issue is clinched through a process of contestation and negotiation. Otherwise, either judicial intervention or intervention by the legislature is too weak to be dismissed as a stray thought!

---

[36] SP Sathe, 'Uniform Civil Code: Implications of Supreme Court Intervention', *Economic and Political Weekly*, 2 September 1995, p. 2165.

[37] *Mohd. Ahmed Khan v. Shah Banu Begam and Others.*

[38] The excerpts of the judgement, pronounced on 8 December 2016 by the Allahabad High Court were given in *The Hindu*, 9 December 2016.

Concluding Observations

The twin goals of gender equality and women empowerment are most critical for inclusive development. As a statement, it makes sense and is easily accepted at its face value; but the trouble starts once efforts are made to implement them in to practice because in a hierarchical society, they are a threat to the prevalent socio-economic and political balances. It is thus obvious that attempts at evolving new social equations reflective of gender equality shall always be opposed vehemently by those upholding patriarchy in its most virulent form. There are two theoretically important points that thus come out: on the one hand, gender equality and women empowerment need to be understood historically given their deeply ingrained socio-economic roots; as the issue is historically textured, it cannot be grasped, let alone conceptualized, on the other, independent of the social context in which it is articulated. To state it simply, the dialectical interconnection between gender equality and women empowerment put in a perspective the twin issues that need to be grappled in a historical context as well. This means that there is hardly a universal model in conceptualizing gender-related issues; but only through context based analyses, they can be comprehended to our satisfaction. What is being reinforced here is the critical role that the context plays in shaping the mind-set supporting or rejecting the prevalent approaches to gender issues. On the whole, it is thus argued that unless linked with the socio-economic and political context, the issues of gender equality and women empowerment can never fully be understood, let alone conceptualized.

Two contemporary issues, namely a uniform civil code and reservation of seats for women in the national Parliament and state legislative assemblies seem to have hogged the limelight in contemporary feminist discourse in India. Conceptually, these twin issues are tuned to the wider concern for freedom and equality. Uniform civil code cannot be accepted so easily since it involves a clear violation of fundamental tenor of the Sharia laws. This thus amounts to a threat to India's secular identity though the continuity of separate civil code for the Muslims negates gender equality in general. The issue has thus created a logjam which none of the political stakeholders are willing to address, presumably due to obvious socio-political repercussions. Similarly, the arguments over the reservation of seats for women in the legislature are justified as essential to fulfil the constitutional goals of freedom and equality. The introduction of the Eighty-First Amendment Bill in 1996 by the United Front government brought back the gender issue to the centre stage of Indian politics. Women needed to be empowered and reservation through a legal enactment was perhaps the most effective device to bypass the patriarchal prejudices responsible for gender discrimination. The efforts have also received severe opposition because it is alleged that a blanket reservation policy is likely to protect the privileged section of women given their instant access to political power due to their specific socio-economic roots. The argument opposing reservation thus draws on the fact that women in India are socially fragmented and it would be conceptually misleading and empirically wrong to conceive of a situation in which women at various social strata articulate a single voice because of their identical biological persona as women. The imbroglio cannot be sorted out so easily. Nonetheless, these debates have established beyond doubt that women are no longer just a voice, but a critical voice challenging the conventional outlook on freedom and equality while providing creative inputs to conceptualize gender equality and women empowerment in the wider social, economic and political context.

Women are disadvantaged due to their gender identity. A blanket legal stipulation may be a necessary, but not sufficient shield against gender discrimination because the degree of women suffering is also contingent on their social location which is conceptually sought to be articulated by the notion of inter-sectionality. As a result, besides being disadvantaged as women, they are also socially deprived due to their social and ethnic identity. In other words, in order to address gender inequality and discrimination, one needs to take into account several other sources which conjointly work to contribute to social exclusion. For instance, women belonging to rural areas, or those who are Muslims or Dalits are naturally underprivileged given the ingrained sectional social prejudices. These women are subject to accumulative dominance which is historically justified and sustained by an appropriate socio-economic and political mechanism. The voice that is raised against the visible sources of gender discrimination is thus rather easily gagged. So, the zeal for uniform civil code or reservation of seats for women in parliament does not seem to completely eradicate gender discrimination or ensure women empowerment in substance unless one is sensitive of the intersectional aspect of women deprivation because of the prevalent mind-set in support of prejudices against gender equality. In that sense, a legal enactment, which is a mere diversional therapy, does not seem to be as decisive as it is projected so long as those who are responsible for implementation hold onto such prejudices.

What is the way out? There is hardly an easy answer because a prejudiced mind cannot be reformed overnight even by applying most stringent coercive measures. One has to constantly attack the sources of prejudices by evolving simultaneously alternative thought processes seeking to bring about changes in the wider social, economic and political environment. This is not a battle between two biologically divided sections of society; but a tussle between two diametrically opposite *weltanschauungs*: one for change, and the other for status quo. Since it is a fight against a mind-set, it cannot be gender-driven, but an encounter involving various sections of society which are persuaded to believe that gender equality is not a charity, but a key to human progress, and hence the sooner it is accomplished, it is better for a society reeling under well-entrenched prejudices depriving half of India's population of equality and fairness.

The Indian feminist discourse confirms once again that there exists the plurality of identities in the single subject: as a woman, she is automatically identified with other women through a blanket description can take us no farther given the embedded diversity due to their specific socio-economic locations. It is therefore theoretically debilitating to essentialize women in view of the deeply ingrained diversity that cannot be ignored in an engagement with gender issues. Women cannot thus be treated as a homogeneous group primarily because their experience as women is determined by their racial, class and ethnic background. Since they are different from one another, the all-inclusive category of woman shall never be an effective aid in understanding the issues of gender equality and women empowerment. Despite being uniform as women, the inevitable differences separating one group of women from another, due to differences around various social, economic and political axes, need to be especially grasped to suggest effective policy solutions; otherwise, there shall hardly be a conclusive end to the debates over gender equality and women empowerment.

Review Questions

1. **What is gender? Elaborate your response.**
2. **How did the founding fathers address the issue of gender in the Constituent Assembly? Elaborate your response.**
3. **Can the issue of gender be conclusively addressed within the constitutional framework? Elaborate your response.**
4. **Gender discrimination is also reinforced by a complementary mind-set. Do you agree with this view? Elaborate your response.**
5. **Gender is also a political question. Explain.**

6. How is gender conceptualized in judicial discourses? Elaborate your response.
7. Constitutional guarantee for gender equality remains vacuous independent of complementary value systems. Do you endorse this view? Elaborate your response.
8. Critically evaluate the 1985 Shah Banu judgement of the Supreme Court of India.
9. Critically assess the constitutional validity of the The Muslim Women (protection of rights on divorce) Act of 1986.
10. How do you assess the argument for and against the Uniform Civil Code? Elaborate your response.

Chapter 11

Right to Freedom of Religion (Articles 25–28)

Learning Objectives

- To understand the importance of the Right to Freedom of Religion as critical to constitutional democracy
- To comprehend the fundamental constitutional values which the founding fathers upheld while framing constitutional provisions to protect the Right to Freedom of Religion
- To grasp the part that the Supreme Court of India had played in seeking to realize the concern that the framers had while devising a specific constitutional design for India in this regard

Religion is both a source of amity and enmity at the same time. As history is a witness to many instances where human beings fought with one another for religious causes, which confirms that religion cements a bond among the socio-economically disparate groups of people. This may appear strange though it is true that regardless of socio-economic differences, people tend to flock together in response to a religious call. Examples are plenty. A cursory look at the socio-political events in India reveals that communal skirmishes leading to riots, on occasions, remain integral to her existence as a polity. It has been established beyond doubt that one of the major causes of the 1947 partition of India was the Hindu–Muslim divide which seemed to have gulfed the nation during the nationalist struggle against the British. As the available literature demonstrates, arguments were marshalled by the respective communities in favour of their claim which they defended by being separate in watertight compartments due to their contrasting religious faiths. What was strange and also conceptually difficult to conceive was the transformation of the communities, engaged in a brutal battle, from 'a class in itself' to 'a class for itself' just because of their distinct religious identity. Religion therefore creates a homogeneous group underplaying the socio-economic differences in specific historical circumstances when religion seems to be privileged over other consideration. Strange as it may sound, it has been true as history is replete with examples. Reasons are not difficult to seek. Because of the peculiar unfolding of communities in the past, religion appears to have created boundary-conscious communities which gain sustenance, if not strength, due to an equally peculiar unfolding of historical processes both during colonialism and its aftermath.

Religion is a consciousness, based on one's subjective understanding of the social reality that one confronts; it is a mirror in which one sees oneself in relation to others. What is puzzling to understand why religion which is a mark of identity becomes divisive in certain circumstances and unifying in another. Here comes the importance of history which enables us to explain the peculiar reality that unfolds especially in circumstances in which, in the name of religion, people behave in a Hobbesian way. The concern here is how to map out the radical transformation of communities as brutal opponents, being placed in watertight compartments despite sharing the same socio-economic space. Being aware of the importance of historical processes in communal divisions, an analyst thus argued that the consolidation of religious animosities 'should perhaps be seen in relation to the long-standing separativeness of religious networks, the acute social distance expressing a high level of social antagonism between [the communities], the lapse of formerly functioning, integrative political and administrative ties and the growth of communally homogeneous groups'.[1] Here too, what is being emphasized is the critical role of social distance in fomenting 'the feeling of being other' in circumstances when there is hardly a channel of communication between the communities. What it confirms is the fact that religion lacks an authority which it gains in specific socio-economic and political milieu. As a consciousness, religion is an ingrained feeling in human beings which cannot be completely washed out. Fundamental here is the point that religion, being largely instrumental in character, is also capable of swaying human action in a specific direction, the nature of which is contingent on circumstances. Two important points need to be kept in mind: on the one hand, while there is no doubt that religion is part and parcel of human existence, and hence it cannot be brushed aside; one should not also miss the point, on the other hand, that there is hardly a universal format in which one can conceptualize religion as a defining influence in case of communal riots since this is context-driven.

This long introduction to the discussion of the Right to Freedom of Religion is neither delinked to the main theme nor unnecessary for our understanding of the situation leading to the incorporation of four Articles (Articles 25, 26, 27 and 28) in the Constitution of India. What governed the founding fathers' choice in favour of these Articles was their concern for sustaining India's socio-cultural diversity, nurtured over generations. For them, this was a necessity not only to maintain India's unique socio-cultural texture, but also to create a harmonious polity in which diversity was privileged over desires for forcible socio-cultural homogeneity. There are two important factors that seem to have influenced the framers of the constitution while they were engaged in discussion in the Constituent Assembly for drafting and also fine-tuning these constitutional provisions. First, despite India's partition on the basis of Hindus and Muslims being two nations in view of well-entrenched cultural separateness, Muslims constitute as high as 12 per cent of the total demography. Apart from Muslims, there were other religious groups who had not had political importance like the Muslims, but remained integral to India's diverse socio-cultural persona. Keen to retain India's unique personality, they were thus persuaded to endorse these provisions. Secondly, being perceptive as they were, the founding fathers had no doubt that the constitutional guarantee of religious freedom was both a powerful critique of the two-nation theory which caused India's vivisection in 1947 and a blueprint of future nation where multiple religious groups would flourish in accordance with their distinctive religio-cultural identities.

Constitutional Roots

No discussion is conceptually persuasive unless one draws on the debates and deliberations in the Constituent Assembly on the Right to Freedom of Religion before that was included in Part III of

[1] Satish Saberwal, 'Elements of Communalism', in *Religion in India*, ed. TN Madan (New Delhi: Oxford University Press, 1991), p. 350.

the Constitution of India. Jawaharlal Nehru while moving the Objective Resolution in the Assembly emphasized the importance of 'the freedom of thought, expression, belief, faith, worship, vocation, association and action, subject to law and public morality'.[2] In his endeavour to create a strong constitutional edifice for India, Nehru further argued:

> The time has come when we should, so far as we are capable of it, rise above our ordinary selves and party disputes and think of the great problem before us in the widest and most tolerant and most effective manner so that whatever we may produce, should be worthy of India as a whole and should be such that the world should recognize that we have functioned, as we should have functioned, in this high adventure.[3]

The message was clear. The aim was to produce a constitution which would take care of the interests of the country men regardless of class, caste, ethnicity or kinship. Primary here was the desire to build a constitutional structure for all. This was stated unambiguously by S Radhakrishnan, the future president of the republic of India in his speech in the Constituent Assembly on 20 January 1947. According to him:

> It is not our desire to establish any sectional Government. We are not here asking anything for a particular community or a privileged class. We are here working for the establishment of Swaraj for all the Indian people. It will be our endeavour to abolish every vestige of despotism, every heirloom of inorganic tradition. We are here to bring about real satisfaction of the fundamental needs of the common man of this country, irrespective of race, religion or community. If the trumpet gives an uncertain sound, we cannot rally the people to our support. It is therefore essential that our bugle call, our trumpet-sound, must be clear, must give people a sense of exhilaration, must give the suspicious and the abstaining a sense of reassurance that we are here pledged to achieve full independence of India, where no individual will suffer from undeserved want, where no group will be thwarted in the development of its cultural life.[4]

What Nehru held while elaborating the Objective Resolution was reverberated by Radhakrishnan who forcefully argued that the proposed constitution was to serve as an instrument to avoid discrimination on any count. There are two important ideas that merit attention. On the one hand, his argument was a powerful critique of those who cast doubts on the entire endeavour for making a constitution for independent India; they were also an endorsement, on the other hand, of what the nationalist leadership postulated for the young nation in the aftermath of decolonization. Basic to his argument was an attempt to chart out a specific course of action rejuvenating the country that was yet to come out of the obvious weaknesses that it had acquired by being a colony. Furthermore, the ingrained social divisions in India which the colonial authority had utilized to its advantage were also a source of concern; it was therefore not surprising that Radhakrishnan strongly felt that the need of the hour was to evolve a constitution for all.

The Nehruvian inputs along with what Radhakrishnan had stated seem to have set the tempo of discussion in the Assembly which was evident in the acceptance of the idea that was upheld by the members

[2] Jawaharlal Nehru, The Objective Resolution, 13 December 1946, *Constituent Assembly Debates*, Book No. 1, p. 59.

[3] Ibid., p. 60.

[4] S Radhakrishnan (from UP general), 20 January 1946, *Constituent Assembly Debates*, Book No. 1, pp. 269–70.

while they were reviewing the Clause for the proposed right to freedom of religion. There was however a view that the Right to freedom of Religion was contrary to secularism which appeared to have been cardinal value for all those involved in the making of the constitution. The view was vehemently opposed. While challenging the idea, Lakshmikant Maitra (Bengal), for instance, argued:

> A secular state is one which does not make any discrimination whatsoever on the ground of religion or community against any person professing any particular form of religious faith [which further] . . . means that no particular religion in the State will receive any State patronage whatsoever.[5]

The idea received further boost from HV Kamath (Central Province and Berar) when he argued that being secular meant the State

> cannot afford to identify itself with the religion of any particular section of the population [though it also did not mean that] state should be anti-religious or irreligious. . . . A secular state [he further clarified] is neither a Godless nor an irreligious not an anti-religious State.[6]

These are important arguments which helped build a support base for the Right to Freedom of Religion which was misconstrued as an effort on the part of the founding fathers to placate the interests of the minorities for partisan ideological gains.

Before the discussion had begun, it was Vallabhbhai Patel who introduced the relevant Clauses for this right. True to his commitment to build an inclusive constitution for the country, Vallabhbhai Patel thus stated:

> All existing laws, notifications, regulations, customs or usages in force within the territories of the Union inconsistent with the rights guaranteed under this part of the Constitution shall stand abrogated to the extent of such inconsistency, nor shall the Union or any unit make any law taking away or abridging any such right.[7]

In his capacity as the Chairman of the Advisory Committee on Minorities and Fundamental Rights, Patel placed the interim report on Fundamental Rights which included (a) rights relating to religion and (b) cultural and educational rights. There were six Clauses: prominent among them were Clause 13 and Clause 18. While the former upheld the view that 'all persons are equally entitled to freedom of conscience, and the right freely to profess, practice and propagate religions subject to public order, morality or health and other constitutional restrictions, as may be required by law, Clause 18 is about the retention of the distinct cultural identity of the religious minorities by agreeing to provide protection to their language, script and culture and it was further assured that there would no laws or regulations that would harm these rights'.[8]

Of all the Clauses, there were two Clauses—Clauses 17 and 18—that provoked heated discussion in the Assembly. While Clause 17 dealt with conversion, Clause 18 referred to the cultural and educational rights

---

[5] Lakshmi Kant Maitra (Bengal), 6 December 1948, *Constituent Assembly Debates*, Book No. 2, p. 831.

[6] HV Kamath (Central Province and Berar), 6 December 1948, *Constituent Assembly Debates*, Book No. 2, p. 825.

[7] Vallabhbhai Patel, 29 April 1947, *Constituent Assembly Debates*, Book No. 1, p. 415.

[8] Vallabhbhai Patel to Rajendra Prasad, the chairman of the Constituent Assembly, Annexure entitled 'Justiciable Fundamental Right', 23 April 1947, *Constituent Assembly Debates*, Book No. 1, pp. 442–43.

for the minorities. According to Clause 17, 'conversion from one religion to another by coercion or undue influence shall not be recognized by law'. In response to this, KM Munshi from Bombay pleaded for adding 'conversion by fraud' to the original Clause because there were instances of conversion by deception. By referring to innumerable case of conversion of minors, Munshi was insistent on putting it in the constitution. Despite having agreed to the basic tenor of the argument, the Christian members, FR Anthony (Bengal) and Reverend JJM Nichols-Roy (Assam) did not seem persuaded by the suggestion that Munshi made since they believed that it was logical for the minors to accept the religion of their parents once they were converted to a new faith. In Anthony's opinion, it was a democratic rights of the adults while, for Roy Nichols, conversion was also an outcome of being spiritually swayed for a particular religion. While elaborating his point, he thus argued:

> Conversion does not mean only that a man changes his form of religion from one religion to another, or adopts a different name of religion, such as, a Hindu becomes a Christian. But there is also the spiritual aspect of conversion, that is, the connection of the soul of man with God, which must not be overlooked by this House.[9]

In the same vein, Reverend Jerome D'Souza stated that since the Assembly was making a constitution for all, some provision must be made which

> will safeguard the authority of the parent, both parents or the surviving parent . . . to the babies in the arms of their mothers. To take them away from the mother or father, who are with them, practically identified physically and juridically with them is to introduce into our legislation an element [he further emphasized] which certainly weakens the concept of authority and sanctity of the family'.[10]

As is evident, both Anthony and D'Souza defended the argument by reference to idea of parents being naturally endowed with authority over their kids. Since this was sacrosanct, no law was justified in this regard.

The tough stance in favour of automatic minority conversion provoked a fierce debate in the Assembly and there were members who forcefully countered the arguments, made by their colleagues belonging to a different religious faith. AR Shastri (Uttar Pradesh), for instance, referred to the history of conversion by force which was contrary to the democratic spirit on which the proposed constitution rested. In an elaborate defence of his contention, he mentioned:

> Wherever the Europeans or white races of Europe, who ruled practically over the whole world, [had gone] they had gone as Missionaries at the outset. . . . The cross was followed by swords which was the pattern everywhere. The Missionaries were followed by the batons, the swords and the guns. It was in this way that they employed coercion for spreading their religions and for extending their Empire. At the same time, they put economic and political pressure on the indigenous tribes and consolidated the foundations on their dominion.[11]

---

[9] Reverend JJM Nichols-Roy (Assam), 11 May 1947, *Constituent Assembly Debates*, Book No. 1, p. 491.

[10] Reverend Jerome D'Souza (Madras), 1 May 1947, *Constituent Assembly Debates*, Book No. 1, p. 496.

[11] AR Shastri (UP), 1 May 1947, *Constituent Assembly Debates*, Book No. 1, p. 497.

By drawing on the history of the expansion of Christianity in India which invariably accompanied the Empire, Shastri justified his argument as integral to basic human instincts. Religious faith was a matter of human conscience which never built up all of a sudden, but over a period of time and after serious pondering over this. Hence he insisted that conversion was justified only when it was based of mutual reciprocity and not forcibly. This was not the case in a majority of the instances of conversion where coercion was indiscriminately applied. As he mentioned, 'you tempt the innocent little ones who you take in your lap, by a suit of clothes, a piece of bread and a little toy and thus you ruin their lives'.[12] By referring to innumerable examples where the minors had no choice but to accept the religion that their parents had accepted, he also justified the contention that most of them later repented because 'they did not get an opportunity to have a religion of their choice'.[13] In view of the obvious anomalies in the arguments that the Christian members put forward in their defence, Shastri supported the amendment justifying the inclusion of a Clause in the Section on Fundamental Rights saying that 'a person who wants to change his religion should be able to do so only after he is convinced through cool deliberation that the new religion is more satisfactory to him that the old one'.[14]

A perusal of the debates shows that the members differed from one another. Apart from the Christian members who hardly supported the suggestion for reconversion, there was unanimity among the members belonging to the other religious groups. As a result, Munshi's amendment was approved and the Clause was referred back to the Advisory Committee for reconsideration. In a similar fashion, Clause 18 upholding the distinct cultural rights for the minorities also led to an extensive discussion in the Assembly. Here too, instead of taking a definite position, those arguing for minority rights defended their point by saying that this needed to be understood contextually. Mahavir Tyagi (Uttar Pradesh) expressed this view by clearly stating that

> in matters like these, i.e., cultural and educational rights, they could be defined only as far as they appertain to individuals and the question of minorities had better be left for the future Governments ... [and] they should be given a free hand to decide according to the times and the situations they face.[15]

This is one aspect of the argument. There is another argument that was also floated, among others by KM Munshi and Mahavir Tyagi, suggesting that the Assembly should not make a definite decision in this regard till 'we see what rights the minorities are given by Pakistan Assembly'.[16] This was based on the media reports coming from across the border which were referred to by these members while defending their respective points of view. Appalled by such an argument, BR Ambedkar thus forcefully stated that 'rights of the minorities should be absolute rights [and] ... they should not be subject to any consideration as to what another party may like to do to minorities within its jurisdiction'.[17] Furthermore, he was also not in favour of strict directions in this regard since it would deprive the legislature of its 'sovereign rights to legislate in areas that it deems appropriate at a particular historical juncture'.[18] Ambedkar's arguments

---

[12] Ibid., p. 499.
[13] Ibid., p. 490.
[14] Ibid., p. 497.
[15] Mahavir Tyagi (UP), 1 May 1947, *Constituent Assembly Debates*, Book No. 1, p. 505.
[16] AR Shastri (UP), 1 May 1947, *Constituent Assembly Debates*, Book No. 1, p. 505.
[17] BR Ambedkar (Bengal), 1 May 1947, *Constituent Assembly Debates*, Book No. 1, p. 497.
[18] Ibid., p. 502.

seem to have clinched the issue that most of the members had supported. The proposed constitutional design might have caused consternation among some members though those who fought strongly for protecting the linguistic and cultural minorities appreciated the endeavour. Jaipal Singh of Bihar thus complimented Ambedkar and his colleagues who did not allow the detractors to prevail by saying that the Clause

> seems to open a new era for India . . . [and he hoped that] the bitterness that there is in the provinces on account of this linguistic warfare may gradually disappear and linguistic minorities may feel that their language will not be victimised, that they may develop their language as they like and that their language has a rightful place in the country.[19]

A scan of the issues that the members had raised while defending their respective positions in the Constituent Assembly reveals that the framers took ample care for protecting the rights of the linguistic and cultural minorities. The reason is not difficult to seek especially in the light of the creation of Pakistan on the basis of two-nation theory which recognized the politico-ideological rights of the minorities in colonial India. As a result, Clause 18, which dealt with the cultural and linguistic minorities, was readily accepted and became an integral part of the future Constitution of India. Clause 17 dwelling on the conversion and other complex religious issues, as shown earlier, was returned to the Advisory Committee for reconsideration.

Actual Provisions

As per the Preamble, the Constitution of India is 'to secure to all its citizens . . . liberty of faith, belief and worship'. This was the ideological inspiration for the provisions that were incorporated in the Constitution to protect the Right to Freedom of Religion. There are four provisions (Articles 25, 26, 27 and 28) for these rights and two for cultural and educational rights (Articles 29 and 30). The Constituent Assembly approved Clauses (from Clauses 13 to 18) had their place in the Constitution of India which also suggests that the constitutional provisions drew on the discussions in the Assembly in which members deliberated on those issues which, they felt, were critical for governance in future India. Of these Articles, Article 25 appears to hold the substance of the Right to Freedom of Religion which is evident in the language in which it was articulated. There is hardly any ambiguity as the Article states very clearly that 'subject to public order, morality and health and to other provisions of this Part, all persons are equally entitled to freedom of conscience and the right to freely profess, practise and propagate religion'. Right that is being given here is not an absolute right but conditional as it is subject to public order, morality, health and other relevant Articles of Part III of the Constitution. True to their commitment to build an inclusive society, the founding fathers left no ambiguity in the Constitution which was further upheld in Article 26 which states that 'subject to public order, morality and health, every religious denomination or any section thereof shall have the right

1. to establish and maintain institutions for religious and charitable purposes;
2. to manage its own affairs in matters of religion;

---

[19] Jaipal Singh (Bihar), 8 December 1948, *Constituent Assembly Debates*, Book No. 2, p. 907–08.

3. to own and acquire movable and immovable property; and
4. to administer such property in accordance with law'.

Article 26 is relatively unambiguous since it ensures that minorities are not restrained in undertaking what they deem relevant for their religious faith, subject, of course, to the conditions that the Constitution has stipulated. This does not hold good vis-à-vis Article 25 which supports only conditional enjoyment of rights because of the well-defined conditions that it has put forward. The Right is not absolute and the State is allowed to intervene if the exercise of such a Right contravenes others' Rights. This can be interpreted in two different ways: one may be persuaded to believe, on the one hand, that it is necessary to endow the state with such an authority to allow minorities to enjoy their constitutionally guaranteed rights meaningfully; hence the restrictions do not appear to be unwarranted. On the other hand, it will also give the state a handle to restrict activities by reference to this provision in circumstances when it tends to deviate from the established constitutional practices for specific ideological reasons. Nonetheless, the constitutional restrictions represent a desire to create a discrimination-free society, as condition (2b) of Article 25 empowers the state to allow all classes and sections of Hindus access to the Hindu religious institutions which was both an attack on the system of denial of access to a section of Hindus because of well-entrenched social prejudices and an endorsement of the ideological keenness of the framers for building an inclusive society by erasing divisions along caste, clan and ethnic axes.

The other important segment of the Right to Freedom of Religion is cultural and educational rights for the minorities which Article 29 and 30 devise. These are provisions guaranteeing specific rights to pursue the distinct religious and cultural ethos which are integral to one's conscience. Article 29 has two clauses: while Clause 1 stipulates that 'any section of the citizens residing in the territory of India or any part thereof having a distinct language, script or culture of its own shall have the right to conserve the same', Clause 2 underlines that 'no citizen shall be denied admission into any educational institutions maintained by the State or receiving aid out of State funds on grounds only of religion, race, caste, language or any of them'. Complementing the effort, Article 30 confirms that 'all minorities, whether based on religion or language, shall have the right to establish and administer educational institutions of their choice' and the state, 'shall not, in granting aid to educational institutions, discriminate against any educational institution on the ground that it is under the management of a minority, whether based on religion or language'. The message is very clear. The state, being nonpartisan, shall not engage in any activities which are clearly tilted in favour of one faith against another. No discrimination is permissible, as per the constitutional provisions. With a proactive judiciary, the ambit of the Right to Freedom of Religion has been, observes the Supreme Court of India, widened by the judicial interpretation that what is guaranteed by Articles 25 and 26 is 'the right of the individual to practise and propagate not only matters of faith and belief but also all those rituals and observances which are regarded as integral parts of a religion by the followers of its doctrines'.[20] Being sensitive to secular values which are ingrained in India and articulated in its unfolding, the Indian judiciary had also played a critical role in defending those constitutional ideas which the founding fathers upheld as concomitant to their desire for making the country a level playing field for minorities. A perusal of the past affirms the assumption that the Constitution champions the minority rights in two ways: by putting a specific constitutional design in place for protecting the rights of the minorities, the Constitution has, on the one hand, contributed to the development of a mechanism which cannot be so easily stifled because of the presence of an alert judiciary, which on the other hand,

[20] *The Commissioner of Hindu Religious Endowment v. LT Swamiar*, AIR, 1954, SC 282.

through its multiple pronouncements, also conveys the message that constitutional values in support of the minorities shall always remain prior to any other considerations. As well as defending the minority rights, the apex court also upheld the view that the state was authorised to put an embargo on religious activities which were repugnant to the values that it nurtured for the sake of peace and tranquillity in the society. It was made amply clear in the 1954 famous case involving the State of Bombay and Bombay Education Society in which the then Chief Justice of India, MC Chagla pronounced:

> It is not as if the State is helpless before minorities who may set up any kind of educational institutions. The important corrective that the State has and possesses is that unless the educational institution conforms to and complies with the proper rules laid down by the State, the State may deny to the educational institutions any aid from its funds. . . . The power of the State to make reasonable regulations for all schools . . . or to prescribe a curriculum for institutions which it supports cannot be questioned. The choice of the minorities is not unfettered and the State can make reasonable regulations.[21]

After having ascertained absolute rights to the State when it funded an educational institution, the Court also reminded that so long as the present Constitution remained, the State needed to take care of the minorities within the constitutional restrictions. As the court upheld:

> So long as the Constitution stands as it is and is not altered, it is, we conceive, the duty of this Court to uphold the fundamental rights and thereby honour the sacred obligations to the minority communities who are of our own. Throughout the ages, endless inundations of men of diverse creeds, cultures and races, Aryans, non-Aryans, Dravidians and Chinese, Scythians, Huns, Pathans and Mughals—have come to this ancient land from distant regions and climes. India has welcomed them all. They have met and gathered, given and taken and got mingled, merged and lost in one body.[22]

The judicial verdict is instructive in two complementary ways: on the one hand, it did not allow the State authority to be infringed when it supports the educational institutions financially for its regular upkeep and functioning. Here, the authority of the State is, in other words, made absolute in a specific context. This does not however, on the other hand, undermine the rights of the minorities to pursue their distinctive cultural and linguistic traits with their own financial means since it conforms to the Fundamental Rights that the Constitution recognizes.

Concluding Observations

In a socio-culturally diverse society like India, the Right to Freedom of Religion is one of the critical Fundamental Rights that the Constitution guarantees for lawful citizens of the country. A perusal of the debates shows that the founding fathers were persuaded to believe that Clauses 17 and 18 were adequately equipped to uphold India's identity as a multicultural socio-political entity. As is argued earlier, the framers

---

[21] *The State of Bombay v. Bombay Education Society*, AIR, 1954, SC 561.

[22] *The State of Bombay v. Bombay Education Society*.

did not appear to have paid enough attention to the issue of religious minority in view of the partition which MA Jinnah defended on the basis of Hindus and Muslims being separate nations. For them, the issue was largely clinched which does not appear to have a solid logical base as India had a substantial Muslim population even after the division of the country along religious axis. Nonetheless, the debates in the Constituent Assembly in which the members addressed the concern in open minds presumably were geared to devise appropriate constitutional provisions for governing a new nation with a long colonial past. The design has its pitfalls though it contributed to the unfolding of processes leading to the creation and also consolidation, in course of time, of constitutional democracy in India.

The constitutional provisions in this section of Part III of the Constitution are very useful in two complementary ways: on the one hand, these provisions provide a solid foundation to the constitutional edifice for the protection of minority rights which are justiciable within the limits that the Constitution sets out. They are also very pertinent, on the other hand, in guiding the judiciary in devising a specific constitutional path for the State. In other words, these Articles, by being both directional and advisory, help the court develop its own responses in accordance with what it deems appropriate in consonance with the inputs from within the socio-political milieu in which it operates. Significant here is the idea that constitution and judiciary are dialectically interconnected which is a powerful theoretical input in reconceptualizing their interconnection in a specific socio-economic and political context.

Review Questions

1. **What is the right to freedom of religion? Elaborate.**
2. **How did the founding fathers conceptualize the right to freedom of religion? Elaborate.**
3. **Critically evaluate the constitutional provisions relating to the right to freedom of religion.**
4. **Do you think that the right to freedom of religion constitutes an important pillar of India's constitutional democracy? Elaborate your response.**
5. **Is this right reflective of a policy of appeasement of minorities or an attempt to realize the fundamental ethos of democratic governance? Elaborate your response.**
6. **How did the Indian judiciary address the concern for the right to freedom of religion? Elaborate.**
7. **Is it fair to argue that the right to freedom of religion is an inalienable right in a democratic polity? Do you agree? Elaborate your view.**
8. **The right to freedom of religion epitomizes a common concern for secular values in collective existence. Explain.**
9. **How do you link the importance of this right in articulating the fundamental democratic ethos for governance? Elaborate your response.**
10. **The right to freedom of religion appears to be futile unless it is complemented by a supportive mind-set. Do you agree with this view? Elaborate your response.**

Chapter

12

Secularism in India

Learning Objectives

- To understand how secularism is critical to constitutional democracy
- To conceptualize the distinctive characteristics of secularism in India with reference to the socio-economic milieu in which it is being constantly reinvented
- To grasp how the judiciary contributes to reconceptualize secularism in the Indian context

Indian variety of secularism is a mixed bag in the sense that it hardly corresponds to the conventional wisdom on the phenomenon. It was creatively articulated underlining the complexities of typical non-western contexts. Broadly speaking, there are two issues that remain critical in the conceptualization of secularism in India: (a) the presence of religion in the public domain and (b) the right of the state to intervene in matters of religion. The reasons why these issues figure prominently in the discourses on secularism need to be located in India's past as a colony. There is no dearth of evidence to argue that religion played havoc in the period leading to the partition of the country following the British withdrawal in 1947. What contributed to the articulation of the two-nation theory which fueled the division is not the concern of this chapter. Nonetheless, it has amply proved how religion shaped public response in a particular historical context which confirms the point that religion had a public presence. That the British state utilized religion to fine-tune its strategy of *divide-et-impera* is also established beyond doubt. This is a testimony to the argument that the state intervenes in a domain which is absolutely private as and when it supports the ideological design that it champions. This chapter thus makes two arguments: first, by drawing on India's distinctive socio-economic and political texture in a historical perspective, this part of the text seeks to understand the processes culminating in a specific type of secularism with almost no similarity with its classical form that had emerged in the Western context. The emphasis here is to understand the distinct character of India's secularism that cannot be conceptualized in a derivative theoretical format. The second argument, a corollary of the first, underlines the fact that since India's secularism defies the pattern that is considered to be universal, it needs to be understood with reference to India's distinct socio-economic and cultural milieu in which it is being articulated and also reinvented. Fundamental here is the point that being organic to the prevalent context, the distinct nature of India's secularism cannot be captured in a theoretical mould, borrowed from the West.

Before we embark on the discussion, it is better to begin with the definition of secularism. Conventionally, secularism is about the separation of religion from public domain which means that the state will remain neutral in so far as its responses in the public domain are concerned. This is being persuasively questioned since in an open society, the state will reflect, argues an analyst, the character of the society. Secularism is therefore 'a social myth' in India seeking to conceptualize a mind-set in accordance with values which are foreign to it; it is 'a vacuous word, a phantom concept' for such people who are instinctively appreciative of multiple religious traditions primarily due to the cultural moorings that they imbibe by being born as Hindus.[1] Being culturally inappropriate, secularism in the Western sense will hardly be of use since tolerance is instinctively ingrained for the majority.[2] Notwithstanding criticism of this point of view, the argument holds water in view of the of available academic treaties showing that religious intolerance is the product of circumstances and is most engineered for the fulfillment of narrow partisan objectives.

Keeping aside the debate over secularism as a process-driven concept, let us concentrate on how it evolved in modern India. There is no disagreement that India is a religious society in which religion remains a powerful marker of one's social identity. Equally important is the idea that religion is exclusively a part of one's private domain. Historically speaking, the idea of secularism in India has drawn on two important conceptualizations that had emerged during the nationalist struggle. On the one hand, there existed the idea that Gandhi and Maulana Azad had offered by devising the notion of *sarvdharma sadbhava* (goodwill towards all religion) which represented an effort to build a goodwill among the socio-culturally diverse Indians by being respectful to one another despite having different religious affiliations. There was, on the other hand, *dharma nirpekshta* (religious neutrality) of Jawaharlal Nehru which was sought to be created in a society, known for privileging religion over other sources of identity. While the former has clear Indian roots the latter is drawn on the Western mode of conceptualizing. In reality however, neither of them does not seem to be as effective as is expected: secular values are always appreciated as integral to the public domain though religious differences continue to cause unbridgeable gulf that manifests in communal riots, the history of which can be stretched back to the British era.

Historical Antecedents of the Idea

Besides the Preamble, which was revised in 1976 with the promulgation of the Forty-Second Amendment Act, there is hardly a specific provision in the Constitution in which the expression 'secularism' figured. There was a serious attempt in the Constituent Assembly to incorporate a provision to that effect. On 3 December 1948, it was KT Shah (Bihar) who moved an amendment in the form of a new Article 18A which stated that 'the State in India being secular shall have no concern with any religion, creed or profession of faith; and shall observe an attitude of absolute neutrality in all matters relating to the religion or any class of citizens or other persons in the Union'.[3] In his explanation of the provision in the Assembly, he elaborated what he meant by 'secularism' as follows:

> By this I do not wish to suggest that the neutrality of the State in matters of religion should mean utter ignorance or neglect of institutions or services which, in the name of religion or belief, be conducted by people professing a particular form of faith. All I wish to say is that

[1] TN Madan, 'Secularism in Its Place' in *Religion in India*, ed. TN Madan (New Delhi: Oxford University Press, 1991), pp. 394–409.

[2] Ashis Nandy, 'The Politics of Secularism and the Recovery of Religious Tolerance' in *Secularism and Its Critics*, ed. Rajeev Bhargava (New Delhi: Oxford University Press, 1998), pp. 321–43; Partha Chatterjee, 'Secularism and Tolerance', *Economic and Political Weekly*, 9 July 1994, pp. 1768–77.

[3] KT Shah (Bihar), 3 December 1948, Book No. 2, *Constituent Assembly Debates*, p. 815.

> with the actual profession of faith or belief, the State should have no concern. Nor should it be, by any action of it, given any indication that it is partial to one or the other. All classes of citizens should have the same treatment in matters of mundane from the State. And, even those who may not be citizens of this State, by living within it, should receive the same treatment.[4]

The amendment that Shah moved was defeated. Nonetheless, it set in motion a perspective in which the debate seems to have acquired the basic conceptual inputs which appeared to have shaped the opinion that the members of the Constituent Assembly had put forward. In his intervention, Tajamul Husain (Bihar) thus argued:

> Religion is a private affair between oneself and his Creator [and] it has nothing to do with others. . . . India, being secular state . . . should not have anything to do with religion [and] the lawful citizens of the country . . . should be allowed to practise and profess their own religion privately.[5]

By reference to the argument, made by Husain, KT Shah further adumbrated the view that he was not actuated 'by any feeling of partiality for one or opposition to another'. He only wished 'that one's religious belief be left as a matter of personal concern'.[6] A perusal of the above mentioned argument confirms the assumption that Assembly members were persuaded to believe that religion or one's professing of a particular faith belongs to an exclusive private domain, within which the individual is free since it causes no harm to others. Core to the argument is the idea that religion is fundamentally a private deed which is consistent with the basic conceptual format of the idea. While there were supporters, there were opponents too who felt that since religious tolerance led to the partition of the country, the arguments for secularism seemed to have lost their viability. So, for them, the issue needs to be understood in a historical perspective which means that one cannot brush aside the historical ambience in which the idea opposed to secularism gains salience. This was the point which Lokenath Misra of Orissa forcefully put across in his defence when he stated:

> For obvious and good reasons, India has . . . to be a secular state. Does it not mean that we have nothing to do with any religion? (. . . the propaganda of religion brought India into this unfortunate state and India had to be divided). If Islam had not come to impose its will on this land, India would have been a perfectly secular state and a homogeneous State. There would have been no question of partition. Therefore, we have rightly tabooed religion. And now to say that as a fundamental right everybody has a right to propagate his religion is not right. . . . Why do you make [India] a Secular State? The reason may be that religion is not necessary or it may be that religion is necessary, but as India has many religions, Hinduism, Christianity, Islam, Sikhism, we cannot decide which one to accept. . . . If you accept religion, you must accept Hinduism as it is practised by an overwhelming majority of the people of India.[7]

---

[4] Ibid., p. 816.
[5] Tajamul Husain, 3 December 1948, Book No. 2, *Constituent Assembly Debates*, p. 818.
[6] KT Shah (Bihar), 3 December 1948, Book No. 2, *Constituent Assembly Debates*, p. 821.
[7] Lokenath Misra, 3 December 1948, Book No. 2, *Constituent Assembly Debates*, p. 822.

This was an extreme position that Misra had held and his colleagues in the Assembly were not persuaded because they endorsed the view of *dharma nirpekshta* which meant that the state should remain neutral and not prejudiced to any of the religious groups. The state 'shall therefore not establish or endow or patronize any particular religion'.[8] Perhaps the most vivid description of secularism was given by Lakshmi Kanta Maitra of West Bengal when he said:

> The State is not going to establish, patronize or endow any particular religion to the exclusion of or in preference to others and that no citizens in the State will have any preferential treatment or will be discriminated against simply on the ground that he professed a particular form of religion. In other words, in the affairs of the State, the professing of any particular religion will not be taken into consideration at all.[9]

This was a strong argument that Maitra made in his defence for secularism. The State should absolutely be neutral to all the communities regardless of their religious affiliation. While insisting on state neutrality in governance, Maitra took ample care in ascertaining individuals' secular rights when he said:

> We must be careful to see that in this land of ours we do not deny to anybody the right not only to profess or practise but also to propagate any particular religion. . . . In the exercise of this Fundamental Right every community inhabiting this State professing any religion will have equal right and equal facilities to do whatever it likes in accordance with its religion provided it does not clash with the conditions laid down here.[10]

Notwithstanding differences of opinion, the Constituent Assembly finally witnessed a consensus on this issue which was supportive of the Nehruvian *dharma nirpekshta*. The idea was unambiguously articulated by BR Ambedkar when he spoke in the Assembly to clarify whether the minority institutions were authorized to conduct religious teaching. According to him:

> Religious instruction has been left free to be taught and given by each community according to its aims and objects subject to certain conditions. All that is barred is this, that the State in the institutions maintained by it wholly out of public funds, shall not be free to give religious instruction.[11]

There was no confusion. The founding fathers were persuaded to accept the idea of state neutrality in governance which was largely a derivative of the Western notion of secularism. The Gandhian insistence on equal respect to religion did not appear to have received the attention that it deserved, according to some of the leading Gandhians who voiced their concern in the Assembly. Nonetheless, this chapter of the Assembly debates is most illuminating in grasping the processes that were critical in the making of the constitutional provisions relating to secularism.

---

[8] HV Kamath (Central Province and Berar), 3 December 1948, Book No. 2, *Constituent Assembly Debates*, p. 826.

[9] Lakshmi Kanta Maitra, 3 December 1948, Book No. 2, *Constituent Assembly Debates*, p. 831.

[10] Ibid., p. 832.

[11] BR Ambedkar (Bengal), 7 December 1948, Book No. 2, *Constituent Assembly Debates*, p. 884.

Unfolding of Secularism in Independent India

As is argued earlier, the Constituent Assembly favoured the Nehruvian ideas of state neutrality to religion which got translated in the constitutional provisions. It was most succinctly stated by Ambedkar in his intervention in independent India's parliament when he was defending the Hindu Code Bill in 1951. According to him, a secular state

> does not mean that we shall not take into consideration the religious sentiments of the people. All that a secular state means is that this Parliament shall not be competent to impose any particular religion upon the rest of the people. This is the only limitation that the Constitution recognizes.[12]

The argument is crystal clear. Parliament is not authorized to intervene in matters of conscience which is exclusively a private domain. The emphasis here is on the public authority which has to be absolutely neutral. In tune with this idea, Radhakrishnan, the future President of India, clarified further as follows:

> When India is said to be a secular state, it does not mean that we reject the reality of an unseen spirit or the relevance of religion to life or that we exalt irreligion. . . . It means that no group of citizens shall arrogate to itself rights and privileges which it denies to others. [Hence] . . . the religious impartiality of the Indian State should not be confused with secularism or atheism. Secularism, as here defined, is in accordance with the ancient religious tradition of India [which draws on] the endeavour to build up a fellowship of believers, not by subordinating individual qualities to the group-mind but by bringing them into harmony with each other.'[13]

Three important ideas are prominent here: first, persuaded to believe that secularism had roots in India's ancient tradition of harmonious existence of multiple religious group, Radhakrishnan argued that it was almost instinctive of the Indians to appreciate the secular values; they thus needed neither to be inculcated nor imposed from above. Secondly, it was made amply clear that the state is not irreligious, as was being propagated during the discussion of this issue in the Constituent Assembly. The constitution gave adequate space and protection to those practising and propagating religion of any denomination. Thirdly, being opposed to majoritarinism, he unequivocally declared that the right to practise and propagate religion was not an exclusive domain of one group or people at the cost of the others. This was a universal right which could never be allowed to be infringed under any circumstances.

Basic to the argument is the idea that secularism is neither foreign nor an alien inclination for the Indians, but is instinctive to them. An integral part of the social ambience, it evolves naturally because of the context which not only sustains but also consolidates the values in its support. Secularism is thus not an ideology but intimately linked with civilized behaviour practised by all except those nurturing exclusive socio-political identity drawing on religion. Nehru explicitly stated this when he declared that it was not a big deal

> by saying that [since] we are a secular state we have done something amazingly generous, given something out of our pocket to the rest of the world, something which we ought not to

[12] BR Ambedkar's statement in Parliament on 5 February 1951, *Parliamentary Debates*, 1951, Vol. III, part II, p. 2466.
[13] S Radhakrishnan, *Recovery of Faith* (New York: Harper Brothers, 1955), p. 202.

> have done, so on and so forth. We have only done something which every country does except a very few misguided and backward countries in the world. Let us not refer to that the word in the sense that we have done something very mighty.[14]

As it is clear, Nehru's strategy could be dubbed as one 'that sought to transcend cultural differences, accommodate conflicts arising out of them, combat parochial and militant Hindu nationalist forces and get on with the business of state as he saw it'.[15] It would be thus appropriate to argue that Nehru saw 'the agenda of the modern state in terms of the transformation of Indian society from one regulated by *dharma* to one of law and instrumental rationality'.[16] This was evident in his argument against the Hindu Code Bill that sought to impose a uniform civil code for the country. Division within the Congress party forced the withdrawal of the bill which ultimately led to the resignation of BR Ambedkar from the Union ministry. In its place, the Hindu Marriage Bill was proposed suggesting a uniform civil code for the Hindus. While criticizing those opposed to the Bill, Nehru emphatically pronounced:

> It is only the women who have to behave like Sita and Savitri [Hindu mythical characters famous for their feminine virtues], the men may behave as they like. ... You cannot have a democracy, of course, if you cut off ... fifty percent of the people and put them in a separate class apart in regard to social privileges. They are bound to rebel against that.[17]

His opposition to the Indian Cattle Preservation Bill, 1955 was also grounded on his faith in 'tolerant pluralism', 'cultural diversity' and 'egalitarianism'. Although the bill was finally shelved because, procedurally, the subject belonged to the state legislature, Nehru argued strongly to knock down the arguments in its endorsement. Those who supported the bill on religious grounds because the importance of cow in Hinduism lost their ground once Nehru exposed the logical incongruity in their arguments. As he elaborated:

> the combination of religion and politics in the narrowest sense of the word, resulting in communal politics is—there can be no doubt—a most dangerous combination and must be put an end to. It is clear ... that this combination is harmful to the country as a whole; it is harmful to the majority, but probably it is most harmful to any minority that seeks to have some advantages from it.[18]

The critical point that emanates from Nehru's intervention on these two bills is linked with his broader ideological vision of a modern state that draws on tradition, but tempered by modern liberal values. Persuaded by the Leninist statecraft, he believed in a strong state capable of guiding human existence in accordance with definite plans. The state emerged as a focal point of social, political and economic

---

[14] Jawaharlal Nehru, 12 August 1949, *Constituent Assembly Debates*, Book No. 4, p. 401.

[15] Paul Brass, 'The Strong State and the Fear of Disorder', in *Transforming India: Social and Political Dynamics of Democracy*, eds. Francine Frankel, Zoya Hasan, Rajeev Bhargava and Balveer Arora (Delhi: Oxford University Press, 2000), p. 79.

[16] Subrata Mitra, 'Desecularising the State: Religion and Politics in India after Independence', *Comparative Studies in Society and History* 33, No. 4 (October 1991), p. 775.

[17] Jawaharlal Nehru's intervention in the Lok Sabha debate on the Hindu Marriage Bill, *The Lok Sabha Debates*, 5 May 1955, p. 7963, quoted in Mitra, 'Desecularising the State', p. 770.

[18] Jawaharlal Nehru's statement, quoted in Bimal Prasad, *Gandhi, Nehru and JP: Studies in Leadership* (Delhi: Chanakya, 1985), p. 136.

transformation. Nehru's historical success therefore lay not in the dissemination of democratic idealism, but in 'its establishment of the state at the core of India's society'.[19] The state remained strong so long as Nehru reigned supreme presumably because of the nationalist sentiments that survived.

The Puzzle

Despite the pronounced commitment of the founding fathers to secularism, it is a puzzle that the expression was nowhere in the Constitution which was promulgated in 1950. It is true that their concern for an egalitarian state was undiluted; nonetheless, they never felt the need of inserting the expression—secular—in the constitution which is a mystery to the students of the Constitution especially in the aftermath of the Partition due to the consolidation of incompatible communal socio-economic and political interests. It took almost three decades since the inauguration of the Constitution when by a decree of the Parliament, the word 'secular' was added to the Preamble to the Constitution during the height of 1975–77 internal Emergency. In the parliamentary debates that preceded the inclusion of the word, it was evident that the parliamentarians supported the Nehruvian model of secularism which entailed that a secular state 'does not obviously mean a state where religion is discouraged; it means, instead, freedom of religion and conscience, including freedom for those who have no religion, subject only to their not interfering with each other with the basic conception of our state'.[20] The Nehruvian spirit was articulated in Article 25(1) of the Constitution which states that the Right to Freedom of Religion is a guarantee of 'freedom of conscience and the right to freely profess, practise and propagate religion'. Secularism thus defined runs counter to its Western connotation which excludes all considerations, drawn on belief in God. There will thus be no discrimination between citizens on the basis of their religion or the form of worship. In the light of this, India ceases to be a secular state despite being defined accordingly in the Preamble to the Constitution of India. There are instances of glaring instances of discrimination which runs contrary to the values of secularism. For instance, notwithstanding the constitutional bar against discrimination, there are separate civil codes and communities are allowed to enjoy protection accordingly though Article 44 of the Constitution of India requires the state to frame a uniform civil code. To deny rights to the Muslim women which are available to women of other faith is a clear violation of the provision of the Constitution insisting on the state not being discriminatory on grounds of religion. There is however a constitutional lapse here. Article 44 is not justiciable since it is included in the Part IV of the Constitution enumerating the Directive Principles of State Policy. Furthermore, the founding fathers seem to have been persuaded not to insist on uniform civil code to convey the message that Muslims would be allowed to nurture their distinctive cultural identity regardless of whether it contradicted the secular persona of the country. This was perhaps a strategic measure in order to bring the Muslims to the mainstream in a context when they felt threatened following the creation of Pakistan which drew on the argument that MA Jinnah forcefully made in favour of Hindus and Muslims being two separate nations due to their unbridgeable religious differences. Acceptance of secularism as a political ideal was therefore a formal registration of a practical necessity in a multi-religious society.

[19] Sunil Khilnani, *The idea of India* (London: Hamish Hamilton, 1997), p. 41.

[20] VC Shukla, the then Information and Broadcasting minister in the Indira Gandhi-led cabinet, defended the cabinet decision in its favour by referring to the statement that Jawaharlal Nehru made in defence of the Hindu Code Bill in 1951. *Parliamentary Debates*, Vol. 18 (June 1976): 2138.

The Judicial Intervention

The Constitution laid out a framework for secularism and the Supreme Court of India refined its texture in a number of remarkable pronouncements which remain critical to our understanding of the idea that founding fathers so assiduously nurtured while devising the rule of law for the country. There are two important judgements which merit attention since they seem to have shaped our approach to secularism. First, the 1994 verdict which also known as the Ramjanmabhumi judgement, in *M Ismail Faruqui and others v. the Union of India and Others* summarized the concept of secularism by underlining that

> it is clear from the constitutional scheme that it guarantees equality in the matter of religion to all individuals and groups irrespective of their faith emphasizing that there is no religion of the State itself. The Preamble of the Constitution read in particular with Article 25 to 28 emphasizes this aspect and indicates that it is in this manner the concept of secularism embodied in the constitutional scheme as a creed adopted by the Indian people has to be understood while examining the constitutional validity of any legislation on the touchstone of the Constitution. The concept of secularism is one facet of the right to equality woven as the central golden thread in the fabric depicting the pattern of the scheme in our Constitution.[21]

Reiterating the idea that was discussed threadbare in the Constituent Assembly, the Supreme Court's division bench made it clear that the State could not afford to be partisan in view of the constitutional values, enshrined in the Preamble to the Constitution and also Articles 25 to 28. By recognizing the declaration in the Preamble as 'touchstone of the Constitution', the apex court left no ambiguity in its understanding of the theme of secularism. This was a follow-up of an earlier judgement of India's Supreme Court which, in its 1975 pronouncement in the *Ziauddin Burhanuddin Bukhari v. Brijmohan Ramdass Mehta and Others*, defended secularism as integral to India's constitutional fabric by mentioning that

> our Constitution-makers certainly intended to set-up a Secular Democratic Republic the binding spirit of which is summed up by the objectives set forth in the Preamble to the Constitution. No democratic political and social order, in which the conditions of freedom and their progressive expansion for all make some regulation of all activities imperative, could endure without an agreement on the basic essentials which could unite and hold citizens together despite all the differences of religion, race, caste, community, culture, creed and language. Our political history made it particularly necessary that these differences, which can generate powerful emotions depriving people of their powers of rational thought and action should be permitted to be exploited lest the imperative conditions for the preservation of democratic freedom are disturbed.[22]

A perusal of the principal points that the apex court made in these two judgements confirms that there was hardly differences of opinion despite the lapse of almost two decades between these two verdicts. As the

[21] The gist of the Ramjanmabhumi judgement was quoted in the 1995 Hindutva judgement, p. 12. http://judis.nic.in/supremecourt/imgs1.aspx?filename=10197 (accessed 8 November 2016).

[22] The gist of the 1975 Supreme Court judgement was quoted in the 1995 Hindutva judgement, p. 14. http://judis.nic.in (accessed 8 November 2016).

Constitution remains the only reference point, the arguments that the Supreme Court made appear to have coalesced to endorse that constitutional values could never be compromised under any circumstances. Basic to their arguments was the concern of maintaining India's multicultural fabric that had evolved historically as intimately connected with her rise as a distinct polity.

While these judgements contributed to the conceptualization of secularism, the 1995 Supreme Court pronouncement, also known as the Hindutva judgement, drew our attention to the changing complexion of India's secularism in the changed socio-political environment in the twenty-first century, especially in the aftermath of the 1992 demolition of the controversial Babri Masjid. The court intervened when it was asked to review whether the term Hindutva was contrary to the spirit of secularism as it evolved in India. Based on its understanding of Hinduism as an inclusive religion, the Court 'conflated Hindutva with Hinduism' by insisting that Hindutva was a way of life and could not be equated with narrow fundamentalist Hindu religious bigotry.[23] In its detailed response, the Court further argued:

> Thus, it cannot be doubted, particularly in view of the Constitution Bench decisions of this Court that the words "Hinduism" or "Hindutva" are not necessarily to be understood and construed narrowly, confined only to the strict Hindu religious practices, unrelated to the culture and ethos of the people of India, depicting the way of life of the Indian people.[24]

This is a clear justification of the fact that as an expression Hindutva is hardly ideological, but an innocent expression of a specific way of life that Hindus seem to have imbibed and also fined-tuned over the years. No fair understanding of the term in a specific historical perspective would allow us to misconceive the notion unless there was an ulterior motive. This was made explicit by the court as follows:

> Considering the terms 'Hinduism' or 'Hindutva' per se as depicting hostility, enmity or intolerance towards other religious faith or professing communalism proceeds form [*sic*] an improper appreciation and perception of the true meaning of these expressions emerging from the detailed discussion in earlier authorities of this Court.[25]

Upholding the view that Hindutva was hardly divisive, the Court justified its stance by reference to its earlier judgements which, despite being products of completely different socio-economic and political circumstances, endorsed the view that the apex court had taken in 1995. With its support to the idea of Hindutva as being entirely free from being an instrument of communalism, which was clear from its opinion that 'misuse of these expression to promote communalism cannot alter the true meaning of these terms', the bench concluded:

> It is indeed unfortunate, if in spite of the liberal and tolerant features of Hinduism recognized in judicial decisions, these terms are misused by anyone . . . to gain unfair political advantage. Fundamentalism of any colour or kind must be curbed with a heavy hand to preserve and

[23] Ronojoy Sen makes this point in his 'Defining Religion: The Indian Supreme Court and Hinduism' (working paper no. 29, Heidelberg Paper in South Asian and Comparative Politics, November 2006), p. 22.

[24] *Dr. Ramesh Yashwant Prabhoo v. Shri Prabhakar Kahsinath Kunte and Others*, 1995, p. 27. http://judis.nic.in/supremecourt/imgs1.aspx?filename=10197 (accessed 8 November 2016).

[25] *Dr. Ramesh Yashwant Prabhoo v. Shri Prabhakar Kahsinath Kunte and Others*, 1995, p. 27.

promote the secular creed of the nation. Any misuse of these terms must, therefore, be dealt with strictly.[26]

The 1995 verdict is a watershed in our thinking on how to conceptualize secularism at a particular point of India's recent political history when the idea of Hindutva seems to have gained political ascendancy, especially in the aftermath of the 1992 Babri Masjid demolition which also created a base for the Bharatiya Janata Party. In three distinctive ways, the Hindutva judgement is most instructive: first, it provides a new perspective for conceptualizing secularism which is usually understood in a derivative, but primarily, Western format. Second, by explaining that Hindutva is a way of life, the bench appears to have endorsed the Gandhian conceptualization of secularism as *sarvdharma sadbhava*. Here, Hindutva, synonymous with Hinduism represents a specific way of life, being nurtured over millennia in India. The idea is just an innocent construct of how the life is seen by those subscribing to a particular religious denomination. Third, under no circumstances, Hindutva can be said to hold, argued the bench, a definite ideological motive to accrue narrow political benefit, which means that only in a specific context it is likely to be distorted. This is 'an aberration' that cannot be taken as 'usual', the court endorses. So, the mere use of the term would, in no circumstances, warrant being charged with communal intention, the bench further underlined.

Although there is not an iota of confusion in the Hindutva judgement, it provoked criticism from various quarters for being 'heavily one-sided' by ignoring the obvious politico-ideological background in which Hindutva was conceptualized and also its contribution to communal divide in contemporary India. According to the contrarians, the judgement is based on two assumptions which are proved to be false at least in the light of the articulation of the political. The *first* assumptions that tolerance is linked with ancient Hindu scriptures and hence Hindus are civilizationally tolerant may not, at all, be consistent with the recent political developments in India. By implication Hindus are, as the *second* assumption underlines, instinctively appreciative of difference within the cultural resources that Indian civilization has already created. Drawn on the cultural logic, reflective of the Savarkarian *pitribhumi–punyabhumi* formula, these two assumptions feed the Hindu sectarian claim of accommodating diversity for a pan-Indian identity. These assumptions also contribute to the view that 'secularism as tolerance is steadfast with Hindu interests, which subsumes other faiths within its philosophy'.[27] This leaves no space for 'plural values' as it engenders one set of values over others. In the 2002 judgement on the text book issue, the Supreme Court seems to have favoured 'a majoritarian views' by glossing over the pluralistic Indian ethos. The argument that in essence there is hardly a difference among various religious faiths is persuasive; the practices are what differentiate one religious faith from another. So, secularism is clearly practice-linked. So far, the Court was insistent on 'tolerance', while in this judgement it appeared to have endorsed the spirit of assimilation which stands in contradiction with the basic notion of Indian pluralism. There is an implicit aim of 'creating oneness' rather that allowing 'a definite space for social and political diversity'. In other words, differences need to be respected with a view to creating a space for inter-religious dialogues. This judgement, by seeking to assimilate differences into one seems to have endorsed the Hindutva judgement by apparently subsuming (?) the majoritarian spirit in its articulation.

---

[26] *Dr. Ramesh Yashwant Prabhoo v. Shri Prabhakar Kahsinath Kunte and Others*, 1995, p. 27.

[27] Sanghamitra Padhy, 'Secularism and Justice: A Review of Indian Supreme Court Judgments', *Economic and Political Weekly* (20 November 2004).

As the discussion made earlier shows, the 1995 Hindutva judgement seems to have contributed to a new wave of thinking leading to reconceptualization of the idea of secularism in the light of the emerging socio-economic context in which the conventional approach to secularism does not appear to be so relevant. What is far more important here is however the critical role of the judiciary in redefining the idea of secularism which does not seem to make sense if it is conceptualized as derivative of the Western politico-intellectual sources. One thus cannot have a persuasive discussion on the theme unless one is drawn to the court decisions. Since courts take into account the prevalent politico-ideological views, their views are usually welcome since they help articulate the sense or mood of the demos in regard to some of important social, economic and political issues. This has emerged as a pattern, as is often exemplified. The latest in these series of endeavours of the apex court is the Supreme Court pronouncement in October 2016 in regard to a petition challenging the 1995 Hindutva judgement. In response to the petitioners' demand for disallowing political parties to resort to religious slogans for political mobilization, the apex court held that 'it is difficult to accept as a proposition that a political party should have nothing to do with religion and those who have something to do with it must cease to a political party'.[28] By dismissing the basic contention of the petitioners, the seven-judge constitutional bench, headed by the Chief Justice of India, now defines what secularism means in India's changed socio-cultural environment as follows:

> Secularism does not mean aloofness to religion by giving equal treatment to every religion. Religion and caste are vital aspects of our public life. Can it be possible to completely separate religion and caste from politics?[29]

In substance, the 2016 Supreme Court judgement is a follow-up of what the apex court held in the 1995 Hindutva judgement, for it also endorses the fact that religion is a part and parcel of India's socio-cultural life that can never be dispensed with while defining secularism as an ideological dispensation for the country. The fact that one is religious does not prevent one from being secular provided one separates one's public concerns from private-ones. The fundamental point that has been emphasized here is that in both these judgements the Supreme Court seems to have been guided by the Gandhian conceptualization of secularism, which is articulated in his belief of *sarvdharma sadbhava* and which also reinforces the argument that tolerance for all religions contributes to social harmony.

Concluding Observations

There is hardly a universal format in which secular values grow and thrive, and this means that one needs to be sensitive to the socio-economic and political milieu while seeking to understand their nature in a specific context. The Indian trajectory is illustrative here. At the dawn of Independence, there had emerged a consensus for the Nehruvian *dharma nirpekshta* (state neutrality to religions) which appeared to have set the tempo when Clauses 17 and 18 (which later constituted the Right to Freedom of Religion in the Constitution) were put to discussion in the Constituent Assembly. The principle of religious liberty to all was the operative norm which the Constituent Assembly upheld while preparing the Constitution for the country. So, communities being separated due to religious identity were to be treated as being equal in

[28] This is drawn on the report of *The Times of India* (28 October 2016).
[29] This is drawn on the report of *The Times of India* (28 October 2016).

the public domain since it was constitutionally endorsed. The Right to Freedom of Religion also ensured that communities were not only allowed to profess, practise and propagate a religion of their choice but also had access to public resources and the freedom to participate in the political arena. The constitutional arrangement that evolved in its wake was undoubtedly secular though there are anomalies, as mentioned earlier, if one draws attention to, for instance, the prevalence of separate civil codes for different communities. Nonetheless, the Constitution of India stipulates, it can be argued, a policy of fairness in dealing with the communities constituting the nation. This has two major implications: on the one hand, the constitutional provisions do not compartmentalize the public and private domains as strictly separate; instead, by recognizing the distinct cultural rights of the communities, they seem to blur the distinction. In order to protect their distinctiveness, the Constitution guarantees, on the other hand, the right to establish institutions to retain their culture and language. This is reflective of the endeavour on the part of the founding fathers to make the Constitution as an instrument which is fair in dealing with different religious communities equally rather than negating or suppressing their religious identities.[30]

There is another point that also merits serious attention. Secularism in India seems to have undergone a sea change in its texture since the 1995 Hindutva judgement which endorses the Gandhian notion of *sarvdharma sadbhava* as being critical to its manifestation in the Indian context. As is shown, the 2016 Supreme Court pronouncement confirms this by forcefully arguing that being religious is not, under any circumstance, an impediment to being secular. This is perfectly possible in a multireligious society like India where religion is dominantly a way of life that shapes individual social choices and preferences. What is most important is the inculcation of values supportive of *sadbhava* or tolerance to all religions with the idea that they are parts of a collectivity. Implicit here is also the idea that despite being different in religious terms, there exists a commonality across communities by virtue of sharing the same socio-cultural universe. So, they are instinctively tied to one another, an idea which Gandhi imbibed with his sustained engagement with a reality that he confronted while devising his unique design of secularism which is neither derivative of the Western experiences nor exactly indigenous, but a creative blending of the two.

Review Questions

1. **Define secularism as a constitutional value.**
2. **How did the idea of secularism evolve in India? Elaborate.**
3. **How did the founding fathers address their concern for secularism? Elaborate.**
4. **Secularism is also a political design. Explain.**
5. **What are the relevant constitutional provisions relating to secularism in India? Elaborate.**
6. **Secularism as an ideology and secularism as a practice are dialectically interconnected. Explain.**
7. **Do you agree with the view that the secularism is a mere top-dressing for the Constitution of India? Elaborate your views.**

[30] This is the argument that Gurpreet Mahajan pursues in her 'Religion and Indian Constitution: Question of Separation and Equality', in *Politics and Ethics of the Indian Constitution*, ed. Rajeev Bhargava (New Delhi: Oxford University Press, 2008), pp. 308–09.

8. **Distinguish between *Dharma-nirpekshta* (religious neutrality) and *Sarvdharam Sadbhava* (equal respect to all religions) with examples.**
9. **Critically evaluate the 1995 'Hindutva' judgement of the Supreme Court of India.**
10. **'Secularism does not mean aloofness from religion but equal respect to all religions'. Do you agree with this view? Elaborate your response.**

Chapter

13

Federalism in India: Redefining the Constitutional Template for Governance

Learning Objectives

- To understand federalism as a conceptual category
- To conceptualize federalism as it had emerged in India
- To grasp the distinctive features of federalism in India with reference to the rapidly socio-economic transformation in the context of globalization

India is a uniquely textured federal polity for a variety of reasons. Prominent among them is the apparent mismatch between Article 1 of the Constitution of India and the actual unfolding of the spirit of federalism in governance. Article 1 endorses the view that India, that is Bharat, is a union of states which clearly privileges the union over the states. The latter remain appendages to the union, at least, as per Article 1. This is a strictly a legalistic interpretation which is however untenable if Article 1 is seen in conjunction with Seventh Schedule enumerating three lists that demarcated domains for the union and constituent provinces. In order to make the states independent in their respective areas of functioning, the founding father felt the need of a separate list of powers for them. However, there is a cautionary note because in case of emergency, these powers are likely to be withdrawn for the sake of sustaining constitutional governance so long as the situation does not improve. It is clear that this is a temporary arrangement which the constitution makers had approved as a precautionary measure. Nonetheless, this clear tilt in favour of unionization of governance makes India 'a quasi-federal state' which is usually justified by reference to the constitutional provisions supportive of unitary tendencies. However, this appears to be simplistic in the light of the functioning of Indian federalism since Independence. It is therefore fair to argue that federalism is a natural outgrowth of constitutionalism in India though under certain extra-ordinary circumstances, the Constitution of India creates conditions for the unitary state to strike roots. Hence India's Supreme Court stated, in a 1962 pronouncement, that 'the evolution of a federal or a quasi-federal structure necessarily involved in the context of the conditions then prevailing, a distribution of powers and a basic part of our Constitution relates to the that distribution with the three legislative lists in the Seventh Schedule'.[1] There are two important points which this judgement endorses: federalism needs to be understood in a specific context; no rigid formulation will therefore work. Equally important is the idea that the Constitution of India, by categorically demarcating powers in three legislative lists, also lays

[1] Quoted from DD Basu, *Introduction to the Constitution of India* (Gurgaon: LexisNexis, 2015), p. 66.

out and justifies the foundation of a federal system. This further confirms that India's federalism defies the universal pattern that had emerged in the constitutional experiences elsewhere. As constitutional arrangements are organic to the society in which it evolves, it will be logically improper and methodologically misleading if Indian federalism is sought to be grasped strictly in a derivative format. One of its unique features is the growth and consolidation of federalism despite India being a parliamentary democracy. In other words, India epitomizes perhaps a rare constitutional design in which federalism flourished in parliamentary democracy which also means an attempt to create an appropriate political structure of governance by appreciating two contrasting tendencies arising out of different socio-economic and political contexts; while the former is usually linked with the US constitutional experiences, the latter is strictly British in its conceptualization. Hence the chapter repeats the clichéd argument that India is neither federal nor unitary, but illustrative of a polity which is federal in a parliamentary set-up and vice-versa. Despite being clichéd, the argument provides us with enough inputs to reconceptualize India's federalism as a unique constitutional design which is not merely contextual but transcendental in spirit and structure. The aim of this chapter is therefore to understand how these two apparently different tendencies gradually evolve in the Indian context as complementary to each other for reasons which need to be located in the peculiar unfolding of socio-political processes in India since the Constitution was inaugurated in 1950.

Constitutional Directions

A typical juridical interpretation of the constitutional provisions relating to centre–state relations confirms that the framers of the Constitution were in favour of creating a strong unitary state in India. There is, of course, the Seventh Schedule which clearly demarcates separate domains of power for the Union Government and constituent units. But the fact that the states do not enjoy absolute authority even in regard to the items in the State List constitutionalizes tendencies towards privileging the Union Government over the constituent states. The Emergency provisions in Part XVIII of the Constitution of India justifies the withdrawal of power that is usually given to the states under normal circumstances, which means that, in case of difficult circumstances, the Centre will be constitutionally empowered to bypass the state while exercising its constitutional authority over the polity. There are innumerable Articles in the Constitution of India which can be cited to make the argument that our Constitution does not seem to be federal in the sense the US polity is. For instance, Article 248 bestows residuary powers of legislation on the Parliament with respect to any matter not enumerated in the Concurrent List or State List. Furthermore, Article 249 allows the Parliament to legislate on matters in the State List,

> if the Council of State has declared by resolution supported by not less than two-thirds of the members present and voting that it is necessary or expedient in the national interest that Parliament should make laws with respect to any matter enumerated in the State List specified in the resolution, it shall be lawful for Parliament to make laws for the whole or any part of the territory of India with respect to that matter while the resolution remains in force.[2]

Though the Constitution accords conditional authority to Parliament to intervene in areas which strictly belong to the State List, Article 249 has a built-in device to undermine the federal balance between the

[2] Constitution of India, Art. 249.

Union and the states. In a similar vein, Article 302 of Part XIII of the Constitution of India allows Parliament 'to impose such restrictions on the freedom of trade, commerce or intercourse between one State and another or within any part of the territory of India as may be required in the public interest'.[3] Here too, the same centralizing tilt is evident which is justified in the name of public interests. There is hardly a shield against the possible misuse of this Article by the Union Government because the Constitution remains silent about what public interest means. In strict constitutional terms, Article 249 also contributes to federal imbalance in governance by ascertaining Parliament's absolute authority under certain specific circumstances.

The earlier discussion of selective Articles of the Constitution of India confirms the apprehension that under given situation, the Union Government is likely to be a bully vis-à-vis the constituent provinces. This is a purely legalistic understanding of the Constitution which does not correspond with its actual unfolding in recent years. Besides decisive judicial interventions seeking to scuttle the tendencies towards unionization of administration, the role of multiple political forces, including political parties and civil society activists, cannot be ignored in conceptualizing the changing texture of Indian federalism in recent years.

Defying the Pattern

India has a hybrid system of government. The hybrid system combines two classical models: the British traditions, drawn upon parliamentary sovereignty and conventions and American principles upholding the supremacy of a written constitution, the separation of powers and judicial review. The two models are contradictory since parliamentary sovereignty and constitutional supremacy are incompatible. India has distinct imprints in her constitution of both the British and American principles. In other words, following the adoption of the 1950 Constitution, India has evolved a completely different politico-constitutional arrangement with characteristics from both the British and American constitutional practices. The peculiarity lies in the fact that despite being parliamentary, Indian political arrangement does not wholly correspond with the British system simply because it has adopted the federal principles as well; it can never be completely American since parliament in India continues to remain sovereign. As a hybrid political system, India has contributed to a uniquely textured politico-constitutional arrangement, described as 'parliamentary–federalism' that had emerged in Canada in the past.[4] Based on both parliamentary practices and federal principles, political system in India is therefore a conceptual riddle underlining the hitherto unexplored dimensions of India's socio-political history imbibing the British traditions and American principles. At the time of the framing of the constitution, political institutions were chosen with utmost care though in their zeal to create a 'modern' India, the founding fathers seem to have been persuaded more by the British Enlightenment traditions which generally treated the indigenous values and practices as erroneous. They also wrongly held the view that 'to rescue people from tradition, their intellectual and practical habitats, all that was needed was simply to present a modern option; people's inherent rationality would do the rest'.[5] As the actual political experience in India demonstrates, this was not the case and traditions reappear in various different forms in the political articulation of, for instance, democracy. Thus, instead of disappearing with the introduction of elections based on universal suffrage, both caste and

[3] Constitution of India, Art. 302.

[4] Douglas V Varney, 'From Executive to Legislative Federalism? The Transformation of the Political System in Canada and India', *The Review of Politics* 3, no. 1 (Spring, 1989): 241–63.

[5] Sudipta Kaviraj, 'Modernity and Politics in India', *Daedalus* 129, no. 1 (Winter 2000): 155.

religion, for instance, continue to cement the bond among the voters both during the poll and its aftermath. The principal argument, the chapter seeks to articulate, is concerned with the complexity of the processes that finally led to the formation of a hybrid political system, influenced heavily by both the British tradition and American principles. In trying to understand the current complexities and future prospects of Indian political system, looking toward European and American precedents is not therefore enough. Instead, it is necessary to conceptualize the historical logic internal to this process. Given the ingrained constitutional peculiarities and their evolution, the chapter further underlines the importance of historical circumstances and socio-economic and cultural distinctiveness in shaping India's political system following the transfer of power in 1947.

Nature of the Indian Union: The Constitutional Inputs

Due to peculiar historical circumstances, the consensus that emerged in the Constituent Assembly was in favour a union with a strong centre. As early as December 1946, GB Pant, one of the important members of the Assembly, thus declared:

> The Constituent Assembly is resolved to set up a suitable republic for independent India. The recognition of the unity of India forms the cornerstone of this scheme. . . . The sentiment of unity will not be impaired in any way. That is first fundamental condition, as without it no constitution can be formulated and none can last for a day.[6]

Arguments were accordingly marshalled for a parliamentary form of government and the colonial experience was a constant reference point. In devising the Union-State relations, the founding fathers were influenced by the principles underlying the Constitutions of Canada and Australia, which had parliamentary federalism and the United States which had presidential system, respectively. The 1935 Government of India Act seems to have influenced the Assembly to a large extent though the 1950 Constitution was substantially different in spirit and ideology. As it finally emerged, the Constitution has important 'federal' features but it cannot be characterized as federal in the classical sense. What it envisages is a unique document, which is, as Ambedkar had articulated, 'unitary in extraordinary circumstances such as war and other calamities and federal under normal circumstances'. Hence, India is described as 'a union of states' where the union is 'indestructible' but not the constituent states because their contour and identity can be 'altered' or even 'obliterated'. There emerged a consensus and the Assembly rejected a motion seeking to characterize India as 'a federation of states'. While challenging the motion, Ambedkar sought to expose the logical weaknesses and practical difficulties of imitating the classical federation like the US as follows:

> [T]hough India was to be a federation, the federation was not the result of an agreement by the States to join in a federation, and that the federation not being the result of an agreement, no State has the right to secede from it. The Federation is a Union because it is indestructible. Though the country and the people may be divided into different States for convenience of administration, the country is one integral whole, its people a single people living under a

[6] GB Pant's convocation address at Allahabad University on 21 December 1946. See *Selected Works of Govind Ballabh Pant*, Vol. 11 (New Delhi: Oxford University Press, 1998), p. 425.

> single *imperium* derived from a single source. The Americans had to wage a civil war to establish that the States have no right of secession and that their federation was indestructible. The Drafting Committee thought that it was better to make it clear at the outset rather than to leave it to speculation or to dispute.[7]

As is evident in the discussion in the Constituent Assembly, the framers refereed mainly to two traditions: the British and the American. But in the background there was always a third stream—understandably downplayed by Ambedkar and other members—the ideas of Ian Coupland and KC Wheare who appeared to have provided the foundational basis of the constitutional experiments in the British Dominions. It is, after all, true that the 1935 Government of India Act laid the foundation for federal structure of governance in India along with an appropriate constitutional edifice for unified legal and financial systems; furthermore, this was the constitutional system that codified distinctive features as group rights, machinery for resolution of inter-state water disputes, state governors and Article 356. There had of course been strong opposition to the 'federal' provisions of the 1935 Act that envisaged the future accession of the princes, including the right of secession that figured unambiguously in the 1942 Cripps Mission proposals. The 1946 Cabinet Mission also endorsed the plan for a Central Government with very limited powers and relatively strong provinces having considerable degree of autonomy with all the residuary powers. Despite inputs supporting a weak centre, the 1950 Constitution provided a scheme of distribution of power that was heavily tilted in favour of a strong centre. The decision to go for a strong centre at the cost of regional autonomy was perhaps conditioned by pragmatic considerations of maintaining national integrity that received a severe jolt with the 1947 partition. Hence there was the deliberate omission of the word 'federal' in the final draft of the Constitution. By accepting the 'federal' form, the framers gave 'recognition' to the multi-dimensional socio-political and geographical Indian reality.

The debates in the Constituent Assembly show that the founding fathers took ample care in creating a constitutional arrangement which is 'federal' in a very specific sense. The system that emerged in India was hardly comparable with any of the prevalent federations. What was critical in their vision was perhaps the fact that federalism is not merely a structural arrangement for distribution and sharing of power between the federal partners, it is also a culture sustaining its very spirit. Its emergence and later consolidation in India is slightly paradoxical since it is the product of two conflicting cultures: one representing the national leaders' 'normative' concern for India's multicultural personality, shaped by its unique history and geography and the other underlining their concern for unity, security and administrative efficiency. While the former led to the articulation of federalism, as laid down in the 1950 constitution and the latter resulted in the retention of the very state machinery, which consolidated the colonial rule in India. The net result was the articulation of a semi-hegemonic federal structure that drew heavily upon the 1935 Government of India Act. Nonetheless, the federal system that supported unwarranted centralization of power appeared to be the most suitable alternative for nation building in India. However, the situation radically changed following the articulation of new demands by hitherto peripheral socio-political groups. The aim here is to grasp the processes that contributed to this significant metamorphosis of India's federal system in the context of constantly changing domestic and global situation.

[7] BR Ambedkar defence of the constitution in the Constituent Assembly on 4 November 1948, *Constituent Assembly Debates*, Book No. 2, p. 43.

Federalism in India

Federalism is not merely a structural arrangement for distribution and sharing of power between the federal partners, it is also a culture sustaining its very spirit. Its emergence and later consolidation in India is slightly paradoxical since it is the product of two conflicting cultures: one representing the national leaders' 'normative' concern for India's multicultural personality, shaped by its unique history and geography and other underlining their concern for unity, security and administrative efficiency. While the former led to the articulation of federalism, as laid down in the 1950 constitution and the latter resulted in the retention of the very State machinery, which consolidated the colonial rule in India. The net result was the articulation of a semi-hegemonic federal structure that drew largely upon the 1935 Government of India Act. Nonetheless, the federal system that supported unwarranted centralization of power appeared to be the most suitable alternative for nation building in India. However, the situation radically changed following the articulation of new demands by hitherto peripheral socio-political groups.

Perspective

Historically, federations have been created in two ways. The first was the coming together of independent units in such a way that each unit surrendered its sovereign status to form a common union. The second path was the opening up of unitary systems, usually old imperial systems, in order to provide representation to territorially based social groups in an effort to create a consensual state system. The first path led to the creation of classical federations such as the USA, Australia and Canada while the latter could be said to include a wide variety stretching from the former Soviet Union to many post-war federations which emerged after decolonization.

There seems to be an inverse relationship between the constitutional arrangement propounding federal structure and its historical evolution. The US and Indian federal system shall be illustrative here. In the case the former, despite the founding fathers' deliberate attempts to make a weak centre with strong states, the constitutional evolution led to the growth of a strong centre and consequently weak states. At present, the US federal government is perhaps the most powerful although the constitution makers intended otherwise. The Indian situation follows the pattern but in a different direction: after the British left, the Indian National Congress took over the administration which was British in tune and spirit. So the strong centre which was created and favoured by the British as an instrument for imperial control was allowed to stay with marginal changes. The government of independent India defended the strong centre in order to maintain national integrity, which was being threatened by fissiparous tendencies in the nascent nation state. Justification of a strong state seems logical and therefore understandable. The situation remained unchanged so long as Jawaharlal Nehru presided over India's destiny as its first premier. There were no dissidents and the Centre–State relations were generally amicable due largely to the historical advantages that the Congress Party had by virtue of being associated intimately with India's freedom struggle. Since 1964, there were occasions when the constituent states openly challenged the centre. The process was articulated in 1967 when non-Congress government assumed power in different states which strengthened regional voice vis-à-vis the hegemony of the centre which continued to be ruled by the Congress party till the capture of power by the Janata Party in 1977. Following the 1998 national elections, the situation became more complex now with the dominant role of different regional parties in the formation and continuity of the coalition governments at the centre. With the demand for regional autonomy, the Union government of India is constantly being challenged and forced to succumb to pressure. This indicates, *inter alia*, the weakening of the centre and the gradual strengthening of the states.

What follows from the previous discussion is that the Indian states are growing stronger gradually and steadily. Not only have they articulated their demands effectively, they have on occasions become decisive in the policy making. Politically, it seems to be a sign of 'adulthood of Indian states' which may create the US confederal type polity with strong units and a centre as a mere monitoring instrument. The concept of adulthood of states does not endorse 'terrorism' at all to snatch statehood; instead, it is premised on a particular variety of 'political consciousness' favouring a strong and healthy India. There are instances which may be cited to substantiate that attainment of adulthood disrupts national integrity but a thorough study of these 'disruptive movements' championing regional autonomy may reveal that the outcome would have probably been otherwise had they been dealt with more seriously at the outset.

The Federal Arrangement

With the above-mentioned perspective in mind, let us dwell on the actual federal structure of governance as it evolved immediately after the transfer of power. For BR Ambedkar, the choice was categorical, since

> the draft constitution is a Federal Constitution in as much as it establishes . . . Dual Polity [with] the Union at the centre and the States at the periphery, each being assigned with sovereign powers to be exercised in the field assigned to them respectively by the Constitution. The States in our Constitution are in no way dependent upon the Centre for their legislative and executive authority. [T]he Centre and the States are co-equal in this matter. [I]t is therefore wrong to say that the States have been placed under the Centre.[8]

On another occasion, when the Assembly members debated on Article 277(A) which later became a part of the Emergency provisions, Ambedkar was far more categorical in ascertaining the importance of the provinces in Indian federalism. As he argued:

> The Constitution is a Federal Constitution [which means] that the Provinces are as sovereign in their field which is left to them by the Constitution as the Centre is in the field which is assigned to it. . . . [w]hen once the Constitution makes the provinces sovereign and gives them Plenary powers to make any law for the peace, order and good government of the province, really speaking, the intervention of the Centre or any other authority must be deemed to be barred because that would be an invasion to the sovereign authority of the province. This is a fundamental proposition which, . . . we must accept by reasons of the fact that we have a Federal Constitution.[9]

As is evident, Ambedkar was in favour of a true federal constitution though there was a strong voice in the Assembly which did not seem inclined to this presumably because of the contextual difficulties confronting the nation just on the eve of its rise as an independent polity. The result was the adoption of stringent Emergency provisions in Part XVIII of the Constitution which drew on section 93 of the 1935

[8] Ibid., p. 33.

[9] BR Ambedkar's response in the Constituent Assembly, 3 August 1949, *Constituent Assembly Debates*, Book No. 4, p. 133.

Government of India Act. What probably conditioned the choice of those who presided over free India's destiny was a pragmatic consideration of transforming India into 'a Union out of the patch work quilt of [British Indian] Provinces and Princely States'[10]. Given the large number of princely states which enjoyed paramountcy during the colonial rule, the task of bringing them under the union was difficult. Moreover, the decision of the Muslim-majority provinces of British India to constitute themselves into Pakistan aroused the apprehension in the minds of the nationalist leadership in India that they might have to face further attempts at secession from a future Indian union. As a result of this fear, 'the Gandhian notion of a truly decentralized and federal India did not receive serious attention in the debate on the Constitution which it otherwise deserved.'[11] However, the very apprehensions that produced a desire for stronger Central authority also led to a counter-tendency in the form of demands from several states for greater autonomy. There were also members who, being inspired by 'the Gandhian tradition for greater decentralization of institutions . . . down to the district and village level' pressed hard for greater autonomy of the states as a precaution to the growth of an authoritarian centre.[12] The argument did not cut much ice since it was believed that the so-called Emergency provisions were 'merely pious expression on the part of the Union government that they are going to try their best to uphold the Constitution and not interfere unduly in the functioning of the provinces.'[13] While justifying these provisions as 'most appropriate', Alladi Krishnaswami Ayyar did not find them incongruent with the federal spirit by stating that 'apart from being an impediment to the growth of healthy provincial and state autonomy, these provisions are a bulwark in favour of provincial and state autonomy because the primary obligation is cast upon the Union to see that the Constitution is maintained.'[14] To protect and safeguard democracy and freedom, the aim was 'to make certain provisions in the Constitution which may stand [the nation] in good stead when unseemly or awkward situations arise.'[15] Perhaps the strongest defence came from Naziruddin Ahmad (West Bengal) when he emphatically declared that 'emergency powers are necessary and I also agree that serious forces of disorder are working in a systematic manner in the country and drastic powers are necessary.'[16] A perusal of these arguments reveal that the voice opposed to the emergency provision for being contrary to federalism did not seem to have gained salience largely because of the uncertainty that had gripped the country with the rising tide of communalism following the partition. Despite having raised their concern at the outset, the Gandhians seemed to have endorsed the provisions since they were shown to have been required due to the exigency of situation.

The Congress System

One of the factors that supported parliamentary federalism in India, as conceptualized by the framers of the constitution was what is popularly described as 'the Congress system' that thrived due largely to a

[10] Mahendra Ved, 'Honouring Sardar Patel: Bismarck of India', *The Times of India*, New Delhi, 22 August 1998.

[11] Ravinder Kumar, 'Securing Stability: No Cause for Constitutional Reforms', *The Times of India*, New Delhi, 15 September 1998.

[12] Paul Brass, *The Politics of India since Independence* (Cambridge: Cambridge University Press, 1990), p. 63.

[13] PS Deshmukh's intervention in the Constituent Assembly debates on 3 August 1949, *Constituent Assembly Debates*, Book No. 4, p. 147.

[14] Alladi Krishnaswami Ayyar's defence of the Emergency provisions in the Constituent Assembly, 3 August 1949, *Constituent Assembly Debates*, Book No. 4, p. 150.

[15] The argument, made by Raj Bahadur (United States of Matsya) in favour of emergency provisions, on 3 August 1949, *Constituent Assembly Debates*, Book No. 4, p. 149.

[16] Naziruddin Ahmad's argument in the Constituent Assembly on 3 August 1949, *Constituent Assembly Debates*, Book No. 4, p. 159.

homogeneous elite in roles of authority and decision making. Rajni Kothari described the Congress system as a huge, hierarchically structured party, broadly rooted throughout the countryside, apparently providing mechanism whereby a plurality of elites, sub-elites and groups could both voice their claims and attempt to realize them. At the same time, the Congress could adequately mediate and settle these multiple and often conflicting claims. If necessary, the Congress High Command could intervene to seal the final bargain. Within this system, the range of social groups represented in the ruling party was considered its most positive feature, making it possible for the opposition parties by forging links with like-minded Congress factions. Thus Kothari concludes that the Congress system was 'a system of patronage [in which] traditional institutions of kin as caste were accommodated and a structure of pressures and compromises was developed' which explains its continuity for almost two decades since Independence.[17] Furthermore, (a) the practice of intra-party democracy, and (b) socially rooted party and political leaders at the state and district levels also account for its sustenance. It is therefore not an exaggeration to suggest that the role of the Congress party in acting as 'a bridge between colonial India and post-colonial democracy is also an important factor that explains India's relative success in transition to democracy' in contrast with her South Asian neighbours sharing the same historical legacy.[18] While reviewing his model in 1974, Kothari reiterated his faith in the Congress system as the most effective means of countering 'the challenges that the country faces'. Hence, his suggestion included, 'rebuild the Congress Party and its regional infrastructure that has become so weak of late, reinvest the electoral process with legitimacy, restore to the opposition parties their due role in parliamentary politics and at regional levels, and restructure the communication linkage between government, party units and the people, so that the system becomes more responsive and has to rely less on coercion'.[19] The scene has undergone a sea change with the consolidation of neoliberalism in the wake of globalization. As Kothari argued, 'an electoral democracy ... [that] broadened its social base and shown special regard for diverse types of minorities and hence gained so much legitimacy got eroded over time and forced the political managers to compromise with and ultimately become party to monied and 'mafia' interests, in the process undermining the autonomy of the state and the political system'.[20]

One of the reasons for its long term viability was probably the success of the post-Independence political process in bringing wide sections of society within the political arena and exposed traditional and emerging elites to both 'the pedagogy and the practice of a democratic polity wedded to an egalitarian ideology'.[21] Underlying this, as the argument proceeds, lay the reasons for relatively smooth functioning of federalism which was never seriously threatened probably because of an effective mechanism of political communication involving various actors at different levels of Indian polity.[22]

Like all ideal types, this schematic picture of consensual politics under the Congress system appeared to be divorced from a much more complex reality which was, *inter alia,* characterized by very low levels of political awareness among the lower castes and poor classes. With the continuity of the major political institutions that held the colonial power even after Independence, it is, in fact, plausible to argue that politics in the Nehru era as a whole is basically 'a continuum with the Raj'. Whatever social configurations

[17] Rajni Kothari, 'The Congress System in India', *Asian Survey* 4, no. 12 (December 1964): 164–65.

[18] Subrata K Mitra, *Politics in India: Structure, Process and Policy* (London and New York: Routledge, 2011), p. 123.

[19] Rajni Kothari, 'The Congress System Revisited: A Decennial Review', *Asian Survey* 14, no. 12 (December 1974): 1052–53.

[20] Rajni Kothari, 'The Democratic Experience', in *Wages of Freedom*, ed. Partha Chatterjee (Delhi: Oxford University Press, 1998), pp. 27–28.

[21] Rajni Kothari, *State Against Democracy: In Search of Humane Governance* (Delhi: Ajanta, 1988), p. 157.

[22] Amal Ray, 'Coordinating Pluralism: The Federal Experience in India', in *Rethinking Indian Federalism*, ed. Rasheeduddin Khan (Shimla: Indian Institute of Advanced Studies, 1997), pp. 98–102.

the Congress party confronted at the various provinces, 'its leader, like the British before them, did not attempt to change the social order but to adapt to it'.[23] Furthermore, it is probably justified to argue that Indian politics in the first two decades after decolonization was built on a kind of consensus based primarily on elite accommodation. The system passed uncontested 'because of its nearness to the mobilization of the national movement, and the relation of implicit trust between its leadership and the masses'. It was a consensus of 'discourse rather than ideological positions'.[24] Soon after Nehru's demise, the system started breaking down—a process that became evident especially from 1969 onwards when Nehru's successor, Indira Gandhi, faced with increasing opposition strength 'rejected the principle of consensus in favour of the majoritarian principle'.[25] Since she carried the masses with her, she ignored the party that had lost its democratic mainspring. Centralization which was once considered as 'an instrument of purposive interventions by a cohesive and disciplined elite' soon turned out to be 'suicidal to the prevalent party system and the federal structure and wider affiliations that were built through them'.[26]

The deinstitutionalization of the Congress party contributed immensely to the erosion of India's federal system by 'dismantling the party's federal structure'.[27] Not only did this decay lead to a massive concentration of power in the Central leadership, it also deprived the party of seasoned national and state party officials. What undermined the system significantly was the conscious endeavour of the top boss within the party of substituting '*loyalists and favourites at state and constituency level for party officials and candidates with local knowledge and support*' (emphasis added).[28] Indira Gandhi could afford to ignore the party since she had established 'a direct and unmediated line with the people who had transposed enormous faith in her charisma and her image as deliverer and secular messiah'.[29] During the 1969–77 period, Centre–State relations were practically reduced to a state of near non-existence and '[u]nitarism triumphed under the aegis of a strong state whose power was controlled by a ruling party which relied exclusively on its leader for its survival'.[30] The 1975–77 emergency was probably the most serious affront to federalism since it led to the consolidation of a puissant centre presiding over a federation of thoroughly enfeebled states.

So, India's federalism had undergone a paradigmatic shift on the eve of the 1977 national elections which replaced the Congress party by a loose-knit Janata coalition representing a variety, if not contradictory, of interests. During the brief interlude of the Janata regime (1977–80), probably because of other preoccupation of the regime, no serious attempt was made to counter the centripetal tendencies which had, by then, firm roots in Indian politics. Indira Gandhi's style of functioning completely destroyed internal democracy within the Congress party. With the disintegration of provincial Congress organizations, the state leaders became mere clients of the central organ of the party. As she became the key to political power and personal gain, there was hardly any challenge to her leadership and the party was reduced to almost a non-entity. The consequence was disastrous. The state tended to ignore the demands of the

[23] Francine Frankel, 'Decline of a Social Order', in *Dominance and State Power in Modern India: Decline of a Social Order*, eds. Francine Frankel and MSA Rao, vol. 2 (Delhi: Oxford University Press, 1990), p. 502.

[24] Sudipta Kaviraj, 'On State, Society and Discourse in India', in *Rethinking Third World Politics*, ed. James Manor (London: Longman, 1991), pp. 87–88.

[25] Rakhahari Chatterjee, 'Democracy and Opposition in India', *Economic and Political Weekly*, no. 17 (23 April 1988): 847.

[26] Kothari, *State Against Democracy*, p. 30.

[27] LI Rudolph and SH Rudolph, *In Pursuit of Lakshmi: The Political Economy of the India State* (Hyderabad: Orient Longman, 1987), p. 99.

[28] Rudolph and Rudolph, *In Pursuit of Lakshmi*, p. 138.

[29] Rajni Kothari, 'Integration and Exclusion', *Economic and Political Weekly*, no. 43 (23 October 1988): 2226.

[30] TV Sathyamurthy, 'Impact of Centre–State Relations on Indian Politics: An Interpretative Reckoning, 1947–1987', in *State and Politics in India*, ed. Partha Chatterjee (Delhi: Oxford University Press, 1997), p. 250.

constituent units and favoured concentration of power simply because those who mattered in political decision making neither questioned nor endeavoured to provide an alternative to centralization.

The breakdown of the consensus model led to the rise of various other strictures, both political and non-political that became formidable in the era of mass politics. Despite Nehru's limitation as a statesman, the Congress party under his tutelage both absorbed new demands and strove to provide avenues for their fulfilment. With the collapse of the party as an effective institution and the inability of the system to create new institutional modes for dealing with newer demands, there emerged 'a new social class of mediators in the political processes'.[31] Kothari draws our attention to the wider implications of this new development in Indian politics:

> The erosion of parliamentary, party and federal institutions and decline of authority of the State and of the national political leadership has also been one of the reasons for the rise of new actors on the scene, new forms of political expression and new definitions of the content of politics.[32]

Historically, federalism in India has undergone radical changes in different phases of its evolution that are linked with the changing nature of the polity. For instance, the first phase is characterised by the single party dominance or the Congress system (1947–66) while following the growth of regional parties, a different type of power relationships emerged between the states and the centre that continued till the rise of the Janata Party coalition in 1977. In the third phase (1978–97), fragmentation of parties brought about significant impact on the nature of federalism that confronted new issues affecting the federal balance. Following the rise and consolidation of coalition government at the centre at the behest of National Democratic Alliance in 1998, the fourth phase of the evolution of India's federalism had begun. The paradox however is that while the centre has steadily declined in the last two decades, the states have also become 'weaker'. A fragmented party politics is likely to give some states greater power depending on the nature of coalition, but the reliance of unstable multi-party coalitions in Delhi on regional parties, even factions, in the states seems to have led to a crisis in the federal system. The system of 'cooperative federalism', envisaged by the Sarkaria commission, with the Inter-State Council as the principal instrument, has failed to strike roots in such circumstances.

The expansion of political participation in the last two decades has placed historically disadvantaged and marginalized groups at the centre of political system and governance at all levels. The rapid politicization and accelerated participation of groups such as OBCs and Dalit raises questions about inclusion, exclusion and varied patterns of empowerment and the impact of the latter on the growth and consolidation of democracy. One aspect of these changes has to do with the processes and strategies that have inspired the induction of marginal groups into the political decision-making process. Though not unique to India, these struggles and contentions have overshadowed the idioms and ideologies that dominated and sustained the post-colonial agenda of social transformation. Many of these are expressions of discontent traceable to the anger of the subalterns against an elite that has cornered the benefits and privileges of post-colonial economic development and have significantly reformulated the political terrain.

---

[31] Subrata Kumar Mitra, 'Democracy and Political Change in India', *The Journal of Commonwealth & Comparative Politics* 30, no. 1 (March 1992): 27.

[32] Kothari, *State Against Democracy*, p. 175.

Federalism in the Changing Socio-economic and Political Milieu

India's political system is in constant flux. Parliament is neither supreme nor sovereign as in the Westminster model of parliamentary democracy. The adoption of the federal principles seems to have 'tempered the unlimited power of Parliament'.[33] Yet, the ruling party, if it masters a stable majority in Parliament, can become an absolute authority under specific circumstances where the legislature will simply act as a ratifying agency. Supported by three major institutions—the Finance Commission, the Planning Commission and the All India Services—the Central Government held in the past the federal balance in its favour. Furthermore, under the changed circumstances of liberalization, the constitutionally guaranteed rights of the constituent States have been significantly eroded. One area that has created consternation among the member states of the Union is whether the Centre is constitutionally authorised to sign treaties with other countries without consulting the affected States. This has become relevant at a time when trade and other international agencies—like those under the Uruguay Round of the General Agreement Trade and Tariff (GATT) are being created in ways that national barriers and sovereignty of the nation state are being assailed. The new GATT is a special instance in question because it is not just concerned with trade in goods but also services (General Agreement on Trade and Services), investment (Trade Related Investment Measures), intellectual property (Trader Related Intellectual Property Rights) and various other aspects of the economy. Apprehending that GATT is likely to curb their power that has been guaranteed by the Constitution, three States, Tamil Nadu, Rajasthan and Orissa, filed suits in the Supreme Court in 1994 against the Union of India 'raising a federal dispute that the new GATT affects their exclusive powers given to them by the Constitution and forces them to share power with the Union in ways that violate the basic structure of the Constitution'.[34] Though the Court verdict is not yet available, the step in indicative of a new trend where the provinces no longer remain the 'silent' observers. Whatever one may think of the desirability of GATT, a powerful argument can be made supporting that it effectively redefines the Centre–State relations in the context of mutual cooperation between the Union Government and States vis-à-vis the imposed restrictions by the international agencies. This is one dimension of federalism in its new form. The other dimension is about the changing nature of Centre–State relations in the changed environment of the 1990s. For instance, the state governments are not dismissed the way they were in the 1970s and 1980s though by being dependent on the Union Government for funds as they do not have adequate sources for raising extra money, they hardly have an effective voice in governance. The situation seems to be worse in a situation when the Union Government, in its keenness to accommodate some of the terms and conditions, imposed by the World Trade Organization (WTO), is authorised to endorse an economic treaty that affects things on the state list (taxation, agriculture) without serious consultation with the States. This is likely to transform the federal balance in favour of the Union Government leading to circumstances when the provinces will just become mere constituents with no substantial power and authority.

The story shall remain incomplete without reference to the changing texture of India's political landscape following the ascendancy of the provinces as important actors in governance. The breakdown of the Congress system and complementary rise of the regional/or state-based political parties seems to have

---

[33] Rudolph and Rudolph, *In pursuit of Lakshmi*, p. 105.

[34] Rajeev Dhawan and Geetanjali Goel, 'Indian Federalism and its Discontents', in *Federalism and Decentralization: Centre–State Relations in India and Germany*, ed. Gert Kueck (New Delhi: Mudrit, 1998), p. 54.

contributed to a process of genuine federalization of the Indian polity that began with the decimation of Congress rule in various states in the 1967 state assembly election. The growing importance of the regional parties, led to the decline of the pan-Indian parties, namely the BJP and Congress. The scene was completely different during the heyday of the 'Congress system' when the Congress Party controlled all the state governments and also the union, the success of which was attributed to consolidation of 'the clientelistic arrangement'[35] that became gradually intrinsic to the party. What was symptomatic in 1967 seems to be a well-entrenched pattern now with the clear political ascendance of the regional parties. The leading member of either of the major coalitions at the pan-Indian level can afford to ignore them only at their political peril.

Following the rise of the regional parties as formidable partners in governance, the constituent states in federal India are growing stronger gradually and steadily. Not only are they now capable of articulating their demands effectively they have, on occasions, become decisive in policy making. Politically, it seems to be a sign of 'adulthood of Indian states' which may create the US confederal type polity with strong units and a centre as a mere monitoring instrument. The adulthood of states is not, at all, a romantic conceptualization of growing importance of Indian states, but is premised on a particular variety of 'political consciousness', drawing on inherent diverse socio-cultural realities of India as a 'nation'. There are instances which may be cited to substantiate that adulthood disrupts national integrity and hence despicable. But a thorough study of the so-called 'disruptive movements' championing regional autonomy may reveal that the outcome would have probably been otherwise had they been dealt with differently at the outset. To put it bluntly, the carefully crafted tendency to 'essentialize' multi-cultural Indian identity boomeranged and the sooner it is understood by those who preside over India's political destiny, it is better for the country. This apart, there is a fairly strong opinion to suggest that political in India continues to be governed by traditional idioms and values. This is probably true if we interpret the growing importance of caste and other primordial loyalties literally without comprehending their articulation in conjunction with the socio-economic and political reality. Caste or religion is representational and hence its importance in political mobilization. And, apart from consolidating a group identity, caste and religion provide a critical meaning to the individuals, located in a wider collectivity. So the idioms which may be mistaken as 'traditional' are actually modern presumably because they are rooted in processes, linked with the growing democratization of the political in its most complex form. It would therefore be wrong to suggest that increasing importance of primordial loyalties in conceptualizing politics in India leaves no scope for modern politics to strike roots. Instead it is fair to argue that modernity in Indian politics is a very complex admixture of various influences, drawn on the past as well as present experiences and there is therefore no straight forward way to easily delimit its domain. This is where the challenge lies.

The 1994 SR Bommai Judgement

No discussion on India's federalism is complete without being engaged with the 1994 SR Bommai judgement of the Supreme Court of India. Opposing the Presidential proclamation, under Article 356 of the Constitution of India, for dismissal of state governments in Meghalaya, Nagaland, Madhya Pradesh, Rajasthan, Himachal Pradesh and Karnataka, the former Karnataka chief minister, SR Bommai challenged

[35] An expression used by Christophe Jaffrelot in his *India's Silent Revolution: The Rise of the low Castes in North Indian Politics* (New Delhi: Permanent Black, 2003), p. 492.

the validity of the decision since it was contrary to the federal spirit of the Constitution of India. Two issues seem to have bothered the division bench of nine judges who, while deciding the justiciability of the dismissal, drew our attention to the increasing importance of the provinces in the federal compact: on the one hand, the division bench paid attention to the constitutionality of the proclamation which also led the apex court to assess its justiciability in the context of India's changing political texture in which states no longer remained mere appendages to the Union. Critical was the concern that the court had expressed in the light of the presidential decision to impose central rule by dismissing the duly elected state governments due to their purported failure to sustain constitutional governance. The basic issue was to ascertain whether the proclamation was meant to serve politico-ideological or constitutionally justiciable ends following the due process.

Legally speaking, the task of the court was made easier with the acceptance of the idea that federalism is part of the basic structure of the Constitution though the points, raised by the division bench, are useful to firmly establish the argument that federalism, being integral to the basic structure, cannot be fiddled with so easily. By drawing upon the conceptualization that AV Dicey had evolved in *The Law of the Constitution*, the bench addressed the concern as follows:

> Federalism is, therefore, a concept which unites separate States into a Union without sacrificing their own fundamental political integrity. Separate States, therefore, desire to unite so that all the member-States may share in formulation of the basic policies applicable to all and participate in the execution of decisions made in pursuance of such basic policies. Thus the essence of a federation is the existence of the Union and the States and the distribution of powers between them. Federalism, therefore, essentially implies demarcation of powers in a federal compact.[36]

India is a federal compact, argued the bench, in which the Union and the States are partners sharing identical concerns for the well-being of the polity. There is hardly a space for confrontation since 'the distribution of the legislative and executive power within limits and coordinate authorities of different organs are delineated in the organic law of the land, namely the Constitution itself'.[37] With the demarcation of authority between the Union and the States, the Constitution created a healthy constitutional arrangement to govern a healthy federal balances. Being aware of the peculiarities of India's federalism that evolved in a parliamentary form of governance in India, the bench also underlined:

> The organic federalism designed by the founding Fathers is to suit the parliamentary form of Government to suit the Indian conditions with the objective of promoting mutuality and common purpose rendering social, economic and political justice, equality of status and opportunity; dignity of person to all its citizens transcending regional, religious, sectional or linguistic barriers as complementary units in working the Constitution without confrontation.[38]

[36] The Supreme Court judgement in the *SR Bommai v. Union of India*, 1994, delivered on 11 March 1994, §14. https://indiankanoon.org/doc/60799/ (accessed 21 October 2016).

[37] *SR Bommai v. Union of India*, 1994, §169.

[38] *SR Bommai v. Union of India*, 1994, §174.

Supportive of hybridization of government, the apex court justified federalism as an appropriate mechanism to realize the constitutional goals that the Preamble enumerates. It was therefore forcefully argued to avoid confusion:

> Institutional mechanism aimed to escape friction to promote harmony, to set constitutional culture on firm foothold for successful functioning of the democratic institutions, to bring about matching political culture adjustment and distribution of the roles in the operational mechanism are necessary for national integration and transformation of stagnant social order into vibrant egalitarian social order with change and continuity economically, socially and culturally.[39]

In strict constitutional terms, there is hardly a threat to the federal compact because the founding fathers, as the bench underlined, took ample care to create a balanced structure of governance for the fulfilment of the politico-ideological aims that they so assiduously nurtured during their confrontation with the alien rule. Nonetheless there are provisions in the Constitution that privileged the Union over the States which is clearly an impediment towards establishing federalism in its true spirit and form. This is clearly evident in the constitutional design of lodging

> in Parliament the residuary legislative powers, and in the Central Government the executive power of appointing certain constitutional functionaries including High Court and Supreme Court Judges and issuing appropriate directions to the State Governments and even displacing the State Legislatures and the Governments in emergency situations.[40]

While being aware that these features are likely to weaken the federal edifice of the Constitution, the bench defended its stance by suggesting that

> the extent of federalism … is largely watered down [in India] by the needs of progress and development of a country which has to be nationally integrated, politically and economically coordinated, and socially, intellectually and spiritually uplifted, [and hence] … the States cannot stand in the way of legitimate and comprehensively planned development of a country in the manner directed by the Central Government.[41]

That India's federalism is peculiar was, according to the apex court, contingent on the historical circumstances in which it had evolved. Being an example of pragmatic federalism, Indian federal structure cannot be conceptualized in the format of classical federalism of the American type. One has to take into account the historical antecedents and also the immediate socio-political instability following the 1947 partition of the country to meaningfully comprehend the so-called deviant features of India's federalism. The bench thus stated that 'federalism in the Indian Constitution is not a matter of administrative convenience, but one of principled outcome of our own historical process and a recognition of the ground realities'.[42]

---

[39] *SR Bommai v. Union of India*, 1994, §174.
[40] *SR Bommai v. Union of India*, 1994, §56.
[41] *SR Bommai v. Union of India*, 1994, §56.
[42] *SR Bommai v. Union of India*, 1994, §276.

Be whatever it is, the bench however affirmed that the presidential proclamation for imposing emergency by dismissing the elected governments could not escape judicial scrutiny because

> federal principle, [along with] social pluralism and pluralist democracy which [forms] the basic structure of our Constitution [demands] that the judicial review of the Proclamation, issued under Article 356(1) is not only an imperative necessity but is a stringent duty and the exercise of power under the said provision is confined strictly for the purpose and to the circumstances mentioned therein and for none also.[43]

Furthermore, seeking to scrutinize 'circumspectly the material on the basis of which the [presidential] power is exercised',[44] the bench reinforces the argument that under no circumstances the federal structure can be allowed to be fiddled with for partisan political gain. Dismissing the proclamation as *ultra-vires* to the Constitution, the bench further affirmed that being integral to the basic structure federal rights of the States could never be violated till all options were exhausted. Here, the judges drew on what BR Ambedkar suggested while defending the Emergency provisions. According to Ambedkar, the President, before suspending the administration of a province, was required to 'issue a mere warning to a province that has erred [and] ... things were not happening in the way in which they were intended to happen in the Constitution'.[45] This was the first step to be followed by holding election to the legislative assembly to provide an opportunity 'to the people of the province to settle matters by themselves'.[46] Once these endeavours yielded no results, the President was authorized to resort to powers, enshrined in Article 356. In the said case, the proclamation for dismissal was issued without exhausting the options that received the approval of the founding fathers. In view of the clear violation of the spirit of the Constitution, the presidential endorsement of the dismissal of the elected state governments was put to stringent judicial enquiry which was justiciable in the light of the deliberate avoidance of the Union Government to act as per the constitutional direction.

The 1994 SR Bommai judgement will go down the history as a landmark event in history of constitutionalism in India for three important reasons. First, by reiterating that the exercise of Emergency powers is permissible once the other constitutionally available options are exhausted. Furthermore, the court has laid down a fundamental principle of constitutionalism that has serious implications: on the one hand, it has now been made amply clear that the President does not have absolute power but enjoys conditional power which can be exercised if the situation so warrants. Second, the verdict emphasizes the limitations within which Article 356 needs to work. As per the apex court, the presidential power is to be exercised sparingly since it is the last resort in cases where it is manifest that there is a complete breakdown of the constitutional machinery in the concerned state. Third, by suggesting that the presidential proclamation is subject to judicial review, the court created a space for itself which is inviolable in this case since it concerned a basic structure of the Constitution of India. Under no circumstances, federal principles can be bypassed or ignored because they are integral to India as a federal compact, the court held. Hence the 1994 SR Bommai judgement is a path-breaking decision in India's constitutional history.

---

[43] *SR Bommai v. Union of India*, 1994, §106.

[44] *SR Bommai v. Union of India*, 1994, §106.

[45] BR Ambedkar's defence in the Constituent Assembly, 4 August 1949, *Constituent Assembly Debates*, Book No. 4, p. 177, quoted in *SR Bommai v. Union of India*, 1994, §106.

[46] Ambedkar, quoted in *SR Bommai v. Union of India*, 1994, §106.

Concluding Observations

Parliamentary federalism that has emerged in India is a unique hybrid system of governance in which the apparently contradictory tendencies are sought to be managed. What has emerged in India during the course of more than half a century does not correspond with any of the classical models of government. Indian political structure is neither strictly unitary nor purely federal; it is a form in which the elements of both are traced and evident. Distinct from the classical types for obvious reasons, Indian political system offers a unique model drawing upon both the British tradition of parliamentary sovereignty and the American federal legacy in which regions seem to be prior to the Centre. This is an essentially a hybrid system of governance that has emerged due to a peculiar unfolding of socio-political processes in the aftermath of India's rise as a nation state. Parliamentary federalism is therefore not merely a structural device for distribution of powers between different layers of government it is also an articulation of a basic philosophy accommodating diverse regional interests in the name of a nation.

As a hybrid political system, India is neither fully parliamentary nor federal. The 1950 Constitution has devised an elaborate system of distribution of powers. So, it is federal following the principles, enshrined in the American Constitution. It is not federal because the Constitution has failed to acknowledge the need to make the central institutions of government fully federal through bicameralism. Instead, the Constitution is clearly in favour of 'an obsolescent' Westminster model of parliamentary government that is clearly 'unitary'. The political processes however have led to the gradual but steady importance of inter-governmental agencies, like the National Development Council (NDC) and Inter-State Council (ISC). Identified as 'federal' agencies, these structures are clearly those with potentials for radically altering the governance format.[47] However, at present these institutions do not appear to be effective in the context of economic liberalization when there is a clear shift from 'inter-governmental cooperation' to 'inter-jurisdictional competition'. While there are institutions like the NDC or ISC to tackle the former, there is no formally constituted agency except the ad-hoc conferences of chief ministers and the inter-state Water Commission to grapple with the emerging tensions arising out of Centre–State relations. In the light of the increasingly competitive patterns of federal relations, this absence creates 'a problem for the horizontal integration of the states in India'.[48]

There is no doubt that India's politico-constitutional structure has undergone tremendous changes to adapt to changing circumstances. Parliament continues to remain, at least constitutionally, supreme though the constituent states have become more powerful than before. In the changed circumstances, what is evident is a clear shift of emphasis from the Westminster to federal traditions, more so, in the era of coalition politics when no single political party had an absolute majority in Parliament. For practical purposes, the scheme the framers had adopted to bring together diverse Indian states within a single authority was what is known as 'executive federalism'—a structure of division of powers between different layers of governmental authorities following a clearly defined guidelines in the form of 'Union', 'State' and 'Concurrent' lists in the Seventh Schedule of the Constitution of India. Due to compulsions of circumstances arising out of coalition politics, the constituent States do not remain mere instruments of the Union; their importance is increasingly being felt in what was earlier known as 'the exclusive' domain of the Centre. A process seems to have begun towards 'legislative federalism' in which the upper chamber

---

[47] Rekha Saxena, 'Role of Inter-governmental Agencies', *The Hindu*, 29 January 2002.

[48] Lawrence Saez, *Federalism Without a Centre: The Impact of Political and Economic Reform on India's Federal System* (New Delhi: SAGE, 2002), p. 158.

representing the units of the federal government is as powerful as the lower chamber. Drawn upon the American federalism where the Senate holds substantial power in conjunction with the House of Representatives, legislative federalism is an arrangement, based on an equal and effective representation of the regions. The decisions, taken at the union level, appear to be both democratic and representative given the role of both the chambers in their articulation. In other words, legislative federalism in its proper manifestation guarantees the importance of both the chambers in the decision-making process that no longer remains 'exclusive' territory of the Lower House for its definite representative character. Not only will the Upper House be an effective forum for the regions its role in the legislative process will also be significant and substantial. If properly constituted, it could be an institution that represented the regions as such, counterbalancing the principle of representation by population on which the Lower House is based. It will also be a real break with the past since India's politico-constitutional structure draws upon the Westminster model with a strong centre associated with unitary government.

Whether 'bicameralism' with a reconstituted Rajya Sabha enjoying equal authority with the Lok Sabha would be desirable is debatable. If the political climate undermines the spirit of coalition, it would increase governmental impotence because what is likely to govern the decisions of the parliamentarians is a design to stall the motions that may not have been inspired out of solicitude for State's rights. So the changed composition of Rajya Sabha may not be a politically appropriate device to creatively fashion the federal balance in India though there have been occasions when the Rajya Sabha has been tough with the Lower House. Its partisanship was, for instance, demonstrated during the brief Janata Party interlude (1977–80) when the Congress-dominated Rajya Sabha thwarted a government-initiated constitutional amendment by refusing to endorse the move for which the support of two-thirds of house was required. The divide between the two houses has become more prominent of late. The Congress majority in the Rajya Sabha appears to have pre-empted several attempts to adopt legislations to fulfil the government's agenda, while in the days before 1967, the Rajya Sabha hardly played a significant role except to corroborate the views expressed in the lower house. Following the installation of non-Congress governments in various states since 1967, the upper chamber seems to have acquired a definite, if not completely new role in the governing processes. The rejection of the Prevention of Terrorism Ordinance (POTO) in early 2002 is an example showing that the Rajya Sabha had asserted its independence by rejecting the Ordinance, already endorsed by the Lower House. In terms of its numerical strength the upper chamber is not simply equipped to stall the acceptance of any bill when the Lok Sabha has adequate numbers to push whatever decisions it adopts. In the case of POTO, the ruling coalition openly challenged the Rajya Sabha that turned down the legislation, already approved by the directly elected representatives.

There is no copy-book conceptualization of Indian federalism since it is being constantly reinvented in response to the changing socio-economic and political reality in which it rests. As is seen, the growing assertiveness of major political institutions holding the federal balance, such as the Supreme Court, the President and the Election Commission have radically altered the centre of gravity. The famous SR Bommai judgement of 1994 in which India's apex court declined to endorse the decision of the Union cabinet to dismiss a duly elected state government in Karnataka by resorting Article 356 of the Emergency provisions. Upholding the view that an elected government in a state cannot be superseded without allowing the ruling party to prove its majority in the assembly, the Supreme Court held that 'states have an independent existence and have as important role to play in the political, social, educational and cultural life of the people as the Union; they are neither satellites nor agents of the Centre'.[49] The idea was unambiguously

[49] *SR Bommai v. Union of India*, 1994, §138.

expressed when the Court stated that both the Union and the constituent provinces 'are coordinating institutions and ought to exercise their respective powers with adjustment, understanding and accommodation to render socioeconomic and political justice to the people, to preserve and elongate the constitutional goals'.[50] The unanimous verdict by the nine-judge constitutional bench is a watershed event in so far as India's federalism in concerned. By emphasizing the importance of the constituent provinces in the federal compact, the Supreme Court of India reaffirmed that federalism is not merely a constitutional template for distribution of power, but a process that is being constantly reinvented in view of the rapidly changing socio-economic and political circumstances in which it is rooted. A context-driven design, it is thus continuously evolving in response to the socio-economic stimulus from the grassroots. Besides contributing to the democratic processes, the trajectory of India's federalism also confirms that notwithstanding its clear colonial roots, it has also created a space in which the Union and the provinces have emerged as partners (not always compatible, as the past has shown) responsible for realizing the aims and objective that the founding fathers set out for the country. Hence, it has been rightly emphasized that apart from devising a constitutional arrangement for demarcation of authority between the two sets of government, federalism seems to have complemented processes towards democratizing governance in India.

Review Questions

1. **Federalism is a contextual phenomenon. Explain.**
2. **How did federalism evolve in India? Elaborate with reference to the past endeavours during the colonial rule.**
3. **How did the founding fathers conceptualize federalism for independent India? Elaborate.**
4. **Distinguish between 'executive' and 'legislative' federalism with examples.**
5. **In what respects, Indian federalism can be said to be a hybrid form of constitutional structure? Elaborate your response.**
6. **The Indian Constitution is a peculiar admixture of both the US federalism with the unitary constitutional scheme that was preferred during the colonial rule. Explain.**
7. **Can Indian federalism be explained as a 'diluted form of federalism'? Explain.**
8. **Critically evaluate the importance of the 1994 SR Bommai judgement of the Supreme Court of India.**
9. **Federalism in India does not conform to a copy-book description of federalism. Do you agree with this view? Elaborate your response.**
10. **Is it fair to argue that federalism needs to be constantly reinvented; otherwise, it will lose its viability. Do you agree with this view? Elaborate your response.**

[50] *SR Bommai v. Union of India*, 1994, §247.

Chapter 14

Emergency Provisions: Part XVIII (Articles 352–360)

Learning Objectives

- To understand the constitutional provisions relating to Emergency
- To evaluate them in the light of the India's past political history
- To grasp whether these constitutional decrees are constitutional or contrary to the Constitution of India

Of all the parts of the Constitution of India, Part XVIII enumerating the Emergency provisions has attracted maximum attention from scholars and practitioners of law and also from the politicians. The reasons are not difficult to seek. For the scholars, this part stands in contradiction with the fundamental democratic spirit on which the constitution rests; for the practitioners of law, it is a part which troubles them when they are engaged in legally defending the exact nature of the constitution though there are enough inputs to justify an emergency to handle an extraordinary situation. To the politicians, the provisions in Part XVIII enable the draconian administration to strike roots in an otherwise democratic polity. There is unanimity here despite the fact that scholars, lawyers and jurists and politicians do not usually share the perspectives in which they tend to defend their respective points of view. Part XVIII comprising nine Articles (from Article 352 to Article 360) is a steppingstone towards creating and also consolidating an authoritarian rule on the basis of the constitutional guarantee that cannot be so easily legally set aside. This is a paradox of India's constitutional history because despite being vehemently opposed to colonialism that deployed multiple constitutional rules and regulations to muzzle the nationalist endeavours, the founding fathers did not seem to have been persuaded enough to completely get rid of these colonial diktats which reappeared in Part XVIII. True, an Emergency cannot be proclaimed at one's whims; there are specific constitutional procedures which need to be followed before it is made a constitutional decree. That the constitutional system can easily be manipulated is beyond doubts, as there are many illustrations from India's recent political history to substantiate the contention. For those supportive of Part XVIII, the state needs to be empowered in case of the outbreak of untoward circumstances which means that it also provides a shield against the distortion in the constitutional fabric of the country. This is a fair argument if it is juridically assessed: an executive feat is justified since it has a wider goal of protecting the system of governance which is tuned to the fundamental democratic values that the founding fathers so assiduously nurtured during their battle against foreign rule. The problem arises when one challenges the foundational arguments that one pursues in favour of the replacement of the normal democratic government by an authoritarian rule. Here comes one's subjective understanding of the situation which provokes the rulers to replace the constitutional governance by a system of authority defying the foundational democratic values on which the constitution is based.

There are two important points that merit attention here: first, the design of Emergence is a constitutionally endowed scheme because it draws its sustenance from the Constitution of India. The withdrawal of normal democratic functioning of public administration is thus justified as per the constitutional directives. In view of their clear constitutional roots, one cannot be dismissive of Part XVIII so easily. Secondly, as per the Constitution, the provisions in this Part are made operational only under the exceptional circumstances. The Constitution is very categorical while delineating the situation which warrants the application of these provisions. There are three specific situations—(a) war or aggression by an external force, (b) breakdown of constitutional machinery in the provinces and (c) threat of financial instability—in which the President is allowed to proclaim an Emergency.

A perusal of the history of Emergency in India shows that it was resorted to by the ruling authority also to fulfil its partisan aims. The 1975–77 internal Emergency is illustrative here. In response to the opposition challenge to the undemocratic deeds of the government, the ruling Congress government hit back by imposing an Emergency. As a result, India's political texture had undergone a sea change. Whether the declaration was justified or not is a subject of fierce debates though there is no doubt that the 1975 proclamation led to, what I call, 'constitutional authoritarianism' in a context when it was alleged that the constitutional machinery had completely broken down. Pushed to the wall, the ruling dispensation of the Congress party had no alternative but to cling to Part XVIII of the Constitution to sustain the integrity of the country which was seemingly threatened. This is not the place to review the system of governance that sprang up during the Emergency though the findings of the 1977 Shah Commission amply prove how Emergency was utilized by those associated with the ruling party for gratifying their personal aims and objectives; it created a system of governance which was distorted to the extent of being highly personalized. What is important here is to understand the concept of constitutional authoritarianism which is an attempt to articulate two contrasting political tendencies in one meaningful theoretical category. An emergency is a constitutional design which is of help in case of a threat to the prevalent constitutional government. Once the provisions of Part XVIII are evoked, the available system of governance is immediately withdrawn, leading to the formation of a centralized and authoritarian administration. So, Part XVIII works both ways: on the one hand, it articulates a constitutional response in case of a breakdown of the constitutional machinery; with the collapse of the system, this Part also endows, on the other hand, the ruling authority to resort to steps and measures to uphold governance in accordance with its priority. As history has shown, these steps and measures that were resorted to during the Emergency were neither democratic nor people-friendly, but were driven by personal whims and motives. Judged from the perspective of both the Constitution and the prevalent politico-ideological context, the idea of constitutional authoritarianism appears to be a meaningful conceptualization to capture the complex texture of Emergency that flourished in India in the wake of the alleged crumbling of governance following the challenge by the opposition.

The Emergency provisions evolved in a historical perspective which cannot be ignored if one seeks to understand them analytically. In other words, since these provisions are exceptional in character, they need to be conceptualized with reference to the historical context in which they became inevitable. Given their exceptional nature, these provisions continue to provoke debates, presumably because of past experiences substantiating the fear that they had caused once they became constitutionally effective. In view of the obvious complexities of provisions of Part XVIII, the aim of this chapter is two-fold: on the one hand, it deals with the constitutional provisions, of course, with reference to their historical antecedents, from both the British initiatives and those the founding fathers had undertaken while defending them in the Constituent Assembly. As is argued earlier, Part XVIII has also been subject to stringent judicial scrutiny.

There are major judicial pronouncements which, by devising various kinds of checks and balances, also strove to evolve constitutional norms and values to restrain the growth and consolidation of constitutional authoritarianism. By focusing on specific court judgements, this chapter thus aims to explore, on the other hand, the changing nature of Part XVIII which is constitutionally entrusted with the responsibility of shaping governance in exceptional circumstances.

Historical Antecedents

Part XVIII of the Constitution of India is a continuity of a constitutional tradition that had its roots in British colonialism. This was not a novel idea that the founding fathers nurtured; instead, they presumably drew on this to evolve a more efficient system to tackle emergency situations in the country. A discussion of historical antecedents confirms this: this is a fairly well-established argument that Emergency provisions in the Constitution are either borrowed or inspired by the efforts that were undertaken earlier in India's political governance.

The British Influence

There is no doubt that Section 93 of the Government of India Act of 1935 provides strong inputs to the India's constitution makers when they were engaged in finalizing Part XVIII of the Constitution. Most controversial for being most draconian, Section 93 of the 1935 Government of India Act endowed the Governor of a province to dismiss an elected government and to bring the administration directly under his control. The legislature would thus automatically become defunct. As it was stated in the Section,

> [It] provides that if at any time the Governor of a Province is satisfied that a situation has arisen in which the government of the Province cannot be carried on in accordance with the provisions of the Act, he may, by Proclamation, assume to himself all or any of the powers exercised by any provincial body or authority. In other words, he may govern the Province himself without the advice of Ministers responsible to the Legislature and without the Legislature.[1]

What is clear here is that absolute authority was given to the Governor in view of the circumstances in which the future of constitutional governance was at stake. This was a contingent measure, necessitated to sustain the rule of law which justifies the application of such a stringent measure. An absolutely temporary measure, Section 93 also provided that such a decision needed to be approved by the both Houses of Parliament. It was made clear with the following stipulation:

> Section 93 further provides that every such Proclamation shall cease to operate at the expiration of six months unless a resolution approving its continuance in force is passed by both Houses of Parliament. Unless, therefore, before the end of this month the necessary resolutions

[1] Hugh O'Neill, the Under Secretary of State for India explained Section 93 in the House of Commons on 28 November 1940 while explaining why Section 93 was proclaimed in Madras on 30 October 1939. http://hansard.millbanksystems.com/commons/1940/apr/18/government-of-india-act-1935 (accessed 13 November 2016).

> are carried in both Houses of Parliament, the Proclamations will cease to have any effect whatsoever.[2]

Similarly, Section 102 of the 1935 Government of India Act remains a critical influence in so far as Article 352 of Part XVIII of the Constitution of India is concerned. According to this Section, 'the Federal Legislature shall, if the Governor-General has in his discretion declared by Proclamation that a grave emergency exists whereby the security of India is threatened, whether by war or internal disturbance, have power to make laws for a province or any part thereof'. The government was authorized constitutionally to suspend the constitution for the sake of handling a bigger danger which was potentially harmful to the maintenance of constitutional governance in the country. In case of war or external aggression, the Proclamation was accepted as a fait accompli given the grave danger that it involved. There were, however, serious dissents when the Proclamation was sought to be justified in the Joint Parliamentary Committee at its meeting in August 1940 as an appropriate means to combat 'internal disturbances' which, the Committee members felt, was an infringement in the domain of provincial autonomy. This was contrary to the fundamental ethos of parliamentary democracy. Despite being aware of the consequences of internal disturbances, for the majority of the members, it was 'a threat to political processes supportive of Westminster model of democracy' and hence it needed to be criticised as 'a derogation from the general plan of provincial autonomy which is so zealously advocated'.[3] Their strong arguments notwithstanding, they had to tone down their criticisms since they were aware that administration needed to be adequately endowed to discharge the responsibility for 'the peace and tranquillity of India'. So, the discussion remained inconclusive except having raised a persuasive point by highlighting the obvious consequences of such a draconian measure if that was indiscriminately resorted to.

The Constituent Assembly Inputs

Emergency provisions were criticised vehemently by a significant section of the members in the Constituent Assembly for being draconian and also contrary to the fundamental ethos of democratic governance that they aimed to establish in India. There were two major criticisms: on the one hand, these provisions were meant to subvert provincial autonomy because as soon as an Emergency was declared, the duly elected provincial governments were constitutionally debarred to exercise their authority in governance. Some of the critics were also apprehensive, on the other hand, that these provisions would endow the political authority to take away democratic rights from the citizens. What was basic to these criticisms was a concern that by resorting to these 'undemocratic steps', the government could be utilized, it was apprehended, for partisan aims, nurtured by the vested interests. In response to the fear that his colleagues in the Assembly expressed, BR Ambedkar, while seeking to assuage their feelings, thus stated:

> If the Centre is to interfere in the administration of provincial affairs, as we propose to authorise the Centre by virtue of [these Emergency] provisions, it must be by and under some obligation which the Constitution imposes upon the Centre. The invasion must not be an invasion which is wanton, arbitrary and unauthorised by law. This is an obligation of the Centre . . . to protect the units or provinces from external aggression and internal commotion. . . . Since the proposed

[2] O'Neill, explaining Section 93.

[3] Cited in SC Dash, 'Emergency Provisions and Union–State Relations in India', *The Indian Journal of Political Science* (January–March, April–June 1961): 57.

> constitution endows the provinces with plenary powers and making them sovereign within their own field, it is necessary to provide that if any invasion of the provincial field is done by the Centre it is in virtue of this obligation. It will be an act in fulfilment of the duty and the obligation and it cannot be treated, so far as the Constitution is concerned, as a wanton, arbitrary and unauthorised act.[4]

The argument was sharp though drawn on Section 93 of the 1935 Government of India Act. For Ambedkar, it was needed to tackle exceptional circumstances and hence the apprehension that the members had was, in his opinion, unfounded. This was made evident when he endorsed even the withdrawal of fundamental rights to enable the state to bring back normalcy. On the surface, the argument is plausible because these provisions aimed at addressing temporary political uncertainties. One had to pay a price for a bigger goal. Hence, for Ambedkar, it was not to be a source of concern at all. Furthermore, he also held the view that given the constitutional checks, it would have been difficult for the Union Government to abuse the authority thus given. There were two important checks: on the hand, the President before taking over the administration of a province, was under a constitutional obligation 'to issue a warning to a province that has erred, that things are not happening in a way in which they were intended to happen in the Constitution; if that warning fails, the second thing for him to do will be to order an election allowing the people of the province to settle matters by themselves'.[5] So, the President was endowed with alternative constitutional options before resorting to what he received by virtue of the Emergency provisions. Hence, he mentioned that 'it is only when these two remedies fail that he would resort this article. It is only in those circumstances he would resort to this article. I do not think we could then say that these articles were imported in vain or that the President had acted wantonly'.[6] Given his faith in liberal democracy of the Westminster variety, Ambedkar seemed persuaded that codified rules and regulations were an adequate shield against the consolidation of authoritarian tendencies although he was aware that 'there is a possibility of these articles being abused or employed for political purposes' which was true, as he further underlined, 'to every part of the Constitution which gives power to the Centre to override the Provinces'.[7] Emphasizing that 'these overriding powers are not the normal feature of the Constitution [and that] . . . their use and operation are expressly confined to emergencies only',[8] he hoped that with the consolidation of democracy in India, 'such articles will never be called into operation', and thus 'they would become a dead letter'.[9] Ambedkar's argument received adequate support from among his colleagues in the Constituent Assembly. Sharing Ambedkar's zeal for Section 93, PS Deshmukh of Central Provinces and Berar seemed to be persuaded in retaining the Emergency provisions. 'Section 93 has worked well for the last so many years', argued Deshmukh. Furthermore, India needed a constitutional shield to take care of emergency situations arising out of 'external aggression or internal disturbances'. Hence there is no need to repeal the section.[10] His colleagues, Raj Bahadur (United States of Matsya), while strongly condemning the accusation that 'this article is merely a subterfuge to nullify the democratic freedom', forcefully made his point by saying that 'it is to protect and safeguard democracy and freedom that such a provision has been made to meet

---

[4] BR Ambedkar's statement in the Constituent Assembly, 3 August 1949, *Constituent Assembly Debates*, Book No. 4, p. 133.
[5] BR Ambedkar's statement in the Constituent Assembly, 4 August, 1949, *Constituent Assembly Debates*, Book No. 4, p. 177.
[6] Ibid., p. 177.
[7] Ibid., p. 177.
[8] BR Ambedkars statement in the Constituent Assembly, 4 November 1948, *Constituent Assembly Debates*, Book No. 2, p. 42.
[9] BR Ambedkar's statement in the Constituent Assembly, 4 August 1949, *Constituent Assembly Debates*, Book No. 4, p. 177.
[10] PS Deshmukh (Central Provinces and Berar), 3 August 1949, *Constituent Assembly Debates*, Book No. 4, pp. 147–48.

certain emergencies' and these provisions, he further added, 'will stand us in good stead when unseemly or awkward situation arise in our land'.[11] Instead of their being merely a guarantee of democracy and provincial autonomy, Alladi Krishnaswami Ayyar justified the inclusion of these provisions in the constitution as follows:

> The primary thing concerning the nation and the Union Government is to maintain the Constitution [and] if the import of that expression is fully realized, it will be noticed that there cannot be any intention to interfere with the provincial constitution because the provincial constitution is a part of the Constitution of the Union. Therefore, it is the duty of the Union Government to protect against external aggression, internal disturbance and domestic chaos and see that the Constitution is worked in a proper manner both in the State and in the Union. If the Constitution is worked in a proper manner in the provinces . . ., that is, if responsible government, as contemplated by the Constitution, functions properly, the Union will not and cannot interfere. The protagonists of provincial or State autonomy will realize that, apart from being an impediment to the growth of a healthy provincial or State autonomy, this provision is a bulwark in favour of provincial or State autonomy because the primary obligation is cast upon the Union to see that the Constitution is maintained.[12]

Unlike the conventional arguments, made by other members in favour of the retention of the Emergency provision, Ayyar drew attention to a fundamental federal principle in which the Union is held responsible for the maintenance of federal balance by ascertaining the autonomy of the constituents which cannot be compromised under any circumstances. Interference by the Union Government is thus permissible for a bigger cause for upholding the constitutional sanctity of the system and the provinces need to endorse such a feat for the sake of nurturing the constitution. With this kind of logic, Ayyar and his colleagues did not find the continuity of Section 93 in India's Constitution as incongruent with democratic governance. For them, these provisions were 'a safety valve which is intended to save the Constitution',[13] as TT Krishnamachari (Madras) mentioned while being critical to those opposed to extraordinary authority, given to the Union Government during an Emergency. He went to the extent of suggesting that

> such dictatorship would be very necessary in order to safeguard the constitution and it is a grim fact from which we cannot escape so long as the world is what it is today with the threat of war, aggression and internal strife, arising out of various causes, mainly economic, . . . that are ever-present.[14]

There was one common thread in all these arguments: Emergency provisions were essentially protective and they needed to be resorted to sparingly. So long as the roots of dissension remained, these provisions were necessary to manage constitutional governance by following the constitution and the practices that followed.

Despite their forceful defence for five Articles (Articles 275–280, which later became Emergency provisions in the Constitution of India), a section of the Assembly voiced its resentment by making

[11] Raj Bahadur (United States of Matsya), 3 August 1949, *Constituent Assembly Debates*, Book No. 4, p. 149.
[12] Alladi Krishnaswami Ayyar (Madras), 3 August 1949, *Constituent Assembly Debates*, Book No. 4, p. 150.
[13] TT Krishnamachari (Madras), 2 August 1949, *Constituent Assembly Debates*, Book No. 4, p. 123.
[14] Ibid., p. 123.

persuasive arguments to suggest that these provisions stood in contradiction with the very ethos of constitutional democracy which India was to adopt following the British withdrawal. What brought Ambedkar's critics together was their concern which they expressed by saying that this chapter of the constitution was to let loose and also consolidate an authoritarian rule under the garb of the maintenance of constitutional governance. One of the first salvos was fired by KT Shah (Bihar) who felt that the Emergency provisions were not only contrary to constitutional democracy but also a threat to its very foundation. In a persuasive manner, he developed his argument as follows:

> Looking at all these provisions and scrutinizing the powers that have been given in almost every article, it seems to me that the name only of Liberty or Democracy will remain under this Constitution. Every one of these articles, and ultimately the article suspending even the fundamental rights and the right of approach to the Supreme Court for the enforcement of those rights, merely on the ground that there is an emergency declared by the Head of the State, is, to my mind, a denial of any right of freedom or civil liberty of any kind that has been conferred on the citizens.[15]

As a disenchanted member of the Assembly, Shah seems to have hit the bull's eye at two complementary levels of thinking: at one level, he had shown the incongruence that this chapter had evinced between the ideal for which the freedom fighters fought the battle for Independence and the proposed constitutional arrangement to govern an independent India; at another, he also conveyed that by depriving citizens of their fundamental rights and also the right to go the court of law for legal redressal, this chapter reduced the fundamental principles of democratic governance—Liberty and Democracy—to mere labels. This was a powerful argument in support of the campaign for the annulment of this chapter in the proposed constitution of India. By endorsing Shah's concern, HV Kamath (Central Provinces and Berar) substantiated the argument that he made, and pursued the point further by saying that this very chapter was 'a negation' of the politico-ideological mission that the nationalists sought to fulfil. According to him, the constitution was founded on

> a Grand Affirmation ... of fundamental rights [on which] the edifice of democracy was [sought] to be built. Now, the process has reversed with the surmounting of that edifice by the consolidation of "the Great Negation". [What it meant was] first the grand affirmation, then that edifice, at any rate that façade of democracy and surmounting that edifice or façade is the great negation of Part XI [enumerating the Emergency provisions]; ... and article 280 of this Part is, to my mind, the keystone of this arch of autocratic reaction.[16]

The adverse implications of Article 280 which later became Article 356 in the 1950 Constitution, were obvious, argued Kamath, for India's democracy since it allowed the ruling authority to suspend democratic rights for the sake of what they would paint as the breakdown of constitutional governance. Hence he said that 'this article ... is fraught with grave danger to the rights and liberties of the individual guaranteed to him under the Constitution.'[17] Characterizing the denial of rights to approach the Supreme Court as 'a slur

[15] KT Shah (Bihar), 4 August 1949, *Constituent Assembly Debates*, Book No. 4, p. 196.
[16] HV Kamath (Central Provinces and Berar), 20 August 1949, *Constituent Assembly Debates*, Book No. 4, p. 533.
[17] Ibid., p. 53.

on our Constitution' Shibban Lal Saksena thus strongly argued for the exclusion of Article 280 from the proposed constitution[18] because this would create conditions for the rise of an authoritarian state, as Kamath apprehended. In an unambiguous way, he thus exhorted that with the incorporation of chapter XI:

> We are seeking to lay the foundation of a totalitarian state, a Police State, a state completely opposed to all the ideals and principles that we have held aloft during the last few decades, a State where the rights and liberties of millions of innocent men and women will be in continual jeopardy, a State where if there is peace, it will be the peace of the grave and the void of the desert.[19]

Warning the members of the obvious adverse impact of this chapter on democratic governance, Kamath characterised the insistence of some members on the Emergency provisions as nothing but a reluctance to learn from history. To substantiate his claim, he referred to the rise of fascism in Germany by drawing upon Article 48 of the Weimer Constitution of the Third Reich (1919–33) which similarly laid down terms and conditions for the growth of an all-powerful administration in case the constitutional governance was at stake. As Article 48 allowed Herr Hitler 'to destroy democracy in Germany and to establish his dictatorship',[20] Part XI too, which bore a resemblance to the Article 48 of the Weimer Constitution, was to be resorted to in India for the establishment of a fascist state. Unless the Emergency provisions were rescinded, 'we are in serious trouble in the future'. This meant that 'we are saying one thing in one article and . . . seeking to annul it by another article'.[21] For Kamath, this amounted to adopting 'subterfuges . . . and crooked business [which neither] behoves us . . . nor does conform to our dignity'. Being unhappy with those strongly defending the chapter on Emergency provisions, Kamath thus argued that 'we are therefore laying ourselves open to snares and traps in our path wherein we shall be caught beyond any rescue'.[22] Condemning those supportive of Part XI, he further emphasized that 'the whole Constitution will be in danger not so much from those who are agitating in the streets as from those who are in power in case these articles are adopted as they are'.[23] The source of concern was the apprehension that these provisions were likely to be abused by the future rulers for narrow and partisan gains. Individuals were to be deprived of their fundamental rights, including the right to approach the court for their reinforcement. So the critics saw in this endeavour of Ambedkar and his colleagues an attempt to lay out the foundation of a draconian state almost in a fascist way. By drawing on how Article 48 of the Weimer Constitution led to the rise of fascism in Germany, HV Kamath and his colleagues defended their arguments by highlighting the adverse consequences of such provisions. They were not persuaded to accept Part XI since it was contrary to the foundational values of democratic governance that the founding fathers so assiduously championed.

The debate over Part XI that dealt with the Emergency provisions is a testimony to a split of opinion among the members of the Assembly on the basis of their well-defined preferences for governance. This is simply, in other words, a division of viewpoints, based on how they conceptualized governance. And, hence it will be a bit overstretching if this chasm of opinion is articulated as being reflective of contrasting ideological perspectives. As is argued earlier, neither Ambedkar nor those endorsing Emergency

---

[18] Shibban Lal Saksena (United Provinces), 20 August 1949, *Constituent Assembly Debates*, Book No. 4, p. 542.

[19] HV Kamath (Central Provinces and Berar), 20 August 1949, *Constituent Assembly Debates*, Book No. 4, p. 539.

[20] HV Kamath (Central Provinces and Berar), 3 August 1949, *Constituent Assembly Debates*, Book No. 4, p. 141.

[21] Ibid., p. 141.

[22] Ibid., p. 141.

[23] Ibid., p. 141.

provisions had ever an inkling to undermine the democratic foundation of India's future polity; in fact, their concern was to strengthen the edifice by evolving adequately strong constitutional devices against the tendencies to the contrary. For them, the Emergency provisions were meant to serve that purpose; they were in place to maintain constitutional governance in case it was threatened by the unfolding of circumstances in which the future of constitutional democracy was at stake. This was, according to them, a pragmatic step which would gradually lose its viability in view of the strengthening of democratic values and principles. Ambedkar thus said that Emergency provisions would become 'a dead letter'. For his detractors, who did not seem to have been persuaded by logic of pragmatism, Part XI was inherently a source of abuse by those holding authority. In case of external aggression, they were partly agreeable since it was an emergency that needed to be tackled in unison with the entire country. Their source of worry was Article 280 of Part XI which allowed the proclamation of Emergency due to internal disturbances. This was a grey area since the individual assessment of the Governor of a province held the key to such a declaration. As there were no specific criteria that the proposed constitution had identified, Shah, Kamath and their colleagues were apprehensive of situations in which these provisions were likely to be abused for fulfilling partisan aims. That their apprehension was not unfounded came true in the period after the inauguration of the 1950 Constitution of India when the provisions for internal emergency were too frequently resorted to for narrow political gain by those holding power.

There were thus two extreme points of view that figured prominently in the debate over these Emergency provisions. A perusal of the debate also reveals that there was a third point of view which endorsed neither of these viewpoints, but drew our attention to an important aspect of constitution building by highlighting the need for evolving a complementary mind-set. BH Zaidi of Rampur–Banams States elaborated the concern in a very persuasive manner as follows:

> Even if we have the finest constitution in the world and if [we] lack the democratic spirit, the Constitution is bound to break down. What do we mean by saying that the President may take the powers into his own hands and may become an absolute dictator? And, will the thirty-two crores of Indians sit quietly and knuckle under? If they would, then they would do that anyhow, no matter what Constitution you frame. We seem to think that our political salvation lies purely in laws, not in a public opinion, which is wide awake, well-informed and vigilant. I feel that if we are going to pin our faith only on the written Constitution without bringing about the education of our new masters—the masses and the people of India then are going the wrong way about it.[24]

Fundamental here is point about the importance of public opinion which needs to be strengthened to make a democratic constitution functional. In Zaidi's concern for making India a truly democratic polity, more than a written constitution what was required was an alert public who, by being the new masters of democratic rule, held the actual authority. Hence so long as the public remained unaware of their legitimate role in democracy, the codified constitution was of no use. It was evident further in his comment to the effect of stating that

> no Constitution which exists only on paper can mean the salvation of a country. What we must [therefore] work for is the proper democratic spirit, the realization that every one of us

[24] BH Zaidi, (Rampur–Banams States), 3 August 1949, *Constituent Assembly Debates*, Book No. 4, p. 145.

> is responsible to see that the country is governed properly along enlightened, progressive [and] democratic lines. If that spirit that vigilant watching of the Government of our country is not there, then no Constitution on Gods earth . . . is going to succeed.[25]

The idea is loud and clear. The success of the constitution is contingent on the people being vigilant of their role in governance. In other words, the written constitutional provisions are vacuous unless there exists an alert public to share their responsibility as important partners in public administration. This is a powerful conceptual formulation that Zaidi put forward while being critical of those Assembly members insisting on including provisions inhibiting tendencies towards abuse of the constitutional prerogatives by those holding important constitutional offices.

Review of the Argument

Majority of the Assembly members were persuaded by the argument that Ambedkar and his colleagues made in favour of the Emergency provisions being incorporated in the 1950 Constitution of India. Nonetheless, the previous discussion of the Constituent Assembly debates shows that it was not a smooth sailing for those supportive of Part XVIII of the Constitution which contains the Emergency provisions. As is evident in the discussion, there were two major arguments: one for the inclusion of these provisions, and the other was opposed to this. For the former, these provisions were necessary for sustaining constitutional democracy under circumstances when its future would be at peril; for the latter, since they were essentially smoke-screens, they needed to be avoided; in certain circumstances, these provisions allowed the public authority to become authoritarian given the suspension of democratic processes to seemingly sustain constitutional governance. There was also a third argument, as is shown previously. This was an argument suggesting that a mere written guarantee or its absence in the constitution hardly makes any difference unless there exists an alert public, being aware of their role and obligation in constitutional politics.

Taken together, these three arguments illustrate the complex unfolding of multiple points of view on a very critical issue of governance in India. What is interesting to note is the fact that the members were almost unanimous in suggesting that maintenance of constitutional democracy was of utmost importance and that cannot be compromised under any circumstances. The difference arose when the arguments were offered by Ambedkar and those holding similar views in favour of diluting constitutional democracy during an Emergency. Without completely dismissing the need for Emergency provisions, the opponents raised their voice for adequate constitutional guarantee against the possible abuse of authority by the rulers once an Emergency declaration was made. It was, therefore, a battle for upholding specific points of view which the respective members of the Assembly pursued in support of their preferences. The third point of view endorsing the necessity for building a strong public opinion is also drawn on the concern for making India a strong and stable democracy. This is a matter of common sense that a written constitution is futile unless it is made to work by an alert citizenry. What is thus important for a true democracy is a well-informed public who, by being alert, never allow those who are constitutionally authorised to govern to deviate from their basic constitutional obligations, namely, maintenance of the constitution. By insisting on this aspect of democratic governance, Zaidi and his colleagues raised a concern which is integrally

[25] Ibid., p. 145.

linked with the articulation of democracy not only as a means to govern but also to make governance participatory and organically linked with the demos.

Constitutional Provisions

Comprising nine Articles (Article 352–Article 360), Part XVIII of the 1950 Constitution of India is perhaps the most controversial segment of the constitution. As is shown earlier, the debates in the Constituent Assembly were a testimony to the strong differences of opinion among the members who were not exactly inclined to altogether abrogate the Emergency provisions, but were keen to impose constitutional restrictions on its application. As a result, Part XVIII was incorporated in the Constitution which was believed to be a shield against efforts towards undermining constitutional governance in India.

There are three types of Emergency, as per the provisions of the Constitution: (a) Emergency due to external aggression (Article 352), (b) Emergency due to the breakdown of constitutional rule in the provinces (Article 356) and (c) Financial Emergency (Article 360). Since the nature of Emergency differs, so do the implications, and the Constitution stipulates them in clear terms. Basic to these provisions is the concern for sustaining constitutional democracy in case it is threatened due to untoward circumstances. As the following discussion will show, these Emergency provisions are nothing but clear constitutional directions in favour of a specific type of governance that draws sustenance from liberal-democratic theoretical postulates.

Emergency due to External Aggression

According to Article 352, 'if the President is satisfied that a grave emergency exists whereby the security of India or any part of the territory thereof is threatened, whether by war or external aggression or armed rebellion, he may, by Proclamation, make a declaration to that effect in respect of the whole of India or of such part of the territory thereof may be specified in the Proclamation'. The President is thus empowered to declare an Emergency on the basis of the inputs from the cabinet; the declaration shall however cease to exist at the expiration of one month unless before the expiration of that period, it has been approved by both Houses of Parliament. In case, the lower House is not in session, it has to be placed before the upper House for approval, and as soon as the session of the lower House is convened, it needs to solicit its approval. The constitutional direction is unambiguous: the President's declaration shall remain transitional unless it is approved by the Houses representing the people which also illustrates the critical significance of the demos in governance even when the need for suspending constitutional democracy arises.

Implications

With the Proclamation of Emergency as per Article 352, the Union Government is empowered, according to Articles 353 and 354, to prevail over the duly-elected governments in the provinces. Article 353 allows the union executive to instruct the state to do what it deems appropriate for governance in case of emergency due to war, external threat and internal turmoil because of armed rebellion. Furthermore, Article 353 increases the judicial authority of the Union Government to legislate even in those areas which are part of the State List. Given the obvious financial burden on the Union Government for such untoward occurrences, which need immediate attention and stern action, Article 354 also allows the President to restrict or prohibit, by order, the distribution of revenues that are to be given entirely to the provinces under normal circumstances.

A perusal of these provisions (Article 352, 353 and 354) confirms that the Union executive is adequately empowered to tackle situation arising out of war, external aggression or armed rebellion. Supported by these provisions, the Union Government acquires unconditional authority which, critics argue, may contribute to the consolidation of a unitary government although this is likely to be scuttled as those supportive of Emergency provisions claim, by the requirement of parliamentary approval for the Presidential declaration.

Breakdown of Constitutional Governance in the Provinces

Article 355, relatively less cited article, is a preface to the Article 356 which justifies the takeover of the state administration by the Union Government in case of breakdown of constitutional governance in concerned provinces. The language is un-ambivalent: 'it shall be the duty of the Union to protect every State against external aggression and internal disturbance and to ensure that the Government of every State is carried on in accordance with the provisions of the Constitution'. This Article bestows the responsibility of maintaining democratic governance in the constituent provinces. In view of the constitutional obligation, Article 356 thus states that 'if the President, on receipt of a report from the Governor of a State or otherwise, is satisfied that a situation has arisen in which the Government of the State cannot be carried on in accordance with the provisions of this Constitution, the President may assume to himself all or any of the functions of the Government of the State' which were deemed to be required for the maintenance of constitutional governance. Similar to Article 352, this Article shall be made operational under certain specific conditions. The President needs to be satisfied by the report that the State Governor sends to prove that the conditions are not propitious for constitutional governance though this is not the only source of information and the President is allowed to justify the Proclamation on the basis of the input that he may derive from sources independent of the State Governor. Like the other Emergency measure, the internal Emergency, guaranteed by Article 356, has to be placed before Parliament if it is to be renewed beyond six months. There is also a constitutional stipulation that the internal Emergency, as per Article 356, cannot be extended beyond three years which is the upper limit in this regard. Whatever may be the restrictions, the fact remains that the Union executive becomes the *de facto* ruler with the suspension of the duly elected State legislature. The constitutional design that emerges as a result also confirms the argument that Article 356 creates circumstances for the consolidation of a centralized government.

Implications

The most controversial section in the Constitution is the one that upholds internal Emergency, justified by Article 356. For the critics, not only is this a slur on the democratic governance, it is also a time-tested device to consolidate fascism in India. Their argument is drawn on Article 358 and 359 which, according to them, are potentially strong enough to evolve a system of governance contrary to what the founding fathers had visualized. In order to bring back constitutional democracy which is being threatened by internal disturbances, Article 358 endows the Union executive with unconditional authority to undertake any steps for this purpose by stating that 'nothing in Article 19 (guaranteeing the Right to Freedom) shall restrict the power of the State as defined in Part III [enumerating Fundamental Rights] to make any law or to take any executive action which the State would . . . would be competent to make or take'. This is a very straightforward constitutional direction to the Union executive in case of the Proclamation for internal Emergency. In order to strengthen the administrative feat in this regard, the Constitution further ensures, as per Article 359, that when the Proclamation is in vogue, the President 'may, by order, declare that the right to move any court for the enforcement of such rights conferred by Part III . . . shall remain suspended for the period during which the Proclamation is in force or for such shorter period as may be specified in the order'. Here too, the stipulations are extremely well-defined: the authority of the Union executive is established beyond doubt; in view of the situations stemming from exceptional circumstances, these constitutional restrictions are perfectly in order. As a system, the mechanism for internal Emergency does not appear to be objectionable though there is an apprehension that these Articles are likely to be misused by those in governance if they are armed with brutal majority in Parliament, as was seen in the 1975–77 Emergency, which will discuss later in this segment of the discussion.

Financial Emergency

Once the financial stability or credit of India or any part of the territory thereof is threatened, the President may proclaim a financial Emergency which entails that 'the executive authority of the Union shall extend to the giving of directions to any State to observe such canons of financial propriety as may be specified in the directions, and to the giving of such other directions as the President may deem necessary and adequate for the purpose'. Again, this is a very well-directed constitutional instruction which is, as per the Constitution, necessary for ascertaining India's financial stability. There is also a specific direction in Clause (b) of Article 360 insisting that the President may 'issue directions for the reduction of salaries and allowances of all or any class of persons serving in connection with the affairs of the Union including the judges of Supreme Court and the High Courts'. This is a step which is felt to be needed to take care of financial crisis, being the result of situations that cannot be meaningfully combatted by adopting normal sets of corrective measures.

Implications

Article 360 articulates certain well-defined constitutional devices to tackle financial Emergency. The implications are obvious: the Union Government is endowed with extraordinary powers and authority to take care of India's financial health which is being affected due to exceptional circumstances. This will again lead to the creation of a centralized authority, at the behest of the Constitution, for maintenance of financial stability and credit of India. A constitutional design, being justified as a contingent measure, the financial Emergency reinforces the argument that since the Union Government is the custodian of India's credit worthiness and financial credibility both internally and globally, the entrusting of absolute authority to the centre does not seem to be unwarranted. Nonetheless, this is a design which complements the processes leading to the consolidation of a centralized authority with no accountability whatsoever due to exceptional circumstances.

Constitutional Amendments

Although, for Ambedkar, Emergency provisions were to be 'a dead letter' soon, India's recent political history proved him otherwise with the consolidation of 'constitutional authoritarianism' in the wake of the 1975–77 Emergency Proclamation. With a post-mortem analysis of the period when constitutional democracy was completely suspended, it is plausible to argue that the ruling authority tends to be dictatorial in certain circumstances, especially when it has brutal majority and is led by individuals with immense popularity and charisma. One of the first assault on the democratic fabric of the polity was the adoption of the Thirty-Eight Amendment Act on 24 July 1975, just one day less than the completion of a month of the Emergency Proclamation on 25 June 1975. Introduced on 22 July the bill received presidential approval in just ten days, this Amendment Act debarred the judiciary to review the Emergency Proclamation whether made to meet external, internal or financial threats. Emergency was an extraordinary measure when the normal constitutional activities were completely withdrawn, and individual had to surrender their fundamental rights for 'a national cause'—an oft-quoted argument that was offered in support of this Amendment by those who mattered in the decision making then. A draconian regime thus set in where neither judiciary nor any other institutions of democracy were allowed to function. This was a significant step to constitutionally strengthen the regime that was believed to have had the required mass support for such a feat! In order to completely decimate the opposition, the then Congress government promulgated the Forty-Second Amendment Act in late 1976 which not only made the judiciary subservient to the executive but also granted unrestrained power to Parliament to amend any parts of the constitution without judicial review. Provinces also lost their distinct constitutional status and were made mere appendages to the Union in a situation in which the Union executive prevailed over the state governments. By reiterating that the President's Proclamation of Emergency was immune from judicial review, the Forty-Second Amendment Act was a reinforcement of what was decided earlier in the Thirty-Eighth Amendment Act of 1975 which consitutionalized the Emergency.

The distortion in India's constitutional framework for democratic governance following the acceptance of the Forty-Second Amendment Act provoked mass consternation, which was one of the factors for the defeat of the Congress government that was instrumental in the 1975–77 Emergency Proclamation. The enactment of the Forty-Second Amendment Act was held responsible for disturbing the constitutional balance in governance. Hence, with the assumption of power by the Janata Party in the 1977 national poll, it had adopted the Forty-Fourth Amendment Act in 1978. In order to contain the rise of authoritarian regimes in future with support from Part XVIII of the Constitution, the Forty-Fourth Amendment Act thus stipulates:

> As a Proclamation of Emergency virtually has the effect of amending the Constitution, it is being provided that the Proclamation would have to be approved by the two Houses of Parliament by the same majority which is necessary to amend the Constitution and such approval would have to be given within a month. Any such Proclamation would be in force only for a period of six months and can be continued only by resolutions passed by the same majority. The Proclamation would cease to be in operation if a resolution disapproving the continuance of the Proclamation is passed by Lok Sabha.[26]

The most disturbing feature of the Emergency which was constitutionally endorsed with the adoption of the Forty-Second Amendment Act in 1975 was the suspension of the right to approach the court for protecting Fundamental Rights. This was also addressed in the Forty-Fourth Amendment Act which put the right to life and liberty 'on a secure footing' by codifying the rule that 'the power to suspend the right to move the court for 'the enforcement of a fundamental right cannot be exercised in respect of the fundamental right to life and liberty'.[27] A bold legislative device, the Forty-Fourth Amendment Act was a watershed in Indian constitutional history because (a) it stopped the so-called devilish endeavours for the establishment of an authoritarian rule by replacing democratic governance and (b) it also reinforced

[26] Forty-Fourth Amendment Act, 1978. http://indiacode.nic.in/coiweb/amend/amend44.htm (accessed 17 November 2016).

[27] Forty-Fourth Amendment Act, 1978.

constitutional democracy as perhaps the only meaningful politico-ideological arrangement for an extremely socio-culturally diverse country like India.

Judicial Interventions

Part XVIII, especially Articles 356, 357, 358 and 359, is one those critical segments of India's Constitution which is both abused and also reinvented by parliamentary means and also by judicial pronouncements. This has also been the case that regardless of their ideological commitment to democratic governance, the ruling parties tend to misuse the Emergency provisions. As is shown previously, the 1975 Forty-Second Amendment Act, while privileging parliament over judiciary, encouraged forces which were contrary to constitutional democracy. As a counter to these endeavours, the Forty-Fourth Amendment Act was a well-planned politico-ideological design to facilitate constitutional governance in India. Nonetheless, this hardly deterred the governing elites from resorting to the powers that they acquire to pursue their narrow ideological mission. Since the Forty-Fourth Amendment Act was an enabling design that guaranteed the right to approach the judiciary for upholding the fundamental constitutional values, the Emergency Proclamations that followed were always subject to stringent judicial scrutiny. There are many cases which illustrate the role of India's judiciary in establishing, beyond doubt, some of the inalienable constitutional principles and mores. Here, we will focus on two major judicial pronouncements: The 1994 Supreme Court judgement in the famous *SR Bommai v. Union of India* and the 1993 judgement of Madhya Pradesh High Court in response to the petition of Sundarlal Patwa against the dismissal of the state government that he led.

With the passing of the Forty-Fourth Amendment Act in 1978 which allowed judiciary to ascertain the justiciability of the Emergency Proclamations, the Indian judiciary was empowered to intervene in case there were complaints by the affected persons. Furthermore, to prevent possible misuses of authority by the ruling dispensation especially with the presence of state governments being run by political parties with incompatible politico-ideological preferences, the role of judiciary becomes far more critical. It was most conclusively addressed by the Madhya Pradesh High Court in its 1993 judgement over the constitutionality of the Emergency Proclamation by arguing that

> the democracy in India can be described as successful when the Government headed by political parties of different ideologies in different States and the Union are allowed to smoothly function within the framework of the Constitution for achieving the constitutional goals. This mixed type of "cooperative federalism" envisaged in the constitutional set up has to be protected to maintain the sound constitutional and democratic traditions. The role of judiciary in a growing democratic society is greater because being a non-political branch of the government of a nation, it is its bounden duty to maintain and enforce the standards of conduct expected of the constitutional functionaries by the founding fathers of the Constitution.[28]

Fundamental here is the idea that provincial governments are as much important for union of India as the Union Government; neither of them can be sacrificed except at the peril of the polity. What it entails is an attempt to inculcate constitutional values supportive of cooperative federalism which also means

[28] *Sundarlal Patwa v. Union of India*, 1993, Madhya Pradesh High Court judgement. https://indiankanoon.org/doc/488734/ (accessed 17 November 2016).

an endorsement of governments drawing on different ideologies in different states and at the union level. This was a conceptual preface to the discourse that judiciary had evolved while being engaged in assessing the constitutional validity of the Emergency Proclamation.

One of the first judicial efforts to oppose the presidential decree for Emergency as it was *ultra vires* to the Constitution was that of the Madhya Pradesh High Court which, in 1993, declared internal Emergency in the state null and void in 1993. Following the agitation that led to the demolition of the Babri Masjid in 1992, the Congress (I) government dismissed three state governments of Madhya Pradesh, Himachal Pradesh and Rajasthan, presumably because they were ruled by the Congress (I) political opponent, Bharatiya Janata Party. The Chief Minister of Madhya Pradesh, Sundarlal Patwa challenged the presidential Proclamation which had had nothing to do with the agitation following the demolition of the mosque, except that he headed a government which was led by the opposition party. The Court examined the validity of the Proclamation in the light of the Forty-Fourth Amendment Act and also the spirit in which federalism was articulated in India. The government decree was set aside and the High Court defended its decision by saying that 'the entire Proclamation is constitutionally invalid for being prejudiced, [and] the ground situation did not warrant such a Proclamation'.[29] Two reasons were put forward: first, by dismissing a government belonging to the opposition, the Proclamation 'intends to achieve the political advantages of conducting the assembly election under the stewardship the State Governor'[30] who was an appointee of the incumbent Union Government. Second, since the presidential proclamation was subject to judicial review as any other government decree, the Court had the jurisdiction, which was constitutionally recognized, to investigate whether this was justiciable. The Court was convinced that the decision was a fallout of ideological differences of the Union Government with the State Government in Madhya Pradesh by saying that because the decision to impose presidential rule was 'virtually taken by the Union Cabinet', there were reasons to accept the charge that the decision was prejudiced to the extent of fulfilling a specific politico-ideological aim. Quoting the minority view in the Minerva Mills case of 1983, the Court further stated that the presidential satisfaction (leading to the Proclamation) was questionable if 'the reasons given are wholly extraneous or based on irrelevant ground for the formation of the presidential satisfaction'.[31] With the enactment of the Forty-Fourth Amendment Act of 1978, 'the scope of judicial scrutiny in relations to the exercise of power by the President under Article 360 of the Constitution has been enlarged and judicial interference on settled principles in such an action is permissible'.[32] Although the presidential decree was not reversed, the High Court judgement established that presidential authority in this regard was not free from judicial enquiry and investigation. If it is found to be mala fide or based on 'wholly irrelevant and extraneous considerations', the judiciary is endowed with constitutional authority to set the decree aside. This was a significant decision that by challenging the authority of the Union Government in this regard set in motion processes for recreating federal balance in India.

Principles that govern the Madhya Pradesh High Court were upheld by the Supreme Court in 1994 when it had an occasion to judge whether the Emergency Proclamation was justiciable. The 1994 Supreme Court judgement which is also known as SR Bommai judgement (since it involved the former Karnataka Chief Minister, SR Bommai who challenged the presidential Proclamation in 1989) is a watershed in India's constitutional history. Challenging the decision of the Congress (I)-led Union Government to dismiss the duly elected state government, led by SR Bommai, the court came out strongly against the Union

[29] *Sundarlal Patwa v. Union of India*, 1993.
[30] *Sundarlal Patwa v. Union of India*, 1993.
[31] *Sundarlal Patwa v. Union of India*, 1993.
[32] *Sundarlal Patwa v. Union of India*, 1993.

Government for being violative of the fundamental constitutional principles. The Supreme Court defended its opinion since Emergency Proclamation was justiciable in the light of the forty-Fourth Amendment Act. Peeved by the implicit political prejudices of the ruling Congress (I) against the Janata Dal Government in Karnataka, the Court characterized the decision bordering on 'satisfying a narrow ideological goal'. Although the dismissed governments were not re-installed, the Court pronouncement resolved some of the vexing constitutional issues in this regard. Of all the points that the Court made in its defence, there were two basic points which appear to be the core of the judgement: on the one hand, the court reconfirmed that the presidential proclamation was not immune from judicial investigation; if the Proclamation was proved to have been derived from the whims of the incumbent government, the judiciary had every right, on the other hand, to decide in accordance what it deemed appropriate under those circumstances. The Court made it explicit in its verdict as follows:

> The validity of the Proclamation issued by the President under Article 356(1) is judicially reviewable to the extent of examining whether it was issued on the basis any material at all or whether the material was relevant or whether the Proclamation was issued in the mala fide exercise of power. When a prima facie case is made out in the challenge to the Proclamation, the burden is on the Union Government to prove that the relevant material did in fact exist [and] such material may be either the report of the Governor or other than the report.[33]

Reinforcing the Court's authority, it further stated:

> If the Proclamation is held invalid, then notwithstanding the fact that it is approved by both Houses of Parliament, it will be open to the court to restore the status quo ante to the issuance of the Proclamation and hence to restore the Legislative Assembly and the Ministry. … In appropriate cases, the court will have power by an interim injunction, to restrain the holding of fresh elections to the Legislative Assembly pending the final disposal of the challenge to the validity of the Proclamation to avoid the fait accompli and the remedy of judicial review being rendered fruitless.[34]

The main concern of the Court is to ascertain that Article 356 should be applied not in the subjective discretion or opinion but on the objective facts in the sense that the circumstances had existed for the declaration of an Emergency; or, in other words, the situation was such that it warranted presidential Proclamation. Reiterating an argument that its Pakistan counterpart had offered while dismissing the presidential decree for dissolution of National Assembly in 1983, the Supreme Court further suggested:

> The President cannot exercise his powers under the Constitution on wish or whim; he has to have facts, circumstances which can lead a person of his status to form an intelligent opinion requiring exercise or discretion of such a grave nature that the representative of the people who are primarily entrusted with the duty of running the affairs of the State are removed with

[33] *SR Bommai v. Union of India*, 1994. https://indiankanoon.org/doc/60799/ (accessed 17 November 2016).

[34] *SR Bommai v. Union of India*, 1994.

> a stroke of a pen. His action must appear to be called for and justiciable under the Constitution, if challenged in a court of law.[35]

By thoroughly subjecting the presidential decree dismissing the Bommai government in Karnataka in 1989, the Supreme Court firmly established that this was contrary to the fundamental ethos of constitutionalism in India. The argument is straightforward and easy to comprehend because that Court believed that

> the federal principle, social pluralism and pluralist democracy which form the basic structure of our Constitution demand that the judicial review of the Proclamation issued under Article 356(1) is not only an imperative necessity but is a stringent duty and the exercise of power under the said provision is confined strictly for the purpose and to the circumstances mentioned therein and for none else.[36]

Reviewing the Judicial Endeavour

The previously stated brief scan of two path-breaking judgements confirms the argument that constitution evolves out of a dialectical interaction with the context which also entails that, except the fundamental constitutional values and principles, there is nothing which is sacrosanct. A watchdog of the system, the court of law is usually hailed as an institution of governance that steers governmental activities in accordance with the rule of law. Being alert and vigilant, it also becomes an instrument for empowering the demos by making them integral to the processes of governance. This was evident, as the previous discussion shows. Armed by the Forty-Fourth Amendment Act of 1978, India's courts, both the High Court of Madhya Pradesh and the Supreme Court of India firmly established that (a) the presidential decree was required to be reviewed because the Constitution said so and (b) the Emergency provisions being special provisions were incorporated by the founding fathers to address the problems arising out of exceptional circumstances; they thus needed to be treated accordingly which entails that they were to be resorted to only sparingly.

Concluding Observations

Emergency provisions are a constant source of contestation, challenge and also despair. As is evident in India's recent political history, there are innumerable instances to show that Part XVIII of the Constitution of India (with nine Articles) has frequently been abused by several Union Governments to pursue their narrow politico-ideological objectives. This is therefore not surprising that whenever occasion arises, the ruling political parties are hardly hesitant to resort to this Part to undermine even the fundamental ethos of India's democratic governance. In other words, since the authority that the ruling party acquires from Part XVIII appears to be unconditional, the ruling party tends to be authoritarian and apparently completely shackle-free, as was visible in the context of the 1975–77 Emergency which the Congress (I) government proclaimed to trounce the opposition. This was thus utilized for a narrow political aim which was clearly *ultra vires* to the Constitution. Both the Thirty-Eighth Amendment Act and Forty-Second Amendment

[35] *SR Bommai v. Union of India*, 1994.
[36] *SR Bommai v. Union of India*, 1994.

Act are a testimony to the authoritarian design that the Congress (I) led government had nurtured during those two years. The Forty-Fourth Amendment Act of 1978 was a counter-response and seemed to have taken a damage control exercise which was further pursued by the court of law, as was shown earlier by reference to two major judicial pronouncements by the High Court of Madhya Pradesh and the Supreme Court of India.

In view of the possibility of Emergency provisions being misused, is it fair to argue that they need to be repealed since they are contrary to the fundamental ethos of democratic governance. There cannot be a conclusive answer to this question because the need for Emergency cannot be completely ruled out especially with the outbreak of politico-ideological movements seeking to destroy India's democratic fabric. So, Part XVIII is an empowering administrative design as it accords constitutional sanction to efforts towards delegitimizing those endeavours striving to undermine democratic governance. This is perfectly understandable. What is alarming is the endeavour that the ruling political parties tend to undertake to realize their narrow political aims, as was evident in so many Emergency Proclamations for dismissing provincial governments simply because they held different political banners. The 1994 Bommai pronouncement is, in this regard, a significant step subjecting presidential decree to judicial review which is the recognition of basic constitutional principles, established by the 1978 Forty-Fourth Amendment Act.

It is true that there are major constitutional hurdles that cannot be overcome so easily, and yet, India is perhaps one of those countries where Emergency provisions are resorted to so often: since the 1950 inauguration of the Constitution, there are more than 100 times when an Emergency was proclaimed. On a surface reading, this is a paradox because constitutional embargos are hardly deterrent to constitutional distortions, which means that mere codified restrictions do not seem to be effective restraints. What is thus required is a strong political will to support the constitution and those propitious constitutional values and mores which are pertinent to the growth and consolidation of healthy constitutional practices. This is where the challenge lies.

Review Questions

1. **How is Emergency conceptualized in the Constitution of India? Elaborate.**
2. **How did the founding fathers justify the Emergency provisions in the Constituent Assembly? Elaborate.**
3. **Write a critical essay on the constitutional provisions relating to the Emergency.**
4. **The provisions in Part XVIII of the Constitution of India stand in contradiction with the fundamental ethos of democratic governance. Do you agree with this view? Elaborate.**
5. **Write a critical note on the provisions for 'internal' Emergency.**
6. **How did the Indian judiciary conceptualize the Emergency provisions? Elaborate.**
7. **Critically assess the period between 1975 and 1977 when an 'internal' Emergency was proclaimed.**
8. **The provisions on Emergency are an attack on India's democracy. Do you agree with this view? Elaborate.**
9. **Is it fair to argue that Emergency provisions are an easy option for establishing constitutional authoritarianism? Elaborate your response.**
10. **Do you support the argument that Part XVIII of the Constitution needs to be deployed sparingly? Give reasons to your answer.**

Chapter 15

Article 370 of the Constitution of India

Learning Objectives

- How does one conceptualize India's federalism in the light of a discriminatory constitutional provision like Article 370?
- How was this Article justified by the founding fathers in the Constituent Assembly?
- How is this Article being justified in contemporary India?

Article 370, which provides special constitutional status to Jammu & Kashmir, is a source of contestation for a variety of reasons. Prominent among them is the argument that guarantee of special status to a constituent state in federal India is constitutionally untenable within the framework of a federal nation. The constitutional sanction for autonomy in certain respects is, in other words, contrary to the ideological mission that the founding fathers had pursued while being involved in the battle for freedom. Ideologically invalid, such a concession did not appear to have been drawn on logic especially in view of the fact that other princely states were simply annexed with the Union following Independence. That the Jammu & Kashmir issue was, however, different and needed to be dealt with differently was the argument that was made in the Constituent Assembly to justify its special constitutional status. This was, thus, a historical necessity which finally persuaded the members to accept a rather discriminatory stance vis-à-vis this state. The aim of this chapter is to understand the processes leading to the articulation of Article 370 in a historical perspective. The question seems to have become far more relevant now with the 2015 judgement of Jammu & Kashmir High Court supportive of Article 370 despite the consolidation of the contrarians who strongly feel that this is ideological indefensible and constitutionally flawed in the present constitutional dispensation for India.

Historical Antecedents

The Constituent Assembly of India which framed the Constitution of India debated the issue. A perusal of the debate shows that this Article was not as intensively debated as other articles in the proposed constitution. It was N Gopalaswami Ayyangar of Madras who held the forte against an equally feeble opposition, led by Maulana Hasarat Mohani of United Provinces. Nonetheless, it was an interesting chapter in the Constituent Assembly debates because it enables us to understand (a) how a special status to a state was justified by the dominant section in the Assembly and (b) how a discriminatory provision in India's federal Constitution helps build a strong political opinion in the state for merger with the Union.

While presenting Article 306A, which later became Article 370 in the Constitution of India, Gopalaswami Ayyangar, minister without portfolio in the interim government attributed the special nature of the Article to 'the special conditions' that existed in the state. Article 306A was, according to him, 'a discriminatory' constitutional design to enable the state to fully integrate with the Union of India in due course. While elaborating his argument for such a discriminatory constitutional provision, he further argued that 'the discrimination is due to the special conditions in Kashmir. This particular state is not yet ripe for this kind of integration. ... There are various reasons why this is not possible now'.[1] One of the important reasons was linked with 'the unusual and abnormal conditions in the state 'due to war' which resulted in 'the capture of part of the state by the rebels and enemies'. The other critical factor supportive of special provision for Jammu & Kashmir was India's commitment to the people of the state for

> an opportunity ... to decide for themselves whether they will remain with the Republic or wish to out of it. [The Indian State was] also committed to ascertaining this will of the people by means of plebiscite provided that peaceful and normal conditions are restored and the impartiality of the plebiscite could be guaranteed. [It was also] agreed that the will of the people, through the instrument of a constituent assembly will determine the constitution of the state as well as the sphere of the Union jurisdiction over the State'.[2]

According to Ayyangar, the discriminatory status to Jammu & Kashmir is attributed to the difficult circumstances in which the local habitat was placed due to war and rebellion. And also, the state was allowed to go for a plebiscite to decide whether it would integrate with the Union or not; there was also a concession for creating a constituent assembly for the state to frame its own constitution.

Being entirely politically expedient, the terms and conditions were clearly discriminatory. Interestingly, Ayyangar's defence of a clearly discriminatory Article 306A did not provoke any of the Assembly members to initiate debates except Maulana Hasarat Mohani who raised his voice by questioning the partiality that the Assembly had shown to the Maharaja of Kashmir at the cost of other princely states. 'Why do you make this discrimination about the Ruler [of Jammu & Kashmir], asked Maulana Hasarat Mohani who further argued that 'if you grant this concession to the Maharaja of Kashmir you should also withdraw your decision about [the merger of other princely states] with the Union of India'.[3] The special status Clause was questioned for being discriminatory; it was unwarranted, as Mohani strongly felt, because it amounted to a serious compromise to India's suzerainty as an independent polity. For him, this concessional provision was thus not justified since no constituent units in federal India had the authority of having either a plebiscite or an independent constituent assembly to frame its own constitution, especially when the Constituent Assembly was already in the process of making one for the Union.

Mohani had hardly had supporters, and Article 306A which later became Article 370 in the 1950 Constitution was approved without a single dissent. Ayyangar thus concluded:

> The effect of this article is that the Jammu and Kashmir State which is now a part of India will continue to be a part of India, will be a unit of the future Federal Republic of India and the Union Legislature will get jurisdiction to enact laws on matters specified either in the

[1] N Gopalaswami Ayyangar (Madras), 17 October 1949, *Constituent Assembly Debates*, Book No. 5, p. 424.

[2] Ibid., p. 424.

[3] Maulana Hasarat Mohani (United Provinces), 17 October 1949, *Constituent Assembly Debates*, Book No. 5, p. 428.

> Instrument of Accession or by later addition with the concurrence of the Government of the State. And steps have to be taken for the purpose of convening a Constituent Assembly in due course to frame a constitution for the state.[4]

Justifying that concessions were absolutely 'temporary' since the Assembly agreed to have a plebiscite to ascertain 'the will of the people' and also the formation of a constituent assembly to devise a constitution for the state, the framers did not pay as much attention to this issue as they did elsewhere. That Article 306A was approved without discussion also confirms that the proceedings of the Assembly were state-managed. As the available media sources suggest that when Article 306A was placed for discussion before the Congress Parliamentary Party, it provoked fierce debate and there was hardly a consensus among the members given the discriminatory nature of Article 306A. Nobody in the meeting could digest the discriminatory treatment that was meted out to the state. Vallabhbhai Patel was reported to have been in accord with the discordant opinion though he hardly spoke since it meant a betrayal to the Congress pledge.[5] Jawaharlal Nehru and Vallabhbhai Patel persuaded the recalcitrant colleagues by saying that the concessional Article 306A was likely to mobilize global opinion in India's favour in the light Pakistan's counter claim for the entire Kashmir.

Article 370 thus became integral to the Constitution of India. In the light of the assurances, given in the Assembly, the Article guaranteed that the power of Parliament to make laws for the state shall be limited to

> (i) those matters in the Union List and the Concurrent List, which, in consultation with the Government of the State, are declared by the President to correspond to matters specified in the Instrument of Accession governing the accession of the State to the Dominion of India as the matters with respect to which the Dominion Legislature may make laws for that State; and (ii) such other matters in the said Lists as, with the concurrence of the State, the President may by order specify.

The second part of the Article is a further endorsement of the distinct constitutional status for the state. As it stipulates:

> Notwithstanding anything in the foregoing provisions of this article, the President may, by public notification, declare that this article shall cease to be operative or shall be operative only with such exceptions and modifications and from such date as he may specify [p]rovided that the recommendation of the Constituent Assembly ... shall be necessary before the President issues such a notification.

Article 370 though titled as 'Temporary Provisions', and included in Para XXI entitled 'Temporary, Transitional and Special Provisions' is a permanent feature of the Constitution of India which embodies the conceptual framework of relationship between of the Union of India and Jammu & Kashmir, and also lays down broad features of special status granted to the State. This is constitutionally guaranteed. In the 2015 judgement on reservation in government jobs, the Jammu & Kashmir High Court articulated its

---

[4] N Gopalaswami Ayyangar (Madras), 17 October 1949, *Constituent Assembly Debates*, Book No. 5, p. 427.

[5] LK Advani, 'When the Congress Party opposed Article 370', *The Indian Express*, 17 February 1992.

response in categorical terms. Very explicit in its articulation, the judgement underlines (a) the State of Jammu & Kashmir retained limited sovereignty and did not merge with the Dominion of India, like other Princely States, that signed Instrument of Accession with the Union. The state continues to enjoy special status of limited sovereignty retained by the state. The limited sovereignty or special status guaranteed under Article 370 of the Constitution—only provision of the Constitution that applied to the State *ex-propriogorige* or on its own. Besides Article 1, no other provision of the Constitution would be applicable to the State except, by presidential order in consultation with the State in case the provision is akin to subjects delineated in Instrument of Accession and with concurrence of the State; and (b) it is beyond amendment, repeal or abrogation, inasmuch as Constituent Assembly of the State before its dissolution did not recommend its amendment or repeal. As per Article 370, the President is conferred with power to extend any provision of the Constitution to the State with 'such exceptions and modifications' as may be deemed fit subject to consultation or concurrence with the State government.[6]

As the judicial pronouncement confirms, Article 370 cannot be abrogated. The division bench of Justices Hasnain Masoodi and Janak Raj Kotwal categorically states that it is 'beyond amendment, repeal or abrogation' as the mechanism provided under Clause (3) of the Article is no longer available with the dissolution of the State Constituent Assembly which was the only authority, endowed with powers to recommend abrogation or amendment in the Article. For the court, the Article does not seem to be an exception because Kashmir had 'limited sovereignty' when the Kashmiri ruler agreed to sign the Instrument of accession following India's Independence from colonialism.

An Article which was accepted because of the exigency of the situation gradually became an integral part of the existence of Jammu & Kashmir as a constituent province of the Union of India with all the special constitutional privileges. With a specific constitutional embargo, the President of India is restrained to act, according to Article 370, without 'consultation' and concurrence of 'the government of the state'. Moreover, the authority of Indian Parliament is further curtailed by Clause (3) of Article 370 which makes the recommendation of the State Constituent Assembly mandatory in case this Article is sought to be changed or repealed.

Constitutional implications notwithstanding, the effort towards abrogating Article 370 will have serious internal political repercussions with global ramifications since strife in Jammu & Kashmir will create a constituency for those anti-democratic forces which are reportedly drawing sustenance from operators, located in different countries. Furthermore, it may not be politically useful for the National Democratic Alliance (NDA) government in Delhi to antagonize its alliance partner, People's Democratic Party (PDP) that is now ruling the state of Jammu & Kashmir because (a) it will allow the opposition to characterize any move towards that as anti-secular and (b) it is likely to alienate the people in the state, especially in the Kashmir valley who always view any attack on Article 370 as debilitating for their identity. So, any kind of fiddling with the Article may mean playing with fire. Neither the NDA nor the PDP can afford to lose out on this count since both these political outfits had to struggle a lot to be in the saddles of power after a long political hibernation. For those living in Jammu & Kashmir that had suffered terribly due to the consolidation of terrorism-engineered anti-democratic forces, Article 370 is no longer as important an issue as in the past simply because it has become part and parcel of their being. There are important socio-economic issues, like poverty, hunger and unemployment that need immediate attention. An opinion seems to have gained momentum highlighting the fact that involvement in the campaign for abrogation

---

[6] *Ashok Kumar and Others v. the State of Jammu and Kashmir*, 2015. http://judis.nic.in/Judis_Jammu/list_new2_Pdf.asp?FileName=1843 (accessed 30 November 2016).

of Article 370 will lead Kashmiris nowhere except fomenting trouble and creating instability in the state. For the rest of India, the campaign for the abrogation of Article 370 will garner support for the NDA's leading partner, BJP, because of its discriminatory nature while in the Kashmir valley, in particular, it will create a fissure between two coalition partners at the cost of those who are fighting for political stability and consolidation of democratic processes at any cost. By highlighting the constitutional validity of Article 370, the Jammu & Kashmir High Court has raised an issue that cannot be addressed as easily as is construed given its obvious implications on what the country stands for.

Concluding Observations

Article 370 is a source of discontent, if not, serious resentment since it constitutionalizes imbalances in India's federal arrangement. It is also a puzzle because Article 370 does not seem to have been grounded on the fundamental principles of federalism; instead, it justifies a constitutional arrangement supportive of a confederal system of government. Whether it is plausible in today's context cannot be decided so easily in view of the specific historical context in which Article 370 was incorporated in the 1950 Constitution of India. There is no doubt that the special treatment that was constitutionally guaranteed for Jammu & Kashmir despite being included in federal India may not appear to be justified in the changed political milieu. An easy option to address this constitutional anomaly is an amendment to the Constitution which, however, does not seem to be plausible given the adverse political implications in the province and elsewhere in the country. A precarious situation has thus emerged in which neither of the options—abrogation of Article 370 or its acceptance—provides an acceptable solution. A careful reading of the debates in the Constituent Assembly also shows that the founding fathers seem to have faced the same dilemma which was evident in their support for making Article 370 a temporary provision; this means that the Article was to be withdrawn if it was needed. As history has shown, it was a hope that dissipated soon due to a peculiar unfolding of socio-economic and political circumstances in the province. In fact, the idea was shelved and Article 370 became an integral part of India's federal arrangement in which the state of Jammu & Kashmir was allowed to retain its semi-independent constitutional identity.

In the constitutional discourse, Article 370 is a new conceptual intervention in the sense that by constitutionalizing the terms and conditions of the accession treaty between India and the erstwhile ruler of this princely state, it contributes to a persuasive argument in favour of autonomy within a federal structure of governance. Here, the argument draws on the principle of accommodation and reconciliation whereby a federal system is both constructed and consolidated. This further confirms that federalism cannot be understood, let alone conceptualized, merely as 'a constitutional design', but also 'a political arrangement' which is hardly static. This is a significant conceptual formulation in two complementary ways: on the one hand, it endows us with persuasive theoretical inputs to enable us to understand the consolidation of federal practices in a socio-culturally diverse polity; it also helps us understand, on the other, the importance of the political will in the shaping of constitutional norms, values and principles in support of an arrangement which is not ordinarily endorsed within the available discursive tools of analysis for federalism. By being deviant from the conventional understanding of federalism as a 'holding together' mechanism, Article 370 is thus a unique constitutional experiment which is academically refreshing, ideologically innovative and politically decisive.

Review Questions

1. **How do you justify Article 370 in the Constitution of India? Elaborate your views.**
2. **How did the founding fathers endorse a discriminatory constitutional provision like Article 370 in federal India? Elaborate.**
3. **Article 370 cannot be abrogated ever. Do you agree with this claim? Elaborate your response.**
4. **Do you think that Article 370 is a concession given to the State of Jammu & Kashmir for sustaining India's unity as a nation? Elaborate your response.**
5. **Article 370 inculcates healthy political practices in a federal India. Do you agree with this view? Elaborate.**

Chapter 16

Election Commission of India

Learning Objectives

- To understand the role of election in democracy
- To grasp the role of the Election Commission of India
- To assess the contribution of the Election Commission in India's constitutional Democracy

Democracy in India is not just an institutional façade, but a reality which is being carefully nurtured amidst myriad crises threatening to weaken its foundation. As history demonstrates, it has become integrally connected with the growth of India as an independent polity following the 1947 partition. This is a remarkable happening in the light of what had happened to other south Asian nations which also had the same colonial legacy. For instance, cleaved from the same geographical entitle, India and Pakistan adopted completely different routes to nationhood: while the former struggled hard to create and also consolidate democratic ethos by building the complementary political institutions the latter not only failed to sustain what it had inherited from the British system of governance but also muzzled the efforts towards democratization. There are many reasons. Prominent among them was the emergence of a mind-set in India that facilitated the consolidation of democratic governance, and its lack explains why it did not happen in Pakistan. What is critical is to understand how a supportive mind-set had developed in India despite the political uncertainty that she confronted due to the Great Divide. The task is made easier by India's founding fathers who really toiled hard for almost three years between 1946 and 1949 to lay out not only detailed rules and regulations but also build those institutions which they felt were required to provide a solid foundation to the India's political future.

A perusal of the past reveals that the framers of the constitution seem to have been persuaded by Enlightenment philosophy of the British variety which shaped their politico-ideological preferences given their critical engagement with the British rule, both as opponents and also supporters, on occasions. Two complementary processes seem to have worked in which liberal democracy prevailed over other alternative forms of governance: on the one hand, the political instability that engulfed the polity immediately after partition left almost no space for the founding fathers to indulge in the out-of-the-box thinking; liberal democracy thus became, in other words, a plausible option since it had organic roots in India. Despite its foreign roots, liberal democracy seems to have had, on the other hand, a natural appeal to the founding fathers as a cementing ideology and also an ideational tool to knit together a nation out of disparate communities and groups. The idea of being governed by clearly coded rules and regulations was readily accepted as being appropriate and politically viable. So, the concern was to develop those institutions which were, according to them, critical to the construction of a genuinely democratic polity. What is also striking is the fact that despite having argued for various alternative forms of governance the members of the Constituent Assembly arrived at a consensus while giving a final shape to the constitution.

As an ideology, liberal democracy is based on complementary institutions which without being dialectically interconnected with the context, cease to be integrally linked with the processes leading to democratic governance in its liberal democratic form and substance. Being sensitive to this interconnection, the constitution makers paid adequate attention to the articulation of supportive values and also founding of those institutions which were to translate them into actual deeds. For liberal democracy to succeed, they devoted wholeheartedly to develop a system to pursue an ideological mission that they so assiduously nurtured during colonialism and its aftermath. Complementary to the system, the Election Commission of India is one of those institutions which was expected to consolidate democracy by discharging its role as an impartial constitutional agency. Whether it was possible for the Election Commission to remain independent of the executive since the latter might bulldoze the former by virtue of holding the popular mandate was a matter of concern to the founding fathers who thus insisted on special constitutional provisions for its independent existence. The outcome was Part XV of the 1950 Constitution stretching between Articles 324 to 329, which is an exhaustive segment dealing with all aspects of elections in India. The role of the founding members was critical because it was they who laid the foundation for the Election Commission. Equally important was the politico-ideological processes in post-Independent India which not only strengthened but also made the Election Commission a watchdog of India's democracy. It is therefore not strange to argue that India's Election Commission performs, by discharging its constitutional obligations, a significant role not only in catapulting the citizens onto the centre-stage of Indian democracy but also making the system vibrant by making them integral to the system. The aim of this chapter is to provide an analytical account of the historical roots of the Election Commission and how it continues to remain perhaps one of the most critical institutions of democracy despite odds. On the basis of the discussion on how the Commission gradually became a fulcrum of India's democratic experiences, the chapter makes a general argument suggesting that democracy as an idea hardly flourishes without being assisted by complementary political institutions. This will be pursued by reference to how the idea of an Election Commission was conceptualized during the discussion in the Constituent Assembly and how it evolved and became stronger as an institution of governance presumably because of the context in which citizens were no longer mere recipients, but instigators of change.

Politico-ideological Roots

Established in 1950, the Election Commission was set up as a constitutional agency and entrusted, according to Article 324 of the Constitution, with the task of superintendence, direction and control of all national and state level elections. The Commission holds substantial power in so far the procedural aspects of the elections are concerned. In fact, it derives its strength from the code of conduct, formulated by the political parties participating in the election generally by consensus. There is no doubt that by its sincere involvement in the processes of elections, starting from the preparation of voters' roll to the declaration of the poll outcomes, the Commission plays a critical role in redefining India's political texture. In view of the importance of these matters in sustaining the democratic values, the Constituent Assembly agreed, at the outset, to include the provisions for elections in that Part on Fundamental Rights. The suggestion was however not endorsed and it was decided that the provisions relating to elections and the institution responsible for holding election needed to be put in a completely separate chapter, which was conceded by the majority of the Assembly members. The members of the Committee on Fundamental Rights, headed by Vallabhbhai Patel had two choices before them: (a) to create a permanent body of impartial individuals, devoted to conduct elections as and when they took place, or (b) to form an ad hoc committee with presidential approval for this responsibility. In the end, the members of the Patel-led Committee favoured the former since election was neither a one-time event after a fixed period nor could be left with an ad hoc body since it required expertise. BR Ambedkar intervened in the debate to further clarify the position that the Committee held as follows:

> It should be recognized that the independence of the elections and the avoidance of any interference by the executive in the election to the Legislature should be regarded as a fundamental right and provided for in the chapter dealing with Fundamental Rights. . . . [It was] affirmed without any kind of dissent that in the interest of purity and freedom of elections to the legislative bodies, it was of the utmost importance that they should be freed from any kind of interference from the executive of the day. . . . It was therefore decided to transfer the superintendence, direction and control of the preparation of the electoral rolls of all elections to Parliament and the Legislatures of States to a body outside the executive to be called the Election Commission.[1]

Being aware of the importance of election as a means to ensure democracy in India, the Assembly members had hardly wavered while they endorsed an independent agency to administer election, both at the union level and also at the level of the state. The outcome was the formation of the Election Commission which was to be entrusted with the sole duty of conducting elections. In order to ascertain its independence, it was further suggested that it was to be an independent institution, free from executive control. The purpose was to evolve an institution of governance which was, in no way, prejudiced and biased, but shackle-free while being engaged in discharging its constitutional obligations.

Here too a perusal of the debates in the Assembly shows how the idea of an independent Election Commission gained ground. With the approval of the Committee on Fundamental Rights, the matter was placed for discussion by Ambedkar on 15 June 1949. The roadmap was clearly stipulated. The Election Commission was entrusted with the task of holding elections which entailed:

1. Election of the President of India.
2. Election of the Vice President of India.
3. The Union Parliament and the composition of the two Chambers.
4. Deciding the eligibility qualifications for the prospective parliamentarians and state legislators.
5. Composition of state legislatures.
6. Duration of Parliament and state legislatures.
7. Fixing the seats in Parliament and state legislatures for the Scheduled Castes and Tribes.
8. The delimitation of the boundaries of the constituencies for both parliamentary constituencies and also those for state legislature.
9. Any other matter that was pertinent to election and other related issues.

Besides the aforementioned identified tasks, the Assembly had three important issues to ponder over: (a) whether there would be two Election Commissions: one for conducting elections to constitute

[1] BR Ambedkar's defence, 15 June 1949, *Constituent Assembly Debates*, Book No. 3, p. 905.

Parliament and another for choosing through election the members for the state legislative assemblies. In other words, the task was to develop appropriate institutions for managing elections to parliament and state legislatures. (b) how to prepare the electoral roll of the voters who were eligible to cast votes in the elections, meant to constitute parliament and legislature for the states, and finally (c) what would be the mode of election was another concern that received adequate attention from among the Assembly members. It was more or less agreed that universal adult suffrage was the preferred mode of election since it was complementary to democracy. There was, however, an opinion for restrictive franchise, given the stunningly high level of illiteracy, which did not receive support as the majority of the Assembly members felt that it was contrary to fulfill their aspired ideal of making India a truly democratic country.

In regard to whether there would a permanent Election Commission or an ad hoc body, appointed at the time of election, the Assembly members steered a middle course. After having an intensive discussion, the majority of the members preferred a middle course which came out very clearly when BR Ambedkar placed his point of view to break the logjam over this issue. As he stated:

> There were two alternatives before Drafting Committee, namely, either to have a permanent body consisting of four or five members of the Election Commission who would continue in office throughout without any break, or to permit the President to have ad hoc body appointed at the time when there is an election.[2]

Members who were not persuaded for a permanent Election Commission argued that it was just not required to have such a body since election was to be held after a gap of five years which means that it was to be held intermittently; those willing to have an ad hoc body were thus of the view that since it was not a permanent feature of governance, an ad hoc body was sufficient to take care of this. There were others who, while arguing for a permanent body, felt convinced that the best option was to have a permanent body to address this issue given the possibility of bye-election time and again. Differences were however bridged and a consensus was arrived at with the intervention of BR Ambedkar who evolved a middle path by suggesting that there would be a permanent Chief Election Commissioner, to be supported by a set of people who would be appointed for the task as and when it was required. Hence he concluded:

> It was therefore felt that having regard to the exigencies of the situation, it would be sufficient if there was permanently in session one officer to be called the Chief Election Commissioner, while when the elections are coming up, the President may further add to the machinery by appointing other members to the Election Commission.[3]

Although opinions varied on whether there would be a permanent Election Commission, the members were unanimous in emphasizing that it should be independent of the executive. Hailing Ambedkar's suggestion as complementary to democracy, RK Sidhva of Central Provinces and Berar argued:

> There is a complete unanimity in this House or outside the House that elections should be fair, pure, honest and impartial. [This] . . . could be achieved only by an impartial agency as has been contemplated in this article. We want the elections to be above-board. Any machinery

[2] Ibid., p. 905.
[3] Ibid., p. 905.

that is to be set up should be quite independent, free from any influence from any agency, executive or anybody'.[4]

The arguments for an independent Election Commission received whole-hearted support from other members of the Constituent Assembly. For instance, Shibban Lal Saxena of United Provinces, who felt that it was necessary to evolve a healthy democratic system. In his opinion, unless the Election Commission was completely independent, democracy was likely to lose its salience. Hence he insisted that the authority for appointing the Chief Election Commissioner and the supporting staff should not rest with the President who, while choosing a person for this position, needed to take the approval of the Prime Minister who, given his party affiliation, was likely to recommend 'a staunch party man' for this constitutional assignment. What was thus required was to devise a mechanism to avoid such an eventuality? Saksena preferred a system whereby the appointment of the Chief Election Commissioner was to be approved by the two-thirds majority of both the Houses. In his words, 'the person who is appointed to the post should be such that he [*sic*] should be enjoying the confidence of all parties—his [*sic*] appointment should be confirmed not only by the majority but by two-thirds majority of both the Houses'.[5] Being aware that a mere simple majority was not a check to a biased appointment since it was easy for the ruling party to muster a majority, he thus argued that 'if it is only a bare majority then the party in power could vote confidence in him but when I want 2/3rd majority then it means that the other parties must also concur in the appointment so that ... real independence of the Commission may be guaranteed'.[6] In support of Saksena, Naziruddin who was from West Bengal exhorted that 'election is a most important item in a democratic setup and it is very necessary that it should be controlled and supervised by a very competent, independent and impartial body'.[7] While the majority of the members endorsed the claim, there was a dissenting voice in support of the argument that independence of the Commission could be a source of serious concern. Hence it was emphasized that the Commission should be 'a subsidiary to Government except in regard to the discharge of the functions allotted to it by law'.[8] While defending the viewpoint, KM Munshi of Bombay thus stated that 'a machinery, so independent, cannot be allowed to sit as a kind of Super-Government. . . . It was not possible nor advisable', he further argued, 'to have a kingdom within a kingdom [and] ... the election matters could not be left to an entirely independent organ of the government'.[9] Regardless of contrary points of view, the arguments endorsing an independent Election Commission received an overwhelming support from among the Assembly members and it was thus readily accepted as integral to the Constitution. The majority of the members seem to have been persuaded to accept the argument for independence for the Commission primarily because it was complementary to the processes of democratization, as per them.

The second important aspect of the debate on the Election Commission relates to the preparation of the electoral roll. While dealing with this issue, the Constituent Assembly laid out a strong opinion in favour of universal adult suffrage. In response to an allegation that those who were linguistically or culturally different from the dominant social group who were the occupants of a particular province, Ambedkar sternly mentioned that this was to be stopped, if necessary, by adopting tough administrative measures.

---

[4] RK Sidhva (Central Provinces and Berar), 16 June 1949, *Constituent Assembly Debates*, Book No. 3, p. 917.

[5] Shibban Lal Saksena (United Provinces), 15 June 1949, *Constituent Assembly Debates*, Book No. 3, p. 908.

[6] Ibid., p. 908.

[7] Naziruddin Ahmad (West Bengal), 16 June 1949, *Constituent Assembly Debates*, Book No. 3, p. 923.

[8] KM Munshi (Bombay), 16 June 1949, *Constituent Assembly Debates*, Book No. 3, p. 925.

[9] Ibid., p. 925.

Appalled by the alleged instruction by some of the provincial governments to exclude these socio-culturally different groups, he thus argued that since

> franchise is a most fundamental thing in a democracy ... [n]o person who is entitled to be brought into the electoral rolls on the grounds which we have already mentioned in our Constitution, namely, an adult of 21 years of age, should be excluded merely as a result of the prejudice of a local Government, or the whim of an officer [because] ... that would cut at the every root of democratic Government.[10]

Despite Ambedkar's unstinted support for universal adult suffrage, the idea appears to have disturbed some of the members who felt that it would not work among the illiterate Indian masses. Political demagogues were likely to, it was apprehended, sway them in accordance with their whims and desires. As a result, universal adult suffrage would become an instrument of personal aggrandizement.[11] This were, however, not the sentiments that the majority of the Assembly members shared, though some of them had cast doubts on this suggestion by saying that the framers needed to take adequate cautions before making universal adult suffrage constitutionally operational. As PK Sen of Bihar argued:

> Before we launch our bark on the uncharted ocean of adult franchise, we have to be careful as to how to proceed. After all, ours is an infant democracy and we have yet to know the shoals and sand banks and all the risks and perils on the voyage. We have yet to know how to find out our coastline when we are in danger and therefore, it is extremely necessary ... to work in such a manner that this Constitution, based upon adult franchise, may really not only turn out a success, but may be an example to all the world.[12]

There was an obvious uncertainty, felt the members, though it was not an impediment to the processes of constitutionalizing India. This was a good beginning in which risks were involved, and these were not unfounded since the adoption of universal adult suffrage was exceptionally a new design of governance. In response to 'fear about adult franchise', P Subbarayan of Madras made a strong case in its favour as follows:

> The Indian humanity is such that they have enough common sense, enough horse-sense, if I may say so, which will make it possible for them to choose their rulers with discrimination, and to choose the people whom they think would be able to carry on the administration in a manner which will be for the benefit of the common man ... [and] the Constitution will stand the test of time and it will lead this country to take her proper place in the comity of nations.[13]

Instead of being cowed down by the apprehension that adult suffrage would not work due to high proportion of illiterate people, the members of the Assembly seem to have been persuaded in its favour since it was a tool to translate democracy (at least, political democracy) in its true substance and spirit. To many it was a risk worth taking. Despite having characterized 'the adoption of the adult suffrage' as having taken

[10] BR Ambedkar, 15 June 1949, *Constituent Assembly Debates*, Book No. 3, p. 906.

[11] B Das (Orissa), 17 November 1949, *Constituent Assembly Debates*, Book No. 5, p. 635.

[12] PK Sen (Bihar), 23 November 1949, *Constituent Assembly Debates*, Book No. 5, p. 830.

[13] P Subbarayan (Madras), 25 November 1949, *Constituent Assembly Debates*, Book No. 5, p. 963.

'the greatest risk', RK Sidhva of Central Provinces and Berar appreciated the effort by saying that it was 'the most appropriate decision'. While defending his stance, he further stated that 'a democracy without adult franchise would have no meaning and, therefore, I am very glad and the House is proud that we have introduced adult franchise in the Constitution'.[14] Addressing those who were critical of adult suffrage since it would enable the illiterate people to dominate the legislatures, both at the national and provincial levels, Sidhva was firm in his opposition which he articulated as follows:

> I do not mind if illiterate people come from the remotest parts of the Indian Union. I have seen that sometimes illiterate people have a power of originality and they argue much more ably than some of us, literate persons. Therefore, I am not, at all, frightened and we have taken the right course and if there is a risk, I know there is a risk, and we have taken it in the right direction.[15]

This was a powerful intervention defending universal adult suffrage as a constitutional mechanism to make people the core of governance regardless of whether they are literate or not. In fact, the statement that Sidhva made in the Assembly is also a testimony to the concern that his other colleagues had expressed for democratizing governance in India. What is admirable is the fact that despite being drawn to the apparent adverse consequences of adult franchise in a country where illiteracy was a serious source of concern, the Assembly members did not seem to have left the mission that they had internalized while challenging the discriminatory governance during colonial rule.

Review of the Argument

The previous discussion of how the Election Commission came into being as integral to India's Constitution confirms two important arguments which remain critical to our understanding of the phenomenon. First, it was firmly established that for conducting elections, there had to be an independent organization, endowed with constitutional authority. An independent Commission was needed to make it universally acceptable. In other words, by ascertaining the Commission's autonomy from the executive, the framers addressed the concern of those who felt that it was to be appropriated by the ruling party if it was made dependent on the executive. As a result, the entire purpose of realizing democracy in its unalloyed form would remain distant. The second argument underlines the sagacity of the Assembly members for their unequivocal support for making the Commission entirely independent of the government of the day. This was a master stroke because it, in one stroke, not only clarified their ideological priorities, but also illustrated their heartfelt desire to evolve a system to translate them into a reality. Since the Election Commission was an aid to the democratic processes, the arguments that the members marshalled in its favour thus provide useful inputs to understand the mind-set that gradually evolved in support of a democratic India.

[14] RK Sidhwa (Central Provinces and Berar), 17 November 1949, *Constituent Assembly Debates*, Book No. 5, p. 624.

[15] Ibid., p. 624.

The Constitutional Design

Articles 324 to 329 of Part XV of the Constitution of India lays out the legal–constitutional framework for holding elections in India. Of these constitutional provisions, Article 324 stipulates a set of functions that are required to be performed by the Election Commission. Hence it is stated:

> The superintendence, direction and control of the preparation of the electoral rolls for, and the conduct of, all elections to Parliament and to the Legislature of every State and of election to the offices of President and Vice President held under this Constitution shall be vested in a Commission (referred to in this Constitution as the Election Commission).[16]

Rest of the Articles in this Part deal with the nitty-gritty of the election processes which need to be respected by the government to retain the Commission's independence. What is important to remember here is the fact that though the Constitution is the supreme guide, we cannot afford to ignore the judicial pronouncements and also the complex unfolding of the political processes in the country to explain the trajectory of its evolution and its distinct nature. For instance, till October 1993, the Election Commission functioned only with one individual who was designated as the Chief Election Commissioner except for a short period between 16 October 1989 and 1 January 1990 when the President of India appointed two Election Commissioners with coordinate powers, besides the Chief Election Commissioner. The presidential decree was challenged in the Supreme Court of India which pronounced[17] that

1. it was desirable that more than one individual should exercise the highly vital functions of the Elections Commission;
2. the creation and abolition of posts was a prerogative of the Executive and Article 324(2) left to the President to fix and appoint such number of Election Commissioners as he may, from time to time, determine; and
3. while it was obligatory to appoint the Chief Election Commissioner, the appointment of other Election Commissioners or Regional Commissioners was left by the Constitution to the discretion of the President.

The Supreme Court judgement was however silent about whether all the Election Commissioners held equal power. The confusion was put to rest with the promulgation of the 1993 Chief Election Commissioner and other Election Commissioners (conditions of service) Amendment Act which gave coordinate powers to the Election Commissioners. This was challenged in the apex court which unequivocally declared that (a) the presidential notification appointing two other Election Commissioners was valid which means that the court endorsed the idea that the Election Commission was a multi-member body, and (b) as far as possible, all business of the Commission shall be transacted unanimously, and in case of differences of opinion, according to the opinion of the majority.[18] What is now clear is that the Election Commissioners are now placed on an equal footing in so far as their authority is concerned. Furthermore, the Court also

[16] Constitution of India, Art. 324.

[17] Drawn on Ujjwal Kumar Singh, *Institutions and Democratic Governance: A Study of the Election Commission and Electoral Governance in India*, NMML Monograph No. 9 (New Delhi: Nehru Memorial Museum and Library, 2004), p. 19.

[18] Singh, *Institutions and Democratic Governance*, p. 20.

devised a system in case there were serious differences of opinion that could be sorted out through dialogue; the Court opted for voting and accepted the majority principle.

Besides the court's stipulations, the Election Commission also derives its authority from the People's Representation Acts of 1950 and 1951. These are important statutory directions which appear to have empowered the Commission to a significant extent primarily because they unambiguously earmarked a specific domain of its functioning in so far the conduct of elections is concerned. Both these Acts are important. The People's Representation Act of 1950 provides the allocation of seats and the delimitation of constituencies for the purpose of election to the Lok Sabha and state assemblies, the qualification of voters at such elections, the preparation of electoral rolls and other matters which are pertinent in the conduct of elections. While the 1950 Act lays out what is basic to the conduct of elections, the 1951 Act accords the responsibility to the Commission for the conduct of election of the Houses of parliament and state assemblies, for deciding the qualifications and disqualifications for the membership of those Houses, for dealing with corrupt practices or offences at or in connection with such elections and also for resolving the disputes arising out of or in connection with such elections. Keeping the fundamental principles as they were in the 1950 and 1951 People's Representation Acts, the amended version of 2010 added further stipulations to streamline the procedures with adequate legal defence.

A perusal of the Representation Acts confirms that (a) the Indian policy makers in independent India, being committed to democratic ethos and values, provided adequate legal protection to those institutions which were meant to sustain democratic governance in India, (b) by providing a detailed methodology of how to manage elections to the legislatures, both at the Union and state levels, they also left no doubt in this regard, and (c) by being aware that the election processes were likely to be jeopardized with the consolidation of corrupt practices, they hardly wavered in suggesting stern measures to weed out the impediments towards realizing the fundamental objective of democratic elections.

The Election Commission: An Aid to Democratization

Democracy is an expansive design of participation that makes the demos the core of the processes whereby it naturally unfolds. Election is one of the critical means in which participation is translated into deeds. Hence it is fair to argue that election is 'a mode of mass participation in policy making at the higher levels in representative democracies' catapulting the voters onto the centre stages of political activities at a particular historical juncture.[19] With the importance of election as the fulcrum of democracy, the Election Commission has gained tremendous respectability in recent years. Given the fact that election is not merely a ritualistic participation, it is also an empowering device in so far the ordinary voters are concerned. This is evident both in the increasing size of the voters and also the proportion of voters who vote in election that has considerably enhanced. This is a testimony to the fact that elections are held by the people as an effective instrument to show their relevance in the political processes. In such circumstances, what is required is an efficient electoral machinery capable of managing such a gigantic exercise, but also allowing the electorates to express their choice without being intimidated or restrained. In other words, not only is the Commission responsible for conducting election, it is also entrusted with the task of ensuring unhindered participation in elections. The growing importance of the Commission as a pillar of democracy in India is also attributed to a situation of 'greater politicization of the socially and economically

[19] Manjari Katju, 'Election Commission and Changing Contour of Politics', *Economic and Political Weekly*, 18 Apri 2009, p. 9.

underprivileged communities'[20] who are not only politically alert but also protective of their rights as part of the citizenry. This is perhaps an important reason as to why the Indian Election Commission is far more proactive than its counterparts elsewhere in the region of south Asia. Not only is the Commission stringent in following rules, there are instances in which it disciplined the errant candidates by adopting severe punitive measures. The Commission holds substantial power in so far as the procedural aspects of the elections are concerned. In fact, it derives its strength from the code of conduct, formulated by the political parties participating in the election generally by consensus. There is no doubt that by its sincere involvement in the processes of elections, starting from the preparation of voters' roll to the declaration of the poll outcomes, the Commission has played a critical role in redefining political in today's India. The role of the Commission in the 2006 state election in West Bengal is illustrative here: with the announcement of the dates of elections, the Commission took control of the election machinery of the state in an unprecedented manner. First, it took ample care to revise the voter's roll since the incumbent Left Front government was charged with manipulating the voters' list The Election Commission found a large number of them in various districts. During the cleanup operation, the observer found 13,00,000 false names[21] in the list of voters, and struck them off. Hence the charge seemed authenticated and media thus attributed the sustained electoral victory of the Left Front to 'the bogus voters'. Second, following its success in Bihar in holding a free and fair election under the strict surveillance of the state-controlled coercive forces, the Commission decided to conduct the poll in five fairly dispersed dates stretching almost two months. The Commission requisitioned police and paramilitary forces from outside the state simply because the state police did not appear to be reliable. Because the dates were dispersed, it was possible to get adequate number of them to supervise the voting on the day of election. It was a remarkable election in West Bengal which was held under the strict control of the Election Commission that implemented its authority strictly in accordance with its constitutional obligation to Indian democracy.[22] Although the electoral outcome brought back the incumbent Left Front government to power in 2006, unlike in Bihar, where a new government was installed replacing the government that held power for more than fifteen years, the Commission provided critical inputs to the processes of democratization by empowering the ordinary voters who now become part of 'the movers and shakers' of Indian democracy which can be ignored only at the cost of the political parties seeking political power. In other words, the voters are not merely seasonal participants; they have also been made to feel their importance in the political processes that hardly mattered so far in their everyday life. In this entire earth-shaking transformation, the Election Commission has discharged a critical role by ensuring that 'democratic ambitions play themselves out in an environment of rules and norms where the underprivileged do not trample upon each other and do not get trampled upon by the powerful'.[23] By being sensitive to its constitutional role, the Commission has thus truly become an instrument for democratizing election which had often been derailed in the past due to money and muscle power and the hegemonic ruling party that tended to flout rules and norms for partisan desires.

---

[20] Manjari Katju, 'Election Commission and Functioning of Democracy', *Economic and Political Weekly*, 29 April 2006, p. 1637.

[21] The figure is taken from Sumanta Banerjee, 'Assembly Polls, 2006: Elections, *Jatra* Style, in West Bengal', *Economic and Political Weekly* 41, no. 10 (11 March 2006), p. 864.

[22] I have dwelled on the role of the Election Commission in 2006 West Bengal assembly election at some length in my 'Left Front's 2006 Victory in West Bengal: Continuity or a Trendsetter', *Economic and Political Weekly*, 12 August 2006.

[23] Katju, 'Election Commission and Functioning of Democracy', p. 1639.

Concluding Observations

The aforecited brief exposition of the trajectory of the unfolding of the Election Commission confirms that it is one of those constitutional organs that stands out presumably because of its rise as a watchdog of democratic values in the midst of the consolidation of tendencies towards demeaning them. This further underlines that mere constitutional guarantee is not an adequate shield against the democratic deficit that usually cripples an otherwise efficient political system. With six constitutional provisions, Part XV resonates with the exuberance that the founding fathers had shown while being appreciative of Election Commission as a powerful organ of what they conceptualized as a vibrant democratic polity. There are no dearth of statutory and constitutional rules and regulations, which ensured, as is argued, 'procedural certainty'.[24] This is an important factor which contributed to the growing importance of the Commission since it was mooted in the Constituent Assembly. The erosion of values in public life, procedural certainty notwithstanding, has created a unique politico-economic circumstances in which even the basic constitutional directions are indiscriminately violated not only by the political parties but also by those individuals interested in narrow personal gain. This is one significant change, being accompanied by the politicization of the peripheral sections of society. So a very complex situation has emerged in which the role of the Election Commission has acquired new dimensions that cannot be grasped entirely in constitutional terms. What it means is the importance of the prevalent political processes which refashion the institutions of governance completely differently defying also the conventional mode of conceptualization. The Commission's peculiar unfolding, especially since 1993, confirms again how, independent of the prevalent political processes, an attempt to understand its changed role will lead us nowhere.

Review Questions

1. **Why is the Election Commission an important instrument for democratic governance? Elaborate your response.**
2. **Critically evaluate the constitutional provisions relating to the Election Commission in India.**
3. **How did the founding fathers conceptualize the role of the Election Commission in democratizing election in India? Elaborate.**
4. **Critically assess the role of the Election Commission as the watchdog of constitutional democracy in India.**
5. **The success of the Election Commission is contingent on the consolidation of a complementary mind-set. Do you agree with this? Elaborate your response.**

[24] Singh, *Institutions and Democratic Governance*, p. 42.

Section C

INSTRUMENTS FOR CONSTITUTIONALIZING INDIA

Introduction to Section C

A constitution provides an institutional framework to achieve the goals that it sets for itself; it is also an executive authority in that respect. In order to fulfil specific politico-ideological missions, the institutions that are integral to the constitutional framework of governance are also supported by well-defined rules, regulations and constitutional norms; otherwise, it would become just a compilation without much substance. Two important ideas are implicit here: on the one hand, it is implied that a constitution ceases to become effective unless it is complemented by a set of institutions seeking to uphold the objectives that it strives to attain. The other idea relates, on the other hand, to the dialectical interconnection between institutions and constitution since they draw on each other, which means that the values enshrined in the latter are futile, independent of adequate institutional back-up.

It is difficult to dwell on each and every institutions shaping governance in India in a single monograph. Hence, this section concentrates on some of the major institutions which remain critical in articulating the constitutional goals that are sought to be realized. In order to purse a pointed discussion on the instruments for constitutionalizing India, this section, besides dwelling on the constitutional position of these earmarked institutions, also focuses on how they evolved as a result of many judicial interventions. For instance, Article 368, which deals with the amendment procedures, was always conditional till the adoption of the Twenty-Fourth Amendment Act in 1971, which allowed Parliament to amend any part of the Constitution. The position was later revised with the intervention of India's Supreme Court through the doctrine of basic structure that cannot, under any circumstances, be fiddled with. The outcome was the passing of Forty-Fourth Amendment Act, which reversed the Twenty-Fourth Amendment Act by restricting parliamentary authority with regard to amending the Constitution to a significant extent. In a similar vein, the panchayati raj institutions which, by being a part of Part IV of the Constitution of India, were never mandatory in India's constitutional governance, but underwent a sea change following the acceptance of the Seventy-Third Amendment Act in 1992 and became integral to rural governance in India.

Besides arguing that institutions are important pillars of constitutional democracy, the section reinforces the claim that they also play a critical role in charting out a specific politico-ideological path for the polity. There are many occasions, as will be shown in the chapters, when these institutions rewrote India's constitutional history by challenging the hegemonic executive which, being armed with its numerical strength in the legislature, resorted to practices which were contrary to the Constitution. The role of the Indian judiciary and the Comptroller and Auditor General are illustrative here, as they, while discharging their constitutional responsibilities, act as shields against the tendencies towards crippling constitutional democracy in India.

Chapter

17

Judiciary in India[1]

Learning Objectives

- To understand how judiciary contributes to the processes of democratization
- To comprehend Indian judiciary with reference to the constitutional provisions
- To grasp its proactive role in being a custodian of the Constitution

Unlike her South Asian neighbours, political institutions have developed organic roots in India. There has been, however, a clear deterioration of Indian Parliament in its role in view of the decline of 'the moral credibility' of the elected representatives. Not only has the quality of the debate on policy issues gone down, the parliamentarians also tend to lose their calm even on the floor of Parliament once they are challenged by their colleagues. The parliamentary decline seems to have matched by the ascendancy of other political institutions of Indian democracy. For instance, the President, the Supreme Court and the Election Commission have, among others, shown a remarkable resilience in upholding some of the intrinsic liberal values.

Like several other institutions under the Constitution, the judicial system of the independent India appears to be a compromise between the two distinct perspectives of judiciary under the parliamentary and federal systems of government. Since, for obvious reasons, India could not have become a unitary system of polity, the colonial rulers tried to introduce some semblance of a federal structure, including a Federal Court to stand at the apex of the judicial system within the country. However, the adoption of the parliamentary system of government based on its functional dynamics in Britain conditioned the extent to which the federal institutions in the country could have been afforded strength and operational autonomy. In other words, under the classical notion of the federal system like in America, the Supreme Court should have been on the one hand, accorded some sort of supremacy amongst the three organs of the government owing to its position as the protector of the Constitution and the people's rights. On the other hand, the imperatives of the parliamentary system as in Britain require the Highest Court to be in a subservient position to the Parliament since the latter is construed to be the sovereign authority in the political system of the country. Now, since the Indian political system was designed to be a half way mark of both the federal as well as the parliamentary systems, the judicial system of India was bound to be an

[1] This chapter is drawn on chapter 6 of my *Indian Government and Politics* (New Delhi: SAGE, 2008), which I wrote in collaboration with Dr Rajendra Pandey.

amalgam of certain features prevalent in both the countries. But how far the judiciary might be permitted to imbibe the characteristics of the two systems to suit the requirements of the Indian polity was a million dollar question bothering the minds of the members of the Constituent Assembly. The aim of the present chapter is, therefore, to present an analysis of the perspectives of the framers of the Constitution on the judiciary and working of the judicial system in the country, with all its pros and cons, in view of the increasing efforts of the judiciary to act as the clearing house for all the mess that the country has been put into. While seeking to understand the rising importance of judiciary in governance, the chapter also argues that with the decline of Parliament as the highest forum of our democracy and the perceived indifference on the part of the bureaucracy to the pressing socio-economic needs of the people, a general distrust of the political executive and the loss of faith in the moral and ideological integrity of those holding power collectively account for an expanded judicial reach.

Historical Antecedents

In their concern for realizing democratic rights, the members of the Constituent Assembly held the judiciary in high esteem. They strongly felt that the courts were to be the watchdogs of constitutional values in case attempts were made to undermine them. The Constituent Assembly thus, argued Austin, 'envisaged the Judiciary as a bastion of rights and of justice'.[2] It was not therefore surprising that the question that bothered them most was 'how to render the fortress impregnable to sapping private interests'.[3] For the judiciary to meaningfully discharge its responsibility, it needed to be kept out of politics, they strongly felt, which is possible with the strengthening of 'the walls of the fortress with constitutional provisions'.[4] There was hardly a difference of opinion in this regard and by insisting on keeping the court of law away from the ambit of politics, the Assembly members sought to demarcate an independent domain for the judiciary. On the basis of their understanding of the role of courts in other federal systems, they had no doubt that a judiciary, equipped with adequate constitutional protections, would enable the new polity to realize the exalted goal of freedom for all. Hence they thus aspired to idealize the courts for the two plausible reasons of giving force to the Fundamental Rights and acting as guardians of the Constitution itself.[5] This idealism guided the framers to design an independent judiciary in the realm of which 'the powers of the Supreme Court and judicial review'[6] emerged as the key issues that loomed large in their minds. The tone and tenor of the judicial system of the country drew on the federal political systems with a strong and independent Supreme Court vested with the responsibility of not only maintaining the sanctity of the federal nature of the polity by keeping the constitutional provisions intact in this regard but also by protecting the Fundamental Rights of the people as the beacon of the modern democratic life. The only concession presumably given to the ethos of the parliamentary system in the country was in terms of the fetters put on the Court's power of judicial review where the rights to property and personal liberty were concerned. Rooted in the desire to facilitate the onset of a social revolution on the one hand, and reiterate the recurrent theme of unity in the Constituent Assembly, on the other, the marginal circumspection of the powers of Supreme Court seemed to be an effort to make the judicial provision of the Constitution congruent with

[2] Granville Austin, *The Indian Constitution: Cornerstone of a Nation* (New Delhi: Oxford University Press, 1966), p. 175.
[3] Austin, *The Indian Constitution*, p. 175.
[4] Austin, *The Indian Constitution*, p. 176.
[5] Austin, *The Indian Constitution*, p. 164.
[6] Austin, *The Indian Constitution*, p. 164.

the broad contours of the parliamentary democracy in the country, lest the supremacy of the judiciary becomes absolute attaining alarming proportions in the absence of a well-placed system of checks and balances as are found in the presidential system of government. This was, however, not a point of concern for the members who seemed to have been reconciled to this position since India's constitutional democracy followed the US pattern in which judiciary was constitutionally recognized as a watchdog of democracy. As KM Munshi (Bombay) elaborated, 'our Constitution is based on an entirely different principles, drawn on the British form of parliamentary democracy [though] we have invested the Judiciary with as much independence as is possessed by the Privy Council in England and to a large extent, by the Supreme Court of America'.[7] The parallel with the US constitutional system stops there because the founding fathers were in favour of an integrated judiciary with the Supreme Court at the apex. It was most succinctly stated by BR Ambedkar when he elaborated his views as follows:

> The Indian Federation though a Dual Polity has no Dual Judiciary at all. The High Courts and the Supreme Court form one single integrated Judiciary having jurisdiction and providing remedies in all cases arising under the constitutional law, the civil law or the criminal law. This is done to eliminate all diversity in all remedial procedure.[8]

This again confirms that the Assembly members were innovative in their approaches to constitutional designs; they were driven by India's peculiar socio-economic needs. Once it was agreed upon, the members argued strongly for judicial independence as it was critical to realizing constitutional democracy in its spirit and substance. The sentiments of the Assembly was unambiguously articulated by KT Shah of Bihar when he said that 'much more important from the point of view of civil liberty and the general democratic character of the governance of the country, is the complete separation of the Judiciary from the Executive in every way that we can possibly guarantee. It is of utmost importance that the Judiciary, which is the main bulwark for civil liberties, should be completely separate from and independent of the Executive, whether by direct or by indirect influence'.[9] In his opinion, which was also endorsed by his colleagues, one of the factors responsible for affecting judicial independence was the possibility of gaining, either monetarily or otherwise, by extending favour while executing justice by the judges. Hence, Shah emphasized that 'the possibility of the translation that has frequently occurred in the past, of high judicial officials being available for promotion or transfer to equally high or even higher executive offices is itself a temptation against which Judges should be guarded'.[10] It was therefore necessary, he argued that the 'judges, by law, should be barred from any such translation from the judicial to executive officers, however eminent, however imposing that office may be, lest, in such a translation, they should be even indirectly influenced, and that they should model their judgements, unconsciously perhaps, in the hope of proper appreciation being shown at suitable moments by the powers that be'.[11] There was hardly a dissent in this regard. Majority of the members arrived at a consensus that judicial independence was of paramount importance in so far as the future of constitutional democracy was concerned. Pursuing his point Shah thus concluded that 'the Constitution should therefore definitely provide that the judiciary shall be completely separate from

[7] KM Munshi (Bombay), 23 May 1949, *Constituent Assembly Debates*, Book No. 3, p. 220.

[8] BR Ambedkar, 4 November 1948, *Constituent Assembly Debates*, Book No. 2, p. 37.

[9] KT Shah (Bihar), 23 May 1949, *Constituent Assembly Debates*, Book No. 3, p. 219.

[10] Ibid., p. 219.

[11] Ibid., p. 219.

and independent of the Executive or the Legislature'.[12] The idea was supported by HV Kamath (Central Provinces and Berar) when he spoke in favour of this motion in the Assembly. In a very categorical manner, he exhorted that 'in the context of the free state that we are going to build, the free democratic state that we are going to build up in our country, an independent judiciary should assume a high priority, before we proceed to confer fundamental rights upon the citizens, or before we allocate various functions and powers between the Centre and the Units'.[13] Alarmed by the rise of State authoritarianism in which individual rights were easily infringed, Kamath thus insisted on an independent judiciary because he felt that 'if the judiciary is not there to protect and safeguard these rights that you confer on the citizens, how are we going to preserve the sanctity of our Constitution?'[14] Kamath's primary concern was to ensure independence for judiciary; otherwise, its role as a watchdog of democracy was likely to be compromised, to a significant extent.

The issue of the independence of the judiciary was so paramount in the minds of the framers that, as Austin complains, they showed disproportionate concern for the administrative aspects of the judicial system, with the tenure, salaries, allowances and retirement age of judges, with the question of how detailed the judicial provisions of the Constitution should be and more pertinently with the mechanism for choosing judges, though with the pious desire to insulate the courts from attempted coercion by forces within or outside the government.[15] This was a source of concern from Alladi Krishnaswami Ayyar of Madras who drew attention to some of the practical difficulties in ascertaining 'absolute' independence to the judiciary given the fact that it carried with itself 'the prevalent socio-economic and political views, prejudices and constraints'. While explaining his position, he thus argued:

> In the interpretation of the Constitution, the Supreme Court will be confronted with apparently contradictory forces at work in society . . . which are likely to have an imprint in the judicial acts and decisions. In other words, it cannot in the discharge of its duties afford to ignore the social, economic and political tendencies of the times which furnish the necessary background. [As a result], on one occasion, it may appear to favour individual liberty as against social or state control and at another time it may appear to favour social or state control. It has [therefore] . . . to draw the line between individual liberty and social control in accordance with the context in which it was to adjudicate.[16]

The idea that Ayyar put forward was drawn on his belief that it was difficult to ignore the contextual compulsions while articulating one's views. Furthermore, it would also be erroneous to think that judicial independence meant complete ignorance of State's social responsibility; the State needed to be sensitive to its social, political and economic obligation to the citizens, especially in a country like India where the state intervention was necessary to bring about the required changes for realizing the ideological goals that the founding fathers nurtured so assiduously during the nationalist phase. The other practical difficulty related to the lack of financial independence of the judiciary; it had to depend on the government of the day for its up-keeping as an instrument of governance. Ayyar thus argued that the maintenance of judicial independence 'may become illusory . . . unless the judiciary has sufficient control over its own

[12] Ibid., p. 219.

[13] HV Kamath (Central Provinces and Berar), 23 May 1949, Constituent Assembly Debates, Book No. 3, pp. 222–23.

[14] Ibid., pp. 223.

[15] Austin, *The Indian Constitution*, p. 176.

[16] Alladi Krishnaswami Ayyar (Madras), 23 May 1949, *Constituent Assembly Debates*, Book No. 3, p. 224.

establishment [and] … if the establishment looks for preferment or for promotion to other quarters, it is likely to sap [its] independence.'[17] This is one part of the argument; in the other part, he referred to the fact that while debating judicial independence one had to take into account that the judges drew their salary and other pecuniary benefits out of the taxpayers' contributions. Once this was taken into account, it brought a new dimension to the entire debate. As he mentioned:

> It has to be recognized that the judiciary and its establishment would have to draw their allowances and their salaries from the public exchequer. The ultimate person who will be affected is the taxpayer. Therefore, while, on the one hand, you must secure the independence of the judiciary, the interests of the taxpayer, on the other hand, will have to be safeguarded in a democracy. That can only be done by giving sufficient control to the Government of the country which is responsible to the House of People in the matter of finance.[18]

In order to break the impasse, Ambedkar moved an amendment to the original provision and suggested that 'the administrative expenses of the Supreme Court shall be a charge on the revenues of India.'[19] This view was further elaborated by TT Krishnamachari in his intervention in its favour. Supportive of Ambedkar, he thus suggested that the judicial expenses

> should be placed outside the purview of the Executive which would otherwise have to take the initiative to include these items in the budget for the reason that independence of the Judiciary should be maintained and that the Judiciary should not feel that they are subject to favours that the Executive might grant to them from time to time and which would naturally influence their decision in any matter they have to take where the interests of the Executive … happens to be concerned.[20]

This was a perfect arrangement, according to Krishnamachari because it would not place the judiciary at the mercy of the Executive. A perfect balance was required in which none of the organs of the government would prevail over others. Highlighting the interdependent nature of the organs, Thakur Das Bhargava (East Punjab) stated that 'it would be a mistake for one to ask as to which of the three is of greater or lesser importance, because all the three, though independent in their respective spheres are component parts of the body politics of the State.'[21] This was corroborated by Krishnamachari in far more clear terms when he mentioned:

> It should be made clear that it is not the intention of this House or of the framers of this Constitution that they want to create specially favoured bodies which in themselves becomes an *Imperium in Imperio* (sovereign authority within the government), completely independent of the Executive and the Legislature and operating as a sort of superior body to the general body politic.[22]

[17] Alladi Krishnaswami Ayyar (Madras), 27 May 1949, *Constituent Assembly Debates*, Book No. 3, p. 391.
[18] Ibid., p. 391.
[19] BR Ambedkar, 27 May 1949, *Constituent Assembly Debates*, Book No. 3, p. 388.
[20] TT Krishnamachari (Madras), 27 May 1949, *Constituent Assembly Debates*, Book No. 3, p. 389.
[21] Thakur Das Bhargava (East Punjab), 27 May 1949, *Constituent Assembly Debates*, Book No. 3, p. 393.
[22] TT Krishnamachari (Madras), 27 May 1949, *Constituent Assembly Debates*, Book No. 3, p. 389.

Addressing his colleague's concern, Ambedkar thus steered 'a middle course' whereby the administrative expenses of Judiciary were to be borne out of the national revenues on the direction of the Chief Justice of the Supreme Court with advice from the President of India. This was an apt arrangement which gave 'the Judiciary as much independence as is necessary for the purpose of administering justice without fear or favour'.[23] The outcome of the discussion in the Assembly was Article 146(3) of the Constitution of India which states that the following:

> The administrative expenses of the Supreme Court, including all salaries, allowances, pensions payable to or in respect of the officers and servants of the Court, shall be charged upon the Consolidated Fund of India, and any fees or other moneys taken by the Court shall form part of that Fund.

This was a clearly stipulated position which left no doubt. The apex court is immune from executive control and its independence is ascertained by ensuring its freedom from the executive in regard to a guarantee of funds which it needs for taking care of the expenses that it incurs for administering justice.

Following the blueprint envisaged by the Sapru Committee and the recommendations of its own ad hoc Committee, the Constituent Assembly broadly agreed to devise such provisions as are prudent in the circumstances peculiar to India, irrespective of their prevalence in Britain or America, to secure the independence of the judiciary. For instance, rejecting the British method of appointment of the Lord Chancellor as too unsupervised, and the American system of confirmation of judicial appointments by Senate as open to politics, the Assembly provided for the appointment of the judges by the President after due consultations with the stipulated judicial officers for the task. The questions of the tenure, salaries and future employability of the judges were also answered on the similar lines.

A remarkable point that arose in the context of the durability of the constitutional provisions safeguarding the independence of Judiciary was their amendability by the Parliament in later years as part of some political maneuvering. The Assembly addressed this issue by entrenching the provisions on judiciary amongst those provisions of the Constitution whose amendability was made the toughest by providing that, among other things, the amendment of such Articles would require the approval of not less than one-half of the legislatures of the states, in addition to the passage by both the houses of Parliament by a two-third majority in each case. Later on, in the judicial pronouncements, the independence of the judiciary was included as part of the basic structure of the Constitution, making it almost an unamendable part of the Constitution.

Anticipating the demerits of dogmatizing the independence of judiciary in ascertaining a cordial and interdependent functioning of the three organs of government, the general mood in the Constituent Assembly was in favour of putting things in perspective, if not to undermine it. Echoing the popular sentiment of the members of the Assembly, Alladi Krishnaswami Ayyar pointed out:

> While there can be no two opinions on the need for the maintenance of judicial independence, both for the safeguarding of individual liberty and the proper working of the Constitution, it is also necessary to keep in view one important principle. The doctrine of independence is not to be raised to the level of a dogma so as to enable the Judiciary to function as a kind of super-Legislature or super-Executive. The judiciary is there to interpret the Constitution or adjudicate

[23] BR Ambedkar, 27 May 1949, *Constituent Assembly Debates*, Book No. 3, p. 397.

> upon the rights between the parties concerned [since the] efficient and proper functioning of our democracy depends on the cooperation between the two.[24]

Couched, therefore, in the guise of social revolution, the powers of the Supreme Court, specially its power of review in cases of right to property and personal liberty were not only circumscribed but also made to obliterate in the times of Emergency when the courts' power of issuing writs get curtailed to a great extent and the Executive's functional domain gets widened enough to suspend the enjoyment of the fundamental rights by the people.

The Supreme Court

Within the framework of a unified integrated judicial system, the Constitution provides for the establishment of the courts at the Central, states and the district levels, with the Supreme Court standing at the head of the system. The founding fathers envisaged the Supreme Court of India as 'an adjudicative bureaucracy, a final architect of the doings of other courts in the hierarchy [and] not as an institutional political actor'.[25] While executing its role as a watchdog of democracy, the apex court appears to have created a new domain which is characterized as *demosprudence* entailing judicial review extending judicial reach-out to areas which were not exactly in its purview in the past. Ordinarily, the judiciary upholds *legisprudence* (the principles or theory of legislation independent of politics) and *jurisprudence* (determining the principles, precepts, standards, doctrines, maxims of law and the concept of law). Based on the dialogue between 'constitutional law and constitutional culture', demosprudence is 'a democracy-enhancing jurisprudence'. While dwelling on the concept which is most appropriate in comprehending the critical role that the Supreme Court plays in reconceptualizing constitutional democracy, a prominent theorist of constitution thus explains:

> Unlike the traditional jurisprudence, demosprudence is not concerned primarily with the logical reasoning or legal principles that animate and justify a judicial opinion; rather it is focused on enhancing the democratic potential of the work of lawyers, judges and other legal elites. Demosprudence through dissent attempts to understand the democracy-enhancing potentials implicit and explicit in the practice of dissent; it describes lawmaking or legal practices that inform and are informed by the wisdom of the people.[26]

This conceptual category is a uniquely textured idea seeking to understand judicial intervention in a completely different theoretical prism. Unlike its conventional role where the procedure established by law is privileged, the court evolves its opinion out of the dissent which, being reflective of contrasting socio-political perspective, articulates an opinion which is not exactly derivative of the established canons

[24] Alladi Krishnaswami Ayyars statement in the Constituent Assembly, 23 November 1949, *Constituent Assembly Debates*, Book No. 5, p. 837.

[25] Upendra Baxi, 'Law, Politics and Constitutional Hegemony: The Supreme Court, Jurisprudence and Demosprudence', in *The Oxford Handbook of the Indian Constitution*, eds. Sujit Choudhury, Madhav Khosla and Pratap Bhanu Mehta (New Delhi: Oxford University Press, 2016), p. 96.

[26] Lani Guinier, 'Foreword: Demosprudence Through Dissents', *Harvard Law Review* 122, no. 4 (2008): 15–16, quoted in Baxi, 'Law, Politics and Constitutional Hegemony', p. 95.

of justice. There are plenty of examples showing that India's apex court is proactively involved in settling issues, not by applying the legally established rules and regulations, but by being attentive to the popular democratic aspirations. Demosprudence provides us with a meaningful conceptual mode to capture the role of the Supreme Court in a mould which does not correspond with what is usually associated with its functioning. This perhaps confirms that judges do not make judicial decisions in isolation. Instead, they are governed, to a significant extent, by the context in which they are nurtured. The idea of demosprudence will help us understand 'how both judges and litigants navigate the system and the context in which the law and the Constitution are ultimately interpreted'.[27] This is an idea in support of context-driven judicial behaviour: the judiciary cannot afford to be insensitive to the efforts being made to democratize governance even when they are not exactly defensible in strict legal terms.

Appointment of the Judges

A successor of the Federal Court of the pre-Independence times, the Supreme Court was inaugurated in 1950 with Chief Justice HJ Kania and seven other judges. Afterwards, owing to the increasing workload of the Court, the Parliament has from time to time increased the number of judges of the Supreme Court which presently stands at 28, apart from the Chief Justice. Interestingly, there exists no stipulation on the minimum number of judges in the Constitution, except for the provision in Article 145 relating to Rules of Court, Clause (3) of which provides that the minimum number of judges who are to sit for the purpose of deciding any case involving a substantial question of law and to the interpretation of the Constitution or for the purpose of having any reference under Article 143 relating to advisory jurisdiction of the Court, shall be 5.[28]

The judges of the Supreme Court are appointed by the President in consultation with such other judges of the Supreme Court and of the High Courts in the states as he may deem fit. Holding office till the attainment of the age of 65 years, a judge cannot be removed from office except for proved misbehaviour or incapacity, the motion for which needs to be endorsed by both the Houses of the Parliament by a two-thirds majority. Proving the cumbersomeness of the process of impeachment of the Judges, in the sixty years of the constitutional history of independent India, only one judge of the Supreme Court, Justice K Ramaswami was impeached by the Parliament in March 1991 for misbehaviour in terms of the alleged financial improprieties while remaining the Chief Justice of the Punjab and Haryana High Court. Despite the committee of enquiry finding Justice Ramaswami guilty of the charges levelled against him, the motion of impeachment fell due to political maneuvering in the Parliament, leading to the absolvent of Justice Ramaswami.

More than the appointment of the Judges, what has created a lot of controversy in the country has been the appointment of the Chief Justice of the Supreme Court, beginning in 1973. Left to the emergence of certain conventions and the good sense of the people that be, the method of the appointment of the Chief Justice has not been provided for in the Constitution. Yet, under the idealistic perspective of the national movement and in honour of the set precedents available in many countries of the world, the convention emerged in the country to appoint the senior most Judge of the Supreme Court as the Chief Justice of India. Like many other things, the discredit for breaking this nascent convention went to the regime

[27] Nick Robinson, 'Judicial Architecture and Capacity', in *The Oxford Handbook of the Indian Constitution*, p. 348.

[28] AC Kapur and KK Mishra, *Select Constitutions* (New Delhi: S Chand and Company, 2001), p. 237.

of Mrs Indira Gandhi when in 1973, superseding three senior judges of the Court, Justice AN Ray was appointed the Chief Justice, in protest against which the three judges resigned at once. Brushing aside the public criticism of the brazen act of undermining the independence of the judiciary in the country, the government defended its action saying that 'it is entirely within the discretion of the government of the day to appoint a person considered in its eyes as the most suitable to occupy the highest judicial office in the country and to take into consideration his philosophy and his outlook of life'.[29] The government of Mrs Gandhi, bent upon reigning in an independent Supreme Court, was so determined to browbeat the independent status of the judiciary that in 1977, on the superannuation of Chief Justice Ray, again violating the precedent of superiority, did not appoint the senior most judge Justice HR Khanna as the Chief Justice of India as a punishment for Justice Khanna to deliver the dissenting judgement in The Habeas Corpus Case in 1976.[30]

With the defeat of Mrs Gandhi's government in 1977 and the inauguration of the Janata government, the wrongs of the past years were corrected in the appointment of Justice YV Chandrachud as the Chief Justice to succeed Justice MH Beg in 1978. Since then, the seniority principle has been scrupulously followed in appointing the senior most judge of the Supreme Court as the Chief Justice of India, even in the cases in which the tenure of the appointee would be as less as just two weeks, as in the case of Justice KN Singh. Crucially, in the wake of relatively weak and coalitional government assuming charge at Centre and the growing respect amongst the masses for the judicial independence, the chances of the well-conceived convention of appointing the senior most judge of the Supreme Court as the Chief Justice of India being broken appears to be bleak, bolstering the prospects of a bright future for the judiciary in the country.

Jurisdiction of the Court

Being the apex court of the country, the Supreme Court has well-defined jurisdictions to ensure that the purpose for which it was constituted is realized. In the Constituent Assembly, it was mentioned that 'the Supreme Court has wider jurisdiction than any superior court in any part of the world'.[31] Reasons are not difficult to seek. Presumably to tackle the contextual difficulties following the 1947 Partition, the founding fathers felt the need for a strong judiciary with wider jurisdiction as perhaps appropriate at that historical juncture. Furthermore, in their concern to build a supportive mind-set for democratic governance in independent India, they seem to have endorsed such a judicial design. It was perhaps believed by them that with the constitutional guarantee of judicial intervention against atrocious and prejudiced social behaviour, a new India was to be ushered in. Be, as it may, the fact remains that the Supreme Court enjoys a jurisdiction that has no parallel in the history of constitutional democracy. In constitutional terms, the jurisdiction of the Court can be divided into three categories: (a) original, (b) appellate and (c) advisory; besides those in which the Supreme Court can intervene *suo motto* to uphold individual rights and constitutional sanctity.

[29] Mohan Kumaramangalam, *Judicial Appointments* (Delhi: Oxford and IBH Publishing Company, 1973), p. 83.

[30] Granville Austin, *Working a Democratic Constitution: A History of the Indian Experience* (New Delhi: Oxford University Press, 2003), p. 243.

[31] Alladi Krishnaswami Ayyar, 3 June 1949, *Constituent Assembly Debates*, Book No. 3, p. 596.

Original Jurisdiction (Article 131)

As the apex court in the country, however, the original jurisdiction of the Supreme Court extends only to the broader issues of protecting the Fundamental Rights of the people, running concurrently with the jurisdictions of the High Courts, as well as adjudicating the issues relating to the federal structure of the Constitution, which happens to be its exclusive jurisdiction. In other cases, the jurisdiction of the Court is mainly appellate.

The original jurisdiction of the Supreme Court has been delineated under the various provisions of the Constitution. Primarily, under Article 131, the Supreme Court has been vested with the original jurisdiction in any dispute (a) between the Government of India and one or more states; (b) between the Union Government and any state on one side and one or more states on the other; and (c) between two or more states, if the disputes relates to any question of law or fact on which the existence or extent of a legal right depends. Such jurisdiction, however, does not extend to disputes relating to water of inter-state rivers or river valleys and it is handled by a special statutory tribunal, provided for under Article 262, matters referred to the Finance Commission (Article 280), adjustment of certain finances between the Union and the states (Article 290), etc.

As a part of its original jurisdiction, the Supreme Court is also vested with special responsibility in the matter of the enforcement of the fundamental rights of the citizens. Running concurrently with the jurisdiction of the High Courts under Article 226, the Supreme Court, under Article 32 of the Constitution, is empowered to issue directions, orders or writs in the nature of *habeas corpus*, *mandamus*, prohibition, *quo warranto* and *certiorari*. Finally, after certain moves and counter moves by way of constitutional amendments, the jurisdiction of the Supreme Court on matters relating to the election of the President or the Vice President has remained intact under the provisions of Article 71(1) of the Constitution.

Appellate Jurisdiction (Articles 132–136)

Placed at the apex of the judicial hierarchy in the country, the appellate jurisdiction of the Supreme Court is so extensive that it practically involves all the cases in the nature of constitutional mattes, civil and criminal cases and the cases where a special leave is granted by the court against any judgement of a court or tribunal in India. Thus, an appeal lies with the Supreme Court from any judgement or order of a High Court in all cases irrespective of being civil, criminal or other proceedings, if, under a certificate of the Court, it is established that a substantial question of law or the interpretation of the Constitution is involved in the case, under Article 132 of the Constitution. However, as per the provisions under Article 133, the appeal to the Supreme Court against the order of the High Court in the civil cases can lie only if the amount involved in the dispute is not less than ₹20,000, as per the certificate issued by the High Court. In criminal cases, Article 134 of the Constitution provides for two types of appeal. First, an appeal as of right would lie in the Supreme Court against the order of the High Court in cases where either the High Court on appeal has reversed an order of acquittal of an accused person passed by the lower court and sentenced him to death, or where the High Court has withdrawn for trial before itself any case from a subordinate Court to its domain and after such trial has convicted the accused to death. Second, an appeal would also lie with the Supreme Court in a criminal case, provided the High Court certified that the case is fit for an appeal to the Supreme Court either on its own volition or on an oral application presented by the convict.

The last category of the appellate jurisdiction of the Supreme Court relates to the appeal by special leave under Article 136 of the Constitution. Usually in the nature of discretionary power conferring quite wide reach to the Supreme Court, this power of the Supreme Court has often been used in cases where the Court finds flaw with the arbitrary acts and unjust decisions of the courts or the administrative tribunals in the matters relating to the domain of welfare of the marginalized sections of the society or the cleansing of the political or administrative system of the country. Laying down the broad principles in the application of the provisions under Article 136, the Supreme Court in the case of *Dhakeswari Cotton Mills Ltd. v. Commissioner of Income Tax*, pointed out that 'it being an exceptional and overriding power, naturally, it has to be exercised sparingly and with caution and only in special and exceptional situations. Beyond that it is not possible to fetter the exercise of this power by a set of formula or rule'.[32]

Advisory Jurisdiction (Article 143)

In addition to the above mentioned jurisdictions, the advisory jurisdiction of the Supreme Court entails a special responsibility on it as per Article 143(1) of the Constitution which states:

> If at any time it appears to the President that a question of law or fact has arisen, or is likely to arise, which is of such a nature and of such public importance that it is expedient to obtain the opinion of the Supreme Court upon it, he may refer the question to the Court for consideration and the Court may, after such hearing as it thinks fit, report to the President its opinion thereon.

Accordingly, a reference may be made to the Supreme Court by the President for its consideration and opinion on any question of law or fact which appears to be of such a nature and of such public importance that it becomes expedient to obtain the opinion of the Court. Such references need not be on a question that has actually arisen but can also be made on the issues which appears apparent to the President to arise in all likelihood. The noteworthy fact in this regard, however, is that neither the Supreme Court is bound to give its opinion on any reference, nor the President is bound to accept the opinion of the Court as it is not in the nature of a judicial pronouncement amounting to be an order of the Court.

The Inherent Power Clause

In the end, the Supreme Court, under Article 137 of the Constitution, has been afforded the power to review its own decisions in the interests of the community and justice. Normally, to press for the review of the decision of the Court, an application needs to be filed before the Registrar of the Court within thirty days after the judgement has been delivered. Such applications, before being looked into by a larger bench than the one that had delivered the judgement, should be accompanied by a certificate by the Counsel that it stands on the sound grounds. Such reviews, carried out in good spirit, may yield a new decision which may go a long way in helping the Court to correct any decision which may have been erroneous. Thus, justice stands to be vindicated in the final analysis, despite certain short term upheavals experienced by

[32] *Dhakeswari Cotton Mills Limited v. Commissioner of Income Tax*, AIR, 1955, SC, p. 65.

the parties aggrieved by the error of judgement by the Court. This is an example of the exercise of 'the inherent power' by the Supreme Court on the basis of the *ex jebito justitiae* doctrine which means that the apex court is authorized by reason or obligation of justice to review its own judgement as and when it feels appropriate. In the Constituent Assembly the idea was floated by Alladi Krishnaswami Ayyar when he stated:

> There is nothing to prevent the Supreme Court from interfering even in a criminal case where there is miscarriage of justice, where a court has misdirected itself or where there is a serious error of law; there is nothing preventing the Supreme Court from developing its own jurisprudence in such a way that it could do complete justice in every kind of cause or matter.'[33]

The doctrine was formally articulated in 1988 in a litigation involving Abdul Rehman Antulay and RS Nayak in which the Supreme Court defended its inherent jurisdiction as being naturally woven around the apex court to ensure that no person suffers as a consequences of its error.[34]

High Courts

Within the framework of a single integrated judicial system in the country, the existence of a High Court in each of the states of the Union provide a sense of completion in the structure of the government at the level of states. The Constitution, therefore, under Article 125, makes provision for the creation of a High Court in each state. Originally, in 1950, the Constitution provided for a High Court only in Part A and Part B states, leaving it on the Parliament to decide on the creation of new High Courts or to extend the jurisdiction of a neighbouring High Court to the other areas. Thereafter, the provision for a High court in all the major states have been made, which in recent years have also been extended to the smaller states such as Uttaranchal, Chhattisgarh and Jharkhand in addition to the National Capital Territory of Delhi, taking the total number of High Courts in the country to 24.

Though existing within the federal system of the country, the position of the High Courts in India differ from the position of the High Courts or the State Courts as existing in other federations of the world, particularly that of the United States. For instance, in the American system, the State Courts, being constituted under the provisions of the State Constitutions, are totally unrelated to the federal judicial system, and the structural features of the courts like the method of the appointment of the judges, their salary structure and service conditions as well as their jurisdiction differ from state to state. On the contrary, in India, all the High Courts are constituted either under the authority of the Constitution or by the Parliament, with the state governments having no substantive say in the creation of a High Court. Being part of an integrated and unified judicial system, the High Courts stand in the hierarchical order below the Supreme Court with an organic relationship existing between the two. The appointment, salary and service conditions of the judges are governed by the laws made by the Parliament with the provision for the transfer of the judges from one High Court to another High Court all over the country.

Consisting of a Chief Justice and such other judges as the President may from time to time determine, a High Court stands at the apex of the judicial system of a state. The method of the appointment of the

---

[33] Alladi Krishnaswami Ayyar (Madras), 6 June 1949, *Constituent Assembly Debates*, Book 3, p. 639.

[34] The argument is drawn on Raeea Vakil, 'Jurisdiction', in *The Oxford Handbook of the Indian Constitution*, p. 349.

Chief Justice and other judges of the High Court was a matter of sufficient controversy in the Constituent Assembly as the suggestion of the Constitutional Advisor BN Rau was that the Governor appoint these judges with the approval of two-thirds of the members of the State Council. However, for the sake of keeping the judiciary above the suspicion of party influence, the present method of appointment by the President was approved. Thus, the Chief Justice of a High Court is appointed by the President by warrant under his hand and seal, after due consultation with the Chief Justice of India and the Governor of the state. However, in appointing the other judges of the High Court, the President is required to consult, in addition to the Chief Justice and India and the Governor of the state, the Chief Justice of the High Court where the appointment of the judges is to be made. The practice has also been evolved to appoint at least one-third of the judges of a High Court from outside the state in order to maintain the impartiality in the functioning of the High Court.[10]

A typical issue that has dogged the independence of the High Courts and impacted on the minds of the judges in recent years has been the transfer of many judges from one High Court to another, with the policy being adopted not to have the Chief Justice from the same state. Beginning in the decade of early 1980s, the policy of transferring the judges had both its opponents as well as the supporters. While the former took the stand that the transfer of judges policy 'aimed at creating fear and a sense of instability' in the minds of the judges, the latter favoured it 'in the interests of sound judicial administration and also the independence of the judiciary'.[35] The practice of bulk transfer of the judges was challenged in the Supreme Court where though the Court decided in favour of the government's right to transfer the judges from one High Court to another, it ruled that such transfer should not be arbitrary and with mala fide intentions prima facie. Consequently, a Peer Committee was constituted by the Chief Justice of India in 1994, consisting of two High Court Chief Justices and three senior Supreme Court judges to look into the matter.

Jurisdiction of the High Courts

Since the High Courts had been functioning in the country, with a fairly satisfactory level of independence and impartiality, for many years by the time India became independent, the founding fathers of the Constitution did not think it fit to put in detail the jurisdiction of the High Courts. It was provided that the High Courts would continue to function with the well-defined jurisdiction as they had been functioning before in the capacity of the apex court in the state, subject to the provisions of the Constitution and the laws made by the Parliament from time to time. However, with the change in the nature of governance in the country, the High Courts, besides the usual jurisdiction in the original and the appellate nature, would be enjoined to four additional powers: (a) the power to issue writs or orders for the enforcement of the fundamental rights or for certain other purpose, (b) the power of superintendence over the subordinate courts, (c) the power to transfer cases to themselves pending in the subordinate courts involving interpretation of the Constitution, and (d) the power to appoint officers.[36]

Though originally endowed with wide ranging original and appellate jurisdiction, The Constitution (Forty-second Amendment) Act of 1976 robbed the High Courts of much of its original jurisdiction. For instance, while they continue to issue prerogative writs like the *habeas corpus*, *mandamus*, prohibition,

[35] Quoted in Austin, *Working a Democratic Constitution*, pp. 516–17.

[36] Kapur and Mishra, *Select Constitutions*, p. 237.

quo warranto and *certiorari* for the enforcement of the fundamental rights, they were restrained from exercising any jurisdiction in cases of the violation of a legal right. The phrase 'for any other purpose' which had a wide ranging connotations, was replaced with a restricted provision limiting it to cases (a) where there happened to be a contravention of a statutory rule causing substantial injury, and (b) where there was an illegality resulting in substantial failure of justice. However, the position was restored by the Forty-Fourth (1978) Amendment to the Constitution. Presently, the original jurisdiction of the High Courts have been confined only to the matters of admiralty, probate, matrimonials, contempt of Court, enforcement of the fundamental rights and cases ordered to be transferred from a Lower Court involving the interpretation of the Constitution to their own file. The High Courts, therefore, have become primarily the courts of appeal.

Substantially, the major power of the High Courts relates to the issue of the prerogative writs under the Article 226 of the Constitution for the enforcement of the fundamental rights, running concurrently with the power of the Supreme Court. Equally, if not more, important power of the High Courts is to superintend over the functioning of all other subordinate courts and tribunals within the territories over the jurisdiction of the Court reaches. Placed in the nature of both administrative as well as judicial, the power of superintendence of the High Courts is unfettered by any constitutional or statutory provision and the Courts are free to monitor the functioning of the lower judicial authorities in order to ensure that the judicial institutions function properly and discharge their duties of delivering justice in accordance with the provisions of law.

The High Courts are made the only authority at the level of state to interpret the constitution and decide the constitutional issues involved in a case. In order to discharge this function, the High Courts have been given the power to transfer the cases to their file if they are satisfied that the case pending in the subordinate court involves a substantial question of law regarding the interpretation of the Constitution. On such transfer, the Court may decide the whole case on its own or it may sort out the constitutional issue involved in the case and hand down the case to the lower court to decide the rest of the case in its own wisdom. The transfer of the cases to the High Court may be on a reference of the lower courts if it finds the involvement of constitutional issue in it, or may also be ordered by the Court to be transferred to it on an application of a party in the case. Once the cases involving constitutional issues are decided, the High Courts act as the Court of Record in such cases. Accordingly, such decisions of the Court can be quoted as evidence without questioning before any other court in the state and the contempt of such decisions may be taken as the contempt of the court, for which the High Court can award exemplary punishment. Finally, the administrative powers of the High Court are vested in the Chief Justice under Article 229 of the Constitution which requires him to appoint the officers and servants of the Court for the efficient functioning of the Court, in addition to the control of the finances of Court, which are charged on the Consolidated Fund of the state.

Judicial Review

In the era of constitutional government bestowed with only limited powers in view of the Constitution acting as the supreme law of the land, the notion of the judicial review has been invented by the Courts in various parts of the world to test the constitutionality of the laws made by the Legislature and the orders issued by the Executive, so that the supremacy of the Constitution may be kept intact. To put it differently, the written Constitution as the fundamental law of the land lays down the basic rules of governance by delineating the functional domain of all the organs of the government, under the broad philosophy of political system of a country. Hence, in order to see that the constitutional scheme of things does not get disturbed and no organ acts in contravention to the provisions of the Constitution, the provisions for a Supreme Court with the power of judicial review have been made in almost all the federal political systems including India.

Conceptually, the notion of judicial review refers to the power of the Court to examine the constitutional validity of the laws made by the Legislature and the orders issued by the Executive, after which if it finds them contrary to the provision of the Constitution, may declare them as null and void. Thus, designed in the frame of facilitating the Court to act as the guardian and protector of the Constitution, the concept of the judicial review has become the hallmark of the federal political systems where the written constitution lays in black and white the powers of the different departments of government so that neither any of the organs of government usurps the powers of others nor the spirit of the political philosophy underpinning the polity gets violated. In the situation of the occurrence of any such impropriety amounting to the violation of the constitution, the Court can step in to set the things in order by declaring such violations as unconstitutional and void.

Owing to certain obvious reasons, the power of judicial review of the Courts has never been explicitly mentioned in the constitution either in the United States or in India. It is by way of implication in either discharging certain functions or interpreting certain provisions of the Constitution that the power of judicial review has been acquired by the Courts. For instance, in the United States, it was in the famous case of *Marbury v. Madison* that the Chief Justice Marshall declared that the Supreme Court determined the constitutionality or otherwise of laws, federal or state, and this power with the Court was a necessary consequence of the Constitution, otherwise declaration of the supremacy of the Constitution had no meaning. Similarly, in the case of Indian Constitution also, the founding fathers avoided the mention of the power of the judicial review of the Court but designed certain provisions of the Constitution in such a way that their implementation would necessarily dovetail on the Courts the power of judicial review to ward off the violations of such provisions.

However, the scope of the power of judicial review is not as extensive as it is in the United States, ostensibly, due to the position of the Parliament as the body expressing the will of the people whose excessive negation would not bear well for the health of the parliamentary system in the country. Hence, instead of following the US pattern of rooting the doctrine of judicial review in the notion of 'due process of law', the framers of the Indian Constitution chose to root in the lenient doctrine of 'procedure established by law.' Consequently, putting fetters on the overreach of the Courts, the Indian Constitution wished the Parliament to define the limits within which the power of judicial review of the Courts would be exercised. Moreover, by drafting certain provisions of the Constitution like the one on fundamental rights, for instance, the founding fathers manifestly circumscribed the areas where the Courts would be well within their rights to exercise the powers of judicial review. Hence the provisions of the Constitution like the laws inconsistent with or in derogation of the fundamental rights (Article 13), remedies for enforcement of the fundamental rights (Article 32), jurisdiction of the Supreme Court (Articles 131–136), power of High Courts to issue certain writs (Article 226), extent and the subject matter of laws made by the Parliament and the Legislatures of the States (Article 245–246), etc. retain the scope for the exercise of the power of judicial review by the Courts. The question of constitutional soundness of the laws and executive orders arises when they are challenged in the competent courts on the grounds of incompetence of the legislature to pass such a law, repugnancy to the provisions of the Constitution and the infringement of the fundamental rights.

With the theoretical aspects of the power and procedure of the judicial review being laid down in the Constitution, the stage was set now for the practical manifestations of the concept as understood by the Courts in the country. The first case in this context happened to be that of *Shankari Prasad v. the Union of India* in 1951, in which the petitioner challenged the first amendment of the Constitution on the ground that it infringed the fundamental right to property which remained unamendable under Article 13(2) of the Constitution. Taking a firm stand rooted in the wisdom of respecting the Parliament's position as representing the will of the people, the Court rejected the contention of the petitioner and held that Parliament is competent to amend any part of the Constitution including that of the fundamental rights. Continuing its confinist approach, the Supreme Court reiterated the same position in the case of *Sajjan Singh v. State of Rajasthan* in which the validity of the Seventeenth Amendment of the Constitution (1964) was challenged on the plea that it violated the fundamental rights under Article 31A. Imbued with the idealism enshrined in the perspective of the Constituent Assembly, the Court mistakenly noted that had the founding fathers of the Constitution intended to subject any further amendment to the provisions on fundamental rights to the provisions under Article 13(2), such provision would have been made explicitly in the Constitution by them.

Significantly, the turning point in the course of the judicial review of the constitutional amendments came in 1967 when neither the political leadership of the country remained restrained in its approach towards other institutions of government nor the Supreme Court sought to avoid a confrontationist attitude towards the Legislative and the Executive branches of the government. Taking a highly conservative position on the amending power of the Parliament, in the case of *Golaknath v. the State of Punjab*, the Supreme Court, with a majority of 6 to 5 held that the Parliament did not have any power to amend any of the provisions of Part III of the Constitution so as to take away or abridge the Fundamental Rights enshrined therein. Putting a blanket ban on the amendability of the fundamental rights created a piquant situation for the government of Indira Gandhi who was bent upon to consolidate her position by taking recourse to populist policies guised in the name of socialism. Hence, after her astounding electoral victory in 1971, she got the Twenty-Fourth and Twenty-Fifth Amendment Acts passed, restoring the amending power of the Parliament in respect of all the provisions of the Constitution.

The constitutional validity of these amendments were challenged in the landmark case of *Kesavananda Bharti v. the State of Kerala*, in which the approach of the Supreme Court appears to be finding a middle ground in its dealings with the Parliament keeping in view of the stubborn attitude of the government in browbeating the independence of judiciary in the country. The Court, therefore, devised the innovative doctrine of 'basic structure' of the Constitution to lay down the far reaching formulation that there exists a basic structure of the Constitution which lies beyond the amending power of the Parliament. Yielding sufficient space for the Parliament to amend the Constitution in order to make it in tune with the changing times, the Court created a sort of fortress in the name of the basic structure to avail an unenviable position in the political system from where it can become the custodian of the Constitution. Interestingly, the Court deliberately avoided defining as to what constitutes the basic structure presumably in order not to frighten the government with the enumeration of the domains which would permanently lie out of bounds for it, in short run, and to keep its options open as to include any provision of the Constitution in the fortress of basic structure to make it immune from amendment. Thus, the Kesavananda Bharti case proved to be win-win situation for the Supreme Court in so far as its power of judicial review is concerned.

Refusing to give up easily, the government started looking up for a way to wriggle out of the uneasy situation created by the Kesavananda Bharti case and finding the answer in the form of the Forty-Second Amendment to the Constitution, which not only enlarged the powers of the Parliament but also put a number of fetters on the power of judicial review of the Courts. Though much of the unsavoury provisions inserted by the Forty-Second Amendment Act were undone by the Forty-Fourth Amendment Act, the remaining portion was challenged in the case of *Minerva Mills Ltd v. the Union of India* in 1980. Consecrating the doctrine of basic structure of the Constitution finally for all times to come, the Supreme

Court reiterated that the Parliament has only limited power to amend the Constitution and in no case the basic structure of the constitution can be destroyed by way of constitutional amendment enacted by the Parliament.

The final hurdle in the unfettered power of judicial review of the Court was cleared by the Supreme Court in 2005 when the constitutional validity of the Ninth Schedule of the Constitution was questioned on the ground that it violates the basic structure of the Constitution by snatching certain laws from the scrutiny of the Court after they are placed in the said Schedule. Taking a bold position, the Supreme Court, exhibiting the middle approach adopted in the case of Kesavananda Bharti in 1973, though did not hold the Ninth Schedule to be null and void, declared that the said Schedule cannot become a shield to hide certain laws passed by the Legislatures from the purview of the judicial review by the Court. Thus, even the last bastion of the Legislature to escape the search light of the judicial scrutiny was demolished by the Supreme Court, taking the power of judicial review to an unprecedented height in the constitutional jurisprudence of the country.

The expanded horizons of the judicial review, which for the time being have overcome all probable stumbling blocks, have raised the heckles of both the political leaders as well as the legal luminaries in the country. Anticipating a highly activist role of the judiciary to the extent of substituting its view for the views of the Legislature and the Executive, the critics call for the formulation of certain norms to act as the guidelines for the Courts to decide the issues of constitutionality involved in the laws. Poised to bear the burden of acting responsibly on their own, the Courts need to be guided by the following maxims in weighing the constitutional validity of the laws:

1. There is a presumption in favour of constitutionality, and a law will not be declared unconstitutional unless the case is so clear as to be free from doubt, and the onus to prove that it is unconstitutional lies upon the person who challenges it.
2. Where the validity of a statute is questioned and there are two interpretations, one of which would make the law valid, and the other void, the former must be preferred and the validity of the law upheld.
3. The court will not decide constitutional questions if a case is capable of being decided on other grounds.
4. The Court will not hear an objection as to the constitutionality of a law by a person whose rights are not affected by it.
5. Ordinarily, the courts should not pronounce on the validity of an Act or part of an Act which has not been brought into force, because till then the question of validity would be merely academic.[37]

Public Interest Litigation

With the growth of the welfarist perspective of state, accompanied by increasing number of civil society organizations and individuals, the new technique of seeking the redressal of grievances through judicial intervention has gained ground in the country. Called as the Public Interest Litigation (PIL), it has emerged as the means of standing for the cause of others because the petitions can be filed by a third party on behalf of the aggrieved or deprived people who are not in a position to seek the intervention of judiciary to right

[37] Quoted in Rumki Basu, 'Changing Role of the Supreme Court in India', in *Essays on Indian Government and Politics*, eds. Meera Verma, Mrinal Mehta and Rumki Basu (New Delhi: Jawahar Publishers, 2004), p. 134.

the wrongs done to them. While accepting such petitions, the Courts usually forgo the observance of the prescribed judicial procedures, mainly the notion of locus standi of the party, and even a post card addressed to the Court can be taken cognizance of. Quite often, the PILs are filed to get the judicial prodding for the executive or the legislature to take certain steps which they have failed to take causing a harm or deprivation to the people. Termed also as social action litigation,[38] the PIL is characterized by relaxation of the rule of locus standi, flexibility in normal judicial procedure, innovative and proactive interpretation of legal and Fundamental Rights of the people, and remedial flexibility marked by ongoing judicial participation and supervision.[39]

Originating in early eighties as a means of ensuring participative public justice, the idea of PIL secured the backing and recognition of the Supreme Court in the case of *SP Gupta v. Union of India*, when the court allowed the petition despite the petitioner not being an aggrieved party on the ground that it seeks to redress the grievances of those people who are not in position to come to the Court to seek justice. At the same time, the Court also noted that the PIL can also be filed in the cases where the interests of the mass of people are at stake, without any discrimination. Since then, PIL is brought before the Court not for the purpose of enforcing the right of one individual against another as happens in the case of ordinary litigation but is intended to promote and vindicate public interest which demands that violations of constitutional and legal rights of a large number of people who are poor, ignorant or in a socially or economically disadvantaged position should not go unnoticed or unredressed.[40] Thus, the numerous PILs filed by the legendary lawyer MC Mehta and institutions like the Centre for Science and Environment (CSE) have thoroughly transformed the way people used to live in Delhi's fast deteriorating environment and depletion of natural resources.

The idea of PIL has been criticized by some people on the counts like interfering in the domains of the executive and the legislature, setting back the pace of development, and burdening the Courts with superfluous matters so much that their core and conventional functions are likely to suffer. However, it needs to be pointed out in this regard that such criticisms appear to be more in the nature of diagnosing the ills rather than curing them. Unfortunately, the PIL syndrome erupted in the country owing to the failure of the executive and the legislature to ensure public well-being. Ironically, while some people charge the Courts with hampering the progress of developmental projects, others accuse the Courts of blindly clearing the completion of the mega developmental projects like the Narmada Valley Project. Finally, the existence of the Courts becomes meaningful only when they act as the institutions to redress the grievances of the people, as the grave issues of constitutional and theoretical nature become absurd for them. The quantum of the PILs can be reduced only by improving the functioning of the executive and legislature in the country, rather than making laws to restrict or outlaw them.

Judicial Activism

Being a natural corollary of the wave of PILs filed frequently by the public spirited people, the idea of judicial activism refers to the practical manifestation of the outcome of the adjudication on the PILs. To

[38] Prakash Chand, *Environmental Protection and Peoples Rights: A Study of the Judicial Decisions Relocating Polluting Industries in Delhi* (Unpublished PhD dissertation, University of Delhi, 2005), p. 76.

[39] Chandra Pal, *Environmental Protection and Development: Environmental Law, Policy and Role of Judiciary*, (New Delhi: Mittal Publications, 1999), p. 226.

[40] SP Sathe, *Judicial Activism in India* (New Delhi: Oxford University Press, 2001), p. 204.

put it differently, the Courts in India have been ordained a defined functional domain, called jurisdiction, to supplement other organs of the government in the smooth working of the democratic polity in the country. But when, owing to certain obvious reasons, the Courts step out of their conventional jurisdiction or domain to seemingly act, if not interfere, in the domains of the other organs of the government, it is construed to be an activist role of the judiciary, known as judicial activism. Judicial activism, thus, though remains within the constitutional limits, militates against the spirit of cordial and coordinated functioning of various organs of government, without any intrusion of one into the domain of others.

The judicial activism has also led to a number of innovations being made by the Courts to equip themselves to meet the unconventional challenges placed before them through the PILs. In fact, without a well-structured investigative machinery at their disposal, the Courts had to enter into new forays like appointing commissioners to investigate, forming committees to deliberate remedies, nominating amicus curiae to assist the Court and directing the national scientific institutions to report on scientific mattes. Based on these, the Courts proceeded to pass wide-ranging orders and directions which are to be obeyed as if they were decrees of the Court. In the process, the judiciary has intervened in matters perceived to be within the domain of the executive, including policy decisions. Courts have, for example, passed orders regarding the criteria for nursery admissions, facilities to be provided by hospitals, conditions of roads and other municipal facilities. However, while recognizing the tremendous efforts made by the judiciary in acting in public interest and without, in any way, detracting from the results achieved, there are a few concerns also to be addressed.[41]

The core concern in this regard is whether the judicial orders are allowed to replace what should normally be conducted by the administrative authorities. Indeed, the move to support that one wing of the state may step into rectify the deficiencies of another is fraught with serious jurisprudential problems. Similarly, there appears to be a real danger that the activism of the Courts may aggravate the in-activism of the administrative authorities. For instance, by leaving the inconvenient decisions to be taken by the Courts, the executive branch of the government seems to be running away from shouldering its responsibilities. Moreover, the extensive use of judicial powers in the administrative domain may well in the long run blunt the judicial powers themselves, which would probably be the saddest day for the health of the democratic and constitutional polity in the country.

Judicial Reforms

In the wear and tear of the Indian democracy during the last sixty years, most of the institutions and organizations seem to have experienced varying degrees of degenerations in their structures and processes due to the factors both inherent and extraneous to them. Hence, while legislature and executive organs of the government have failed utterly to stand up to the expectations of the people, the judiciary has also not remained immune from a number of flaws, though it is still held in high esteem by the people in comparison to the position of the other two organs. As a noted legal luminary points out succinctly,

> in its performance the judiciary suffers less from the pathological infirmities of the other two wings. Indeed, the nation holds the judicature high in its esteem since some luminous members on the Bench are as good as the best in the Commonwealth or the US. Even so, while a critical examination of the judicial process reveals a remarkable level of creativity and humanity, it is at times marred and mangled by grave and goofy theatricality, blatant deviance and daring delinquencies. The fundamental values of the Constitution and the autonomy implicit in

[41] Dipankar Gupta, 'Hanging in the Balance', *Hindustan Times*, 15 June 2007.

parliamentary jurisprudence and cabinet initiatives are often ignored. These are instances but spoil the majesty of law. The country has a non-negotiable and none-too-late obligation to scotch lazy litigative locomotion, judicial somnolescence and administrative pachydermy.[42]

In a nutshell, the broad limitations of the judiciary as experienced over the years relate to:

1. The slowness and inaccessibility (due to the heavy cost of legal services and ignorance of the general public about their rights and obligations and their enforceability) of the judicial process;
2. The antiquated nature of court procedures and management practices;
3. Flaws in procedural laws, lack of effective control of court proceedings and availability of multiple remedies at different rungs of the judicial ladder which enables dishonest and recalcitrant suitors to abuse the judicial process; and
4. The lowered standards of conduct, character and competence of the legal profession and judges.[43]

In view of the growing uneasiness of the people with the tardy pace of functioning of judiciary, the urgency of reforms in the judicial system has been felt for quite some time.

The judicial reforms suggested from various quarters usually fall into two categories: creation of an alternative system of delivering justice in those cases which does not require an interpretation of law or defining certain constitutional issues involved in the case; and reforms in the structures and functioning of the mainstream judicial system of the country. In the first category, the reforms have generally boiled down to the creation of Lok Adalats, in the main, to deal with the issues arising out of disputes on the subjects pertaining to day to day activities of life, in addition to the other mechanisms such as the Consumer Disputes Redressal Forums and Central Administrative Tribunal. These alternative methods of adjudication have, no doubt, been able to lessen the burden of the judiciary proper, yet the trend which seems to have rendered the efforts of these mechanisms futile is the tendency on the part of losing party to appeal in the higher court against the verdict of these tribunals which brings the whole problem back to square one.

At the level of the judiciary proper, the essence of reforms lies in an effort on the part of the presiding officers to narrow down the disputes by means of a preliminary hearing and suggesting reasonable settlements to avoid prolixity of evidence and procrastination of arguments. Such an effort of the judicial officers need to be supplemented by the legislature and executive to simplify the judicial procedures by substantially amending the Civil Procedure Code, the Code of Criminal Procedure and the Evidence Act which still remain so archaic and arcane in the age of technology. Another substantive in-house reform of judicial process can come in the form of the judges while disposing of cases should try to sort out the real issue involved in the matter which would not only discount the possibility of a rebirth of the case but also act as the law of land for similar cases at other times.

Reviewing the Argument

An independent judiciary is a *sin qua non* in a democratic polity drawing its sustenance from the rule of law. In other words, the constitution remains a reference point for the judiciary to function as a watchdog

[42] VR Krishna Iyer, 'The Patchy Indian Judicial Record', *The Hindu*, 6 September 2007.

[43] PD Desai, 'Reforms in Administration of Justice', quoted in Ramesh Thakur, *The Government and Politics of India* (London: Macmillan, 1995), pp. 65–66.

of democracy. As is argued previously, the Constituent Assembly members took ample care to ascertain independence to judiciary although they were aware that independence in its absolute sense was illusive because it could hardly be immune from the contextual compulsions. What they meant by independence was that judiciary was free from executive or legislative control; otherwise, they would be constrained to objectively test the constitutional validity of the decisions, taken by the executive or legislature. This is the crux of the argument in favour of judicial independence which was most eloquently articulated by an eminent jurist, Krishna Iyer J in his pronouncement in the *Union of India v. Sankalchand Himmatlal Sheth* case of 1977. According to him:

> In a dynamic democracy, with goals of transformation set by the Constitution, the Judge, committed to uphold the founding faith and fighting creeds of the nation set forth, has to act heedless of executive hubris, socio-economic pressure, and die-hard obscurantism. This occupational heroism, professionally essential, demands the inviolable independence woven around the judiciary by our Constitution.[44]

Independence of judiciary is guaranteed once the judges avoid being influenced. This is easier said than done because judges are also the product of specific socio-economic and political circumstances. Neither constitutional guarantee nor statutory provisions can ever be an effective means because 'the best guarantee of judicial independence is the character of the person holding the office' and hence judicial independence is argued to be 'directly proportional to the value attached by the citizens of the country and the judges to that signal virtue'.[45] Virtues do not fall from heaven; instead, they are nurtured in our worldly existence which confirms the importance of the context in their conceptualization. In the ultimate analysis, judicial independence is thus context-specific and hence it cannot be universally formatted since situation varies from one context to another.

Concluding Observations

In a way, for the transitional societies like India which had embarked on an ambitious path of practicing the democratic system of governance even in the face of a number of hindrances emanating from the socio-economic and politico-cultural milieu of the country, the existence of an independent institution was a prime guarantee for India's constitutional democracy. As the Constituent Assembly debated on judiciary show, the members argued strongly for judicial independence for they believed that

> the Judiciary, though without purse and sword, was the most august wing because it had paramount corrective power over the Executive when it violated constitutional prescriptions, and over the Legislature when it transgressed the provisions of the *suprema lex* as interpreted by the judges, . . . and vigilantly functioned as *qui vive* with respect to every Indian's human rights.[46]

---

[44] Quoted in BN Srikrishna, 'Judicial Independence', in *The Oxford Handbook of the Indian Constitution*, p. 349.
[45] Srikrishna, 'Judicial Independence', p. 366.
[46] Iyer, 'The patchy Indian Judicial Record'.

With their commitment to constitutional democracy, they endeavoured hard to translate their ideological priorities into reality by devising specific measures for ascertaining judicial independence. Despite adopting the parliamentary system of governance of the British mould in its letter and spirit, to the extent possible, they also went against the conventions of the parliamentary system of governance; being sensitive of India's peculiar socio-economic and political texture in which the role of an independent constitutional institution was most crucial, they not only provided for an strong and formidable judicial system but also ensured that the fine web of the parliamentary government does not get broken by ensuring adequate checks and balances for all the three organs of government.

The multiple viewpoints that had emerged during the course of debates in the Constituent Assembly reveal that the founding fathers were keen to develop a unique system of judiciary which was compatible with India's peculiar socio-economic needs. Their effort was thus directed to evolve a structure for administering justice which was not only 'competent ... but was also suited to the conditions of the country'.[47] The idea was inspirational to those who held the judicial authority in independent India. For instance, Justice Kania who was the first Chief Justice of India spoke in his inaugural address to highlight the point that 'with the establishment of the Supreme Court of India, we shall develop our own jurisprudence based on our historical background [and] we will make substantial contribution toward the formation of India into a great country retaining its own civilization, traditions and customs'.[48] The focus here was to build a system of judicial adjudication with reference to the prevalent socio-economic context in which it was to function. Being organic to the Indian reality, the Supreme Court, while administering justice, also appears to have taken a lead in creating new areas of engagement which did not traditionally fall under its domain. For instance, the constitution of social justice bench comprising two senior jurists of the Supreme Court by the former Chief Justice of India, HL Dattu, in 2014 was one such initiative to play a proactive role in expeditious resolution of social problems affecting the lives of the voiceless and marginalized sections of the population. The bench was slotted to meet every Friday at 2 pm to hear PILs raising a wide range of issues such as human trafficking, tracing missing children, providing hygienic midday meals, welfare of construction workers, rehabilitation of acid attack victims and protecting women's dignity by reining in the lumpen elements circulating pornographic materials online. With the withdrawal of the bench in 2016, an interesting chapter in the unfolding of the judicial trajectory in India came to an end though it corroborates the point, being made earlier, emphasizing that Indian judiciary keeps on experimenting with new idea in accordance with what it deems appropriate in rendering justice to the demos.

During the early years of the functioning of the judicial system in India, the judicial process, attuned to the principles of natural justice, adopted the well-established adversarial system of adjudication. The pattern of the court, in its ascending order, followed the hierarchical structure and was accessible, under the Constitution, to every citizen of the country. The courts on rare occasions defaulted, delayed and deviated from the desirable path. But such instances have been rectified later by the larger benches or criticized by jurists or set right by means of the constitutional amendments. Thus, despite all odds, the Indian judicial system remained stay put by and large within the broad jurisdictional domains set out by the Constitution. In recent times, owing to the lack of functional vibrancy on the part of the other two organs of the government, the judiciary has been called upon by the people by way of PILs to perform such functions which would have in proper scheme of things remained within the scope of activities of

[47] Alladi Krishnaswami Ayyar (Madras), 6 June 1949, *Constituent Assembly Debates*, Book No. 3, p. 639.

[48] Quoted in MV Pylee, *Constitutional Government in India* (London: Asia Publishing House, 1965), p. 504.

the executive or the legislature. The prudence of the judiciary, however, lies in not getting too much into such extra-jurisdictional domains and transfer back the issues to the nodal agencies for the discharge of such functions, for the strength of the judiciary is secure and enhanced only when the other organs of government remain vibrant and supplementary to one another in realizing constitutional democracy in letter and spirit.

Review Questions

1. **Why is judiciary critical to constitutional democracy? Elaborate.**
2. **Critically trace the evolution of judiciary in India since it arrived on the scene in the wake of colonialism.**
3. **An independent judiciary is a *sin qua non* in a democratic polity. Explain.**
4. **How did the founding fathers conceptualize the role of judiciary in India in their deliberations in the Constituent Assembly? Elaborate.**
5. **Critically evaluate the historical genealogy or antecedents of Indian judiciary.**
6. **Write a critical essay on the jurisdictions of the Supreme Court of India.**
7. **Critically evaluate the judicial system that had emerged in India following her Independence in 1947.**
8. **What is the 'Inherent' clause in the judicial discourses? Elaborate with examples.**
9. **Critically evaluate the jurisdictions of the High Courts in India.**
10. **Write a critical essay on Indian judiciary in the light of both 'judicial activism' and 'judicial overreach'.**

Chapter 18

Amending Procedures[1]

Learning Objectives

- What is an amendment?
- How do you understand the role of amendment in constitutional democracy where constitution reigns supreme
- How to conceptualize constitutional amendments in India especially when there are allegations that these are means to violate the Constitution?

Amendment of the constitution is critical to its survival. Constitution is a lasting document and it needs to be adapted to the changing socio-economic circumstances. If the procedure is very rigid, the constitution will become futile to address the concerns of the day; if the amendment procedures are too flexible, it is likely to become an instrument of gratification of personal whims. So, this is a tricky issue that is required to be handled most carefully. The framers of the US Constitution thus put a number of conditions in the Article 5 of the Constitution for its amendment. This is not true of the Indian Constitution which is neither stringent nor terribly flexible with regard to the procedures for amendment. By reviewing the constitutional design for amendment to the Constitution, this chapter seeks to provide a threadbare discussion in the Constituent Assembly of the processes leading to the adoption of the provisions in this regard, accompanied by an analysis of these stipulations.

Historical Antecedents

The issue of amending procedures of the Constitution happened to be one of the least debated and controversial issues dealt with by the Constituent Assembly due, probably, to the less importance attached to it by the members on the one hand and the lack of adequate knowledge and 'immediate experience' amongst the average members of the Assembly, on the other. Although it was a limited discussion, it was very rich in terms of ideas and viewpoints. It was Jawaharlal Nehru who set the ball in motion by laying out certain fundamental principles which one should not forget while being involved in devising ways of means for this task. In his words:

[1] Drawn on Chapter 1 of my *Indian Government and Politics* (New Delhi: SAGE, 2008), which I wrote in collaboration with Dr Rajendra Pandey.

> A Constitution is something which should last a long time, which is built on a strong foundation, and which may, of course, vary from time to time—it should not be rigid—nevertheless, one should think of something which is going to last, which is not a transitory Constitution, a provisional Constitution, a something which you are going to change from day to day, a something which has provisions for the next year or the year after next and so on and so forth.[2]

Here, Nehru argued for a stable constitution which would last long; otherwise, the system of governance would suffer in view of the failure to develop sets of rules governing the system. While he was in favour of a stable constitution, he also felt that it had to be changed to keep pace with history. Hence he argued:

> It may be necessary to have certain transitory provisions; it will be necessary because there is a chance to have some such provisions, but so far as the basic nature of the Constitution is concerned, it has to be maintained by devising appropriate constitutional devices, to be applied on rarest of rare occasions.[3]

With the above-mentioned prefacing remark, Nehru got into the crux of the issue by stipulating what was most appropriate in regard to our Constitution which was meant to serve a young nation like India. In a very perceptive way, he thus offered his argument as follows:

> While we want this Constitution to be as solid and as permanent a structure as we can make it, nevertheless there is permanence in Constitutions. There should be a certain flexibility. If you make anything rigid and permanent, you stop a Nation's growth, the growth of a living vital organic people. Therefore it has to be flexible. So also, when you pass this Constitution, you will, and I think, lay down a period of years—whatever that period may be—during which changes to that Constitution can be easily made without any difficult process. This is a very necessary proviso [to enable] the newly elected House to [have] the opportunity to make changes as it wants to. . . . We should not therefore make a Constitution such as some other great countries have, which are so rigid that they do not and cannot be adapted easily to changing conditions. Today, especially, when the world is in turmoil and we are passing through a very swift period of transition, what we may do today may not be wholly applicable tomorrow. Therefore while we make a Constitution which is sound and as basic as we can, it should also be flexible for a period we should be in a position of change it with relative flexibility.[4]

Nehru's concern was to leave a space for the future decision makers to revise or adopt new legislations to address the concerns of the emerging circumstances. If the procedures were made rigid, it would have put the prospective rulers in serious trouble. Being a democrat and a statesman with an acute pragmatic sense, Nehru seems to have set the tempo for debate on this issue in the Assembly, as was evident in the interventions by his colleagues that followed. Taking cues from him, Ambedkar thus pursued the point as follows:

> The Draft Constitution has eliminated the elaborate and difficult procedures [for] amending the constitution. The powers of amendment are left with the Legislatures: central and

---

[2] Jawaharlal Nehru, 25 November 1948, *Constituent Assembly Debates*, Book No. 2, pp. 588–89.

[3] Ibid., p. 589.

[4] Jawaharlal Nehru, 8 November 1948, *Constituent Assembly Debates*, Book No. 2, pp. 322–23.

> provincial. It is only for amendments of specific matters—and there are only few—that the ratification of the State Legislatures is required. All other Articles of the Constitution are left to be amended by Parliament. The only limitation is that it shall be done by a majority of not less than two-thirds of the members of each House present and voting, and a majority of the total membership of each House. It is difficult to conceive of a simpler method of amending the Constitution.[5]

The amending procedure that he favoured was not, at all, rigid. However, there were areas in the Constitution, which upheld its spirit, that needed to be protected; otherwise, the Constitution would, he apprehended, lose its sanctity. So, the Constitution was neither extremely rigid nor terribly flexible which Ambedkar defended as follows:

> The Assembly has not only restrained from putting a seal of finality and infallibility upon this Constitution as in Canada or by making the amendment of the Constitution subject to the fulfilment of extraordinary terms and conditions as in America or Australia, but has provided a most facile procedure for amending the Constitution.[6]

As is evident, Ambedkar and Nehru held identical views in regard to the amendment procedures since they felt that a living constitution needed to be adapted to the changing socio-economic milieu to remain viable; otherwise, it would just be a text of rules and regulations with no substance. What was critical to them was to devise a mechanism for amendment which was not too rigid, nor too flexible, but was conditional; as regards the basic features of the Constitution, the formula followed a strictly rigid procedure, but for the rest, it was relatively flexible.

A perusal of the debates show that the terms and conditions that were already set by Nehru and Ambedkar seem to have critically governed the discussion that followed in the Assembly on this theme. Barring a few customary references in the Reports, prepared by Nehru and TB Sapru as well and the draft Constitutions of KM Munshi and KT Shah, KM Panikkar and others, a well thought out scheme of amending procedures was not available to the framers till mid of 1947 when BN Rau presented his framework of amending procedure providing for two fold procedures for amending the Constitution.

First, the amendments should first be passed by a two-thirds majority in both houses of the Parliament and then ratified by a like majority of provincial legislatures. Second, the transitional provisions may be amended by simple majority in Parliament. However, the main dilemma before the framers was, presumably, to reconcile between the competing allurements of amending the Constitution by simple majority to keep the Constitution dynamic, living and serving the needs of the society with the changing times and circumstances on the one hand; and making its amending procedure rigid enough to thwart any frivolous attempt to alter the basic framework of the federal polity of the country, on the other. After due deliberations on the practices followed in the American, the Australian and the Irish Constitutions, the Constituent Assembly agreed to provide for a threefold method of amending the Constitution under the provisions of Article 368, drawing appreciation from the experts like KC Wheare who complimented the framers

---

[5] BR Ambedkar, 4 November 1948, *Constituent Assembly Debates*, Book No. 2, p. 43.

[6] BR Ambedkar, 25 November 1949, *Constituent Assembly Debates*, Book No. 5, p. 976.

for striking a balance by protecting the rights of the states while leaving the rest of the Constitution to be amended easily.[7]

Labeled as 'one of the most ably conceived aspects of the Constitution',[8] the provisions under Article 368 appear to be able to meet the aspirations of the framers to make the Constitution a living document while making it extremely difficult to rob it of its basic characteristics. Of the three methods of amending the Constitution, two have been specifically provided for in Article whereas the third has been provided for in about 22 other Articles. Thus, first, the Constitution can be amended by introducing an amending Bill in either house of Parliament which needs to be passed by a majority in each house with two-thirds of the members present and voting, after which it is sent for the presidential assent, at the receipt of which it becomes an amendment.

The second method relates to the Articles enumerated under the proviso to Article 368 items (a) to (e), dealing with the subjects of the method of election of the President of India; distribution of legislative powers between the Union and the states; extent of the executive power of the Union and the states; representation of the states in Parliament; provisions relating to the Supreme Court and the High Courts; and the amendment of the Constitution itself. To amend any of these Articles, the amending bill is not only to be passed by a majority of total membership in each house and majority of not less than two-thirds of the members present and voting in each house but also ratification by at least one half of the state legislatures.

Third, the Constitution can be amended by a simple majority vote in the two houses of Parliament, followed by the assent of the President. The basic percepts, with which this provision deals with, such as formation of new states, alteration of state boundaries, changing name of states, delimitation of constituencies, qualifications for citizenship, quorum in Parliament, and so on, to name a few, are to remain in force until the Parliament brings about changes in them. Though a formal amendment in all such cases is not effected, yet they have the effect of making changes in the constitutional law.

In view of the overt provisions made in Article 368 on the methods of amending of the Constitution, a subtle debate emerged amongst the scholars regarding the scope and nature of Parliament's power to amend the Constitution. One school of thought, rooted in legal positivism, contended that, owing to the elaborate provisions made in the Constitution, the Parliament must confine itself to what is provided for in this regard, without any attempt to derive implied powers of amendment. Responding, in a way, to the provisions of Article 13(2) which bars the state from making any law which takes away or abridges the Fundamental Rights, the other school of thought holds that the amendment of the Constitution should be viewed in the context of the requirements of socio-economic needs of the country, instead of the strict legal provisions provided for in this regard. These two contrasting, if not conflicting views on the amendability of the Constitution have found their reflection in the ongoing game of one-upmanship between the Parliament and the Supreme Court even till today.

Though the questions on the limits of amending power of Parliament were raised very soon after the inauguration of the Constitution in the case of *Shankari Prasad v. the Union of India* in 1951, the Supreme Court took the position till 1967 that Parliament has unfettered powers to amend the Constitution. This position was dramatically reversed by the Supreme Court in the case of *Golaknath v. the State of Punjab* in 1967, ruling that the Parliament has no power to amend the provisions on Fundamental Rights, leading

[7] KC Wheare, *Modern Constitutions* (New Delhi: S. Chand and Co, 1988), p. 143.

[8] Quoted in Granville Austin, *Working a Democratic Constitution: A History of the Indian Experience* (New Delhi: Oxford University Press, 1999), p. 264.

to serious resentment in the political circles that started groping to find a way out of this all imposing judgement. Responding by way of Twenty-Fourth and Twenty-Fifth Amendments, the government sought to turn the table on the Supreme Court by not only nullifying what the Court had provided for in the Golaknath case but also extending the whip to the office of the President by providing that when a constitutional amendment is presented to him for his assent, he shall give his assent and that he would not have any discretion in this regard. Creating again an opportunity for a standoff between the government and the Supreme Court, the Twenty-Fourth and Twenty-Fifth Amendments were challenged in the Supreme Court in the case of *Kesavananda Bharti v. State of Kerala* in 1973. The historical judgement in the Kesavananda Bharti case tried to restore the precarious balance between the government and the judiciary on the issue of amendability of the Constitution by rejecting Golaknath verdict, upholding the Twenty-Fourth and Twenty-Fifth Amendments and striking down the 'escape clause' in the Twenty-Fifth Amendment which, by revising Article 31C, justified the right to property under certain circumstances. Core of the judgement of the division bench of nine judges[9] was the reconfirmation of the idea that Article 368 did not authorize the Parliament to alter the basic structure of framework of the Constitution. The Court, thus, through the doctrine of implied limitations and doctrine of basic structure, tried to ensure the permanence of the basic constituent aspects of the Constitution, on the one hand, and give the maximum possible leverage to Parliament to amend the socio-economic provisions to usher in an era of welfare state in the country, on the other.

The concern that the division bench in the Kesavananda Bharti case had shown was reiterated by the Supreme Court in the case of *Minerva Mills Ltd v. the Union of India*, thereby asserting the irreversibility of the doctrine of basic structure in relation to the amendability of the Constitution. However, an aberration, in the form of the Ninth Schedule of the Constitution, existing since 1951, which made certain laws and amendments immune from judicial review after they are placed in the said schedule by Parliament, created an anomalous situation in which Parliament was accorded an indirect escape route to amend the basic structure of the Constitution and shield it from the scrutiny of the Court. Removing this anomaly, the Supreme Court, in the case of *IR Coelho v. the State of Tamil Nadu* (2007) held that the Ninth Schedule was created for a specific purpose and not to be used as a shield to keep certain laws and amendments out of the purview of judicial review, which may even have the propensity of subverting the basic structure of the Constitution.

Reviewing the Argument

In the contemporary times, the issues regarding the amending procedure and ancillary questions appear to be settled in favour of a dominating position of the Supreme Court, which has progressively attained the position of commanding heights in the constitutional framework of governance in the country, partly due to the pernicious acts of commissions on the part of the government, on the one hand, and deplorable acts of omissions by the government, on the other; in both cases the people have to move the Court to get the wrongful undone and the rightful done through the judicial pronouncements. This unsavoury predicament of the constitutional framework needs to be cleared in favour of the reasoned balance in the jurisdictions of various organs of government. The doctrine of basic structure of Constitution had thus

[9] The bench comprised 13 judges: while nine endorsed the judgement, the remaining four remained absent.

emerged as the reference point for amendments which are justified provided they do not adversely affect the Constitution's basic identity, as per the apex court.

Concluding Observations

The constitution is a living organism; it needs to be reinvented in the light of the newer social, economic and political demands. The process is required to be institutionalized in conjunction with the prevalent politico-ideological preferences that, if compromised, will strike at the foundation of the constitution. Two important ideas are thus critical: on the one hand, the values, norms and principles, which are considered fundamental to the existence of a particular constitution can never be bypassed; in view of the changing socio-economic circumstances and political predilections, there should also be a scope, on the other, for introducing newer ideas to the constitution. This is of utmost importance for the survival of the constitution. Here comes the criticality of amendments as mechanisms for revision, repeal and also addition to the existent constitutional provisions; these are important devices to keep the constitution in correspondence with the changing reality. This is also important from the point of view of constitutional democracy in the sense that amendments to the constitution are also constitution-compliant instruments for incorporating newer concerns and conceptualizations. Fundamental here is the idea that amendments remain integral to the processes of constitutionalization and democratization of the political practices which also means that they are contextual responses as well. So, there is a dialectical interconnection between amendments and the contextual priorities which the constitution does not always reflect. By arguing that amendments are context-propelled and vice versa, this is also to suggest that they are also an offshoot of dialogues and deliberations at various levels within specific socio-political boundaries. What it means is that, at one level, amendments are a general mechanism of change; at another, they are context-specific and hence they cannot be conceptualized in a universal or derivative theoretical format. The argument in support of the amendment-context dialectical interpenetration also identifies in other words, the inherent limitations of the one-size-fits-all formula, which also reinforces the idea that independent of the context an amendment ceases to be organic to the constitutional practices.

Amendments are also legitimizing designs in the sense that they, while responding to the compulsions of the day, are also specific measures to address the concerns within the framework that constitution endorses. The idea is simple. An amendment is one which follows those steps which are constitutionally recognized and justified. There is no short-cut and the procedures that are laid down need to be adhered to. Once these procedures are complied with, an amendment is recognized as being part of the constitution. This is common to all written constitutions. Procedures, however, vary: in the US Constitution, the procedures are very rigid while the Indian counterpart endorses a system which is both rigid and flexible depending on the issue in question. As shown previously, the Indian founding fathers did not seem to have favoured rigid amendment procedures since that would not, as they strongly felt, allow the Constitution to adapt to the changing socio-economic priorities of the people. Implicit here was the concern that the Constitution should not be an impediment towards incorporating newer provisions in case they were pertinent in the changed environment.

Since amendments are strictly procedure-driven, they cannot thus be arbitrary; they are required to be justified with reference to both the constitutional principles and also practices. This was the primary concern of the founding fathers who qualified their arguments in favour of amendments by underlining that they were mere devices for making the constitution pertinent to the changing/changed socio-economic and political milieu. As demonstrated previously, the amendment procedures of the Indian Constitution are both rigid and flexible: they are rigid if the amendment involves change of the fundamental character of the Constitution; they are flexible once they simply seek to add or alter or repeal the prevalent provisions/ Articles which seem to have exhausted their utility, or, in simple terms, they are irrelevant. This is one side of the story; there is another side as well. As per Article 368 of the Constitution of India, the amendment procedure is very rigid with regard to certain Parts and the Seventh Schedule of the Constitution. Furthermore, in view of the constitutional salience of the doctrine of basic structure, the executive cannot amend any of those Parts of the Constitution which constitute the basic structure. What it confirms is the idea that the amendment cannot be arbitrary and has to be defended as perhaps the most needed at a particular point of time.

In constitutional democracy, amendments are, in the final analysis, a bridge between the executive and other important organs of government, namely legislature and judiciary. While judiciary reviews the amendments to ascertain their constitutionality, the legislature plays a role in their making when they are placed for deliberations before the legislators. This is a very clichéd description. A careful study of some path-breaking pronouncements by the Indian judiciary, however, reveals that some important Parts of India's Constitution can never be fiddled with since they are identified as its 'basic features'. In other words, by conceptualizing these features as 'basic' to the Constitution of India, the Indian judiciary restricted, to a considerable extent, the executive authority in so far as amendment was concerned. Being integral to India's constitutional practices, the basic structure doctrine cannot thus be ignored if one seeks to understand Article 368 as a mechanism for amending the Constitution in conformity with the available politico-ideological inputs.

There is another aspect which we should not lose sight of. Amendments are also a means to elicit public opinion as soon as they are placed in the public domain. An alert citizenry acts as a shield against endeavours towards undermining the fundamental constitutional ethos, as was evident in the context of the 1975–77 Emergency when there were series of campaigns against arbitrary amendments which the government adopted contrary to the spirit in which constitutional democracy was articulated in India. With the repeal of the draconian amendments that were adopted during the Emergency, it was again established that constitutional democracy had deeper roots in India and amendments were accepted as appropriate mechanisms for ushering in significant constitutional changes. So, amendments were not merely a pathological exercise to make a constitution sensitive to the contemporary politico-ideological priorities, they are also indispensable, if not most pertinent, designs of a dialogue in which the role of the governed is as critical as that of the formal institutions of governance.

Review Questions

1. **In what respects, amendments are critical to constitutional democracy? Elaborate.**
2. **How did the founding fathers conceptualize the amendment procedures during their deliberations in the Constituent Assembly? Elaborate.**
3. **Critically evaluate Article 368 of the Constitution of India.**
4. **Identify two major amendments to the Constitution of India which, according to you, radically altered its texture and also nature.**
5. **Can a democracy function if the constitutional provisions for amendments are completely removed? Give reasons for your answer.**

Chapter 19

Comptroller and Auditor General of India[1]

Learning Objectives

- How does one conceptualize audit as critical to constitutional democracy?
- How was the Comptroller and Auditor General instituted in India?
- To evaluate its role as one of those constitutional agencies which are critical to democratic governance in India

The Comptroller and Auditor General of India (CAG) is one of the most important institutions of governance. In order to ascertain accountability in the spending public funds, the founding fathers felt the need for an independent agency for auditing the government expenditure. This is a post-mortem exercise since the CAG is allowed to intervene once the expenditure is incurred. Being a constitutional agency, it performs those roles which are critical to a stable constitutional democracy; its independence is also ensured by categorical constitutional provisions, ensuring its existence as an agency completely separate from other constitutional agencies. Besides constitutional guarantee, the CAG derives its strength from the public given the important role that it discharges while executing its functions in accordance with the Constitution. This is a watchdog of India's constitutional governance. Hence it has been argued that 'by performing such an important function the Comptroller and Auditor General makes himself [*sic*] an indispensable instrument in the proper working of a parliamentary government'.[2] Being indispensable to constitutional governance in India, the CAG is thus a constant check on those tendencies which are likely to cripple democracy. In that respect, not only is this integral to the Constitution of India, it is also a significant politico-ideological institution that acts both as a guardian and also custodian of constitutional values that have flourished in the wake of constitutional democracy in India. The aim of this chapter is to understand CAG as an institution of governance with reference to the constitutional provisions and practices. With its growing importance in India's constitutional democracy in recent times, this segment also concentrates on the trajectory of its unfolding by reference to its contemporary manifestation.

[1] This segment of the discussion is drawn on Sadhna Gupta, 'Comptroller and Auditor General in India' (M. Phil dissertation [in Hindi], University of Delhi, 2014), unless otherwise indicated.

[2] MV Pylee, *Constitutional Government in India* (London: Asia Publishing House, 1960), p. 665.

Historical Antecedents

There is nothing strikingly original in the provisions of the Constitution dealing with the CAG. It had its earlier incarnation in British India. The Comptroller and Auditor General of India as a head of Supreme Audit Institution of India (SAI) has a long history. The office of the Auditor General had already been in existence in India since 1919 with the promulgation of the Montague–Chelmsford Reforms. The idea came from England where it was installed in the early part of the nineteenth century. In India, it has evolved through the practice and tradition of governance in British India. Just prior to the Mutiny of 1857, Lord Canning had initiated a major administrative reorganization. As a part of this reorganization, for the first time, a separate department with an Accountant General was established. He was responsible for the accounting and auditing of the financial transactions under the East India Company. After the mutiny, the British Crown took over the administration of India and passed the Government of India Act 1858. This Act introduced a system of an annual budget of Imperial income and expenditure in 1860. The budgeting system laid the foundation stone of Imperial Audit. Sir Edward Drummond took charge in November 1860 as the first Auditor General. Therefore, originally it was designated the Accountant General to the Government of India and later designated as the Auditor General of India in 1860. The term Comptroller and Auditor General of India was first used in 1884. Under the Montague–Chelmsford Reforms of 1919, the Auditor General became independent of the government. The Government of India Act 1935 strengthened the position of the Auditor General by providing for provincial Auditor General in a federal setup. He was given the status of a judge of a federal court in regards to the security of his service. The legacy of the 1935 Act continued in the period following Independence. Till 1947, when the last British Auditor General, Sir Bertie Monro Staig, handed over the reins, the department remained an integral part of British administration.

Realizing the critical importance of an independent agency in parliamentary democracy, the founding fathers were keen to make it completely separate from executive and legislative control. To enable the Auditor General work fearlessly and efficiently, they devised various constitutional means while debating on its nature in the Constituent Assembly. The idea was naturally appealing to all the members regardless of their ideological preferences. Instead of having an Auditor General, they insisted on a Comptroller as well, which meant that they agreed to endow the Auditor General with extra authority of 'controlling irregular expenses and also designing how this could be stopped'. Hence the Indian version of Auditor General is known as the Comptroller and Auditor General. It was BR Ambedkar who is credited with this idea which entails that 'he will have all the powers as far as audit is concerned'.[3] It was favoured also because

> the Auditor General is not an accountant per se; he has a number of duties to perform and in so functioning he has got to have a knowledge of the entire administration [which] is possible only with the extension of authority beyond being a mere auditor.[4]

Once this was settled, the founding fathers were concerned with evolving a mechanism for its independence, since

---

[3] RK Sidhva (Central Provinces and Berar), 30 November 1949, *Constituent Assembly Debates*, Book No. 3, p. 412.

[4] TT Krishnamachari (Madras), 30 November 1949, *Constituent Assembly Debates*, Book No. 3, p. 410.

> the post of Auditor General is so very important that it needs to be protected from undue influences; [being] the watchdog of our finances, his position should be made so strong that he cannot be influenced by anyone, howsoever great he may be; he should be independent of either the legislature or executive.[5]

This was a common concern, being shared by the members. In an identical fashion, B Das of Orissa, thus, stressed:

> It is necessary for the maintenance of the integrity of the Government of India in public expenditure that the Auditor General should be placed in the status wherein we have placed the members of Federal Public Service Commission and also the Chief Justice of the Supreme Court of India.[6]

The idea was unanimously endorsed. While being appreciative of the suggestions of his colleagues, Ambedkar pursued the point forcefully as follows:

> I am of the opinion that this dignitary or officer is probably the most important officer in the Constitution of India. He is one man who is going to see that the expenses voted by Parliament are not exceeded, or varied from what has been laid down by Parliament in what is called the Appropriation Act. If the functionary is to carry out the duties—and his duties . . . are far more important that the duties even of the judiciary—he should have been certainly as independent as Judiciary, [and ideally speaking], he ought to have far greater Independence than Judiciary itself [which the proposed constitution] has not guaranteed.[7]

Not only did Ambedkar demarcate the domain of its functioning, he also argued strongly for its independence which was not ascertained as per his preferences. Nonetheless, what came out of the debates seemed to have satisfied the members. One of them was B Pattabhi Sitaramayya of Madras who admired his colleagues for having made the Auditor General one of the strongest institutions of governance in independent India. It was clearly stated when he said:

> We have done a great thing, in respect of the position that we assigned to the Comptroller and Auditor General. No matter how perfect your Constitution may be, no matter how numerous may be the checks and the balances and safeguards for the right conduct of business of the future, it is money that counts, . . . and if all this money is not spent alright, and if the people deliver cheap gibes at [the authority], . . . then, there is no government at all worth mentioning; it is anarchy, it is chaos, it is loot, it is dacoity. The Comptroller and Auditor General must thus be made as supreme and independent as the Judges of the Supreme Court perhaps even more so. He is not merely an Accountant General, but he represents a judicial authority with a judicial frame of mind, and his acts must be acts of justice between what he considers to be right and

---

[5] RK Sidhva (Central Provinces and Berar), 30 November 1949, *Constituent Assembly Debates*, Book No. 3, p. 405.

[6] B Das (Orissa), 30 November 1949, *Constituent Assembly Debates*, Book No. 3, p. 405.

[7] BR Ambedkar, 30 November 1949, *Constituent Assembly Debates*, Book No. 3, pp. 407–08.

what is actually done by the executive. This is achieved only by making him as the supreme arbiter of Indias finances and then alone our Swaraj will be a proper Swaraj.[8]

A careful analysis of the issues raised in the Assembly reveals that the concern for an independent audit seems to have become primary to the members. They were unanimous in their assessment that the proposed CAG needed to be independent; otherwise, the purpose of having such an institution was sure to be defeated. As a moral custodian of public purse, the CAG was expected to act as an impartial observer to ascertain that no money was spent improperly and without authorization.

Theoretically, the Indian Constitution establishes an independent CAG that ensures guarantee to its people that government is accountable and responsive to Parliament. It is the foundational principle of parliamentary system of government that Executive will be responsible to Legislature and the essence of such control lies in the system of financial control by the legislature. To discharge this function, it is important that Legislature has some kind of agency which should be fully independent from the Executive, who would scrutinize the financial transactions of the government. Therefore, it is important to asses this very important institution in contemporary times. CAG is not only an institution but also a tool to maintain governance and to empower people.

A Brief History

After Independence, in a federal set-up, a unitary Audit System was established, which meant that the Comptroller and Auditor General of India will audit the Central as well as state governments. Before adopting this system in the Indian Constitution, a huge debate was taken up in the Constituent Assembly. The draft constitution prepared by the Constitutional Advisor in October 1947 contained separate provisions for the appointment of the Auditor General of the Federation and auditor generals for the provinces. The Auditor General for the Federation was to be appointed by the President, and would have the same security of tenure as a judge of the Supreme Court. It was open to a Provincial Legislature to provide by law for the appointment of an Auditor General for the province. Appointment to the office of the Provincial Auditor General was to be made by the Governor in his discretion and he could be removed from office only in the same manner as a High Court judge.[9] The Expert Committee on the financial provisions of the Union Constitution observed that the provisions of this draft were 'adequate for the purpose of securing the independence of the Auditor General'. The committee, however, favoured the continuance of a single Auditor General for the Government of India as well as for the provincial governments.[10] Later, this advice was accepted by the Drafting Committee.

Position in Indian Constitution

Our constitution makers, realizing the importance of an independent agency for audit under the parliamentary form of government, made the CAG fully independent so that it could function efficiently.

[8] B Pattabhi Sitaramayya (Madras), 25 November 1949, *Constituent Assembly Debates*, Book No. 5, p. 945.

[9] Subhash C. Kashyap, ed., *The Framing of India's Constitution: A Study* (revised edition, New Delhi: Universal Law Publishing Company Private Ltd., 2004), p. 414.

[10] Kashyap, *The Framing of India's Constitution*, p. 414.

In Part V of the Constitution of India, Articles 148, 149, 150 and 151 form the basic structure of the institution of CAG of India. As stated in Article 148(1):

> There shall be a Comptroller and Auditor General of India, who shall be appointed by the President by warrant under his hand and seal and shall be only be removed from office in like manner and on the like grounds as a Judge of the Supreme Court.

With this, his salary and other conditions of service may be determined by Parliament, but once appointed neither his salary nor his rights in respect of leave of absence, pension or age of retirement can be varied to his disadvantage. After retirement or resignation, he will be not eligible for any office under the Government of India or any state government. His salary and other expenses of his administration or office are charged upon the Consolidated Fund of India; it means they are not subject to vote.

Independent CAG in Independent India

As shown earlier, one of the primary concerns of the founding fathers was to guarantee independence to the CAG by providing adequate constitutional protection. Being aware that unless the CAG was put above board, the call for independence was to be a farce. It was endorsed by almost all the members that there should be clearly worded constitutional provisions for ensuring that neither Legislature nor Executive was in a position to control and influence the CAG. Keeping this in mind, our constitution framers have made this institution autonomous from the government so that it could discharge its functions free from the pressure of government. The Constitution guarantees independent audit by the CAG by the following provisions:

- Appointment by the President of India.
- Special procedure for removal like that being followed in regard to a Supreme Court Judge.
- Salary and other administrative expenses be charged on the consolidated fund of India, which means they are not subject to vote.
- He/she cannot hold any other government office after his/her term expires.

Powers and Duties of the CAG

Articles 149 and 150 of Constitution of India deal with the power and duties of CAG. According to Article 149:

> The Comptroller and Auditor General shall perform such duties and exercise such powers in relation to the accounts of the Union and of the States and of any other authority or body as may be prescribed by or under any law made by Parliament and, until provision in that behalf is so made, shall perform such duties and exercise such powers in relation to the accounts of Union as of the States as were conferred on or exercisable by the Auditor General of India.

Beside the Constitution, the Comptroller and Auditor General of India (Duties, Powers and Conditions) Act, 1971 also talks about the duties and powers of CAG in detail. This Act has identified the various subjects and items which come under the scrutiny of CAG. According to this Act, it shall be the duty of CAG:[11]

1. To audit all expenditure from the consolidated fund of India.
2. To audit all transactions of the union and the states relating to contingency funds and public accounts.
3. To audit all trading manufacturing, profit and loss accounts and balance sheets and other subsidiary accounts kept in any department of the Union or of a state.
4. Audit of receipts and expenditure of bodies or authorities substantially financed from Union or state revenues.

In 2007, the CAG issued, under section 23 of the DPC Act, 'Regulations on Audit and Accounts', which define in detail the scope, manner and extent of his auditing and accounting mandate.

Types of Audit

There are mainly three types of audit which the CAG handles:

1. Compliance Audit
2. Financial Audit
3. Performance Audit

Apart from these traditional forms of audit, the CAG is now engaged in auditing activities relating to the information technology systems and environment.

What Happens to the Audit Reports?

The reports prepared by CAG are submitted to the President in the case of Union and to the Governor in the case of the state. Article 151 of the Constitution says: (a) the reports of the Comptroller and Auditor General of India relating to the accounts of the Union shall be submitted to the President, who shall cause them to be laid before each House of Parliament; (b) the reports of the Comptroller and Auditor General of India relating to the accounts of the state shall be submitted to the Governor of the state, who shall cause them to be laid before the Legislature of the state. Once submitted in the respective houses, the reports are referred to the Central and state-related Public Accounts Committee and Committees on Pubic Understandings (COPU). These specialized committees scrutinize these reports and select those paragraphs/findings that are to be most critical to the public interest. In this process, CAG provides them technical assistance. On the basis of their study, these committees prepares a report with recommendation and submit them to their respective houses for further discussion.

[11] Comptroller and Auditor-General's (Duties, Powers and Conditions of Service) Act 1971 (Government of India). http://saiindia.gov.in/hindi/home/about_us/mandate/DPC_act/DPC_act.html (accessed 3 December 2016).

Changing Role of the CAG

Over a period of time, the CAG has changed itself. We have already discussed the mandatory provisions relating to the CAG and its importance to maintain democracy. As per the Constitution, the CAG is an autonomous institution; this is made so to enable the institution to have surveillance on the government through its audit reports. In course of time, it has redefined its role by being proactive and sensitive to its constitutional obligations. It was like the Election Commission which was inefficient till 1990s. Till the early 1990s, the Election Commission, despite being a 'constitutional' authority, functioned more or less as a wing of the executive branch—a friendly agency sympathetic to the party in power, unwilling to express itself strongly to fulfil its defined role as 'the guardian of purity in the electoral process.'[12] But in the 1990s, this situation underwent a sea change. The Election commission reinvented itself in accordance with the spirit of the Constitution rather than acting as a mouthpiece of the party in the power. In this process, the Election Commission became an important institution in India's constitutional democracy. With TN Seshan becoming the Chief Election Commissioner of India, the Election Commission became an active, independent, strong-willed umpire to oversee fair play in the electoral process. He is said to have given teeth to the organization; it is widely perceived now that the Commission has a strong bark and a vicious bite when occasion demands it.[13] The radical change in the nature of the Commission is attributed to the personality of the holder of the office; being a very assertive officer, TN Seshan rearticulated the role of this constitutional agency in a different light which was refreshing and also constitutionally reassuring for a vibrant democracy like India. This is also the case in regard to the CAG, being headed by Vinod Rai, a former Indian Administrative Service officer who came out strongly in his audit reports against the incumbent government even in adverse political circumstances. The CAG in the pre-Rai era did bark now and then, though it never went to the extent of implicating the prevalent government; it was as it were a toothless tiger which was threatening at the very sight of its appearance though not so harmful in real terms. With Rai as the head of the organization, it became a powerful institution which not only upheld its constitutional role but also endeavoured to act fiercely as a watchdog of public interests by subjecting the government income and expenditure to serious scrutiny. By transforming the CAG into a meaningful institution of authority in governance, the role of the erstwhile CAG, Vinod Rai, is being compared with that of earlier Election Commissioner, TN Seshan, who had, as argued previously, radically altered the nature of the Election Commission by exercising his authority as per the Constitution. Being dubbed as the 'Seshan of CAG,'[14] Rai is thus credited with noticeable changes in the institution of audit in India which was not as proactive in the past as the founding fathers expected it to be.

The CAG audit is a routine matter which allows citizens to assess whether government expenditure is incurred as per the well-established norms and values, as upheld by the constitutional practices and legislative initiatives. In its audit report, the CAG indicted the Rajiv Gandhi-led Congress government in 1986 because of the evidence that it received kickbacks over the purchase of Bofors Guns from Sweden. Later on, the media brought out evidence to prove that the charge was not, at all, fabricated. In a similar vein, the CAG's scrutiny of the expenditure in the Commonwealth Games (CWG) of 2010, and soon thereafter the analysis of the 2G spectrum allocation, had put the government in the defensive. It was the

---

[12] TSR Subramanian, 'CAG: A Necessary Evil or a Bulwark?' *Economic and Political Weekly*, 27 October 2012, p. 19.

[13] Subramanian, 'CAG: A Necessary Evil or a Bulwark?' p. 19.

[14] Subramanian, 'CAG: A Necessary Evil or a Bulwark?' p. 19.

outcome of the CAG report which shook the UPA-II government on the basis of the evidence to substance the charge of the government of being consisted of corrupt ministers. The CAG became a face of anti-corruption campaign in India. Vinod Rai reinvented the role of the CAG not merely as an expert of postmortem audit, but also a powerful device to weed out corruption in governance by exposing the corrupt deeds of those holding even the ministerial positions. According to him, CAG is not merely an accountant. It has not been made merely to conduct audit and prepare a report and place it in Parliament. During a lecture at Harvard Kennedy School in the US, he reconceptualized CAG's role by saying:

> The question that continues to repeatedly arise in our minds is whether the Parliament, and in fact, the public at large, expect us to be mere accountants and do arithmetic over government expenditure? If it was so, then why constitutions worldwide should—appoint such high dignitaries as Auditors General and give them independence, freedom from the executive and accord them a constitutional position. Evidently what was envisioned in the constitution was more than expecting them to be mere accountants.[15]

This is not the story of one day which suddenly changed this institution; there are so many factors that contributed to this change. Vinod Rai has effected important changes but this change was initiated much earlier, as India's politico-administrative history has shown. There are two completely different phases of the working of the CAG since it was instituted with the introduction of the 1950 Constitution: the phase between 1950 and 1991 and what followed after 1991. There were so many economic and political changes which also had manifestation in CAG's functioning as well. In his own assessment, Rai attributed the CAG's transformation to the changes in the wider socio-economic circumstances following the consolidation of globalization especially after the adoption of the 1991 New Economic Policy in India. According to him, besides being accountable, efficient, transparent, responsive, equitable, inclusive and bound by the rule of law, governance

> has assumed such critical proportions that it appears too important to be left only to the government. The stakeholders in governance have expanded beyond the executive, legislature and judiciary to civil society, social organizations, media and the public. Apart from the base expanding, each new stakeholders has become very vociferous and demanding.[16]

In view of the growing importance of civil society in governance, the CAG is being constantly monitored by forces other than the government. A non-Weberian development since government is held accountable not merely internally but also externally in the sense that for decisions relating to public are being continuously assessed. In the changed environment, it is obvious that CAG cannot escape public attention, given its critical role to ascertain that the rules, regulations and norms are respected and not violated.

[15] The speech of Vinod Rai at the Kennedy School of Government, 8 February 2013. http://www.ndtv.com/article/india/govt-auditor-cag-vinod-rai-s-speech-at-harvard-kennedy-school-327674 (accessed 3 December 2016).

[16] The speech of Vinod Rai.

Major Changes in CAG's Organization during 1990s[17]

The period between 1990 and 2010 marks an era of multi-faceted developments in CAG's organization.

1. The year 1990 witnesses initiatives to reduce the importance of the Indian Audits and Accounts Department (IA & AD), since a considerable portion of their responsibilities has already been transferred to the state governments.
2. The period was characterized by very significant growth in computerization and information technology applications in the age of ICT (information and communication technology), tremendous improvements in infrastructure and other facilities and modernization of office systems and procedures.
3. The IA & AD has assumed several entirely new kinds of audit functions following the government instruction of auditing the expenditures of Panchayati Raj institutions; it has been added further with the expansion of its duties in view of the creation of new states.
4. New systems and procedures were introduced, such as system of peer review, strategic plan and perspective plan. The department is expected to prepare the mission statement as well as the vision statement for the department. A trend was sought to be established to experiment with innovative designs of audit and also to draw upon the best practices in audit, being practised elsewhere.
5. A development of great significance was the decision of the former CAG, VN Kaul, to issue the Regulations on Audit and Accounts in pursuance of powers vested in him under Section 23 of the CAG's (DPC) Act, 1971.
6. The period will also be known for the entry of India's SAI into international auditing scene for the first time with its election as a member of the United Board of Auditors in 1992. The 1990s also marked the entry of India in the international forum like International Organization of Supreme Audit Institutions (INTOSAI) and the Asian Organization of Supreme Audit Institutions (ASOSAI). The period also saw the growing CAG participation in these two global forums for SAI.
7. In the field of government auditing, the era is marked by several very momentous developments. Most significant of these were the new audits that came up as a result of the major liberalization reform that was ushered in since 1991. In the audit department, a wave of globalization has started. The IA & AD has made efforts to integrate with the best global auditing standards and practices. New areas of audit sprang up as a result of the government policies on privatization. Performance audit has become more accentuated by completely rebuilding its structure and methodology and defining the tools more clearly and objectively.
8. In the field of audit practices and procedures, several new systems were tested; these included the concept of outsourcing of certain field workers for carrying out beneficiary surveys. Also, the department has begun hiring experts and consultants to help in complex technical areas.
9. This was also the era of building up several new institutions. An autonomous institution under the aegis of CAG was set up in 1996 called 'Institute of Public Auditors of India' as a 'think tank' in audit, accounting and accountability matters. The CAG also set up an Audit Advisory Board in March 1999. It has 14 members from various fields, including those from the academia,

[17] This section presents a summary of the major developments in the CAG's organization during 1990s. The material is based on Vijay Kumar's book *The Comptroller and Auditor General of India: A Thematic History, 1990–2007*, Vol. 1. New Delhi: APH Publishing Corporation, 2008).

engineering, civil service, medical practitioners, defence personnel and the corporate world—a new group which was instituted to provide intellectual and technical support to the top management team responsible for devising appropriate policy designs.

The transformation within the CAG has resulted in visible changes; it is being viewed as one of the most effective governance mechanism to ensure transparency, accountability and probity in dealing with public funds. By exposing the scams, it has also acquired the reputation of neither being influenced not subservient to the government in power. The growing salience of the CAG in the last decade of this century cannot be attributed to an individual, but the processes of democratization leading to intense participation by the demos in processes of governance. The 2011 drive against corruption at the behest of the India Against Corruption group was a momentous event which unleashed a very organized campaign involving people from various walks of life. A new era was ushered in and this explains partly the proactive nature of the CAG, which was also inspired to utilize its constitutional role to contribute to public well-being by charting a clearly independent course of action. The change was possible with the involvement of the actors from outside the government; the civil society rose to prominence in the wake of the 2011 Anna Hazare movement which took up the cudgels against constitutional derailment of governance. The purpose was to make government accountable for its deeds. Young people joined this movement for a transparent and accountable government. Social media played an important role to spread the information quickly. Speaking at the third anniversary of the Moneylife Foundation in Mumbai, the former CAG Vinod Rai says that 'the year 2012 will go down in the history of Indian democracy as a defining year. A year in which citizen came to the center-stage [of politics] and debunked the old age myth of the silent majority'.[18] In his lecture at Harvard Kennedy School, he reiterates how the civil society and the citizens of India have supported this institution. He says that 'today's youth is discerning, demanding and believers in respecting Institution created by the constitution. He is not willing to see politicians subvert these institutions [defying the myth] that he is not a mere mute observer of what is happening around him'. The CAG is not a mere accountant, he further adds, but also 'an instrument for sensitizing people of their responsibilities in democratizing governance'.[19]

The administrative changes that Rai had brought about seem to have streamlined the functioning of the CAG by reference to its primary commitment as a constitutional authority. These are not merely directed to bring about a structural change, but they are also an attempt to transform the mindset that appears to have become hegemonic in governance. Some of the major changes are as follows:

1. Now CAG has engaged itself in the business of upgrading governance as any other agency in the administration. In the changed perception, one of the important features of the CAG audit report is to focus on the good practices and also to devise techniques to avoid further decline.
2. The CAG has started to convert the salient observations of their reports into small booklets to facilitate easy understanding of the complex issues relating to financial governance. With the distribution of pamphlets, christened as 'Noddy' (the character which the author Enid Blyton had popularized) books, to the media, colleges, citizen's groups, non-governmental organizations, the CAG seeks to spread awareness among the wider society of how important postmortem audit is for democracy and a corruption-free government. This is being undertaken in the firm belief that

[18] 'Vinod Rai is the Face of a New, More Assertive Even Aggressive, Comptroller and Auditor General', *Mint*, 2 April 2013.
[19] The speech of Vinod Rai.

an awakened citizen, once sensitized about the inadequacy of government departments, would exert pressure on these departments and maintain vigilance on what they undertake, and this will ensure a better delivery of government services.

3. Now the institution of CAG supports the concept of social audit for a more widespread coverage of social sector issues. As a majority of the Indian population, mostly in rural areas, remains in the dark about government welfare schemes, social audit will act as an effective mechanism both for making them aware and also allowing them to be part of the processes of governance. By creating 'credible citizens' groups', especially in rural areas which are endowed with local knowledge, the CAG took a meaningful step in setting up institutions for dialogues among the villagers over issues which are relevant to them; they are asked to prepare a blueprint for what is needed for development in their villages, which provides specific inputs to the policy makers while designing policies for village-uplift. This has given the CAG 'a better outreach, and also provided these agencies with a more credible voice in legislative designing of policies and programmes'.[20]

Evaluative Remarks

As a constitutional agency, the CAG in India has changed its role since it was instituted. Although it has been constitutionally empowered to discharge its independent role, there were occasions when it was vitiated by heavy political interference. As a result, its independence was questioned and it was criticized as nothing but an appendage to the ruling party. There are, however, instances when the CAG rose to the occasion and performed its role as an independent agency, which acted as a conscience keeper of the government by adopting adequate steps to avoid financial impropriety. The audit of government expenses by the CAG, thus, became a powerful constitutional instrument which also brought the tax payers as stakeholder in the reckoning.

While evaluating the role of the CAG as an assessor of how the government spends tax payers' money, one should also be sensitive to the context in which it functions. If it was a hegemonic role of a single political party, it might not have been possible for the CAG to remain true, for obvious reasons, to its constitutional obligation. Furthermore, the individual integrity of the CAG cannot be ignored. Despite the fact that the selection process is quite rigorous, there have been many instances of individual follies that did tamper CAG's reputation as a public institution. Nonetheless, the CAG is probably one of those few constitutional bodies that has still been respected presumably because of its constant vigil on government spending.

Besides its role as an auditor, the CAG also puts the government on alert by raising issues in the public domain. As Rai argues:

> Once citizens are sensitized about [CAG's] findings, they get empowered to hold the custodian of the public purse accountable. In a parliamentary democracy, it is critical that the citizens of a country are able to hold their representative accountable; democratically elected representatives can only be held accountable if they, in turn, can hold accountable those who implement their decisions. An important ingredient of this accountability cycle is an

[20] The speech of Vinod Rai.

> independent and credible Supreme Audit Institution capable of scrutinizing the stewardship and use of public resources. It is incumbent on [the CAG] to show our efficacy by appropriately responding to the concerns of citizens.... [By] communicating and promoting the values of [probity, the CAG has become] an effective instrument for catapulting citizens on the centre stage of public governance.[21]

By creating public opinion in case the government violates the constitutional norms, the CAG has acquired a distinct voice in consolidating constitutional democracy in India. With its defined constitutional role, it has thus not only put the government in checks but has also created an environment in which citizens are given an equally important role in governance. With the exposure of several scams in which even the ministers are involved, the CAG has gained reputation as a tough instrument of governance that cannot so easily be ignored given its constitutional power and also its ability to consolidate mass opinion against the government follies. This is a remarkable achievement of a constitutional agency that, despite being identified as a government-appendage in the past, has gradually become a powerful public voice even in the midst of the consolidation of forces challenging democracy.

Concluding Observations

No discussion on financial administration in India shall remain complete unless one takes into account the role of the CAG in the post-mortem of the government expenses and spending. With its constitutional responsibility, the CAG has perhaps become the most reliable instrument to establish integrity in administration that cannot be ignored. Given its vibrant nature in India, it has also fulfilled its political role in raising public opinion when the government or the spending authorities deviate from what is considered 'proper' in the lexicon of financial administration. As the discussion has shown, the CAG, by being always alert to its constitutional obligation, appears to have surpassed, in recent times, its institutional role of a mere auditor; it has become one of the constitutional agencies that is critical to India's democracy. In other words, the CAG, while fulfilling its constitutional role, has set in motion processes protecting its sanctity in conjunction with India's democratic ethos.

Review Questions

1. **Critically trace history of the growth of the Comptroller and Auditor General of India.**
2. **How was the concern for an Auditor General conceptualized in the Constituent Assembly debates? Elaborate.**
3. **Critically elaborate the constitutional provisions relating to the Comptroller and Auditor General.**
4. **What are the major changes in the 1990s that enabled the Comptroller and Auditor General to meaningfully discharge its constitutional obligations? Elaborate.**
5. **The Comptroller and Auditor General is an important pillar of constitutional democracy. Explain.**

[21] The speech of Vinod Rai.

Chapter 20

Governor: A Constitutional Functionary with Political Aims or a Political Functionary with Constitutional Goals (?)

Learning Objectives

- To understand the role of governor as a constitutional functionary in India's federal governance
- To review the role of governor in the changing socio-economic and political milieu following the rising importance of constituent provinces
- To conceptualize the viability of a gubernatorial position in India's constitutional democracy

The governor of a state is a unique office in India's constitutional governance. As per the Constitution, the governor is the executive head of the state because 'the executive authority of the State shall be vested in the Governor and shall be exercised by him (*sic*) either directly or through officers subordinate to him in accordance with the Constitution'. Appointed by the President who holds the office during his/her pleasure, a governor is usually chosen by the Union Government, which precludes the possibility of the governor being an absolutely non-partisan individual. In fact, this was one of the issues that is being raised continuously by those state governments which are ruled by a party other than the one at the centre. The Sarkaria Commission that looked into the Centre–State relations in India made several suggestions to address this constitutional lacuna which, in its views, was a deterrent towards realizing federalism in its true spirit and substance. The issue received adequate attention in the academic discourse but did not result in any substantial changes in the constitutional position of the governor in the overall set-up of state administration. Instead of being a constitutional functionary who is primarily a facilitator, the governor, on many occasions, became a stumble block for smooth functioning of a state government; governors are, thus, a source of discontent in the state. This is, however, one part of the story. The other part is usually told by reference to the various instances showing how a governor, despite not being associated with the state in any way before the appointment, gradually became a centre of activity which is politically rewarding for the state and constitutionally supportive of the role that he/she is charged with. With the growing politicization of the processes of appointment of governors, following the consolidation of personality or dynasty-driven politics in the 1970s, governors hardly have freedom of action as soon as the appointment is made. Governors, instead of being the bridge between the elected representatives belonging to parties with contrasting ideological perspectives, act in a way which is contrary to how the founding fathers conceptualized their role in independent India.

The growing politicization of governors has to do with the politicization of the constitutional processes which do not seem to draw on the Constitution but on the governing political ideologies of the political parties holding the fort in the state. Constitution seems to have lost its salience to a significant extent and it becomes a hostage due to peculiar socio-economic and political churnings that India as an independent polity has confronted so far. There is, thus, a very powerful point when it is argued that with the gradual decline of the fundamental constitutional values and principles, individual preferences seem to have gained ascendancy in governance. This is constitutionally debilitating and politically degenerating in any system of governance; it is more so in a constitutional democracy like India where the Constitution is also a social document seeking to create a society of equals irrespective of socio-economic differences.

A note of caution is however necessary. The visible decline of constitutional values appears to have created several alternative avenues of political empowerment leading to what is described as massive democratization of those who remain peripheral in governance. The role of the governor needs to be conceptualized in such a changed socio-economic circumstances in which citizens are not mere recipients of change but are its instigators. A governor is not merely political, but holds a constitutional office which is meant to uphold the Constitution in its true spirit and content. In other words, being a constitutional functionary, a governor is expected to govern in accordance with the constitutional stipulations, and not in accordance with the whims of the appointing authority. This is easier said than done in the changed environment when the constitutional functionaries do not seem to have been as sincere to their constitutional obligations as is expected. The obvious result is the declining importance of constitutional values in governance. A governor cannot be entirely immune from the distortion in constitutional governance where Constitution appears to have significantly lost its salience. This is, at one level, definitely a source of disenchantment with constitutional democracy in India; at another, this has created a space for forces which, so far, remain peripheral but have gained ascendancy as a result of growing democratization of political processes. Governance is no longer the exclusive domain of the elites; it has become a space for interaction, both at the formal and informal levels of decision making, involving various strata of society.

As governor is part of the politico-constitutional processes, this chapter is directed to understand his/her role with reference to (a) the debates in the Constituent Assembly, (b) the provisions of the Constitution and (c) the changing socio-political and economic circumstances. The aim here is to conceptualize the role of the governor not merely as a constitutional functionary but also as a political authority that derives its sustenance from the Constitution, which will definitely help us comprehend the transforming nature of the office in contemporary India. What is required to be understood is how the office articulates its role in a context in which political calculations seem to have been critical both in the appointment of governor and also how he/she should chart out courses of action for the fulfilment of his/her constitutional obligations.

Historical Antecedents

In the proposed system of governance, the members of the Assembly agreed to have a governor for the provinces to act as a constitutional head. The idea was readily accepted, presumably because of the ideological continuity between the erstwhile form of governance and the one that was in the offing. Differences of opinion, however, surfaced as soon as the Assembly started debating on the provisions for the appointment and powers to be allocated to the governor as per the Constitution. BN Rau, the constitutional advisor, for instance, suggested that the governor should be elected by the provincial legislature by secret vote according to the system of proportional representation by the single transferable votes. This was carried forward by the recommendations of the Union and Provincial Constitution Committee[1] in its meeting of 7 June 1947. It was suggested that (a) there should be a governor as the head of the province, (b) the governor should be appointed by the province and not by the Central Government, and (c) the governor should be appointed by direct election on the basis of adult franchise through a special electoral college.

The arrangement did not find favour from the members of the Assembly since it was contrary to the spirit of the parliamentary form of government. Four reasons were offered for rejecting the proposal:

First, the members did not get persuaded because election for gubernatorial position was simply incompatible with the system of governance that the new constitution was contemplating. While defending nomination for the post of governor, Alladi Krishnaswami Ayyar of Madras argued that this was the most judicious means to select a governor. As he elaborated, nominating a person for being a governor was the best option because

> if the choice is left to the President and his cabinet, the President may, in conceivable circumstances, with due regard to the conditions of the province, choose a person of undoubted ability and position in public life who at the same time has not been mixed up in provincial party struggle or factions. Such a person is likely to act as a friend and mediator of the cabinet and help in the smooth working of the cabinet government in the early stages.[2]

Two considerations seem to have been important to Ayyar: (a) the governor should be above petty party politics to discharge his/her constitutional obligation in the best manner possible and (b) nomination by the President was preferred since he/she was immune from partisan considerations arising out of the provinces. The governor should be free from the vicious influences since he/she, argued Ayyar,

> is to be a constitutional head, a sagacious counsellor and adviser to the ministry and one who can throw oil over troubled water. Hence . . . the governor, chosen by the Government of India, presumably with the consent of the Provincial Government, is likely to discharge his functions better than one who is elected on a party ticket by the province as a whole based upon universal suffrage or by the legislature on some principle of election.[3]

Ayyar was not alone who opposed election and argued for nomination. He was supported by his colleague, KM Munshi of Bombay. In his defence, Munshi raised a powerful theoretical argument by drawing on a fundamental assumption on which the proposed constitution rested. According to him, given the conceptual grounding of independent India's governance on the Westminster form of parliamentary democracy election was not only 'absurd' and 'contrarian', it was also politically 'impractical'. As he elaborated,

> After we have adopted the British model, the election of the governor by adult franchise in the province remained an anomaly, a completely out-of-date and absurd thing. Imagine a governor being elected by adult franchise of all the citizens in a province. The persons who are at the top of the political life of the province would sooner prefer to be the Prime Minister

[1] Drawn on KP Singh, 'The Governor in the Constituent Assembly', *The Indian Journal of Political Science* (October–December 1965): 39.

[2] Alladi Krishnaswami Ayyar (Madras), 30 May 1949, *Constituent Assembly Debates*, Book No. 3, p. 431.

[3] Ibid., pp. 431–32.

> and Ministers with effective power in their hands. Therefore, the party in power when it goes to the election will put up a person who is not as outstanding as the prospective ministers for the office of the governor, with the result that the best man in the party will not be available for it.[4]

Apprehending that direct election was likely to undermine the authority of the council of ministers in the provinces, Munshi was not in its favour. Furthermore, in view of the possibility of the rise of two power centres, the provincial administration was certain to get adversely affected if the relationship between the governor and the council of ministers soured. Once the governor was directly elected, that would give him/her far more confidence which might lead him/her 'to override the elected prime minister'. He was convinced that nomination was the best option, which he illustrated by stating:

> Take the case where there is no majority party or the majority party is split into two or more factions and there is a rivalry for premiership.... It would lead to unnecessary complications in the affairs of the province. It would be much better that person is nominated and thus cut away from party politics of the province, so that the competition or the race between the rival groups is conducted in a fair, responsible and constitutional manner. All things considered, it would be better to have a governor nominated by the centre, who is free from passion and jealous of local party politics.[5]

What Munshi apprehended was also shared by HV Kamath of Central Provinces and Berar. He too defended his opinion in terms of the foundational ethos of parliamentary democracy with the cabinet being endowed with substantial constitutional authority. It was evident in his views which he articulated by stating:

> It is an admitted fact that one of the essentials of successful cabinet government in a province ... is the existence of a fairly impartial constitutional head, who is more or less a symbol of a constitutional figure head. If the governor were to be elected by the direct vote of all voters in a province he is very likely to be a party-man with strong views of his own and considering that he will be elected by the whole province—by the entire adult population of the province —he will think that he is a far superior man and a far more powerful than the Chief Minister/ premier of the state.... There will thus be two conflicting authorities in the State, both of them are elected [which] will create unnecessary complications [affecting] governance of the province.[6]

The same argument prevailed. Election would endow the governor with substantial political authority which was not permissible due to its debilitating effect on provincial governance. Highlighting that an elected governor was likely to be deterrent by also creating 'mischief', BG Kher (of Bombay), thus, endeavoured to persuade his colleague to accept nomination by suggesting that 'to have as a governor a person who is elected on a wider franchise to have at the head of the province a person who is supposed

[4] KM Munshi (Bombay), 31 May 1949, *Constituent Assembly Debates*, Book No. 3, p. 452.
[5] Ibid., p. 452.
[6] HV Kamath (Central Provinces and Berar), 30 May 1949, *Constituent Assembly Debates*, Book No. 3, p. 428.

to be more representative than the premier would be a mistake'.[7] The situation could be worse if there were two sets of political parties ruling at the Centre and the provinces. Rohini Kumar Chaudhuri of Assam drew the attention of his colleagues to this aspect by suggesting if the party that ruled at the Centre did not govern the province, the governor, appointed by the Union Government would find it difficult to even survive. 'Will a governor who is selected by the Congress Party act in harmony with the ministry of a province the premier of which belongs to another party?'[8] asked Chaudhuri. He was convinced that this was not the right option as it would lead 'to constant friction between the premier of the province and the governor'.[9] Supportive of nominating the governor, PK Sen (Bihar) also shared the views that seem to have persuaded most of the Assembly members. In his words, 'in the best interest of democracy, in the best interest of parliamentary form of government which has been decided upon as the basis of the Draft Constitution, the election of the Governor by adult suffrage is uncalled for and inappropriate'.[10] There was, however, a lone dissenting voice in support of election. Based his argument that the concern for the nation and a deep sense of patriotism, Shiban Lal Saksena, for instance defended his position by stating:

> Both these elected persons will be patriots and will love their province, and the country. They will try to show, when they work, that they can work in the interest of the province. They will show that, when they occupy these high offices, they can adjust their personal predilections and work in the interest of the province.[11]

Nonetheless, there had emerged a consensus in the Assembly in favour of nomination to avoid the provincial administration being paralyzed due to the rise of two conflicting centres of authority. The debate was finally concluded with the intervention of Jawaharlal Nehru who said:

> This was unnecessary [because], apart from leading to conflict and waste of energy and money [the election of governor] will lead to certain disruptive tendency in this big context of elective governor plus parliamentary system of democracy. Therefore, I should like support the [contention] that the Governor should be a nominated Governor.[12]

A major source of conflict was conclusively addressed; it was agreed upon that instead of being elected, a governor was to be nominated by the President out of the names, chosen by the Union Government for this position. The President did not have a choice to add or delete names, given his role as a titular head of the State.

The second set of argument relates to the concern of the Assembly members to have a person as a governor who was endowed with impeccable qualities and is above petty political calculations. He/she had to be impartial and was immune from being ideologically biased. Two major suggestions were placed before the Assembly: on the one hand, there were some who wanted the President to have an absolute authority in selecting a person of his/her choice; there was also a demand, on the other, for choosing a governor from a different province than the one in which he/she would be appointed as the governor. As regards the first, it was Brajeshwar Prasad of Bihar, who was a lone voice: he insisted that the President

[7] BG Kher (Bombay), 30 May 1949, *Constituent Assembly Debates*, Book No. 3, p. 434.
[8] Rohini Kumar Chaudhuri (Assam), 30 May 1949, *Constituent Assembly Debates*, Book No. 3, p. 436.
[9] Ibid., p. 436.
[10] PK Sen (Bihar), 31 May 1949, *Constituent Assembly Debates*, Book No. 3, p. 445.
[11] Shiban Lal Saksena (United Provinces), 31 May 1949, *Constituent Assembly Debates*, Book No. 3, pp. 450–51.
[12] Jawaharlal Nehru, 31 May 1949, *Constituent Assembly Debates*, Book No. 3, p. 456.

should be given a free hand, so that a person without any political baggage could be selected. Once the names came from the Union Government, it would be difficult to avoid a prejudiced choice. Hence he was in favour of 'giving unrestricted and unfettered choice to the president'.[13] The other suggestion was to make a person ineligible to become the governor of a state to which he/she belonged. This was endorsed by the Assembly because it was felt that 'a man from a province should not be appointed in the same province [for the post of governor] because it gives encouragement of fissiparous tendencies'.[14] In other words, the feeling that a governor, if he belonged to the same province in which he was to hold the highest constitutional authority, was likely to be less impartial for obvious reasons. In consonance with this sentiment, it was Jawaharlal Nehru who clearly stated the position that the Assembly had held with regard to who would be eligible to be appointed as a governor. Emphasizing that a person was ineligible to be appointed in a state to which he/she belonged, Nehru thus mentioned that he should be

> a detached figure . . . who is not intimately connected with local politics [and] is also acceptable to the province, otherwise he could not function there; he must not be known to be a part of the party machine of that province itself. . . . On the whole, it would probably be desirable to have people from outside, eminent in something, education or other fields of life who could naturally cooperate fully with the Government in carrying out the policy of the Government . . . and represent before the public something above politics.[15]

For Nehru, to be eligible to be a governor, the person had to fulfil two qualifications: on the one hand, he had to be a man of eminence and also a person who was, on the other, above party politics. Insisting on these qualifications, Nehru felt that these qualifications were critical for the governor to effectively discharge his/her role as a constitutional head of the province.

While Nehru identified 'the normative qualifications', PK Sen of Bihar drew out attention to those functional attributes which one needed to be efficient in a context where multiple socio-political ideas jostled for prominence. As the governor was to discharge his role as a major constitutional functionary in the state, he/she has to, as per Sen,

> fulfil the function of a lubricator [which means] that he is not to interfere, but he has just to smooth matters. If there are factions, if the different sections of the community are at loggerheads with each other, it is for him to act more or less as a lubricator, a cementing factor. He is to help the machinery of Government which is in the hands of the Prime Minister and the Council of Ministers; he is not to interfere and cause confusion or chaos; he would be the person really to lubricate the machinery and to see to it that all the wheels are going well by reason not of his interference, but his friendly intervention.[16]

What was emphasized here was the concern for nominating a person as a governor who was to rise above narrow sectional interests. A governor was not to be partisan while discharging his/her constitutional responsibility. It was believed by almost all the members that for the fulfilment of the constitutionally assigned tasks, a governor had to be absolutely independent which, they also felt, was not beyond realization in view of the ideological goal that the founding fathers had set out for them for building the nation.

---

[13] Brajeshwar Prasad (Bihar), 30 May 1949, *Constituent Assembly Debates*, Book No. 3, p. 426.

[14] Brajeshwar Prasad (Bihar), 30 May 1949, *Constituent Assembly Debates*, Book No. 3, p. 426.

[15] Jawaharlal Nehru, 31 May 1949, *Constituent Assembly Debates*, Book No. 3, p. 455.

[16] PK Sen (Bihar), 31 May 1949, *Constituent Assembly Debates*, Book No. 3, pp. 445–46.

The third set of factor drew on the concern of the founding fathers for making the governor a true bridge between the Centre and provinces. A seamless web was to be struck to maintain the federal balance in governance. Being above petty party politics, a governor was likely to be far more acceptable than the elected premier of the provinces in case the scope for a dialogue was completely missing. Hence, it was insisted in the Assembly:

> We must try every method by which harmony could be secured between the Centre and provinces. If you have a person who is not elected by the province or the State but you have a person appointed by the President of the Union with the consent . . . of the provincial cabinet, you will add a close link between the Centre and the provinces and clash between the provinces and the Centre will be avoided which will otherwise occasionally result.[17]

The argument is simple and clear. Apprehending the possible clash of interests between the Centre and the constituent provinces, the founding fathers sought to evolve a constitutional agency capable of acting as a link between them. A governor, nominated by the President in consultation with the provincial cabinet, was preferred because it was believed that nomination by the President would give him/her a national perspective and the approval of the provincial cabinet makes the nominated person acceptable to the state. With a creative blending of national with provincial perspectives, the governor would emerge as perhaps the most authentic source of inputs for the Union as well the provinces.

The final set of factors for making the governor a constitutional head of the provinces was based on the founding fathers' apprehension that an elected governor was likely to be a source of conflict which was to be avoided at any cost for the sake of nation's progress. Two sets of arguments were made: on the one hand, it was believed that in a responsible government, since the elected representative held substantial authority, backed by the constitution, the presence of another elected constitutional functionary was likely to be a source of friction and thus undesirable. In other words, since the elected representatives held substantial authority, there is nothing that the governor could do except perhaps acting as a guide in case the provincial governments deviated from the constitutionally recognized principles of governance. So, the governor was a figure head with no substantial authority at his/her disposal. Being a constitutional head, his/her role was that of a referee who was charged with the responsibility of ascertaining that those involved in governance followed the constitutional rules and regulations. That being so, 'it would not be correct to ask the people to take the trouble of going through a huge election on a gigantic scale to elect a person who would be merely a figure head'.[18] This did not, of course, mean that people would be deprived of their democratic rights of electing their own representatives; they would exercise their rights to vote in choosing periodically their own representatives as and when election to the provincial assembly took place. As PS Deshmukh eloquently put, the decision to go for a nominated governor did not take away people's democratic rights since they

> will have periodically to choose on the basis of adult franchise their own representatives in the provincial assemblies, a majority of whom will form the Provincial Ministry which will rule the province and exercise all the powers which the Constitution provides for.[19]

---

[17] Alladi Krishnaswami Ayyar, 30 May 1949, *Constituent Assembly Debates*, Book No. 3, p. 432.

[18] PS Deshmukh (Central Provinces and Berar), 30 May 1949, *Constituent Assembly Debates*, Book No. 3, p. 433.

[19] PS Deshmukh (Central Provinces and Berar), 30 May 1949, *Constituent Assembly Debates*, Book No. 3, p. 433.

It seems that there was a consensus and the Assembly members had agreed to the idea that the governor needed to be nominated for effective governance. There was an implicit assumption that the arrangement was purely temporary in view of the unforeseen circumstances following the partition. Nonetheless, the system that evolved in the Assembly was for nomination and not election of governor for reasons connected with the fear of creating an alternative power centre which was likely to hamper the normal functioning of constitutional governance in India. Hence BR Ambedkar mentioned:

> According to the principles of the new Constitution, he (governor) is required to follow the advice of his Ministry in all matters. Having regard to this fact it was felt whether it was desirable to impose upon the electorate the obligation to enter upon an electoral process which would cost a lot of time, a lot of trouble and . . . a lot of money as well. It was also felt that nobody, knowing full well what powers he is likely to have under the Constitution, would come forth to contest an election. [Given the fact that] the powers of the Governor were so limited, so nominal, his position so ornamental, that probably very few would come forward to stand for election.[20]

Concurring with his colleagues, Ambedkar made a powerful argument for nominating the governor, and not for the election which he justified by reference to equally persuasive pragmatic arguments. As he felt, the lack of substantial power and authority was probably a serious factor in discouraging many from contesting election; so the demand for election had its serious limitation. In his words, in view of the governor being essentially an ornamental functionary, 'how he comes into being, whether by nomination or by election is purely an academic question . . . which should not bother the members in the Assembly'.[21] What was critical to him was to decide the nature of authority that the governor held. In other words, what power and authority the governor was expected to have to meaningfully discharge his/her responsibility as a constitutional head of the province. Besides being a conscience keeper in the province, the governor was also responsible to see that the constitutional values and principles were upheld in governance. The ministry was thus not entirely independent, it had to work along with the governor within the well-defined constitutional framework.

Gubernatorial Power and Authority: Constitutional Provisions

The issue was amply discussed in the Constituent Assembly. At the end of the debate on this, it was BR Ambedkar who most clearly summarized the discussion by identifying the duties that the governor was expected to discharge which should, he felt, commensurate with the power and authority that he/she needed to have. In his speech before the Assembly on 2 June 1949, he submitted that the duties of the governor

> may be classified into two parts: one is that he has to retain the Ministry in office. Because the Ministry is to hold office during his pleasure, he has to see whether and when he should exercise

[20] BR Ambedkar, 31 May 1949, *Constituent Assembly Debates*, Book No. 3, pp. 467–68.
[21] Ibid., pp. 468–69.

> his pleasure against the Ministry. The second duty which the Governor has, and must have, is to advise the Ministry, to warm the Ministry, to suggest to the Ministry an alternative and to ask for reconsideration of decisions which are not constitution-driven.[22]

Both these duties are interrelated: while the former entrusts the governor with the duty to act as a guardian of the ministry in power the latter makes him/her the custodian of the Constitution in the province. On the whole, the governor represents an epitome of constitutional, moral and ethical values which are considered integral to 'perfect' governance. It was explicit when Ambedkar further argued:

> It is in the name of the people that he carried on the administration; he must see that administration is carried on a level which may be regarded as good, efficient [and] honest administration. Therefore having regard to these [above] two duties which the Governor has namely, to see that the administration is kept pure, without corruption, impartial and that the proposals enunciated by the Ministry are not contrary to the wishes of the people.[23]

The crux of the argument that Ambedkar pursued relates to two basic qualities that a governor should have: besides being eminent and morally incorruptible, he/she should possess the capacity to carry the province with him/her in accordance with constitutional stipulations. On the basis of elaborate discussions in the Assembly, the 1950 Constitution incorporated eleven provisions (Articles 152–162) in Part VI of the Constitution. The governor holds executive power. As Article 154 states, 'The executive power of the State shall be vested in the Governor and shall be exercised by him either directly or indirectly through officers subordinate to him in accordance with this Constitution'. In discharging his/her executive power, the governor is authorized to appoint his/her Council of Ministers, the Advocate-General of the state and members of the Public Service Commission; they hold the office during his/her pleasure though he cannot remove them without the concurrence of the President of India. As regards the legislative powers, the governor is a part of the State Legislature (Article 164) just as the President of India is a part of Parliament. He/she has a right of addressing and sending messages, and summoning, proroguing and dissolving the legislature, as is true of the President of India who is also constitutionally authorized to undertake these functions. He has the authority to ask the state government to place the annual financial statement (budget) in the state assembly and also to recommend money bills. The governor has judicial powers to grant pardons, reprieves, respites or remission of punishment or suspend, remit or commute the sentences of any person convicted of any offence against any law with regard to any matter within the state's jurisdiction (Article 161). Finally, the governor also holds authority when an emergency (Part XVIII) is proclaimed. A governor is authorized to send a report on the basis of which the President is allowed to exercise authority in the state; in that case, the governor acts on behalf of the President. The Constitution stipulates that even during Emergency, the governor does not possess absolute authority; he/she is authorized to discharge the responsibility according to the presidential directives.

The Constitution does not sanction 'discretionary power'; a governor has to abide by the constitutional stipulations. The Assembly, after having extensively debated on this, came to the conclusion that 'the governor is not, at all, vested with any discretion'[24]; or, as Ambedkar suggested, 'there was no room

[22] BR Ambedkar, 2 June 1949, *Constituent Assembly Debates*, Book No. 3, p. 546.

[23] BR Ambedkar, 31 May 1949, *Constituent Assembly Debates*, Book No. 3, p. 546.

[24] TT Krishnamachari (Madras), 1 August 1949, *Constituent Assembly Debates*, Book No. 4, p. 61.

for the Governor acting on discretion'.[25] This means that the governor lacks the discretionary authority that the President has vis-à-vis his /her Council of Ministers, although at the outset a separate schedule (Schedule IV) was suggested to govern the relationship between the President and governors and the ministers. It was, however, justified that in independent India

> it has now been felt that the matter should be left entirely to convention rather than to be put into the body of the Constitution as a Schedule in the shape of an Instrument of Instructions, and there is fairly large a volume of opinion which favours that idea.... [A separate Schedule], it now felt to be entirely unnecessary and superfluous to give such directions in the Constitution which really should arise out of the convention that grow up from time to time and the President and the Governors in their respective spheres will be guided by these conventions.[26]

The idea thus became redundant in the changed politico-ideological environment following India's Independence. There should not be a manual to instruct how the President or the governor should behave in relation to their Council of Ministers. The Instrument of Instructions were devised by the colonial rulers to give certain directions to the head of the states as to how they should exercise their discretionary powers that were vested in them. With Independence, a new system of governance had emerged in which the need for discretions had disappeared.

> It was therefore felt that ... they are useless and can serve no particular purpose; ... they are useless and it is not desirable to have such Instrument of Instructions which really can be effective in a different set of circumstances which can by no stretch of imagination be deemed to exist after the new Constitution comes into existence.[27]

In legal–constitutional terms, the withdrawal of the Instrument of Instruction is a significant development, for it re-established constitutional democracy in its spirit and substance. The nominated governor has no discretionary authority. That he/she is a constitutional head is established beyond doubt by according primacy to the council of ministers comprising the elected representatives. In order to ascertain that the governor is constitutionally subservient to the ministry in the provinces, the Constitution leaves no space for uncertainty by suggesting that the governor (a) is appointed by the President in consultation with the Union Council of Ministers and (b) holds the office during the pleasure of the President (Article 156). What it means is that the President can remove a governor if he/she so desires and is also a competent authority as far as the appointment of a governor is concerned. These are constitutional restrictions on the governor who does not wield absolute authority in governance in the provinces; he/she has to work within the constitutional parameters that have been very clearly stipulated. These constitutional restrictions are useful but may not be adequate if 'a bad person becomes a governor ... he can do a great deal of mischief, in spite of the very little power given to him under the Constitution'.[28] So, in the ultimate analysis, what matters is the individual quality of being sensitive and respectful to the fundamental ethos of constitutional democracy, and only then the foundation of a democratic State will be strong and stable.

---

[25] BR Ambedkar, 30 July 1949, *Constituent Assembly Debates*, Book No. 4, p. 41.
[26] TT Krishnamachari (Madras), 11 October 1949, *Constituent Assembly Debates*, Book No. 5, p. 114.
[27] BR Ambedkar, 11 October 1949, *Constituent Assembly Debates*, Book No. 5, pp. 115–16.
[28] BG Kher (Bombay), 30 May 1949, *Constituent Assembly Debates*, Book No. 3, p. 435.

Gubernatorial Independence

As argued previously, the governor is not an independent functionary despite having been identified as a constitutional authority. The reasons are not difficult to seek: as per Articles in Part VI of the Constitution, he/she owes the appointment to the President and continues in office as long as the President desires. The very process of the appointment and continuity of a governor put obvious restrictions on the nature of the assignment; he/she cannot be independent, at all. Hence, governors were identified as 'the errand boys of Prime Minister'[29] or '*chaprasis* (servants) of the Home Ministry'[30] who always remained at the beck and call of their political masters. This is, therefore, an age-old phenomenon: as they owe their position to the Union Government, it is but natural that the governors will invariably act as agents of the Union Government by being its 'eyes and ears'. This was most vivid when an Emergency is proclaimed according to Article 352 and 356 during the two-year period between 1975 and 1977. The Union Government acted havoc in almost all the Indian provinces by operating through the governors who were appointed largely because of their expressed loyalty to the incumbent Indira Gandhi-led Congress government. The Shah Commission that came into being in 1977 to probe into the excesses during the 1975–77 Emergency illustrated the contention by referring to 'the abuse' of constitutional authority by many governors. It was, therefore, not surprising that the appointment of governors received adequate attention when the Sarkaria Commission was appointed to review Centre–State relations in 1983 and suggested changes within the framework of the Constitution of India. With regard to the appointment of governor, the Commission prescribed 'effective consultation between the Union Government and the chief ministers of the provinces' before choosing a governor. Besides arguing this, the Commission further recommended that a governor should be eminent in any field of human betterment, should be from outside the state of his/her appointment, should not be 'not too intimately connected with its politics', and had not taken 'too great a part in politics generally'. It was also suggested that a politician of the party in power in New Delhi should not be appointed as a governor to a state, governed by another party. The Commission felt that one of the major reasons for governors being subservient to the Union Government was the absence of a fixed tenure for the office. In a very revealing manner, the Commission thus described its take on the issue:

> The ever-present possibility of the tenure being terminated before the full term of five years can create considerable insecurity in the mind of the governor and impair his (*sic*) capacity to withstand pressures, resist extraneous influences and act impartially in the discharge of its discretionary functions.[31]

Hence it strongly recommended that a governor should have a fixed tenure and should not be replaced except for extremely compelling reasons, and without the concurrence of both the Houses of Parliament. The servility of those holding a gubernatorial post was attributed, by the Commission, to their greed for another office of profit under the Union or state government. The Commission thus suggested that unless this possibility was completely foreclosed, no constitutional design for securing governor's independence was likely to succeed.

---

[29] M Ruthanaswamy, 'Errand Boys of Prime Minister', *The Times of India*, New Delhi, 26 February 1970.

[30] Piloo Mody, 'Chaprasis of the Home Ministry', *The Statesman*, New Delhi, 27 March 1974.

[31] *The Report of the Commission on Centre–State Relations* (also known as the Sarkaria Commission as the Commission was headed by Justice Ranjit Singh Sarkaria, a retired jurist of the Supreme Court of India), Vol. 1 (Delhi: Government of India Press, 1988), p. 125.

Summarizing the Argument

The structure of governance that the 1950 Constitution sought to build did not seem to be different from the one that evolved out of the 1935 Government of India Act. The similarity ends there since the governor in the Constitution for independent India does not hold any substantial authority, like his/her counterpart under the British suzerainty had held. Constitutionally, the governor is a titular head of the province with mere ceremonial powers and authority; the chief minister and the council of minister are the de facto ruler of the province while the governor is a de jure head of the provincial administration. For good reasons, the Constituent Assembly favoured the arguments for governors being a figure head to avoid unnecessary complications in governance. Even the Congress Working Committee that dealt with the issue before it was placed for deliberations in the Assembly also endorsed the idea that a constitutionally strong governor was likely to be stumble block in constitutionalizing governance. There was a consensus among the members who found the idea congruent with what they fought for in colonial India. The outcome was the articulation of the provisions in Part VI of the Constitution which supported the concern by diluting the gubernatorial authority to a substantial degree.

By clipping the wings of the governor, the 1950 Constitution provided solid foundation to democratic–federal governance in India. As shown previously, the founding fathers did not support election of the governor since it would contribute to the creation of a parallel power centre in the provinces, which would be unwarranted since it was already accepted that only the elected representatives from within the province were to govern. The method did not seem persuasive in view of the obvious complications in governance with the presence of an elected governor. But, as a constitutional head of the province, the importance of a governor was always emphasized. By being a bridge between the Union and the provinces, the governor was considered to be a significant agency in federal governance; not only does a governor act as a custodian of constitutional values and principles, he/she will also be useful in sustaining the administrative link with the Union on behalf of the provinces which is relatively easier for him/her, under normal circumstances, given the prerogative of the former in choosing someone as a governor.

As per the Constitution, a governor is merely a ceremonial head to the extent of being 'a little more than a puppet controlled by chief minister, on the one hand, and by the President, that is to say, virtually by the Prime Minister on the other'.[32] This was the point that the Sarkaria Commission (1988) raised while reviewing the Centre–State relations in India. The issue, however, remains unresolved since the system of nomination continues to govern the selection of governor in India. Nonetheless, the description of the governor being a puppet for reasons explained earlier has triggered a new debate in India's constitutional discourses, which may lead us to reconceptualize the role of governors in India's constitutional democracy differently.

Concluding Observations

Governor is a constitutional functionary; Part VI of the Constitution earmarks a specific domain for the office of governor. The language is explicit: the governor is just a titular head. A careful reading of the provisions indicates that there are grey areas in the provisions which can be interpreted differently.

---

[32] HV Kamath, 'Should the Office of Governor be Abolished?' *The Illustrated Weekly of India*, 18 August 1957, p. 27.

In normal circumstances, a governor is constitutionally obliged to discharge his/her role within the boundaries, set out by the Constitution which means that he/she will merely be a signatory authority of the decisions that the state chief minister adopts in consultation with his/her council of ministers. This further entails that a governor is just a rubber stamp who hardly has an independence as far as governance is concerned. Similarly, when the state assembly is in suspended animation or dissolved or when an emergency is proclaimed, the governor has to work in accordance with the direction of the President, à la, the Union Government, led by the Prime Minister. Here, too, the governor is a mere post office acting without being independent. This is how the role of the governor is conceptualized in the 1950 Constitution. The Supreme Court, however, gave a respite to governors by endorsing that they cannot be dismissed without providing solid arguments and reasons in a writ petition, filed as a public interest litigation in the wake of the removal of the governors of the states of Uttar Pradesh, Gujarat, Haryana and Goa on 2 July 2004 by the President of India on the advice of the Union Council of Ministers. In the oft-quoted 2010 *BP Singhal v. the Union of India* case, the apex judicial authority in India categorically endorsed that the power to remove a governor under Article 156(1)

> cannot be exercised in an arbitrary, capricious or unreasonable manner. The power will have to be exercised in rare and exceptional circumstances for valid and compelling reasons. … What would be compelling reasons would depend upon the facts and circumstances of each case.[33]

The court also clarified the doctrine of pleasure that needed to be interpreted in the democracy was governed by rule of law where arbitrariness in any form was eschewed and no government or authority had the right to do what it pleased. The concern was to restrict the application of constitutional authority by other governmental functionaries on whimsical grounds. It was also a source of irritation for the judiciary, which was drawn to the idea that the constitutional provisions were being misused to pursue partisan agenda. Hence, by clearly articulating the doctrine of pleasure, the apex court underlines that it

> does not mean a licence to act arbitrarily, capriciously or whimsically. It is presumed that discretionary powers conferred in absolute and unfettered terms on any public authority will necessarily and obviously be exercised reasonably and for public good.[34]

Being the occupant of a constitutional office with important constitutional functions and duties, the governor should be given independence to act as per what he deems appropriate in accordance with the constitutional stipulations. This concern was raised in the Constituent Assembly by KT Shah of Bihar as follows:

> We must not leave the Governor to be entirely at the mercy or the pleasure of the President; while he (*sic*) is acting correctly, in accordance with the Constitution following the advice of his ministers, he should not be at the mercy of the President who is away from the Province and who is a national and not a local authority.[35]

---

[33] *BP Singhal v. the Union of India*, 2010. https://indiankanoon.org/doc/1471968/ (accessed 22 December 2016).

[34] Ibid.

[35] KT Shah (Bihar), 31 May 1949, *Constituent Assembly Debates*, Book No. 3, p. 471.

On the basis of a thorough probing of the relevant constitutional provisions by reference to the political processes, the Court also concluded that 'a governor cannot be removed on the ground that he is not in sync or refuses to act as an agent of the party in power at the Centre'.[36] The 2010 judicial pronouncement reinvents the governor's position in India's constitutional framework: it is now established beyond doubt that the governor is not, at all, a stooge of the Union Government which cannot dismiss him/her in case there exists a serious and unresolvable differences, if not dispute, that cannot be sorted out within the constitutional references. In view of the judicial clarification that the authority to remove a governor needs to be exercised sparingly, the judiciary appears to have been influenced by the 1983 Sarkaria Commission which expressed a serious concern at the numerous instances of unceremonious dethroning of governors by the Union Government for fulfilling narrow ideological aims.

In federal India, the role of a governor cannot, at all, be dispensed with. Besides constitutional functions, being largely ceremonial, a governor also represents the state in which he holds the gubernatorial post. While discharging the constitutional obligations, he/she can provide leadership in areas that may not have received adequate attention in the current political dispensation. What it means is that he/she can act as a statesman seeking to chart out a different course of action for the state to pursue. This was perhaps the reason as to why the 1988 Sarkaria Report emphasized that a governor needed to be selected from among the eminent persons from any walks of life. Whether it can be followed without being diluted is a difficult question to respond, since gubernatorial appointment cannot be totally insulated from the political calculations, as the past has shown. What it confirms is a fundamental theoretical predisposition in contemporary political processes, namely, being a politico-constitutional agency, a governor cannot be entirely 'neutral' or 'free' from the prevalent socio-economic compulsions. In other words, the existing power relationship shall remain pre-eminent and critical in shaping the institutions of governance. This is simply unavoidable if one seeks to understand politics as reflective and also dependent on the on-going politico-ideological churnings. Therefore, the role of a governor has to be understood in keeping with the prevalent socio-economic and political context in which he/she discharges the responsibility. Only then, a near objective assessment of the institution of governor in the Indian context is possible.

Review Questions

1. **The governor represents a continuity of the colonial system of governance. Do you agree with this? Elaborate your response.**
2. **Why did the founding fathers justify the office of governor despite its clear colonial roots? Elaborate your view.**
3. **Critically evaluate the relevant constitutional provisions relating to the governor.**
4. **The governor can never be independent in India's constitutional structure. Do you agree with this? Elaborate.**
5. **In what ways the office of the governor can be a blotch to India's federalism? Elaborate your views.**
6. **The governor is a critical player capable of creating and maintaining a healthy federalism in India. How do you justify the contention? Elaborate your response.**
7. **What are the major recommendations of the 1988 Sarkaria Commission relating to governor? Elaborate your response.**

[36] *BP Singhal v. the Union of India*, 2010.

8. **The office of the governor is a political one. Do you endorse this view? Elaborate your answer.**
9. **In federal India, the role of a governor cannot, at all, be dispensed with. How do you justify the argument? Elaborate your response.**
10. **In India's constitutional democracy, a governor is neither a titular head of the province nor an effective administrative agency. Do you agree with this assumption? Elaborate your response.**

Chapter 21

Local Governance in India

Learning Objectives

- To understand local government as a phenomenon
- To comprehend the historical evolution of local government in India with reference to India's colonial past and its aftermath
- To evaluate the latest constitutional amendments relating to local government in India

Localizing governance is a critical area of discussion following the consolidation of neoliberal ethos and values, especially in the domain of public policy. The State has become 'an enabler' and not 'a doer'—an assumption which not only has altered our perception of the State but also made the State subservient to other actors, involved in the delivery of public services. Whether this is good or bad is debatable, though it has contributed to a situation in which local governance has gained tremendous attention not only from the analysts but also from the practitioners of governance. There are now concerted endeavours to understand the phenomenon in the changed contexts. It is, therefore, not surprising that the panchayati raj governance has acquired salience not only among the policy makers but also among those who always felt that India's salvation lies in regenerating this system of governance. Inspired by Gandhi, the Gandhians argued strongly in favour of making the villages as the unit of governance in opposition to those who insisted on making the individual as primary. As is well-known, the 1950 Constitution did not favour the Gandhians and local governance lost the importance that it deserved. The scene had, however, undergone a sea-change, especially in the wake of the consolidation of globalizing neoliberal trends. The outcome was the adoption of the Seventy-Third and Seventy-Fourth Amendment Acts in 1992 to revitalize local governance in rural and urban areas, respectively. A revolutionary step undoubtedly, these Acts are a watershed in our understanding of governance and its articulation; in conceptual terms, the Seventy-Third and Seventy-Fourth Amendment Acts have also created an identifiable space for arguments questioning the Weberian format of governance supportive of pyramidal structure of bureaucracy. With an in-depth analysis of local governance in India that had emerged with the adoption of the aforementioned Amendment Acts, this chapter seeks to make two major arguments: first, localizing governance is a definite step towards revitalizing a system of governance that has roots in India's traditional system of governance, as the available literature illustrates. As the texts that Gandhi left for posterity amply show, the panchayati raj governance is perhaps one of those mechanisms which will ensure efficiency and also make governance inclusive by being open to the demos regardless of socio-economic and cultural differences. The second argument strives to conceptualize the apparent theoretical weaknesses of the theoretical format that Max Weber, designed in the light of the growing dissatisfaction of a hierarchical and centralized form of administration. With the consolidation of the image of bureaucracy being 'a rent-seeking organization', the idea gains ground that it is no longer 'a benevolent guardian of society', as Jeremy Bentham had suggested. In such a context, the arguments supportive of decentering of administration by revamping institutions of grassroots governance appear to be far more persuasive than in the past. The concern here is to conceptually capture the theoretical preferences in conjunction with the contextual necessity for redrawing the theoretical premises independent of the Weberian model of the ideal form of organization.

Debates in the Constituent Assembly

Two important ideas of participatory democracy and localizing governance seem to have shaped the tenor of the arguments that the Constituent Assembly members offered. At one level, there were hardly disagreements because the Assembly members were unanimous in their support for participatory democracy. Adult suffrage was thus readily accepted. At another level, dissension surfaced when a group of Assembly members, especially the Gandhians, insisted on making the villages as the basic units of governance. While seeking to substantiate their points of view, they drew on Mahatma's notion on village swaraj. They were persuaded to believe that with villages being the basic units of administration, the State could not only be well-equipped to discharge its responsibility efficiently, but also enable the people to get connected with others by virtue of being integral to the oceanic circle. Organically linked, such an administrative set-up would create an environment of mutual give-and-take which would ensure and also strengthen, on the one hand, the communal bond among the villagers and also, on the other hand, make the State accountable, given the powerful voice that the villagers would generate by virtue of being united. This was also a model of social engineering since through intensive social interaction most of the forces alienating one community from another were likely to lose steams in course of time. It was, therefore, not odd when L Krishnaswami Bharati of Madras expressed his sentimental attachment with Gandhi's belief by exhorting that

> in my opinion, it is very necessary that this sovereign body [Constituent Assembly] should enunciate and give its views on the fundamental tenet of Mahatma Gandhi, his idea being that there must be decentralization and the village must function as an economic unit [because] ... India dies if villages die, India can live only if the villages live.[1]

As argued, Ambedkar, the chairman of the Drafting Committee, did not seem persuaded by this argument because of the prevalence of caste-brutality in villages which he suffered himself all through his life. He thus felt that the arguments in favour of making villages as basic units of governance were supportive of the continuity of the rigid caste system which was simply not acceptable in democratic India. Condemning the villages 'as dens of ignorance, brutality and oppression', Ambedkar took up the cudgels against the Gandhians who marshalled arguments in its favour. Besides his unhappy past when he witnessed the brutal manifestation of caste bias, the influence of John Dewey, his teacher at Columbia University, cannot be

[1] CA Debates, Vol. VII, 4/11/1948 – 8/1/1949, p. 527, L Krishnaswami Bharathi, 22/11/1948.

ignored. It was Dewey who persuaded him to believe that individual-centric liberalism was an effective instrument to combat social prejudices.[2]

That the Assembly members arrived at a consensus on the inclusion of what later became Article 40 in Part IV of the 1950 Constitution of India is also a testimony to their wider concern of democratizing governance by making the villages as units of administration. It is true that the Gandhians lost and individuals became the basic units of governance, as Ambedkar preferred. Nevertheless, the founding fathers left a space for these Gandhian ideas to strike roots by incorporating Article 40 in the final document. Here, the Assembly members seem to have been unanimous in their perception because they were aware that the Constitution, in order to remain relevant in the days to come, needed to be accommodative of newer demands to sustain being democratic and inclusive in its character. Jawaharlal Nehru expressed this sentiment most explicitly when he exhorted his colleagues to remain united for protecting 'the basic democratic nature' of the Constitution. As he unambiguously stated:

> So far as the basic nature of the Constitution is concerned, it must deal with the fundamental aspects of the political, the social, the economic and other spheres, and not with the details which are matters for legislation. You will find if you go into too great detail and mix up the really basic and fundamental things with the important but nevertheless secondary things, you bring the basic things to the level of secondary things too. You lose them in forest of detail. The great trees that you should like to plant and wait for them to grow and to be seen are hidden in a forest of detail and smaller trees.[3]

This was a clearly stated position that Nehru held while endorsing the fundamental values that the Constitution of India sought to achieve. He left the space open for future generations to work on the details to accomplish the constitutional goals that the founding father had preferred. As a living organism, the Constitution needed to be responsive, which he articulated as follows:

> A Constitution is something which should last a long time, which is built on a strong foundation, and which may, of course, be varied from time to time–it should not be rigid–nevertheless, one should think of it as something which is going to last, which is not a transitory Constitution, a provisional Constitution, a something which you are going to change from day to day, a something which provisions for the next year or the year after next and so on and so forth.[4]

The idea is very clear. Nehru tackled the dissension at two levels: at one level, by referring to the basic nature of the Constitution, he upheld the importance of fundamental constitutional ideals which remained sacrosanct even in the years to come. The nationalist movement was directed to achieve democratic form of governance to articulate popular aspirations. Seeking to involve people in governance, the Constitution makers remained committed to this ideal which was never compromised. At another level, he allowed the future generations to accommodate the newer popular aspirations to sustain participatory democracy that the founding fathers so assiduously sought to build at the dawn of India's rise as an independent polity. Futuristic in his vision, Nehru can thus be said to have laid the foundation of a system of governance that

[2] I have pursued this argument in my 'BR Ambedkar and the History of Constitutionalizing India', *Contemporary South Asia* (New Delhi: Taylor and Francis, forthcoming).

[3] CA Debates, Vol. VII, 4/11/1948 – 8/1/1949, p. 589, J Nehru, 25/11/1948.

[4] CA Debates, Vol. VII, 4/11/1948 – 8/1/1949, p. 589, J Nehru, 25/11/1948.

was rooted in his urge for participatory democracy. In other words, he might have endorsed what Ambedkar stood for in the Assembly debates by supporting the liberal faith in individualism though he prepared the ground for decentralization of authority by insisting on the basic nature of the Constitution. Implicit in his argument was the idea that democracy needed to be reinvented to retain its vitality; otherwise, it would become a mere structure of governance without much substance.

There are two fundamental points that are critical in conceptualizing the processes that finally culminated in localizing governance in independent India. First, the idea that government needed to be de-centred, which was mooted during the early years of colonialism, had begun unfolding with the intervention of those colonial rulers who believed in participatory democracy in its most rudimentary form. It was perhaps a strategic decision on the part of the British, nonetheless, though it triggered those forces which, in course of time, contributed to and also consolidated nationalist aspirations for change. As various colonial legislations illustrate, attempts were regularly made to localize governance which, despite having benefitted the British government by creating an interface between the ruled with the ruler, also made the people at the grassroots realize their importance as stakeholders of the system; the idea that they were significant in governance was what prepared them to shoulder bigger responsibility if need arose. Second, a perusal of the past initiatives show that efforts towards localizing governance appeared to have been ingrained in the processes towards constitutionalizing India. The very idea of 'detached administration' (entailing independence of each layers of administration with an identical politico-ideological goal) that the British government upheld seems to have significantly altered the complexion of local government by creating a space for the local populace to take part in the decision making at the grassroots. A remarkable feat which gradually transformed the texture of governance since it allowed the local voice to get articulated and heard, which was a meaningful step as far as localizing governance was concerned. There were challenges notwithstanding, the voice became stronger with the passage of days, and, in independent India, as the chapter shows, the panchayati raj governance (with its conceptual roots in Gandhian village republics) fulfilled the aspirations that the Gandhians in the Constituent Assembly so effusively expressed when they argued strongly for Gandhi's village swaraj. The issues that the Assembly members had raised during the debates thus remain very useful in conceptualizing the common urge for de-centring and also decentralizing governance—an urge that gradually became not only sources of radical constitutional transformations at the grassroots governance but also provoked socio-ideological movements for democratic and participatory governance.

Early Efforts

In tune with the provisions of the Directive Principles of State Policy suggesting the establishment of village panchayats as units of self-government, an ambitious plan for rejuvenating rural society, the Community Development Programme (CDP) was undertaken in 1952. The primary aim of the CDP was to secure socio-economic transformation of village life through people's own democratic and cooperative organizations with the government giving technical services, supply and credit. The main thrust of the programme is to make a community self-reliant by utilizing its internal resources and the State provides the necessary support as and when it is needed. The CDP initiatives were supplemented in 1953 by the creation of National Extension Service (NES) which aimed at transferring scientific and technical knowledge to agricultural, animal husbandry and rural craft sectors. The objective was to support the innovative pilot projects that the government devised for rural development. Run by government functionaries, the NES also created new zeal among the villagers who got drawn to this when the project was launched. The CDP and NES were important pillars in India's journey towards localizing governance.

By 1956, it was accepted that village panchayats should be made the focal point of local governance; in course of time, these elected bodies should take over, it was further emphasized, the entire general administration and development of the districts excluding functions such as law and order, administration of justice and selected administrative responsibilities pertaining to revenue administration. Such a governmental initiative led to the appointment of the Balwant Rai Mehta Committee in 1957 to translate the idea into a reality. Though the committee was constituted to assess the community development initiatives and to recommend improvement measures thereon, the findings, however, suggested the necessity of strengthening of panchayats for institutionalizing community participation in CDP because the Committee found that it created enthusiasm among the villagers to participate in activities pertaining to community development. One of the constraints, as the Committee noted, was largely due to the ad hoc nature of those bodies responsible to manage CDP and NES programmes. Since these bodies were largely nominated, the villagers were hardly forthcoming when they undertook activities for development, which means that they failed to generate enough enthusiasm for the programmes among the stakeholders. Hence, the Committee lamented by saying:

> So long as we do not discover or create a representative and democratic institution which will supply the local interest, supervision and care necessary to ensure that expenditure of money upon local objects conforms with the needs and wishes of the locality . . . we will never be able to evoke local interest and excite local initiative in the field of development.[5]

Aware of the weaknesses of the earlier efforts, the Committee thus insisted on creating statutory bodies, which were to be endowed with necessary executive powers and adequate resources. In order to make these bodies 'an instrument of expression of local people's will in regard to the local development',[6] the Committee came out strongly against government interference, which hampered the growth and consolidation of the spirit towards democratizing governance at the grassroots. Instead of supporting delegation of power, the Committee was categorical in its preference for decentralization in its true sense. It was further underlined that decentralization was 'a process whereby the Government divests itself completely of certain duties and responsibilities and devolves them on to some other authority [and] . . . devolution of responsibility cannot be completed without a complete devolution of all the control over the necessary resources'.[7] The committee had recommended a three-tier system of rural local government, i.e., village panchayats at the village level, the panchayat samiti at the intermediate level and Zilla Parishad at the district level, with panchayats samitis being the most effective body. Essential for democratic decentralization, this structure, the Committee felt, 'can alone lead to effective rural development'.[8]

Efforts towards streamlining the instruments of local governance were again undertaken in 1977 when the Ashok Mehta Committee was appointed. In its report, which was submitted in 1978, the Committee reiterated the argument made by its predecessor, the Balwant Rai Committee, by saying that panchayati raj should emerge as 'a system of democratic local government discharging developmental, municipal and

---

[5] *Panchayati Raj: Concept and Approach* (Report of the Balwant Rai Mehta Committee, 1957), reproduced in P Satyanarayana, *Towards New Panchayati Raj: Critical Perspectives on the Reorganization of Rural Local Government* (New Delhi: Uppal Publishing House, 1990), p. 139.

[6] *Panchayati Raj: Concept and Approach*, p. 141.

[7] *Panchayati Raj: Concept and Approach*, p. 141.

[8] *Panchayati Raj: Concept and Approach*, p. 158.

ultimately regulatory functions'.[9] The Committee was persuaded to believe that in order for democratic devolutionary decentralization to strike roots in governance, an appropriate organizational structure needed to be put in place which would not only create a space for the stakeholders' participation but also a device to undertake administrative measures which appeared to be attentive to their needs. The main aim was to design a system of governance to bring about development in rural areas. With the involvement of the people, the panchayats would therefore become empowering instruments which would work for them in accordance with their priorities. Despite being optimistic, the Committee was appalled, given the failure of available panchayat institutions to become meaningful institutions of governance due to a wide range of factors, including the deliberate negligence of those holding power. It was evident when the Committee stated:

> The activities of PRIs [panchayati raj institutions] were meagre, their resource base weak and the overall attention given to them niggardly. The functioning of the Panchayati Raj system thus became discouraging. As if this was not enough, some of the State Governments would postpone holding of elections or supersede some of the important tiers of PRIs for one reason or the other. The lukewarm attitude of the political elite at higher levels towards strengthening of the democratic process at the grassroots was generally the crux of the matter. Of particular significance in this connection is the relative cooling off of enthusiasm of [Members of Parliament] and [Members of Legislative Assemblies] in State towards Panchayati Raj, because they would perceive a threat in emerging Panchayati Raj leadership to their position in their respective constituencies. In the ultimate analysis, all this led to a weakening of political support to PRIs and of the administrative will to work through them.[10]

Born out of the mass euphoria for democracy following the electoral defeat of the Congress Party in the aftermath of the 1975–77 Emergency that established Indira Gandhi's constitutional authoritarianism,[11] the Ashok Mehta Committee recommendations were a class apart for three important reasons: first, reiterating the importance of basic democratic values in governance, this 1978 Report was a powerful statement re-establishing that democracy being organic to India as a nation could never be compromised. By recommending democratically elected local bodies at the grassroots, the Mehta Committee translated the popular urge for democracy into a reality. Second, the Mehta Report also re-emphasized the Gandhian arguments for village swaraj as perhaps the only means to democratize administration and to make Indian villages inclusive in the real sense of the term. An idea that the Gandhi-followers pursued in the Constituent Assembly finally gained acceptance as integral to policy making, which did not receive as much attention in the past as was expected. Finally, the Mehta Report was a giant step because it (a) put a system of democratic governance at the sub-state level by devising specific mechanisms and (b) sought to create an environment in which democracy was to emerge as inevitable. As the following discussion will show, in the light of its contribution to participatory democracy, the Mehta recommendations can be said to have ushered in a new era in governance in India.

---

[9] *Local Governance: An Inspiring Journey into the Future* (Sixth Report of Second Administrative Reforms Commission), October 2007, p. 5.

[10] *Panchayati Raj: Review and Evaluation* (Report of the Ashok Mehta Committee, 1978), reproduced in P Satyanarayana, *Towards New Panchayati Raj*, pp.165–66.

[11] I have dealt with the nature and adverse consequences of Emergency (1975–77) in my *Ethics in Governance in India* (Oxford, UK: Routledge, 2016), chapter 5, pp. 129–38.

The 1978 Mehta Committee did not seem to have had the impact on the policy makers that it had anticipated, presumably because panchayati raj institutions (PRIs) lacked justiciability by virtue of being part of non-enforceable segment of the Constitution of India. The issue was addressed again in 1985 when another committee—GVK Rao Committee—was appointed to suggest how to re-galvanize grassroots democracy. According to the Rao Committee, the key to effective and meaningful rural development was the revitalization of the PRIs that hardly received adequate attention in India's policy making. It was also noticed that the stakeholders had no voice as far as planning for rural areas was concerned. Like the earlier committees, the Rao Committee expressed the same concern by saying that unless the PRIs were revamped, the basic objective of participatory democracy would remain distant. Unlike the committees of the past, the 1986 LM Singhvi Committee accepted Gandhi's model of panchayati raj as a reference point since it was potentially useful to rejuvenate rural India, which needed immediate attention to ensure national well-being. At the outset, while elaborating its conceptual foundation of the recommendations that were to follow, the Committee underlined three important ideas[12]: (a) panchayati raj institutions as basic units of self-government; (b) Indian villages and Gram Sabhas (village panchayats) as the republican base of India as a democratic nation; and (c) Gram Sabha as the embodiment of direct democracy. Drawn on its commitment to revitalize the PRIs as instruments for localizing governance, they held the view that 'villages may be reorganized and many of them may in process be groups and enlarged in order to make for viable village panchayats and enlarged villages should continue to be the primary and homogeneous units of self-government with a measure of direct democracy'.[13] Critical of bureaucratic intervention in planning for rural development, the Committee strongly argued that 'bureaucratic structure and mechanical devolution of power cannot achieve people's participation in a meaningful manner'.[14] Hence the PRIs should be, the Committee further underlined, 'organized as part of the process of democratic decentralization for building up the institutional edifice from the grassroots upwards and not as a gift of devolutionary processes'.[15] For the Committee, the panchayat system was not merely a structure of governance, but a definite mechanism for realizing participatory democracy in its true spirit. This was evident when it had emphasized that 'the operational dynamics of panchayati raj should be directed to achieve community and social mobilization, transcending the barriers of caste, religion, sex and disparities of wealth and surmounting social disabilities and disadvantages'.[16]

Given the critical importance of the 1992 Amendment in establishing the PRIs as effective instruments for localizing governance, this chapter is directed to comprehend its nature and consequences along with the context in which it became more or less fait accompli in the light of growing democratization across the length and breadth of India. In order to bring government closer to the people, the Congress leadership, which held power during the period from 1984 to 1989, introduced the Sixty-Fourth Amendment Act in 1989, which was defeated in Parliament due to some technical snags. Nonetheless, the idea was highly appreciated and, in 1992, the bill was approved and made a law by the Congress-led government following the acceptance of the content of the Sixty-Fourth Amendment Act, which became Seventy-Third Amendment Act.

---

[12] *Revitalization of PRIs for Democracy and Development* (Report of the LM Singhvi Committee, 1986), reproduced in P Satyanarayana, *Towards New Panchayati Raj*, p. 220.

[13] *Revitalization of PRIs for Democracy and Development*, p. 221.

[14] *Revitalization of PRIs for Democracy and Development*, p. 222.

[15] *Revitalization of PRIs for Democracy and Development*, p. 222.

[16] *Revitalization of PRIs for Democracy and Development*, p. 222.

Conceptually, the entire exercise was directed to redesign governance by insisting simultaneously on localization, externalization and de-bureaucratization.[17] With the devolution of power at the grassroots, the PRIs would automatically become de facto authorities with adequate constitutional protection for their functions. The instant outcome of this process was the flow of power from the top to the bottom where actual decisions were executed. It was an attempt to establish an intimate relationship between the administrators and the recipients who so far remain peripheral in decision making. This is a reiteration of the Gandhian notion of participatory democracy, which Gandhi had articulated through the concepts of *swaraj* (self-government) and *swadeshi* (community's control over resources) and by invoking the imagery of the village republic (*gram swaraj*) as representing India's democratic tradition.[18] Localization was, therefore, a significant process with far-reaching consequences at the grassroots, transforming both the existent power structure and the processes in which power was exercised. Implicit in these processes was also the roots of externalization which, in contemporary management vocabulary means 'contracting-out' to non-public agencies. This also entails that besides the government-sponsored public authorities, there are numerous other agencies which also have a stake in governance. By being critical to grassroots decision making, the local populace thus become not only recipients but also instigators of change. So, power is externalized to make participatory democracy real in its manifestation and also execution. Localization and externalization hardly make sense without governance being substantially de-bureaucratized. As argued previously, one of the principal factors for the decline of PRIs was the hegemonic control of public bureaucracy that flourished with the connivance of the local vested interests. The aim of the Seventy-Third and Seventy-Fourth Amendment Acts was thus to destroy this evil and also the well-entrenched nexus that appeared to have crippled participatory democracy to strike organic roots in rural areas. With governance being democratically decentralized, following the creation of institutional spaces for participation, a parallel process begins whereby the peripheral sections will get drawn to decision making by being sensitive to their roles and responsibilities as members of the localities. As a result, governance that so far remains distant will become closer to the people which will automatically reduce the so-called dependency syndrome and make governance a people-centric and largely de-bureaucratized exercise.

Rural Local Governance[19]

Panchayati Raj Institutions

PRIs, as stated earlier, are the institutionalized pan-Indian forms of rural local governance that came into existence with the passage of Seventy-Third Constitutional Amendment Act in 1992. This legislation has heralded a three-tier structure of rural local governance—gram panchayats at the bottom level, Panchayat Samiti at the intermediate level and Zilla Parishad at the highest level.

---

[17] Arvind Sharma, 'Administrative Reforms in India during 1990s: A Synoptic View', in *Governance and Development: Issues and Strategies*, eds. Pradeep Sahni and Uma Medury (New Delhi: Prentice-Hall of India, 2003), pp. 110–19.

[18] DL Seth, 'Globalization and New Politics of Micro-movements', *Economic and Political Weekly* 39, no. 1 (3 January 2004), pp. 45–58.

[19] The entire discussion of Seventy-Third and Seventy-Fourth Amendment Acts, 1992 is drawn, unless otherwise stated, on chapter 6 of my earlier book entitled *Indian Administration: Evolution and Practice* (New Delhi: SAGE, 2016), which I wrote with Prakash Chand.

The Seventy-Third Constitutional Amendment Act, 1992

The Seventy-Third Constitutional Amendment Act, 1992 is considered to be a watershed in the history of local government in India. It has virtually salvaged the age-old tradition and institution of local governance from a dependent status to one of self-reliance by conferring the much-coveted constitutional status on it. Until the passage of the Seventy-Third Constitutional Amendment Act, states were the only sub-national units officially recognized by the Indian Constitution. The provision for local government remained under the state list and, hence, there was no uniform pattern of it across the country. The Act has heralded a three-tier PRIs across the country. The functional domain of rural local bodies was limited largely to the provision of some core services such as water supply, sanitation, local roads, etc. The 'developmental' activities were limited to the role of implementing developmental schemes sponsored by either the Central or state governments. The passage of the Act has empowered the local bodies to formulate and implement development plans of their own.

Main Features of Seventy-Third Amendment Act

Whatever be the motive behind the constitutionalization of panchayats, the Act has changed the very contour of local governance at the rural level. Some of the redeeming features of the Act are as follows:

- The Act has heralded a three-tier PRIs with Zilla Parishad at the top, the panchayat samitis at the intermediate level and village panchayats at the bottom.
- The Act has clearly devolved power, authority and responsibilities to rural local bodies to enable them to function as the institutions of self-government (Article 243G).
- The Act has made it mandatory for all levels of PRIs to conduct periodic elections in every five years. In case of early or premature dismissal of PRIs, elections are to be held within a period of six months, with the newly elected members serving out the remainder of the five-year term (Article 243E).
- The Act has also made provisions for the reservation of seats for SCs and STs in all panchayats at all levels in proportion to their respective shares in the panchayat concerned. In addition to that, the Act has also made mandatory reservation of one-third of all seats in all panchayats at all level for women, of which one-third is to be reserved for the women belonging to SC and ST. The constitutional provision for the reservation of seats for SC and ST also extends to position of panchayats chairperson at all the three tiers of PRIs and one-third mandatory reservation is earmarked for them.
- The Act has stipulated the constitution of a state-level Election Commission for a period of five years to ensure free and fair elections in local bodies.
- The Act has also empowered the state government to constitute another independent state-level commission, namely, the Finance Commission, for five years to review the overall financial position of local bodies and recommend the principle that should govern the allocation of funds and taxation authority to local bodies. The governor of the state is entrusted with the power of constituting the finance commission, which will review the financial positions of the panchayats and make recommendations thereon to the governor.
- The Act has also made provision for the constitution of Gram Sabha, the body of the electorate of the gram panchayats, and established a more direct channel of people's participation. The underlying rationale was that Gram Sabha would function as a fulcrum of developmental process, where the community would participate both at the formulation and the implementation of developmental plans. Moreover, this body will also function as an organ of local accountability and oversight.

- The XI schedule (Article 243G) has been added which gives the list of 29 functions to be performed by PRIs.

According to Article 243(G) of the Act, 'Panchayats shall be given powers and authority to function as institutions of self-government'. This would be done by delegating powers and responsibilities to panchayats at the appropriate level such as: (a) preparation of plan for economic development and social justice and (b) implementation of scheme for economic development. Article 243(H) authorizes a panchayat to levy, collect and appropriate taxes, tolls and fees. These two Articles clearly lay out the powers, authority and responsibilities of panchayats vis-à-vis state governments. They empower rural local bodies to play a pivotal role in the provision of public services, creation and maintenance of local public goods and planning and implementation of developmental activities and programmes to alleviate poverty and promote distributive equality. Unlike in the past, the PRIs are now constitutionally authorized to act in those areas which are earmarked as their domain in the Eleventh Schedule of the Constitution of India. The Ninth Plan (1997–2002) clubbed these areas under five broad categories,[20] which are as follows:

First, Agriculture and Allied Activities:

- Land improvement, implementation of land reforms, land consolidation and soil conservations
- Minor irrigation, water management and watershed development
- Animal husbandry, dairying and poultry, fisheries
- Social forestry and farm forestry
- Minor forest produce and fuel and fodder

Second, Rural Industrialization:

- Small-scale industries, including food-processing industries
- Khadi, village and cottage industries

Third, Infrastructure Development:

- Rural housing, drinking water
- Roads, culverts, bridges, ferries, waterways and other means of communication
- Rural electrification, including distribution of electricity, non-conventional energy sources
- Markets and fairs, maintenance of community assets

Fourth, Human Development:

- Technical training and vocational education, adult and non-farm education, primary and secondary education, cultural activities
- Health and sanitation, including hospitals, primary health centres and dispensaries
- Family welfare
- Poverty alleviation programme

[20] Rural Development, The Ninth Five Year Plan (1997–2002), Government of India, 2002, Appendix 1, p. 191. http://planningcommission.nic.in/plans/stateplan/sdr_punjab/sdrpun_ch5.pdf (accessed 23 December 2016).

Finally, Social Welfare and Gender Development:

- Women and child development
- Social welfare, including welfare of the handicapped and mentally retarded
- Welfare of weaker sections and in particular of SC and ST
- Public distribution system

The above-mentioned list contains all those critical activities which need to be meaningfully attended to bring about inclusive rural development. What is striking is the idea that rural development does not necessarily mean economic prosperity, but also human development, for instance, for which one is required to devise effective policies. Hence, the goal that has been constantly emphasized both by the stakeholders in villages and the policy makers is to localize governance, whereby governance emerges as an instinctive design for the villagers to fulfil their aspired goal by dint of their own endeavour.

Working of the Panchayati Raj System

It is evident from the preceding discussion that there are some radical provisions in the Seventy-Third Amendment Act. They seek to address some of the problems encountered by PRIs in the past; for example: (a) granting PRIs constitutional status, (b) empowering socially and economically disadvantaged groups, i.e., Dalits, Adivasis and women (c) ensuring free, fair and regular elections, (d) keeping terms of PRIs fixed, (e) identifying a list of items which would fall under the jurisdiction of PRIs and (f) addressing the issue of PRI finances.[21] Thus, the Act has provided for a significant degree of fiscal, administrative and political decentralization from the state to local levels.

Now that the democratic decentralization experiment is with us for more than two decades, it is necessary to evaluate it, which is often euphemistically called as 'silent revolution'. In this section, we will interrogate the democratic decentralization experiment by asking a few important questions: Are we really ready for decentralization? Is democratic decentralization an end in itself? Does democratic decentralization truly empower local community? These questions require a lot of introspections. In this section, we will critically appraise the role of democratic decentralization in delivering development and social justice.

Weaknesses of the Panchayati Raj System

Despite much accolade and fanfare, PRIs fail to bring about much needed transformation in Indian society and polity. In fact, several shortcomings have surfaced within a decade of its functioning. First, panchayat as an institution of local self-government has been suffering from an identity crisis as the meaning of self-government has not been clearly articulated. Second, the PRIs have inherited a culture of subservience, deliberately inculcated by the colonial era, which has gone against the fullest realization of decentralization in the post independent India. Third, though this new form of PRIs has an avowed stand on gender empowerment, as the Seventy-Third Constitution Amendment Act has envisaged one-third reservation for women, in actuality, panchayats are witnessing a typical phenomenon of proxy participation, where male members of the women candidate wield power on her behalf. The infamous *pradhan-pati* syndrome is a case in point. Fourth, another major weakness of this system is the over-politicization of the panchayats. In a parliamentary democracy, thanks to being in power for many years, often panchayats administration

[21] Peter Ronald deSouza, 'Decentralization and Local Governance: The Second Wind of Democracy in India', in *India's Living Constitution: Ideas, Practices and Controversies*, eds. Zoya Hasan, E Sridharan and R Sudarshan (Ranikhet: Permanent Black, 2002), p. 379.

and party administration have become identical and inseparable, leading thereby an overlapping of responsibilities. Consequently, panchayat administration became the extended branch of party administration, with the same set of persons simultaneously discharging both the duties, leading thereby to a lot of confusion. However, politicization is nothing unique, as Indian panchayati raj system has allowed political mobilization. In a democratic system, competitive political mobilization could have enhanced the status of the community, if political parties are allowed to mobilize freely. For, in this system, political parties always wanted to outpace their contenders by improving the quality of services. Distortions occur only when any political party or combination of parties hold powers unilaterally for a long time. Fifth, the over-reliance on PRIs as institutions of local governance often leads to 'system overload', with too many developmental projects vying for attention in panchayats. Finally, a strong centralizing tendency with the centrality of development state has been implicit in the decentralization initiatives in independent India. Starting from the Balwant Rai Mehta Committee to the recent Seventy-Third Constitution Amendment Act, there has been a distinct tradition of centrality.

The functioning of new panchayati raj system reveals the fact that though the legislative and electoral formalities have been completed in almost all the states, at the operational level, there are large variations among them. The 29 subjects mentioned in the Eleventh schedule do not give power of legislation to the local bodies, but only to take decisions. The State Finance Commissions' recommendations are not mandatory in nature. It is completely up to the state government to devolve or not to devolve functions, functionaries and resources on the local bodies as per the constitutional scheme. As of 2007, only three of India's 28 states had passed executive orders devolving all 29 functions to the local level, as required by the constitutional amendment. The high handedness of bureaucracy, with a few exceptions, over the local autonomy still prevails. The experience gained so far is that, at the district level, various department and agencies still implement programmes and function under the overall supervision and control of the District Collectors. The PRIs, therefore, have to be content with backseat driving.[22]

The experience of democratic decentralization makes it clear that it cannot be a solution to one and all ills of governance. Rigid patriarchal structure inhibits the participation of backward castes and women in village governance. The Seventy-Third Amendment stipulates that one-third of all panchayat seats are 'reserved' for women, with a similar provision for SC and ST. In North India, where caste and gender inequalities are particularly resilient, the local elites have tended to adapt to this requirement by putting up 'proxy' candidates from the required group, and are continuing to wield power through them. The submissive female chairperson or *sarpanch*, sitting quietly in a corner while her husband (often initially mistaken for the *sarpanch*) answers the questions, is a familiar figure in the critical literature on panchayati raj in North India.[23] Moreover, a majority of the elected representatives are first timers with little or no prior knowledge of the functioning of PRIs. It is not easy for the rural weaker section to actively participate in the development process. The literacy level among SC, ST and women are quite low. The distribution of rural assets and powers is heavily skewed in India—the bottom 39 per cent of rural households (belonging to lower castes) own only 5 per cent of all assets, while the top 5 per cent own 46 per cent. This makes the opportunities and social choice shrink for the really deprived villages at the grassroots.

Inadequate financial resources are another crucial constraint in the effective functioning of decentralized governance. The panchayats have to depend on the devolutions and the grants-in-aid from the state

[22] BPR Vittal, 'Evolving Trends in the Bureaucracy', in *State and Politics in India*, ed. Partha Chatterjee (New Delhi: Oxford University Press, 1997).

[23] Jean Dreze and Amartya Sen, *India: Development and Participation* (New Delhi: Oxford University Press, 2002), p. 362.

governments as they have not developed any independent sources to raise revenues. Besides, most of the states have not transferred funds for the areas that have been given to these local bodies. A study of 12 states has shown that, in nine of these, the tax revenue of the local bodies (both panchayats and urban local bodies) was less than 5 per cent of the total tax revenue of the state government.[24] The limited fiscal autonomy of panchayats renders them excessively dependent on the Central and State governments.

The constraints and problems that mark democratic decentralization initiatives are myriads but should not create a panic, as we are passing through a transitory phase, and any kind of transition takes time to show positive results. It is a fact that a silent revolution is taking place in rural India where people are becoming conscious of their rights. One of the most heartening aspects of the panchayati raj experiment has been the inclusion and participation of variously disadvantaged groups such as Dalits, Adivasis and women. It is arguable that the provision of quotas has generated widespread awareness. Studies have shown that the developmental outcomes in panchayats headed by women are impressive, even if empowerment impacts have been rather slow in materializing what is expected.[25] The renewed movement towards democratic decentralization has eroded the bureaucratic monopoly over the development processes and has shifted the locus of power to those who matter at the grassroots level.

The new panchayati raj system represents an institutional watershed which has bought 'the people' back into the political process at grassroots level. People have been given a voice. This voice, even in a situation of pervasive asymmetric power, will result in a flattening of the asymmetry, a process that can have only emancipatory consequences. To quote BS Baviskar, 'the Seventy-Third Amendment Act can rightly be termed as "a silent revolution," which in many respect salvaged the institution of self-government from a mere "agent" of provincial government to one of "self-reliant" one'. In spite of all these positive developments, the panchayat members belonging to SC and ST have, warns Baviskar, 'miles to go before achieving full and meaningful inclusion' and, in some case, he further adds, 'the power enjoyed by them is often symbolic'.[26] This is, however, not a mean achievement given the fact that in the past they were completely ostracized even for social communication. In that respect, the amended constitutional provisions can easily be identified as a harbinger of significant socio-economic transformations at the grassroots.

Urban Local Governance

Structure

Unlike the rural governance, urban governance is not hierarchical. Article 243Q of the Seventy-Fourth Amendment Act, 1992 (that came in force in 1993), stipulates that there shall be three types of urban local bodies (ULBs) in India, namely, Nagar Panchayat for the transitional areas, municipal councils or municipalities for smaller urban areas and municipal corporations for larger urban areas. State governments are allowed to design their own municipal acts in accordance with the broad parameters outlined in the Seventy-Fourth Amendment Act of 1992.

---

[24] Report of the *National Commission to Review the Working of the Constitution of India*, 2001, p. 29, Ministry of Law, Justice and Company Affairs, Department of Legal Affairs, Government of India, New Delhi, 2002.

[25] Niraja Gopal Jayal, Amit Prakash and Pradeep K Sharma, *Local Governance in India: Decentralization and Beyond* (New Delhi: Oxford University Press, 2006), p. 13.

[26] Introduction in BS Baviskar and George Mathew, *Inclusion and Exclusion in Local Governance: Field Studies from Rural India* (New Delhi: SAGE, 2009), pp. 10–11.

Functions

Article 243W of the Constitution deals with the 'power, authority and responsibilities of municipalities', which clearly lays out the functions of municipality including the list of functions enumerated in the Twelfth Schedule. The detail of those functions, stipulated in the Twelfth Schedule of Constitution[27] can be organized around the following major concerns:

First, Urban Well-being:

- Planning for social and economic development, regulation of land use and construction of buildings, planning for urban poverty alleviation, slum improvement and upgradation.

Second, Infrastructure Development:

- Building of roads and bridges, water supply for domestic, industrial and commercial purpose, public amenities including street lighting, parking lots, bus stops and public conveniences.

Third, Human Development:

- Public health; sanitation, conservation and solid waste management; urban forestry; protection of the environment and promotion of ecological aspects; safeguarding the interests of weaker sections of society, including the handicapped and mentally retarded; provision of urban amenities and facilities such as parks, gardens and playgrounds; promotion of cultural, educational and aesthetic aspects; burial and burial grounds, cremations, cremation grounds and electric crematoriums.

Fourth, Concomitant Requirements:

- Cattle pounds, prevention of cruelty of animals, vital statistics including registration births and deaths, regulation of slaughter houses and tanneries.

Similar to the Eleventh Schedule, the Twelfth Schedule is also a check-list of items which are necessary aids for inclusive urban development. Here, too, the idea is to encourage participation by the local populace in activities which they deem appropriate for their own benefit. As the list shows, an attempt is made to bring about an all-round urban development by addressing those major concerns which need to be conclusively addressed to make urban life better and also humane. By encouraging participation of the stakeholders in urban affairs and also by creating a supportive institutionalized system of governance, the Seventy-Fourth Amendment Act, similar to the Seventy-Third Amendment Act, radically changed the texture of urban governance by making it responsible, accountable and sensitive to the constituents. In that respect, this legislative design can be said to have ushered in a new era of the state–citizen interface in the context of growing democratization in India.

---

[27] Prepared on the basis of the inputs available in the Twelfth Schedule that was added to the Constitution of India by the Seventy-Third Amendment Act in 1992.

The Seventy-Fourth Amendment Act, 1992: Main Provisions

The Seventy-Fourth Amendment Act, 1992 has ushered in a new phase of urban governance in India. However, it has a striking similarity with the Seventy-Third Constitutional Amendment Act, 1992. This Act is incorporated in Article 243 Part-IX A of the Indian Constitution. Major provisions of the Act are as follows:

- ULBs, to be known as Municipal Corporation, Municipal Councils and Nagar Panchayat, depending on the population, shall be constituted through universal adult franchise in each notified urban area of the country.
- These shall be constituted for a period of five years.
- Not less than one-third of total number of seats in each urban local body shall be reserved for women.
- These bodies shall be endowed with power and authority to formulate and implement schemes for economic development and social justice on 18 subjects.
- In order that the ULBs can perform the functions assigned to them, the legislature of a state shall assign them specific taxes, duties, tolls and levies and authorize them to impose, collect and appropriate the same.
- Each state shall also constitute a finance commission which shall review the financial position of the ULBs and recommend the principles that should govern the devolution of resources including grant-in-aid from the consolidated fund of the state of these bodies.
- The superintendence, direction and control of the preparation of electoral rolls for, and the conduct of, all election to the ULBs shall vest in the State Election Commission.
- The Act has made provision for the constitution of Ward Committee in all municipalities with a population of three lakhs and more.
- District Planning Committee and Metropolitan Planning Committee shall be constituted to prepare a development plan.

The Seventy-Fourth Amendment Act provides ULB with legitimacy through regular elections and devolution of functional and financial powers. In order to make these ULBs forums for inclusive governance, the Act earmarks specific domains for them. Seeking to ensure people's participation in civic affairs at the grassroots, the Act also suggests the creation of Ward Committees in ULBs with a population of 300,000 or more. The Ward Committee is 'the most promising institution in which citizens from all sections of society can take part in local governance'.[28] Being an important mechanism to achieve this goal, the Ward Committee is hailed as an instrument with 'the potential to introduce participation, partnership, proximity, transparency and accountability in urban governance'.[29]

By guaranteeing constitutional status to the municipalities the Act seeks to redefine their role—power, function and finances. This has ushered in a new era of urban governance and urban management in India. The Act is significant because, apart from the traditional functions, it has allocated the municipal bodies the function of economic development and social justice, which suggests their elevation from mere instrumentalities for 'agency functions' to responsible bodies for development planning. The provision of state-level finance commission is a landmark step in the direction of providing financial autonomy to the

[28] A Ghosh and M Mitra, 'Institutionalizing People's Participation in Urban Governance: An Inter-city Perspective of Ward Committees in West Bengal', in *New Forms of Urban Governance in India*, eds. ISA Baud and J DeWit (New Delhi: SAGE, 2008), p. 85.

[29] Ghosh and Mitra, 'Institutionalizing People's Participation', p. 86.

ULBs. Reservation of seats, especially for women, ensures the participation of socially deprived sections of the society. The new Act has become an instrument of political education. In the context of urban politics, people are learning to organize, question established patterns of authority, demand their rights, resist corruption, and so on. This learning process enhances their preparedness not only for local democracy alone but also for political participation in general.

Major Challenges Before Urban Local Governance

The Seventy-Fourth Amendment Act has surely revived the ULBs in India, but they still face a number of problems. The first and most serious problem facing the ULBs is the acute scarcity of finance. In the absence of proper funds, powers become meaningless because the same cannot be translated into real efforts and outcomes. The new Act provides for the constitution of a State Finance Commission to look into the financial sources of local bodies, but the recommendations of the Commission are not binding on the respective states. People's participation in urban bodies is still negligible. Major cause of this attitude is that people look towards the municipal bodies with inherent suspicion and take it for granted that their problems and grievances will not be taken care of. Moreover, like the eleventh schedule, there is no clear demarcation of functions between different local units of the urban local government, leaving it to the respective state. This has given the states the liberty to impose their own choices in this regard, which has at times created more confusion than order regarding what is to be delegated and otherwise.

In the changing scenario, the ULBs need to exclusively devote themselves to the task of development and, therefore, should enjoy a large measure of autonomy. But the ground reality depicts a different picture. Criticizing the Seventy-Fourth Amendment Act, Nirmal Mukarji argues that 'it is almost a carbon copy of the Seventy-Third Amendment Act' and 'a hasty afterthought'.[30] Comparing with the Seventy-Third Amendment Act, he further notes that 'it looks as if some independent thinking went into the panchayat law and then, one day, the *municipalitywallahs* suddenly woke up and said "we too, please" and were simply served the panchayat dish with municipal sauce'.[31] Second, it thoughtlessly 'constitutionalizes an artificial dichotomy between rural and urban when all previous thinking has stressed a continuum between the two'.[32] Apart from the above mentioned issues, urban governance is facing the new challenges as a result of the process of liberalization, privatization, globalization and urbanization. Besides certain obvious limitations for structural and socio-political reasons, the ULBs also present two contrasting patterns. On the one hand, there is a conventional model which seeks to organize ULBs in accordance with the constitutional guidelines, while, on the other hand, there is another model which allows the state government to be drawn on informal networks among the urban dwellers to evolve their own forums. As a recent study shows,[33] the Kerala model of urban governance is a state-induced participatory exercise in which the state formulated the policies of participation of the local population and facilitated this process through official channels within constitutional provisions. In contrast, there is a unique design of urban governance that Delhi has crafted, by drawing upon informal networks across various segments of Delhi's population, build institutional forum for people's participation in civic governance by creating Residents' Welfare Associations (RWAs), which are democratic grassroots-level agencies dealing with planning and implementation of projects as per peoples' aspirations. Delhi's Bhagidari is neither constitutionally

[30] Nirmal Mukarji, 'The Third Stratum', *Economic and Political Weekly*, 1 May 1993, p. 860.

[31] Mukarji, 'The Third Stratum', p. 860.

[32] Mukarji, 'The Third Stratum', p. 860.

[33] N Sridharan, 'New Forms of Contestation and Cooperation in Indian Urban Governance', in *New Forms of Urban Governance in India*, pp. 307–10.

supported nor has emerged as a legislative design, but was formed out of an executive decision to create an alternative administrative set-up for urban well-being.

Implications of Seventy-Third and Seventy-Fourth Amendment Acts

The Acts as mentioned earlier are phenomenal in many respects. Besides setting a three-tier system of governance, what is most distinctive about these Acts is the establishment of a district planning committee as per Article 243Z to consolidate the plans prepared by both panchayats and municipalities for the district as a whole. It is true that the district authority is responsible for finalizing the plan though the inputs that it receives from the panchayats and municipalities remain its core. As a result, the district plan is expected to be inclusive in its goal and objective. In this section, we will specifically highlight some of the implications.

Constitutional Status

The first and foremost implication of the Seventy-Third and Seventy-Fourth Amendment Acts is the conferment of constitutional status on local government. Initially, the Constitution of India did not confer any special status on local government, except an entry in the State List of the Seventh Schedule of the Constitution and a specific article in the Directive Principles of State Policy, expecting state governments to take initiatives for organizing panchayats.

Until recently, there was no uniform pattern of local self-governments across the country. Formation and nurturing of local government was absolutely a matter of goodwill on the part of state governments. With the passing of these Acts, it has become mandatory for state governments to construct rural and urban local governments. Hence, the constitutionalization of rural and urban local governments has engendered an exclusive legislative domain for the local governments, or what is known as a 'third stratum' of government,[34] paving the way for a direct linkage between the governance process and the community per se.

Administrative Powers

The Acts have provided the much-needed administrative autonomy in terms of functional devolution of power to both the urban and rural local bodies. For long, local bodies were considered as the mere 'agents' of the state governments. They did not have any authority of taking administrative decisions independent of state control. But the new Acts have enabled the local governments to manage their own affairs. For instance, the authority of local bodies to superintend overall development of the area concerned may be mentioned, which includes, among others, the preparation of plans for economic development and social justice, implementation of various developmental schemes or any other developmental initiative as the local bodies deem necessary.

Financial Autonomy

Another important implication of the said Acts is the financial autonomy. Financial autonomy is the sine qua non of any organization. Local bodies in India were known for their perennial financial stringency. The Acts have virtually salvaged the cash-strapped local bodies (including both the urban and rural institutions) with substantial financial authority. For example, the new Acts have allowed panchayats and municipalities to mobilize their own resources, apart from the normal sources of finance, that is, the grants-in-aids, which they usually receive from the government.

[34] Mukarji, 'The Third Stratum', p. 859–62.

The Acts have also the provisions for mandatory constitution of State Finance Commission by the state governments once in every five years to review comparative financial positions of the local bodies and to make recommendations to the state government on the following issues: (a) the distribution between the state and the local bodies (panchayat and municipalities) of the net proceeds of the taxes, duties, tolls and fees leviable by the state, which may be divided between them under this Act and the allocation of resources between these local bodies shall also be governed by the same stipulation; (b) the determination of the taxes, duties, tolls and fees which may be assigned to, or appropriated by the local bodies (panchayats and municipalities); (c) the grants-in-aids to the local bodies (panchayats and municipalities) from the consolidated fund of the state.

Transparency in Governance

Nowadays transparency has become a buzzword. It is now considered to be a necessary precondition for ensuring integrity in local government and is an inseparable element of good governance. By making open deliberation on the issues of governance, the decision making at the grassroots has become transparent, which was simply inconceivable in the past when it was clearly bureaucracy-centric. The Acts under consideration have also given due importance to this transparency factor. Article 243 J of the Seventy-Third Amendment Act and the Article 243 Z of Seventy-Fourth Amendment Act have mentioned the provisions for the mandatory audit of accounts of panchayats and municipalities, respectively.

Accountability in Governance

As a result of these amendments the local bodies are now accountable to fulfil the aspirations of the people. They have been assigned powers and functions to solve the problems at the grassroots level.

Deepening of Democracy

It is often said that the secret formula behind the success of Indian democracy lies in the embeddedness of democratic spirit of Indian society. The new Acts, by setting up of an all-inclusive popular body, i.e., Gram Sabha at the bottom level (and Gram Sansad below the Gram Sabha in case of West Bengal) of panchayats and Ward Committee in case of municipalities, have paved the way for greater penetration of democracy into interstices of Indian society. It has, thus, been commented that 'a virtual democratic revolution has been brought about with the promulgation of these Amendment Acts'.[35] Moreover, the new Acts have regularized the election process across the country. Prior to the Acts, elections in these local bodies were more or less voluntary. Barring a few instances, it was occasional and sporadic in most cases. The new Acts have clearly stated that the elections to the local bodies are to be held every five years. If a panchayat or municipality is dissolved prematurely, elections must be held within six months, with the newly elected members serving out the remainder of the five-year term.

Gender Empowerment

Another redeeming feature of the new Acts is the institutionalization of women participation via reservation of seats at the local bodies. Women folk in India, especially in rural India, have been subject to a systematic and systemic exploitation of the patriarchy. They have been systematically 'excluded' from the corridors of power. The Acts have substantially elevated the status of Indian women from a subjugated status to a self-reliant one. The Acts have stipulated in categorical terms that 'not less than one third of the total number

[35] Kuldeep Mathur, *Panchayati Raj* (New Delhi: Oxford University Press, 2013), p. 37.

of seats to be filled by direct election in every panchayat shall be reserved for women'. It was thus observed by one of the working groups on decentralized planning and PRIs:

> One of the significant achievements of the provisions of the 73rd Amendment Act concerning reservation of seats and political offices in favour of women and the disadvantaged sections of the rural community is that it had improved their awareness and perception levels and has created an urge in them to assert their rightful share in the decision making process at the local level.[36]

The Seventy-Third Amendment was a threat to the prevalent socio-economic dispensation since it challenged the male-chauvinistic mindset that always remained a stumbling block towards realizing gender equality.[37] The policy of reservation was a powerful legislative design that sought to replace the mindset supportive of gender prejudices; most of the earlier efforts towards making local governance inclusive were scuttled since the vested interests played a critical role in panchayat affairs, which allowed neither women nor the underprivileged to participate as equal partners. It is true that the situation has undergone a sea-change since seats are reserved for women, SC and ST in the PRIs in proportion to their share in India's demography, though the effectiveness of these provisions is very uneven. There are instances showing that seat reservations have 'provided underprivileged groups with increased visibility and an opportunity to influence local affairs'.[38] In many panchayats, women managed to direct local affairs in accordance with their priorities by marshalling adequate financial resources and lobbying bureaucrats and politicians at higher levels.[39] We have also reasons to be alarmed because there are panchayats where elite dominance continues to prevail and the traditional caste leaders and landed elite 'dominate decision making by proxy or manipulations'.[40] A recent study, thus, shows that female *pradhans* (head of gram panchayats) usually act as proxies for husbands, sons or powerful neighbours, which means 'functions of the gram Pradhan are performed by husbands, brothers-in-law, fathers-in-law [and their] role is ... limited to household chores'.[41] In his study of panchayats in western Uttar Pradesh, GK Lieten has shown how a typical patriarchal mindset stood in the way of realizing gender parity in local governance. As he mentioned:

> Most male members [insist] that girls should go to school, but only to learn and write, and there is no need for them to go for higher education, for in that case they "go and sit on the head" of the males. Their freedom should be limited and they should not indulge too much in

[36] *Report of the Task Force on Panchayati Raj Institutions (PRIs)*, Planning Commission, Government of India, New Delhi, 2001, cited in Mahi Pal, 'Panchayati Raj and Rural Governance: Experience of a Decade', *Economic and Political Weekly* 39, no. 2 (10 January 2004), p. 142.

[37] Nirmala Buch pursues this argument in her 'Women and Panchayats: Opportunities, Challenges and Supports', in *Decentralization and Local Governance*, ed. LC Jain (Hyderabad: Orient Longman, 2005), pp. 343–65.

[38] Mark Robinson, 'A Decade of Panchayati Raj Reforms: The Challenge of Democratic Decentralization in India', in *Decentralization and Local Governance*, p. 20.

[39] My on going study of self-help groups in Uttar Pradesh confirms this. In two districts of Uttar Pradesh, Sultanpur and Raebareli, women members in PRIs who are also members of self-help groups play critical roles in decision making, and there are examples to show that they also took decision in opposition to their male counterparts.

[40] Robinson, 'A Decade of Panchayati Raj Reforms', p. 20.

[41] Buch, 'Women and Panchayats', p. 351.

> public activities. They are regarded as not knowing anything, and of not being of much use in panchayats: "she should take proper care of the house only" is an often heard proposition.[42]

Hence, the hope that the PRIs are effective challenges to the well-entrenched gender-basis seems to be overstretched. The argument goes because 'the pious hopes of some members [of panchayats], including female members, of furthering human, social and economic development through the panchayats have proven to be out of touch with reality'.[43] The scene does not seem to be as disappointing as it is made out to be, as studies of women panchayats in Madhya Pradesh, Rajasthan and also some parts of Uttar Pradesh provided inputs challenging 'the myths about rural women's lack of interest in politics, their passivity and nonparticipation in local political institutions, proxyism by male relatives, women's universal political connectivity and women's entry into panchayats from only well-off sections'.[44] Limitations notwithstanding, these amendments provoked processes of significant socio-political changes at the grassroots by making the PRIs 'a democratic forum to grapple with social and political issues in the open [and] churning process will continue'.[45] These amendments are, thus, the beginning of the era of empowerment of women and underprivileged when social, economic and political hegemony of the privileged is being questioned justifiably to fulfil the aspired goal of making India an equitable society, free from prejudices of any kind. There is no denying that in an unequal patriarchal society like ours, reservation of seats for women has invariably uplifted the status of women. However, it should not be taken as *the* way of empowering women. It is only a step towards empowerment, not the empowerment in itself, as it is often mistakenly equated. The issue of reservation boils down to an irreducible duality between differences versus equality. The feminist epistemology seems to have been caught in this perennial dilemma. Putting it bluntly, the debate is centering round whether women should struggle for equal rights or they valorize their differences from men folk and thereby asking for preferential treatment.

Empowerment of Disadvantaged

It is quite fashionable these days to talk about 'inclusive development', which calls for an all-embracing formula and framework of development, so that the disadvantaged section should not be left out at the margin. Modern political philosophers such as Ronald Dworkin, John Rawls and others have justified, at least in essence, the necessity of an inclusive development in their argument for equity and social justice. The Constitution of India has devoted considerable portion of it for the upliftment of SCs, STs and OBCs. In addition to that, the new Acts have enabled the least advantaged section (i.e., the SCs and STs) to have the greater chance of representation at the local bodies by reserving one-third seats for them in both the urban and rural local bodies. It has thus been rightly observed:

> The political space given to marginalized section has, to some extent, dealt a blow to the asymmetrical social structure at the local level and given greater space for their participation and involvement in decision making.[46]

---

[42] GK Lieten, 'Panchayats in Western Uttar Pradesh: Namesake Members', *Economic and Political Weekly*, 28 September 1996, p. 2704.

[43] Lieten, 'Panchayats in Western Uttar Pradesh', p. 2705.

[44] Nirmala Buch, *From Oppression to Assertion: A Study of Panchayats and Women in MP [Madhya Pradesh], Rajasthan and UP [Uttar Pradesh]*, Centre for Women's Development Studies, New Delhi, 1999 (mimeo).

[45] Lieten, 'Panchayats in Western Uttar Pradesh', p. 2705.

[46] Pal, 'Panchayati Raj and Rural Governance', p. 142.

A new, perhaps powerful, voice was articulated with the acceptance of the Seventy-Third Amendment Act; it was a voice which was, so far, suppressed under age-old social prejudices that always privileged one's ascribed identity over any other considerations. These constitutional amendments can thus be said to have introduced newer ways of conceptualizing human relations, though that is not enough since the constitutional amendment alone cannot bring about the expected transformation unless the demand for 'defacto decentralization does not arise from the grassroots'.[47] Nonetheless, the Seventy-Third Amendment Act stands out as one of these radical pieces of legislations that not only created newer parameters of conceptualizing interpersonal relationships but also initiated movements for inclusive growth of communities in the midst of well-entrenched divisions along caste, class and ethnic axes.

Popular Participation

The said Acts have institutionalized the popular participation in local governance. The introduction of 'participatory development' as an alternative paradigm of development in the Seventy-Third and the Seventy-Fourth Constitutional Amendment Acts, 1992 is a case in point. The Acts have formalized popular participation through the mandatory construction of Gram Sabha or Ward Committee at the bottom level.

Decentralized Planning

Another important hallmark of the new Acts is the introduction of decentralized planning process. For long planning was couched as a highly technical job to be done by a group of seasoned mandarins. But of late, the notion of planning has undergone a sea-change, as we are now favouring 'bottom-up' approach to the conventional paradigm of 'top-down' model. The efforts of the government towards decentralizing the planning process are evident in both rural and urban local bodies. In case of rural local bodies, the state-initiated rural development through scheme-based activities with the participation of the people in implementing the activities has been reversed and replaced by people-initiated rural development programmes with the participation of the government.[48] People are now couched as the stakeholders of development. Article 243G, for example, has recognized the panchayats as 'institutions of self-government' and entrusted them with the responsibilities of preparing plans for promoting economic development and social justice.

The State Panchayat Act has, at least, formally given necessary powers and functions to the panchayats to formulate plans. However, barring a few states like Kerala, Karnataka and Tamil Nadu, the track record of grassroots planning in the rest of the country is not inspiring. In fact, Kerala has taken a giant stride in this direction. For example, Kerala's much-hyped 'people's campaign for the Ninth Plan' may be mentioned. Under the programme, the panchayats have been entrusted with the responsibility to prepare and prioritize projects in an integrated and scientific manner. The programme also ensured maximum participation of local people at every stage of the planning process. The decentralized planning model is not confined to panchayats alone. The Seventy-Fourth Amendment Act has also made some provisions for decentralized planning via a few structural innovations like the formulation of Metropolitan Planning Committee and District Planning committee.

---

[47] Pal, 'Panchayati Raj and Rural Governance', p. 142.

[48] G Palanithrai, 'Development Roles Reversed: People's Initiative and Government's Participation', in *Decentralization and Local Governance*, pp. 459–78.

Civil Society: Facilitating People's Participation in Local Governance

As discussed in the available literature, civil society is an important actor of local governance. They ensure people's participation in the local governance. The following section deals with the crucial role played by the civil society actors.

Role of Civil Society in Rural Development

Rural development has a typical statist bias. Until recently, it was considered as a state-led and state-induced development programme. But of late, courtesy of the neo-liberal 'recipe' of rolling back the state and the consequent unification of market, it was found that state was no longer in a position to carry forward the huge task of community development single-handedly. Confusions reigned supreme as a virtual battery of scholars soon plunged into the scene. A host of possibilities were conjured up, which were ranging from 'rural development sans state paradigm' to an eventual eclipse of rural development. But history proved those 'prophecies' false as rural development as a policy had shown no sign of recession, even though countries such as India had already entered the third generation of her economic reform. Quite to the contrary, rural development in India has been experiencing an altogether new paradigm of people centric model, ever since she has plunged into a free market economy.

Under the new circumstances, the importance of non-governmental organizations (NGOs) or civil society organizations has increased exponentially. Under the new paradigm, NGOs and people are taken as joint stakeholders of development along with its seasoned campaigner state. Traditionally, the interaction between the state and voluntary organizations was either absent or was more of a regulatory nature. They were not considered as 'equal partners' in the nation-building process. Their activities remained confined to relief and welfare activities alone. However, the new paradigm calls for a consortium of government and non-governmental institutions with their common pool of resources to cater to rural people. NGOs are therefore supposed to supplement and complement the state in the process of rural development. Together, they can effectively attain the larger goal of people's empowerment and integrated rural development for which the country has been struggling for decades. The Seventy-Third Constitutional Amendment Act 1992 (with effect from 1993) further endorsed 'the complementarities' between voluntary organizations and panchayats in rural development.

Role of Civil Society in Urban Development

The very contour of urban governance has also undergone a sea change over the last couple of decades, thanks to the sweeping economic, political and social transformation in the wake of globalization. With the progressive dissolution of trade and tariff barriers across the globe and the resultant networking of global market, cities are now emerging as 'management hubs' or 'logistic centres'[49] in this 'Borderless World.'[50] Hence, urban governance, which has so long been considered as an exclusive preserve of the state, is now being seen as a collaborative effort of all the stakeholders in the urban space, having their respective

[49] Nigel Harris, 'Globalization and the Management of Indian Cities', *Economic and Political Weekly*, 21 June 2003.

[50] Kenichi Ohmae, *The Borderless World: Power and Strategy in Global Marketplace* (London: HarperCollins, 1994).

roles to assert.[51] The underlying impetus, however, is coming from the *New Right Movement* and its prescription of 'rolling back the state'. Hence, there has been a partnership between the state and the market and the NGO sector in the name of public–private partnership (PPP).

New Dimensions of Local Governance

In the wake of globalization, the local democracy is facing new issues and challenges. The following section deals with such issues and the response of the local institutions and people to the new challenges.

Global–Local Debate

The global–local debate refers to an ongoing debate regarding development at the local levels. The basic debate is about what should be the guiding principle of local development—the local ideas and innovations or the external technology and expertise? There are two views. According to the first group, locally developed technology and arrangements are more convenient to the local development. They believe that local arrangement is based on the idea of immediateness and relevance. They argue that local requirements vary from place to place. There are different cultures, traditions and ways of life, and so a uniform arrangement is not applicable to all.

Supporters of the idea of localism believe that locally developed solutions gain high acceptance and suit the local requirements. In such an arrangement, people feel a sense of belongingness, and so they are always ready to implement the idea. Their active cooperation, readiness and enthusiasm become the main vehicle of implementation of the programmes. In this system, local knowledge and resources are employed in a more meaningful way, which saves the time and resources on training for implementation of the programmes. Locally arranged models ensure greater participation and give a feeling of empowerment to the people. Thus, under this scheme, problems can be identified quickly and responsive and sensitive solutions can be found out.

The supporters of the global idea believe that today the world is like a global village and we can solve local problems more effectively and economically with the help of external expertise and technology. They argue that local efforts are not sufficient for rapid development, which is the need of the hour. Thus, to fulfil the requirements of the growing population, we need new and advanced technology, which is only possible from global support and collaboration. If we keep ourselves within our boundaries and never think beyond that, we are depriving ourselves of new experiences, knowledge and innovations. Such kind of approach will keep us backward in our approach and action, which is not fruitful for local development.

The preceding debate makes it clear that local problems can be solved better with local solutions. Local arrangement has a better acceptability among people, which ensures greater participation and effective implementation of the programmes. There is a sense of belongingness and participation among the people. So, this approach is more participatory, effective and economical in addressing local issues. But, at the same time, we have to keep in mind the changing circumstances. Today we are in a globalized world; today's citizens are global citizens. There are a number of problems and challenges which can only be resolved by the global efforts and cooperation. Terrorism, global warming, climate change, border conflicts, new

[51] Amitabh Kundu and Debolina Kundu, 'Urban Local Government and Private Sector Partnership in Gujarat', in *Pro-Poor Growth and Governance in South Asia: Decentralization and Participatory Development*, ed. Ponna Wignaraja Susil Sirivardana (New Delhi: SAGE, 2004).

diseases such as cancer, AIDS and swine flu are a few examples in this regard. These issues can only be resolved by international efforts. So, today, we cannot keep ourselves aloof.

As far as application and adoption of external technology and resources at the local level is concerned, we can take some precautions. We can adopt those technologies and knowledge which suit our local needs and circumstances. These have to be in accordance to our culture, values and traditions. Before adopting such a technology, local people should be taken into confidence. It should be implemented only when local people are convinced that it is going to help them. Thus, global ideas and experiences have to be participatory, sensitive and accommodative to the local needs and requirements. In this way, the local–global debate can be converted into a fruitful, productive and constructive approach in promoting the development of the local area.

New Localism

The concept of 'New Localism' owes its popularity to the UK and to the policy changes announced by former Prime Minister Tony Blair in the early 2000s. It represented devolution of power to local governmental agencies, but only within a framework of national priorities and goals. What has particularly characterized the movement as new, is the continued primacy of the Central Government in setting the agenda that would surround 'local autonomy and action'.[52] Thus, it was introduced as a cautious devolution of power to the local level in an attempt to implement the national goals in a better coordinated and uniform way.

'New Localism' primarily evolved to provide a uniform agenda and framework for local governance throughout the nation in the UK. Specific focus of localism in the UK included freedoms to meet central goals in health care, education and in improving the overall responsiveness of public services to children and family needs. Accompanying elements in the new localism are the notions that there should be reduction in Central governmental approval functions, much more neighbourhood governance and direct engagement in implementing national goals, responsiveness to client needs and desires and an encouragement of local authorities to wrap multiple services around shared problems, such as health, employment, police, education and police.

Thus, New Localism is a cautious devolution of power to the local bodies in order to implement the national policies in a better way. It is new in two aspects. First, it recognizes the role of the Central Government in bringing changes at the local level, which was strongly resisted by the local people in the 1980s in the UK. Second, besides the local institutions, it involves the local communities and voluntary agencies in the provision of services to the people. Thus, it is more accommodative and participatory in nature.

Thus, the concept of New Localism is not a denial and refutation of national goals, policies and reform measures. It is rather a refocusing of attention upon local districts, communities and neighbourhoods in the context of national and even global objectives. In this sense, it is an arrangement where urban local governance is seen to be provided with a uniform framework under an order of the Central Government. Thus, New Localism emerged from the realization of the limitations of centrally driven policy implementation. It recognizes that local problems could not be solved by standardized policy imposed from above and that local institutions needed space to adapt and innovate within the public policy process. Thus, it is a pragmatic response to the complexities and diversities at the grassroots.

---

[52] Robert L Crowson and Ellen B Goldring, *The New Localism in American Education* (San Francisco, CA: Wiley-Blackwell, 2010), p. 2.

Urban Development Dynamics

There are a number of factors and forces which have changed the nature and character of the cities in the last three decades, particularly in India. Liberalization, privatization, globalization and urbanization are the significant ones. Different studies indicate the new development dynamics and its ramifications on the cities and its people. Some of the work locates the intensification of urban exclusion as a result of systematic deployment of neo-liberalism as structural adjustment policies,[53] others understand it within the rubric of socio-economic changes ushered in by globalization[54] and yet others see it as the rise of a new bourgeois governmentality in urban governance.[55] While assessing the neo-liberal impact of urbanization especially in the developing countries, Mike Davis argues that structural adjustment policies imposed forcibly on the Third World have destroyed import substitution industrialization, shrunk public-sector jobs by ushering in waves of privatization and decimated rural sectors as well.[56] The result is an increase in urban unemployment, rural to urban migration and further pressure on urban informal jobs. The result is the emergence of a new form of imperialism that colonizes the urban poor of the world through joblessness, poverty and informalization of the processes, which were considered integral to human development in not so remote past.

Within India, as Madadevia describes by drawing upon her extensive study of the city of Ahmedabad in Gujarat, there is a desperate entrepreneurial urge on the part of civic governments to become 'World Class' by emulating the cityscapes of the First World. She indicates a rapid transfer of municipal budgets from social infrastructure towards beautification and slum eviction, a trend representing steady state withdrawal from social sector and more funding for modernization and beautifications of cities,[57] leading to 'the institutionalization of exclusion of [the underprivileged sections of the population] in the 1990s when [Ahmedabad] was integrated with the global entrepreneurial forces through the initiatives of the bureaucrats and some international development agencies'.[58] On the basis of her extensive study of a riot-torn Ahmedabad (in Gujarat), she thus concludes:

> Globalization ... at the behest of the global capital ... does lead to exclusion of the local population, whose life spaces start shrinking. In such circumstances, globalization also brings a perceived threat of the invasion of the other in the life spaces of the people, which, in fact, happens, and a community can be made to be the "other" with systematic propaganda by an organized force.[59]

---

[53] M Davis, 'The Urbanization of the Empire: Mega Cities and the Laws of Chaos', *Social Text* 81, no. 22 (4) (Winter, 2004): 9–15; DF Harvey, 'Right to the City', *New Left Review* 53 (September–October, 2008): 23–40.

[54] A Appadurai, 'Deep Democracy: Urban Governmentality and the Horizon of Politics', *Public Culture* 14, no. 1 (2002): 21–47; A Broudehoux, 'Seeds of Dissent: The Politics of Resistance to Beijing's Olympic Redevelopment', in *Dissent and Culture in Asia's Cities*, eds. M Butcher and S Velayutham (London and New York: Routledge, 2009), pp. 14–32.

[55] BS Baviskar, 'Between Violence and Desire: Space, Power and Identity in the Making of Metropolitan Delhi', *International Social Science Journal* 55 (2003): 89–98.

[56] Davis, 'The Urbanization of the Empire', pp. 9–15; Harvey, 'Right to the City', pp. 23–40.

[57] Mahadevia, 'Communal Space over Life Space', *Economic and Political Weekly*, 30 November 2002, pp. 4850–51.

[58] Mahadevia, 'Communal Space over Life Space', p. 4858.

[59] Mahadevia, 'Communal Space over Life Space', p. 4858.

The 'purified spaces' of the 'beautified city' normalize a 'bourgeois urbanism'[60] that informalizes labour, legitimizes the downward spiral of wages, sharpens socio-economic inequalities and institutionalizes displacement and social exclusion of minority groups. Another study shows that in the name of making the capital city clean and green, lakhs of industries were closed and relocated from Delhi. The process has made majority of workers jobless, reduced their bargaining capacity, forced the workers to work in a more exploitative market economy and brought with it isolation, frustration and social tension for working class and their family.[61] Thus, workers had to pay a high price for a 'clean' Delhi.

Concluding Observations

The 1992 constitutional amendments created a new set of political opportunities for deepening of democracy by creating a space for participation by the majority of the population, especially the underprivileged, in governance. By creating supportive political institutions for constitutionalizing devolution of power at the grassroots, these legislative stipulations stand out in India's long history of democracy. There are problems and occasional hiccups; nonetheless, these amendments set in motion processes whereby the citizens are empowered to understand their rights and also duties to make the country a viable democracy.

As the fundamental impulse of policy making moves away from centralized state institutions towards market, these amendments, in principle, should facilitate the creation of structures that devolve power to the localized bodies. As per the Seventy-Third Amendment Act, the underlying principle of panchayati raj is the use of local knowledge, popular experience and participation in the making of decisions that affect local people. There is no doubt that the reformed panchayati raj institutions are supposed to reconstitute the decision-making processes on the basis of local participation on a continuous basis and, thus, in principle, represent an institutionalized shift in power towards lower, hitherto 'disempowered', sections of rural population. The only flaw in this argument is that the village-based institutions continue 'to reflect unequal social and economic structures . . . and higher castes and economically powerful groups within the village continue to be the de facto leaders in panchayats; while the women, despite the reservation, remain "proxies" to male counterparts who participate in panchayat affairs and decisions'.[62] Notwithstanding the obvious structural constraints, the panchayati raj institutions provide a form of governance that is based on community resources. At the grassroots, community is the organic unit of cultural, social, economic and political organization. In view of the growing popularity of the panchayat institutions, there is no doubt that a better administration can easily be achieved by building on the community resources rather than trying to import 'managerialization' of public services. Similarly, by empowering the ward committees as the locus of decision making in wards, the Seventy-Fourth Amendment Act created a space of participatory democracy which is complementary to localizing governance. A constitutional structure, these ward committees, acting as nurseries of civic virtues, have become proactive in urban affairs by being involved in both planning and its implementation. With reservation for women and the socially underprivileged, the ward committees, like the PRIs, are also a stepping stone towards building inclusive urban governance.

---

[60] Partha Chatterjee, *The Politics of the Governed: Reflections on Popular Politics in Most of the World* (New Delhi: Permanent Black, 2004), pp. 1–25.

[61] Prakash Chand, 'Implications of Industrial Relocation on Workers in Delhi', *Social Change* 42, no. 1 (March, 2012), pp. 49–68.

[62] Supriya Roychowdhury, 'Globalization and Decentralization', *The Hindu*, 5 January 2002.

With regard to both these amendments, the primary aim was to make participatory democracy realistic and realizable. It is therefore valid to argue that unlike in the West, where the imperative of the devolution of power was clearly administrative, in India, what contributed to the promulgation of Seventy-Third and Seventy-Fourth Amendment Acts was the politico-ideological momentum at the grassroots, built by processes of contestations and challenge against forces circumscribing popular democratic aspirations. Hence, it is further stated that the Indian experiment at democratic decentralization is one of 'the normative-political projects of greater inclusion and the representation of the historically disadvantaged and marginalized groups'.[63] So, there are two objectives that are sought to be attained by incorporating these momentous pieces of legislations: on the one hand, these amendments were clearly devices for democratization since they created spaces for representation of people regardless of caste, income or ethnicity; they also put, on the other hand, development as the topmost priority in circumstances when the state-led centralized planning appeared to have completely lost its salience. Arguments for democratic decentralization, thus, gained credibility presumably because they fashioned an alternative developmental paradigm, which is also people-centric because (a) it is based on what people deem to be of use for them and (b) it also sets in motion processes of coming together of people regardless of socio-economic schisms to rise as an inclusive community.

Notwithstanding the shortcomings of the prevalent system of local governance, which are linked with the existing social and economic bases of power, these amendments, especially the Seventy-Third Amendment Act, provide an alternative to the state-led and re-distributive developmental models. The renewed movement towards democratic decentralization and citizen-centric government has eroded the bureaucratic monopoly over the development processes and has shifted the locus of power to those who matter at the grassroots. This has been a reality due to variety of factors. With constitutional recognition to rural and urban local bodies, state-level election commissions and also finance commissions and granting of mandatory status to the Gram Sabhas, the bureaucrats are seen as mere facilitators and promoters of development and not regulators and directors. Within the theoretical format of democratic decentralization, bureaucracy is a catalyst for change rather than agents of change. So, it is a significant step in eroding the overwhelming paternalistic authority hitherto enjoyed by bureaucracy.

Having crafted a qualitatively different role for the PRIs, the Seventy-Third Amendment Act has substantially circumscribed the bureaucratic power, especially in the developmental plans at the grassroots. In states like Maharashtra, Gujarat and West Bengal, the district collectors/magistrates are, for instance, totally kept out of the Zilla Parishads, while in Uttar Pradesh and Bihar, they are allowed to attend meetings of the panchayat samiti and its standing committees without any right to vote. Furthermore, the statutory recognition of Gram Sabhas as the locus of the local governance has radically altered the power structure at the grassroots. Now, these Gram Sabhas are authorized to discuss and suggest policies for development, identify beneficiaries for various development programmes, discuss panchayat budget and review and monitor the implementation of various developmental programmes. Moreover, the government decision to implement various development programmes, including Jawahar Rozgar Yojana from the Eighth Five Year Plan onwards, through the panchayat has legitimized its role further. Involved in both the planning and execution of the programmes, relevant to the local needs, the Gram Sabhas have become significant instruments diluting the bureaucratic monopoly in the localities. The growing involvement of the people in the PRIs and Ward Committees has made the concept of 'peoples' audit' meaningful, which serves as a powerful check on the aberrations in bureaucratic functioning in the development sphere, be it the

[63] Niraja Gopal Jayal, 'Introduction' to *Local Governance in India: Decentralization and Beyond*, p. 5.

misappropriation of funds, false reporting or wrongful identification of beneficiaries. These amendments are, therefore, not just pieces of legislations but revolutionary legislative outcomes of sustained struggles against vested interests that did not appear to have been challenged in the past to the extent it was expected, presumably due to circumstances which were in their favour!

Review Questions

1. **Critically trace the evolution of local governance in India.**
2. **What is 'new localism'? Elaborate with examples.**
3. **How do you conceptualize panchayati raj governance as theoretical category? Elaborate your response.**
4. **How did the founding fathers articulate their views vis-à-vis localizing governance in India?**
5. **How did Mahatma Gandhi conceptualize rural governance? Elaborate.**
6. **Write a critical essay on the contribution of the Balwant Rai Mehta Committee Report (1957) and Ashok Mehta Committee Report (1978) on the growth and consolidation of panchayati raj governance in India.**
7. **Localizing governance is an offshoot of democratic decentralization. Explain.**
8. **Critically evaluate the Seventy-Third Amendment Act of 1992.**
9. **Critically assess the Seventy-Fourth Amendment Act of 1992.**
10. **The Seventy-Third Amendment Act of 1992 brought about radical changes in rural governance especially with the guarantee of 33 per cent reservation of seats for women in panchayat elections. Do you agree with this view? Elaborate your response.**

Conclusion

I

The constitution of a country is a purposeful text; besides being a guide for governance, it also charts out a specific politico-ideological course for the country in question. There are also multiple ways in which a constitution is made. In the historical past, the responsibility of making a constitution was largely the prerogative of a law-giver or constitution-maker; the famous law-givers were, to name a few, Aristotle, Thomas Aquinas and Jean Jacques Rousseau. They framed constitutions of their choice in accordance with their distinct ideological preferences. In modern times, it is usually a group of people who is entrusted with the task. The famous example is the 1787 Philadelphia Convention that framed the Constitution for the United States of America in 1789. The deliberations in the Convention was certainly important in comprehending the nature and also texture of the Constitution; what is also important is the text of *The Federalist Papers*, which Alexander Hamilton, James Madison and John Jay had prepared in favour of federalism in the US as opposed to confederation that some of their fierce critics insisted. While seeking to establish social pluralism, constitutionalism and federalism, the authors of *The Federalist Papers* seem to have built their defence on the assumption that in order to evolve the post-colonial America into a strong nation state, the critical alien voice needed to be respected. At a critical juncture of the American history, they wisely felt the necessity of being appreciative of trust and truthfulness in order to create and also sustain the required confidence among the states, supportive of a confederal America. What seems to have brought them together was free and frank dialogue in an environment of trust and truthfulness, and the idea of federalism appears to have become handy in articulating participation in the decision-making processes in its real and substantive sense. There is a moral dimension as well, since the Federalists also believed that '[p]rovidence has in a particular manner blessed it with a variety of soils and productions and watered it with innumerable streams for the delight and accommodation of its inhabitants'.[1] It was also believed that the providence had also contributed to the emergence of America as

> one connected country with one united people—a people descended from the same ancestors, speaking the same language, professing the same religion, attached to the same principles of government, very similar in their manners and customs, and who, by their joint counsels, arms

[1] Alexander Hamilton, James Madison and John Jay, *The Federalist Papers*, with an introduction by Clinton Rossiter (New York, NY: New American Library, 1961), p. 38.

> and efforts, fighting side by side throughout a long and bloody war, have nobly established their general liberty and independence.[2]

So, the federalists 'converted federalism from an expedient into an article of faith, from an occasional accident of history into an enduring expression of the principles of constitutionalism'.[3] For the federalists, federalism was not about the distribution of power among the constituent units; it, being reflective of its providential goal, created a political platform for protecting 'the inalienable rights of the lawful citizens'. The very description of federalism being an interactive platform confirms the importance of participation in the constitutional processes.

In substance, there are three important points that the federalists made while conceptualizing participatory governance in a context of political uncertainty in the wake of the threat for a confederal US. First, in their judgement, representative democracy was an acceptable system of representation since it allowed the citizens to select a chosen few for governance on the basis of their 'wisdom'. As they were wise, felt the federalists, they were not likely to be swayed by passion, which would keep the government in right tract. Second, by suggesting that representation needed to be extended to reach out to a greater number of citizens, they endeavoured to conceptualize democracy in an expansive sense. Implicit here is the idea that democracy is not merely structural, but also a device enabling citizens to express their priorities in response to what they gather out of their interactions with the prospective representatives. Finally, the federalist provided a complex model of democracy which was also republican. Dialectically conceptualized, democracy and republicanism are complementary to each other, as experiences of democratic governance from across the globe reveal. Since direct democracy is not feasible, republican design of democracy gains precedence. By insisting on indirect democracy, the federalists not only added a new dimension to participatory governance, but also reinforced the idea that the final authority rests in the citizens who exercise their power not only during the election but also in different fora for discussion on public issues.

As shown previously, the US Constitution owed a great deal to *The Federalist Papers*, which appears to have set the tone for deliberations in the Philadelphia Convention of 1787. Similar processes seem to have been followed in India. Founded in 1946, the Constituent Assembly framed the Constitution of India through intensive deliberations in which contrasting points also surfaced. Like its US counterpart, the Constituent Assembly drew on some of the texts, prepared by the nationalists. Two prominent texts were (a) the 1928 Motilal Nehru Committee Report and (b) the 1945 Sapru Committee constitutional proposals. Besides these, the suggestions of BN Rau, who was appointed as the Constitutional Advisor to the Constituent Assembly, were also of help to the members when they embarked on this exercise. There was, however, a major difference in the approaches that these two aforesaid committees held while suggesting specific constitutional designs for India. The Nehru Committee did not insist on independence; it simply wanted India to be a dominion within the British empire with the same status as Canada, Australia, New Zealand, South Africa and the Irish Free State, demanding a parliament with powers to make laws for the 'peace, order and good government of India and an executive responsible to that parliament'.[4] So, there was no doubt in the minds of the nationalists that it would be better off if India was given the power and authority as other dominions in the empire had enjoyed. The structure of governance followed the Westminster model of parliamentary democracy with no substantial power, as India continued to be ruled

---

[2] Hamilton et al., *The Federalist Papers*, p. 38.

[3] Hamilton et al., *The Federalist Papers*, p. xii.

[4] *The Nehru Report, 1928*, reproduced in *The Framing of India's Constitution: select documents*, Vol. 1, ed. B Shiva Rao (Delhi: Universal Law Publishing House, 1967), p. 59.

by the British Parliament. It is perfectly understandable why the Nehru Committee took such a stand as Congress was still divided as to whether a demand for independence was appropriate in 1928. The scene, however, changed in 1929 Lahore Congress when the resolution for Swaraj was adopted. Unlike the Nehru Report, the 1945 Sapru Committee upheld the view that it was constituted to frame a constitution for independent India. It was not an easy task for the committee either, given the growing support for the Partition of India into two independent nations. The Committee was, however, firm in its commitment to prepare 'a Constitution for a single state' which was evident when it stated:

> We, as a committee, have emphatically pronounced ourselves against the division of India into two or more independent sovereign states and, as a necessary corollary thereto, we accept the Cripps proposal, viz., the setting up of one constitution-making body charged with the function of framing a constitution for a single union for all India, but with no option to any of the units to back out of it after the final terms have been settled by the body.[5]

Along with these two nationalist alternatives that left a blueprint, the Constituent Assembly members also had another proposal prepared by BN Rau, the Constitutional Advisor to the Constituent Assembly. This was far more realistic, presumably because of the historical context of 1946 when the proposal for Pakistan was conceded. As for the structure of governance, Rau suggested that 'India is to be a Federation which may be called the "United States of India" [which entailed] that the units, as in a confederal system, are in a sense sovereign states'.[6] In Rau's scheme, the proposed federation comprised three groups: Group A includes the existing British Indian provinces of Madras, Bombay, the Central Provinces and Berar, Orissa, the United Provinces, Bihar, Delhi, Coorg, Panth Piploda and Ajmer-Merwara; Group B consists of the frontier regions comprising the British Indian provinces of the Punjab, the North-West Frontier Province, Sind and British Baluchistan on the west and Bengal and Assam and Andaman and Nicobar islands on the east; Group C contains the existing Indian states which may be expanded in case any of the provinces belonging to Group A and Group B are keen to join Group C.[7]

The scheme that Rau had proposed was also an endeavour to prevent India's partition. Hence, he was roughly in favour of a confederal arrangement in which the constituent units were to remain sovereign, which he articulated when he said that 'the particular Federation here outlined concedes the substance of the Pakistan demand'.[8] The idea did not appear to be realistic given the intransigence that the Muslim League had shown for its demand for Pakistan. Nonetheless, the constitutional design that Rau had left was referred to by the framers while being engaged in deliberation in the Assembly for preparing an appropriate constitution for independent India.

What is significant here is to highlight the issues that figured prominently in both Nehru Report and Sapru Committee Report, and also in the Rau constitutional proposals. A perusal of these report shows that, in their recommendations, both the committees felt the urgent need of addressing the specific communal concerns of the minorities, especially the Muslims. The Assembly members, particularly BR Ambedkar, insisted on giving adequate constitutional protection to the minorities because unless they were integrated with the nation, India's political freedom would just become vacuous. What is also striking is the acceptance by the Constituent Assembly of the structure of governance that these two reports had

---

[5] *Constitutional Proposals of the Sapru Committee, 1945*, reproduced in *The Framing of India's Constitution*, Vol. 1, p. 156.
[6] BN Rau, *The Outlines of a New Constitution*, reproduced in *The Framing of India's Constitution*, Vol. 1, p. 159.
[7] Drawn on Rau, *The Outlines of a New Constitution*, pp. 159–60.
[8] Rau, *The Outlines of a New Constitution*, p. 159.

laid out. It will, thus, not be an exaggerated claim to say that independent India's Constitution had its roots in earlier nationalist efforts at constitutionalizing India.

II

A careful analysis of the Constituent Assembly debates suggests that the draft constitution was not an outcome of consensus among the members; instead, there are many members who held completely different views which they supported by providing persuasive arguments. The most scathing criticism was made by Hukum Singh of East Punjab; he had no qualms to say that since

> in this Constitution no particular pattern has been followed ... it will not endure because it is neither indigenous nor a complete copy of any other single type. It is neither federal nor unitary. It is an enigmatic production, with every part stranger to the other.[9]

He pursued his argument further by being far more critical when he mentioned that

> the English make of Indian frame was already there as the Government of India Act, 1935. We have substituted an American head in the form of a President, replaced the old limbs by an English Parliamentary system, poured Australian flexibility in bones and flesh, infused Canadian look of a single judiciary and added an Irish appendix of Directive Principles and thus brought out a hybrid which we have been pleased to name the Indian Constitution.[10]

For Singh, the Constitution was a direction-less document since it was based on other constitutions, which was not going to work in the Indian context in which a strictly liberal constitution in the Western mould was bound to fail. Unhappy with the structure of the Constitution, which hardly gave 'anything substantial to the individual', Singh further warned that the imposed structure was hardly democratic. With the declining importance of common man in politics and the establishment of the President-driven rule, there was every possibility, he apprehended, that 'an ambitious President would discover a rich find in this Constitution to declare himself as a dictator and yet apparently be acting within this Constitution.'[11] Hukum Singh was not alone in criticizing the Constitution; he was supported by another member from West Bengal, Arun Chandra Guha. Like Singh, Guha also expressed his discomfort since the Constitution had, in itself, elements of contradictory constitutional designs. According to him:

> This Constitution is something like a hybrid Constitution. It is a Federal Constitution but it has started at the top, not from the bottom, as all Federations should start. It is the Centre that is delegating some of its powers to the federating units—not that the federating units who are enjoying sovereign powers are surrendering some of their sovereign powers to the Centre as was the case in the USA. So naturally the Centre which is devolving some powers must be stingy in this revolution of power. And, in the present context, it is in the fitness of things that the federating units have not their full privileges that in a Federation they ought to have.[12]

---

[9] Hukum Singh (East Punjab), 21 November 1949, *Constituent Assembly Debates*, Book No. 5, p. 749.
[10] Ibid., p. 749.
[11] Ibid., p. 753.
[12] Arun Chandra Guha (West Bengal), 21 November 1949, *Constituent Assembly Debates*, Book No. 5, p. 728.

Guha was critical of the draft constitution for being heavily tilted in favour of being a unitary State leading to the Centre being hegemonic in governance. To him, it was unacceptable since it was contrary to the very spirt of federalism. The same concern was expressed by PS Deshmukh of Central Provinces and Berar. Amused at the blending of different constitutional designs, he thus argued that although 'we have adopted a parliamentary democracy modelled on the British constitution . . . we have also decided to encroach on the sovereignty of our parliament in various ways by incorporating Fundamental Rights and many other matter of like nature'.[13] There were, therefore, serious anomalies in the structure of governance that was preferred.

As shown earlier, some of the members expressed their reservation since the Constitution, instead of being a federal constitution, became completely unitary. There was another viewpoint, mainly nurtured by the Gandhians, who felt alienated because the draft constitution did not pay adequate attention to the fundamental Gandhian ideals. One of the powerful critics in the Gandhian mould was Jaspat Roy Kapoor of United Provinces. While charging the members for having framed 'a completely alien constitution', he argued:

> Our Constitution is a miserable failure [because] . . . the spirit of Indian culture has not breathed on it; the Gandhism by which we swear so vehemently at home and abroad, does not inspire it. It is just a piece of legislation like, say, the Motor Vehicles Act'.[14]

The argument that Kapoor advanced was pursued further by Nandkishore Das of Orissa, who was also appalled since the constitution makers had hardly paid adequate attention to the Gandhian values while preparing the Constitution. As he emphatically declared:

> I do not, at all, feel disappointed that this Constitution is not moulded on Gandhian ideal, inasmuch as I least expected a Gandhian Constitution from our constitution-makers. We all swear by the name of the Father of the Nation [Gandhi], but how many of us have been able to assimilate his teaching in our personal activities of the day-to-day life? How many of us have that undying faith in the refashioning of our society on the old village self-sufficiency model? A Gandhian constitution is not to be produced by a mere mechanical process but must grow out of deepest convictions and a determination to shape our society strictly and meticulously in conformity with his ideals. The determination is to be found nowhere in the country. Hence evolving of a Gandhian constitution out of non-Gandhian brains and minds is quite out of the question.[15]

This was a clear attack on BR Ambedkar and his colleagues in the Assembly who did not seem to have been persuaded by the Gandhian insistence on making village as the primary unit of governance. It was, thus, obvious for the Gandhians to be unhappy with the constitution in which Gandhian ideals remained marginalized; it was inevitable, they felt, because the Constitution was framed by what Das characterized as 'non-Gandhian brains and minds'. A careful study of the above-mentioned points that the Gandhians made while defending their support for a Gandhian constitution reveals that the Assembly was sharply

[13] PS Deshmukh (Central Provinces and Berar), 22 November 1949, *Constituent Assembly Debates*, Book No. 5, p. 776.
[14] Jaspat Roy Kapoor (United Provinces), 21 November 1949, *Constituent Assembly Debates*, Book No. 5, p. 760.
[15] Nandkishore Das (Orissa), 23 November 1949, *Constituent Assembly Debates*, Book No. 5, pp. 851–52.

divided and the members of the Drafting Committee, including BR Ambedkar, failed to assuage their sentiments and feelings. The Constitution had thus become anything but Gandhian.

Division among the members notwithstanding, the draft constitution was finally approved in the form that the Drafting Committee had suggested. Constitutional democracy was sought to be established and the Constitution was considered to be an important tool in this respect. The success of constitutional democracy was contingent on, as Jadubans Sahay of Bihar explained,

> the character of a nation, the integrity, the honesty, our love for democratic principles and our zeal to pursue and follow them which can make or mar a constitution. The constitution of a country does not depend upon the cold letters, however beautifully or brilliantly printed in a book. It depends for its growth and development upon the character of a nation. It is the soil —the character of a nation—upon which the seeds of the constitution have got to germinate. If the soil is rocky and barren, then certainly howsoever good the constitution might be and in howsoever grand language it may be worded, it is sure that the constitution cannot lead us to our goal.[16]

This was a fundamental concern, being shared by the members of the Assembly. To be an effective guide for governance, the Constitution needs to be upheld by a complementary mindset in support of the values that it represents. A brilliant constitution is futile unless it is made to be functional by those who remain committed to the values, norms and ideals that it seeks to fulfil. Hence, Sahay further argued:

> No amount of guarantees in the Constitution or the filling up of the omissions mentioned will carry us to the goal. It depends upon those who work the Constitution. It depends on how we develop the spirit of tolerance and not on Constitution or the letter of the law. It depends on the spirit of love towards those that are down-trodden, . . . those who call themselves minorities and "have-nots". It does not depend on the Constitution or its articles. It depends upon our own character, our own vitality as a nation.[17]

So the basic point that comes out of Sahay's intervention was the need for developing a complementary mindset in support of a liberal constitution seeking to direct the nation towards those politico-ideological goals that the founding father had set for themselves. It was Ambedkar who also drew our attention to this aspect when he emphatically argued that

> the Constitution is workable, it is flexible, and it is strong enough to hold the country together both in peace time and in war time [and] . . . if things go wrong under the new Constitution, the reason will not be that we had a bad Constitution, but will have to say that Man was vile.'[18]

The same point was reiterated. A constitution succeeds if it is endorsed by the people supportive of values on which it rests. What is emphasized by Ambedkar was the importance of a complementary mindset which drew on constitutional morality. A challenging task no doubt, though the members were confident

[16] Jadubans Sahay (Bihar), 22 November 1949, *Constituent Assembly Debates*, Book No. 5, p. 800.
[17] Ibid., p. 800.
[18] BR Ambedkar, 4 November 1949, *Constituent Assembly Debates*, Book No. 2, p. 44.

to sail through all the difficulties in view of the determination that the nation had shown while fighting for freedom. Now, the time had come to work for those unrealized socio-economic goals. Hence, Independence, despite being 'a matter of joy, has', argued Ambedkar,

> thrown on us great responsibilities [because] . . . we have lost the excuse of blaming the British for anything going wrong. If hereafter things go wrong, we will [have] nobody to blame except ourselves. . . . If we wish to preserve the Constitution in which we have sought to enshrine the principle of Government of the people, for the people and by the people, let us resolve [to] not be tardy in the recognition of the evils that lie across our path and which induce people to prefer Government for the people to Government by the people, nor to be weak in our initiative to remove them. This is the only way to serve the country.[19]

There are three important points that appear to have been reinforced in what Ambedkar had suggested. First, like his colleagues with similar kind of ideological inclinations, he strongly felt that the success of a constitution was dependent on the socio-economic context in which it evolved. Unless a supportive mindset was created, the Constitution would merely become a compilation of rules and regulations with no substance. Being a victim of a highly regimented social system, he was aware that the task of creating a complementary mindset was not an easy one especially when inequality was well-entrenched in India's social and economic life. Nonetheless, the need for a constitution could not be negated since it was certain to contribute to processes for change and reform in the prevalent socio-economic circumstances. Second, by codifying rules and regulations against socio-economic discrimination due to the accident of birth, he also championed the idea of substantial equality which needed to be realized to bring about noticeable changes in the mindset that so far remained committed to birth-driven inequality. This was a great achievement for him, especially when feudal socio-economic values did not seem to have lost their steam, presumably because of the prevalent milieu in which they continued to receive endorsement. Finally, there is no doubt that with its support for liberal democracy, the Constitution initiated processes for change by giving a jolt to the existent socio-economic values, shaping inter-personal relationships. Once the Constitution was inaugurated in 1949, it was easier for the socially and economically peripheral groups to assert their rightful existence on an equal footing with other socio-economically privileged sections of the demography. This was a revolutionary change not only in their own perceptions, but also in how others viewed them as integral to the same social space which, so far, remained out of their reach due to the accident of birth. It is in this sense that the 1950 Constitution of India is not only an empowering instrument but also a significant determinant of change in independent India.

III

In the evolution of a constitution, the role of amendment is of immense significance. In fact, an amendment to the constitution is potentially strong enough to change the nature of the constitution. Hence, it is considered to be an effective tool to make a constitution relevant to the changing socio-economic and political context. There is, of course, an ethical question relating to the indiscriminate use of this tool to fulfil partisan aims and goals of the ruling authority. If that is the case, then the constitution will lose its

[19] BR Ambedkar, 25 November 1939, *Constituent Assembly Debates*, Book No. 5, pp. 980–81.

sanctity as the rule of law. One can seal that possibility by making the procedure most stringent which, however, shall be futile unless there is a mindset to back the prevalent constitution. In other words, what is important is the political will, adequately supported by the demos, to sustain a constitution. That is possible once the constitution is held by all as an instrument both empowering the people and ensuring a fair play of rules and regulations irrespective of social, economic and ideological considerations. Without the possibility of amendments whenever required, it is difficult for a constitution to keep pace with the changing socio-economic milieu, contributing to newer politico-ideological preferences. Of course, there is judiciary to interpret the constitutional provisions in case they are infringed. This is certainly one of the most effective means of retaining the constitutionality of the constitution; but, it is not enough in radically altered socio-economic circumstances. Hence, there is the importance of amendments as perhaps the most important tool of making the constitution consistent with the changing socio-economic and political realities.

The purpose of amendments is to accommodate newer politico-ideological demands arising out of the prevalent socio-economic circumstances. One cannot, however, rule out the possibility of amendments being misused for narrow political gains. Nonetheless, amendments are, in conceptual terms, an effective mechanism to articulate and constitutionalize newer ideas which are absolutely critical for sustaining the constitutional fabric of a polity. The point can be substantiated by drawing upon the US Constitution, one of the oldest written constitutions of the world that has been functional since 1789. Comprising seven articles and 27 amendments, the US Constitution wields sovereign authority as far as governance is concerned, and amendments are sparingly resorted to accommodate pressing socio-economic demands as and when they are absolutely necessary. Of all the amendments, the Thirteenth Amendment (1865) and the Twenty-Fourth Amendment (1964) are revolutionary in the sense that they radically altered the prevalent texture of American society by removing slavery and restrictions on voting, respectively. While the former abolished 'slavery and involuntary servitude', the latter established the universal civil rights by making racial discrimination ultra vires to the Constitution. Being complementary to the 1865 Amendment, the Twenty-Fourth Amendment led to two revolutionary legislations: the 1964 Civil Rights Act and 1965 Voting Rights Act. Both these important pieces of legislation ushered in a new era in which racial segregation was, at least legally, abolished. By forcing the State to accept universal franchise, these Acts translated into practice the core values of American constitutionalism, enshrined in the Declaration of Independence and the 1863 Emancipation Proclamation, which helped in getting rid of slavery and involuntary servitude.

This is also true of the Constitution of India that also evolved over the years in response to some of the path-breaking amendments with significant socio-economic and political implications. There are more than one hundred amendments to the Constitution that was inaugurated in 1949. To substantiate the point, we will confine ourselves to three major amendment acts, which however does not belittle the impact of other amendment acts in bringing about radical socio-economic and political changes. Within two years after the Constitution was put into effect, the first Amendment Act was adopted in 1951. The main objective of the amendment was to constitutionalize the validity of Zamindari abolition laws in general. Article 19 guaranteeing the Right to Freedom was amended; it was further stated that the State is authorized to make special provisions for the educational, economic and social advancement of any backward classes of citizens or for the Scheduled Castes and the Scheduled Tribes. This was a revolutionary step which reinforced some of the concerns that the founding fathers expressed while debating on the Directive Principles of State Policy. Not only was the amendment an attack on one foundational pillar of feudal land relations, but it also set in motion processes of empowerment of the socio-economically peripheral sections of the population. It also established 'the precedent of amending the Constitution to overcome judicial judgements impeding fulfilment of the government perceived responsibilities to the seamless web and to particular policies and programmes'.[20] Furthermore, by creating the Ninth Schedule, which was safeguarded from judicial review, the First Amendment Act ensured an extra protection to the government of the day. In view of its adversarial constitutional implications, the first amendment can be said to have prepared the ground for future political authority to fiddle with the fundamental character of the Constitution, as history has shown.

While the First Amendment Act was a step towards making the Constitution more democratic, the Twenty-Fourth Amendment Act, 1971 threatened to overturn some of its fundamental politico-ideological values. It was a reaction of the ruling authority in response to the 1967 Golak Nath case ruling which debarred Parliament from amending all parts of the Constitution including Part III relating to Fundamental Rights. The amendment was justified as necessary to give effect to the Directive Principles of State Policy for the attainment of the socio-economic objectives, set out in the Preamble to the Constitution. The primary goal was to abolish property rights which stood in the way of fulfilling 'a public purpose'. It was therefore considered 'necessary to provide expressly that Parliament has power to amend any provision of the Constitution so as to include the provisions of Part III with the scope of the amending power'.[21] Furthermore, it was also stipulated that the President was bound to give assent to an amendment when a constitution amendment bill was passed by both Houses of Parliament. This was a draconian Amendment Act which established parliamentary supremacy by violating the sovereignty of the Constitution. By conferring unquestionable authority on the Parliament, the Act became a powerful constitutional instrument to transform even basic character of the Constitution. The implications were, noted *The Statesman*, 'breath-taking because Parliament now has the power to deny seven freedoms, abolish constitutional remedies to citizens, and to change the federal character of the Union'.[22] What is distinctive was the effort on the part of the government of the day to undermine the fundamental character of the Constitution: India is a constitutional democracy in which Constitution remains supreme and endeavour at privileging the Parliament over the Constitution amounts to surpassing its basic structure.

The effort at changing the basic structure of the Constitution was carried forward in the Forty-Second Amendment Act of 1976. It was justified as needed 'to spell out expressly the high ideals of socialism, secularism and integrity of the nation ... and make the directive principles more comprehensive and given them precedence over those fundamental rights which have been allowed to be relied upon to frustrate socio-economic reforms for implementing the directive principles'.[23] The amendment was thus considered to be highly appropriate for removing 'the difficulties which [had] arisen in achieving the objective of socio-economic revolution which would eradicate poverty and ignorance and disease and inequality of opportunity'.[24] On the surface, the amendment may appear very innocent; but a deeper reading of the text reveals that it was an attempt to instil parliamentary sovereignty as opposed to constitutional supremacy.

With 59 Clauses in the above-mentioned amendment, almost all parts of the Constitution, including the Preamble and amending procedures, were changed. As per the revised Preamble, the aim was to constitute India into a Sovereign Socialist Secular Republic and not merely Sovereign Democratic Republic,

---

[20] Granville Austin, *Working a Democratic Constitution: A History of the Indian Experience* (New Delhi: Oxford University Press, 1999), p. 97.

[21] The Constitution (Twenty-Fourth Amendment) Act, 1971. http://indiacode.nic.in/coiweb/amend/amend24.htm (accessed 6 January 2017).

[22] *The Statesman*, Calcutta, 6 August 1971.

[23] The Constitution (Forty-Second Amendment) Act, 1976. http://indiacode.nic.in/coiweb/amend/amend42.htm (accessed 6 January 2017).

[24] The Constitution (Forty-Second Amendment) Act, 1976.

as in the past. Not only did it strip the Supreme Court of its authority to review the justiciability of legislations, which were considered appropriate for fulfilling the socialistic objective of the government, it also gave Parliament unrestrained power to amend any parts of the Constitution without judicial review and also to make the laws passed in pursuance of a Directive Principles immune, from scrutiny by the Supreme Court. It made the state subservient to a significant extent by transferring more power to the Union Government from its counterparts in the constituent provinces, which also threatened the federal system of governance, being nurtured so assiduously since the inauguration of the Constitution in 1949. Even a cursory look at these changes reveal that the principal aim of this Amendment Act was to overhaul the system of governance in which the Constitution reigned supreme; it was an effort to put, in its place, the parliamentary hegemony in governance. It was also apprehended that the Forty-Second Amendment Act was a just a stepping stone towards establishing a regime of constitutional authoritarianism. Austin thus argued that 'the Forty-Second Amendment, with [Indira] Gandhi's justification ... in nationalist, unity-integrity and social revolutionary terms joined classic examples in Italy and Germany of socialist-nationalist rhetoric put at the service of the authoritarian intentions of a few'.[25] This was slightly over-stretched given the well-entrenched roots of constitutional democracy in India, since following the 1977 national poll, most of the changes that this Amendment Act had brought about were reversed in the Forty-Fourth Amendment Act of 1978. Nonetheless, the Forty-Second Amendment Act remains a watershed in India's constitutional history, showing that an amendment could easily be utilized to radically alter the texture and also the nature of the Constitution.

In a different way, the Seventy-Third Amendment Act of 1992, for instance, brought about a noticeable metamorphosis in India's constitutional structure. An imperative need was felt, as per the objective of the Amendment, 'to enshrine in the constitution certain basic and essential features of Panchayati Raj Institutions to impart certainty, continuity and strength to them'.[26] By inserting Part IX in the Constitution and endowing the panchayats with such powers and authority as may be necessary to enable them to function as institutions of self-governance, the Amendment Act laid out an alternative structure of governance in contrast with the one that tended to centralize authority. Being given constitutional guarantee, these local-level institutions of self-governance have become integral to India's constitutional democracy which now percolates down to the grassroots.

The implications of this Amendment Act for constitutional governance are far-reaching. Besides making the PRIs important stakeholders at the grassroots, the Amendment has also evolved a constitutional mechanism for making democracy not merely an aspirational ideological goal, but also a means to translate into reality the founding fathers' desire of truly democratizing governance by devolving power and authority to the grassroots. A revolutionary step nonetheless, it has also its pitfalls though there is no denying that it gave a jolt to the age-old governance system in which local vested interests remained hegemonic, which is not a mean achievement.

This section reinforces the argument that amendments are an essential component of the evolution of constitutional democracy in India. Amendments expand, abrogate and reinterpret the available constitutional provisions, of course, within the well-set parameters, to retain the fundamental ethos, values and principles which the constitution represents. As is evident in India's constitutional history, amendments seeking to radically alter the texture of the Constitution—as was the case in both Twenty-Fourth

[25] Austin, *Working a Democratic Constitution*, pp. 388–89.

[26] The Constitution (Seventy-Third Amendment) Act, 1992. http://indiacode.nic.in/coiweb/amend/amend73.htm (accessed 6 January 2017).

Amendment Act (1971) and Forty-Second Amendment Act (1976)—were immediately reversed and this confirms that the zeal for democracy is deeply rooted in India. Fundamental here is the point that amendments form the backbone of the constitution because they contribute to its adaptation to the changing socio-economic milieu and also prevalent politico-ideological preferences of the governing elites. And, in that respect, the significance of amendments, even if they are undesirable in constitutional terms, as a bridge between the constitution and the governed can never be belittled.

IV

The judiciary is an important pillar of constitutional democracy in India. Being entrusted with the responsibility of ascertaining the justiciability of legislative stipulations, Indian courts have contributed immensely to the reinforcement of politico-ideological values that are critical to the Constitution of India. Indian judiciary can both be reactive and proactive in its deeds in the light of the growing importance of the doctrine of judicial activism. Whether it is defensible or not is not the question; what is important here is to assess the role of the judiciary in sustaining the constitutionality of the Constitution and also to create its new domains by way of being innovative in its interpretations of legislative acts and designs. So, the judiciary is an important partner, along with other institutional and non-institutional actors, in India's constitutional democracy.

There are many significant judicial interventions, especially by the Supreme Court of India, which led to the consolidation of constitutional values that, so far, remained either peripheral or insignificant in constitutional governance. Examples are in abundance. To substantiate the argument, this section concentrates on some of the major judicial pronouncements, which are not only constitutionally creative but also illustrative of efforts towards constitutionalizing governance within the acceptable limits that the constitution has demarcated.

Of all the judicial efforts which are constitutionally significant, the series of judgements by the Supreme Court of India on the idea of basic structure remain most significant in constitutional discourses. The idea had its first appearance in the 1951 *Shankari Prasad v. the Union of India* case, when the apex court was asked to adjudicate whether one's right to property could be annulled if it stood in the way of radical land distribution that had wider socio-economic goals. The court held the view that as per Article 13 of the Constitution, laws violating one's fundamental rights are ultra vires to the Constitution. The view was reiterated in the 1965 *Sajjan Singh v. the State of Rajasthan* case; the majority of the judges in the division bench felt that not every part of the Constitution was free to be amended since there are parts within the Constitution that holds the spirit which is fundamental to its core. The next important milestone in this regard was the 1967 Golak Nath case in which the Supreme Court endorsed the view that parliamentary authority of amending the Constitution was not absolute. Since amendments were just like other laws, passed by Parliament, they could not 'encroach upon the rights guaranteed by the Constitution [and] ... rights formed the inviolable core of the Constitution [and needed to be] kept beyond the reach of parliament'.[27] This was reiterated in the 1973 Kesavananda judgement of the Supreme Court which was endorsed by a group of six judges, led by the Chief Justice of India.

[27] Madhav Khosla, 'Constitutional Amendment', in *The Oxford Handbook of the Indian Constitution*, eds. Sujit Chowdhury, Madhav Khosla and Pratap Bhanu Mehta (New Delhi: Oxford University Press, 2016), p. 238.

The apex court held that the Fundamental Rights, being part of the essential elements or basic structure of the Constitution could not be abrogated or 'emasculated by the exercise of the power of amendment under Article 368'.[28] Even of the dissenting judges, the idea was also upheld. For instance, Justice J Khanna defended the point that the Constitution could be amended subject to the retention of its basic structure or the framework. Despite persuasive critiques, the idea of the basic structure of the Constitution appears to have become integral to constitutional democracy in India. The Supreme Court in the *Indira Gandhi v. Raj Narain* case (1975) also held the importance of the doctrine in its pronouncement stating that democracy is the basic structure of the Constitution and it includes free and fair election, which cannot be abrogated. In continuity with its earlier stance, the Supreme Court, in its pronouncement on the 1980 Minerva Mills case, declared that Parliament was not authorized, under Article 368, to expand its amending power so as to acquire itself the right to repeal or abrogate the Constitution or to destroy its basic and essential features. By insisting that the Parliament had 'unlimited' power as far as the basic structure was concerned, the apex court privileged the essential features of the Constitution by making them sacrosanct.

The preceding brief account of several judicial pronouncements underlines that the basic structure doctrine has become a unique feature of India's constitutional history; these judgements also confirm that the judiciary in India remains a proactive instrument of governance which neither the legislature nor the executive can afford to bypass. A significant development undoubtedly, the basic structure doctrine seems to have created conditions in which the Parliament appears to have become dwarfed, which is indicative of another major shift, namely, from a regime endorsing parliamentary sovereignty to another appreciative of constitutional supremacy. Therefore, there is substance when it is claimed that 'the Indian Constitution clearly adopted the American model of constitutionalism with limited government and strong judicial review'.[29] Be that as it may, the fact remains that the basic structure doctrine is a powerful judicial input to reconceptualize the form of democracy that India had opted for following the British withdrawal. It has its pitfalls as well because allowing the judiciary to prevail over parliament, which is a representative body, may not be justified in a democratic framework of governance. Nonetheless, the doctrine of basic structure is justified as having put a brake on the parliamentary authority in case it is exercised arbitrarily and with an ulterior motive. In other words, by identifying an illustrative list of essential features, the apex court fulfilled its role as a guardian by being sensitive to the constitutional values that are being nurtured since the inauguration of the Constitution in 1949. In that respect, the doctrine is not only an appropriate one but also an important device to redraw the contour of constitutional governance in the changed socio-economic and political environment.

In a 2017 path-breaking judgement on the Section 123(3) of Representation of People Act, 1951, the Supreme Court raised some important constitutional issues relating to secularism, election and democracy, which are also useful in conceptualizing the Constitution in a different light. The basic contention in this case was whether the candidates contesting election are allowed to appeal the voters by reference to their primordial identities based on religion, race, caste, community and so on. The majority of the judges of a division bench of seven judges held the view that the appeal to caste, religion, language and community should be kept out the electoral processes since it vitiates the democratic processes by drawing upon 'the divisive markers of identity' which are an impediment to realize the democracy in its substantive form. Furthermore, democracy entails that voters exercise their franchise 'on the basis of rational thought and

[28] PK Tripathi, 'Kesavananda Bharati versus the State of Kerala: who wins?' http://www.supremecourtcases.com/index2.php?option=com_content&itemid=1&do_pdf=1&id=407 (accessed 7 January 2017).

[29] Sudhir Krishnaswamy, *Democracy and Constitutionalism in India: A Study of the Basic Structure Doctrine* (New Delhi: Oxford University Press, 2009), p. 218.

action, appeals to religion, language and caste are inherently emotive and irrational in nature',[30] and hence are contrary to the fundamental ethos of constitutional democracy. In the words of the Chief Justice:

> Religion will not play any role in the governance of the country which must at all times be secular in nature. The elections to the State legislature or to the Parliament or for that matter or any other body in the State is a secular exercise just as the functions of the elected representatives must be secular in both outlook and practice. Suffice it to say that the Constitutional ethos forbids mixing of religions or religious considerations with the secular functions of the State.... An appeal in the name of religion, race, caste, community or language is impermissible under the Representation of People Act, 1951 and would constitute a corrupt practice sufficient to annul the election in which such an appeal was made.[31]

The argument which the majority of the judges pursued defends the view that in the public sphere, we must leave our 'messy markers of personal identity at the door ... to participate as rational individuals, ... unencumbered by the baggage of our religion, caste, language or community'.[32] The argument was challenged by the dissenting judges of the division bench on the basis of their different understanding of India's constitutional democracy in which identity was differently constituted. Not only has the state recognized one's identity on the basis of one's religion, caste, language, race or community, the constitutional provisions were also articulated accordingly. It is thus emphasized that the Constitution recognizes 'religion, caste, language and gender in the social life of the nation' which was made clear by Justice DY Chandrachud who further underlined that the Constitution deals with them and contains

> provisions for the amelioration of disabilities and discrimination which was practised on the basis of those features. These are matters of concern to voters especially where large segments of the population were deprived of basic human rights as a result of prejudice and discrimination which they have suffered on the basis of caste and race. The Constitution does not deny religion, caste, race, community or language a position in the public sphere. Discussion about these matters – within and outside the electoral context—is a constitutionally protected value and is an intrinsic part of the freedom of speech and expression.... A sense of inclusion can only be fostered by protecting the right of citizens freely to engage in dialogue in public spaces. Dialogue and criticism lie at the heart of mobilizing opinion. Electoral change is all about mobilizing opinion and motivating others to stand up against patterns of prejudice and disabilities of discrimination.[33]

The dissenting view is far more persuasive since it acknowledges the importance of primordial loyalties in the existence of Indians as Indians. Religion is a critical marker of identity which cannot be so easily dispensed with. Secularism in India needs to be conceptualized accordingly. The majority view thus appears to be very idealistic in the sense that it endorses a vision of 'a pure electoral process shorn of caste, religion and presumably other things that matter to Indians [and] elections for them must be limited to purely

---

[30] Gautam Bhatia, 'Two Takes on Democracy', *The Hindu*, New Delhi, 4 January 2017.

[31] *Abhiram Singh v. CD Commachen (dead) with Narayan Singh v. Sundarlal Patwa*, 2 January 2017. https://indiankanoon.org/doc/85515763/ (accessed 7 January 2017).

[32] Bhatia, 'Two Takes on Democracy'.

[33] *Abhiram Singh v. CD Commachen (dead) with Narayan Singh v. Sundarlal Patwa*, 2 January 2017.

secular concerns'.[34] Despite having conceptualized their viewpoints in contrasting perspectives, both the dissenting judges and their counterpart reinforced the claim that the judicial pronouncements allow us to see the Constitution in different lights. Being reinvented regularly, the Constitution needs to be conceptualized regularly which, however, does not mean that its essential features can be fiddled. In that respect, this judgement serves two clear purposes: on the one hand, it reemphasizes that being secular does not mean that one cannot be religious; in conceptualizing one's identity, the Constitution too factors in religion, race, language and community which are integral to one's existence as an Indian. In elections, the appeal to the voters in terms of their primordial identities does not, on the other hand, constitute a violation of the fundamental principles of constitutional democracy. This is a realistic assessment of the circumstances in which Indians exert their Indian identity in practice.

This segment has shown that the role of the judiciary is as critical as the constitutional provisions in comprehending the Constitution as a living organism. The Constitution needs to be updated, and the task is accomplished by judicious judicial interventions, besides, of course, the law makers who regularly intervened by devising legislative means to make the Constitution pertinent to the changing socio-economic circumstances. A note of caution is also required here. With the basic structure doctrine in place, the Constitution cannot be indiscriminately amended, and by its constant vigil, the Indian judiciary also plays a critical role in sustaining constitutional democracy in India despite occasional hiccups. This further confirms that constitutional democracy is not merely a top-dressing, as Ambedkar had apprehended during the making of the Constitution, but has also become organic to India's socio-economic and political practices, which is not a mean achievement in a polity divided on various axes around religion, caste, race, language and so on and so forth.

V

Politics and constitution are intricately enmeshed; they are dialectically linked. A constitution evolves in a political context and a political context remains critical in conceptualizing a constitution. What is important is, therefore, to understand the complex interrelationship between politics and constitution which means that the nature of one cannot be properly conceptualized independent of the other. This also means that being organic to a specific socio-political milieu, a constitution is largely a contextual text at one level; at another, it also epitomizes some of the universal politico-ideological values and principles which are significant in both creating and consolidating a social compact. Basic here is the idea that a constitution is a design of governance which also draws on the political processes and vice versa. A perusal of India's recent political history confirms that the Constitution always remains a source of empowerment to both its supporters and detractors: that the supporters are inspired is obvious; for the detractors, the Constitution of India provides sources of strength within the same constitutional parameters, which is not a puzzle given the peculiar character of the Constitution.

As argued previously, the Constitution is simultaneously a source of democratic aspiration and also inspiration for distorting democracy. It is a paradox especially when the Constitution is hailed for being clearly democratic; nonetheless, there were events in India's recent political history demonstrating how the constitutional values were undermined to endorse individual whims and fancies and also how the same Constitution had inspired campaigns for constitutional democracy regardless of consequences.

[34] Arghya Sengupta, 'The Belly of Democracy', *The Times of India*, New Delhi, 5 January 2017.

To make and defend the argument, this segment focuses on two major events—the campaign against the 1975–77 Emergency which led to the establishing of a constitutional authoritarianism in India and the campaign against corruption in 2011.

The 1975–77 Emergency was proclaimed due to pressing circumstances, as Indira Gandhi stated to defend her action. Critical of such an interpretation, the Shah Commission that was constituted to probe into the excesses committed during the period, charged her for violating constitutional propriety even while she was preparing the ground for the declaration on 26 June 1975. The proclamation of Emergency was not a knee-jerk reaction, but one that was based on serious thinking, which was supportive of Indira Gandhi's design for personalizing authority at the cost of the fundamental values of parliamentary democracy and collective responsibility of the Westminster form of authority. It was possible for her to bypass the constitutional checks and balances, presumably because the institutions holding India's democratic structure of governance were too weak to contain authoritarian tendencies and also because of the fact that those associated with her did not find it prudent to challenge her decisions. Nothing was thus reason-driven but was governed by power, which created a different kind of politics where values became less significant and hardcore pragmatism seemed to have ruled the roost. A new era had thus ushered in when an individual, if endowed with extraordinary personality, could easily be authoritarian within the constitutional boundary of the 1950 Constitution of India, as Indira Gandhi had shown during the two-year period of Emergency.

The Emergency was a wake-up call for the citizens because it alerted them of the adverse consequences of personalization of administration at the cost of the core principles of democratic governance being nurtured in independent India. Democracy is 'an ethic' and not 'just a machine', and the core of democratic politics is to create the conditions for individuals in a society to develop to their fullest potentials. Although the core loses salience on occasions, history has shown that it is revived by the people once they understand the importance of democratic principles as perhaps the best shield for protecting individual rights against ruling authority's hegemonic design. The Emergency was an occasion when individual rights were taken away, which perhaps contributed significantly to the endeavours for getting them back through sustained politico-ideological movements. Thus, a commentator metaphorically suggested that although 'the fragile balance between reason and power was jolted during the Emergency, [the fact that] ultimately reason returned'[35] due perhaps to the campaign drawing on the public concern for democracy and prejudice-free governance. The Emergency is also about human existence appreciative of contrasting tendencies. It had shown 'how easily [Indians] could accept the loss of their freedoms and how obediently [they] agreed to being herded into submission'.[36] The Emergency was a peculiar experience that Indians had undergone following the 25 June proclamation. It prepared India for democracy which, unless properly nurtured, loses its vitality, as the Emergency had shown. The real legacy of the Emergency has thus been wholly unintended because, as argued by an analyst, 'it has made India conscious, as never before, of civil liberties, of the right to freedom of expression; the Emergency by robbing India a while of the soul of republicanism, has made it a truer Republic than it was before 1975' when Emergency was put into effect.[37] It was thus a defining moment not only for citizens who, by confronting a systemic attack on their rights, learnt that rights needed to be protected but also for the nation which was likely to be subservient to the political authority if it lost its vitality.

---

[35] Krishna Kumar, 'Conscience and the Body Politics', *The Hindu*, New Delhi, 10 July 2015.

[36] Santosh Desai, 'Trivial Tales of Emergency', *The Times of India*, New Delhi, 29 June 2015.

[37] Gopalkrishna Gandhi, 'Mastering the Drill of Democracy', *The Hindu*, New Delhi, 26 June 2015.

What accounts for the complete collapse of democratic governance in India during the Emergency was not a systemic failure, but the capacity of the ruling authority to utilize the prevalent constitutional arrangement to its advantage. This is an important lesson of Emergency for what had happened in the wake of the June proclamation was endorsed by the 1950 Constitution of India. The Emergency was not, at all, an extra-constitutional design, but one that was justified by the provisions of the Constitution. It has thus been aptly characterized as a regime of constitutional authoritarianism. Being armed with constitutional guarantee, those who had ideologically sponsored the Emergency utilized the legally backed available rules to fulfil their partisan goals. It is argued that the horrors of mass detention during Emergency was indeed 'built into the preventive detention legislation initiated by [India's first Prime Minister], Jawaharlal Nehru'.[38] Underplaying this aspect of governance, the Shah Commission attributed the Emergency to the abuse of the system by an individual and coterie around her. What had happened was not the subversion of a system of administration, 'but its apotheosis,'[39] and the misuse of authority sprang directly 'from the very provisions and rules and traditions built into that system'.[40] This is a conundrum that cannot be resolved easily because it is surprising that democratic governance was made to disappear during the Emergency by the same Constitution that protected and nurtured its well-being. What it suggests is perhaps the fact that constitutional guarantee, by itself, can never be an adequate safeguard unless the institutions are strong enough to stand by the constitution which is not merely a codified version of the rule of law, but also holds its spirit. The Emergency was undoubtedly a constitutional design, but clearly an aberration of the processes of governance challenging the very foundational values informing the Constitution of India. And, an analytical scan of the period thus reveals how constitutional values lost their viability because of constitutional reasons, and the consolidation of an authoritarian regime was also justified as possibly the best shield against the opposition-engineered efforts towards undermining those very constitutional values.

The second event was the one that defended the campaign for a strong Ombudsman for India, which is, in Indian parlance, defined as 'the Lokpal'. By creating the institution of CAG (Articles 148–151), the Constitution provided a mechanism for ascertaining accountability in the spending of public funds. But there is nothing in the Constitution to put a brake on the malpractices in governance. There is hardly, in other words, a conscience keeper in the Constitution. The need was strongly felt with the growing incidence of corruption in the last few years leading to mass disenchantment with the system of governance. Outraged by the inept government which was charged with being complicit with the corrupt forces, citizens joined the campaigners in large numbers with the hope that it would not only expose the deviants, but also lay the foundation of an ethically sound political system.

The 2011 Anna Hazare movement unfolded in a context when several scams had already rocked India. It was easier for the organizers to mobilize in the light of a popular demand for an end to corruption. There was a common feeling that since the government connived with vested interests, it simply became inept to effectively combat corruption in governance. Added to this feeling was 'the discovery of the loot in the upper echelons of governance, by top politicians, senior bureaucrats and even the judges in the higher courts'.[41] Hazare's solution was to create a strong Lokpal to contain corruption which was all that was needed 'to unleash the full benefits of liberalization in India'.[42] The institution of Lokpal was first suggested

[38] 'Shah Commission's Final Report III', *Economic and Political Weekly*, 6 October 1978, p. 1839.

[39] Shah Commission's Final Report III, p. 1839.

[40] Shah Commission's Final Report III, p. 1839.

[41] Sumanta Banerjee, 'Anna Hazare, Civil Society and the State', *Economic and Political Weekly*, 3 September 2011, p. 12.

[42] Mathew Jenkins, 'Anna Hazare, Liberalization and the Careers of Corruption in Modern India: 1974–2011', *Economic and Political Weekly*, 16 August 2014, p. 48.

by the first Administrative Reforms Commission in 1968 and the first Lokpal bill was immediately introduced in that year. Since then, it has been introduced nine times, but was never passed. Essentially a technocratic solution, the Lokpal was thus assumed to be adequately equipped to completely root out corruption. Insisting on a legislation for a strong Lokpal, Anna Hazare and his colleagues appeared to have expressed complete faith in a panoptical institution, capable of fulfilling their ideological mission. Those supporting the campaign were persuaded to believe that a parliamentary law had the capacity to effectively mitigate corruption in public life. The creation of an effective Lokpal, it was believed, was an antidote to corruption. The followers of Anna Hazare were led to believe, a commentator thus argues, that 'a powerful individual with a reputation of honesty [with substantial power] would eradicate corruption, without the need for changing the prevailing system.'[43] The idea seemed to have created a hope, which was reflected in the swelling of mass support that was witnessed during the fast that Hazare had undertaken to force the government to initiate steps for an effective legislation.

The movement fizzled out and the goal remains elusive. Nonetheless, the 2011 Anna Hazare campaign is a milestone in contemporary India because not only has it brought the issue of corruption in public life for common reckoning, it has also created a demand for Lokpal as a constitutional authority. Despite being exhaustive, the 1950 Constitution is lacking in this respect. Hence, the demand received attention beyond what was expected at the outset. While the excesses of the Emergency led to the Forty-Fourth Amendment Act in 1978, the massive campaign that Anna Hazare led did not seem to yield results, though the Supreme Court suggested various stringent measures to curb corruption in public life while pronouncing its verdicts. Be that as it may, there is no denying that efforts are being made to develop an all-powerful Lokpal within the constitutional format of governance, which again confirms the argument that the constitution expands in response to demands arising out of the prevalent socio-economic and political circumstances.

By drawing upon two selective instances, the segment substantiates the argument that being a living organism, the Constitution is being constantly reinvented. Here lies the reason as to why a constitution survives and remains relevant to the changed milieu. This is an organic text which is being regularly revised to accommodate the newer socio-economic and political demands. Unless this process is allowed to prosper, the constitution will just become an inert set of rules and regulations with no substance at all. The US Constitution, which was inaugurated in 1789, is illustrative here. Following a mass campaign against slavery which led to the 1863 Emancipation Proclamation, the law makers were forced to adopt the 1865 Thirteenth Amendment Act which constitutionally abolished slavery and involuntary servitude. The 1789 Constitution did not, thus, remain the same. Similarly, in India the adoption of the Forty-Fourth Amendment Act in 1978, following the campaign against the excesses of the 1975–77 Emergency, put a brake on the possibility of the rise and consolidation of an authoritarian regime within the constitutional framework. It is now established both by this Amendment and many judicial pronouncements that Constitution is sovereign and parliamentary supremacy is to be conceptualized accordingly. The Lokpal is yet to be constitutionalized. Nonetheless, the contribution that the 2011 Anna Hazare movement made towards building a campaign for a strong Lokpal cannot be belittled. There is no denying that the voice for a competent constitutional authority is now too strong to be so easily dismissed, and, in that respect, the Hazare campaign is a watershed in India's constitutional history.

[43] Banerjee, 'Anna Hazare, Civil Society and the State', p. 13.

VI

Like any other stable constitution, the 1950 Constitution of India is not just a text of rules and regulations, but a guide for a specific type of constitutional democracy that arose in the aftermath of the British withdrawal in 1947. Strangely enough, the Constitution drew its sustenance from the politico-ideological ideas of liberalism that also defended colonialism. In view of stronger liberal roots of the Constitution, it is not conceptually improper to argue that it was rooted in those ideas of liberalism which also inspired the nationalists to launch a fierce campaign against the alien State. It is also now established that the efforts by the nationalists towards constitutionalizing India both during the colonial rule and its aftermath drew on the core principles of the philosophy of Enlightenment. The 1928 Motilal Nehru Report and the 1945 Sapru Constitutional Proposals are illustrative here. These are useful inputs for the Constitution besides, of course, the British initiatives at organizing governance in India by following, in steps, the structure of the Westminster form of constitutional democracy. By being engaged in debates, deliberations and contestations for close to three years, the Constituent Assembly gave a final shape to the Constitution which hardly remains a static document as legislative and judicial interventions keep on expanding (and also restricting) its sphere of functioning. The Constitution also draws on inputs from the public domain, as the campaign against the Emergency and later against corruption in 2011 show. Keeping all these inputs in view, the book concludes with a significant statement by arguing that the Indian Constitution is a continuous journey in which multiple ideas, practices, values and norms are constantly being creatively blended and absorbed which allows it to remain living, vibrant and receptive to the rapidly changing socio-economic and political milieu. Being salient in the past, the Constitution thus continues to remain relevant for the present despite being designed in the remote past when India was passing through perhaps the most tumultuous phases of her history.

Select Bibliography

The 1950 Constitution of India has received extensive scholarly attention. Besides scholarly works, there are many significant judicial pronouncements which are very useful to understand the nature and texture of the Constitution. An analytically persuasive study needs to take into account both the academic and judicial inputs; otherwise, the effort will not only be futile but also academically sterile. Since the literature is available in abundance, it is difficult, if not impossible, to prepare an exhaustive bibliography on this theme. So the aim is different here: This select bibliography includes books that are easy to understand and, at the same time, are well-researched and lucidly written. By drawing attention to some of the basic books on the Constitution of India, this bibliography shall thus be an intellectual aid for those seeking to unravel the dynamics of the Constitution of India.

The literature on the Constitution of India can be divided into three analytical categories. The first category includes books that are very legalistic in approach and tenor. These books are important in their own right, but may not be so useful to understand the Constitution as a political treatise, being constantly reinvented since socio-economic circumstances in which it evolves never remain static. Books in the second category are different from legally moulded texts. There are many conceptually challenging monographs which, while seeking to understand the constitution as a contextual response, draw our attention to the socio-political and economic milieu. The endeavour is directed at conceptualizing the constitution not merely as a compilation of rules and regulations but also an offshoot of the contextual inputs. Finally in the third category, we have a number of monographs that seek to creatively blend both legalistic and political (for want of a better expression) approaches to the Constitution. This is useful because for an analytically persuasive understanding of the Constitution, one needs to be acquainted with the provisions per se and how they evolved in a specific context.

Since the book is also about India's constitutional democracy, the Constitution is required to be understood as integral to democratic governance that the founding fathers so assiduously nurtured while battling for freedom. The bibliography is structured accordingly, which means that the books listed in the bibliography dwell on how the Constitution is both a critical and an unavoidable input for the constitutional democracy in India. Implicit here is an important idea that the Constitution, besides nurturing fundamental constitutional values, is also an important pillar of the system of governance that derives its sustenance from a complementary mindset in its support.

Before putting the titles, let me end this brief bibliographical note by suggesting that the first important text in this regard is the 1950 Constitution itself. Comprising 395 Articles, 12 Schedules and more than 100 Amendments, the 1950 Constitution is a very useful text for not only will it acquaint the readers with the actual provisions, but will also enable them how they were articulated in a language which is both lucid and purposive. There is another important source for the study of how the Constitution evolved in the

Constituent Assembly during the course of little less than three years. The five volumes of the *Constituent Assembly Debates*, published by the Lok Sabha Secretariat, provide very useful, and also critical, inputs to conceptualize how the founding fathers chose what they finally chose while being engaged in making what BR Ambedkar defined as 'the bulkiest constitution'.

Austin, Granville. *The Indian Constitution: The Cornerstone of a Nation*. New Delhi: Oxford University Press, 1966.

———. *Working a Democratic Constitution: A History of the Indian Experience*. New Delhi: Oxford University Press, 1999.

Basu, D. D. *Introduction to the Constitution of India*. Gurgaon: LexisNexis, 2015.

Bhargava, Rajeev, ed. *Politics and Ethics of the Indian Constitution*. New Delhi: Oxford University Press, 2008.

Bhatia, Gautam. *Offend, Shock or Disturb: Free Speech under the Indian Constitution*. New Delhi: Oxford University Press, 2016.

Bombwall, K. R. *Indian Constitution and Administration*. Ambala Cantt: Modern Publication, 1978.

Chakrabarty, Bidyut. 'BR Ambedkar and the History of Constitutionalizing India'. *Contemporary South Asia* 24, no. 2 (2016): 133–149.

———. 'BR Ambedkar: A "Rebel" Liberal in the Gandhian Universe'. *Indian Historical Review* 23, no. 2 (2016): 289–315.

Chaube, Shibanikinkar. *Constituent Assembly of India: Springboard of Revolution*. New Delhi: Manohar, 2000.

———. *The Making and Working of the Indian Constitution*. National New Delhi: Book Trust, 2009.

Chopra, Pran, ed. *The Supreme Court versus the Constitution: A Challenge to Federalism*. New Delhi: SAGE, 2006.

Chowdhruy, Sujit, Madhav Khosla, and Pratap Bhanu Mehta, eds. *The Oxford Handbook of the Indian Constitution*. New Delhi: Oxford University Press, 2016.

Dasgupta, Sandipto. 'A Language which is Foreign to Us: Continuities and Anxieties in the Making of the Indian Constitution'. *Comparative Studies of South Asia, Africa and the Middle East* 34, no. 2 (2014): 228–242.

Elangovan, Arvind. 'The Making of the Indian Constitution: A Case for a Non-nationalist Approach'. *History Compass* 12, no. 1 (2014): 1-10.

———. 'The Road Not Taken: Sir Benegal Narsing Rau and the Indian Constitution'. In *Decolonization and the Politics of Transition in South Asia*, edited by Sekhar Bandyopadhyay. New Delhi: Orient Blackswan, 2016.

———. 'Constitutionalism, Political Exclusion, and Implications for Indian Constitutional History: The Case of Montagu Chelmsford Reforms (1919)'. *South Asian History and Culture* (2016): 1–18.

———. 'Provincial Autonomy, Sir Benegal Narsing Rau, and an Improbable Imagination of Constitutionalism in India, 1935–38'. *Comparative Studies of South Asia, Africa and the Middle East* 36, no. 1 (2016): 66–82.

Hasan, Zoya, E. Sridharan, and R. Sudarshan, ed. *India's Living Constitution: Ideas, Practices, Controversies*. Ranikhet: Permanent Black, 2002.

Jayal, Niraja Gopal. *Citizenship and its Discontents: An Indian History*. Ranikhet: Permanent Black, 2013.

Kashyap, Subhash C. *Our Constitution: An Introduction to India's Constitution and Constitutional Law*. New Delhi: National Book Trust, 2015 (reprint).

———. *The Indian Constitution: Conflicts and Controversies*. New Delhi: Vitasta Publications, 2010.

Khosla, Madhav. *The Indian Constitution*. New Delhi: Oxford University Press, 2012.

Krishnaswami, Sudhir. *Democracy and Constitutionalism in India: A Study of the Basic Structure Doctrine*. New Delhi: Oxford University Press, 2009.

Legg, Stephen. 'Dyarchy: Democracy, Autocracy and the Scalar Sovereignty of Interwar India'. *Comparative Studies of South Asia, Africa and the Middle East* 36, no. 1 (2016): 44–65.

Noorani, A. G. *Constitutional Questions in India: The President, Parliament and the States*. New Delhi: Oxford University Press, 2000.

Pylee, M. V. *Constitutional Government in India*. London: Asia Publishing House, 1965.

Ramnath, Kalyani. 'We the People: Seamless Webs and Social Revolution in India's Constituent Assembly debates'. *South Asia Research* 32, no. 1 (2012): 57–70.

Rau, Benegal Narsing. *Outlines of a New Constitution*. 1946. Reproduced by B. Shiva Rao, ed. *The Framing of India's Constitution*, Vol. 1. Delhi: Universal Law Publishing House, 1967.

Roy, Anupama. *Mapping Citizenship in India*. New Delhi: Oxford University Press, 2010.

———. *Citizenship in India*. New Delhi: Oxford University Press, 2016.

Saez, Lawrennce. *Federalism with a centre*. New Delhi: SAGE, 2002.

Saxena, Rekha. *Situating Federalism: Mechanisms of Intergovernmental Relations in Canada and India*. New Delhi: Manohar, 2006.

Seth, Sanjay. 'Rewriting Histories of Nationalism: The Politics of "Moderate Nationalism" in India, 1870–1905'. *American Historical Review* 104, no. 1 (1999): 95–116.

Sharma, Brij Kishore. *Introduction to the Constitution of India*. New Delhi: Prentice Hall of India, 2005.

The Constitutional Proposals of the Sapru Committee. 1945. Reproduced by B. Shiva Rao, ed. In *The Framing of India's Constitution*, Vol. 1. Delhi: Universal Law Publishing House, 1967.

The Motilal Nehru Committee Report. 1928. Reproduced by B. Shiva Rao, ed. In *The Framing of India's Constitution*, Vol. 1. Delhi: Universal Law Publishing House, 1967.

Index